TEACHING SECONDARY SCHOOL MATHEMATICS

Techniques and Enrichment Units

2nd Edition

Alfred S. Posamentier
Professor of Mathematics Education
The City College
The City University of New York
New York, New York

Jay Stepelman
Supervisor, Mathematics
George Washington High School
New York, New York

Charles E. Merrill Publishing Company
A Bell & Howell Company
Columbus   Toronto   Sydney   London

Published by Charles E. Merrill Publishing Co.
A Bell & Howell Company
Columbus, Ohio 43216

This book was set in Times Roman and Helvetica Bold.
Production Coordination: Rex Davidson.
Cover Design: Cathy Watterson.
Cover Photo: Stephen Park.
The illustration on the cover is a computer-generated
image of the magic square found on page 208 of
the text. The magic square appeared in an
engraving entitled "Melancholia" by the German
artist and mathematician Albrecht Dürer.

Library of Congress Catalog Card Number: 85–62655
International Standard Book Number: 0–675–20422–4
Printed in the United States of America
    4 5 6 7 8 9 — 91 90 89 88

CONTENTS

PART 1
TEACHING MATHEMATICS   1

1   Planning a Lesson   3
The Unit Plan   4
The Daily Lesson Plan   4
Types of Lesson Plans   7
More Developmental Lessons   12
Strategies for Discovering Generalizations   17
Individualized Lessons   21

2   Classroom Questioning   27
Ten Types of Questions to Avoid   28
Classroom Questioning Features to Develop   31

3   Techniques of Motivation   37
Motivating Students   38

4   Assigning Homework   45
Assigning Homework   46
Format of the Homework Assignment   52
Reviewing the Homework Assignment   53
Checking Homework Assignments   54

5   Constructing Tests   59
Constructing a Class Test   60
Administering a Test   66
Grading a Test   68
Interpreting Test Results   69
Multiple Choice Tests   70

6   Evaluating Student Performance   73
Student Responsibilities   74
Parental Responsibilities   74
Determining the Course Grade   75
Determining the Course Grade in Honors
    or Slow Classes   76
Other Grading Systems   77

**7   Professional Growth and Evaluating
Teacher Performance**   79
Professional Growth   80
Informal Evaluations   81
Formal Observations   82
Evaluation Towards Tenure   84
Formal Evaluation After Tenure   84

8   Remediation   91
Basic Mathematics Curriculum   92
Minimum Competency Tests   92
Who Needs Remediation?   92
Diagnostic Procedures   93

Methods of Remediation   94
Computer Assisted Instruction (CAI)   99
Physical Arrangements for Remedial
    Instruction   100
The Traditional Classroom   101
Individual Tutoring   102
Handicapped Students   102

9   Problem Solving   105
A Psychological View of Problem Solving   106
Problem Solving in Mathematics   107
Strategies for Solving Problems   111
Standard Algebraic Problems   114
Standard Geometric Problems   116
Non-Routine Problems   120
Creating Mathematical Problems   122
Creativity in Problem Solving   123

**10   Using Calculators and Computers in
the Classroom   127**
Calculators   128
Computers   130

**11   Enriching Mathematics
Instruction   139**
Enriching Mathematics Instruction with an Historic
    Approach   140
Enrichment Techniques for All Ability Levels   147
The Slow Learner   147
The Average-Ability Student   148
The Gifted Student   149

**12   Extracurricular Activities in
Mathematics   155**
The Mathematics Club   156
Mathematics Teams   156
Mathematics Contests   159
Mathematics Projects   159
The Mathematics Fair   159
Topics for Mathematics Projects   160
The School Mathematics Magazine   161
Mathematics Assembly Program   161
Guest Speakers Program   162
Class Trips of Mathematical Significance   162
Peer Teaching Program   163
The Computer   163
The Bulletin Board   163

13   Classroom Management   173
Classroom Practices   174
Discipline   176
Administrative Details   178

14   Preparing for a New Course   181
Long-Range Preparation   182
Short-Range Preparations   183
Selecting a Textbook   183

15   Using Performance Objectives   187
Performance Objectives   188
How to Write Performance Objectives   189
Using Performance Objectives   189

**16   Overcoming Mathematics
Anxiety   193**
Sources of Mathematics Anxiety   194
Strategies for Preventing Failure   194
Overcoming Mathematics Anxiety   195

**PART 2
ENRICHMENT UNITS FOR THE SECONDARY
SCHOOL CLASSROOM   199**

1   Constructing Odd Order Magic Squares   206
2   Constructing Even Order Magic Squares   208
3   Introduction to Alphametics   210
4   A Checkerboard Calculator   212
5   The Game of Nim   214
6   The Tower of Hanoi   216
7   What Day of the Week Was It?   218
8   Palindromic Numbers   223
9   The Fascinating Number Nine   224
10   Unusual Number Properties   226
11   Enrichment with a Hand-Held
        Calculator   228
12   Symmetric Multiplication   230
13   Variations on a Theme—Multiplication   232
14   Ancient Egyptian Arithmetic   234
15   Napier's Rods   236
16   Unit Pricing   237
17   Successive Discounts and Increases   238
18   Prime and Composite Factors of a Whole
        Number   240
19   Prime Numeration System   241
20   Repeating Decimal Expansions   243
21   Peculiarities of Perfect Repeating
        Decimals   245
22   Patterns in Mathematics   246
23   Googol and Googolplex   248
24   Mathematics of Life Insurance   250
25   Geometric Dissections   252
26   The Klein Bottle   254
27   The Four Color Map Problem   255
28   Mathematics on a Bicycle   257
29   Mathematics and Music   260
30   Mathematics in Nature   262
31   The Birthday Problem   264
32   The Structure of the Number System   265
33   Excursions in Number Bases   267
34   Raising Interest   269
35   Reflexive, Symmetric and Transitive
        Relations   271
36   Bypassing an Inaccessible Region   273

37 The Inaccessible Angle   274
38 Triangle Constructions   276
39 The Criterion of Constructibility   278
40 Constructing Radical Lengths   280
41 Constructing a Pentagon   281
42 Investigating the Isosceles Triangle Fallacy   282
43 The Equiangular Point   284
44 The Minimum Distance Point of a Triangle   285
45 The Isosceles Triangle Revisited   287
46 Reflective Properties of the Plane   289
47 Finding the Length of a Cevian of a Triangle   291
48 A Surprising Challenge   293
49 Making Discoveries in Mathematics   295
50 Tessellations   296
51 Introducing the Pythagorean Theorem   298
52 Trisection Revisited   300
53 Proving Lines Concurrent   302
54 Squares   304
55 Proving Points Collinear   305
56 Angle Measurement with a Circle   307
57 Trisecting a Circle   309
58 Ptolemy's Theorem   310
59 Constructing π 312
60 The Arbelos   314
61 The Nine-Point Circle   316
62 The Euler Line   317
63 The Simson Line   319
64 The Butterfly Problem   320
65 Equicircles   322
66 The Inscribed Circle and the Right Triangle   324
67 The Golden Rectangle   326
68 The Golden Triangle   328
69 Geometric Fallacies   330
70 Regular Polyhedra   332
71 An Introduction to Topology   334
72 Angles on a Clock   335
73 Averaging Rates—The Harmonic Mean   337
74 Howlers   339
75 Digit Problems Revisited   341
76 Algebraic Identities   342
77 A Method for Factoring Trinomials of the Form: $ax^2 + bx + c$ 344
78 Solving Quadratic Equations   345
79 The Euclidean Algorithm   347
80 Prime Numbers   349
81 Algebraic Fallacies   351
82 Sum Derivations with Arrays   353
83 Pythagorean Triples   355
84 Divisibility   357
85 Fibonacci Sequence   359
86 Diophantine Equations   361
87 Continued Fractions and Diophantine Equations   362
88 Simplifying Expressions Involving Infinity   364

89 Continued Fraction Expansions of Irrational Numbers   366
90 The Farey Sequence   368
91 The Parabolic Envelope   370
92 Application of Congruence to Divisibility   372
93 Problem Solving—A Reserve Strategy   374
94 Decimals and Fractions in Other Bases   377
95 Polygonal Numbers   378
96 Networks   381
97 Angle Trisection—Possible or Impossible?   383
98 Comparing Means   384
99 Pascal's Pyramid   386
100 The Multinomial Theorem   388
101 Algebraic Solution of Cubic Equations   390
102 Solving Cubic Equations   392
103 Calculating Sums of Finite Series   394
104 A General Formula for the Sum of a Series of the Form $\sum_{t=1}^{n} t^r$ 396
105 A Parabolic Calculator   399
106 Constructing Ellipses   401
107 Constructing the Parabola   403
108 Using Higher Plane Curves to Trisect an Angle   405
109 Constructing Hypocycloid and Epicycloid Circular Envelopes   407
110 The Harmonic Sequence   409
111 Transformations and Matrices   410
112 The Method of Differences   413
113 Probability Applied to Baseball   414
114 Introduction to Geometric Transformations   416
115 The Circle and the Cardioid   418
116 Complex Number Applications   421
117 Hindu Arithmetic   423
118 Proving Numbers Irrational   425
119 How to Use a Computer Spreadsheet to Generate Solutions to Certain Mathematics Problems   426

PREFACE

How to teach secondary school mathematics well is what this book is all about. It is specifically written for pre-service mathematics teachers, yet it is designed to be useful for in-service junior and senior high school teachers as well.

The fact is, there is no dearth of books on virtually every aspect of education. The education section may even be one of the largest in a college library. We believe this text offers an alternative to others available with respect to both style and coverage. The style is direct and to the point, with a minimum of theory and a maximum of practical information from experienced teachers.

The book was written in two parts. Part 1 is a clear guide to daily teaching. It is, in effect, a handbook on how to prepare lessons, motivate young people, design homework assignments, prepare tests, evaluate student performance, and organize a classroom. The role of routine and challenging verbal problems and the role of calculators and computers as well as extracurricular activities are also considered. In addition, thoughts on how a teacher's performance may be evaluated and some reflections on the problem of pupil anxiety in a mathematics classroom are offered.

Part 2 is a unique section containing a wealth of enrichment ideas designed to be used by both junior and senior high school mathematics classes. Each enrichment unit is self-contained and includes performance objectives, preassessments, motivation ideas, teaching strategies, and postassessments. A cross-reference table relating the enrichment units to the appropriate topic, grade level, and ability level is provided at the start of Part 2. This table will facilitate the selection of an enrichment activity appropriate for a particular class.

The introductions to Part 1 (page 1) and Part 2 (page 199) develop the presentation of the contents of each part in more detail. It is recommended that you read these introductions at this point so that you may more fully appreciate what the authors are striving to achieve.

In recent years the national shortage of mathematics teachers has been gradually worsening. More new mathematics teachers are entering the classrooms without the traditional preparation formerly provided. At the same time there seems to be a dual thrust in mathematics education aimed at improving the mathematical skills of secondary school students and enriching the instruction of all ability levels of these students. With this Second Edition we have recognized this new audience of mathematics teachers, while at the same time addressing these two current emphases of instruction. In Chapter 1 we added a section on strategies for discovering generalizations in mathematics, while Chapter 8, Remediation, was updated with a discussion of computer assisted instruction. Sections were also added on professional development and responsibilities of the inservice teacher and a topic of concern to many inservice teachers: selecting a textbook for their classes. Also helpful are the newly added reading lists provided at the ends of chapters. Chapter 16 was almost entirely rewritten to reflect current research.

The book may be used as a text for both undergraduate and graduate courses in the teaching of secondary school mathematics as well as for an inservice course on topics in mathematics for secondary school teachers. The inclusion of the enrichment units (Part 2) makes this a valuable source of special topics and ideas for enriching mathematics instruction. The book is thus designed to play an active role in the mathematics teacher's professional library for many years to come.

ACKNOWLEDGMENTS

A book of this scope requires input from a wide variety of professionals. Many secondary school teachers participated in the preparation of the enrichment units, a majority of which were originally published by Croft-NEI Publications (Waterford, Connecticut). We extend our sincere gratitude to these fine teachers: Renee E. Baxter, Peter Catranides, Beatrice F. Cohen, Steven Colello, Joyce A. Dato, James DeMetro, Benito Gomez, Adele Hayda, Cynthia Horvath, Howard Kale, Gladys Kornfield, Arlene Kuperberg, Susan Loeb, David Martinez, Robert Parisi, Patricia Pearson, Steven Pottash, Soraida Rivera, Amelia O. Roges, Howard Sardis, Verna Segarra, Max Sharf, Malcolm Singer, Joseph Skittone, Jon Sontz, Daniel Stolnitz, Richard A. Vitulli, Stanley Weinstein, Barbara Winters, and Betty York.

We appreciate the assistance of two educational psychologists: Professor Robert H. Ellis of the State University of New York, College at Fredonia, made contributions to Chapter 16, "Overcoming Mathematics Anxiety." Professor Alfred Weiss of the City College of the City University of New York contributed "A Psychological View of Problem Solving" in Chapter 9 as well as the section on "Creativity in Problem Solving," also in that chapter.

We also received some expert criticism and input for two specialized chapters. Gerald H. Elgarten, former Director of Mathematics at the New York City Board of Education, and now Assistant Professor of Mathematics Education at The City College of the City University of New York, made some valuable contributions on microcomputers in Chapter 10, "Using Calculators and Computers in the Classroom." Steven Conrad, a well-known problem-solving expert, a leader in national and local mathematics contests, and a mathematics teacher at Benjamin Cardozo High School (New York City), offered some valuable comments on Chapter 9, "Problem Solving." Both have our thanks for their assistance.

Special thanks are offered to Jacob Cohen, assistant principal in charge of mathematics at Theodore Roosevelt High School (New York City), for his careful reading of the entire manuscript and for the very insightful comments he offered throughout. In particular, his work on Chapter 5, "Constructing Tests," and contributions to Part 2 were greatly appreciated. Thanks are also extended to Peter Catranides, teacher of mathematics at George Washington High School (New York City), for drawing some of the more complex geometric figures in Part 2.

Many of the revisions in the Second Edition resulted from comments generously offered by Professor Miriam E. Connellan (Marquette University), Professor William M. Waters, Jr. (North Carolina State University), Professor Claire M. Newman (Queens College, CUNY), and Professor Max Sobel (Montclair State College). We are grateful to these mathematics education experts for reviewing the text and providing their insights.

In the preparation of a manuscript two important services are required, typing and proofreading. For these services we extend our sincere thanks to Norma Levy, Yolanda Lora, Noreen Posamentier, Lisa Posamentier, and Deborah Stepelman.

We are also grateful to our editor, Beverly Kolz, for providing valuable support services and generally allowing us to work in a pressure-free atmosphere.

PART 1 TEACHING MATHEMATICS

Part I offers "no-nonsense" suggestions covering the entire range of classroom related activities. We begin with one of the most essential skills in teaching: lesson planning. Following the rather detailed overview of the topic, the "nuts and bolts" of this skill are considered. Specifically, Chapters 2–5 discuss classroom questioning, motivation, assigning homework, and test construction in a very practical and easily adaptable manner. For example, the chapter on motivation describes (with lots of illustrative examples) eight techniques for motivating a lesson.

To function effectively in a school setting a teacher must not only be able to evaluate student performance, but also be aware of how his or her performance is evaluated. This is discussed in Chapters 6 and 7.

The first three "Recommendations for School Mathematics of the 1980s" set forth by the National Council of Teachers of Mathematics (*An Agenda for Action,* 1980) are that:

1. Problem solving be the focus of school mathematics in the 1980s.
2. Basic skill in mathematics be defined to encompass more than computational facility.
3. Mathematics programs take full advantage of the power of calculators and computers at all grade levels.

Each of these recommendations is thoroughly treated in a useable manner in Chapters 8–10 of the book. Of particular note is the chapter on problem solving, which contains implications for all levels of students and provides an extensive list of sources of non-routine mathematics problems.

By convention, enrichment and extracurricular activities are generally reserved for gifted students. We try to show in the next two chapters that this need not necessarily be the case. We discuss enrichment for the slow, average, and gifted students separately, with the hope that *all* students will eventually receive enriched instruction in mathematics. Extracurricular activities are often viewed as a burden by mathematics teachers. We address this problem by offering a wealth of ideas. Lots of activities are presented, including some useful notes for a mathematics team, and an extensive bibliography to assist in establishing extracurricular activities.

Chapters 13 and 14 presuppose an acquisition of the skills and concepts discussed in earlier chapters. They are intended to prepare and assist teachers in the organizational aspects of teaching. Chapter 15 is principally provided to buttress and sharpen the process of planning a lesson.

Chapter 16 is designed to make the teacher aware of possible causes of mathematics anxiety, so common among today's students. It offers some suggestions on how to deal with this problem and is specifically relegated to the end of this part of the book, so that it will remain clear in the reader's mind when he or she departs for the classroom.

Throughout Part 1 of the book samples of real, as well as ideal, teaching situations, strategies, lessons, tests, activities, and so on are offered in as practical and useful a manner as possible. This approach has frequently resulted in a diminution of explicit theoretical bases for many suggestions offered. This was done with the intention of not detracting from the usefulness of the book. End-of-chapter exercises are offered to allow readers to check their understanding of the skills and concepts discussed as well as provide an opportunity to expand their consideration of the topic.

CHAPTER 1 PLANNING A LESSON

A successful teacher instinctively possesses certain traits. He is capable of making simple and clear that which is complex and clouded. He enjoys what he is teaching and is an inspiration to those he is teaching. In addition, he should possess skills that may be acquired through training. For example, he should be capable of planning, organizing and presenting a formal lesson to a class of young people.

How does one acquire the skills to plan and organize a lesson? In this chapter we will show you some techniques for preparing several types of lessons. You will study a variety of actual lesson plans, some good, some not so good, taken from teachers' files. Through evaluation of these plans, you will gain insight into the thinking that goes into preparation, organization and execution of a lesson.

Can you imagine an actor without a script? A musician without a score? A speaker without an outline? A teacher without a lesson plan? These are anamolies indeed, for in every case it is as if the heart is removed from the soul. Because of the formal structure of our schools, every teacher is expected always to be well prepared, and entering one's classroom without a planned lesson is not tolerated. In fact, it may become grounds for severe warning, reprimand or dismissal if the pattern becomes a regular one. The teacher who walks into a classroom and begins a lesson with "Where did we end yesterday?" or who begins a lesson by taking out the text and merely reading from it to the class, or who teaches "off the cuff" from memory, performs a gross disservice to the young people in his charge. Such actions show that the teacher has a lack of concern, perhaps even disdain for them, that might easily be construed as unprofessional conduct.

THE UNIT PLAN

While it is most desirable that daily lesson plans be prepared on a day-to-day basis, they can be prepared as much as a week in advance. Of course, the probability of any individual lesson following the script exactly as written is small, so that when long range plans are written, adjustments must be made on a daily basis. Teachers should not be reluctant to make modifications just because it is easier to leave the original plan as written.

No meaningful daily lesson can be prepared in a vacuum, for the whole unit of work is the sum of its specific lessons. Each lesson plan should be prepared with the intent of meeting unit goals. Suppose that you are teaching a unit on ''Radicals'' in the first year algebra course. After reading the course of study and the appropriate material in texts, and after seeking guidance from experienced colleagues, you must decide on a sequence of logically arranged lessons that will cover all relevant topics. A review lesson and time for an examination should be included. Following is an example of such a unit:

UNIT: RADICALS

1. Powers and roots; square-root table
2. Pythagorean theorem; quadratic equations of the form $x^2 = 9$ and $x^2 = 3$
3. Square root algorithm
4. Simplifying radicals
5. Adding and subtracting radicals
6. Multiplying radicals
7. Dividing radicals
8. Rationalizing denominator
9. Radical equations
10. Review
11. Test

THE DAILY LESSON PLAN

You should plan in advance, in writing, every detail of your classroom activities. The amount of written detail versus the detail kept in the memory of the teacher will vary with the teacher and the number of years of experience as well as the number of times the particular course has been taught. But in any event you must know what you are going to do and what you expect to have your pupils do throughout the period. You must think through the statements you are going to make, the questions you will ask, and the answers you expect to get. You should try to anticipate incorrect answers so that you may prevent a lesson from going astray. An unexpected wrong answer or a sudden question by a slow learner, both of which might require extensive explanation by the teacher, can easily upset a lesson for the entire class. The beginner, in particular, should include the wording of his statements and questions in the written lesson plan, for it is so easy to forget the exact phraseology when you face a class.

A lesson may not turn out as planned for reasons you could not foresee. When this happens once in a while, there is no harm done. It merely supports the contention that every lesson must be carefully thought through.

Just as a successful performer spends lots of time rehearsing a performance, a teacher needs to rehearse a lesson. But the practical way for a teacher to rehearse is ''mentally.'' You can best achieve this by planning your ''performance'' (lesson) on paper. Writing a good lesson plan will force you to go through a detailed ''mental dry run'' of the lesson. This activity not only allows you to crystallize your thoughts but also to anticipate possible pitfalls in the actual lesson.

Lessons should be written in a ''plan book'' so you will have an organized daily record of the work your classes have done every day of the term. This book can be used as a guide for you in the future, or as a record for your supervisors, or the parents, and as an aid to a substitute. Yet it is advisable to write new plans each time a course is taught. This will not only allow you to tailor each lesson to the specific class being taught, but it should go far in keeping your mind continuously stimulated.

The script that an actor uses follows a certain format, with appropriate variations which are determined by the nature of the performance itself, whether comedy, tragedy, musical, and so on. Similarly, the teacher's lesson plan follows a certain basic format. These plans will also vary somewhat, depending on the nature of the lesson being planned.

Following is the basic format of a lesson plan. Not all parts of this suggested arrangement need be included in every lesson. Following the chart are details and explanations of specific items found in this suggested format.

Topic

By stating the topic at the beginning of each lesson plan your focus becomes clear when you are planning the lesson as well as when you are simply filing it or looking for it.

Apperceptive Basis

This section calls for a listing of the previously learned material which is required for the present lesson and for which the students are responsible. Although the experienced teacher may frequently omit this section, it is useful for the starting teacher.

A SUGGESTED FORM FOR A LESSON PLAN

Class: _____   Date: _____

TOPIC:

APPERCEPTIVE BASIS (Previously learned knowledge):

AIM:

MOTIVATION:

DO-NOW EXERCISE:

DEVELOPMENT AND METHODS:

DRILL:

MEDIAL SUMMARY:

APPLICATIONS AND DRILL:

FINAL SUMMARY AND CONCLUSION:

HOMEWORK ASSIGNMENT:

SPECIAL EQUIPMENT NEEDED:

IF TIME:

Aim of the Lesson

1. Should be stated succinctly and written near the top of the lesson plan.
2. Should be made clear to the class early in the period, preferably elicited from the students as a result of a "need" you have demonstrated for topic (see Chapter 3, "Motivating Students").
3. May be written on the board, depending on teacher preference, school requirement or the particular lesson.

Motivation

This portion of the lesson channels student interest toward the topic to be learned. A common medium to achieve this is the do-now exercise. Further discussion of techniques of motivation is left to Chapter 3.

Do-Now Exercise

1. Is a class exercise, written in the same section of the board every day. It helps pupils settle down at the beginning of the period. It does indeed set the tone for the lesson and is therefore a most important part of the lesson.
2. Might serve the purpose of reviewing and reinforcing a previously learned topic, motivating the lesson, helping to develop a new topic or assessing the class' achievement.
3. Might also serve as a managerial device, allowing the teacher the time needed to perform the multitude of "little" chores needed to be done at the beginning (open or shut windows, clean boards, take attendance, return test papers, have students write homework solutions on the board, etc.). It could take five minutes, or ten or only three.
4. Could consist of examples made up by the teacher, or taken from the text, or it could be a brief selection to be read silently or aloud or a quiz to be collected and graded.
5. Should usually be discussed upon its completion, before the class moves on to the next phase of the lesson. Yet, occasionally its review could become part of the lesson.
6. May be omitted when the lesson does not require it. Beginning teachers, however, are best advised to use the do-now exercise regularly to achieve a smoother transition into the lesson than they might otherwise get. More experienced teachers may have developed techniques that don't rely so heavily on the do-now exercise.

Development and Methods

This is the heart of the lesson. The ability to develop and implant a new idea in students' minds distinguishes the teacher-skilled craftsman from the teacher-unskilled laborer. Just as in formal painting classes one can learn techniques and styles of painting, so in education courses one can learn techniques and styles of teaching. In neither course will you learn to be an "artist," for it is only after the training in these courses that your talent takes over. Thus, your first two or three years as a teacher are critical ones in your development. The hours you spend planning a lesson, the thinking you do about creating ways to introduce new topics, the reading you do to broaden your mathematics background, the enjoyment you derive from working with teenagers—all these will enrich you in the years ahead to make you the kind of teacher you want to be. Your attitude towards your teaching will set the tone for your performances and their results.

1. Major questions and statements should be recorded. These should be written in the order they will be asked, at the appropriate points in the lesson plan. You may refer to the plan book on your desk, or hold it with you, if you wish, as you walk about the room. (While holding the plan with you may indicate some insecurity on your part, if you, as a new teacher, feel that it will provide you with some confidence during a particularly difficult development that you want to do "just right," you should not hesitate to do so.)
2. Boardwork should be planned so there will be no crowding and ample room to write all elements of the lesson. The teacher ought to know such details as where the do-now will be written, where the development will take place, where the previous day's homework will be written, whether solutions to certain algebraic problems should be arranged horizontally or vertically, and finally, which drill exercises students will be asked to write on the board.

   The boardwork serves as a model for students. If you are neat, write legibly, are well organized and use a straightedge and compasses for diagrams, the chances are they will, too. This is an opportunity to help develop work habits that will benefit them (as well as you, when you mark their test papers) for the remainder of their lives.

Drill

The drill work, coming after the developmental portion of the lesson, is where theory yields to practice. The lesson is "clinched" at this point. Model solutions are demonstrated by the teacher and are followed by having students work on their own. At this point in the lesson, drill may be provided which involves *only* the newly developed concept or topic, not yet integrated with other previously learned material.

Medial Summary

This is a rather brief summary of the key points of the topic developed earlier. Among the many functions this medial summary can serve is allowing a student who is not quite clear about the aim of the lesson, or the nature of what was developed and its significance, or who may have simply daydreamed for some key moments at the early part of the lesson and is now lost, to catch up with the rest of the class and benefit from the remainder of the lesson.

Applications and More Drill

Now that everyone, hopefully, is caught up to the appropriate part of the lesson, and everyone has had an opportunity to practice using the new concept or topic in very simple drill exercises, this section provides for applications and drill which integrates the new concept or topic with other previously learned concepts or topics. These applications or drill exercises will be more complicated and more embedded in other topics than the first set of drill exercises. Naturally, the specific nature of the topic under consideration will determine the type of problems included in this or the other drill section; sometimes there may be little difference between the two sections.

Final Summary and Conclusion

The final summary is a brief review of the highlights of the lesson. Here the teacher should tie together all the parts of the lesson. This summary, as is the case with prior summaries as well, may likely be in the form of pointed questions from which students will provide the summary of the lesson, or simply statements of the summary, or combinations of both. Sometimes a simple question to the class such as "Suppose your classmate was absent and called you on the phone to ask what today's lesson was about; what would you tell him about the lesson so that he would get a clear idea of the topic he missed?" will elicit a summary.

Homework Assignment

Chapter 4 is devoted entirely to the nature of homework assignments. Since most mathematics lessons require some follow-up homework, it is necessary to include the assignment in each lesson plan. Any remarks you wish to make about any particular part of the assignment should be noted here.

Special Equipment to be Used

Special equipment to be used may be listed. These include items such as board compasses, graph chart, geometric models, overhead projector, etc. This list serves the purpose of reminding you what you must order from the supply room before the lesson. The special equipment to be used need not always be listed as part of the teacher's actual lesson plan. It might be listed, however, if one desires to present to an outside observer a complete picture of the lesson planned.

If Time

Every lesson plan should end with an "if time" section, which may include either additional drill exercises, or enrichment, or any other useful time filler. Also, you should plan to cover more than can be done in one period rather than find yourself with everything done several minutes before the bell is to ring. Those moments can be horribly long and uncomfortable!

TYPES OF LESSON PLANS

The most common types of daily lessons used by teachers in high school mathematics classes are described as "developmental," "lecture," "drill," "review," "mathematics-through-reading," and "individualized." The term "guided discovery" is also sometimes used in connection with "developmental" or "individualized" lessons. The names of the lesson types describe their purpose, and they will be discussed in the remainder of this chapter.

The Developmental Lesson

The *developmental lesson* technique may be used when you want to develop a new topic. It is probably the most difficult lesson of all the lesson types to present well, for it requires planning and a series of questions through which the new concepts are developed. It usually requires the longest preparation time, achieves the best results when done properly, and offers the greatest personal satisfaction to the teacher when it is completed. New teachers as well as experienced ones are capable of presenting this type of lesson well.

Following are two model developmental lesson plans for use with a high school geometry course. These plans demonstrate two types of strategies to direct the class towards discovering conclusions. Other strategies are, of course, possible.

Model Lesson Plan 1, pages 8–10, illustrates how a set of carefully worded, sequentially written questions can guide pupils to discover a proof of the Pythagorean Theorem.

Model Lesson Plan 2, pages 10–11, shows how, through a series of strategically placed (mostly oral) questions, all major properties of a parallelogram can be elicited and proved. Using the suggested technique of listing students' ideas, this lesson plan affords the opportunity to try to *prove* things that are, in fact, false and has the students discover where the proof breaks down and why, therefore, the propositions are false.

Model Lesson Plan 1   *Comments*

TOPIC: The first lesson on the Pythagorean Theorem

For the high school geometry course.

APPERCEPTIVE BASIS: Similarity, mean proportional theorems for the right triangle.

These are the primary topics which the students need to know to be able to handle this topic.

AIM: To introduce, prove and apply the Pythagorean Theorem.

DO-NOW EXERCISE:
In the figure below, $\overline{CD}$ is an altitude of right $\triangle ABC$ with right angle at C. The lengths of the segments are marked. Referring to the figure, complete each of the following:

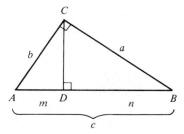

This set of exercises will be distributed on spirit duplicator sheets.

1. AC is the mean proportional between __(AB)__ and __(AD)__.

2. Therefore $\dfrac{c}{(b)} = \dfrac{b}{(m)}$, or $b^2 =$ __(cm)__. Why?

3. __(BC)__ is the mean proportional between AB and BD.

4. Therefore $\dfrac{(c)}{a} = \dfrac{(a)}{n}$; or $a^2 =$ __(cn)__. Why?

5. Adding the results of Exercises 2 and 4, we get $a^2 + b^2 =$ __(cm)__ $+$ __(cn)__ $=$ __(c)__ $(m + n)$.

6. But $m + n =$ __(c)__.

7. Therefore $a^2 +$ __(b²)__ $=$ __(c²)__.

N.B. Circles indicate correct answers, which are obviously not included on actual answer sheets.

Notice also that these exercises review the mean proportional theorems while at the same time permit the student actually to prove the Pythagorean Theorem. Although students may not realize this at first, they will be lead to see this during the development of the lesson.

DEVELOPMENT AND METHODS:

1. Ask the class (make up a story) if they can get a 10 ft. diameter circular table top through a door which is only 8 ft. high and 6 ft. wide.

Do not rush through your story in an effort to get to the "meat" of the lesson. This will diminish the effectiveness of this approach.

2. Use the prepared overhead transparency to review to do-now exercise with the class.

This previously prepared transparency should be just like the copy of the do-now exercise given to the class.

3. Indicate to the class the significance of the do-now exercise. That is, *they* have just *proved* the Pythagorean Theorem.

This must be carefully presented so as to reap the full impact intended from these exercises.

4. Ask the class what Euclid and President James A. Garfield had in common. Now give the class some historical notes about the Pythagorean Theorem (such as the Egyptian "rope stretchers," the 360+ proofs, and so on).

Both proved the Pythagorean Theorem.

This brief discussion should generate some extra interest for this topic.

5. Discuss an application of the Pythagorean Theorem with the class (see Item 1 above).

Visual aids would be quite helpful here.

6. Find the length of the hypotenuse of the right triangle shown below:

This is a very simple application and should be done together with the class.

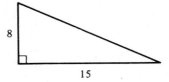

DRILL: Find x in each of the following (send students to chalkboard):

These are simple exercises which only apply the Pythagorean Theorem and require no other prior knowledge.

1.

2.

3.

Students will be asked to place their correct solutions on the chalkboard. These correct solutions will be detected by the teacher during his walk throughout the classroom while the students are working on these exercises.

MEDIAL SUMMARY (ask the following questions):
1. State the Pythagorean Theorem.
2. For what can we use the Pythagorean Theorem?
3. Can the Pythagorean Theorem be applied to any triangle where the lengths of two sides are given?

These questions should elicit the key points of the previous part of the lesson and thus serve as a summary to this point in the lesson.

APPLICATIONS AND DRILL:
Find x in each of the following (send students to the chalkboard when assigning the problems to the class):

Students should be assigned to do their work on the chalkboard immediately, rather than first to work the problems at their seats and then just to copy them over onto the board. The class can learn from classmate errors as well as from correct solutions.

1.

2.

3.

4. *Given*: $\overline{PS}$ is an altitude of $\triangle PQR$
   Prove: $PQ^2 - RP^2 = QS^2 - SR^2$

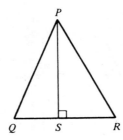

Comments

FINAL SUMMARY (ask the following questions):
1. State in words the Pythagorean Theorem.
2. How can the Pythagorean Theorem help us find the length of a diagonal of a rectangle when we are given the length of the sides of the rectangle?
3. What would you guess to be true about a triangle whose sides have lengths 3,4, and 5?
4. State the converse of the Pythagorean Theorem.
5. Is it true?

HOMEWORK ASSIGNMENT:
1. Four exercises similar to those in the application and drill section of the lesson plan.
2. One proof involving the Pythagorean Theorem.
3. One exercise using the mean proportional theorems.
4. One exercise on similar triangles.

IF TIME (discuss the following problem with the class):
In the figure, $\overline{PC} \perp \overline{BD}$ at C and $\overline{PB} \perp \overline{AB}$. $AP = 17$, $AB = 8$, $BC = 9$, and $CD = 3\frac{1}{2}$. Find PD. $\left(12\frac{1}{2}\right)$

EQUIPMENT NEEDED:
Spirit duplicator copies of the Do-Now Exercises as well as a transparency of them, an overhead projector, colored chalk, and ruler (or some sort of chalkboard straightedge).

This summary is intended to review the topic of this lesson, and allow students to show that they really understand what it is and how it can be used.

Questions 3–5 foreshadow the next lesson on the converse of Pythagorean Theorem.

This homework assignment is a spiralled assignment which reviews previously learned material as well as the newly presented topic. (See Chapter 4 on homework assignments.)

This problem involves numerous applications of the Pythagorean Theorem. It is a departure from the previously simpler applications.

Let us now consider a second model lesson plan. Notice the style is somewhat different. Remember there is no one "perfect lesson plan." Each plan must conform to the personality and needs of the teacher using it.

Model Lesson Plan 2

TOPIC: Introductory lesson on properties of the parallelogram.

AIM: (a) To learn and prove the properties of a parallelogram;
     (b) To do simple algebraic applications of these properties.

PREVIOUSLY LEARNED: (a) Properties of angles formed when parallel lines are cut by a transversal;
                    (b) Methods of proving triangles congruent;
                    (c) Definitions of quadrilateral and diagonal.

DO-NOW:

GIVEN: Quadrilateral $ABCD$
$\overleftrightarrow{AB} \parallel \overleftrightarrow{CD}$; $\overleftrightarrow{AD} \parallel \overleftrightarrow{BC}$

QUESTION: What relationship exists between $\angle A$ and $\angle B$? Why?

DEVELOPMENT AND METHODS:

(Students are not to write in their notebooks until told to do so by the teacher. All proofs of theorems that are elicited from the class will be done orally. Record all responses in tabular form as shown at the end of the plan.)

1. Define "parallelogram." (Head the table "In a parallelogram:" and elicit the aim of the lesson.)
2. Discuss the do-now. (Elicit: "Consecutive angles are supplementary," and prove.)
3. Question: What must be true about $\angle A$ and $\angle C$? Why? (Elicit and prove: "Opposite angles are congruent.")
4. Draw $\overline{BD}$
5. Question: What new things can you see in the diagram as a result of having drawn $\overline{BD}$? (Elicit and prove: "Two congruent triangles are formed, and opposite sides are congruent.")
6. Erase $\overline{BD}$; Draw $\overline{AC}$.
7. Question: Does drawing $\overline{AC}$ yield anything new that we can prove?
8. Medial Summary: Have students read and explain the list developed so far and copy it into their notebooks.

DRILL:

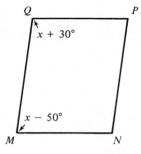

ABCD is a parallelogram.
Find *x*. (Reason?)

PQRS is a parallelogram.
Find *x*. (Reason?)

Parallelogram *MNPQ*.
Find m $\angle P$.

DEVELOPMENT (continued):

9. Draw both diagonals;
10. Question: State and prove a conclusion you might reach about the two diagonals that appear together in the diagram. (Answer: "Diagonals bisect each other.")

DRILL:

ABCD is a parallelogram
Find *DE*.

SUMMARY: Erase the table from the board and ask, "List in your own words the properties of a parallelogram that we discussed earlier."

HOMEWORK: (a) Six examples in textbook, similar to drill that was done in class;
           (b) Several other examples from a previous topic.

IF TIME: As many examples as time permits on the same topic. (Specific examples should be listed here.)

Table (on side of front board:)

	IN A PARALLELOGRAM:
(Definition)	1. Opposite sides are parallel.
(Theorem)	2. Consecutive angles are supplementary.
(Theorem)	3. Opposite angles are congruent.
(Theorem)	4. Diagonal divides it into two congruent triangles.
(Theorem)	5. Opposite sides are congruent.

(Theorem)	6. Diagonals bisect each other.

MORE DEVELOPMENTAL LESSONS

The five developmental plans that follow are from actual lessons taken from various teachers' records. They were created by teachers for the purpose of using them in their own classes, rather than to serve as the models that are often the only ones discussed in teacher training courses. Among the minor adjustments made for printing purposes are:

1. The versions you will see may be more neatly arranged than the teachers' written plans. (In the haste of lesson preparation, and in the course of developing a lesson, deletions and insertions may tend to make the handwritten plan a bit sloppy.)
2. Whenever the writer of the lesson referred to specific examples in a text, the examples and page numbers listed in the illustrations are fictitious; they are listed for illustrative purposes only.
3. A "comments" column appears on the right side of each plan. These are *our* comments on the plans being exhibited.

If you study, analyze, discuss and comment on these lessons, you can learn what is right from the strong ones as well as what is wrong from the weak ones.

Sample 1.   (A detailed plan for an elementary algebra lesson)

Comments

AIM: To recognize quadratic equations and learn how to solve them by factoring.

DO-NOW: When a number is multiplied by 3 more than itself, the result is 0. Find the number.

$$x = \text{the number}$$
$$x + 3 = 3 \text{ more than the number}$$
$$x(x + 3) = 0$$

These are the answers the teacher expects to elicit when reviewing the do-now.

Let's stop for a moment and see if we can discover something which will help us solve this equation. Everybody, think of two numbers whose product is 0. (Write answers on board.)
What do you notice about each pair of numbers?
Who can say in words what we just noticed? (Write on board: If $ab = 0$, then $a = 0$ or $b = 0$.)
Now, let's use this fact to solve our equation:

These are the major questions and comments, written in the same order they were asked by the teacher.

x	$(x + 3)$
$x = 0$	$x + 3 = 0$
	$x = -3$

How would you use this same fact to solve: $x(x + 4) = 0$?
How would you solve $x^2 + 4x = 0$? (Elicit "factoring.")
What about this one: $x^2 + 5x + 6 = 0$?
How would you solve this: $x^2 - 4 = 0$?

This question was not asked because the teacher saw that the lesson was running too long and wanted to begin to cut out some parts of the prepared lesson.

Looking back at the equations we've just solved, who can tell us the steps we used? (Elicit the following.)
(Write on board)

1. Factor.
2. Set each factor $= 0$.
3. Solve each linear equation.
   Now use these steps to solve the following:
   (a) $x^2 + 5x = 0$ (b) $x^2 + 6x + 8 = 0$ (c) $x^2 - 16 = 0$
   (Go over solutions.)

Developing steps used in solving a quadratic serves as a medial summary.

Example (c) was cut out of the class presentation to save time.

How are these equations different from the ones you've learned to solve before today? ("degree 2," "two answers," etc.)

A pivotal question comparing students' new knowledge with previous knowledge.

These equations are called QUADRATIC EQUATIONS.

Which of the following are quadratic equations?
(a) $x^2 + 7x + 12 = 0$ (b) $x^2 - 2x = 0$ (c) $x^2 = 2x$ (d) $x^2 + 7x = -12$ (e) $x + 3 = 0$

The teacher wrote on the board the aim of the lesson: How to Solve Quadratic Equations.

Compare (a) and (d); (b) and (c).

Who can summarize for us how we go about solving quadratic equations? (*Note*: Extra step of gathering all terms on one side in descending powers.)

HOMEWORK: Study pages 157 and 158.

　　　　　　　Do examples 3, 5, 7, 11, 13, 17, 19.

Comments

Students were asked to read the text explanation of the same topic and to do practice examples.
NOTE 1: The homework assignment was not spiral;
NOTE 2: Although the assignment was written last in the plan, it was written on the board FIRST by the teacher. At the end of the period, the teacher changed the assignment by eliminating the types of examples that were not discussed.

Go over homework today. Page 140/ 2, 3, 4, 6.

This was not done in class because of insufficient time.

IF TIME: Solve each quadratic equation:

　　　　(a) $x^2 + 8x + 15 = 0$　　(b) $x^2 - 64 = 0$　　(c) $a^2 = 7a$　　(d) $B^2 + 6B = -8$

This also was not done in class.

Boardwork (front):

PANEL I	PANEL II	PANEL III
DN	(1) If $ab = 0$, $a = 0$ or $b = 0$	Solve: $x^2 + 5x = 0$
$x(x + 3) = 0$	(2) Steps to solve (quadratics)	$x^2 + 6x + 8 = 0$
$x(x + 4) = 0$	a) Collect terms on one side.	$x^2 - 16 = 0$
$x^2 + 4x = 0$	Set = 0.	Which are quadratics?
$x^2 + 5x + 6 = 0$	b) Factor	$x^2 + 7x + 12 = 0$
$x^2 - 4 = 0$	c) Set each factor = 0	$x^2 - 2x = 0$
	d) Solve linear equations	$x^2 = 2x$
	(3) Facts about equations:	$x^2 + 7x = -12$
	a) degree 2	$x + 3 = 0$
	b) two answers	

The classroom has three front board panels, and the teacher planned where he wanted everything to be written.

　　　　　　Note: Homework on side boards.

Sample 2.　(A detailed plan for a remedial mathematics class)

Comments

TOPIC: Addition of simple arithmetic fractions.

APPERCEPTIVE BASIS:

1. Students are familiar with the basic concepts of fractions.
2. Students have studied multiplication and simplification of simple fractions.

This refers to previously learned material relevant to this lesson. It is usually one of those details kept in back of the teacher's mind rather than recorded in the plan.

DO-NOW:

Use this diagram:

How many parts are shaded? (4)
Not shaded? (8)
What are the total number of parts? (12)

The expected answers are circled.

Write the following fractions:

$\dfrac{\text{shaded}}{\text{total}} = \left(\dfrac{4}{12}\right)$

$\dfrac{\text{not shaded}}{\text{total}} = \left(\dfrac{8}{12}\right)$

Reduce each fraction to lowest terms:

$\dfrac{4}{12} = \left(\dfrac{1}{3}\right)$

$\dfrac{8}{12} = \left(\dfrac{2}{3}\right)$

Review procedure for simplifying fractions:

$$\frac{4}{12} = \frac{\cancel{2} \times \cancel{2}}{\cancel{2} \times \cancel{2} \times 3} = \frac{1}{3}$$

$$\frac{8}{12} = \frac{\cancel{2} \times \cancel{2} \times 2}{\cancel{2} \times \cancel{2} \times 3} = \frac{2}{3}$$

CHALLENGE: What must $\frac{4}{12} + \frac{8}{12} = ?$ Why?

Use diagram to illustrate answer.

What must $\frac{1}{3} + \frac{2}{3} = ?$ Why?

Look at next diagram:

Name the fraction in each diagram:

What topic will we learn today?

Write: *Addition of Fractions* on board

The aim of the lesson is elicited here. It was written on the board well into the lesson.

CHALLENGE:

(1).   (2).

Name the fraction in each diagram.

$\left(\frac{3}{9}\right)$ and $\left(\frac{1}{9}\right)$

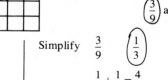

Simplify $\frac{3}{9}$ $\left(\frac{1}{3}\right)$

$\frac{1}{3} + \frac{1}{9} = \frac{4}{9}$

$\frac{3}{9} + \frac{1}{9} = ?$ $\left(\frac{4}{9}\right)$

Look at the two examples:

$$\frac{1}{4} + \frac{1}{2} = \frac{3}{4} \Longleftrightarrow \frac{1}{4} + \frac{2}{4} = \frac{3}{4}$$

$$\frac{1}{3} + \frac{1}{9} = \frac{4}{9} \Longleftrightarrow \frac{3}{9} + \frac{1}{9} = \frac{4}{9}$$

What must be true about the denominators of fractions when we add? $\boxed{Same}$

PRACTICE:

$\frac{3}{5} + \frac{1}{10}$ Are the denominators the same or different?

Name the common denominator. ⑩

The teacher demonstrated the addition in a vertical as well as horizontal arrangement.

$\frac{3}{5} = \frac{6}{10}$ Why? $\boxed{\frac{3 \times 2}{5 \times 2} = \frac{6}{10}}$

$\frac{6}{10} + \frac{1}{10} = \frac{7}{10}$

MORE PRACTICE: $\frac{4}{7} + \frac{1}{21} = ?$

CHALLENGE QUESTIONS:

$\frac{3}{5} + \frac{2}{3}$ What is the common denominator?

$\frac{1}{2} + \frac{2}{3} + \frac{5}{6}$

$\frac{2}{5} + \frac{1}{2} + \frac{2}{3}$

Comments

*These are really ''if time''
questions, and in fact only the
first was done.*

FINAL SUMMARY: What have we learned today?

HOMEWORK: Page 157: ex. 2, 3, 5, 7, 9, 11, 12, 13, 15, 18.

Sample 3. (This plan is considerably less detailed than the previous ones. It was written by a teacher of experience having confidence in his ability to think on his feet while in front of a class. It was a successful lesson in a slow geometry class.)

Comments

HOMEWORK: p. 212/ 2, 4, 7; p. 208/ 8, 11

DO-NOW:

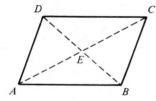

Rhombus *ABCD*

AC = 10

BD = 8

(1) What kind of angle is *AEB*? Why?

(2) Find area of △ *AEB*

(3) Find area of entire rhombus.

*The aim of the lesson was to
derive the formula for the
area of a rhombus in terms of
its diagonals.*

Then: Let *AC* = *x*, *BD* = *y*

Show Area = $\frac{1}{2}xy$

DRILL: p. 212/ 3, 5, 6

*The do-now leads into the
new work. This is the
development.*

*The teacher demonstrated the
first example on the board.
The remaining two were done
by students themselves at
their seats and reviewed by
the teacher.*

Review homework.

*Examples were assigned to be
written on the board while
class was working on the
do-now.*

''If time'' is missing.

Sample 4. (This was written by a competent geometry teacher of several years experience. Only highlights of the lesson were included in her plans, such as the precise wording of several theorems that were to be used, some diagrams and proportions. Also, specific examples and pages in the text to which pupils referred during the lesson were listed.)

Comments

Return test.

*The test had been reviewed
previously.*

Recall theorem about line parallel to one side of triangle.

*Students are reminded of
previously learned relevant
material.*

Theorem: If a line parallel to one side of a triangle intersects the other two sides, then it cuts off segments proportional to those sides.

*This is the theorem that was
recalled.*

Theorem: If a line intersects two sides of a triangle and cuts off segments proportional to those two sides, it is parallel to the third side.

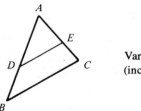

Various proportions
(include addition)

Page 192/ ex. 13, 14

Theorem: The bisector of an angle of a triangle separates the opposite side into segments whose lengths are proportional to the lengths of the adjacent sides.

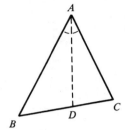

$$\frac{BD}{DC} = \frac{BA}{CA}$$

Page 193: ex. 1, 3, 4

IF TIME: Page 192: ex. 17, 18

HOMEWORK: Page 192: ex. 11, 12, 15, 16
                        Page 193: ex. 5, 6

Comments

The converse of the theorem above was discussed and explained but there is no indication in the plan how this was done.

"Addition" refers to
$\frac{AD}{DB} = \frac{AE}{EC}$ *and implies that*

$$\frac{AD + DB}{DB} = \frac{AE + EC}{EC}$$

Two algebraic applications.

The teacher knew the proof well and did not find it necessary to write it out in the plan.

Three drill examples, algebraic and geometric.

Sample 5. (This is a poorly written second year algebra lesson plan. There seems to have been some thought put into its preparation, but planning was nevertheless poor and constant referral to textbook pages and examples make this plan awkward to follow while teaching.)

Comments

Page 138/ ex. 17, 18.

This is a "warm-up" exercise consisting of 2 fractions that use the principle $\frac{a - b}{b - a} = -1$ in their simplification.

Check homework.

Teacher walked around during the "warm-up" to check if students did the homework.

Any questions?

The teacher asked for homework questions the students wanted to have explained, which he then proceeded to do.

Do this: $\dfrac{2}{3} \div \dfrac{3}{4}$; $\dfrac{3}{4} \div \dfrac{2}{3}$

Another sign to indicate division.

Take LCD of denominators:

$$\frac{\cancel{12}^{4} \cdot \dfrac{2}{3}}{\cancel{12}^{3} \cdot \dfrac{3}{4}} = \frac{8}{9}$$

$$\frac{\cancel{12}^{3} \cdot \dfrac{3}{4}}{\cancel{12}^{4} \cdot \dfrac{2}{3}} = \frac{9}{8}$$

Page 157: explain ex. 4.

Do ex. 3, 5, 9, 11, 12.
Explain ex. 10.
Do ex. 13, 15, 16, 17.

IF TIME: p. 103, explain equations.
Solve by LCD method.
Do ex. 2, 3, 4.

HOMEWORK: page 157: 6, 7, 8, 20
page 103: 5, 6, 7

Comments

This is the beginning of the new topic, but less than fifteen minutes remained in the period.

The teacher asked, ''What is another way to indicate division?''

Students are told what will work if they are to simplify complex fractions. No development is indicated.

The teacher demonstrated simplification of an algebraic complex fraction.

Sufficient drill is provided in the plan but there was barely enough time to do more than three examples.

Even though this was not done, it is better to overplan than to underplan. This lesson, however, was much too overplanned for a forty-minute period.

The homework assignment required readjustment as a result of not having done all the topics that were planned.

STRATEGIES FOR DISCOVERING GENERALIZATIONS

Devising strategies for discovering generalizations are a challenge for the teacher. For example, you might ask a class to work out several numerical problems involving rate, time, and distance before the class will conclude that rate $\times$ time = distance. You may have pupils toss coins before they will conclude that there is a relationship between the coefficients of the terms of a binomial expansion and probability theory.

Comparing tables of values, studying graphs, using protractors and compasses, using calculators, as well as using your own imagination are all suitable tools for discovering generalizations. Here are two different strategies.

Illustration 1. Use your protractor to measure each angle in each diagram. What conclusions do you reach?

After appropriate class discussions, the following generalizations should come forward:

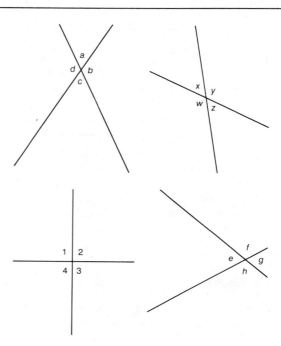

1. Vertical angles are congruent.
2. The sum of the measures of the angles about a point (in a plane) is 360°.
3. The sum of the measures of the angles about a point on one side of a straight line (in a half-plane) is 180°.

In junior high school, these generalizations need not be proven.

Illustration 2. To elicit properties of an indirect proof.

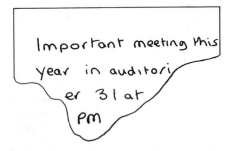

This notice was sent home to your parents near the beginning of the school year. It got torn in the mail. Which month is the meeting?

1. List the months ending in -er and the last day of each:

   September   30 days
   October   31 days
   November   30 days
   December   New Year's eve

2. Eliminate all but one.
3. Therefore, the meeting is in October.

In each case, you must supplement your questions with diagrams, activities, historical embellishments, clarifications, and so forth, and these should all appear in your plans. Depending upon the level and type of class, these generalizations sometimes must be proved after they are "discovered," whereas other times the mere discovery itself will suffice.

Yet, in spite of your best efforts in planning a good lesson, the words of the Scottish poet Robert Burns ring loud and clear, "the best laid plans of mice and men 'gang aft agley.'" Even after a defeat, and you will have them, your plans must be studied and analyzed so you will not repeat past mistakes.

The Lecture

The lecture technique is most suited to a mature audience, one which has a reasonably long attention span.

College students, as well as those in the more advanced high school mathematics classes, are most often exposed to this type of lesson.

While active pupil involvement is sought in a developmental lesson, pupils who rarely interrupt the lesson are the "ideal" participants in a lecture. In fact, the active student in a lecture situation, who constantly questions and probes, is often viewed by both lecturer and fellow students as an irritant who delays the lecture and prevents the teacher from delivering his planned lesson fully.

The lecture approach is probably the most efficient one when a complex body of material requiring pupil thought and concentration is to be presented. For example, the epsilon-delta method of finding limits, the "fundamental theorem of integral calculus," and the theory behind mathematical induction might very well lend themselves to the lecture approach. But it is also most appropriate when a skill is being taught, such as how to operate a calculator or a key-punch machine.

Many of the same features found in a developmental lesson plan might be found in a lecture lesson plan—the aim, do-now exercise, homework, summaries and drill. The difference occurs in the actual development of the new material—*lecture* versus *guided discovery*.

It is not always possible to determine whether the teacher plans to present a lecture or a developmental lesson by merely studying the plan. Thus, sample lesson 4 was implemented as a developmental lesson by the teacher, although the same plan might have been written to be delivered as a lecture.

The Drill Lesson

Practice by repetition is an important technique in the teaching of mathematics. It reinforces previously learned skills while developing new ones via the nuances that are bound to arise from doing a large selection of examples. It may well lead to better understanding of the theory.

A drill lesson may last the entire period, or it may be an adjunct to a developmental or lecture lesson. Thus, for example, a lesson on factoring trinomials into a product of binomials in first-year algebra may begin as "developmental" and end as "drill." In this case the teacher could develop patterns which the youngsters can follow, and spend the remainder of the period practicing what they have just been shown. The philosophy is one of "practice makes perfect."

Sample lesson 6 that follows illustrates just such a "developmental-drill" lesson. Note that the very large selection of drill examples are *not all mere repetitions* of each other. They are a series of graded exercises which demonstrate many of the subtle variations that may arise in factoring examples. Even this list is by no means complete.

Sample 6.

TOPIC: Introductory lesson on factoring trinomials into a product of two binomials.

AIM: To learn to factor trinomials of the form $x^2 + bx + c$.

APPERCEPTIVE BASIS: Pupils can multiply binomials by inspection.

DO-NOW: (Assign four groups of students to get the answers for each set below and select one from each group to write them on the board.)

Set 1	Set 2	Set 3	Set 4
$(x + 3)(x + 2)$	$(x + 5)(x - 2)$	$(x - 3)(x + 2)$	$(x - 3)(x - 5)$
$(x + 1)(x + 7)$	$(x - 3)(x + 5)$	$(x + 1)(x - 6)$	$(x - 1)(x - 8)$
$(x + 4)(x + 3)$	$(x + 5)(x - 1)$	$(x - 4)(x + 2)$	$(x - 7)(x - 2)$

DEVELOPMENT:
1. Discuss patterns in each group of answers;
2. Demonstrate how patterns can be used to work back to factors using the product $x^2 + 8x + 15$.
   2a. Always begin with the parentheses ( )( );
   2b. Factor the constant term so that the sum of the factors is equal to the coefficient of the middle term.

DRILL:

1. $x^2 + 7x + 10$
2. $x^2 - 5x + 6$
3. $x^2 - 7x + 6$
4. $x^2 - 2x + 15$
5. $x^2 + 5x - 14$
6. $x^2 - x - 20$
7. $x^2 + 3x - 40$
8. $x^2 - 6x + 9$
9. $x^2 - 64$
10. $x^2 + 4x - 12$
11. $x^2 - 81$
12. $49 - x^2$
13. $x^2 - \frac{25}{36}$

SUMMARY: Review each pattern type as shown in the four sets

HOMEWORK: Should consist of about fifteen trinomials to be factored, as an extension of the drill in class, in addition to any other appropriate examples that would "spiral" the assignment.

Review Lesson

At the end of a unit of work, usually preceding an examination on that unit, the teacher may desire to spend a full period or two reviewing the material and preparing students for the examination.

Suppose we consider the unit on radicals presented earlier in this chapter. After nine days of work the teacher is ready to spend one full period reviewing the material in preparation for the test to follow the next day.

Things you should remember before planning the review lesson:

1. Homework assignments were spirally arranged throughout the unit, so there was "built-in" review daily.
2. The review should be appropriate to the examination you plan to give the next day. Thus, the examination should have been prepared *before* the review lesson is presented.
3. Those topics that, in your judgment, need most reinforcement should take priority over the other topics.

The review lesson should consist of a variety of examples carefully selected for their instructional value. Thus, for the unit on radicals, one series of questions might be:

1. Use the Pythagorean theorem to find x. (Your answer may be left in radical form.)

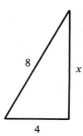

2. Express x in the above in simplest radical form.
3. Evaluate x in the above to the nearest tenth.
4. Compare and discuss the three forms of the same answer that were just found.

Note that the review lesson and drill lesson differ in that a drill lesson focuses on a limited number of topics, usually only one, and focuses on a skill; whereas the review lesson ranges broadly over the entire unit and is concerned with tying concepts together as in question 4 above.

Note also that the format of the review-lesson plan will include an aim (to review the unit on radicals), a do-now exercise (such as question 1 above), several practice examples, and homework (to study specific pages and examples for the test).

Mathematics Through Reading

College teachers of mathematics often have been known to advise high school teachers, "You teach the young people how to read mathematics, we'll do the rest." This is an important thought.

Teaching young people to read and understand mathematical material is more often than not a neglected aspect of secondary mathematics teaching. Yet, whether pupils are poor or good readers, we need to teach them

how to read a mathematics book. They must learn that because of the extensive symbolism, it is not like reading a novel and that it usually requires several readings before they can expect reasonable comprehension of the material. Furthermore, a pencil and paper must always be at hand while reading mathematics. Because of this, mathematics reading is slow reading.

If pupils are to be properly trained in the learning of mathematics, they must learn to resort to the textbook to supplement the activities of the classroom. It is certainly helpful to no one when a teacher suggests, "Pupils can't even read so how can they possibly study from the textbook by themselves?" He might even be surprised at the positive results when he tries to train his pupils to read the text by using it in the classroom in connection with the presentation of new work, drill or review.

Sample Lesson 7 is a sample mathematics-through-reading lesson in which the open textbook is used in class. Pupils should be directed to read the material silently for a few minutes. This should be followed by oral questions and answers by pupils and the teacher. No written boardwork is needed.

Sample 7. (This portion of a geometry lesson is for demonstration purposes only. While major questions ought to be planned in advance, most questions will be an outgrowth of the answers given by pupils.)

Students are directed to study the following outline of a proof found in the textbook, and are told that after a few minutes they will be questioned on what they read.

Proposition: If a diameter of a circle is perpendicular to a chord, it bisects the chord and its arcs.

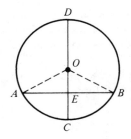

HYPOTHESIS: In circle 0, diameter $\overline{CD} \perp \overline{AB}$ at E.
CONCLUSION: $\overline{AE} \cong \overline{EB}$;
$\qquad \overset{\frown}{AC} \cong \overset{\frown}{CB}$
$\qquad \overset{\frown}{AD} \cong \overset{\frown}{DB}$

1. Draw $\overline{OA}$ and $\overline{OB}$.	1. A straight line may be drawn between two points.
2. $\triangle OAE \cong \triangle OBE$	2. Give full proof.
3. $\overline{AE} \cong$?	3. Why?
4. ? $\cong \angle AOE$	4. Why?
5. $\overset{\frown}{AC} \cong$?	5. Why?
6. $\overset{\frown}{CAD} \cong \overset{\frown}{CBD}$	6. Why?
7. $\overset{\frown}{AD} \cong$?	7. Why?

Questioning begins:
When the author prepared the diagram for this proposition, what did he draw first?
Then what did he draw?
What else did he draw?
How was the diameter drawn?
Then what did he draw?

Why are radii $\overline{OA}$ and $\overline{OB}$ needed in the diagram?
What information can we get from the two triangles?
Why are the arcs AC and CB congruent?
What follows from the fact that $\overset{\frown}{CAD} \cong \overset{\frown}{CBD}$?

Comments: Thus pupils are given practice in reading material involving mathematical symbols and expressions. The answers to questions asked by the teacher show whether or not the pupils have understood what they have read, and the discussion between the various answers helps in further clarification.

INDIVIDUALIZED LESSONS

Many individualized teaching programs, under various names, are available commercially. And some schools have developed their own individualized programs to best suit their own needs. Whatever variations and gimmicks these programs have, there is one feature common to them all—they permit pupils to advance at their own pace. These programs run the gamut from remedial arithmetic to advanced mathematics, though the lower end of the mathematics ladder is by far the more popular area of individualized use.

The commercially prepared programs are usually arranged so that the teacher (as well as the student) has a well-ordered predetermined series of steps he must follow. Little is left to the imagination and skill of the teacher.

While these programs may be beneficial to certain types of pupils who need an alternative to traditional classroom techniques, there is a potential danger in some of them. The danger is in the loss of what is commonly called "socialization" in the classroom. This is the interaction between and among students and the teacher that often leads to the development of a class "spirit" which fosters healthy growth in the subject. Thus, for example, the teacher's humor in the classroom or his reaction towards a pupil who came without his homework are all part of growth and development in the learning process for the students.

So, for those of you who will one day be involved with an "individualized" program, our recommendation is:

Within the confines of the particular program you have, try to devise some plan whereby students in a room get to know others in the same room, and get to know you. Perhaps it means that the class will work as a unit for a few minutes each day on a do-now exercise or for one period per week on a common lesson. Thus you will have an opportunity to be creative and imaginative so that even within the individualized setting there may be room for a little development, a little guided discovery, and so on.

Some topics that might be developed in a small amount of time over a period of days or weeks include:

sequences (arithmetic, geometric, harmonic, Fibonacci, etc.)

graphs (line, bar, etc.)

volume (prisms, cylinder, etc.)

magic squares

history of mathematics (biographies of famous mathematicians, ancient Greeks, etc.)

mathematical puzzles and games

modular arithmetic

Individualized lessons based on prescriptions that are developed as a result of standardized testing are common. Sample Lesson 8 is an example of such a prescription:

Sample 8. (An Individualized Remedial Prescription Lesson.)

This is part of a plan which a teacher may develop for use in remedial classes. The form lists the skills which are to be mastered for a particular topic, as well as space for pages and examples to be taken from two workbooks, a commercially prepared kit and with use of a calculator. After the teacher administers and analyzes a diagnostic test, teacher-prepared or standardized, he will fill in the pages and examples of the particular items needing remediation. Each youngster then follows the plan on a daily basis. (Thus the term "prescription.") The teacher checks on the pupils' progress as frequently as possible, and provides personal assistance when it is needed.

This is a unit on decimals. Other units might include addition, multiplication, percent, measurement, and so on. This plan is not prepared daily by the teacher. It is a long-range plan prepared by the teacher, which pupils work on daily. Every day they simply continue where they left off previously. More on this can be found in Chapter 8, ''Remediation.''

STUDENT ASSIGNMENTS—DECIMALS

Topic	Workbook Assignment 1	Workbook Assignment 2	Kit Assignment 3	Calculator Assignment
1. Place Value				
2. Rounding Off Decimals				
3. Changing Decimals to Fractions				
4. Comparing Decimals				
5. Adding Decimals				
6. Adding Decimals Horizontally				
7. Subtracting Decimals				
8. Subtracting Decimals Horizontally				
9. Progress Test				
10. Whole Number × Decimal Number				
11. Decimal × Decimal				
12. Rounding Off to Nearest ¢				
13. Decimal × 10; 100; 1,000				
14. Dividing Decimals by Whole Numbers				
15. Dividing Decimals 10; 100; 1,000				
16. Dividing Decimals by Decimals				
17. Dividing Smaller by Larger Numbers				
18. Changing Fractions to Decimals				
19. Progress Test				

SUMMARY

No performer enjoys playing the same role day in and day out. It kills initiative and dulls the imagination. So too with the teacher who might, for example, lecture every day to every class (except for examinations, of course). Variety is what makes the learning process, as well as the teaching aspect of that process, a pleasant one. Thus, the developmental, lecture, drill, review, mathematics reading, and individualized lessons must all be part of the mathematics teacher's repertoire.

Distinctions between lesson types are not always sharp. They might in fact be so blurred that only a slight shift of emphasis in one aspect of a lesson could cause the description of that lesson to change from one type to another—for example, from developmental to lecture; from lecture to reading; from developmental to drill, and so forth.

Every lesson ought to contain all or most of the standard features of aim, do-now, development, drill, summary and some review if needed.

When you plan, do so carefully and imaginatively. You have a wide range of options for planning lesson types, so use them all at various times throughout the semester.

EXERCISES

1. Select one of the topics from the unit plan on ''radicals'' given on page 4 and write a lesson plan for it. What type of lesson plan did you write? Why did you choose that particular type for your topic?

2. a. What are the key features found in most lessons?
   b. What types of lessons lend themselves to the ''developmental'' technique?
   c. *True or false*: Every lesson can be developmental. Discuss.

3. Select a topic from first year algebra and write a developmental lesson plan for it.

4. a. Find a section in a first year high school algebra textbook to teach as a mathematics-through-reading lesson. Write a list of ten questions you plan to ask the class after they read the section.

   b. Do the same in a geometry text.

   c. Do the same in a second year algebra text.

   d. Do the same in an eighth grade mathematics text.

5. Write a lesson plan for the day before a long vacation, featuring mathematics puzzles and games.

6. Write a lesson plan for the first day of any mathematics class.

7. Select a topic from an advanced mathematics course and prepare a lecture on it.

8. Write a drill lesson plan for each of the following:

   a. fractional and negative exponents

   b. simple trigonometry (sin, cos, tan)

   c. the distance and midpoint formulas in coordinate geometry.

   d. the L.C.M. and G.C.D. in the eighth grade.

9. Prepare a review lesson plan for the topic "percent" in a remedial arithmetic course.

10. What are the strengths and weaknesses of the following review lesson on congruent triangles presented to a high-ability geometry class:

Do-Now: State the congruence postulate illustrated:

(1)   (2)   (3)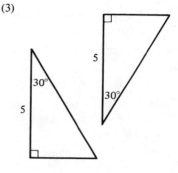

Then: Discuss with class using AAA or SSA (explain ambiguity in using SSA).

Then: Do the following proofs:

Given: $\overline{BD} \perp \overline{AC}$
       $AD \cong DC$
Prove: $\triangle ABD \cong \triangle CBD$

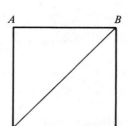

Given: $\angle ADB \cong \angle CDB$
       $\angle ABD \cong \angle CBD$
Prove: $\triangle ABD \cong \triangle CBD$

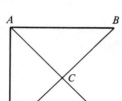

Given: $\overline{AB} \cong \overline{AD}$
       $\overline{BC} \cong \overline{CD}$
Prove: $\triangle ABC \cong \triangle ADC$

11. Prepare a developmental lesson on:
    a. The first lesson on simultaneous equations for a first year algebra class.
    b. The first lesson on trigonometric curves.
    c. The first lesson on the Law of Sines.
    d. The first lesson on addition and subtraction of signed numbers in a junior high school class.
    e. The first lesson on changing fractions to decimals in a high school remedial class.
    f. The first lesson on changing fractions to a middle school class.

12. Develop a series of eight ten-minute presentations on the following topics to be made to a class that does individualized work for most of the period:
    a. sequences
    b. history of mathematics
    c. patterns in mathematics
    d. recreational mathematics

13. How would you differentiate between a formal lesson plan one might discuss in a college methods course and a plan you might write for a secondary school class you are teaching?

14. Suppose you were asked to develop a unit on truth tables for an eighth grade junior high school mathematics class. Such concepts as negation, conjunction, disjunction, and truth values are to be included. Indicate
    a. What steps you would take to set up such a unit.
    b. The topics you would include.
    c. How many lessons this unit would require.

15. Select one topic from the truth-table unit you prepared for Exercise 14 and write a developmental lesson for it.

16. Prepare a lesson for a seventh grade mathematics class that develops the mean, median, and mode in one period. Allow sufficient time for practice exercises.

17. Write a lesson plan for teaching an introductory lesson in BASIC on a microcomputer for a remedial mathematics class. Assume the class has microcomputers available for each pupil and that the students know how to handle the machine.

18. Find four mathematics teachers who are willing to cooperate with you on a small research project. Two teachers should be very experienced and two should be relatively inexperienced. Ask each to write a lesson plan on a topic in secondary school mathematics. If possible, have them all work on the same lesson and then observe each teach that lesson, having the lesson plan in hand. Write a critique of both the lesson and the lesson plan based on information you learned in this chapter. (Promise each of the subjects that you will not share your critique with anyone and that it will be destroyed after use with this project.)

SUGGESTED READINGS

Johnson, Donovan A., and Rising, Gerald R., *Guidelines for Teaching Mathematics*. Belmont, California: Wadsworth Publishing, 1972.
This text provides some interesting alternatives to this chapter.

National Council of Teachers of Mathematics. *The Learning of Mathematics, Its Theory and Practice*, Twenty-first Yearbook. Washington, D.C.: NCTM, 1953.
Although most of this book contains useful articles, the article by Irving Allen Dodes, Planned Instruction *specifically addresses the topic of this chapter.*

National Council of Teachers of Mathematics. *The Teaching of Secondary School Mathematics*, Thirty-third Yearbook. Washington, D.C.: NCTM, 1970.
This book provides some outstanding discussions about teaching mathematics. Most articles are clear, crisp, and provide useful examples. Particularly appropriate is Part Three, Classroom Applications, *especially the lead article by F. Joe Crosswhite,* Implications for Teacher Planning.

ADDITIONAL READINGS

Davidson, Neil. "A Demonstration of Terrible Teaching Techniques." *The Mathematics Teacher,* 70 (1977): 545.

Henderson, Kenneth B. "Anent the Discovery Method." *The Mathematics Teacher* 50 (1970): 287.

————. "A Model for Teaching Mathematical Concepts." *The Mathematics Teacher* 60 (1967): 573.

Jones, Phillip S. "Discovery Teaching—from Socrates to Modernity." *The Mathematics Teacher* 65 (1970): 501.

Kinney, Lucien B., and Davison, Dan J. "Mathematics In The Junior High School." *The Mathematics Teacher* 49 (1956): 548.

Laing, Robert A., and Peterson, John C. "Assignments—Yesterday, Today, Tomorrow." *The Mathematics Teacher* 66 (1973): 508.

The Mathematics Teacher 69 (1976). Special Edition—Individualized Instruction.

Ortolan, Cathy, and Camp, Carol. "Meet the Challenge—Individualize." *The Mathematics Teacher* 73 (1980): 588.

Schmalz, Rosemary. "Categorization of Questions that Mathematics Teachers Ask." *The Mathematics Teacher* 66 (1973): 619.

Schoen, Harold L. "A Plan to Combine Individualized Instruction with the Lecture Method." *The Mathematics Teacher* 67 (1974): 647.

Swireford, Edwin J. "Ninety Suggestions on the Teaching of Mathematics in Junior High School." *The Mathematics Teacher* 54 (1961): 145.

Wilkinson, Jack. "Teaching General Mathematics: A Semi-Laboratory Approach." *The Mathematics Teacher* 63 (1970): 571.

CHAPTER 2 CLASSROOM QUESTIONING

Every good teacher strives to make her classroom a place where students will enjoy the learning process. Active student learning is usually a concomitant goal. Certainly, the manner in which new material is presented to a class will determine the true learning atmosphere. If students are *told* all the information they are required to know about a topic, they will inevitably become bored, lose interest and ultimately "tune out." Thus, the teacher must constantly try to promote an exciting learning atmosphere in the classroom. One way of achieving this is to set a tone of constant mental stimulation throughout the lesson. This can be done regularly by offering moderate mental challenges in the form of carefully thought out questions presented in a non-threatening manner.

By asking a class well-constructed questions, the teacher encourages active learning on the part of the students. What should the goal of such questioning be? Classroom questioning should elicit student responses consisting of information which would have otherwise been presented by the teacher. (Sometimes some valuable "original" comments are also received!) Although this is, in fact, quite difficult to fully achieve, it is a goal for which to strive.

To begin, consideration must be given to the construction of a good question. Good questioning is an art and is one of the most important elements of good teaching. As a result, it is either a great strength or a serious weakness in classroom work. Questions must be conscientiously prepared and patiently practiced. There are a number of pitfalls to avoid in asking classroom questions. We shall begin by considering these pitfalls, then examine some guidelines to follow.

TEN TYPES OF QUESTIONS TO AVOID

In any sequence of questioning a few weak questions may be asked without harm, but many poor questions will weaken a lesson. Following are ten types of questions a teacher should consciously avoid, for they may be counterproductive.

Overlaid Question

Often teachers, in the midst of asking their classes a question, find that the question is not specific enough to elicit the desired response. Rather than let the original question ride on its merits and give students a chance to answer it, the teacher may augment the question before students have even had a chance to answer the original question. When this happens, students who may have understood the original question may now hesitate to answer, since they are uncertain about their understanding of the entire question. Thus, by elaborating on a question which she felt was unclear, the teacher may have caused confusion by tagging on an additional thought.

> **EXAMPLE:** What method shall we use to solve this problem, and which will make our solution elegant?

Even if a student knows which method to use to solve the problem in question, he may avoid answering the question because of uncertainty about the second part of the question; namely, whether his method will produce an ''elegant solution.'' An improved way to ask this question is: ''What method shall we use to solve this problem (pause) Noreen?'' ''Is this the most efficient way to solve this problem (pause) Yolanda?''

> **EXAMPLE:** Which two triangles are congruent and also share a common angle?

Students might be ready to answer the first part of the question, but then may hesitate upon hearing the second part, for an inspection of the ''common angle'' would require further thought. Furthermore, some students may simply be overwhelmed with the question and shy away from it. This question may be asked as: ''Which two triangles sharing a common angle are congruent (pause) Mabel?'' You may also choose to ask the question as two separate questions.

In each of the two examples of an overlaid question, an elaboration of an original question was tagged on. This had exactly the opposite effect of what was intended.

Multiple Question

A multiple question is formed by asking two related questions in sequence without allowing for a student response until both parts of the question have been asked.

> **EXAMPLE:** Which triangles should we prove congruent and how will they help us prove $\overline{AB}$ parallel to $\overline{CD}$?

Although a student may know which triangles need to be proved congruent, he may not know how congruent triangles will help prove $\overline{AB}//\overline{CD}$. This student will probably not answer the question. On the other hand, if the question had been asked in two parts, allowing for an answer to the first part before the second part was asked, then more students would be likely to respond. This may be done as follows: ''Which triangles should we prove congruent (pause) Henry?'' ''How will these congruent triangles enable us to prove $\overline{AB}//\overline{CD}$ (pause) Evelyn?''

This type of question is similar to the overlaid question in that it also has two parts. It differs from the overlaid question by asking two questions which could actually stand as separate questions. Teachers often resort to multiple questions when they feel that the time remaining for a lesson is too short, or when they get somewhat impatient and want the lesson to move along more rapidly. As before, students easily can be discouraged from answering this type of question. In order for a student to provide a correct response he must be able to answer correctly *both* parts of the question. Thus a student who can correctly answer only one part of the question will not volunteer to respond. By reducing the pool of students who will respond to questions, the teacher has diminished active learning throughout the class:

> **EXAMPLE:** What is the discriminant of this equation (pointing to a quadratic equation) and what type of roots does it have?

As separate questions the multiple question above could stand, but in its present format it would most likely discourage students from responding. The same information can be elicited by asking: ''What is the discriminant of this equation (pointing to a quadratic equation) (pause) Alice?'' and ''Based on the value of the discriminant, what type of roots does this equation have (pause) Jordan?'' By stifling student responses, multiple questions reduce the effectiveness of a lesson and should therefore be avoided.

Factual Questions

There is certainly nothing wrong with asking a question which has a simple factual response if the question is part of a build up of a series of sequential facts necessary for the solution to the problem under consideration. Otherwise, isolated factual questions do little to stimulate student thinking.

EXAMPLE: What is the Pythagorean Theorem?

Not much thought is required to respond to this question. A student either knows the answer or does not know it. If we agree with our original premise regarding classroom questioning, then aside from being a part of a sequence of questions, factual questions contribute little to an active learning environment in the classroom.

Elliptical Questions

Questions which are unclear because the teacher has omitted specifics offer nothing to a lesson. Although not particularly harmful to a lesson, use of an elliptical question is simply an unnecessary waste of time.

EXAMPLE: How about these two angles?

Teachers frequently have a habit of thinking aloud. They may be looking at a pair of angles and thinking of what to ask about them, such as "What is their relationship?" or "Which angle has the greater measure?" In any case, the teacher may instead first voice her thought: "How about these two angles?" By verbalizing this thought into a question which has no answer, classroom time is wasted. The teacher might have wanted to ask, "What is the relationship between these two angles (pause) Gil?" where a definite answer is required.

Had the teacher wanted to say something (so as to avoid a lull in the lesson) when she was thinking about the two angles, a statement such as, "Consider these two angles," could have been made. This would have served the intended purpose and not wasted classroom time with possible student wise-crack answers such as, "How about them!"

EXAMPLE: What about these two parallel lines?

As before, this elliptical question asks for either nothing or more than most students are prepared to offer. At any rate, because of the omission of specifics, it leaves itself open for wise-crack responses. The teacher may wish to say something such as, "Which angles can we prove congruent using these parallel lines (pause) Laura?"

The teacher does not have to overreact to avoid lulls. Instead, she should stop and give some thought to a question rather than ask it in a form which has no clear response.

Yes-No or Guessing Questions

For the most part there is little value in a yes-no or guessing question. With few exceptions a yes-no question can be easily transformed into a good thought question.

EXAMPLE: Is $\overline{AB}$ perpendicular to $\overline{CD}$?

A student attempting to answer this question takes a very small risk. His chances of being correct are actually better than 50 percent. The teacher asking the question more often than not is seeking a positive response. In addition, the diagram to which this question relates should also offer assistance. Thus the question becomes somewhat rhetorical. This question might be transformed to read, "What is the relationship between $\overline{AB}$ and $\overline{CD}$ (pause) Stephanie?" This would require the student to scan the possible relationships which two line segments may have and then choose the one which she feels is appropriate. In its transformed state, the question provokes active learning among the students.

EXAMPLE: Is triangle *ABC* isosceles?

Why would a teacher ask this question if the triangle were, in fact, not isosceles? Unless the teacher were set to trick the class, students would be correct to assume that the teacher is simply seeking an affirmative response. Why then ask the question? The question would be far more productive when asked as, "What type of triangle is $\triangle ABC$ (pause) Ernie?" It is therefore a good practice to avoid yes-no or guessing questions whenever possible.

Ambiguous Questions

Occasionally, a teacher may seek a response which may require a specific interpretation of a situation. Here the questioner, trying to get her desired response with one question, may likely ask an ambiguous question, one that could have a variety of different, yet correct, answers. The desired response would be more easily attained by a series of short sequential questions.

EXAMPLE: How does the law of sines differ from the law of cosines?

Many different correct answers to this question could be given. Certainly the context in which this question was asked will help narrow the choices among the correct responses. Students will tend to shy away from responding to this question, however, out of obvious confusion caused by its ambiguity. Among many forms of confusion generated by this question, students may be wondering if the question refers to the difference in appearance of the two laws, the difference in application, the difference in derivation, and so on. One possible form in which this question may be asked is, "Under what different circumstances are the laws of sines and cosines used (pause) Lynn?" Because such confusion is obviously counterproductive, ambiguous questions should be consciously avoided in classroom questioning.

EXAMPLE: What is the relationship between the area of a circle and the circumference of a circle?

Once again this question has lots of correct answers. Is the questioner concerned about the numerical relationship, the physical relationship, the dimensional relationship, or some other less obvious relationship? Although the context in which the question was asked will assist students in responding to the question, confusion rarely is avoided when an ambiguous question is asked. One specific way of asking this question is, "What is the numerical ratio between the area and circumference of a circle (pause) Carol?" (Note: it is not necessarily a bad or undesirable feature to pose questions having several correct answers. We are considering the "ambiguous question" rather than this type of question here.)

Before asking a question that is likely to be ambiguous, set the specifics about the situation. Then ask short simple questions to elicit the desired response instead of asking the ambiguous question.

Chorus Response Questions

Although a question calling for a chorus response may be good, the chorus response often provides little value to the lesson. When a class responds in chorus to a question, the teacher usually cannot determine which students are answering incorrectly and which students are not responding at all. Furthermore, a chorus response can become too unclear for students eager to learn from the answer to hear the answer correctly. By missing the answer to a question, a student could be missing an important link in a chain of reasoning, resulting in damage to the learning process for this student.

> **EXAMPLE:** What type of quadrilateral is *ABCD*, class?

If we assume that not everyone in the class knows the correct answer to the question, some students will be shouting an incorrect answer while others will be answering correctly. Should one student not respond, but instead listen for the correct answer, he may hear an incorrect answer (because a wrong response may have come from someone close by) and then try to learn a concept with an incorrect piece of information. The time lost in correcting this error is certainly undesirable.

A preponderance of chorus response questions will allow some students to glide through the lesson without actually learning the subject matter presented. The teacher in this situation will be unable to detect individual difficulties since they are likely to be clouded by the chorus responses. This gives further reason to avoid the chorus response question as much as possible.

But an occasional use of this type of question may be acceptable if the response is not too crucial to a development and if it is necessary to involve the entire class, even for the sake of variety. A change of style, offering variety to the lesson, may be a healthy feature.

When used for this purpose, however, the chorus response question should be used sparingly.

Whiplash Questions

A whiplash question usually is not planned by the teacher. It comes about when a teacher decides to make a question out of a statement midway through it.

> **EXAMPLE:** The slope of this line is, what?

Aside from possibly frustrating students, little harm is caused by this type of question. Perhaps its greatest flaw is its uselessness. By catching students off guard, not expecting a question, the students must first mentally rephrase the question before attempting an answer. Under normal circumstances the beginning key word of a question (e.g., why, when, what, how, etc.) puts the students in a psychological set, ready to receive and process a question. The whiplash question does not provide this readying process and thereby wastes time and loses much of the student audience. A more productive way to ask this question would be, "What is the slope of this line (pause) Fred?"

> **EXAMPLE:** We now have $\overline{AB}$ parallel to $\overline{CD}$ because of which theorem?

This question would have been much more effective had the key word announcing a question been at the beginning of the question. It would then read, "Which theorem justifies the fact that $\overline{AB}$ is parallel to $\overline{CD}$ (pause) Edith?" In this form, the student knows from the first word that a question is being asked. The second word has him focus on the various theorems learned while he listens to the remainder of the question. At the completion of the question the student is ready to respond without wasting time to rephrase the question. This latter form of the question is clearly more efficient than the whiplash format, and a teacher need not turn every statement into a question just for the sake of producing student participation. Such an attempt at increasing student participation could easily become counterproductive.

Leading Questions

A leading question is one which tugs the desired response from the student. This type of question serves no reasonable function.

> **EXAMPLE:** Wouldn't you say that $\triangle ABC$ is equilateral?

Most students would be quite reluctant not to agree with the teacher asking a question as the example above. Thus the question does not provoke much thought, since the student is more than likely to simply respond in the affirmative.

EXAMPLE: Seven is a factor of 35, isn't it?

Again, there is no need to turn the statement "Seven is a factor of 35" into a question. The teacher would be better served by either leaving the statement stand as is, or by asking a question such as, "What are the factors of 35 (pause) Walter?" or "By what number must 7 be multiplied to yield 35 (pause) Larry?" Each of these questions requires some thought on the part of the student before answering. In addition to replacing a time-wasting question, active learning is induced.

Teacher-centered Questions

It is generally desirable to have students consider the teacher as part of the class. Although students are well aware of the different roles of the teacher and the student, when addressing the class it is more effective for the teacher to use the first person plural (i.e., we and us) where appropriate. For example, "Let us consider the following. . ." rather than "I have the following. . ." would make the class feel that they are all part of one group working on a common problem together. They do not need a constant reminder that they are the students and the teacher is quite distinct from them. Regular use of the first person singular (i.e., I and me) could create an invisible shield between the teacher and the class, a possible detriment to a healthy active learning environment.

EXAMPLE: Give me the solution set of $3x - 5 = 2$.

A better way to ask this is: "Give us the solution set of $3x - 5 = 2$ (pause) Al."

EXAMPLE: What must I do next in solving this problem?

This question ought to be asked as: "What must we do next in solving this problem (pause) Jack?" Each of the examples above illustrates the sort of teacher comment which seeks to set apart (albeit subconsciously) the teacher from the students, not particularly conducive to a good classroom learning situation.

CLASSROOM QUESTIONING FEATURES TO DEVELOP

Besides avoiding the pitfalls of poor classroom questions, teachers must consciously develop habits of questioning which will strengthen their teaching performance. Each of the following suggestions for developing an effective style of classroom questioning should be carefully practiced, for their implications go beyond classroom questioning and can have a substantial impact on the teaching-learning process.

Direct and Simple Language

Classroom questions should be direct and simple in language. The student focus on a question should be on its content, not on the language used in its delivery. That is, if the language is such that it distracts students from the content, either by being too complex, or perhaps too humorous, the potential effectiveness of a question may be lost. By using direct and simple language (i.e., appropriate for the level of the intended class) a teacher can use classroom questions to fulfill their desired function.

Definite and Clear Meaning

Classroom questions should be definite and clear in meaning. If a question lends itself to various interpretations, students may be reluctant to respond. To maximize the number of volunteer respondents, ambiguities should be avoided. Often shorter questions are less confusing.

A question should call for only one or two points in a line of reasoning. A teacher should ask more questions, rather than try to limit the number of questions and lengthen each one. By trying to ask too much in a single question, the teacher may become prone to asking multiple or overlaid questions (see page 28).

Logical Sequence

Questioning should develop a train of thought in logical sequence. An inexperienced teacher's impatience with the developmental process may cause her to rush to the pivotal (or prime) question of a lesson without spending enough time leading up to it by shorter preparatory questions. This impatience often diminishes the ultimate effectiveness of the pivotal question. Since the pivotal question generally elicits a highlight of the lesson, its effectiveness should not be weakened. Thus teachers should give special attention to all parts of a line of questioning which develops a train of thought in logical sequence. This means that the same care should be given to the early, perhaps almost trivial, or review questions, as is given to the pivotal and culminating questions. Remember, the pivotal question is rarely effective if it is not properly built up through a carefully developed sequence of subordinate questions in predetermined order.

Questions Keyed to Class Ability

The level of ability of a class should determine the language and complexity of the classroom questions used. It is easy for a teacher to use the same questions during two consecutive class periods, especially when the same lesson is being used. Yet if the ability levels of the two classes are different, this practice should be consciously avoided. For the slower or perhaps less sophisticated class, simpler language might be used than with a class comprised of more able students. When planning classroom questions, every effort should be made to prepare questions for each class appropriate to their level of ability. Teachers should not use condescending language, while at the same time the teacher should not conduct the class with language beyond the students' ability to grasp the content comfortably. By asking questions properly suited for the intended audience, communication with classes at all levels will be improved.

Questions Stimulating Effort

Questions should arouse an effort. While gearing the phrasing of a question to the appropriate level for a class, a special effort must be made to prepare questions which are sufficiently difficult to arouse an effort, yet not too difficult to stifle the class. Good classroom questioning should create a moderately challenging atmosphere throughout the lesson. Classroom questions should be short and crisp and arranged in a logical sequence building up to the desired point. A sequence of questions might well consist of a blend of factual and thought questions, with a majority of the latter kind. Included would be a balanced mixture of some short, yet challenging questions, along with other review or connecting questions. Such a blend should go far to stimulate active learning.

Maintaining Student Interest

Classroom questioning should hold student interest throughout a lesson. A few important points should be included regularly.

Every effort should be made to call on as many different students throughout a lesson as possible. Try to avoid predictability in your calling on students. Mix calling on non-volunteers with calling on volunteers. This will keep everyone attentive. If a teacher begins a course by requiring students to give complete answers to classroom questions, she is helping to insure that such a practice will eventually become habitual in the class.

It is a good habit to praise students (with tact) for correctly answering a question. It is equally important, however, for a teacher to handle incorrect answers properly. With classroom time permitting, the teacher may guide the student to realize his error through a series of questions specially tailored to this discovery. Alternatively, the teacher may choose to refer the question to the rest of the class. And student questions may be answered by other students. The teacher should not feel that only she should provide the answers to student questions. Very often some interesting things result from peer interaction.

For example, by answering another student's question, the first student can better learn the concepts under

consideration. Teaching usually allows the teacher to better understand the subtleties of subject matter being taught. The same can be true when one student explains a concept to a classmate.

When students are expected to respond to one another's questions, there is a greater degree of alertness throughout the classroom, since students cannot predict precisely when they will be called on to correct or answer another student. This alertness should go far to enliven the class.

The best treatment for an incorrect answer depends on the type of class and the time available in the lesson. Under no circumstances should the teacher be abrupt to or scold a student for giving an incorrect answer. This would likely have an adverse effect on the student's learning and inhibit his future willingness to respond to the teacher's questions.

Avoiding Repetition

The teacher's question should generally not be repeated. Naturally, if for some unusual reason the question was inaudible, repetition may be necessary. Variety can be provided by having a student repeat a question when it was not heard by some students. Habitually repeating a question can make the class inattentive, however, since they can rely on the question being repeated. Students also may call continually for the repetition of a question in order to waste class time. Yet, if they know that the repetition of a question is not easily obtained, this scheme will not work. The result will be an attentive class, with no time wasted.

Sometimes just after the teacher has asked a question of the class, she may repeat the question in perhaps a rephrased form before the class has even had a chance to respond to the question. An uncertainty, on the part of the teacher, about the clarity of the question will provoke this immediate repetition of the question. Very often only the teacher finds the question unclear. The class may have been ready to respond to the original question, but after hearing the rephrased question may be somewhat confused. The teacher should let the original question stand, give students sufficient time to respond, and only if no correct response is forthcoming should the question be rephrased. Students often have an unsuspected ability to properly interpret a teacher's question, even if it is a bit unclear. At such times teachers should not be overly critical of their own questions. Proper questioning preparation could avoid this entire situation.

Avoiding Repetition of Student Answers

The teacher should not repeat student responses. For reasons similar to those discussed above, teachers should make a conscious effort not to repeat student responses.

If students can rely on the teacher to repeat most of the more important student responses to teacher questions, they may eventually not even listen to their classmates. This would greatly inhibit active student interaction throughout a lesson. If, in the teacher's judgment, a student's response is inaudible, then the teacher should have the student or another student repeat the response. Consistency with this procedure will eventually cause students automatically to speak loudly and clearly just to avoid having to repeat their responses (or hear other students do so).

Some teachers have a habit of "mentally processing" a student's response aloud. This results in a repetition of the student's response. Most teachers, when made aware of this habit, can curtail it. Tape recording a teacher's lesson would be helpful in demonstrating this flaw in a teacher's performance. If a teacher cannot avoid such repetitions, however, she should at least try to incorporate this repetition into her next statement or question. This way it may not appear as a simple repetition of what has already been said.

Teacher repetitions of student responses are also caused by the teacher's fear that unless a substantive statement is made by the teacher, the class will not note it properly. This, too, will only be so if the teacher allows it to happen. The teacher sets the class tone and routines and the manner in which classroom questioning and the resulting student responses are handled.

Calling on Students

Another way to generate constant student attention is to call on a particular student for a response after a pause at the end of a question.

> **EXAMPLE:** Why is $\overline{AB}$ the perpendicular bisector of $\overline{CD}$ (pause) David?

If the class is accustomed to having the teacher call on a student to respond to a question after it has been asked, each student will be attentive just in case he is the one selected by the teacher to respond. On the other hand, if a teacher addresses David before asking the question, perhaps only David will be attentive, since the rest of the class will know they are not being asked the question. This latter situation does not promote an active involvement in the learning process. Thus the teacher is advised to ask classroom questions addressing particular students at the end of the question and thereby assuring student attention throughout the lesson.

It is sometimes helpful to discover which students in your class are trying to avoid being called upon. There are times when it may be wise to call on them or simply meet with these students after class to discuss their apparent avoidance. The question is, how can the teacher discover which students are trying to avoid being called upon? Experience has shown that if, after the teacher asks a question of the class and pauses to look around for a student to call upon for a response, a student appears to make a conscious effort to avoid eye contact with the teacher, the teacher can assume that student does not want to be called upon. This avoidance sometimes manifests itself in the student appearing to be very "busy," where the teacher's calling on him would be seen as in interference of his "concentration." Sometimes the teacher can discourage this by making a general statement to the class about this type of avoidance. Done properly, the class may find this humorous (since many of the students may have been guilty of this type of behavior at one time or another) and realize that this teacher must be very clever and is not easily fooled. However, you then must be watchful for other, perhaps more creative, techniques which some students may use to avoid your questions (especially when they feel they cannot properly answer them).

Wait-Time After Asking a Question

Allowing students sufficient time to think about a teacher-posed question is a very important aspect of classroom questioning. One of the leading researchers in the area of the questioning behavior of teachers is Mary Budd Rowe. Her findings over the years have had a significant impact with teacher performance in the classroom. In her extensive analysis of classroom performances, she has found that most teachers, on average, wait less than one second for students to respond to their questions. On the other hand, there are some teachers who wait an average of three seconds for students to reply. When she compared student responses with different wait-times, she found that the longer wait-times (three seconds or more) produced more thoughtful responses, increased classroom discussion, and enabled students to analyze a situation more critically than was the case with shorter wait-times following the teacher's questions. Dr. Rowe also found that teachers who waited an average of more than three seconds before calling for a response enjoyed the following results:

- the length of student responses increased 400%–800%
- the number of voluntary, yet appropriate, responses increased
- failure to respond decreased
- student confidence increased
- students asked more unsolicited questions
- weaker students contributed more (increases ranged from 1.5% to 37% more)
- there was a greater variety of student responses. Creative thinking increased!
- discipline problems decreased

One effective technique to determine the wait-time following your class questions is to make a tape-recording of your lesson and then during the playback, time the periods of pause following each question. Try increasing your wait-time if it is too short and again tape the lesson to inspect for an increase of wait-time. Such an exercise ought to produce favorable results.

Once you have succeeded in increasing the wait-time following your classroom questions, you might try to pause briefly after a student has responded to allow for reflection or to permit a student to add more information onto his first response. This second type of wait-time has similar effects on the learning environment as the first type of wait-time. This has been shown by an analysis conducted by Dr. Rowe of more than 800 tape recordings of lessons in urban, suburban, and rural schools.

Variety in Questioning

Perhaps one of the most important elements in good classroom questioning, as in most aspects of good teaching, is variety. Variety can refer to the types of questions asked, to the manner in which questions are asked, to the way students (with volunteers and non-volunteers) are called on to respond to questions, and to the procedure by which responses are handled. Variety reduces

predictability, which in turn ought to promote continuous stimulation. When teachers vary the type of questions asked, students constantly are required to be alert to more than simply the content of the questions. This additional alertness should have a refreshing spin-off toward improved learning. In addition to providing students with a more interesting experience, teachers also are more apt to be aroused by the challenge of creating continuous variety in their questioning.

SUMMARY

In this chapter we have considered one of the important elements of classroom teaching: questioning. Ten types of questions to avoid were presented and analyzed, after which numerous suggestions for effective classroom questioning were discussed. Although many points have been made in this chapter, you should practice them in small doses, for considering them all at once could become overwhelming and as a result not very useful. Remember, when asking a classroom question *listen to your own question* with a critical ear. You may be one of your own best critics. Should more careful self-analysis be desired, a video-tape recording would be helpful. Constant self-assessment of one's teaching performance should have rewarding results.

EXERCISES

1. State whether or not each of the following is a good classroom question; if it is not, explain why.
   a. "What is the solution set for the equation $3x - 5 = 8$, and how will it help us solve the problem (discussed earlier with the class) Lisa?
   b. "How about this set of numbers . . . Daniel?"
   c. "Why is $\triangle ABC$ isosceles, Noreen?"
   d. "Yolanda, wouldn't you say these triangles are congruent?"
   e. "Class, is this curve a parabola?"
   f. "The discriminant of this equation is what?"
   g. "What is my next step in solving this problem?"
   h. "What is the greatest common factor of these two numbers and how can we be sure that there is no greater common factor, Joshua?"
   i. "How can we change this equation $\dfrac{x}{3} + \dfrac{5x}{7} = 2$ to one without fractions, Henry?"
   j. "For what conditions will the roots of this equation (pointing at the chalkboard) be imaginary and how will this help solve our problem, Evelyn?"
   k. "Who can tell me what the solution to this equation (pointing to the chalkboard) is?"
   l. "Which is the longest side of this triangle (pointing to right $\triangle ABC$), class?"
   m. "How does solving a linear equation differ from solving a quadratic equation, Lynn?"
   n. "Am I correct in dividing both sides of this equation (at chalkboard) by five, . . . Sue?"
   o. "What is $\sqrt{196}$, class?"
   p. "If we apply the Pythagorean Theorem to this triangle we find AB equals what, Alice?"
   q. "Why is there only one acceptable answer to this problem, Fred?"

2. Rephrase each of the questions in Exercise 1 which are not good classroom questions.

3. Explain why it is more desirable to call on a student after the question has been asked rather than before.

4. Explain how you would react to the following student responses to your question.
   a. "I didn't hear the question."
   b. "I was absent yesterday."
   c. "I don't know."
   d. silence

5. Choose a short topic from the secondary school mathematics curriculum. Prepare a series of questions which you may use to develop this topic (through guided discovery) with your class.

6. What are some of the changes you can make in your questioning technique if you find that you have few volunteers responding to your questions?

7. Have a videotape made of one of your lessons (an audio tape will suffice if a videotape is impractical).
   a. Write an analysis of your classroom questioning by categorizing each of your questions according to the types of questions indicated in this chapter.
   b. Analyze the students' response patterns. That is, were you calling only on volunteers, only on non-volunteers? What percent of the students used simple yes, no answers, etc.?

8. Ask an experienced mathematics teacher if he or she would be willing to have you either audiotape or videotape one lesson. Take this audio tape and perform the same analysis required for Question 7.

9. Review the tapes made for Exercises 7 and 8 and gauge the wait-time after each question. Analyze and compare your results with the findings of Mary Budd Rowe.

SUGGESTED READINGS

Bell, Frederick H. *Teaching and Learning Mathematics in Secondary Schools*. Dubuque, Iowa: William C. Brown Company, 1978.

Hunkins, Francis P. *Questioning Strategies and Techniques*. Boston: Allyn and Bacon, 1972.

Rowe, Mary Budd. *Teaching Science as a Continuous Inquiry: A Basic*. New York: McGraw-Hill, 1978.

ADDITIONAL READINGS

Davidson, Neil. "A Demonstration of Terrible Teaching Techniques." *The Mathematics Teacher* 70 (1977): 545.

Henderson, Kenneth B. "Anent the Discovery Method." *The Mathematics Teacher* 50 (1970): 287.

Jones, Phillip S. "Discovery Teaching—from Socrates to Modernity." *The Mathematics Teacher* 65 (1970): 501.

Schmalz, Rosemary. "Categorization of Questions That Mathematics Teachers Ask." *The Mathematics Teacher* 66 (1973): 619.

Swireford, Edwin J. "Ninety Suggestions on the Teaching of Mathematics in Junior High School." *The Mathematics Teacher* 54 (1961): 145.

CHAPTER 3
TECHNIQUES
OF
MOTIVATION

One of the more difficult tasks teachers of mathematics face is that of motivating students for a particular lesson. Planning motivation requires creativity and imagination. The needs and interests of students must be carefully considered. This will naturally vary with the many student characteristics found in today's schools.

It would appear that geometry, because of its visual nature, would readily generate interest among students. Unfortunately, this is not always the case. Much of the course deals with proving theorems and then applying these theorems to artificial problems. Interested mathematics students will be excited by this as they would be by almost any other mathematical activity. We must focus our attention on less interested students, however, in planning appropriate motivation, since they will not be enchanted with such concepts as the postulational nature of geometry.

To motivate students is to channel their interests to the specific topic to be learned. In this chapter we shall consider some techniques which can be used to motivate secondary school students in mathematics. Specifically, eight different techniques will be presented. For each, a number of examples from algebra and geometry will be provided. (Note that the technique is the important part to remember. The examples are merely provided to help understand the technique.)

MOTIVATING STUDENTS

Indicate a void in students' knowledge. Students usually have a natural desire to complete their knowledge of a topic. This technique of motivation involves making students aware of a void in their knowledge and capitalizes on their desire to learn more. For instance, you may present a few simple exercises involving familiar situations followed by exercises involving unfamiliar situations on the same topic. Or you may mention (or demonstrate) to your class how the topic to be presented will complete their knowledge about a particular part of mathematics. The more dramatically you do this, the more effective the motivation. Often, guiding students to discover this void in their knowledge is effective. Following are some examples of how this technique may be used.

> **EXAMPLE:** (Introducing the general angle—second year algebra.) Present the following questions to your students:
>
> Find the value of each of the following:
> 1. Sin 30° = ?
> 2. Cos 60° = ?
> 3. Cos 75° = ?
> 4. Sec 75° = ?
> 5. Cos 105° = ?

Students familiar with the 30-60-90 triangle ought to be able to answer the first two questions easily. The third question easily can be answered with the aid of a table of trigonometric functions. Recognizing the reciprocal relationship between questions 3 and 4 should yield a quick answer to question 4. The fifth question will cause students some discomfort, however. Since their trigonometric tables do not show measures greater than 90°, students will most likely speculate about the correct answer. You should now have students realizing that there is a void in their knowledge. They are now moti-vated to learn how to find the values of trigonometric functions of angles greater than 90°.

> **EXAMPLE:** (Introducing the measures of angles with their vertices outside a given circle—geometry.) Suppose students have learned the relationships between the measures of arcs of a circle and the measure of an angle (whose rays determine these arcs) with its vertex *in* or *on* the circle, but not outside the circle. A possible set of exercises is shown below.

Find the value of x in each of the following:

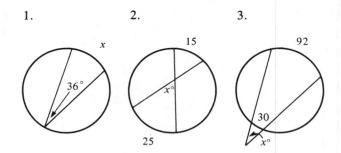

After completing the first two exercises, students should *want* to learn the relationship exhibited in the third exercise. This should serve as a good springboard into the lesson. (For an interesting alternative to teaching this unit, see Enrichment Unit 56, "Angle Measurement with a Circle."

Show a sequential achievement. Closely related to the technique above is that of having students appreciate a logical sequence of concepts. This differs from the previous method in that it depends on students' desire to increase, but not complete, their knowledge. A chart may be useful in applying this method of motivation.

> **EXAMPLE:** (Quadrilaterals—geometry.) In the development of the properties of quadrilaterals, a chart such as the following may be developed.

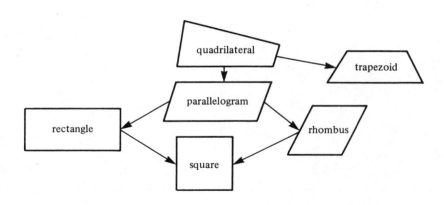

Students could be led to want to reach, sequentially, various levels of this diagramed development. The chart must be developed carefully with its intended purpose clearly in focus.

Present a challenge. When students are challenged intellectually, they react with enthusiasm. Great care must be taken in selecting the challenge. The problem (if that is the type of challenge used) must not only definitely lead into the lesson, but it must also be within reach of the students' ability. A challenge should be short and not complex. It should not be so engrossing that it may detract from the intended lesson. This would certainly defeat the purpose for which this challenge was intended. Thus, challenges providing motivation for one class may not do so for another. Teacher judgment is most important here.

> **EXAMPLE:** (Properties of tangents—geometry.) Suppose you wish to motivate your students to learn a lesson on tangents to a circle. Have students consider the following problem:
>
> *Given:* $\overline{AQP}$, $\overline{BRP}$, and $\overline{QTR}$ tangent to circle O at A, B, and T, respectively. $AP = 18$.
> *Find:* The perimeter of $\triangle PQR$.

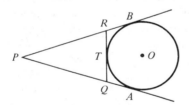

Students may feel that insufficient information was supplied. To solve this problem, they need know only the relationship between the lengths of two tangent segments to a circle from a common external point. Once the need for this theorem has been established (via this little challenge), students ought to be able to solve the problem by noting the equalities $AP = BP$, $AQ = TQ$, and $BR = TR$. That is, the perimeter of $\triangle PQR$ = PR + PQ + TR + TQ = PR + PQ + BR + AQ. Also, AQ + PQ = AP = 18, and BR + PR = BP = 18. Therefore the perimeter of $\triangle PQR$ = 36.

> **EXAMPLE:** (Concurrency of angle bisectors of a triangle—geometry.) Another possible challenge may be used when introducing the idea of concurrency of the angle bisectors of a triangle. The student is asked to determine (or draw) the angle bisector of an angle whose vertex is located within an inaccessible area. Students should be familiar with constructions that require the use of straightedge and compasses.

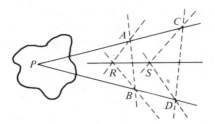

One desired solution requires drawing any lines $\overleftrightarrow{AB}$ and $\overleftrightarrow{CD}$ intersecting the rays of the angle, which is inaccessibly located at P. Angle bisectors of the four angles (as shown above) are drawn, and the two points R and S determine the desired angle bisector. Students should notice that since the bisectors of the angles of a triangle are concurrent (here considering $\triangle APB$ and $\triangle CPD$ separately), both points R and S *must* be contained in the bisector of the inaccessible angle. After witnessing this solution, students should want to prove the concurrency of the angle bisectors of a triangle. (For a more in-depth consideration of this problem see Enrichment Unit 37, "The Inaccessible Angle.")

> **EXAMPLE:** (Introducing the sum of a geometric series—second-year algebra. Present the following challenge to your students:
>
> What would you rather have?
> A. $100,000 per day for 31 days; or
> B. 1¢ the first day
>   2¢ the second day
>   4¢ the third day
>   8¢ the fourth day
>   16¢ the fifth day
>   . . . and so on for 31 days?

Most students will opt for choice A, since that seems like a lot of money. After 31 days, $3,100,000 will have been attained. The job of adding the 31 terms in B will be somewhat exhausting. Students should now be motivated for a short-cut for this addition. After they have developed the formula for the sum of a geometric series, the students can apply it to this problem. They may be surprised to discover the large number resulting: $21,474,836.47.

Indicate the usefulness of a topic. Here a practical application is introduced at the beginning of a lesson. The applications selected should be of genuine interest to the class. Once again the applications chosen should be brief and not too complicated so that they motivate the lesson rather than detract from it. Student interest must be considered carefully when selecting an application. Remember *usefulness* is only appropriate when a student has a prior knowledge of the topic involving the application. The following examples are offered to illustrate this technique.

EXAMPLE: (Properties of a line perpendicular to a plane—geometry.) In erecting a flagpole, students will be interested in knowing how to assure perpendicularity. Hence, a natural motivation for the theorem: "If a line is perpendicular to each of two intersecting lines at their point of intersection, then the line is perpendicular to the plane determined by them." Further elaboration on the flagpole problem depends on the ability level and interest level of the class. (This is true with all methods of motivation presented here.)

EXAMPLE: (Relationship between the segments of two intersecting chords of a circle—geometry.) Finding the size of a cracked plate in which the largest remaining piece is a small segment of the original circle is an application in which students are required to find the diameter of the circle of which $\overset{\frown}{ACB}$ is a minor arc. Perhaps couching this problem in a story might be even more motivating.

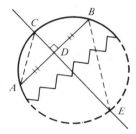

Draw any chord $\overline{AB}$ of the arc and the perpendicular bisector $\overline{CDE}$ of that chord (where C is on the arc). Measure $\overline{AD}$ and $\overline{CD}$. Then use similarity to establish the proportion: $DE/AD = BD/CD$. Thus $\overline{DE}$ and then $\overline{CE}$, the desired diameter, may be found easily. This problem can serve as motivation for the theorem which states, "If two chords intersect in the interior of a circle, thus determining two segments in each chord, the product of the lengths of the segments of one chord equals the product of the lengths of the segments of the other chord." Although students may be able to solve the problem in the manner shown above, they would welcome a shorter method. Hence the problem has created a need for establishing the relationship $AD \cdot BD = DE \cdot CD$. The proof of the theorem is embedded in the solution above.

EXAMPLE: (Properties of similar triangles—geometry.) When introducing properties of similar triangles, ask the class how the "cross-legs" of an airplane service truck have to be positioned so that the plane of the box will be parallel to the plane of the truck.

As the "cross-legs" shift position, it should be noticed that the legs must always partition each other proportionally if the plane of the box is to remain parallel to the plane of the truck. This ought to motivate students to prove this fact.

Use recreational mathematics. Recreational motivation consists of puzzles, games, paradoxes, or facilities. In addition to being selected for their specific motivational gain, these devices must be brief and simple. A student should realize the "recreation" without much effort in order for this technique to be effective.

EXAMPLE: (Area of a circle—geometry.) When beginning the study of the area of a circle, students may be presented with five concentric circles (the smallest has radius one unit) whose radii differ by one unit, respectively, and asked to compare *intuitively* the areas of the two shaded regions (see diagram.)

Most students conclude that the "inner region" has a greater area than the region of the "outer ring." Consideration of the area of a circle yields the true relationship. Students are generally astonished to find that the two regions have equal areas.

EXAMPLE: (General.) Such topics as division by zero, betweenness, definitions such as $\sqrt{ab} = \sqrt{a} \cdot \sqrt{b}$ when a and b are non-negative, and the existence of reflex angles are often dramatically presented via mathematical fallacies. Many books contain such fallacies which involve these topics as well as many other topics. Four of these are listed below.

Ball, W. W. Rouse. *Mathematical Recreations and Essays.* Revised by H. S. M. Coxeter. New York: Macmillan, 1960.

Dubnov, Ya. S. *Mistakes in Geometric Proofs*. Translated by A. K. Henn and O. A. Titelbaum. Boston: Heath, 1963.

Maxwell, E. A. *Fallacies in Mathematics*. London, England: Cambridge University Press, 1959.

Northrup, E. P. *Riddles in Mathematics*. Princeton: Van Nostrand, 1944.

EXAMPLE: (Introduction to digit problems—algebra.) Begin your presentation by asking your students to select any three-digit number in which the hundreds digit and units digit are unequal. Then have them write the number whose digits are in the reverse order from the selected number. Now tell them to subtract these two numbers (the smaller number from the larger one). Once again tell them to take this difference, reverse its digits and add the "new" number to the *original difference*. They *all* should end up with 1,089.

For example, suppose a student selected the number 934. The number with the digits reversed is 439. Her computation would appear as:

$$
\begin{array}{ll}
934 & \\
439 & \\
\hline
495 & \text{(difference)} \\
594 & \text{(reversed digits)} \\
\hline
1089 & \text{(sum)}
\end{array}
$$

When students compare results they will be amazed to discover the uniformity in their answers. At this point they should be quite eager to find out *why* they all came up with the same result. A detailed discussion of this unusual number property is presented in Enrichment Unit 75, "Digit Problems Revisited."

Tell a pertinent story. A story of a historical event or of a contrived situation can motivate students. All too often teachers, already knowing the story they are about to tell, and eager to get into the "meat" of the lesson, rush through the story. Such a hurried presentation minimizes the potential effectiveness which the story may have as a motivational device. Thus a carefully prepared method of presentation of a story for motivating a lesson is almost as important as the content of the story itself.

EXAMPLE: (Introducing the sum of an arithmetic series—algebra.) Tell your students about young Karl Friedrich Gauss who at age 10 was in a class which was asked by its instructor to add the numbers from 1 to 100. Much to the astonishment of the instructor, young Gauss produced the correct answer immediately. When asked how he arrived at the answer so quickly, he explained that

$$
\begin{array}{l}
1 + 100 = 101 \\
2 + 99 = 101 \\
3 + 98 = 101 \\
\text{and so on.}
\end{array}
$$

Since there are 50 such pairs, the answer is $50 \times 101 = 5{,}050$.

This scheme can be used to develop the formula for the sum of an arithmetic series.

EXAMPLE: (Various topics—geometry.) For the study of parallel lines, the story of Eratosthenes measuring the circumference of the earth might be appropriate (see Posamentier, Banks and Bannister. *Geometry: Its Elements and Structure*. New York: McGraw-Hill, 1977, p. 226).

Before proving that the base angles of an isosceles triangle are congruent, the teacher may find a brief discussion of *Pons Asinorum* appropriate. Telling students that during the Middle Ages this proof separated weak students from better students should provoke attempts toward solution by all students.

An endless number of stories, historical and otherwise, can be used for motivational purposes. Some of these include the following topics. (After each we offer references.) Many other references can be found in *A Bibliography of Recreational Mathematics* (4 vols.) by William L. Schaaf (Washington, D.C.: National Council of Teachers of Mathematics, 1970(2), 1973, 1978):

1. The origin of certain symbols or terms to be introduced
   Cajori, Florian. *A History of Mathematical Notations* (2 Vol.). La Salle, Ill.: Open Court, 1952.

2. The history of π
   Beckmann, Petr. *A History of π*. New York: St. Martin's Press, 1971.

3. The Golden Rectangle
   Posamentier, Alfred S. *Excursions in Advanced Euclidean Geometry*. Portland, Maine: J. Weston Walch, Publisher, 1979.
   Runion, Garth E. *The Golden Section and Related Curiosa*. Glenview, Ill.: Scott, Foresman, 1972.

4. Ancient measuring devices
   Kline, Morris. *Mathematics: A Cultural Approach*. Reading, Mass.: Addison-Wesley, 1962.

Polya, George. *Mathematical Methods in Science*. Washington, D. C.: Mathematical Association of America, 1977.

5. Major breakthroughs in mathematics
Smith, David E. *A Source Book in Mathematics*. New York: McGraw-Hill, 1929.
Newman, James R. *The World of Mathematics* (4 Volumes). New York: Simon and Schuster, 1956.
Bunt, L., Jones P., and Bedient, J. *The Historical Roots of Elementary Mathematics*. Englewood Cliffs, N. J.: Prentice-Hall, 1976.

6. Pertinent biographical notes
Bell, E. T. *Men of Mathematics*. New York: Simon and Schuster, 1937.
Coolidge, Julian L. *The Mathematics of Great Amateurs*. New York: Dover, 1963.
Turnbull, Herbert W. *The Great Mathematicians*. New York: New York University Press, 1961.

7. Pertinent anecdotes
Aaboe, Asger. *Episodes from the Early History of Mathematics*. Washington, D.C.: Mathematical Association of America, 1964.
Eves, Howard. *In Mathematical Circles* (2 Volumes). Boston: Prindle Weber and Schmidt, 1969.
Eves, Howard. *Mathematical Circles Revisited*. Boston: Prindle Weber and Schmidt, 1971.

Get students actively involved in justifying mathematical curiosities. One of the more effective techniques for motivating students is to attempt actively to justify a pertinent mathematical curiosity. The students should be comfortably familiar with the mathematical curiosity before you "challenge" them to justify it. Although this could consume more time than may be normally allotted for a motivational activity, to proceed with a justification before sufficient exposure has been achieved would be counterproductive.

EXAMPLE: (Introducing the midline of a triangle—geometry.) Suppose students are about to study the properties of a midline of a triangle. As motivation, they may be asked to draw any five quadrilaterals and then in each quadrilateral to join the midpoints of the adjacent sides with line segments. Much to their amazement, they will find that they have drawn five parallelograms.

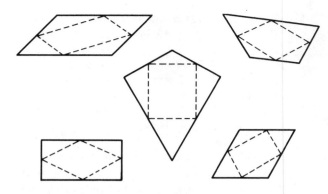

A request for a proof of this can be expected from the class. One of the more elegant proofs is based on the properties of a midline of a triangle. Thus the teacher has an excellent opportunity to introduce the midline and its properties.

EXAMPLE: (Similarity—geometry.) Another geometric curiosity is the *pantograph,* an instrument used for drawing similar plane figures. Students can construct this instrument at home. At the beginning of the lesson in which similarity is to be considered, the operation of the pantograph can be justified.

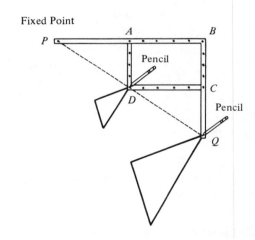

The pantograph consists of four bars hinged at points A, B, C, and D. Point P is fixed, and pencils are inserted in holes at D and Q. Various holes may be provided on the bars for other ratios of similitude, BC/BQ.

Use teacher-made or commercially prepared materials. Here motivation can be achieved by presenting the class with material of an unusual nature. This may include teacher-made materials such as models of geometric shapes, or specifically prepared overhead transparencies, or practical "tools" which illustrate a specific geometric principle. Some fine commercially prepared materials are available, ranging from geometric models to films of various kinds. Materials selected should be reviewed carefully and their presentation carefully planned so as to motivate students for the lesson and not to detract attention from it.

SUMMARY

Remembering a few general rules for using these eight motivational techniques will make them more effective.

1. The motivation should be brief.
2. The motivation should not be overemphasized. It should be a means to an end, not an end in itself.
3. The motivation should elicit the aim of the lesson from the class. This is a fine way of determining how effective the motivation actually is.
4. The motivation should be appropriate for the class—their interest and level of ability.
5. The motivation should draw upon motives actually present in the learner.

Although planning the motivation for a lesson is challenging, and at times difficult, the rewards are immeasurable. The higher degree of student learning resulting from a well-planned and well-executed activity will make this additional work worthwhile.

EXERCISES

1. How can you determine whether or not your motivational activity was successful?
2. For each of the following topics, prepare a motivational activity using one of the techniques presented in this chapter.
   a. The introductory lesson on area (tenth grade).
   b. The introductory lesson on solving factorable quadratic equations.
   c. The introductory lesson on reducing fractions (arithmetic).
   d. The introductory lesson on multiplication of signed numbers.
   e. The introductory lesson on mathematical induction.
   f. The introductory lesson on solving simultaneous equations algebraically (addition method).
   g. The introductory lesson on locus.
   h. The introductory lesson on truth tables (tautologies).
   i. The introductory lesson on parallelograms.
   j. The introductory lesson on proving trigonometric identities.
   k. The introductory lesson to bases of other than 10.
   l. The introductory lesson to the metric system.
   m. The introductory lesson on measurement.
3. Prepare a second motivational activity for each of the topics in Exercise 2.
4. Suppose you prepared a motivational activity which so captured the class interest that they did not want to leave the topic. What would you do to make this activity serve its intended purpose, that is, exciting students about the topic of the lesson? Justify your answer.
5. Select a topic in the secondary school mathematics curriculum and prepare two different motivational activities using the techniques presented in this chapter.
6. Repeat Exercise 5 using another topic from the secondary school mathematics curriculum.
7. Prepare three motivational activities for the same topic in the secondary school mathematics curriculum. After incorporating these motivational activities into the same lesson plan, teach this lesson (each of course with a different motivational activity at the beginning) to three different classes. If you cannot videotape these three lessons, have an experienced mathematics teacher observe the three classes. At the completion of this activity, analyze the three lessons with an experienced mathematics teacher and determine which of the three motivational devices worked best and why it worked best. Such factors as the appropriateness of the technique, the type of class it was used with, and the personality of the teacher using the technique should be addressed in the analysis.
8. Repeat Exercise 7. This time the teacher of the three lessons should be a volunteer, an experienced teacher of mathematics. However, the planning of the motivational devices can be done cooperatively.

SUGGESTED READINGS

Kolesnick, Walter B. *Motivation, Understanding and Influencing Human Behavior.* Boston: Allyn and Bacon, 1978.

Swireford, Edwin J. "Ninety Suggestions on the Teaching of Mathematics in Junior High School." *The Mathematics Teacher* 54 (1961): 145.

Wlodkowski, Raymond J. *Motivation and Teaching: A Practical Guide.* Washington, D.C.: National Educational Association, 1978.

CHAPTER 4 ASSIGNING HOMEWORK

The regular assignment of homework for a mathematics class is accepted almost universally among mathematics teachers. Many teachers consider the homework assignment as important as, if not more important than, the classwork. Unfortunately, some teachers lose sight of the purpose for assigning homework. When this happens, all aspects of the homework assignment are weakened.

After a brief discussion of the purpose for assigning homework, we shall consider the many questions a new teacher is likely to have about homework assignments. Some of these questions are

Why assign homework?

What should be involved in preparing the homework assignment?

What should be the nature of the homework assignment?

How much work should each assignment require?

Should all students be assigned the same work?

How frequently should homework be assigned?

When in the lesson should homework be assigned?

How should the assignment be made?

How should long term assignments be given?

How should the homework be arranged?

Where should the homework be written?

When should the homework be reviewed?

How should the homework assignment be reviewed?

How much of the homework assignment should be reviewed?

How frequently should the homework assignment be reviewed?

Should homework be collected?

How should the homework assignment be collected?

What should be done with the collected homework assignments?

How should the teacher deal with students who copy homework from others?

Should quizzes be used to check if homework assignments have been mastered?

We do not pretend to provide all the answers to these questions; however, we shall present some possible responses with the hope that others might be generated by the reader. Our intention is to provide the reader with enough information to formulate her own strategies for providing classes with meaningful and effective homework assignments. Remember, there is no one correct answer to these questions. Since teaching is generally tailored to the particular personality of the teacher and the type of class being taught, so too must a homework assignment strategy be somewhat consistent with the teacher's style and the class's needs.

ASSIGNING HOMEWORK

Questions About Homework Assignments

Why assign homework? Many reasons exist for assigning homework regularly to a mathematics class. Perhaps the most important reason is to provide for all students an active role in the learning process. Some educators think that although the classroom may provide an active learning environment, the "real learning" takes place when the student works alone at his own pace outside the classroom. This is not meant to minimize the importance of the classroom teaching process, but to accentuate that of the assigned homework. In the classroom, the teacher generally paces the instruction for the average student, with some accommodation for the weaker and stronger students, but there still may be many students for whom the instruction was not precisely paced. For these students the classroom instruction may serve as a forum for exposure to new material, while the time spent on homework would provide the genuine learning experience.

Homework assignments provide the students an opportunity to gain a broader understanding of topics and concepts taught in class, and also provide them a structure for deeper analysis of the subject matter. This is rarely possible in the classroom where the teacher is moving along at a predetermined pace. The homework assignment allows time for a student to reflect on the work at his own pace, so that creative work can germinate.

Another important reason for assigning homework is to motivate students for further learning. By allowing students to expand on what has been taught in class, students may be inspired to extend their knowledge. Occasionally a teacher may choose to foreshadow the next day's classwork. By having students work on this type of carefully prepared assignment at home, where they can work alone, a real desire to move ahead in the subject area can be developed.

Perhaps one of the most common reasons for assigning homework is to provide practice in a newly developed skill. If planned properly, such drill of necessary skills could be quite effective. Unfortunately, this type of assignment is often abused. When used as punishment for some disciplinary reason, such a homework assignment not only becomes ineffective but may become counter-productive. A well-planned and effective teaching performance usually requires no special consideration of discipline. Weak teaching, however, which often promotes discipline problems, is damaged further by a punitive homework assignment given to solve these discipline problems.

The homework assignment is an integral part of the entire learning process and consequently must be handled properly. The remainder of this chapter is designed to allow the teacher to focus on the key aspects of homework assignments and then formulate a personalized plan.

What should be involved in preparing the homework assignment? It is helpful for both the teacher and the students to anticipate the homework assignment. The teacher, as part of the preparation of her lesson and homework assignment, should work out all of the exercises being assigned to the students for homework. Not only would this be useful in more accurately determining the time required for a student to complete the assignment, but it would also enable the teacher to alert students about potential trouble spots in the homework assignment before they encounter them at home. By telling the class beforehand what is expected of them with regard to the homework assignment, the assignment should become a more meaningful part of the total learning process.

What should be the nature of the homework assignment? Many types of homework assignments are possible in a mathematics class. No one is necessarily better than another. The content and the nature of the class should determine the type of homework. Perhaps the key thought to keep in mind when preparing a homework assignment is *variety*. Monotony is likely to be the chief factor influencing students to abandon their homework assignment.

Teachers should try to provide different kinds of exercises. For example, some of the types of exercises to choose from would include: drill exercises, verbal problems, proofs, construction exercises, thought questions, applications of newly taught principles, and reading assignments. Particularly in a mathematics class, a reading assignment needs lots of student motivation, since a non-written assignment is likely to be omitted, being deemed unnecessary by the students.

In addition to varying the type of exercises offered, assignments may also vary in nature. For example, one assignment may be intended entirely for review of previously studied material, while another may include some discovery questions. Included in a review assignment may be a variety of different kinds of exercises. The assignment may simply offer exercises which review the previous lesson's work, or it may provide exercises which will assist the student to review for a test on an entire unit's work.

Another type of homework assignment may involve a discovery approach. Here the student is given a series of exercises which foreshadow the ensuing lesson. The questions are usually arranged in an order which will permit the student to discover a new idea after completing the sequence of questions. A few examples of this type of exercise follow.

EXAMPLE: The homework assignment just prior to a discussion on the slope relationship between two parallel and perpendicular lines might include the following:

1. Find the slope of the lines represented by each of the following equations:
   a. $5x + 3y = 15$
   b. $-3x + 5y = 10$
   c. $5x + 3y = 5$
   d. $5y = 3x + 20$
2. Graph each of the equations in Exercise 1 with the same set of coordinate axes.
3. Which lines appear perpendicular? What is the relationship of their slopes.
4. Which lines appear parallel? What is the relationship of their slopes.
5. Make a generalized statement regarding the slopes of parallel or perpendicular lines (based on the above exercises).

This set of exercises provides review of a skill learned earlier, then requires the student to make some simple generalizations from the specifics presented.

EXAMPLE: The homework assignment the day before introducing the Pythagorean Identity to a trigonometry class might include the following:

Complete the following chart (use the radical relationships):

θ	Sin θ	Cos θ	Sin² θ	Cos² θ	Sin² θ + Cos² θ
30					
45					
60					

What generalization seems to be true about $\text{Sin}^2\theta + \text{Cos}^2\theta$?

Although completing the chart ought to be relatively simple for students, it should lead them to discover an interesting relationship.

EXAMPLE: The homework assignment immediately preceding the lesson which will introduce the topic of angle measurement with a circle to a geometry class might include the following set of exercises.

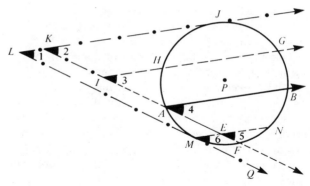

In the figure, consider all lines parallel that appear to be so. The answers to questions 2 through 8 are arcs.

1. Why are angles 1–6 congruent?
2. $m\angle BAF = \dfrac{1}{2}$ m $\overset{\frown}{BF}$
3. $m\overset{\frown}{BN} = $ m $\overset{\frown}{AM}$ = m $\overset{\frown}{MF}$
4. **$m\angle NMQ = m\angle BAF = \dfrac{1}{2}(mBN + $ m $\overset{\frown}{NF}) = $**
   $\dfrac{1}{2}(m\overset{\frown}{MF} + $ m $\overset{\frown}{NF}) = \dfrac{1}{2}$ **m** $\overset{\frown}{NM}$
5. **$m\angle NEF = m\angle BAF = \dfrac{1}{2}(m\overset{\frown}{BN} + $ m $\overset{\frown}{NF}) = $**
   $\dfrac{1}{2}($ **mAM + m** $\overset{\frown}{NF})$
6. **$m\angle GIF = m\angle BAF = \dfrac{1}{2}$ m $\overset{\frown}{BF} = \dfrac{1}{2}($ m $\overset{\frown}{BF} + $**
   $m\overset{\frown}{BG} - m\overset{\frown}{BG}) = \dfrac{1}{2}($m $\overset{\frown}{BF} + mBG - $ m $\overset{\frown}{NA})$
   $= \dfrac{1}{2}($ **mGBF − m** $\overset{\frown}{HA})$
7. **$m\angle JKF = m\angle BAF = \dfrac{1}{2}$ m $\overset{\frown}{BF} = \dfrac{1}{2}($ m $\overset{\frown}{BF} + $**
   $m\overset{\frown}{JB} - m\overset{\frown}{JB}) = \dfrac{1}{2}($m $\overset{\frown}{BF} + mJB - $ m $\overset{\frown}{JA}) = $
   $\dfrac{1}{2}($ **mJBF − m** $\overset{\frown}{JA})$
8. **$m\angle JLM = m\angle NMQ = \dfrac{1}{2}$ m $\overset{\frown}{NM} = \dfrac{1}{2}($ m $\overset{\frown}{NM} + $**
   $m\overset{\frown}{JN} - m\overset{\frown}{JN}) = \dfrac{1}{2}($m $\overset{\frown}{NM} + mJN - $ m $\overset{\frown}{JM}) = $
   $\dfrac{1}{2}($ **mJBM − m** $\overset{\frown}{JM})$
9. Express verbally the bold-printed relationships in Exercises 4–8.

These exercises succinctly develop all the angle measurement theorems related to the circle which are generally taught in the high school geometry class. Students are led through a series of simple questions which, because of their structure, essentially prove the sought-after relationships. Discovery here should be a natural result.

We suggest interspersing discovery exercises with others, since their function satisfies only some of the purposes for assigning homework.

One of the more popular types of homework assignment is often called a *spiraled* assignment, since it spirals back over previously learned material. Perhaps it owes its popularity to its ability to satisfy two homework assignment functions. In addition to enabling students to reinforce the current classroom instruction, a spiraled assignment provides review of previously taught topics. For example, suppose you are assigning homework after a lesson on ''angle measurement with a circle'' in the high school geometry course. As part of this assignment, you might include one exercise reviewing similarity, one proof involving a parallelogram, and one construction. Regardless of which previous topics are selected for inclusion in a particular assignment, the selection ought to be done in an organized and orderly fashion.

One convenient method for spiraling the homework assignments is to mark dates of assignment in the margin next to the exercises in the teacher's copy of the textbook. This will assist her to keep a record of which items have or have not been assigned. The extent and degree of the spiral depends on each individual class's needs. This further reinforces the idea that lesson plans (including homework assignments) should not be used from one year to the next without making substantial adjustments for each class.

Many other types of homework assignments may be used for a mathematics class. These may include home experiments of some mathematical principle (e.g., coin tossing to compute probabilities empirically); short essays on famous mathematicians or some other vignette out of the history of mathematics (e.g., how Eratosthenes measured the circumference of the earth); library assignments (e.g., to find the origin of the $\sqrt{}$ symbol or the first use of the letter π to represent the ratio of the circumference of a circle to its diameter); and brief papers on some topics related to, but not included in, the curriculum (e.g., a paper on applications of parabolas and parabolic surfaces).

Whichever assignment a teacher chooses to use for a particular situation, the key to success is variety. Not only should the types of exercises be varied, but also the types of assignments should be dictated by the subject matter and therefore should change as needed. Although some teachers assign homework which consists of mixtures of the types of assignments described here, others exhibit no creativity in their homework assignments. Such teachers' assignments simply read ''Do page 353, ex. 1–29, odd numbers only.'' It does not take long for students to react in kind to this type of homework assignment. The result is a lost opportunity to achieve meaningful learning in mathematics outside the classroom. Remember, the needs of the class determine the type of homework to be assigned.

How much work should each assignment require? The answer to this question must vary with each intended audience. We can answer this question only by providing guidelines for setting the proper assignment length for a particular class.

Each homework assignment will have specific objectives based on the needs of the class. The knack for preparing an appropriate assignment is to accomplish the objectives with the least amount of student work time. Unnecessary repetition should be eliminated, or at least minimized. The exercises should be carefully selected so that each one is highly effective in meeting the objectives of the particular homework assignment.

Students are quick to realize when an assignment is time-efficient and when it is loaded with superfluous material. When the exercises are largely repetitive, students can easily get bored and distracted. As a result, they may either do the work ''just to get it done,'' or they may copy the work from a classmate and submit that. Naturally this results in a waste of student time with little or no learning being accomplished. Therefore, the homework assignments should be succinct, properly covering the intended content in the minimum time.

It is difficult to specify a time limit to a mathematics homework assignment. The mathematics teacher obviously would prefer giving the class a longer homework assignment just to make sure everything is thoroughly covered. But she must remember that mathematics is only one of several courses each student must take. Therefore, the time allotted to mathematics homework should generally be kept to at most about one-half hour per assignment. (This is merely a guide and can vary with individual circumstances.)

Should all students be assigned the same work? Once again (and at the risk of repetition) the answer to this question depends on the type of class for which the homework assignment is intended. If the class is purely homogeneous with respect to student mathematical ability and achievement, then perhaps a uniform homework assignment for the entire class would be appropriate. In reality, classes generally do not have this sort of uniform composition. Therefore an alternative to uniform assignments may be sought.

The best instruction is tailored to each student's individual needs. Unfortunately, it is not always practicable to satisfy such a desirable objective in the regular secondary school classroom. Perhaps one of the few ways of approaching such a goal is through the homework assignment. The homework assignment provides a useful means for adjusting class instruction to meet students' individual needs.

Special enrichment assignments can be provided for the more able students, while they can be excused from some drill or review exercises. On the other hand, students needing more drill and review of some necessary skills could be given exercises designed for this purpose. The mathematics teacher should not neglect this fine opportunity to individualize at least a part of the learning process.

How frequently should homework be assigned? Since one of the basic functions of the homework assignment is to reinforce the classroom instruction, a homework assignment should follow each classroom lesson. Naturally, there may be some lessons which may not require a follow-up homework assignment. Then either no assignment may be made or a review assignment might be useful.

Some teachers feel that no homework assignments should be given on the weekends. Others feel that homework should be assigned only four out of every five days, but the one day where no homework is assigned should vary according to the class's instructional needs.

Either of these two rather liberal plans have pitfalls. It is usually better to start off a course with a stringent attitude regarding the frequency of the homework assignments, and then later make some adjustments where appropriate, than it is to begin with a ''promise'' to provide days where no homework will be assigned and then have to renege on this ''promise'' when instructional considerations demand a change to more frequent homework assignments. Students will always welcome a change to a more relaxed pace rather than the reverse.

The question regarding frequency of homework assignments also can refer to the frequency with which assignments are presented to the class. Should they be given to the class on a daily, weekly, bi-weekly, or monthly basis? Once again, each teacher must decide which system (or combination of systems) is best suited for her classes or teaching style. There are probably equally good arguments for many plans.

Those who favor assigning homework on a daily basis would probably argue that this is the only way in which the homework can be regularly tailored to instructional needs. Each day when a new lesson is planned (based on the experience of the previous lesson) a homework assignment is prepared based on the immediate needs of the students. Such precisely fitted assignments are far more difficult (if at all possible) to achieve when assignments are given a week at a time. For one thing, teachers who have planned a week's assignments and have given them to the students may find altering them inconvenient, and may therefore not only be reluctant to make changes based on instructional needs but also may try to pace their lessons (to a degree) to this predetermined plan. Consider the case in which a teacher finds that, midway through a week's assignments, a class needs some drill on a particular skill. The class may be resentful at a last minute augmentation of the assignments. This negative student attitude could adversely affect the educational benefits which were intended by this additional work. Even if some previously assigned work is deleted from the assignment to accommodate the additional work, the resulting assignment may still not be as effective as if it were planned on a daily basis to meet the ongoing needs of the class. Thus a daily planned assignment has as its chief advantage the ability to meet the regularly assessed needs of the students based on classroom experiences and previous homework performance.

Seemingly equally convincing arguments support weekly planned homework assignments. Here teachers will argue that by assigning homework a week (or more) at a time, they can better plan and spiral their homework assignments. They would also point out that by making the assignments only once every several days, they save classroom time otherwise taken up by giving out new assignments. In addition, proponents of weekly homework assignments would indicate that by having a week's assignments in their possession, students who are absent from school could without much inconvenience try to keep up with the rest of the class.

The weekly assignment also enables a student to accelerate his homework by going ahead of the class (if he is able to). This has both advantages and disadvantages. For example, if a student finds that, say on a Wednesday, he will not have time to do his homework assignment, he might complete (if capable) this assignment on Tuesday. Although this is not an ideal practice, it is better than coming in to his Thursday class unprepared. The disadvantage to knowing future assignments is that the surprise factor is gone. There is some motivational advantage to having students discover new concepts. By knowing what future assignments are planned, students also know which topics are going to be studied and when. The removal of this element of discovery could be a weakness for the instructional plan.

The question of frequency of assignments, like many others in this chapter, is one that can be answered only by the individual teacher. We present the chief arguments for the various positions and leave the choice to the reader. Whatever the choice, substantial justification should be consistent with a teacher's personality, teaching style, and educational philosophy, and with the nature of the class.

When should homework be assigned? Perhaps an ideal time to give a homework assignment is at the point in the lesson which naturally leads up to the work to be assigned. For example, a teacher may say, ''Now that you know how to solve a quadratic equation, try the following for homework.'' It can be argued, however, that this approach breaks the continuity of the lesson and for this reason should be avoided.

Once again, for the teacher who elects to assign homework daily, there is probably no single ''right time'' to assign the homework. Those who argue for assigning the homework at the beginning of the lesson may say that asking students to write their assignment when they enter the room assures that they are occupied as soon as they enter and that they will not forget to write their assignment.

Others may argue that by assigning the homework at the beginning of the lesson, the teacher may reveal the topic of the ensuing lesson and thereby eliminate the effect or impact of a discovery approach. It is also possible that when an assignment is given out at the beginning of the lesson, some students may begin to work on it *during* the lesson just to "get it over with early" and as a result miss the new work presented during the lesson. This should certainly be discouraged.

Opponents may respond that a teacher could become so involved in the lesson that she may forget to assign the homework, or possibly give it to the students when the period-ending bell sounds and students are in the process of leaving the room. This would not give the teacher an opportunity to explain the homework assignment to the class. In addition, some students may miss receiving the assignment by exiting too quickly. At any rate, a rushed assignment is not desirable.

In response, the proponents of the end-of-lesson assignment would argue that by assigning homework at the end of the lesson, the teachers would be able to make adjustments in the originally planned assignment based on the class performance during the lesson without the class knowing it. This way no ill feeling on the part of the class can result.

Many more arguments can be offered for the "best time" to assign homework. We have simply presented a sample of the options available so that the reader can make a decision. Whichever time the teacher finds best suited for both herself and her class, the assignment must be reviewed carefully with the class. Ambiguous parts should be clearly explained and potential tough spots anticipated. This should also make students aware of the purpose of the particular homework assignment.

How should the assignment be made?   This will depend on the way in which the homework is being assigned. If the homework is being assigned on a weekly basis, then the assignments ought to be written on a stencil, duplicated (perhaps on a spirit duplicator machine) and passed out to the class. A typical assignment sheet might include the assignment number, the topic of the lesson, the date, the actual assignment, and some of the highlights of the lesson which ought to be studied. One possible arrangement is shown in the sample Weekly Homework Assignment Sheet.

For the student, such a homework assignment sheet can also serve the function of reinforcing the objectives of the lesson. In addition, this sheet can serve as an on-going form of communication with the parents. It will allow them to be aware of the direction of the course and where possible offer some assistance to their children. The direction of the course will also become more clearly focused for the students as a result of using these homework assignment sheets.

A small, but potentially important benefit of using homework assignment sheets, is that it avoids the possibility of students accidentally writing a wrong assignment. Such can be the case if they must copy it from the chalkboard or from teacher dictation.

Homework assignment sheets also can be used by a teacher giving out the assignments on a daily basis. This time the sheets would probably be cut into individual assignments or run off daily. A difficulty with using any assignment sheet for daily assignments is that if a teacher must make adjustments in the assignment, she must involve the class in this assignment change. This procedure could have a negative effect among the students, although if handled properly, the negative effect could be minimized or even eliminated.

A popular way of giving out homework in the mathematics class is on the chalkboard. Some teachers, fortunate enough to have their own classroom, may write the assignments for all their classes on the chalkboard so that when each class enters the room, the students may simply copy the assignment into their notebooks. In this case it is possibly better to use the side chalkboard (if one is available) rather than the front chalkboard, reserving the front chalkboard for the regular classwork.

The teacher who assigns homework at the end of the lesson can use the chalkboard for this purpose. In this case, the front chalkboard would be more desirable since it would be no longer needed for classwork. The assignment is better seen at the front chalkboard and therefore less apt to be overlooked by the students.

Assignments may also be given orally, but this is usually not the most effective way. A student can miss hearing a portion of the assignment or possibly hear a part of the assignment incorrectly. The result may have negative effects on the learning process. Giving a homework assignment orally could require several repetitions and still cause confusion. When handled improperly, the oral assignment could leave students with the impression that the assignment is either optional or not too important.

Regardless of the manner in which the homework is assigned, the teacher should make every effort to be certain that there are no ambiguities. For example, if there are similarly numbered exercises at the top and bottom of a given textbook page, the location, top or bottom, should be specified in the assignment. Each assignment should be properly identified by class, date and topic, as well as any other relevant information. Above all, the manner in which the homework assignments are presented should be consistent with the teacher's instructional style and properly suited for the type of class.

Weekly Homework Assignment Sheet

_____
(Class)

_____   _____   _____
(Assignment No.)   (Topic)   (Date)

Book / Page / Exercises
"   "   "
"   "   "

Concepts and Relationships to Remember:

_____   _____   _____
(Assignment No.)   (Topic)   (Date)

Book / Page / Exercises
"   "   "
"   "   "

Concepts and Relationships to Remember:

_____   _____   _____
(Assignment No.)   (Topic)   (Date)

Book / Page / Exercises
"   "   "
"   "   "

Concepts and Relationships to Remember:

_____   _____   _____
(Assignment No.)   (Topic)   (Date)

Book / Page / Exercises
"   "   "
"   "   "

Concepts and Relationships to Remember:

_____   _____   _____
(Assignment No.)   (Topic)   (Date)

Book / Page / Exercises
"   "   "
"   "   "

Concepts and Relationships to Remember:

Some teachers feel that a weaker mathematics class is more apt to require homework assignments presented on sheets because they could copy their assignment incorrectly or simply forget to copy it. Thus the type of class might well be an important consideration in selecting the best format in which to present the homework assignment.

How should long term assignments be given?

Occasionally a long term assignment may be appropriate for a mathematics class. A teacher may decide to assign a report on a famous mathematician; students also may be assigned a geometric construction project or may be asked to conduct a statistical experiment. For any of these long term assignments, the manner in which the assignment is presented to the class is important.

The possibility of a long term assignment should be announced to the class at the beginning of the course. When the teacher is ready to formally assign this project to the class, she must be sure to include the following:

> The extent of the work that will be required (specific topics should be listed).
> The specific guidelines for choosing a topic (if a choice is called for).
> The scope and limitations of the project.
> The format for submission of the work.
> The time table for the assignment.
> Available resources (i.e., school, department or public library).

After a reasonable period of time, the teacher should monitor the students' progress. Those students who are floundering should be assisted and encouraged, while those students who are working in the wrong direction should be redirected. At this time, the teacher may discuss with the class difficulties some students may have encountered in the process of working on the assignment, possibly helping others facing similar problems.

Midway through the project, the assignment format should be reviewed with the class. Students should be reminded about resources available (e.g., mathematics department library, school library, etc.).

To make a long term assignment as meaningful as possible, students should be scheduled for individual conferences with the teacher to get on-going assistance. This not only provides a necessary input for direction but also a usually much needed stimulus for further work.

Unlike the regular homework assignment, the long term assignment requires continuous monitoring, guidance, assistance and assessment. Unless special care is taken to prepare and assist students in these endeavors, such an assignment is likely to be ineffective.

FORMAT OF THE HOMEWORK ASSIGNMENT

Much to the amazement of the beginning teacher, students seek out direction from the teacher in almost every aspect of school work. This certainly includes direction regarding the format of the homework assignment. Two basic questions come up in this respect: How should it be arranged? and Where should it be written? Although the responses to these two questions are closely related, we shall discuss them separately.

Questions about Arrangement of Homework

The format of the homework, if uniform among the students, is useful to the teacher when reading individual assignments. Endless options exist for selecting a convenient format for students to follow when writing their homework. We shall indicate some, with the hope that this discussion will generate other, perhaps more useful, ideas for the reader. In deciding on a format to have your students follow, you ought to consider *your* work with these homework assignments as well as the students' eventual use for them.

Both Sides of Paper? Perhaps one place to begin is by asking yourself if you find it more convenient to have students write their work on only one side of the paper or on both sides. Except for special situations (e.g., an unusual proof, problem or report to be submitted), requiring students to write on only one side of a sheet of paper is perhaps wasteful and costly. Yet some teachers may prefer to do so, and with adequate justification.

Identifying information? The teacher should specify what information should be written on the homework paper. In addition to the student's name, should his subject class, homework assignment number, date, etc. be included? Should each assignment be numbered in a particular way? Whatever the teacher chooses to require should be uniform throughout the class.

Writing the questions? Another issue on which the teacher must decide is whether or not students should copy a homework question before answering it. Many teachers consider this a poor use of a student's time. Yet, some feel that if students have the questions before them, the homework assignment papers become a better source from which to study.

Margins? Any teacher who has gotten a homework assignment paper from a student who left no margins on her paper, will appreciate having students leave sufficient margins for teacher comments. Students may also like to use this space to make necessary corrections after listening to a class review of the homework assignment.

Framing answers? Some teachers require students to frame in (with a rectangle) their answers to a question to separate them from the rest of the work. This makes the teacher's work easier when reading many papers. An extra benefit derived from this practice is that it requires students to identify the answer to a question, a skill often taken for granted but sometimes not so trivial. After working a problem, students sometimes lose sight of what exactly was being asked and, having worked the problem correctly, do not submit the proper answer.

Format of the paper? For some short problems in algebra or arithmetic, a teacher might want her students to fold a sheet of paper into a specific number of rectangles. This not only may result in a neater paper, but it also allows the student to get more work onto a sheet of paper. A similar effect can be obtained by ruling lines on the paper instead of folding it.

Teachers often insist on a format for working particular types of problems. For example, when solving equations it is desirable to have students line up the equal signs vertically. Students may simplify radicals by working horizontally. Special directions may be given when the homework assignment involves graphing functions or proving geometric theorems. Since both of these latter types of exercises usually require using a full page for each problem, a more efficient format would involve

folding a piece of 8½″ × 11″ paper in half to form a "booklet" (5½″ × 8½″) of four pages, each of which can accommodate one problem. (See figure below.) This format allows a student to place four, instead of two, longer problems (such as a geometric proof or a graph of a function) on a sheet of paper. Teacher handling also should be easier.

Regardless of which format a teacher chooses to use, uniformity among the students serves two useful functions. It gives the students the direction they desire, and it makes the teacher's job of reading the papers much easier.

Where should the homework be written?

Depending on the type of class involved and the subject matter being taught, a uniform arrangement should be worked out for the class. For example, for a high school geometry class, the teacher may require a loose-leaf or spiral notebook (8½″ × 11″) with a clip or large envelope fastened to the inside back cover. This will enable the students to keep their notes along with their homework in folded booklets together.

Teachers may instead ask students to keep a separate homework section in their loose-leaf notebook (of a specified size) so that after it is collected by the teacher it can be reinserted in the notebook.

There are lots of useful ways to have students keep their homework. The exact manner should be determined by the teacher and may vary with each class, considering such things as subject matter, class discipline, student work habits and so on.

REVIEWING THE HOMEWORK ASSIGNMENT

A teacher must answer several questions about the review of homework. The teacher must decide when and how the homework is to be reviewed. She must also consider how often she ought to go over the homework with the class and how much of it should be discussed. That is, should every exercise be reviewed or only a representative few? We will discuss these questions in this section.

Questions about Reviewing Homework Assignments

When should the homework be reviewed? There is probably no "best time" during a lesson for discussing the previous night's homework. Some teachers feel that every lesson must begin with a review of the previous lesson's homework assignment. They

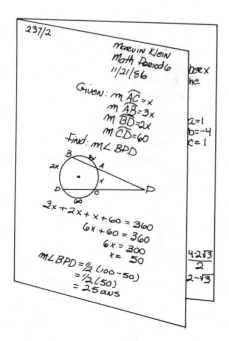

Sample Homework Format

argue that new work should not be presented until the previous work (in the form of the homework assignment) has first been mastered.

On the other hand, other teachers review the previous lesson's homework at the end of the lesson so as to allow the new lesson to get off to a crisp and motivating start. These teachers prefer to begin the lesson with a motivating activity leading into the development of the lesson. Only after the new topic has been completely discussed do they want to go over the past homework assignment.

A teacher certainly could adopt both systems and even include one which calls for a review of the previous homework assignment at a point in the class period at which it most naturally fits! In the case of a discovery-type homework assignment, it might be appropriate to discuss the homework just before introducing a concept or relationship which may come up in the middle of the lesson. Here the homework would be useful to elicit from students the desired mathematical relationship. When used in this way, various parts of the homework might well be reviewed at different times throughout the class period. Although this variety is nice, the final determination should be based on the individual class's needs and the appropriateness for the lesson.

How should the homework assignment be reviewed? Different kinds of homework exercises require different methods of review with the class. Some homework exercises can be gone over orally; one example of this is exercises which call for single word (or short phrase) answers.

Using the chalkboard is one of the most popular methods of reviewing homework in a mathematics class. The chalkboard can be used in a number of different ways. The teacher may write correct solutions on the chalkboard, or students may be assigned to write particular problems from the homework on the chalkboard. One popular way to review homework at the chalkboard is to assign students to write the solution to a particular homework problem at the side chalkboard when they enter the room. It is usually better to make these chalkboard assignments as students walk in, rather than when the homework is first assigned, so that, while doing their homework, students do not concentrate only on the chalkboard-assigned problem at the expense of the rest. At the appropriate time of the lesson, these students should explain their work to the rest of the class and answer any questions their classmates might have. Occasionally it may suffice simply to have the class read the chalkboard work and ask the writer questions if something is not clear. This should not be done on a regular basis unless the teacher feels sure that no student lets a problem's solution go by without question when it is still unclear to her. Oftentimes, some teacher questions regarding the homework exercises will help determine the extent to which students understand the work. Only in special circumstances, such as when there is little remaining time in a lesson, should the teacher explain the students' chalkboard work. Students may at first show reluctance at having to explain their own chalkboard work to the rest of the class, but after a while they will begin to enjoy it, taking pride in their own work. This sort of procedure goes far to promote an active learning environment for the class.

Another way of reviewing homework is to have previously selected students prepare model solutions on spirit duplicator stencils. At some time before the mathematics class, these students make enough copies on a spirit duplicator machine for the rest of the class. These sheets are then passed out to the class at the appropriate time in the lesson. The main advantage to this procedure is that no students are taken away from classwork at the beginning of the class period to write solutions to a part of the previous homework assignment on the chalkboard. All necessary corrections on these papers would be made when reviewing the work with the class. This procedure is costly and inconvenient since it requires a substantial amount of extra time to make duplicates; however, it allows students to leave the class with a correct copy of the homework and with a minimum of writing when the problems are being reviewed in class.

One way of avoiding the inconvenience mentioned above, but still deriving many of the advantages this scheme has to offer, is to have the specially selected students write their work on overhead projector transparencies rather than on spirit duplicator stencils. Then when the teacher is ready to have the class review the previous day's homework, these specially selected students would simply exhibit their work on an overhead projector. For this system, each student in the class would have a supply of these reusable acetate transparencies so that when assigned specific problems from the homework for the next day's review, these students would merely copy the solutions to these selected problems on the transparencies after they have completed their entire homework assignment. This method includes many of the desirable features of the other methods described and in a rather efficient manner. The only difficulty with this method is the continuous need for an overhead projector and the comparatively short time that the class sees the work flashed on the screen.

Certainly there are other methods for reviewing homework assignments which were not discussed here. We simply chose a few proven methods to give the reader some ideas. An imaginative teacher will develop numerous variations.

How much of the homework assignment should be reviewed? Teacher judgment is probably the only way to determine how much of the homework assignment should be reviewed. The teacher must consider the subject matter involved, the class level and their ability to learn the particular topic, the type of students, and their achievement. If the class is a high ability mathematics class, then perhaps only a representative sample of the homework needs to be reviewed. If the teacher can ascertain that no one in the class had any difficulty with the assignment, then perhaps no review may be necessary, although in this case the teacher might just spot-check with some pointed questions to see if, in fact, the entire class really did have no difficulty with the homework.

On the other hand, a low ability mathematics class could very likely require a complete review of the homework assignment. Many of the students may have missed some of the homework questions and would greatly benefit from a comprehensive review of the homework.

How frequently should the homework assignment be reviewed?

In most cases, the homework assignment should be gone over with the class during the lesson following the assignment. Naturally, there are exceptions to this. For example, if a homework assignment has nothing to do with the succeeding lesson but does relate to a lesson a few days in the future, it might be more advisable to defer a discussion of this homework assignment until the later lesson.

The ability level (or achievement level) of a class can also be a determining factor in the frequency of a homework review. A gifted class may not require a daily review; here it might be done only on request. A teacher should be cautious about not reviewing homework daily. Students could give a teacher a false sense of security, saying they do not need to discuss the homework when, in fact, such a review might help them.

Generally, it is best to review a homework assignment immediately after it has been done by the students, for this insures that it is still fresh in their minds and remains part of the total learning process.

CHECKING HOMEWORK ASSIGNMENTS

Once the homework has been assigned and completed according to a prescribed format, the teacher should lead a review of this work. At the same time, the teacher must grapple with the issue of checking each individual's homework. The questions arise: "Should the homework be collected?" "From whom?" "How regularly?" "Should it be graded?" "Aside from reading a student's homework, how can the teacher determine the level of student mastery of the homework?" We shall now consider these and other questions about checking homework assignments.

Questions on Checking Homework Assignments

Should homework be collected?

Although some teachers collect homework daily, it is quite a chore for the teacher carrying a full teaching load to read so many papers. Suppose a teacher has five classes, each consisting of thirty students. If this teacher were to collect each student's paper daily, she would have to read 750 papers per week! If she spent just one minute on each paper (far too little time to offer meaningful comments), she would be spending 12½ hours per week reading homework assignments. This is an inordinate amount of work, especially when coupled with the chores of planning lessons, preparing tests, and caring for other school-related matters. Unless a teacher is willing to devote these vast amounts of time to reading students' homework papers, it is probably better to collect fewer papers but to read them more carefully.

If the homework is important enough to assign, then it is important enough to check. Therefore, whatever homework is assigned should also be checked. Since we see the gargantuan chore involved in reading and making meaningful comments on each student's homework paper every day, it would be advisable to collect only a small portion of the class's homework daily. By reading a different sample of student homework papers each day, the teacher ought to get a reasonably good feeling for the progress of all the students in the class.

For some classes, it may not be necessary to actually collect homework papers for some topics. The teacher may walk about the room during the lesson, when students are working on a classwork problem, and quickly check some of the students' homework papers. This sort of homework reading might be possible when the assignment involves graphing some functions, which can be checked quickly by inspection.

Constructive criticism as well as complimentary remarks should be made to the students whose papers are looked over. Remember, this process is part of the learning process.

How should the homework assignment be collected?

Students should not be able to predict when their homework papers will be collected by the teacher. Otherwise they may avoid doing their homework on days when they feel reasonably sure that their homework papers will not be collected. The teacher should set up a random selection, noting in her record book when each student's work was read.

The teacher may collect one row's homework on one day, then a diagonal the next day, then perhaps a column of students the following day. Such a system would allow the teacher to collect the homework from one particular student in need of extra help on two or three consecutive days without embarrassing him before the class. This would be the student who could be made to be at the intersection of a row, column and diagonal of students in the room. The student may just view his multiple collections as "bad luck" when, in fact, it was deliberately planned. The teacher now has the opportunity to give this student extra help with his homework.

What should be done with the collected homework assignments?

There is a wide range of choices of what might be done with collected homework assignments. On the one hand, a teacher may do nothing with the collected work, while on the other, the teacher would do an in-depth evaluation on every homework paper with comments and a grade. Both extremes are not very advisable. Doing nothing with the homework collected is dishonest to the students. If homework is collected, the student expects that it will at least be looked at, and rightly so.

The other extreme is ill-advised from the point of view of the workload consideration discussed earlier. In addition, this extreme also introduces the question of grading homework papers. This is generally a bad practice to follow since it brings a potential punitive aspect to the homework assignment. When homework papers are graded, students are likely to go out of their way to get the right answers. They may go to classmates, parents, friends or even other teachers and have these people do the homework assignment for them. Although this sometimes has educational value (such as when students actually learn the material as a result of seeing it done correctly by others), the concern usually lies with getting the correct answer down on paper to show to the teacher rather than learning how to correctly solve the problem.

Those homework papers which have been collected should be read for completeness and accuracy. Where appropriate, detailed comments should be made and complimentary remarks should be offered for encouragement. Having read some sample homework assignments, the teacher is far better equipped to teach the class, for she will now know more precisely the weaknesses and strengths of the students. Such information can improve the learning process significantly.

There may be situations when the teacher wishes to check a class's homework in detail. She may want to determine whether a particular difficult point was properly mastered, or whether her students are preparing themselves for an upcoming examination (such as the Advanced Placement Examinations given by the Educational Testing Service). Generally, however, one would not check all homework daily and in great detail, since this would be too time-consuming.

Remember, the primary value of a homework assignment is the students' work on it. The teacher checking the homework serves as motivation for the student for the next lesson. This ought to be kept clearly in mind when comments are offered on the students' papers.

How should the teacher deal with students who copy homework from others?

Traditionally the student who copied the homework (if this can be proved) is penalized in some manner. If he is desperate, he may try again at some future date. He may feel that rather than be penalized for not having done the homework assignment, he would take a chance copying it from his classmate's work. An effective way to deal with this problem is to "dry-up the source." By penalizing the student who *gave* the homework assignment to the other student to copy, the giver will be far more reluctant to repeat this incident and therefore not let anyone copy his homework. Thus, by attacking the source, the problem of copied assignments should be eliminated.

Another effective way to handle this problem is to speak to both students involved. Confront them with the "evidence" and discuss the virtues of honesty. After a second occurrence parents of the copier should be notified. An initial warning to the class of this plan at the beginning of the course could avoid the problem entirely.

Should quizzes be used to check if homework assignments have been mastered?

As long as a quiz is not given for primarily punitive reasons, it could be sparingly used to determine the true level of mastery of the class on a particular homework assignment. The quiz should be brief and should consist of material covered in the homework (if that is the area of concern). The questions on the quiz should be simply stated with no complications so as to avoid confusion. The extrinsic motivation presented by the expectation of a quiz could also be a useful factor in the total learning process.

SUMMARY

This discussion on homework assignments is not intended to be all-inclusive. It should serve as a guide to the various aspects of assigning homework. To keep some basic principles as a ready reference, consider the following:

1. Homework should be assigned regularly.
2. All homework should conform to a uniform format.
3. The homework assignment should be planned so that students do not have to work more than thirty minutes on mathematics each evening. (Occasional exceptions are acceptable.)
4. Homework assignments may be varied for a single class to meet individual student needs.

5. Homework should be assigned daily, with adjustments in this routine made only after the daily pattern has been well established.

6. The homework assignment should be properly motivated, making the class aware of its purpose.

7. The homework assignment should be clear and unambiguous.

8. The content of the homework assignment should be revised as needed, based on classroom experiences and made meaningful to the students.

9. Attempts should be made to vary the type of homework assignments.

10. Homework should never be considered as punishment.

11. Homework should be reviewed daily.

12. Various methods for reviewing the homework may be used.

13. A system should be established to select a sample of different students (daily) to submit their homework for teacher reading and comments.

14. Grading homework assignments could be counterproductive.

15. Short quizzes might be used to measure mastery of a homework assignment.

This list should serve as a brief review of some of the questions raised and comments made in this chapter. Assigning homework is a personal thing, which, following some of the suggestions here, ought to be an important component in the learning process.

EXERCISES

1. For each of the following topics write a homework assignment for an average ability class. You may use any appropriate mathematics textbook to assist you. Try to make a provision for both ends of the ability spectrum in this class.
   a. The first lesson on the quadratic formula.
   b. The last lesson before a test on special parallelograms.
   c. The first lesson on multiplying signed numbers.
   d. The first lesson on the law of sines.
   e. A lesson on the greatest common factor (eighth grade).
   f. The first lesson on the Pythagorean Theorem (high school geometry).
   g. The first lesson on metric measures (seventh grade).

2. Suppose you are teaching a mathematics class at the high school level. The principal asks the faculty to assign a short term project to each class. Describe the project you would have your students do in each of the following courses. Then discuss how you would handle this project with the class. Include in your discussion the amount of class time you would devote to it, credit allotted, penalties for failure to do a creditable job or failure to do it at all, and uses to which student research would be put (follow-up activities).
   a. Elementary algebra.
   b. Second year algebra.
   c. Trigonometry.
   d. Geometry.
   e. Consumer mathematics.
   f. Senior mathematics.
   g. General mathematics.

3. React to the following student reasons for not doing homework:
   a. "I did not have time last night since I had too much homework in my other subjects."
   b. "I work after school and do not have much time to do homework."
   c. "I have to do various housework chores and care for my younger brothers and sisters after school and have no time for my homework."
   d. "I didn't understand the homework."
   e. "I forgot to copy my homework assignment yesterday."
   f. "I lost my (1) assignment pad, (2) textbook, (3) completed homework."
   g. "I didn't do my homework."
   h. "I left my homework home."
   i. "I did the wrong assignment and threw it away this morning when a classmate told me I did the wrong work."
   j. "I forgot I had homework last night."

4. Select a unit of study in the secondary school curriculum and prepare a review homework assignment.

5. Prepare three different discovery homework assignments. You may choose any three topics from the secondary school mathematics curriculum.

6. Indicate the topics which would be useful to review through ''spiraling'' in a homework assignment in each of the following areas:
   a. A first lesson in factoring polynomials.
   b. A lesson on the area of a trapezoid.
   c. A lesson on the reduction formulas (the general angle) in trigonometry.
   d. A lesson on solving third- and fourth-degree equations having rational and irrational roots.
   e. An introductory lesson on irrational numbers in elementary algebra.

7. Prepare one enrichment problem for inclusion in a homework assignment on each of the following topics:
   a. Multiplication and division of monomials in elementary algebra.
   b. Operations with complex numbers in second year algebra.
   c. Proving triangles congruent in plane geometry.

8. Select any topic from secondary school mathematics and show how the homework assigned to prepare the class for a unit test differs from the homework assigned elsewhere in the unit.

9. React to the following student complaints:
   a. ''You give too much homework.''
   b. ''The homework is too hard.''
   c. ''My other teachers don't give homework on weekends.''
   d. ''You collected my homework assignment three times this week and you didn't collect Jay's homework even once!''
   e. ''I do my homework in a hard cover (bound) notebook and having to tear it out to hand it in is messing up my whole notebook!''
   f. ''You didn't go over the problems in class that I didn't understand.''
   g. ''You don't *look* at the homework I hand in. All you do is place a check mark on it.''

10. Develop a questionnaire to be administered to at least twelve mathematics teachers that asks the following questions.
   a. How frequently are students required to do homework?
   b. What type of assignments are required? What kind of questions are asked? How long are the assignments?
   c. Are assignments made on a daily, weekly, or monthly basis?
   d. How are assignments checked by the teacher or by other students?
   e. How are assignments reviewed for quality and completeness?
   f. What is the required format for these assignments?
   g. Does the respondent ever assign research projects or term papers in the mathematics class?
   After you collect the completed questionnaires, analyze the responses to see if there is agreement among the respondents on any of the issues or if there is total disagreement on some of the issues raised in the questionnaire. What can you conclude from this analysis?

SUGGESTED READING

Swireford, Edwin J. ''Ninety Suggestions on the Teaching of Mathematics in Junior High School.'' *The Mathematics Teacher* 54 (1961): 145.

CHAPTER 5 CONSTRUCTING TESTS

Testing is the primary means through which many teachers evaluate the work of their students, although most teachers take into account such other factors as classwork, homework, notebooks, and perhaps attitude and attendance. Nevertheless, class testing remains the foremost factor in student evaluation. Teachers use tests both to check on student learning and understanding of the material being tested and to measure the success of the teacher in conveying information to the class. In effect, the teacher is checking on himself as well as on his students when he gives his class a test. Accordingly, it is most important that tests be carefully constructed, administered, graded, and interpreted. We shall consider each of these aspects of the testing process after presenting a variety of sample examinations early in the chapter.

CONSTRUCTING A CLASS TEST

The art of constructing a good class test is mastered over a period of time and with help from as many sources as possible. The beginning teacher can draw on the experience of others as well as on his own early ones, and he should not hesitate to do so. Teachers should consult with their supervisors and their colleagues, especially those who have taught or are teaching the same courses being taught by the new teacher, and they should check files of old examinations for style, content, format, and so on. Many department offices contain these files for reference purposes, and the new teacher should not hesitate to make use of them. Other members of the mathematics department often will be happy to share their experiences with new colleagues. Their suggestions on the preparation of class tests are often most helpful, and the new teacher should draw on them to as great an extent as possible. In this way, he can at least avoid making the same mistakes made by others in the past.

How to Begin

The first step in preparing a test, of course, is to determine what is to be tested. Every test has an objective, whether it be narrow or broad, and the teacher must have this purpose clear in his own mind in order to prepare a test which is appropriate for his class.

A test may be very limited in scope, covering only one or two topics and being of short duration—perhaps five or ten minutes. Such tests are usually referred to as quizzes, and they often contain only a single question or perhaps a few simple ones. Quizzes often are designed to measure student understanding of a topic taught the previous day. Or they may be given to determine whether or not the students in a particular class have done their assigned homework for the day! In this case, the quiz question(s) would most likely be very similar to the ones assigned the day before for homework. A quiz is usually not announced in advance. Following are some sample quizzes.

Sample 2. Plane Geometry Quiz (5 minutes)

The measure of an exterior angle at the base of an isoceles triangle is 105°. Find the measure of the vertex angle of the triangle.

Sample 3 Second Year Algebra Quiz (8 minutes)

Given the equation $2x^2 - 3x - 7 = 0$

1. Calculate the value of the discriminant.
2. Describe the nature of the roots of the equation.

Sample 4 Eighth Grade Quiz (5 minutes)

1. What is 20% of 40?
2. Express 7% as a decimal.
3. What percent is equivalent to $.3\overline{3}$?

A more comprehensive examination would be designed to measure the extent of student mastery of several topics and would most likely be planned to require a full class period for its completion. Such tests are generally administered upon completion of a unit of work in the classroom. They should be announced several days in advance to enable students to prepare, through review of their text sections, notes, homework assignments, class exercises, etc. Topics should be listed on the board and typical test questions given the day before. Such tests carry much more weight in student evaluation than do single quizzes, and students may be expected to devote

Sample 1. First Year Algebra Quiz (10 minutes)

SHOW ALL WORK

1. Express as a trinomial $(2a + 5)^2$.
2. For which value of the variable is the fraction $\dfrac{x+2}{3-x}$ meaningless: (a) 3 (b) 2 (c) −3 (d) −2
3. Express in lowest terms $\dfrac{x^2 - 4}{3x - 6}$:
4. Factor completely $3ax + 6a$.
5. The product of two factors is $2x^2 + x - 6$. One of the factors is $(x + 2)$. What is the other factor?

Name: _____

Answers
1. _____
2. _____

3. _____

4. _____

5. _____

much effort to preparing for them. The scope of full-period tests is generally quite broad. Following are three more sample tests; two are actual full-period tests and one double-period (midyear) examination. Study carefully their layout of questions, point values, types of questions, use of extra credit, and so on.

Sample 5.   Geometry Test: Parallelograms Plus Review (full period)

Name: _____

I. Place the answer in the space provided (5 points each).

1-5. Indicate whether Always, Sometimes or Never true.

_____   1. Diagonals of a rhombus bisect each other.

_____   2. If two lines are perpendicular to the same line, they are parallel.

_____   3. An equilateral quadrilateral is equiangular.

_____   4. If the diagonals of a quadrilateral are $\perp$, it is a rhombus.

_____   5. Opposite angles of a parallelogram are supplementary.

6-9. Choose the best answer.

_____   6. An exterior angle at the base of an isosceles triangle is
(a) acute (b) obtuse (c) right (d) dependent upon the type of triangle.

_____   7. If the measures of the angles of a triangle are represented by x, y, and $x + y$, the triangle is
(a) isosceles (b) equilateral (c) right (d) unknown—depends on x and y.

_____   8. Which of the following is used to prove that the accompanying construction (of a line parallel to a given line through a given point) is correct: (a) Through a given outside point only one line can be constructed || to a given line (b) If two lines are parallel their corresponding angles are congruent (c) Two lines are || if their corresponding angles are congruent.

_____   9. In $\triangle ABC$, $\overline{BC}$ is extended through C forming $\angle x$. Which of the following must be true?
(a) $m \angle x > m \angle c$ (b) $m \angle x < m \angle C$ (c) $m \angle x > m \angle B$ (d) $m \angle x < m \angle B$

10-13. If always true write TRUE, otherwise write FALSE.

_____   10. Two lines are either parallel or intersecting.

_____   11. If a diagonal divides a quadrilateral into two congruent triangles, it is a parallelogram.

_____   12. The bisectors of a pair of opposite angles of a parallelogram coincide.

_____   13. If the diagonals of a quadrilateral are both congruent and perpendicular, then the quadrilateral is a square.

14-16. Numericals

_____   14. Find the perimeter of a triangle formed by joining the midpoints of the sides of a triangle with sides of length 5, 12, 13.

_____   15. Given rhombus $ABCD$, $AB = 5$, $m \angle ABC = 120°$, find BD.

_____   16. Given parallelogram $ABCD$, $m \angle A = 50$, $m \angle ABD = 75$, find $m \angle CBD$.

(Sample 5 continued on next page.)

II. (20 points)

Given: parallelogram *MOTE*
      $\overline{HO} \cong \overline{AE}$
Prove: MATH is a parallelogram.

Statements | **Reasons**

Fold here and continue proof on other side.

FOR EXTRA CREDIT (show work on other side):
Prove: If the diagonals of a trapezoid are $\cong$, it is isosceles.

Sample 6. Remedial Math Test—Fractions and decimals (full period)

Name: _____   Date: _____

1. Find the area:

13.1

8.02

2. Find the perimeter:

12

8.03

3. From 269 subtract .33.

4. Divide:

  (a) $7\overline{)14.35}$ (b) $.5\overline{)51.510}$

5. Make a circle around the fractions equivalent to the first fraction in each of the following:

  (a) $\dfrac{1}{2}$ | $\dfrac{3}{5}, \dfrac{4}{8}, \dfrac{5}{10}, \dfrac{7}{15}, \dfrac{20}{40}$

  (b) $\dfrac{2}{5}$ | $\dfrac{4}{9}, \dfrac{3}{8}, \dfrac{8}{20}, \dfrac{7}{15}, \dfrac{14}{35}$

6. Simplify:

  (a) $\dfrac{9}{24}$ (b) $\dfrac{8}{56}$ (c) $\dfrac{5}{45}$

7. Use the symbols $<$ and $>$ between the two given numbers:

  (a)   8   3   _____

  (b) $\dfrac{3}{5}$ $\dfrac{4}{7}$ _____

  (c) $\dfrac{1}{2}$ $\dfrac{2}{5}$ _____

8. Draw a diagram to illustrate the fraction $\dfrac{2}{3}$

9. In the fraction $\dfrac{9}{4}$, the number 9 is the _____.

10. Find the missing number:

  (a) $\dfrac{2}{3} = \dfrac{}{12}$ (b) $\dfrac{4}{5} = \dfrac{}{100}$

11. Add (simplify your answers):

  (a) $\dfrac{2}{3}$ (b) $\dfrac{3}{10}$ (c) $\dfrac{1}{2}$

     $+\dfrac{1}{3}$ $+\dfrac{1}{10}$ $+\dfrac{3}{2}$

12. Find the missing number:

   (a) $\dfrac{13}{8} = 1\dfrac{?}{8}$ (b) $\dfrac{13}{4} = \underline{?}\dfrac{1}{4}$

13. Add (simplify):

   (a) $\begin{array}{r} 2\frac{3}{8} \\ + 3\frac{5}{8} \\ \hline \end{array}$ (b) $\begin{array}{r} 5\frac{7}{10} \\ + 4\frac{9}{10} \\ \hline \end{array}$

14. Change to a mixed number:

   (a) $\dfrac{38}{5}$ (b) $6\dfrac{29}{4}$

15. Write equivalent fractions with the lowest common denominator for each pair:

   (a) $\dfrac{3}{8}, \dfrac{3}{4}$ (b) $\dfrac{1}{6}, \dfrac{2}{9}$

Sample 7.   Second Year Algebra—Midyear Examination (80 minutes)

DO NOT WRITE ON THIS PAPER.   *SHOW ALL WORK ON YOUR ANSWER PAPER.*   *WRITE NEATLY.*

Part I: Answer all questions (5 points each).

1. Express in terms of i the sum of $5i$ and $3\sqrt{-100}$.

2. (a) If $93{,}000{,}000 = 9.3 \times 10^n$, find the value of n.
   (b) If $0.0000286 = 2.86 \times 10^k$, find the value of k.

3. Simplify: $\dfrac{\dfrac{a}{b} - 2}{4 - \dfrac{a^2}{b^2}}$

4. If $\log x = a$, $\log y = b$ and $\log z = c$, express $\log \dfrac{\sqrt{xy}}{z^3}$ in terms of a, b and c.

5. Write the quadratic equation whose roots are $1 + i$ and $1 - i$.

6. If $\log x = 8.4365 = 10$, find x.

7. If $x = 7$, find the value of $3x^\circ + (x + 2)^{\frac{1}{2}} - 49x^{-2}$.

8. If $R = \{(1,2), (-1, 5), (6,2), (3,-7)\}$ find R^{-1} and state whether R and R^{-1} are functions.

9. Solve for x: $3^x = 9^{x-1}$

10. Find the value of k such that the following equation will have equal roots: $x^2 - 4x + k = 0$

11. If $f(x) = x^2 - 4x + 1$, find the value of $f(\frac{1}{2})$.

Part II: Answer only three (3) questions (15 points each).

12. Find the roots correct to the nearest tenth: $2x^2 - 3x - 1 = 0$

13. Evaluate using logarithms: $\sqrt[3]{\dfrac{(67)(.0973)}{100}}$

14. Solve the following for a, b and c and check in all three equations:

   $a + 3b - 4c = -13$
   $2a - b + 2c = 4$
   $4a - 6b + c = -1$

15. Write an equation or system of equations that would be used to solve the following problems. In each case, state what the variable(s) represent. (*Solution of the equation(s) is not required.*)

   a. A motorboat travels 8 miles downstream in $\frac{1}{3}$ hour and then returns upstream to its starting point in $\frac{1}{2}$ hour. Find in miles per hour the rate of the boat in still water and the rate of the current.

   b. A two-digit number is 2 less than 5 times the sum of its digits. If the digits are reversed, the new number will be 9 more than the original number. Find the original number.

Whether the examination is a short quiz or a lengthy midyear examination, certain procedures should be followed.

In selecting topics and questions, the teacher should try to include a number of questions similar to those done in class or as part of homework assignments, and the typical question should be of moderate difficulty. A test which is as important to most students as a full period class test should not be filled with surprises (unexpected or novel questions). It should be designed so that a student who has done her work conscientiously and has a reasonably good grasp of the subject will pass.

A sample test might be presented and discussed the day before the real test. This is so that the test format and type of questions do not come as a complete surprise, thus allowing students to focus on the content.

Test papers should be marked promptly by the teacher. Using student assistants as markers is dangerous because of errors they might make, and possible partiality to friends. Student markers should be used only when they can be supervised carefully. Furthermore, it is best when a teacher marks the exams himself because only in that way can he become sensitive to the types of errors students are making. Ideally, the papers should be marked and returned to students the next day while the test is still fresh in their minds.

If the tests are returned at the beginning of the period, be prepared to review the test for most of that period (except for quizzes which might have already been reviewed immediately after they were given). If papers are returned at the end of the period, students can be assigned to correct their papers at home and thus be prepared for the in-class review of them the next day. An advantage of returning papers at the end of the period is that the commotion caused by returning tests at the beginning is avoided, as students are often more interested in what grade their classmates earned on the test than on why they themselves got something wrong.

Selecting Priorities Among Topics and Concepts Taught

No test, no matter how broad its scope, can test everything. When we remember that most tests administered by teachers during the course of a school term or year are limited to single class periods, we realize that priorities must be established. The teacher must select from among all the topics that have been taught to his class in a given interval of time and determine which to include and which to omit on a given test. This does not mean that the latter topics will never be tested. They may be tested on a future class test, especially one of a cumulative nature, and they may certainly appear on midyear or final examinations, whether teacher prepared or uniform throughout a department. The teacher must decide to what extent he wishes to "spiral" back to topics taught

earlier in the term on a given test, if, indeed, he wishes to do so at all.

Types of Tests

The type of test presented to a mathematics class depends, of course, on the purpose for which the test is being given. Most often, the teacher will be seeking to measure student achievement. Achievement tests may range in scope and length from brief quizzes to comprehensive midyear and final examinations. A quiz may be prepared to test student understanding of just one or two concepts, or it may be designed to achieve a prompt start of a lesson, to check student comprehension of a homework assignment or of the work taught the previous day, or even to provide additional grades for students to assist the teacher in evaluating their work accurately.

Comprehensive tests of student achievement include full period class tests on work covered over an extended period of time, perhaps two weeks or longer, unit examinations, midyear examinations, and final examinations. Final examinations may be prepared by individual teachers for administration in their own classes or they may be prepared by committees of department members for uniform usage. In any case, they must be constructed carefully to measure the objectives of the unit or course and the extent to which students have mastered these objectives.

Teachers of mathematics are sometimes called upon to prepare other types of tests. Diagnostic tests are used to identify student strengths and weaknesses in a particular area of mathematics, so that the teacher may build on the strengths and plan remedial activities to overcome the weaknesses. These tests are used frequently in remedial mathematics courses, and they will be discussed further in the chapter on remediation. Although many such tests are commercially prepared, the teacher may wish to prepare his own test to measure some specific aspect of student background or to supplement the information provided by standardized tests.

Types of Questions

The types of questions to be included on any test are determined by a number of factors, including the ability level of the class, the nature of the material to be tested, the time available for the test, and so on. The following are illustrations of some types of questions commonly found on mathematics tests.

True-false questions may involve only a simple decision one way or the other. The teacher may require that an answer of "false" be accompanied by a correction of the statement offered.

Always-sometimes-never questions are modifications of true-false questions, since they require a determination as to whether a statement is always true (indicated by a response of "true" if in true-false form) or only sometimes true or never true (both of the latter require responses of "false" on true-false tests). A decision with two options now becomes a decision with three options.

Multiple choice questions are more challenging than either of the two types mentioned, since they require selection of a correct answer from four or five responses offered.

Completion questions reduce many aspects of guessing. They require a student to supply a correct response to an incomplete statement.

Matching questions permit some guessing, but this can be minimized by providing more choices in the column from which selections are being made than in the other column.

Numerical and algebraic exercises are objective questions which may be used to test understanding of principles, recall and application of formulas, and so on.

Types of questions mentioned thus far are essentially objective. *Geometric proofs* fall more into the subjective category, corresponding to essay questions in other subject areas. Like an essay question, a proof can often be done in a variety of ways and still be correct (i.e., there may not be only one correct solution). They require recall of postulates, definitions, and theorems proved in earlier work. They also may call for some degree of memorization, since some theorems are of such major importance that, although their proofs are included in the textbook, their recall may be expected of students. Other theorems whose proofs are called for on examinations may measure the ability to reason sequentially and logically better than those which are often memorized.

EXAMPLE: (Geometry.)
(1) Prove that the sum of the measures of the angles of a triangle is 180°.
(2) Given $\square$ *ABCD*, *M* is the midpoint of $\overline{AD}$, $\overline{BM}$ intersects diagonal $\overline{AC}$ at *E*.
    Prove: (a) $\triangle BEC \sim \triangle MEA$.
           (b) $AE \times BE = ME \times CE$.
           (c) If $BE = 8$, what is the length of *ME*?

The first example is a theorem whose proof is found in every textbook on plane geometry. The second example might be considered an "original" one. It challenges students to draw and label properly an appropriate diagram and to reason logically. The second part of the question asks for further recall of the properties of similar triangles and proportions, and the final part reviews the concept of ratio of similitude. Finally, the question combines geometry and algebra, as well as arithmetic.

Questions requiring sequential reasoning through several parts must be carefully constructed. If possible, the parts should be somewhat independent of each other. Otherwise, an early error in the work results in a string of errors and perhaps a situation in which it is impossible for a student to work subsequent parts of the question at all.

EXAMPLE: (Trigonometry.) A flagpole 40 feet high is anchored to the ground by a wire extending from the top of the pole to a point 30 feet from the base of the pole. The pole is perpendicular to the ground,
(a) Find the measure of the angle made by the wire with the ground, to the nearest degree.
(b) Find the length of the wire, to the nearest foot.

A student who uses the result of part (a) to answer part (b), using the sine or cosine function, gets a slightly different result from that obtained by the student who does part (b) independently, by the Pythagorean Theorem. As a matter of fact, the latter may wonder why the specification "to the nearest foot" is made when she gets an answer of exactly 50. The other student accepts this specification as something to be expected, and rounds off his answer to 50 also, unless he has made an error in part (a), in which case he will have an error in part (b) also. This difficulty could have been avoided easily by reversing part (a) and part (b) and phrasing the new part (a) unambiguously: (a) Find the length of the wire.

Writing a Good Question and Arranging Questions

Writing a good test is indeed an art. The questions must be prepared carefully and arranged on the test paper to enable students to achieve to the limit of their abilities. Before actually constructing the exam, the teacher should list the topics and concepts to be tested, including all major ideas, principles and skills. Clear, concise, straightforward questions should then be prepared for each of these areas. Guidelines used in preparing good classroom questions (discussed in chapter 2) apply in writing test questions as well. For example, test questions should be simple in structure and precisely phrased; if multiple concepts are involved in working particular questions, they should be included in separate parts of each question. Test items should test students' abilities to think as well as to merely recall information. Types of questions will vary with the content being tested and the ability of the class, but an effort should be made to include both objective questions and subjective ones, such as problems and proofs, especially in the area of geometry. Examinations may be filed for future use in the teacher's personal file or in files maintained in the department office. New teachers are advised to have their tests critiqued in advance by more experienced colleagues and/or by their supervisors. In this way, unanticipated "traps," pitfalls, inconsistencies in questions, etc. can be caught before they reach the students. The new teacher will soon learn how often a question which appears straightforward to the teacher may seem ambiguous or unclear to a student.

> **EXAMPLE:** Find the slope of each of the lines whose equations follow: (a) $y = 3x - 5$
> (b) $2x + y = 3$ (c) $y = -7$ (d) $x = 2$

The question tests understanding and recognition of slopes of straight lines from their equations. However, the line whose equation is given in part (d) has no slope. From the wording of the question, however, students may feel that each of the lines given *must* have a slope, and therefore search fruitlessly or incorrectly for a number which does not exist for the slope of (d). Better wording of the question, that would avoid this problem, might be, "Find the slope of each of the lines whose equations follow. If no slope, write 'none'."

An effort should be made to arrange questions so as to proceed from the simple to the more complex. This helps to build student confidence and encourages poorer students to do their best, since they encounter the simpler questions first. Teachers sometimes wonder whether it is wise to provide students with a choice of questions on a test. Choices are most often found on final examinations, especially if they are uniform throughout a department. This provides students with some latitude to compensate for different depths of treatment of various topics by different teachers, different emphasis, different amounts of time spent, and so on. When these reasons are pertinent, choice of questions may be appropriate. For relatively short (one period or less) class tests, however, providing a choice of questions is not recommended, since students often waste inordinate amounts of time browsing among questions, making poor starts and then abandoning questions, and losing valuable time.

Assigning Point Values to Parts of the Test

Credit for each question should be determined by the teacher before the test is administered to a class. Students are always interested in knowing how much each question on a test is worth. This serves as somewhat of a guide to them as to how to apportion their time. Credit values should be assigned in proportion to a number of factors, including the relative importance and difficulty of each question and the time expected to be required by an average student to work each question. For a single-period test, less challenging questions requiring little time, such as objective questions of a factual or simple computational nature, true-false questions, and always-sometimes-never questions, should generally be assigned little credit, such as three to five points each. Fill-ins might be worth five or six points. More time-consuming numerical and/or algebraic exercises are generally weighted at perhaps ten to fifteen points. Geometric

proofs and verbal problems may deserve fifteen or even twenty points.

The teacher should work the test himself in order to check its time requirements before administering it to his class. A test designed to be done by a class in a forty-minute period should not take the teacher more than seven or eight minutes to complete.

Presenting the Test

Tests may be written on the chalkboard, projected on a screen with the help of an overhead projector, or individual copies may be produced for each student on mimeograph or spirit duplicator machines. Most teachers prefer the latter method whenever possible, since it provides each student with her own copy of the test. This minimizes (but does not eliminate altogether) errors in copying questions, reading symbols, reading directions, following instructions, etc. A single quiz exercise, however, might well be simply written on the board and students given a few minutes to write their responses on plain sheets of paper. The overhead projector might be used, for example, to project a partially completed geometric proof on a screen and students could be asked to complete it on plain sheets of paper. If he writes a test on a duplicator master or stencil, the teacher should work out the test from the stencil before administering it to the class. He will catch typos that way—before students get frustrated trying to do impossible questions. Also, proofread a test from the board.

ADMINISTERING A TEST

The primary concern of the teacher in administering a class test should be to provide optimum conditions so that each student may have the best opportunity to demonstrate his knowledge. To achieve this objective, the teacher can follow a number of simple principles in presenting any class test.

Alternatives for Administration

Every test should begin promptly so that students have the full time promised to them for working on the questions presented. A late start, for whatever reason, both upsets students and deprives them of working time. Whether a test is to be written on the chalkboard by the teacher (a slow, less desirable practice) or distributed to all students through mimeographed or spirit duplicated sheets of questions, the questions should be made available to the students very soon after the period begins. This is particularly important if the test is scheduled for a full period, since time lost at the beginning of the period can never be made up later.

The teacher must decide whether students are to answer questions and work problems directly on the question paper, in spaces provided, or on separate sheets of plain paper. Sufficient space must be provided for students to work each question and write an answer for it. If there are to be uniform formats for answer sheets, and if students must prepare these themselves, the time spent doing this must be considered when preparing the test. Also, students must be told in advance of any special equipment they are expected to bring to the test, such as rulers, compasses, calculators, and graph paper.

Classroom Arrangement

Teachers often are concerned with the problem of obtaining honest results when they give tests. Students who are unsure of themselves or who actually have little knowledge of the material being tested may be driven to desperate measures. Of course, it is better for the teacher to anticipate such problems and prevent them from happening than to deal with them after the fact. If the class is not too large and empty seats are available in the room, students can be separated from each other. An empty seat on each side of a student (and perhaps in front of him and behind him) is clearly a good deterent to cheating during a test. Or, if classroom furniture is movable, it is easy to arrange the students so that they are reasonably well "spread out." Every effort should be made to remove temptation from students. If they have no opportunity to cheat, their test results will be as truly representative of their abilities and achievements as possible.

Some teachers reorder questions on test papers so as to present students with what appears to be two different tests, and these are used in alternate rows to minimize cheating problems or with different classes in the same subject meeting at different times of the day. This procedure may be effective for a time, but students often become aware of what is being done and then they easily can defeat this technique. A somewhat better approach, especially for classes meeting at different times and being tested on the same material, is for the teacher to prepare alternate forms of each question and, in effect, prepare two different versions of the same test. This is only fair to the extent that the alternate forms of the questions are of equal difficulty and the tests are truly equivalent. Otherwise, the fate of a particular student is dictated by the seat he chooses or to which he is assigned in the classroom during the test. Clearly, this is grossly unfair!

Alertness During Proctoring

Even the most experienced and skilled teacher sometimes encounters the problem of cheating in spite of all precautions taken to prevent it. Presumably, the class members have been cautioned at the beginning of the testing period to do their own work and keep their eyes on their own papers. As long as this warning has been issued, what action should a teacher take when a violation occurs?

Most teachers who observe attempts at cheating on a test usually speak quietly to the offender first. He is warned, without making a scene which would disturb other students while they are trying to concentrate on their work, and perhaps his seat is changed. The teacher also may make a notation on his test paper to indicate at which point in the test the cheating occurred; presumably, work following that point may be considered the student's own (if no further attempts at cheating are observed). Penalties for cheating must be decided upon by each teacher. It is a good idea to consult a supervisor on these matters. Experience will help the teacher to formulate his own philosophy and practices with regard to this problem, and to refine these as circumstances change.

Cheating discovered only after a test is over, during the course of grading papers, is a different and more difficult problem with which to deal. Identical errors on papers of students who were seated adjacent to each other during a test suggest a lack of vigilance on the part of the teacher. Accusations at this point may accomplish little more than to build bad feelings; students will deny wrongdoing and one student actually may be innocent! It is possible for one student to copy from another without the knowledge of the latter. Some teachers may be tempted to re-test the suspected parties, but many will prefer just to minimize the significance of these particular grades for the students involved and to make a mental note to themselves to be more alert next time. In effect, the teacher learns from his own experiences as much as his students do, whether these experiences are good or bad.

Early Finishers

A test should be so constructed as to require the time *planned* for its completion from almost all of the students in a given class. If a great many students finish early, the test was too short! Some students in every class, however, will work faster than their classmates and will, accordingly, finish a given test before the time allotted. Such students may be kept busy by offering optional or honor problems for extra credit while their classmates are completing the required part of a test. These problems should be available to all students, of course, but the likelihood is that only the best students will have the time to attempt them or to complete them successfully. In any case, perfect papers with additional problems correctly completed may be given grades such as 100+ or grades based on more than 100 points or separate extra credits or any other credit allowance the teacher considers appropriate. Rewards for such credits presumably would include higher grades at the end of given rating periods or at the end of the school term.

Absentees

The problem of dealing with students absent from a test is a perennial one which has no simple or entirely satisfactory solution. The best advice to the beginning teacher simply is to evaluate each case on its own merits and discuss the situation with the supervisor. The primary concern is to be fair to all students involved.

GRADING A TEST

Marking test papers is a time-consuming task, but it is a most important one for the teacher. Not only does he arrive at an evaluation of the work of his students, but in a very large sense, he does so for his own work as well. By studying student techniques and errors, the teacher can measure the success of his own teaching program. He may also be in for a number of surprises, involving student misunderstandings, when he grades a set of test papers.

Assigning Partial Credit

Partial rather than full credit should be given for a student's answer that indicates some but not complete understanding of how to arrive at that answer. Also, a student who makes an obviously careless error fully deserves most of the credit the problem is worth. Many questions, indeed, do not lend themselves to the assignment of partial credit. Included in this category are true-false questions, always-sometimes-never questions, and factual questions (e.g., Write the quadratic formula). On the other hand, more lengthy problems which involve numerous calculations in sequence (any one of which a student might inadvertently perform incorrectly, leading to an incorrect final result) would certainly be deserving of partial credit. Geometric proofs done with a substantial degree of accuracy and with only minor errors by a student also deserve some recognition. Experience and consultation with others will help the beginning teacher to formulate policies on partial credit and to modify these as circumstances dictate.

Students often have much correct work in connection with a test exercise, but a blunder somewhere along the way leads to an incorrect final result. On the other hand, students may have little, if any, correct work on a particular exercise, but they may have the correct final result. Consider the following examples.

> **EXAMPLE:** (Elementary algebra.) Reduce the fraction:
>
> $$\frac{x^2 - 25}{x - 5}$$
>
> Correct procedure: $\dfrac{(x + 5)(x - 5)}{(x - 5)} = x + 5$

Student's incorrect procedure:

$$\frac{x + 5}{\frac{x^2 - 25}{x - 5}} = x + 5$$

Here the student has obtained the correct answer by an outrageous procedure.

Such a procedure, although it delivered the correct result, clearly shows no understanding of factoring of binomials or of reduction of algebraic fractions, and deserves no credit of any kind. In the normal course of grading, a teacher would see the answer, not the method, and give credit.

> **EXAMPLE:** (Trigonometry.) Find the value of sin 75° in radical form.
>
> Student response:
>
> $$\sin 75° = \sin (45° + 30°)$$
> $$= \sin 45° \cos 30° + \cos 45° \sin 30°$$
> $$= \frac{\sqrt{3}}{2} \cdot \frac{1}{2} + \frac{\sqrt{3}}{2} \frac{\sqrt{2}}{2}$$
> $$= \frac{\sqrt{3} + \sqrt{6}}{4}$$

Here a student clearly deserves some partial credit, although he has confused the radical forms of the values of the trigonometric functions. Credit is deserved for realizing that sin 75° can be written as the sine of the sum of 45° and 30°, for knowing the correct expansion of sin $(A + B)$, and for knowing how to multiply and add fractions properly, albeit the wrong fractions. Thus if the question were worth ten points, it might be given six points of credit.

In geometry, students are called upon to write proofs of theorems on examinations. The teacher must first glance at the entire proof to see if it makes any sense at all. Many students make errors in some of the statements and/or reasons in these theorems. If the errors are so numerous and the reasoning so poor as to show little understanding on the part of the student, then perhaps no credit at all is deserved. When the student shows a good deal of knowledge, however, but perhaps he has an error here and there or some of his steps are not properly sequenced, then certainly, some partial credit is deserved. Generally speaking, a minor error of the mechanical type might be penalized to the extent of a ten percent deduction, while a major error in theory might result in deductions ranging from thirty to fifty percent of the credit value of a given problem, depending on its significance. These are only general guidelines; the beginning teacher will want to refine them as he gains experience.

Can a Wrong Answer Not Result in a Deduction?

Often, a student will obtain an incorrect answer to a problem by using a correct procedure and making no mechanical errors. How is this possible? Quite simply. The student is working on a problem involving sequential reasoning and several steps, some of which make use of answers obtained in earlier steps. The student should be penalized for his original error(s) only. Deductions should not be made twice because of the one, initial error.

> **EXAMPLE:** (Trigonometry.) In $\triangle ABC, \angle C$ is a right angle, $m\angle A = 37°$, $BC = 6$. Find, to the nearest integer, AC and AB.
>
> Student response:

$$\tan 37° = \frac{6}{x}$$

(error: student read table incorrectly—sin 37° instead of tan 37°)

$$.6018 = \frac{6}{x}$$

$$x = 10, \text{ to the nearest integer}$$

The student thinks she has found AC, but she has actually found AB. If she now tries to find AB by the Pythagorean Theorem, obtaining an answer of 12, to the nearest integer, she has made what is called a "consistent error." There should be only one deduction, since there was only one error.

Rounding off of answers in early parts of a problem, can lead to numerous errors later on in the same problem. Problems should be formulated so as to minimize the effects of such procedures. Alternate approaches to some problems (e.g., using the Pythagorean Theorem or using trigonometry of the right triangle to find the lengths of the legs or the hypotenuse of the triangle) may result in slightly different results; if these results are then to be used in subsequent parts of the same problem, difficulties may arise. The teacher must be alert to all of these possibilities.

What to Look for in Grading a Test

The teacher must make every effort to grade each test paper carefully and fairly. Students compare graded test papers to those of their peers and will be upset if they feel that they were not treated equitably. They also may compare their papers to tests they took earlier in the term to measure their own improvement.

Generally speaking, the teacher will examine test papers to determine the depth of student understanding of the concepts being tested, their ability to reason logically and sequentially and to solve problems, and their ability to carry out numerical calculations and algebraic procedures carefully and correctly. In grading papers, the teacher discovers the most common errors made by students and can then plan appropriate remedial or re-teaching activities. These errors should be explored carefully with the class, to minimize the likelihood that they will be repeated on the next test. It is wise to review the entire test with the class after it has been returned to them, corrected and graded. Reviews may be accomplished by having students place their solutions to individual questions on the board and then explaining their procedures to their classmates and answering questions posed by the latter. When time is an important factor, a review may also be accomplished by the teacher distributing to all students mimeographed or spirit duplicated sheets containing correct and complete solutions to all test questions, and then answering student questions on these solutions after they had some time to study them. Although this procedure does save some time, it also reduces student participation in the review (and the learning) process.

INTERPRETING TEST RESULTS

After a test has been given to a class, graded, and reviewed with the students, the teacher should examine the test closely to interpret the results. He can then plan the teaching of future units more carefully, plan for necessary remediation or complete re-teaching of certain material, and plan for better construction of his next test if the present one contained surprises or unexpected problems (misunderstanding of questions by students, insufficient time).

What the Test Results Indicate

Tests are measurement devices. As such, they indicate the degree to which students understand the material being tested. A test may measure the amount of attention students paid, whether they grasped the concepts being taught, their ability to apply these concepts to solving problems of various types, and whether they did the assigned homework.

Tests also provide the teacher with information about himself and his teaching. They often reflect the degree to which he was understood. The new teacher who feels most frustrated and concerned that students are not performing well enough is usually the one who ends up being a fine teacher, for he is constantly seeking the means to do better.

Analyzing Individual Items or Parts of a Test

Item analysis of test questions after the test has been marked is a valuable technique in improving construction of tests. It helps the teacher to determine which questions are too simple, too difficult for the average student but perhaps suitable as honor or extra credit questions, too difficult for almost all students, too short, too long, unclear, confusing, subject to misinterpretation because of the use of poor terminology or notation, and perhaps unfair as far as the assignment of appropriate credit is concerned.

It can help a teacher to determine which topics were best understood by the class and which were least understood. Item analysis is a question by question analysis of student responses. It will often lead to a conclusion concerning the significance of the particular question on this test. A good question is an effective discriminator between the more and less able students.

MULTIPLE CHOICE TESTS

With the ever-increasing availability of computers in schools, short response tests are being used where in earlier years they may have been avoided. The most popular test is the multiple choice (or response) test. Computer use is most convenient here since the respondent must only give one-letter answers. To make such an examination effective, certain care must be taken in preparing and interpreting these instruments.

When writing test items, care must be taken (as always) to ensure against ambiguities. If one has the luxury of time, it is wise to write the test one day and then set it aside for a few days. A second reading of the item (after a period of time) usually will reveal any possible ambiguities.

The multiple choice item is not a particularly easy item to write, because part of its effectiveness rests on the writer's ability to construct good "distractors"—incorrect responses to a multiple choice question. Although they are incorrect, the test constructor should try to anticipate the kinds of errors students might commit in each item and derive these distractors from these incorrect procedures.

Naturally, if one has time available, an item analysis ought to be done for each item before the test is administered. This, however, requires administering the test to a representative student group and analyzing the effectiveness of each item as a discriminator between high, average, and low achieving scorers. An item is deemed effective if the high scorers answer correctly and the low scorers do not. An item analysis is not usually practicable for regular classroom tests since administering a test twice is usually not possible. For major school-wide tests, such a procedure might be reasonable, especially if the test is to be used for more than one semester.

The question about how a multiple choice test should be scored is sometimes controversial. Some educators claim that the number of items answered correctly should determine the test score, whereas others hold that a multiple choice test should be "corrected for guessing." That is, the test score (or raw score) should be obtained from the formula:

$$\text{raw score} = R - \frac{W}{n-1}$$

where R is the number of correct items, W is the number of incorrect items, and n is the number of choices provided for each item. The number of items omitted does not directly figure into the calculations.

Although multiple choice tests are easier to score (especially with the help of a computer), when properly prepared they are much more difficult to construct, since there is more to writing the item than just constructing a question. Searching for good "distractors" can be quite time consuming.

SUMMARY

The goal of teaching is learning. Every teacher wants his students to master as much of the material being taught as possible. Since class tests are a major means of measuring the degree to which students have learned what has been taught, the teacher is naturally drawn to examining test results to help him to determine the success of his teaching program.

If the results on a test are good, and the teacher feels that the test was a fair measure of achievement (appropriate in difficulty level, comprehensive in scope, of suitable length for the time available), then he can be reasonably satisfied with his performance and that of his students. Apparently, they are learning the material being taught, and they are ready to continue with their studies. If the opposite is true, however, then the teacher must seek to determine the causes of whatever shortcomings the students demonstrate through the test. Is it the fault of his own teaching techniques, of students' poor learning habits or other problems (inadequate backgrounds for learning the material presented, distaste for or fear of mathematics in general, poor study techniques, etc.), or of the test itself? Generally, a combination of factors is involved. If teaching techniques and/or student learning habits are problems, then, of course, remedial action in these areas must be undertaken, and these aspects of the learning process are considered elsewhere in the text. If the test itself is the primary source of difficulty, then every effort must be made to remedy the problem before the next test is given, lest the same mistakes be repeated in constructing that test, leading to another set of poor papers. The teacher must examine the test in depth to determine the causes of the poor results. If the test was too long, it can easily be shortened. If its scope was too broad (students were not able to retain all of the material expected of them), perhaps their strength in this respect can be built up through a series of shorter tests, each covering a more limited amount of material, until the class is ready to cope with more comprehensive testing. If the test was too difficult, then a number of simpler questions can be included on future tests to build student confidence, encourage students to attempt all questions, and achieve a broader spectrum of grades. If some of the questions were misinterpreted or not understood at all, then the teacher should either discard those questions altogether or rewrite them more clearly so that all the students will interpret them correctly. If the test contained too many objective questions and not enough non-objective ones (proofs, sequential problem solving situations), or vice versa, the balance easily can be adjusted before the next test is prepared. In short, the test should be written so that it is a fair measure of the extent to which students have mastered the work taught in the class and reinforced by study at home. A test so constructed will be a good indicator to the teacher of the learning achieved thus far. He can then make the determination as to whether the class requires re-teaching or review of any part of the material tested, or whether it is ready to move on to more advanced material.

In conclusion, we note that testing is a vital part of teaching, and that each teacher must develop his own philosophy with regard to testing and marking. Examinations must be carefully planned. They must test skills, content, concepts, facts, and comprehension of the structure of mathematics rather than merely isolated segments of it. Reading and problem solving techniques should be strengthened through the testing process. Tests can be used to identify student weaknesses as well as to measure the extent of their mastery of particular topics. As individual differences of students are determined, the teacher can then plan his teaching program so as to help each student develop his abilities to the limit of his capacity.

EXERCISES

1. Prepare a five- to ten-minute quiz on each of the following topics:
   a. Converting from a base 10 number to one expressed in base 2; base 8.
   b. Using formulas for angle measurement with the circle for angles whose vertices are on the circumference of the circle.
   c. Recalling the values of the trigonometric functions of 30°, 45°, 60° in radical form (without the use of tables).
   d. Determining the sum and product of the roots of a quadratic equation.
   e. Determining the union and intersection of sets.
   f. Converting fractions to decimals (seventh grade)

2. Discuss the three tests shown earlier in this chapter (pp. 61–63) with respect to
   a. Variety of questions.
   b. Level of difficulty.
   c. Repetition of concepts.
   d. Format.
   e. Challenge.
   f. Point values.

3. Prepare a full-period test on each of the following topics:
   a. Area formulas for the rectangle, square, parallelogram, and triangle.
   b. Equilateral triangle, and trapezoid.
   c. Operations with radicals (simplification, four fundamental operations) in elementary algebra.
   d. The unit on trigonometric graphs, including amplitude and period.
   e. Metric measures.

4. Comment on the quality of each of the following test questions:
   a. *True or false:* $\tan 90° = \infty$
   b. *True or false:* $x^2 - 4x + 4 = 0$ has two roots.
   c. *Always, sometimes, or never:* If the opposite angles of a quadrilateral are supplementary, the quadrilateral is a parallelogram.
   d. Complete the following: A triangle is _____
   e. Simplify the expression: $\dfrac{\dfrac{3x}{2}}{5}$

f. Find the measure of an angle whose supplement exceeds its complement by 90°.

g. How does the measure of an inscribed angle of a circle compare to that of a central angle?

h. Arrange in order so that each set of figures is a subset of the preceding set: rhombus, square, parallelogram, rectangle, quadrilateral.

5. React to the following comment made by a teacher of geometry: "My students always do much better with numerical and algebraic exercises than they do with proofs. They just don't know how to proceed with a proof after they write the hypotheses as the first step. I give as few proofs as possible on my tests."

6. On a test on the topic of areas and circumferences of circles, different students in a class obtained varying results to test questions by using different approximations of π, such as $\frac{22}{7}$, 3.14, 3.1416, or simply leaving their results in terms of π. How should the teacher grade these answers?

7. The question of permitting the use of calculators by students during class tests is one which is currently of some concern to teachers. Discuss the pros and cons of such usage on tests in (a) algebra, (b) geometry, (c) trigonometry, (d) arithmetic (remedial).

8. Some teachers like to "drop" students' lowest test grades when making their determinations of final course grades. Discuss the advantages and disadvantages of this policy and decide whether you favor the policy.

9. Discuss your feelings on the granting of partial credit in each of the following situations:
   a. When asked to solve a quadratic equation by the method of completing the square, the student merely used the quadratic formula.
   b. When asked to solve a system of simultaneous linear equations graphically, the student used algebraic techniques of substitution or addition-subtraction.

10. A student complains to you that you graded his test paper unfairly. He points out that on a particular question his neighbor had exactly the same errors as he had, but received more partial credit than he did. Discuss the implications of the complaint and your reactions to it.

11. Find a commercially prepared multiple choice test appropriate for the subject you are teaching (this need not be a standardized test, but can be one provided by a publisher as a supplementary item of a textbook series). Administer the test to about forty students, then analyze the responses as follows: tally the number of responses for each choice of each question, then determine whether the majority of students answered the item correctly, only the high scorers answered an item correctly, or only low scorers answered an item correctly. Draw conclusions from your analysis of the responses on each item as discussed in the chapter.

12. Write a ten-item, multiple choice test with five choices for each question. Pay particular attention to writing effective distractor choices. Administer this test to about forty students and then analyze the items in a way similar to that required for Exercise 11.

SUGGESTED READINGS

Swadener, Marc, and Wright, Franklin. "Testing in the Mathematics Classroom." *The Mathematics Teacher* 68 (1975): 11.

Swireford, Edwin J. "Ninety Suggestions on the Teaching of Mathematics in Junior High School." *The Mathematics Teacher* 54 (1961): 145.

Troutman, Andrea, and Lichtenberg, Betty P. "Problem Solving in the General Mathematics Classroom." *The Mathematics Teacher* 67 (1974): 590.

Walter, Marion I., and Brown, Stephen I. "Problem Posing and Problem Solving." *The Mathematics Teacher* 70 (1977): 4.

Williams, Irene S., and Jones, Chancey O. "Multiple Choice Mathematics Questions." *The Mathematics Teacher* 67 (1974): 34.

CHAPTER 6 EVALUATING STUDENT PERFORMANCE

Consider this conversation between two students at the end of the term:

Manny: How did you do in math?

Luis: I passed. How did you do?

Manny: She failed me. I don't know why. I came every day and I did all my work.

Typically, Manny places the responsibility of his having failed on the teacher, while Luis places the responsibility for his having passed on himself! The fact is that *both* teacher and student share responsibility for the grade a pupil receives.

Responsibility is a two way street. Part I of this book is devoted to a discussion of how a teacher's responsibilities toward her students ought to be fulfilled in order to maximize their educational growth and development. In this chapter, however, we will add a dimension to this discussion by presenting the often neglected or overlooked sides—the student's responsibilities toward himself, and parental responsibilities. We also will analyze the factors a teacher may use to make a judgment about a pupil passing or failing for the semester.

STUDENT RESPONSIBILITIES

Students should be made aware of their responsibilities at the beginning of the term, for their passing or failing the course depends on their successful fulfillment of these responsibilities.

The impression that passing or failing a course depends only on the average of test marks, or on attendance in class, must be altered so that students know that those are only *two* factors of several which help determine a final grade. The effort to have a youngster succeed in a course is a joint teacher-student-parent one. The teacher will try to live up to her end of the deal by preparing and presenting good lessons, giving fair tests, and so on. The student must also live up to his responsibilities if he expects to succeed. But what exactly must the student do? Some of his responsibilities include the following.

1. *Homework assignments*
   Students are responsible for
   a. Getting the assignment accurately.
   b. Following directions in the homework examples.
   c. Working honestly and accurately.
   d. Doing every assignment completely.
   e. Making an effort to get assistance if it is needed.
   f. Doing assignments even on days when they are absent.
   g. Periodically reviewing previously done homework assignments (as required).
   (For more details, see Chapter 4 on Assigning Homework.)

2. *Class Participation*
   In the classroom, students should always
   a. Get ready quickly at the start of the lesson.
   b. Have all necessary equipment: notebook, text, pencils, etc.
   c. Try to concentrate on the material being taught.
   d. Ask questions pertinent to the day's lesson.
   e. Listen to the questions and answers of others.
   f. Take an active part in the discussion.
   g. Volunteer to do work at the board or answer questions at their seats.

3. *Tests*
   Test results can be maximized if students
   a. Review far enough in advance so they can do an unhurried, thorough job on the test to reflect their true ability.
   b. Read appropriate sections and model exercises in the textbook.
   c. Believe in their ability and remember that the final mark will be determined on the basis of an entire term's work and not only one test.
   d. Have all necessary equipment—pencils, compasses, etc.
   e. Follow directions and read instructions carefully.
   f. Show all work clearly.
   g. Make an all-out effort to prepare well for every exam. (For more details see Chapter 5 on Constructing Tests.)
   h. Do their homework regularly.

4. *Attendance in class*
   Students should be reminded that
   a. Each day's absence from a mathematics class is especially serious because it means a real loss of two days' work—the day they were absent as well as the day they return (since they may not have a full understanding of what the teacher will be doing upon their return to class).
   b. Cutting a class is a breach of school discipline, besides the loss of a day of instruction.
   c. Coming late to class means loss of valuable time during which they might have learned something significant. In addition, lateness is disruptive to the class and teacher. Regular lateness reflects students' attitude towards the subject.

5. *Discipline*
   Improper behavior in the classroom is disruptive to everyone. It cannot help but influence the teacher to develop a negative feeling towards the student, which, even in an indirect way, may affect the final grade.
   (For more details, see the section in Chapter 13 on Classroom Management.)

6. *Attitude and Effort*
   The student must show that she cares about doing well by seeking extra help when she needs it (from the teacher, from a classmate, or from a tutorial group in or out of the school), by doing extra credit work when it is assigned, by not walking into the class late or with a preconceived negative attitude towards mathematics, and by living up to the responsibilities listed previously.

PARENTAL RESPONSIBILITIES

Every young person has two hands. The teacher ''holds'' one to help guide and direct the student in the educational process, as the teacher is trained to do. The other hand is ''held'' by the child's parents who have the moral, as well as legal, obligation also to guide and direct, to the best of their ability. Thus, parents share the responsibility for a student's performance in class. Although they may have fewer responsibilities and although these responsibilities may differ somewhat from those of the pupil and those of the teacher, they are no less important. In fact, the parents' responsibilities are more in the nature of overseer, confidant and encourager.

Parental Responsibilities
1. Check that students do their homework completely and conscientiously whenever it is assigned.
2. Show a genuine concern in their child's test results, providing encouragement and support when appropriate.
3. Contact the teacher occasionally to check on the student's progress.
4. Discuss with their son or daughter problems which may be affecting the learning process.
5. Provide for additional assistance when needed.

DETERMINING THE COURSE GRADE

Your Grading Philosophy

Before you consider the question of determining grades, you ought to know your own philosophy about the grading of students. But you must realize that just as there is no point in trying to arrive at a "right" or "wrong" view in politics or religion, so, too, with marking philosophies.

Are you a "hard-nosed type" who will stick strictly to "averages" on tests with no room for emotionalism or feeling in determining a grade? Do you feel that this is the only way to "maintain standards" and raise the level of performance that has "dropped" so low in the public schools? If so, you will tend to give your students "low" grades.

On the other hand, are you a "bleeding-heart type" who feels that everyone's marks are affected by background as well as ability? Do you feel that those factors that are beyond the student's control and that he possesses merely by accident of birth should not be used to determine grades that may affect his future—whether it be college or employment? If so, you will tend to give your students "high" grades.

While arguments can be presented for either point of view by adherents of those views, it is probably best to set for yourself a middle-of-the-road course. A balance should be sought in which sensitivity to students and their backgrounds as well as firmness in requiring evidence of satisfactory performance should be considered when determining students' grades.

Techniques for Determining Grades

Once the responsibilities of student, parents and teachers in the educational process have been considered, both pupils and parents will be ready to understand how a teacher arrives at a report card grade. This report card rating, sent to students and parents several times a year, is the culmination of a process of evaluation. At these times, the teacher examines her records of such items as the quality and quantity of the students' homework, every aspect of their classwork, their test marks, attendance, discipline in class and overall attitude (the items listed above as "student responsibilities").

In other words, you will attempt to determine whether the student is fulfilling his responsibilities and how extensively he is doing so. You must examine each of his responsibilities and arrive at a judgment as to how successful the student is in fulfilling them. Finally, in some "mysterious" way (to be described soon) you arrive at a grade—either a letter:

> A = outstanding level of performance
> B = good level of performance
> C = satisfactory level of performance
> D = poor but minimally acceptable level of performance
> F = failing level of performance

or a number:

> 91–100 = A
> 81–90 = B
> 71–80 = C
> 65–70 = D
> Below 65 = F

The ways of arriving at a grade are "mysterious" because they are often not understood by either student or parent. In addition, they have a degree of subjectivity and are often arbitrary. Even test scores reflect a certain degree of subjectivity since they often result from a teacher-made test, a somewhat subjective instrument itself. Although attempts have been made to determine a "scientific" or objective way of arriving at report card ratings, no one has ever succeeded in doing so. No one has succeeded in replacing the teacher's professional judgment with an objective formula.

Some of the mysterious ways of arriving at a grade, described more fully in the paragraphs that follow, include

1. Using a "scientific" formula.
2. Comparisons with other students in the class.
3. Determining the amount of improvement.
4. Anecdotal record rather than grade.
5. "Pass" or "Fail" grade only.

Consider the following ''scientific'' formula where certain categories are a percentage of the final grade:

test average	60%
classwork	10%
homework	10%
final exam	20%

You may feel that this is a reasonable rule or guideline for determining grades. In fact, a similar formula is used by many teachers. Yet, consider the subjectivity involved in such areas as preparation and grading of tests, as well as in the determination of the percentage values assigned. Furthermore, the non-included items of punctuality, attendance, attitude and discipline ultimately must affect the teacher's decision in a subjective way, so that even after the formula has been applied the mark so determined may be adjusted up or down as the teacher sees fit.

A second ''mysterious'' technique of determining a rating for a student is his actual performance as compared to the performance of other students in his class. Thus, students doing best on test results, homework, etc., (as decided by the teacher) are rated A, the next category is rated B, and so on. This technique is best for ''honors'' or ''slow'' classes rather than ''average'' classes. A more extensive explanation of this technique follows later in this chapter.

A third technique used is that of determining the amount of improvement that has occured during the period of time involved. For example, in a remedial class, where a student who began with a fifth grade equivalent arithmetic level (according to standardized tests) but ended the term with a seventh grade equivalent arithmetic level, should get a certain grade to reward the two years of growth in one semester. In this type of situation, school philosophy will determine whether such a youngster shall pass the course, even though the work he is doing is below his appropriate high school level. School policy will determine whether such a mark should be included in the student's overall high school average (on a par with courses such as English and social studies).

The anecdotal record type of report to students and parents has gained popularity in some school districts. The teacher is thereby relieved of determining a numerical or letter grade, but instead submits a written description of the pupil's attitude, test results, homework, behavior, etc. This technique is sometimes combined with a numerical or letter grade at least once a year.

''Pass–Fail'' reports gained widespread popularity in the 1960s and early 1970s. This was merely a judgment by the teacher of whether the pupil should ''pass'' the course and receive credit for it or not. While many are vocal advocates of this system, only small pockets of school systems continue to use it. It was dropped mainly because it seemed to place academic mediocrity on the same level as real achievement. The lack of recognition of talent, ability and scholarship was not acceptable to many people.

Assigning grades is one of the most difficult tasks confronting teachers, since so many subjective decisions must be made. How can a teacher determine objectively whether a student is working to capacity or what her attitude toward the subject is? Furthermore, the grade itself varies in meaning to a great degree. An ''A'' could mean ''genius at work'' or ''plugger at work.''

Yet, those of us who are a product of our school systems, as well as those who are still involved in it, have learned, through some sort of ''sixth sense,'' what a grade means. If you were to ask a student in your class to rate herself before you did, she would likely do so with a grade reasonably similar to one you might expect to give her. Teachers who have asked for their students' own assessment of their progress and achievement in class at the end of the term know this. Things are not as haphazard as they might seem after all, for there appears to be an unwritten understanding among students and teachers regarding what mark a particular student ought to get for his work in a course.

Nevertheless, the grade a student is determined to have earned in a course may be unreliable as an indicator of ability and achievement. Yet, it is precisely this grade which is supposed to inform the student, parents, colleges, employers of the student's success or failure in a course. It is even sometimes used to predict possible success or failure in a wide range of future activities. With such a large potential impact on a student's career, much care must be taken in preparing these student assessments.

DETERMINING THE COURSE GRADE IN HONORS OR SLOW CLASSES

Special conditions exist in both extremes of honors and slow classes.

Students in honors classes receive more extensive and lengthy homework assignments than students in other classes. They also get more difficult tests. More is expected of them in the form of attitude, overall effort, attendance, and so on. In addition, ''extra credit'' work is usually expected of students in honors classes. The average of test scores, which is usually the single factor that contributes most to a report card grade or rating, will thus probably be lower than that same student might have attained on tests in a regular class. He is thus, in effect, being ''punished'' for his willingness to participate in a more rigorous academic program. The possible lower grades might well affect his college admission. This problem occasionally results in a reluctance of parents and students to accept participation in an honors track.

One simple solution to this problem that has been successfully used by some teachers. It involves several steps.

1. The concept of the traditional 100% as an indicator of a perfect test paper would be discarded. In fact, some tests are more difficult, more comprehensive or more mathematically significant than others. Thus, to rate all types of tests on the basis of 100% may be blatantly unreasonable, especially if all are equally weighted when they are averaged. Tests might be made to total *any* number of points, depending on the teacher's judgment about the point value for each question.

2. At the end of the marking period, everyone's test points are totaled. In addition, a teacher-determined "formula" of the type described earlier, which would include homework, classwork, attitude, attendance, etc. also can be used to determine a "grade" for these non-test aspects of the pupil's total evaluation. A grand total of test and non-test scores is then calculated.

3. A list of pupils written in order of highest grand total first, down to lowest, is then made. Thus the youngster ranked first may receive a grade of 99% (or 100%, or 95% if the teacher so judges.) Other grades will vary accordingly down to, say, 85%. (In letters, honors marks should be *A* or *B*.)

4. After the grading is completed, a final check by the teacher is necessary to determine if the scheme used produced no glaring inequities to any student, giving her an unjustifiedly low grade, or one that is too high. Thus, for example, while a student might have been performing poorly for the first half of the marking period, she might be performing superbly during the second, perhaps more important, half. The teacher might want this fact reflected in the student's final grade and she would thus adjust the grade accordingly. This is another example of the subjective judgments used by teachers to determine grades.

A similar scheme can be devised for grading students in slow classes. The difference is that *here* the maximum

mark for a student ranked first might be 80%. Other marks will, accordingly, vary down to a failing grade. (In letters, slow class marks should be *C, D,* or *F*.)

OTHER GRADING SYSTEMS

Other types of grading systems are available for teacher use in some schools. For example, there is a criterion-referenced system (in contrast with the norm-referenced system described above) which allows the teacher to assess the extent to which the student has met specific objectives. These are usually itemized by skill or concept. The primary advantage to this system is that students (as well as their parents) are appraised of the student's particular strengths and weaknesses within a given course, as opposed to a "blanket" grade for the entire course. The latter does not provide any breakdown by skill, which the former does. Unfortunately, the decision of the type of grading system is not up to the teacher. Such decisions are generally made by the administration, yet a teacher's knowledge of the various options can be useful if called upon by the administration for input into the decision-making process.

SUMMARY

What does "passing a course" mean? It means that the student has fulfilled all of his responsibilities concerning such items as homework, class participation, attitude, discipline, and satisfactory test results. Parents as well as teachers have a role to play in assisting the student to fulfill his responsibilities: the parent as an overseer, the teacher as a guide.

Similarly, "failing a course" means that the student's responsibilities have not been discharged, and certainly it is not the teacher alone who shoulders the responsibility for this occurrence.

The teacher evaluates a student on the fulfillment of these responsibilities several times a semester, rating him with a numerical or letter grade, or with a written report, depending on school policy. In spite of efforts to place grading of students on a scientific basis, the subjective judgment of the teacher is bound to play a decisive role in the evaluation process.

In the matter of grading youngsters, some have viewed the role of the teacher as that of a "scribe" who merely records the student's performance. This is a rather narrow view, for it limits the role that the professional judgment of the teacher must play in the process.

EXERCISES

1. Consider these "special cases" and determine the final rating you might make in each. Support your answer with appropriate reasons.

    a. Robert is a very bright boy in a high school first year algebra class who learns the mathematical material very well on his own. He was absent from class thirty days, has a 94% test average on the three tests he took, but was absent from three others. He is never a discipline problem, but rarely does his homework. At a meeting with his mother, she admitted that she is not capable of assisting or even speaking to him in a meaningful manner.

    b. Joanne's behavior in a remedial mathematics class is very volatile. Her mother forces her to attend school and she does so regularly. She has a 59% test average and behind her tough facade she seems to want to pass the subject and even studies at home, on occasion.

    c. Paula is an eighth grade student who does all the extra credit work she can, and seeks more. Her attendance and homework are excellent, though you have suspected for some time that she copies the homework from someone. Her test average is 52%. She always comes to you for help outside class and tells you how much she loves the subject.

    d. Suppose David were your best student in geometry and earned 100% on every exam throughout the term. Would you give David a 100 as a report card mark if his class work were also very good? Or would you assign him a 99 since "no one is perfect" enough to earn 100, a "perfect" mark? Would you do the same if this were a remedial mathematics class?

2. Suppose you used the scheme described in the section Determining the Course Grade in Honors or Slow Classes. After giving the first test of the term to your honors class, you returned the papers and students found that their marks ranged to a maximum of 37 points for a perfect paper. How would you explain the rating scheme to the class? How would you overcome the tendancy of youngsters to "convert" their score to a "mark" on the basis of 37 points = 100%?

3. What changes, if any, would you make in the "scientific" formula suggested in the section on Determining the Course Grade? Explain the reasons for your changes, or lack of them.

4. What is your opinion about the grade you should give to a sixteen-year-old student who managed to raise his arithmetic grade equivalent level from sixth to seventh grade in six months? This increase was due to intensive remediation efforts on your part.

5. Suppose you were a parent who received an anecdotal type report card from your youngster's school, with this report from his teacher:

    ATTITUDE: Poor, lazy
    TEST RESULTS: 68%
    HOMEWORK: Incomplete
    BEHAVIOR: Needs improvement

    What could you learn from this report card? What more would you like to know? What additional details should the teacher have included?

6. Based on your own experience as a student and/or teacher, what method of determining grades would you like to have put into effect?

7. Earlier in this chapter, the "Pass–Fail" method of grading students was mentioned. What are some positive features of this method?

8. Prepare a well-structured interview guide which you will use to interview six mathematics teachers, three relatively inexperienced and three experienced teachers. Focus your interview on eliciting their methods of evaluating student performance. Write a short report to summarize your findings.

CHAPTER 7 PROFESSIONAL GROWTH AND EVALUATING TEACHER PERFORMANCE

Some teachers evoke strong, emotional reactions by pupils: "He's great" or "he stinks" sometimes describe the same teacher as seen by two different students sitting in the same room! More often than not, however, pupils' evaluations of a teacher are fairly consistent, whether favorable or not.

Although regular, formal evaluations and ratings by certified supervisors are usually mandated by school boards, informal assessments of teacher performance also may be made to guide the teacher towards improving his teaching skills. Pupils, parents, other teachers, as well as the teacher himself can all participate in this type of evaluation process.

Is the classroom the only stage where the teacher's performance is judged? No, indeed! How the teacher affects student performance and attitude, both inside and outside the classroom, his skill in managing a classroom situation, as well as his professional and personal qualities also ought to play a role when judging his overall performance.

Professional growth is generally the responsibility of each teacher. This chapter provides a broad overview of this responsibility and ways it can be met successfully.

In this chapter we shall also discuss those details of the evaluation process that a teacher ought to know about, for it is precisely that process that will examine the teacher's growth to date, as well as help chart a course for growth in the future. A sample teacher rating form will be shown in addition to typical supervisor evaluation reports of observed lessons.

PROFESSIONAL GROWTH

As with all major professions, teachers of mathematics must constantly upgrade their teaching skills and their knowledge of mathematics. This can be done in several ways. Some are quite formal, whereas others are rather informal. On the more formal level, mathematics teachers should seek out courses which pique their interest. These courses can be offered by local colleges, teacher organizations, or local school districts. They might focus on content, methodology, or both.

The undergraduate preparation of prospective mathematics teachers merely qualifies them to enter the profession: it is by no means a complete and all-inclusive preparation. For this reason most school systems encourage their teachers to take further courses. This encouragement may come in the form of tuition reimbursement or higher salary scales based on the number of courses taken beyond the baccalaureate degree. The individual mathematics teacher needs to make the most of these incentives but not abuse them. Courses should be chosen which complement their prior education. Often a mathematics teacher is wise to obtain a *broad* exposure in mathematics rather than a very *concentrated* exposure in one branch of mathematics. This would imply graduate work in several areas of mathematics, such as algebra, geometry, probability, statistics, number theory, and analysis, rather than concentrating study in only one or two areas. One could easily make the argument that the secondary school teacher of mathematics is more resourceful to students as a "jack of all subjects" rather than a "master of one"!

The professional upgrading of mathematics teachers is not limited to taking in-service courses, nor does it end when a teacher reaches the highest available salary scale. It is an on-going professional obligation for all mathematics teachers.

One rather pleasant way to stay current with developments in mathematics education is to attend professional meetings and read professional journals and books. The leading organization devoted to the improvement of classroom instruction at all levels is the National Council of Teachers of Mathematics (1906 Association Drive, Reston, Virginia 22091). The NCTM sponsors several regional conferences each year along with its annual convention, which is held in a different region of the country each year. This convention includes more than five hundred sessions with leading mathematics educators and is specifically designed for teachers at all grade levels. Extensive commercial exhibits of mathematics books and materials provide teachers with an easy way to see what is currently on the market. Teacher and student exhibits are also on display at these conventions.

The regional meetings, coordinated by NCTM local affiliates in conjunction with the headquarters office at Reston, Virginia, are similar to the annual convention, though smaller in scale. They offer a greater outreach to teachers who might not be able to travel to the annual convention, while at the same time providing more frequent professional activities, since they are spread out throughout the academic year. Attending sessions at these meetings should be a fine stimulus for mathematics teachers to constantly re-tool themselves in both mathematics and methods of instruction.

The NCTM also publishes various journals which allow teachers to stay current. *The Mathematics Teacher* and *The Arithmetic Teacher* are each published monthly from September to May. The former is primarily intended for secondary school and two-year college teachers, whereas the latter is for elementary school teachers. News items are published five times a year in the *News Bulletin*. In addition to many professional books the NCTM publishes an annual yearbook on an appropriate theme and *The Journal for Research in Mathematics Education,* which, with five issues each year, covers comprehensive reports of empirical studies, summaries of major mathematics research studies, and articles about current research in mathematics education.

Although the NCTM offers more than enough activities and materials to keep teachers current in the field, there are other organizations that provide activities of interest to the mathematics teacher. One such is the Mathematical Association of America (1529 Eighteenth Street, N.W., Washington, D.C. 20036), which is more directed towards the interests of college professors but still has features that ought to be of interest to secondary school teachers.

Another organization concerned in part with issues in mathematics education is the School Science and Mathematics Association (Bowling Green State University, 126 Life Science Building, Bowling Green, Ohio 43403). It, too, publishes a journal with articles of interest to the mathematics teacher and sponsors an annual convention.

In addition to these professional opportunities, many colleges and regional school organizations offer in-service programs for mathematics teachers. Some are sponsored by the National Science Foundation or other governmental agencies and frequently offer additional incentives. However, with all the available opportunities for mathematics teachers to constantly up-grade their knowledge and skills in their profession, the primary responsibility for making these activities worthwhile lies with each individual mathematics teacher. It is the mathematics teacher's *professional* responsibility to take advantage of these opportunities!

INFORMAL EVALUATIONS

The pupils' judgments of a teacher, especially when taken over a period of time and in different situations are often very meaningful. That judgment determines the teacher's "reputation" and is arrived at "informally," by word of mouth among students. Teachers may try to gain some insight into their reputation by asking students to express their opinions anonymously, in writing. A prepared form which includes a well-constructed checklist as well as some space for general comments might be a useful instrument for soliciting these feelings.

Sample 1 is an evaluation form similar to what some teachers have distributed to their students at the end of the term. These may be completed and returned anonymously. The results are seen only by the teacher who may then use them to adjust his teaching patterns. It is the kind of analysis that every young teacher should implement early in his career. Perhaps the adage about self-recognition being the first step towards improvement is what may motivate this exercise.

Sample 1.   Pupil's Evaluation Survey

TEACHER _____   DATE _____

Instructions:

Place a check (✔) in the appropriate space on the right.

The Teacher:	Usually	Usually Not	Comments (If Any)
Explains the work well			
Answers questions thoroughly			
Explains a second time if necessary			
Helps students outside class			
Knows the subject well			
Is always prepared			
Wastes time in class			
Gives unfair tests			
Prepares class for tests or quizzes			
Returns marked tests the next day			
Gives too much homework			
Reviews homework			
Is too strict in class			
Has a friendly personality			
Has a sense of humor			
Grades fairly			
Explains to class how grades are determined			
Meets pupils outside class to discuss problems			
Makes me like to go to math class			
I feel that I would like to have him again.			

OVERALL RATING: Satisfactory   Unsatisfactory

(circle one)

Comments or suggestions:

After analyzing the data in the form above, the teacher can determine the areas which might be in need of changes. For example, if his tests are judged to be unfair, a supervisor or colleague might be asked to help write them for a while. (If students feel that he has a poor sense of humor, a Hollywood gag writer might help!) The only pressure to implement the findings of the survey is the teacher's own professional conscience. Very often this force promotes genuine concern and ultimately real change follows.

Another type of informal evaluation technique is available in schools which have portable video-tape equipment. This usually can be borrowed by the teacher for use in a class. Seeing oneself as others do affords the opportunity for self-analysis that is often more meaningful than the report or comments of others. With the assistance of a student (or teacher) "technician," it is possible to video-tape an entire lesson as it unfolds before your own class. The picture can be viewed at the teacher's leisure and the tape can then be erased if he so desires.

For some, the experience of being video-taped is so intimidating and frightening, even if no one but the teacher's own pupils are in the room, that they may reject this method of evaluation outright. For those who choose to participate in this type of self-analysis, a video-taped record of a teacher's performance will be most effective when viewed by the teacher together with several experienced colleagues who can point out what was done well, what was done poorly, and what corrections ought to be made. For a dramatic example, one teacher, after viewing himself on the video, remarked, "I didn't know I was so bald! (The next day he began parting his hair differently.) Another was astonished that she so frequently pushed her hair back during the lesson. This was apparently done unconsciously. Naturally the primary benefit of this immediate feedback is to enable the teacher to critically observe himself interact with the class. This could be an extremely worthwhile activity.

Other informal evaluation techniques are available to those interested in using them. Take time out to answer the following questions honestly. Your answers should help guide you towards achieving the goal of excellence for which you ought to be striving.

1. Do I study more mathematics so that I will become a more competent and knowledgeable teacher?
2. Do I evaluate my classroom problems with fellow teachers at seminars, in-service courses or even at the lunchroom table while offering opinions to, and receiving advice from others?
3. Do I offer my services as an extra-curricular advisor? Do mathematics teams, clubs, newspapers, speakers, interest me?
4. Do I attend professional meetings of local and national mathematics teacher associations? Am I familiar with relevant professional literature as well as recent periodicals?
5. Do I observe other classes and ask other teachers to observe me for their reactions?
6. Do I inform parents or guidance counselors of students who have special problems?
7. What new and creative ideas have I offered lately to my colleagues, supervisor or students?
8. Do I show an interest in the life of the school other than in the area of mathematics?

FORMAL OBSERVATIONS

In many school systems, a teacher's overall performance is rated yearly. The rating, especially during the early non-tenured (probationary) years, is taken very seriously, for it is often on that basis that tenure is granted or denied. While many aspects of the teacher's performance are considered when granting or denying tenure, the ability to teach a lesson well is of prime importance.

Whether a teacher is tenured or not, the formal observation is the technique used by supervisors to help formulate their opinion concerning a teacher's skill in the classroom. This observation may be an announced or unannounced visit to the classroom. It is sometimes preceded by a pre-observation conference at which time the teacher and supervisor discuss the nature of the class to be observed, the topic to be taught, the type of lesson the teacher expects to teach, and the reason why the teacher selected that particular type of lesson. The supervisor may help the teacher plan the lesson by suggesting an interesting motivation, key questions, types of drill exercises, etc. It is then up to the teacher to implement that plan when the supervisor observes. The pre-observation conference is usually held several days before the lesson is actually taught.

The observation is usually followed by a post-observation conference at which the lesson is discussed, suggestions are offered, criticisms are made and alternatives are presented. A detailed written report on the observation will follow this conference, and the report usually becomes part of the teacher's official record of performance in the school. While the tenured teacher may be formally observed once or twice a year, the non-tenured teacher may be seen as many as six or even eight times annually, depending on the district's policy or the supervisor's determination of need.

Observation Reports

The two sample observation reports that follow (Sample 2 on page 83 and Sample 3 on page 85) will give you some general ideas of what supervisors look for in formal observations. Both are actual reports.

Sample 2. Observation Report of a First Year Algebra Class

Teacher_____ Class_____ Date_____

Description of the Lesson

As the pupils entered the room, they found a do-now exercise on the board, asking them to express algebraically four statements involving number relationships, using ''x'' to represent the number in question in each example. Thus, the attention of the class was directed to the work of the lesson immediately and no time was wasted. After reminding the class that pupils needing extra help were urged to attend the after-school study sessions, the teacher circulated about the room to check on the quality of pupil work on the board exercises. A reasonable time was allowed for the class to do this work; then the teacher called on several pupils for their answers. These were given correctly in each instance: $x + 6$, $6x + 5$, $6x + 5 = 35$, and $7x - 4x = 24$.

Referring to the original statements, the teacher asked the class to distinguish between those which are sentences and those which are merely phrases. The pupils were able to do this, and the teacher emphasized that the last two were sentences, and therefore led to equations when translated into algebra, because of the presence of the verb ''is'' in their statements. The first two statements, both phrases, possessed no verbs in their statements. The teacher capitalized on a good opportunity here, both to link the study of mathematics with the work of his pupils in English and to introduce the concept of the mathematical sentence. The latter idea was carried further when the teacher elicited the solution of the equation $6x + 5 = 35$ from the pupils and then had a pupil point out that the number ''5'' makes the sentence ''true.'' The use of the concept of the mathematical sentence is most valuable as a unifying device in the teaching of mathematics, especially in future work, where ''sentences'' include inequalities as well as equations.

After requiring the class to check the result of the solution of this equation in the original problem, a commendable procedure, the teacher paused to elicit a medial summary from the pupils, and he listed the steps for solving verbal problems on the board: 1. Read (the sentence), 2. State the unknown, 3. Set up equation, 4. Solve, and 5. Check. A pupil was then sent to the board to solve the equation $7x - 4x = 24$, while the rest of the class worked at their seats and the teacher circulated about the room to assist where help was needed. The work on the board was discussed and checked.

The remainder of the lesson was devoted to the solution of two additional problems of the same type as those already solved. These application exercises were considered carefully, the pupils working on them at their seats, the teacher checking their work, and then the class discussing and checking the solutions placed on the board. All checks were made orally in the original statements of the problems.

Commendations

The pupils were required to begin work immediately upon entering the room, since the do-now exercises were already on the board. Thus, no time was wasted in beginning the lesson.

The teacher repeatedly circulated about the room while the pupils were working on problems at their seats, thereby maintaining a continuous check on the quality of pupil work.

The work of the pupils in their English classes was brought into the lesson in connection with the recognition of phrases and sentences. The concept of the ''mathematical sentence'' also was introduced in the lesson and carefully illustrated.

Questioning was generally good. Non-volunteers were frequently called upon to answer questions. In addition to distributing questions widely, the teacher made an effort to increase pupil participation in the lesson by having pupils place their solutions to problems on the board.

The teacher elicited a medial summary from the pupils and wrote it on the board. This was the list of five steps to be taken in solving simple verbal problems. Applications of these steps were provided in subsequent problems. Of the five steps, the teacher especially stressed reading the problem (so important for all pupils, but especially for many of the slower ones in ninth year mathematics) and checking in the original statement of the problem.

Suggestions

Although the aim of the lesson became clear to this observer as the lesson unfolded, it would have been desirable to state it in concrete terms for the pupils, to enable them to take clearer and more meaningful notes. The aim could have been elicited from the class by asking for a title to the list of five steps presented as the medial summary. These pupils could have been expected to contribute a statement such as ''Steps in solving problems,'' which the teacher could have refined, if he thought it necessary, before writing it on the board.

When teaching a lesson on problem solving, one must make a special effort to present at least some problems which will command considerable pupil interest and yet be simple enough for them to solve at their level. Most of the problems presented in this lesson were of the straight textbook type and lacked this special ''spark.'' The teacher could have had an effective motivation problem in the do-now set and more interesting problems throughout the lesson by relating them more closely with the pupils' experiences, such as their classroom test grades, their work experiences, their financial and earnings experiences, and so on.

Although the teacher attempted to elicit much of the material of the lesson from the pupils, he also gave them information in many instances which he could have obtained from them. Efforts should always be made to elicit the maximum amount of information from the class.

As with many new teachers, the teacher has a tendency to repeat most pupil answers. This practice should be avoided as much as possible, since it tends to foster pupil inattention to the original responses by fellow pupils. If it is necessary to have any pupil answers repeated, either because of inaudibility or because of a need for clarification, the pupil giving the answer or another pupil should be asked to repeat it.

Summary   Although new to the profession, Mr. X has been doing a very conscientious job with a program of generally weak classes. He has managed to maintain the interest of his pupils in their work and he has made every effort to have them do their work faithfully. He has shown many signs of becoming a fine teacher, and I am certain that his techniques will improve as he becomes more experienced. It is a pleasure to welcome him to the department.

_____

Supervisor

Teacher's Signature: _____

Although it is possible to incorporate more rating categories, such as "excellent" and "poor," into an observation form (see Sample 4 on page 86), such a refinement could make an "average" rating appear to be worse because it would then be further from the highest rating. Sample 4 is merely one possible variation. Both, items to be ranked as well as ranking intervals, are usually developed by supervisors to meet specific school needs.

EVALUATION TOWARDS TENURE

The granting of tenure to a teacher is a serious matter to boards of education, for they and the state are thereby making a commitment to invest a large sum of money in a person over a span of many years. They would like to "get their money's worth" by acquiring the best "product" possible. The sums often include pensions, death benefits, health plans and sick benefits, in addition to salaries.

In addition, a tenured teacher has certain legal and academic protections so that removal from the job for any reason must be well documented. In these matters, unions and professional associations such as the National Education Association and American Federation of Teachers are vigilant in protecting the rights of teachers against unscrupulous supervisors.

By granting tenure only after careful scrutiny, the state is thus not only protecting itself but also the children involved.

The probationary period for a teacher (often three years) is that time when a board of education, through its staff of administrators and supervisors, determines whether an individual merits tenured service. This determination is based on observations of classroom teaching techniques and classroom management, participation in school activities, and possibly in community activities. Professional, as well as personal, qualities are assessed. Willingness to accept and implement suggestions offered by supervisors, as well as overall attendance patterns also are considered. Supervisors assess a teacher's overall cooperative effort as well as his suitability to the school district.

Rating Checklist

Sample 5 on page 87 is a checklist that might be used by a school board (through its superintendent) when rating a probationer.

FORMAL EVALUATION AFTER TENURE

The process of evaluation and teacher growth is expected to continue throughout the teacher's professional career. Yearly ratings of "satisfactory" or "unsatisfactory" are often given. As in the case of non-tenured teachers, evaluations of tenured teachers are also based on formal observations of the type described earlier, though they are not nearly as frequent. The purpose, here, is to keep teachers on their professional "toes," through periodic evaluation of their performance. To make this a meaningful activity, recommendations are made and assistance is offered if it is determined that change is needed.

Sample 3.   Observation Report of a Regular High School Geometry Class

Teacher _____   Class _____   Date _____

Aim of Lesson: Introduction to parallel lines and corresponding angles formed by a transversal.

Procedure: The homework assignment for the following day was on the side board and the classroom exercise:

Given: $\angle 3$ ╳ $\angle 1$ $\angle 2$ $\angle 4$ $m\angle 1 = 80°$

Find: $m\angle 2$, $m\angle 3$, $m\angle 4$

was at the front. After a few minutes, you told all students to stop writing and insisted that they put down their pens and pencils and listen to the discussion of the classwork exercise. You then stated that the topic to be discussed was "parallel lines." The definition and properties of parallel lines were stated, with emphasis on the importance of the two lines lying in the same plane. A transversal crossing two parallel lines was then drawn on the board, and the students were asked to guess which angles were equal in measure. After relating this diagram to the classwork exercise, you gave the pupils several appropriate exercises. The lesson ended with a review of the new work.

Commendations:

1. This was a well-prepared lesson.

2. Many students appeared to be eager to learn and followed instructions well.

3. The boardwork was generally clear and the use of colored chalk was effective.

4. Several excellent techniques were employed during the course of the lesson, especially when you had the students state the various properties of parallel lines which they knew from past experience; when you emphasized the possibility of two lines not meeting and yet not being parallel (skew lines); when you asked the students to "guess" which angles are congruent when a transversal is drawn; when you gave illustrations with two horizontal and two vertical parallel lines cut by a transversal; when you referred to the homework for the following day at appropriate times during the lesson; and when you summarized the lesson at the end of the period.

5. You praised students when their replies were correct, and when a particularly important answer was given such as, "We can't prove lines parallel because the angles (in a certain diagram in the textbook) are not corresponding angles," you asked another student to repeat it.

Shortcomings and Suggestions:

1. Avoid statements which are vague, unclear, and which may not be understood by the pupils. For example, after parallel lines were defined, you said, "The definition is not believed to be true by all people." You apparently had in mind one of the non-Euclidean geometries. Yet this statement, at this particular time, can only serve to confuse the students. In any event, the concept of truth or falsity does not apply to a definition. Also, after the class was able to conclude that "If two parallel lines are cut by a transversal, the corresponding angles are congruent," you should have told the pupils to simply postulate this, as has been done with other statements in the past. Instead, you said, "People have attempted to prove they are congruent and have succeeded. We won't prove it. It's an assumed proof." All this was unnecessary, for it was meaningless to the students.

2. You should not have attempted to illustrate skew lines with your drawing of two highways. You should only have referred to the diagram in the textbook instead of using a rather poor blackboard drawing.

3. At the beginning of the period when a boy walked in late, you said, "Oh my! Do you have a pass?" The boy answered, "No!" and you replied, "I'll have to mark you late. That's the second time—watch it!" While it was appropriate to ask for a pass, the "punishment" of marking him late, and the threat to "watch it!" were meaningless. You should simply have told him to explain his lateness at the end of the period, and if the explanation was not a satisfactory one, you would have to report it to the dean.

4. You should not wait to collect the homework until after the period has ended. This creates confusion. The collection should have been done earlier.

5. With more experience, you will realize that the lesson would have been more meaningful to the students if you had discussed not only the corresponding angles, but also the alternate interior angles and interior angles on the same side of the transversal, all in a single period. You should also realize that these angles are formed if two *non*-parallel lines are cut by a transversal.

General Estimate: Satisfactory

Teacher's Signature: _____   Supervisor _____

Some supervisors prefer to use a simple form similar to this one to record their observation:

Sample 4.   Observation Report with Rating Categories

Teacher_____ Class_____ Date_____

A. *Brief Description of the Lesson:*

	Good	Average	Needs Improvement	Comments
B. *Methods of Teaching:*				
1. Motivation				
2. Connection with Pupils' Previous Knowledge				
3. Use of Illustrative Material				
4. Skill in Questioning				
5. Continuity and Development				
6. Conveying of Information				
7. Stimulation of Thought				
8. Summary or Generalization				
9. Drill				
10. Effective Use of Textbook				
11. Homework Review				
C. *Responsiveness of Class*				
1. Attentiveness and Interest				
2. Participation by Students				
D. *Qualities of Teacher*				
1. Quality of Voice				
2. Use of English				
3. Appearance				
E. *General*				
1. Talking too much?				
2. Repeating Pupils' Answers?				
3. Effective Use of Time				
4. Holding and Reaching Entire Class				
5. Knowledge of Subject				
6. Classroom Management				
7. Rating of Lesson				

F. *Favorable Comments*

G. *Some Basic Suggestions*

Teacher's Signature: _____   Supervisor_____

In recent years some have suggested that teachers be rated on the performance of their pupils on standardized tests (or minimum competency examinations). This has been rejected by most knowledgeable professionals in the field of education in favor of a multiple indicator of pupil progress designed to help determine a teacher's effectiveness. These multiple indicators would involve such items as observation of the teacher's relationship with students, student performance on tests, cumulative pupil records, informal and formal observation of the teacher's classroom performance, receptivity to suggestions and so on.

Ultimately, the purpose of teacher evaluation programs is to improve student growth and learning. All the means used have that end in mind.

SUMMARY

Those teachers who are interested in growing professionally will find ways to do so. They become the "great" or "pretty good" teachers. They are usually teachers who actively participate in professional organizations, meetings, and programs and regularly read professional journals. Those who pay mere lip service to their development (or who are honest enough to do not even that) become the teachers who are just passable or who, as described earlier in this chapter, "stink."

While continued self-analysis and evaluation ought not to become an obsession with a teacher, it ought to be a serious concern. Analyses result from informal

Sample 5. Rating Checklist

Name _____

School _____

Date _____

Lateness Record:

Attendance Record:

	Outstanding	Satisfactory	Unsatisfactory	Comments (If Any)
A. *Classroom Instruction and Management*				
1. Control of class				
2. Maintenance of a wholesome classroom atmosphere conducive to the learning process				
3. Planning and preparation of work				
4. Skill in adapting instruction to individual needs				
5. Effective use of appropriate methods				
6. Skill in making lessons attractive and interesting to pupils				
7. Evidence of pupil growth in knowledge, skills, appreciations, and attitudes				
8. Attention to pupil health, safety and general welfare				
9. Attention to physical conditions of the classroom				
10. Housekeeping and appearance of room				
11. Care of equipment by teacher and students				
12. Attention to records and reports				
13. Attention to routine matters				
B. *Professional Qualities*				
1. Professional attitude				
2. Understanding of students				
3. Effect on character of students				
4. Resourcefulness and initiative				
5. Evidence of professional growth				
6. Willingness to accept special assignments in connection with the general school program				
7. Effort to establish and maintain good relationships with parents				
8. Maintenance of good relationships with other teachers and with supervisors				
C. *Personal Qualities*				
1. Appearance				
2. Voice, speech, English usage				

evaluation that one's students can provide, video-tape recording of a lesson (if such is available), classroom observations by colleagues, critical questioning of one's role and effectiveness as an educator, and comments and suggestions made after formal observations by one's supervisor.

The post-observation conference consists of a serious and critical analysis of the lesson that was just presented. The written observation report is the written synthesis of this conference. This report becomes a permanent record of the description of the lesson, its strong and weak points, as well as suggestions and recommendations for future improvement.

The observation process continues throughout a teacher's career, for no one is immune to occasional slippage in technique, lesson presentation, classroom management, etc. A few reminders are often all that is needed to return the teacher to his previously high standards.

One experienced teacher, a former professional actor, always appreciated being observed, for he recalled its importance in his acting days when he would hire people to sit in the audience to observe his performance in the show. They would then report on every aspect of his performance, down to the most minute detail. It made him a better actor. He was an excellent teacher!

EXERCISES

1. Periodically, a teacher might send a student to the board to act as teacher for a portion of a lesson, while he sits in that pupil's seat. Comment on this as a type of teacher evaluation.

2. Some supervisors prefer to make *un*announced observations to see what a teacher's performance is "really" like. What are the merits of *announced* and *unannounced* visits?

3. "If a teacher gives the entire class high report card grades, all his students will like him, and this will be reflected in their evaluation of him." Comment on this.

4. Prepare a lesson from the unit plan on radicals for a first year algebra class (see p. 4, Chapter 1) and present it to your colleagues in this class. Have them evaluate your presentation

5. Try to remember your own favorite high school mathematics teacher. What qualities impressed you most? Use the Pupil's Evaluation Survey in this chapter as a guide.

6. Suppose you are teaching in a high school and you find that one of your colleagues has aroused a strong negative feeling among his students. What would you do about this situation when one of his students comes to you for help (both in mathematics and in general regarding his classroom situation)?

7. After teaching for five years you find yourself teaching the same courses each year. You feel you are not being properly stimulated and are getting bored with your work. Explain how you might go about solving this dilemma.

8. The superintendent of your school district has come to observe you with an eye towards the granting of tenure. After the lesson, his comments to you are simply, "I see all this audio-visual equipment lying around the room and you used none of it. If you don't use it from now on, we'll take it from you and pass it on to someone in another school." Comment on your probable feelings at that moment and your use of audio-visual equipment in the future.

9. A few days after a supervisor observes you, she sends you a report of the lesson that, in your judgment, is filled with inaccuracies and untruths. For example, she says you had no prepared lesson plan when indeed you did; she says you called on only a few students in class when, in fact, you involved virtually everyone. What is your reaction to this type of observation report, and what could you do?

10. Write to the National Council of Teachers of Mathematics (1906 Association Drive, Reston, Virginia, 22091) to request sample copies of *The Arithmetic Teacher* and *The Mathematics Teacher* journals along with membership application (half price for students). Read an article in each journal and write a brief review.

SUGGESTED READINGS

Kenney, Robert. "Basic Competencies in Vermont." *The Mathematics Teacher* 71 (1978): 702.

National Council of Teachers of Mathematics. *Guidelines for the Preparation of Teachers of Mathematics*. Washington, D.C.: NCTM, 1981.
This booklet provides the NCTM's position on what the preparation (both inservice and preservice) of mathematics teachers should entail.

Schult, Veryl. "A Giant Step for NCTM." *The Mathematics Teacher,* 66,5 (1973): 391–92.
A brief history of the National Council of Teachers of Mathematics is given here.

Shuard, H., and Quadling, D. *Teachers of Mathematics, Some Aspects of Professional Life.* London: Harper & Row, 1980.
This book describes the professional life and responsibilities of the mathematics teacher in the United Kingdom. One can get an interesting perspective of one's professional position by viewing its analog in another country.

Taylor, Ross. *So You're a Mathematics Supervisor?* Washington, D.C.: NCTM, 1982.
Although addressed to the mathematics supervisor, the teacher of mathematics can benefit greatly from knowing what the supervisor expects and what the supervisor is trying to achieve within the profession.

CHAPTER 8 REMEDIATION

Our objective in this chapter is to offer various alternatives for remediation in arithmetic skills at the secondary level. The term *remediation* implies that a remedy is being offered to correct that which is in need of repair. The student who has somehow not developed these mathematical skills in his early, formative years in school is the focus of attention in mathematics remediation programs. The deficiency may have occurred in the past because of ineffective teaching, inadequate curriculum, repeated failure, poor work habits, dislike of school, slow maturation, oppressive or non-supportive environment, or simply because the child may be a slow learner or one with emotional or physical problems.

The goal of remediation programs is, at the very least, to raise the student's mathematical performance to an "acceptable" level some time before he graduates from high school. This is a desirable goal because the student will then be employable as a mathematically literate high school graduate, and may even be able to handle college preparatory work in mathematics.

For the readers of this book who are mathematically mature, an understanding of "acceptable" high school performance level might include, at the very least, the traditional algebra, geometry and trigonometry, as well as the accompanying arithmetic skills. But realistically, this is not a universally attainable goal. If the students had mastered much of what they were taught through the eighth grade (before coming to high school), there would be no need for remediation programs, for everyone would be at the proper starting point for high school mathematics. However, many students reach junior and senior high school already improperly prepared, which we will define specifically as being two or more years below grade level in arithmetic skills and in general mathematical knowledge. As teachers we must find ways to help these students.

BASIC MATHEMATICS CURRICULUM

What is an average pupil, on grade level, taught in elementary school and junior high school before arriving at the senior high school? While courses of study do vary in various parts of the country, basically, you can expect a youngster's background through eighth grade to include exposure to many, if not all, of the following topics:

   I. Sets
       A. Concept
       B. Notation
       C. Kinds (finite, null, etc.)
       D. Union, intersection, complement
  II. Real numbers
       A. Integers
          1. Positive, negative
          2. Order of operations
          3. Properties (closure, commutative, associative, distributive, etc.)
          4. Prime and composite numbers
          5. Factors
          6. Linear open sentences
       B. Rationals
          1. Decimals
          2. Scientific notation
          3. Properties (commutative, identity, inverse, etc.)
          4. Simplifying expressions
       C. Terminating and repeating decimals
       D. Irrationals (square root)
 III. Ratio, proportion, percent
  IV. Geometry
       A. Point, line, plane
       B. Angles
       C. Polygons
       D. Perpendicular lines
       E. Parallel lines
       F. Congruence
       G. Similarity
       H. Polygons
          1. Triangle properties
          2. Quadrilateral properties
          3. Perimeter and area
       I. Circles
          1. Arc length and measure
          2. Circumference
          3. Area
       J. Solids
          1. Surface area
          2. Volume
   V. Coordinate geometry
       A. Plotting points
       B. Pythagorean Theorem
       C. Graphing
       D. Inequalities
  VI. Statistics
          1. Interpretation of data (including graphing)
          2. Mean, median, mode
          3. Probability

From ninth grade through twelfth grade the exposure to mathematics becomes much more specialized, to include algebra, geometry, trigonometry, possibly some calculus, computer programming, and more. While exposure to the mathematics of the early grades is universal, the remaining high school grades see fewer and fewer pupils electing to continue their mathematics studies.

MINIMUM COMPETENCY TESTS

Recent trends, which are perhaps more the result of public pressure than educational leadership, are in the direction of preventing a student from graduating from high school with a diploma if she has not mastered the basic mathematical skills and concepts that are usually taught through eighth grade (listed above). (Reading, writing and sometimes speaking are generally also included as the required basic skills for graduation.) Thus, many communities have established minimum competency or minimum proficiency requirements, usually at the eighth grade level of work, before the student can receive a high school diploma.

An understanding of what minimum competency or proficiency exams are like ought to prove helpful to teachers who are faced with the problem of providing remediation for students who must pass such an examination in order to graduate. Sample 1 (see page 94) is a partial set of questions one might find on a minimum competency test. A full examination may contain twice as many questions as this set. A student might need to answer 60% to 70% of the questions correctly to be considered as having "passed" the examination and thus be entitled to receive a high school diploma.

WHO NEEDS REMEDIATION?

Several categories of students, at some time in their secondary school career, may be in need of some form of remediation service. These are:

1. Students who are two or more years below grade level in mathematical skills (as determined by standardized tests).

2. Students who are chronic failures in mathematics.

3. Students who are unable to score a passing

grade on a minimum competency or proficiency examination.

4. Pupils whose family, friends, neighborhood and culture do not encourage success in school and who are therefore not succeeding in their mathematics work.

5. Students with interfering physical or learning disabilities.

6. Students who transfer from one school to another and who are having adjustment problems (perhaps because of poor coordination between the two schools involved).

7. Recent foreign immigrants who may be having language and other adjustment difficulties.

DIAGNOSTIC PROCEDURES

A guidance counselor may identify a student as belonging to one or more of the categories above by checking previous records, interviewing her teachers, speaking to the child and her parents, and finally, by administering, or having the mathematics teacher administer and interpret, a diagnostic test. The results of some or all of these efforts will lead to a determination of whether or not placement in a remedial program is justified. This procedure may also help determine which program is most appropriate if several are available.

Several diagnostic procedures are available to the counselor or mathematics teacher.

Teacher-made Materials

One appropriate type of examination may cover typical seventh or eighth grade topics similar to the sample minimum competency test shown earlier. Every well-managed mathematics department office has records of examinations of this type that might have been used in the past. A comprehensive examination, even though not scientifically prepared and tested for statistical validity, can provide the teacher and counselor with immediate and reasonable insight into the student's mathematical ability, as well as her areas of strengths and weakness.

Standardized Tests

The California Achievement Tests (Level 5, Form B) published by McGraw-Hill is but one example of the type of standardized test that is not only easy to administer and interpret but also comprehensive, testing computation, understanding of mathematical concepts, and problem solving. Your supervisor should be able to provide you with a packet of this or some other standardized tests that contain answer keys, grade equivalency conversion tables and other pertinent analyses of the test. Hopefully, someone has already selected the test deemed most appropriate for your district's students while at the same time providing you with the specific information required.

For example, after administering a standardized test as part of a diagnostic procedure, you may wish to be able to determine (easily!) the areas, if any, in which a student is deficient. Some such tests will provide the teacher with an analysis of the student's strengths and weaknesses in the various key mathematical skills and concepts. Such analyses can be extremely helpful in designing a remediation program for the individual student.

Thus the standardized test can, and should, be used to identify candidates for a mathematics remediation program, as well as be used to design and prepare the individual programs based on each student's needs.

Survey Tests

Survey tests are found in all mathematics textbooks and workbooks that deal specifically with arithmetic skills. (See books listed on p. 100.) Although these tests generally do not give you norm-referenced data, they might well provide you with a good idea of a student's mathematical strengths and weaknesses. In addition, the results of this type of test should guide you to the appropriate part of the textbook for each pupil tested.

Pre-test Cards

Pre-test cards are similar to the survey tests described above and are usually found in commercially prepared mathematics kits. (Several recommended kits are listed on p. 100.) Their primary purpose is to assist the teacher in ascertaining an individual student's mathematical strengths and weaknesses in order to guide the teacher to the appropriate activity in the mathematics kit.

Criterion-Referenced Tests

Criterion-referenced tests also provide a form of diagnosis. Here the diagnosis is more in the form of an assessment of specific previously taught skills and concepts than one of a general, all-encompassing, survey of abilities. Whereas the previously mentioned tests essentially inventory a student's general (and required) mathematical knowledge, the criterion-referenced test is an instrument designed to assess specific learning goals prescribed prior to instruction. Both types of assessment play an important role in assessing student mathematical ability or achievement.

Attitudinal Assessment Instruments

Very often assessing a student's attitude toward mathematics, school, discipline, society, and so on can reveal some interesting notions about groups of students as well as about individual students. Information of this sort can have a profound effect on a remediation program. Although at first thought the extra work involved in either selecting an instrument or developing one might not appear to be worth the investment in time, teachers who have taken the time to inspect apparent remedial problems from the point of view of a student's attitude towards related factors have found such additional insights useful in preparing a remedial program.

Much time has been devoted to studying various aspects of attitude measurement. An excellent source from which a teacher can learn about the different kinds of attitude scales as well as ways to construct these instruments is *Scales for the Measurement of Attitudes* by M. E. Shaw and J. M. Wright (McGraw-Hill, 1967).

In addition to assessing attitude, teachers might also find it useful to determine their students' interests. For this purpose various interest inventories have been prepared and are readily available. Some of these inventories attempt to measure a student's tendency to like and choose from among some specific activities. Other inventories correlate a student's interests in school, recreation and work. Much can be learned about a student's interests from such inventories. The teacher who takes the time to view all possible factors (including attitude and interests) which may affect student achievement in mathematics is probably most likely to design and prepare a meaningful program for her remedial students.

Mathematical Retardation

Mathematical retardation will probably manifest itself in any one of the diagnostic procedures just outlined. Although retardation may be a result of environmental factors or inherited traits, these diagnostic testing procedures are usually not adequate to determine the specific causes of the slow learner's problems. Possible causes may range from limited manipulative abilities to sight and hearing disabilities, as well as other physical problems. Family-related educational pressures and other emotional problems may also adversely affect student achievement.

If the retardation is innate or permanent, the student may never be able to reach his appropriate grade level in mathematics achievement, regardless of the intensity of remedial work being offered. If, on the other hand, the retardation is related to external factors, it may be remediable. Thus the curriculum and methods of instruction must be adapted to a level of achievement that is realistic for the individual. Every teacher of a remedial class must be aware of the limitations of each child so that her expectations for that child's mathematical performance are consistent with the student's abilities and problems.

METHODS OF REMEDIATION

Individualization

Many individualized programs use a diagnostic-prescriptive approach for the remediation of skill deficiencies in mathematics. A standardized mathematics diagnostic test (such as the California Achievement Test mentioned earlier) may be administered at the beginning of the school year to determine each pupil's specific skill

Sample 1. Mathematics Competency Test

---

(1) Add:

$$835$$
$$218$$
$$81$$

(2) Subtract:

$$3016$$
$$- \ 259$$

(3) Multiply:

$$259$$
$$\times \ 63$$

(4) Divide:

$$34 \ ) \ 2476$$

(5) Reduce the fraction:

$$\frac{12}{16} =$$

(6) Express as an equivalent fraction:

$$\frac{3}{5} = \frac{}{15}$$

(7) Add:

$$\frac{1}{2}$$
$$+ \frac{1}{3}$$

(8) Multiply:

$$\frac{2}{3} \times \frac{3}{5}$$

(9) What is $\frac{2}{3}$ of 24?

(10) Multiply $3 \frac{1}{3} \times 2 \frac{1}{2}$.

(11) Round 2.37 to the nearest tenth.

(12) Divide $\frac{2}{3} \div \frac{1}{3}$

(13) Subtract 3.51 from 20.20.

(14) Find 12% of 8.

(15) Add −5 and −6

(16) Divide .03$\overline{)4.215}$

(17) Solve for *x*: $2x + 4 = 10$

(18) Find the average (mean) of 62, 70, 70, 88.

(19) A woman buys an air conditioner for $500. The sales tax is 8%. How much sales tax must she pay?

(20) What is the circumference of a circle whose radius is 10. (Use the formula $C = 2\pi r$. Use $\pi = 3.14$.)

(21) What is the length of the line segment joining *A* and *B*.

(22) On the graph below plot the point (2,3)

(23) What is the perimeter of a triangle whose sides are 5, 12 and 13?

(24) Which angle best approximates 30°?

    (a)   (b)   (c)   (d)

(25) What is the area of a rectangle whose length measures 10 *m* and whose width measures 8 *m*?

(26) In the circle, what is the line segment *AB* called?

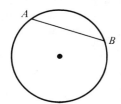

(27) Write $\dfrac{3}{5}$ as a percent.

(28) Express $\dfrac{3}{25}$ as a decimal.

(29) Express $\dfrac{37}{7}$ as a mixed number.

(30) José earns $4.50 per hour. How much does he earn for working 6 hours?

(31) Solve for *x*: $\dfrac{4}{7} = \dfrac{x}{14}$

deficiencies and the areas in which he needs work. In addition, the teacher may interview the pupil to further focus on his areas of difficulty.

The teacher can then analyze the test results more carefully and prescribe remediation activities using workbooks, arithmetic skill kits, calculators and teacher-prepared materials. These materials are most efficiently organized in individual folders which contain a continuous record of each pupil's work. Such folders may include the diagnostic test results, the prescribed remediation plan, progress tests, and the student's actual work as she completes each assignment.

Each folder will be complete at the end of the term only when a post-test is given and its results compared to the pre-test results to determine the progress made. Comparing the end-of-year results with those of the same diagnostic test given at the beginning of the year provides a sound basis for judgment of the overall success of the individualized remediation program for that youngster.

If you refer to Sample Lesson 8 (Chapter 1), you will find a sample individualized remedial prescription lesson on decimals. To make the listing of appropriate remediation topics more complete, and for your information and guidance when you teach this level remedial class, we suggest the following topics, in addition to the one on decimals.

1. *Whole numbers*
   Place value: reading and writing whole numbers
   Rounding off
   Addition
   Subtraction
   Multiplication
   Order of operations
   Prime and composite numbers
   Division
   Exponents

2. *Fractions*
   Comparing fractions
   Reducing fractions
   Improper fractions and mixed numbers
   Ratio, proportion
   Least common multiple; lowest common denominator
   Adding and subtracting fractions
   Multiplication of fractions
   Reciprocals
   Division of fractions

3. *Decimals*
   (already listed previously)

4. *Percent*
   Changing decimals and fractions greater than

100%; less than 1%
Finding percent of a number

5. *Algebra*
   Signed numbers
   Evaluating formulas (including exponents)
   Solving simple equations

6. *Graphs*
   Plotting points
   Linear graphs
   Reading and interpreting graphs: bar graphs, line graphs, circle graphs and pictographs

7. *Geometry*
   Definitions
   Figures (recognition and parts)
   Area, perimeter

8. *Measurement*
   Ruler
   Time
   Conversion of units
   Metrics
   Scale drawings

9. *Statistics*
   Mean, median, mode
   Probability

10. *Problem Solving*
    Word problems
    Arithmetic
    Algebra
    Writing your own problems

Each pupil's progress should be tested frequently with a ten- to fifteen-minute quiz. These regular assessments can be incorporated into the individualized program in such a way as to enable the pupil to take this quiz and demonstrate some accomplishment of the unit tested before moving on to the next programmed item. If the pupil does not succeed, a second prescription may have to be written by the teacher for that particular topic. As an example, we show here Sample 2, a progress test.

Sample 2. Progress Test—Division of Fractions

1. Write the reciprocal of each

$$\frac{4}{7}; \quad 3\frac{1}{2}; \quad 2;$$

2. Divide each pair of numbers as indicated:

$$\frac{3}{5} \div \frac{9}{15}; \quad \frac{1}{2} \div 3; \quad 20 \div \frac{5}{9}; \quad 3\frac{1}{2} \div 2\frac{3}{5};$$

3. $8\frac{1}{3}$ yards of cloth are divided into five equal pieces. How many yards long is each piece?

Students may be held accountable for the quality as well as the quantity of work they do based on their individual prescriptions. They might be asked to record satisfactorily completed assignments on a personal progress record such as Sample 3.

Sample 3. Personal Progress Record

Student _____

Class _____

Unit	Date Started	Topic	Progress Test	
			Mark	Date
1		Whole numbers —place value —rounding off —addition —subtraction . . . etc.		

In a typical individualized remedial class, when a student walks into the room, she picks up her folder, returns to her seat, opens her folder and checks the individualized prescription (see Sample Lesson 8, p. 21) assigned to see what she completed the day before, along with the teacher's comments or assessments of this work, and what she should be doing today. She should then determine the materials she needs for that session. She would then pick up that material from the appropriate place in the classroom (where it has already been laid out in advance by the teacher), and return to her seat and begin working. The teacher and/or teacher's assistant in the room should check her progress regularly during the period and assist her when needed.

This "typical" day has many variations which the teacher will implement as required. Some of these are listed below and include a variety of activities that add many new dimensions to the individualized lesson.

Small Group and Whole Class Instruction

Even in the individualized type of class just described, some small group and whole class instruction may be conducted to teach specific skills when a general weakness is exhibited among a number of students.

If the remedial program in your school is not set up with individualized classes, you will find that students' abilities at that level vary so greatly that you will be forced to offer, at the very least, some form of small group instruction to young people with similar deficiencies. It is no simple matter to break up the class into several groups, each with similar skill deficiencies. While assignments are given to the rest of the class, a group you select to work with for a portion of the period may sit around you as you demonstrate a specific skill which the members of this group lack. An educational assistant would be helpful in such a class to check on others while you are busy with the one group. Such assistants are not always available, however, in which case you might have better mathematics students assigned to assist the poorer ones. These better mathematics students might be taken from this or other classes.

Even if you are assigned a non-individualized remedial mathematics class with a specific textbook that you are asked to use, you will find it beneficial and useful to administer some type of diagnostic test so you can at least determine the direction you will follow for the term. Appropriate topics in such a class would include the same ones listed previously for individualized classes. Activities such as mathematical games and use of calculators, as well as some form of "camouflaged drill" can be used to motivate students and help them understand mathematical concepts. These activities will be explained further in the following sections.

Student Projects

In any type of class, you may develop activities which will enable students to apply their skills in a variety of interesting and motivating ways. Project activities are generally long range, perhaps two or three months. They require planning by both pupils and teacher. In addition, regular meetings between individual pupils and the teacher must be arranged so that progress can be monitored and evaluated.

You may propose a list of topics for the class to consider and have them construct, build, draw and/or write something on one topic they select. They must be encouraged to use mathematics books and encyclopedias from the school or public library.

Following are some ideas that suggest possible topics for remedial mathematics class projects. The teacher's assistance is vital in having a student select the area of research most appropriate for him.

Abacus	Magic Squares
Altitude	Möbius Strip
Angles	Negative Numbers
Calendar	Parabola
Clocks	Pi (π)
Computer	Prime Numbers
History of Mathematics	Repeating Decimals
Hypotenuse	Square Root
Infinity	Volume

Mathematics Games and Puzzles

As a supplement to mathematics instruction, whether individualized, small group or whole class, games and puzzles that challenge students and make them think are appropriate for periodic use in the class. A detailed listing and discussion of appropriate games appears on p. 95 of this chapter. Above all, remember that games should be selected to meet both the deficiency needs of the youngster and his recreational needs.

Field Trips

Field trips should relate directly to instruction in order to provide motivation for learning and should be correlated with classroom learning activities. Planning a trip to such places as a computer center, a television or radio studio, a newspaper office, or a bank should always be done with an eye towards highlighting the mathematics applications appropriate for the remedial audience. Arithmetic computations may even be used by the class in preparing for the trip in such activities as calculating the cost per student and calculating the distance to be traveled. Scale maps may be drawn where appropriate. Letters, charts and tables for every possible aspect of the trip should become a learning experience for the students. Above all, whatever experiences are encountered as part of the field trip should be used to motivate further remedial instruction.

Camouflaged Drill

All too often students in remedial classes are "turned off" to the instruction. Most often the reason for their dislike for the remediation is that they feel bored with learning the same mathematics topics year after year in a similar way each time. Sometimes students find instruction in arithmetic degrading, and as a result avoid it in whatever way they can, leading to discipline problems or truancy.

One way of avoiding this dislike for remediation among students is to camouflage the drill work in a meaningful setting. There are countless ways to offer practice in arithmetic skills in such a way as to camouflage the intent of the exercise. Drills can be camouflaged by:

1. Having the student take an active role in planning a field trip. Here the arithmetic applications would have to be carefully planned and not appear to be artificial.
2. Requiring each student to bring to school a supermarket receipt, together with an analysis of the items purchased, price per item, total cost, change given, etc. Once again a specific plan must be in hand before this is tried with a

class. All arithmetic applications would have to be anticipated and careful directions provided for the students.
3. Suggesting that pupils keep a record of daily Fahrenheit and Centigrade temperature readings, comparing accuracy by using the appropriate conversion formula.
4. Computing the cost of maintaining a family car, including computing gas mileage, cost of gas, insurance, repairs, etc. Comparisons between this cost and the cost of public transportation also should be made.
5. Involving students in simple probability games such as computing probabilities which require the addition and multiplication of fractions. This provides a fine camouflage of these often "meaningless" arithmetic processes.

The purpose of camouflaging drill is to generate a genuine enthusiasm for learning some of the arithmetic skills which students have often shrugged off as boring or unattainable. Usually when the skills are placed in a "real world" context, students are more apt to want to learn information which has evaded them for years. Various (funded) remediation programs have been conducted around this theme and have met with encouraging success.

Peer Group Tutoring

Tutoring by one's peers who are more mathematically advanced may be effective when a professional teacher's efforts may not be. Many schools have organized peer tutoring programs in which youngsters receive remedial assistance which is supplementary to the work they receive in their regular mathematics classes. This applies to remedial work at every level of secondary mathematics, and such a tutorial service is often available whether the remediation is needed in arithmetic, algebra or geometry. The initial diagnostic testing, as well as progress and post-testing is often supervised by a teacher-in-charge. The peer tutors are often directed to follow a particular course of action or plan with the pupil seeking assistance. Training of peer tutors is usually an integral part of such a program. Such training sessions involve discussions of methods and techniques of presenting the material to be covered as well as alerting the tutors to the various resources available to them. This experience can be enlightening to the peer tutors. In addition to learning and developing "new" methods of communication, they are provided with an opportunity to better understand the mathematics they are assigned to teach, since whenever one teaches a topic she is provided with an opportunity to crystalize her thoughts on that topic, and as a result, she obtains a better grasp of the topic. Thus a peer tutoring program benefits the tutor as well as the remedial student being tutored.

Relevant Applications

Mathematics may be made meaningful and relevant to the student when it is in some way tied to his own experiences, hobbies and interests. Thus, for example, a youngster's interest in art might suggest that the teacher develop a program for that youngster and others like him, in the following areas:

1. Geometric patterns that may be created with compasses and straightedge. This might lead to measurement of segments and angles, properties of the circle and regular polygons, and much more, depending on the students' interests, as well as the imagination of the teacher. The teacher must always remember the specific intent of the unit so that the art does not become an end in itself but remains a means to an end.

2. String designs that may be created by connecting appropriately located points (or holes in cardboard) such as the points A_1 and B_1, A_2 and B_2, etc.,

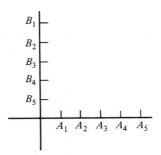

thereby forming an envelope for a parabola (see Enrichment Unit 91, "The Parabolic Envelope"). Other conic sections may be similarly constructed (see Enrichment Unit 106, "Constructing Elipses.") Before advanced work can be done in this unit, students learn about measurement on a ruler (both inches and centimeters), acute, right and obtuse angles, names of conic sections, etc. Once again, this is limited only by the teacher's imagination and student's interest. While at first thought some of these examples may appear too ambitious, actual experience with them has proved otherwise.

An investigation of some relevant topic through arithmetic applications can be extremely fruitful in motivating students towards mathematics. Lots of possible topics are available, yet the main criterion for this selection is the interests already present among the intended audience. A proper topic selection together with a creative and imaginative teacher should insure success in this mathematical endeavor.

Computer Assisted Instruction (CAI)

The computer will probably prove to be the most revolutionary teaching aid ever. In the case of remedial instruction it is but one more tool to supplement individualized, small group or large group lessons.

Well-written programs that result in a high degree of student interaction and involvement are becoming increasingly available for all the popular microcomputers found in schools these days. It is not unusual to find a computer lab with youngsters doing remedial work in arithmetic (any of the four operations), problem solving, and algebra (solving first or second degree equations, multiplying binomials, factoring, graphing, and so forth).

Programs are available to teach, reteach, reinforce, drill, and practice. Many also take into account such factors as learning rates and ability levels.

Frequently the software allows pupils to select the topic as well as the level of difficulty by themselves. Of course, the teacher might prefer to make that decision for the youngster.

One problem with CAI is that there is sometimes no place for a student to go after completing a unit of study. In other words, the structure and inflexibility of most curricula is such that it is difficult to individualize only the remediation aspect of a particular topic. If you have an opportunity to work with CAI, you will handle both fast and slow individuals, as well as those with needs that cannot be predicted.

Your mathematics department office is a good place to obtain catalogs, brochures, and other information regarding available software. Unfortunately, it is not always easy to check a software's quality before it is purchased. In any event, you must preview all software before you offer it for pupils to use.

The variety of topics and techniques is vast. One can easily obtain software dealing with:

>   basic number facts
>   whole numbers
>   fractions
>   decimals
>   arithmetic drill and practice
>   introduction to algebra
>   learning first year algebra
>   selected topics in algebra
>   introductions to geometric concepts
>   logic
>   fundamental concepts in trigonometry
>   introductory ideas in calculus

Computer games that reinforce specific skills are especially popular among pupils and make the business of learning mathematics a pleasant one.

PHYSICAL ARRANGEMENTS FOR REMEDIAL INSTRUCTION

The Mathematics Skills Laboratory

Physical settings are important regardless of the educational objectives. This is particularly true for the remedial class. A room appropriate for and conducive to the intended instruction can be instrumental in the success of a remedial program.

Wherever possible, a *mathematics skills laboratory* room should be made available to serve as a resource center and exclusive classroom for students in remedial mathematics classes. The purpose of such a room is, first of all, to provide a pleasant atmosphere for the students, and second, to have readily available in one location all the software and hardware that may be needed for remedial instruction.

Following are suggestions for some of the features that should be included in an effective mathematics skills laboratory. You may augment or delete from this list according to your needs. For the most part, remedial mathematics classes are wholly or partially individualized, and these features are suggested in that spirit.

Textbooks, Workbooks, and Kits. A display table containing available textbooks, workbooks and kits should be a prominent feature of this laboratory. Among the many such materials available are the following recommended items. (When available, answer keys might be displayed along side their respective books so that students may have them available for checking their work).

> Any appropriate recreational mathematics books (these may include puzzle books, activity books, etc.) and any good algebra or geometry texts.
> Jones, Wilmer, L. *Learning to Compute, Books 1 and 2*. N.Y.: Harcourt Brace Jovanovich, 1973.
> Goozner, Calman. *Arithmetic Skills Workbook*. N.Y.: Amsco School Publications, 1973.
> Rasmussen, Peter-Steven. *Key to Algebra*. Berkeley, Calif.: *Key Curriculum Publications,* 1972.
> Tobin, Alexander, and Sass, Kailly. *Systemathix*. N.Y.: A. E. Sadlier, 1973.
> Schlegel, Albert G. W. *A New Look at Fractions; Decimals; Percents*. Elgin, Ill.: Continental Press, 1966.
> Dressler, Isidore. *Preliminary Mathematics*. N.Y.: Amsco School Publications, 1965.
> Stein, Edwin I. *Refresher Mathematics*. Boston: Allyn & Bacon, 1970.
> Mathers, McCormick, *Cross Number Puzzle, Books A-D*

> Henney, R. Lee. *Systems for Success,* Book 2. Chicago: Follett Publishing Co., 1972.
> Wallace, Mary C. *Figure It Out*. Chicago: Follett Publishing Co., 1971.
> Computation Skills Development Kit. Chicago: Science Research Associates.
> Arithmetic Skills Kits. N.Y.: Random House.

In addition, a wide variety of fine materials is available from J. Weston Walch, Publisher, Portland, Maine.

Calculators and Computers. A second display table (or tables) should contain calculators and microcomputers. These might include:

> Electronic printing calculators (any simple types would be satisfactory)
> Display calculator (here, too, any simple types with at least the four basic operations would be satisfactory)
> Monroe Classmate 88 (a simple programmed calculator designed to assist in arithmetic drill). Game-like programs will improve understanding of basic concepts.
> Commodore PET, Radio Shack TRS-80, or the APPLE II computer with a video screen (CRT) can offer a variety of basic skills programs which provide challenge, stimulation and novelty to students required to do remedial work.

Cassettes and Tape Players. A third display might consist of cassettes and tape players, frequently a useful addition to any remedial mathematics program. The tapes usually direct pupils to perform certain exercises in conjunction with a workbook. They will guide them to follow a certain path if they are succeeding in getting correct answers and will direct them to another path if they are not succeeding.

Many textbook publishers also produce this type of material. For example:

> Addison-Wesley currently has available a series of tapes called "SKILLSEEKERS"
> Innovative Sciences of Stamford, Connecticut, produces a comprehensive package for mathematics remediation called "Intuitive Math"
> Educational Development Laboratories/McGraw-Hill also has similar materials available.

Television. An ordinary UHF/VHF television receiver is sometimes useful, especially if you live in an area that has an educational television station. There are occasions when interesting mathematics programs are broadcast and pupils should certainly be given the opportunity to view them as part of their remediation program.

Work Folders. Student work folders containing all relevant data (such as diagnostic test results, teacher prepared prescriptions, progress reports and student work) should be easily accessible. Here, too, laying them out on a table for individual student accessibility is probably best. However, storage in a file cabinet at other times is probably advisable.

Bulletin Boards. An ample number of bulletin boards should be available in the room so that student work may be exhibited. These bulletin boards may also be used for weekly mathematics contests. Here, too, the answers to past contests and the names of winners should also be displayed. Interesting professional or student-made posters may also be exhibited here, along with announcements for the students.

Storage Facilities. It is essential that adequate storage facilities be available, such as supply cabinets, file cabinets, closets, book cases (for supplementary texts and workbooks, as well as for teacher resource materials).

Storage facilities are vital so that the room will not acquire the atmosphere of a storage room and the materials will be better protected from vandalism and theft. In addition, adequate storage facilities will encourage the teacher to gather as much useful material as possible without fear of becoming overcrowded and unable to make these materials easily accessible.

Chalkboard. A chalkboard must be available in the room for any classwork you may present to the entire class as well as for small group lessons, or to display the daily mathematics puzzle (if you want to have your class involved in this type of competitive activity). These puzzles can consist of relatively simple questions involving a bit of thought and leading to some discussions, such as:

What is the next number in the series 1, 1, 2, 3, 5, 8, 13, —?

What is the smallest number of coins you need to make 61¢?

The chalkboard can be used for many other functions and is therefore an indispensible part of a mathematics skills laboratory.

Cubicles or Carrels. Individual work cubicles (or carrels) are built into some laboratory-type classrooms to provide students with as much privacy as possible. Here they can listen to tapes or whatever individualized work has been assigned to them with minimum distraction. A disadvantage of this is that the student may not feel that he is part of a class in this seclusion of his own cubicle.

Teacher awareness of this possible problem usually rectifies any difficulties which may arise in this respect.

Games. No laboratory would be complete without a mathematics recreation section which may be accessible to youngsters periodically (as determined by the teacher). Games that might improve arithmetic skills or mathematical thinking include:

> Backgammon
> Billionaire (Parker Brothers)
> Chess
> Checkers
> Division, Multiplication flash cards (Milton Bradley)
> Master Mind (Invicta Plastics)
> Multifacto Producto (Scott Foresman)
> Tridominoes
> Concentration
> Treasure Hunt
> (Many games are listed in the catalogues of Nimble, Mind/Matter Inc., Creative Publications, and other similar companies)

If you are even a bit creative and imaginative, you will discover and devise additional appropriate recreational games.

Some teachers we know, who have used games that have a more or less mathematical content, have found their value to lie in areas other than skill or concept building. Yet, there is always some positive spin-off resulting from playing games involving strategy or other mathematical or logical skills. The value seemed to lie in providing a break in the daily class routine as well as to provide time for some youngsters to "catch up" to others in the class or to do extra work if they desired.

Pupils should be allowed to select the games they prefer (dominoes and backgammon are two favorites in one school we are familiar with.) Other pupils will learn the games by asking those who are knowledgeable with the rules to teach them, or by watching pupils play against each other. The interaction is often lively and tends to breathe some life into a class, and could leave a "halo" effect for several days afterward.

THE TRADITIONAL CLASSROOM

The traditional classroom is, of course, the "old reliable" standby if a laboratory room is not available. Nevertheless, even in this type of class setting, many of the features mentioned earlier may be employed, depending on the type of traditional classroom available (presumably containing built-in storage space, bulletin boards and chalkboards). As in the mathematics skills laboratory, instruction can be individualized, in small groups, or as a whole class. Once again, a great deal depends on the teacher's creativity to develop a pleasant atmosphere conducive to learning and appropriate for the remedial program designed. Your supervisors and the school custodian may be helpful in arranging for any physical changes you believe to be reasonable and necessary.

A drawback of using such a classroom is that other classes may be likely to use it during the day, thus seriously limiting the amount of materials that can be on regular display and limiting any significant reconstruction.

INDIVIDUAL TUTORING

Individual tutoring is a commonly used method for remedial instruction, either by a teacher or by another student. The student in need of remediation receives one-to-one assistance which should be based on the results of diagnostic examination and his record of previous performance. Many of the materials used will be the same as those used in the individualized approach. The advantage of such an approach is obvious—the student receives immediate corrective action in the event he makes a mistake while solving a problem. Perhaps the disadvantage (if any actually exists) is the large number of personnel required for an individualized tutoring program. The cost is high for what may perhaps be one of the best remedial approaches.

HANDICAPPED STUDENTS

Recent directives by federal authorities require schools to consider more carefully than ever before the individual strengths and weaknesses of students with handicapping conditions. Individualized programs for such youngsters must be developed by the schools, and one aspect of such a program is to mainstream them into regular classes whenever it is deemed feasible by school personnel.

Thus, teachers will often find students with mild handicaps and special needs who have been programmed into their regular math classes. Such students often receive additional services such as mathematics remediation, psychological counseling, and so on. As the class teacher of one or more such pupils, you may be called upon to advise and assist the counselors in determining their mathematics program.

As a consultant, you will attempt to draw upon information from a variety of sources, including aptitude and achievement tests, teacher recommendations and social or cultural background. You will be informed of the student's specific physical condition as well as adaptive behavior.

The disabilities you might encounter include poor health, poor vision, hearing loss, social and emotional maladjustment, low general intelligence, and communicative and motor disabilities. As the student's classroom teacher, you must learn to deal with his or her special needs within the context of a regular class. Some direction and guidance for teachers is usually provided within the school.

SUMMARY

The slow learner who is in need of remediation is most likely to be the pupil who is a chronic mathematics failure. Some success in mathematics is needed so he can reverse this syndrome by seeing that failure is, indeed, not inevitable. Placement in appropriately designed remedial programs may be just what he needs. The counselor and/or mathematics teacher may administer one or more diagnostic instruments (standardized tests and/or teacher-made tests) to determine correct placement in such a program.

Generally, students who are two or more years below their grade level are candidates for remedial instruction. Also, those students who are unable to pass a minimum competency examination in mathematics some time before graduation might well be potential members of a remediation program.

The most common type of remediation program is the individualized approach to instruction. This usually consists of a "diagnostic-prescriptive" program, where a student's weaknesses are first diagnosed and then, for each deficiency detected by this diagnosis, an individualized "prescription" of corrective work is provided. However, small group instruction, formal classes, and peer-group tutoring are also frequently used methods of teaching remediation classes. Within these classes one can occasionally find in use such items as mathematical games, computers, calculators and arithmetic kits when the necessary drill work may be camouflaged in a form that permits variety and interest.

The physical setting in which remedial instruction can occur may vary from the traditional classroom to the fully furnished mathematics laboratory which contains such items as calculators, pre-programmed microcomputers, audio cassette activity kits, workbooks, reference books, mathematical games, and other related materials.

The basic idea behind this is that secondary school remediation should generally not resemble the elementary school methods. Since these students obviously met with much frustration at the elementary levels, every effort should be made to provide a fresh, new start in attaining mastery of the basic mathematics skills.

EXERCISES

1. Suppose your remedial mathematics class just completed the unit on all operations with fractions. Write a "camouflaged drill" lesson related to this topic while using
   a. Perimeter and area formulas.
   b. Calculators.
   c. Some aspect of probability.

2. In your remedial mathematics class, you ask students to add $\frac{1}{2} + \frac{1}{3}$ and many of them write $\frac{1}{2} + \frac{1}{3} = \frac{2}{5}$. You then present the same problem vertically

$$\begin{array}{r} \frac{1}{2} \\ + \frac{1}{3} \\ \hline \end{array}$$

and most of those who did it incorrectly the first time write

$$\begin{array}{r} \frac{1}{2} = \frac{3}{6} \\ + \frac{1}{3} = \frac{2}{6} \\ \hline \frac{5}{6} \end{array}$$

Explain how this phenomenon will have an impact on your teaching this class.

3. Suppose you are teaching in a large urban high school and you find that most of the students in your remedial mathematics class are from minority backgrounds (i.e., Blacks and Hispanics) with parents whose incomes are below the poverty level. How would the topics you present to this class differ from the topics you would present to a remedial mathematics class composed primarily of middle income white students?

4. Find some mathematically relevant recreational games, either those listed in this chapter or others, and determine how they can be effectively used in a remedial class. State the specific topic with which they are to be used.

5. Determine a set of appropriate activities with which you would involve a remedial mathematics class during the course of planning a trip to a local factory. Specify the destination of the trip.

6. Obtain three sixth grade arithmetic textbooks or workbooks and use these (as well as a calculator) to write an individualized prescription for a student having trouble with any form of long division.

7. Develop ten brief, simple-challenge exercises that could be used in a "puzzle for the day" section of the chalkboard or bulletin board in your remedial arithmetic class. Indicate the particular benefit which may be derived from each exercise.

8. Describe an activity (besides a trip) that would fall into the category of "camouflaged drill."

9. Discuss how the attendance patterns of students in a remedial mathematics class will very likely determine the methods of remediation used with this class. First specify the attendance in the hypothetical class.

10. A computer laboratory with one machine per student is available for your remedial mathematics class one day each week. A sufficient amount of computer assisted instruction software is available.
    Prepare a long range strategy for using this laboratory for your class.

11. Write a plan for a typical computer assisted instruction lesson in the computer laboratory described in Exercise 10. Assume a laboratory assistant is available to work with you.

12. Suppose you are a teacher in a high school assigned by your supervisor to teach a full program of remedial mathematics classes. Since your school has no special mathematics laboratories, your supervisor asks you to redesign a conventional classroom to best suit your needs for a remedial class. She further indicates that the school is prepared to obtain whatever furniture you may need and make whatever physical alterations you desire.
    Prepare a detailed plan for this remedial mathematics laboratory. Include a floor plan, a list of materials and equipment (and furniture) to be purchased and any other work which may be required (e.g., electrical alterations).

13. Visit three secondary schools and observe the remedial program in each. Write a brief report on each program, pointing out what, in your judgment, are the strengths and weaknesses of each program. As a summary to this assignment, compare the three programs with regard to their similarities, differences, and highlights.

SUGGESTED READINGS

Beckmann, Milton W. "Teaching The Low Achiever in Mathematics." *The Mathematics Teacher* 62 (1969): 443.

Boyer, Lee E. "Provisions for the Slow Learner." *The Mathematics Teacher* 52 (1959): 56.

Fremont, Herbert, and Ehrenberg, Neal. "The Hidden Potential of Low Achievers." *The Mathematics Teacher* 59 (1966): 551.

Haitt, Arthur A. "Basic Skills: What Are They?" *The Mathematics Teacher* 72 (1979): 141.

Herman, Maureen L. "Hopeless in Mathematics? It's Too Soon to Say." *The Mathematics Teacher* 76 (1983): 515.

Kenney, Robert. "Basic Competencies in Vermont." *The Mathematics Teacher* 71 (1978): 702.

Maor, Eli. "The Pocket Calculator as a Teaching Aid." *The Mathematics Teacher* 69 (1976): 471.

The Mathematics Teacher 69 (May 1976). Special Issue—Individualized Instruction.

The Mathematics Teacher 71 (February 1978). Special Issue—Minimum Competency.

Ortolan, Cathy, and Camp, Carol. "Meet the Challenge—Individualize." *The Mathematics Teacher* 73 (1980): 588.

Paul, Frederic. "New York Basic Competency Examination." *The Mathematics Teacher* 71 (1978): 767.

Proctor, Amelia D. "A World of Hope—Helping Slow Learners Enjoy Mathematics." *The Mathematics Teacher* 62 (1965): 118.

Rauff, James V. "Minimum Mathematical Skills." *The Mathematics Teacher* 72 (1979): 50.

Sasse, Katherine J.S. "Mathematics for the Non-College Bound in Junior High School." *The Mathematics Teacher* 58 (1965): 232.

Turner, Linda M. "GCM + TC + PR—A Formula for Survival in a Non-Academic Mathematics Club." *The Mathematics Teacher* 72 (1979): 580.

Vogel, James R., and Gentry, Dale. "Remediation of Number Facts Using Finger Multiplication." *The Mathematics Teacher* 73 (1980): 118.

Wilkinson, Jack. "Teaching General Mathematics: A Semi-Laboratory Approach." *The Mathematics Teacher* 63 (1970): 571.

CHAPTER 9 PROBLEM SOLVING

What is a problem? The psychiatrist may have one answer to this question, the scientist a second, and the mathematics student a third. In algebra when we use the word "problem" we usually mean "verbal problem" as opposed to, say, the problem of how to find the value of $\sqrt{17}$ to the nearest tenth. In geometry, a problem may be an "original" proof or construction. In general, a problem poses a situation in which there is something you want but don't yet know how to get. So the "problem" is how to go about getting it!

The National Council of Teachers of Mathematics identified problem solving as a primary goal for mathematics education. In its *Agenda for Action,* teachers are urged to

1. Create a classroom environment and develop appropriate curricular materials in which problem solving can flourish
2. Give priority to the identification and analysis of specific problem solving strategies
3. Develop examples of "good problems"
4. Encourage students to question, experiment, estimate, explore, and suggest explanations

Before exploring problem solving in mathematics, we shall discuss the general topic of problem solving from a psychological standpoint.

A PSYCHOLOGICAL VIEW OF PROBLEM SOLVING

All problem solving involves some form of information (perceptual, physiological, sensory) and use of that information to reach a solution. Given the individual differences we find on a developmental level as well as the varieties of content and levels of complexity of problem situations, a single, simple approach to problem solving would be difficult to discover (let alone implement).

As far back as 1910, John Dewey, in a book titled *How We Think* (Boston: D.C. Heath), outlined five steps for problem solving. They were presented in the following order.

1. Recognizing that a problem exists—an awareness of a difficulty, a sense of frustration, wondering or doubt.
2. Identifying the problem—clarification and definition, including designation of the goal to be sought, as defined by the situation which poses the problem.
3. Employing previous experiences, such as relevant information, former solutions, or ideas to formulate hypotheses and problem-solving propositions.
4. Testing, successively, hypotheses or possible solutions. If necessary, the problem may be reformulated.
5. Evaluating the solutions and drawing a conclusion based on the evidence. This involves incorporating the successful solution into one's existing understanding and applying it to other instances of the same problem.

While not all problem solving would necessarily follow this order, Dewey's analysis of the thinking process in problem-solving has not been improved upon yet. Note that it involves both the intake or reception of information and discovery learning in an interrelated process—one in which the learner is an active participant in his own learning.

In terms of mathematics, the work of George Polya in *How To Solve It* (Princeton, N.J.: Princeton University Press, 1945) presents techniques for problem solving which are not only interesting but are also meant to insure that principles learned in mathematics courses will transfer as widely as possible. His techniques are called *heuristics* (serving to discover), strategies that aid in solving problems. He says that there is a "grain of discovery" in the solution of any problem. "Your problem may be modest; but if it challenges your curiosity and brings into play your inventive facilities, and if you solve it by your own means, you may experience the tension and enjoy the triumph of discovery."

He suggests the following heuristic methods.

1. Understand the problem. What is the unknown? What are the data? What is the condition? Draw a figure, introduce suitable notation. Separate the various parts of the condition.
2. Devise a plan: Find the connection between the data and the unknown. Have you seen it before? Do you know a related problem?
3. Carry out the plan. Check each step. Can you see that each step is correct? Can you prove that it is correct?
4. Look back. Examine the solution obtained. Can you check the result? Can you check the argument? Can you derive the result differently? Can you see it at a glance? Can you use the result, or method, for some other problem?

In 1974, a study revealed that teachers asked for rote responses in all but 5 percent of classrooms observed. Such teaching methods tend to promote habitual, rigid thinking. Such "set" thinking interferes with more effective problem-solving techniques.

As an example, examine this series of problems presented by Luchins and Luchins in their book, *Rigidity of Behavior* (Eugene, Oregon: Univ. of Oregon Press, 1959). Pupils were given the following chart and asked to solve each problem regarding water jars. Given three jars with listed capacities, they were asked to measure the amount of water requested in a fourth column. (Only three of the seven problems will be listed here.)

Problem Number	Jar Capacity (quarts)			Quarts Needed
	A	B	C	
1	29	3	0	20
4	18	43	10	5
7	23	49	3	20

In each of the first six cases, the largest jar is filled first and emptied into the smaller jars until the required amount is obtained. Most pupils attempt to solve the seventh problem in the same way, even when they are cautioned to "look carefully."

Polya presents many aspects of mathematical problem solving—from induction to working backwards. Let us illustrate his approach with a problem similar to the one above that he presents to illustrate working backwards.

1. Let us try to find an answer to the following tricky question: *How can you bring up from the river exactly six quarts of water when you have only two containers, a four-quart pail and a nine-quart pail, to measure with?*
   [He proceeds immediately to visualize the pails with no scale markings (what is given).]

[Then] We do not know yet how to measure exactly six quarts; but could we measure something else? (If you cannot solve the proposed problem, try to solve first some related problem. Could you derive something useful from the data?) [He notes that most people, when confronted with a puzzle, work forwards, trying this or that and goes on to say:]

2. But exceptionally able people, or people who had the chance to learn in their mathematics classes something more than mere routine operations, do not spend too much time in such trials but turn around, and start working backwards. [Polya notes that the Greek mathematician, Pappus, gave an important description of this method. See Enrichment Unit 93, ''Problem Solving—A Reverse Strategy.'']

What are we required to do? (What is the unknown?) Let us visualize the final solution as clearly as possible. Let us imagine that we have here, before us exactly six quarts in the larger container and the smaller container is empty. (Let us start from what is required and assume what is sought as already found, says Pappus). (pp. 198–199)

Polya goes on to demonstrate the subsequent steps in solving the problem. He asks, ''From what antecedent could the desired result be derived?'' and notes that if the larger container were filled and exactly three quarts poured out we would achieve the result. How to do that? Well, if only one quart were left in the smaller container, then we could pour out exactly three (''let us inquire into what could be the antecedent of the antecedent''). He notes that this may be encountered accidentally, possibly seen before. Certainly by pouring four quarts from the large container twice in succession, ''we come eventually upon something already known (these are Pappus's words) and following the method of analysis, working backwards, we have discovered the appropriate sequence of operations.''

As the fine teacher he is, Polya uses problem-solving techniques which include both associative and insightful learning. He adds an ingredient of personal enthusiasm for his subject and a respect for the capacities of his students. One could ask little more of a teacher in any subject—that he be informed, use his information in a skillful manner in sharing with students, and provide them an opportunity to explore, analyze and demonstrate their own skills.

PROBLEM SOLVING IN MATHEMATICS

A mathematical problem may be described as ''challenging'' if its solution requires creativity, insight, original thinking, or imagination. To each person, some problems are found to be considerably more challenging than others. In fact, what may be challenging for one person may be quite routine to another. Thus, consider this problem:

PROBLEM: If it takes Big Ben 5 seconds to strike 6 o'clock, how many seconds will it take to strike 12 o'clock?

If you present this problem to a group of people you will undoubtedly find that some will ''see'' the answer immediately while many others will ''struggle'' for a while before arriving at a solution, if they ever do. (Ten seconds is NOT the correct answer.*)

On the other hand, the problem:

PROBLEM: If 5 is subtracted from three times a number the result is 8. Find the number.

may be a bit challenging to the uninitiated student in first-year algebra, but is trivial to anyone well versed in even the most elementary aspects of the subject.

Another facet of problem solving is that the challenge which may be inherent in solving a problem may not be apparent at the outset. The following problem appears to be harmless enough, but turns out to be one of the most complex in elementary Euclidean geometry! It is called a ''classic'' problem and is often named ''The Internal Bisectors Problem.'' It has been discussed in *Scientific American*'s ''Mathematical Games'' section. To see how difficult this problem is, try it! The problem may be stated as follows:

PROBLEM:

Given: $\overline{AE}$ bisects $\angle BAC$
$\overline{BD}$ bisects $\angle ABC$
$\overline{AE} \cong \overline{BD}$
Prove: $\triangle ABC$ is isosceles

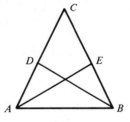

SOLUTION:
Here's one solution of this problem:

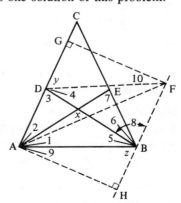

*Since it takes 5 seconds for 6 strikes, 5 seconds are required for 5 intervals (assuming no time for a strike). Therefore each interval between strikes is one second. Thus at 12 o'clock there are 11 intervals for the 12 strikes which require a total of 11 seconds to be completed.

$\overline{AE}$ and $\overline{BD}$ are angle bisectors, and $AE = BD$. Draw $\angle DBF \cong \angle AEB$ so that $\overline{BF} \cong \overline{BE}$; draw $\overline{DF}$. Also draw $\overline{FG} \perp \overline{AC}$, and $\overline{AH} \perp \overline{FH}$. By hypothesis, $\overline{AE} \cong \overline{DB}$, $\overline{FB} \cong \overline{EB}$, and $\angle 8 \cong \angle 7$. Therefore $\triangle AEB \cong \triangle DBF$, $DF = AB$, and m $\angle 1 = $ m $\angle 4$.

$m\angle x = m\angle 2 + m\angle 3$
$m\angle x = m\angle 1 + m\angle 3$
$m\angle x = m\angle 4 + m\angle 3$
$m\angle x = m\angle 7 + m\angle 6$
$m\angle x = m\angle 7 + m\angle 5$
$m\angle x = m\angle 8 + m\angle 5$

Therefore, $m\angle 4 + m\angle 3 = m\angle 8 + m\angle 5$
Thus $m\angle z = m\angle y$.
Right $\triangle FDG \cong$ right $\triangle ABH$, $DG = BH$, and $FG = AH$.
Right $\triangle AFG \cong$ right $\triangle FAH$, and $AG = FH$.
Therefore, $GFHA$ is a parallelogram.
$m\angle 9 = m\angle 10$ (from $\triangle ABH$ and $\triangle FDG$)
$m\angle DAB = m\angle DFB$
$m\angle DFB = m\angle EBA$ (from $\triangle DBF$ and $\triangle AEB$)
Therefore, $m\angle DAB = m\angle EBA$, and $\triangle ABC$ is isosceles.

Textbook problems, especially algebraic ones, are normally routine and repetitive. Their greatest challenge often lies in the attempt to unravel the wording of the problem so that it may be made to fit a predetermined "mold" which will then lead to the solution.

Here is a typical digit-problem like so many hundreds of others found in algebra textbooks.

> **PROBLEM:** The sum of the digits of a two-digit number is 7. If 9 is added to the number, the result is a number with the digits of the original number reversed. Find the original number.

The predetermined mold is *always* to begin a digit problem this way:

> Let t = tens' digit
> u = units' digit
> $10t + u$ = original number
> $10u + t$ = original number reversed

This is followed by the appropriate pair of simultaneous equations to solve the problem.

Another standard type is this uniform-motion ("upstream-downstream") problem.

> **PROBLEM:** A boat travels 16 miles downstream in 2 hours. It then travels the same distance upstream in 8 hours. What is the rate of the boat in still water and what is the rate of the current?

Another favored type of predetermined mold is this table which is set up to help solve uniform motion problems:

> Let x = rate of current
> y = rate in still water

	RATE $\times$	TIME	= DISTANCE
Upstream	$y - x$	8	16
Downstream	$y + x$	2	16

This is followed by the appropriate pair of simultaneous equations to solve the problem.

These problems are so typical of all others of the same type that if a pupil studies the solution of only one or two of them he should be able to devise a similar solution for all of them. The challenge (if any) exists only in the formulation of the solution to the first problem of the type with which the student is confronted. One mark of a good textbook is that it offers a reasonable number of "nonroutine" problems in addition to the standard ones.

In this chapter we will discuss why problem solving should be taught and offer some guidelines which may be used for teaching problem solving. We also will show how mathematics problems may be created by pupils. Finally, we will present some "nonroutine" problems that, over the years, have been shown to possess sufficient challenge and interest to be worthy of being called "classics."

Why Teach Problem Solving?

Students will learn to read mathematics. They will learn to develop and use models for standard type problems and not be frightened away from the more challenging ones.

Mathematics textbook authors and teachers have often found it convenient to arrange their material as follows:

> First, develop a specific skill (for example, how to solve simultaneous linear equations.)
> Second, assign an exercise set of straightforward drill examples (for example, fifteen pairs of simultaneous equations, usually arranged in ascending order of difficulty).
> Third, solve a variety of verbal problems (for example, digit, coin, uniform-motion, etc.) which will lead to a pair of simultaneous equations that need to be solved in order to find the solution to the problem.

It often seems that verbal problems in textbooks are merely vehicles through which additional practice exercises may be presented, in "disguised" form. While verbal problems may indeed serve as such a vehicle, this is by no means their exclusive purpose.

Many teachers agree that most standard textbook problems are not "challenging." These problems are often taught so they will be solvable by merely following a previously developed model, as shown earlier. Nevertheless, there is still some value that may be derived from their study.

In order for students to handle even standard problems effectively, they must be taught how to read mathematics (see sample mathematics reading lesson, page 19). They must learn that even a single phrase or sentence may contain a great deal of significant information. Even a student who may be a rapid reader in other areas should read mathematics slowly. Specifically, the student must read the verbal problems slowly, pausing at commas or at the end of an idea. The student must reflect on what has been read, must determine what it means, and should reread and re-examine the problem as often as necessary. Skimming has little value in reading a mathematics problem.

Some students may eventually become quite adept at solving standard problems. But these problems rarely lead to discovery of new generalizations or unusual insights because they are basically repetitive in nature. They may, however, be a source of valuable potentially challenging problems if you consider the possibility of organizing them heterogeneously rather than by type. Pupils would then be challenged to first read the problem, then determine the type, and finally write the solution. This mix might also be treated as a collection of word puzzles which students who might have difficulty recognizing a type problem will be encouraged to solve by any means possible—arithmetic, algebra, geometry, or intuition. With this approach, correct solutions may be harder to come by initially because the student will have a choice of many "means" before reaching the desired "end."

Students will develop a sense of pride. They will be enthusiastic, seeing how their skills have grown and developed over the years of mathematical training.

Situations often arise in which students face the same problems in their later secondary school years as in their earlier ones. The approaches used in solutions should prove enlightening to both pupil and teacher and serve as an indicator of the student's growth and increased mathematical maturity over the period of years they spend in secondary school. Students will also recognize that as their knowledge of mathematics expands, so does their ability to devise problem-solving strategies.

To better understand this point, consider the following examples.

PROBLEM: Find the number of diagonals in a convex polygon of n sides.

The advanced eleventh or twelfth grade secondary student might determine the number of diagonals, d, the following way:

SOLUTION:

$$d = {}_nC_2 - n \quad \text{or} \quad \binom{n}{2} - n$$

$$= \frac{n!}{2! \, (n-2)!} - n$$

$$= \frac{n(n-1)}{2} - n$$

$$= \frac{n^2 - 3n}{2}$$

$$= \frac{n(n-3)}{2}$$

However, the geometry student, usually a tenth grader, might use a diagram and might realize that $n-3$ diagonals may be drawn from each of the n vertices. Since each diagonal passes through two vertices, the number of diagonals is $\frac{n(n-3)}{2}$.

The arithmetic or algebra student, at eighth or ninth grade level might first prepare the table of values

n	3	4	5	6	. . .
d	0	2	5	9	. . .

He would then spend some time "guessing" a formula relationship between n and d until he "struck" on $d = \frac{n(n-3)}{2}$ or some variation thereof. A proof of the formula might not be his major concern at this point but he would "feel" darn sure that was correct!

A second situation in which students can appreciate how their increased knowledge has improved their problem-solving skills is when they are asked to do the following problem.

PROBLEM: Show that $\sin (x + y) = \sin x \cos y + \cos x \sin y$, for appropriate x, y and $x + y$.

In a tenth grade geometry course, students with some knowledge of elementary trigonometry would appreciate this solution for acute angles x, y and x + y. (An outline of the derivation is shown.)

SOLUTION:

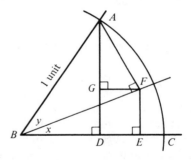

B is the center of a circle with radii AB and BC.

I

In $\triangle ABD$

$$\sin(x + y) = EF + AG$$

II

In $\triangle AGF$
$$m\angle GAF = x$$
$$AG = (\cos x)(AF)$$

In $\triangle BAF$
$$AF = \sin y$$
$$AG = (\cos x)(\sin y)$$

III

In $\triangle BFE$
$$EF = (\sin x)(BF)$$

In $\triangle ABF$
$$BF = \cos y$$
$$EF = (\sin x)(\cos y)$$

Incorporating the results of Part II and Part III into Part I, we get the required formula.

In an eleventh or twelfth grade trigonometry course the same formula can be derived for x, y and $x + y$ in any quadrant (i.e., any size, as opposed to the restriction of an acute angle of the earlier derivation) by using the law of cosines, and identities for functions of negative angles. (This derivation is lengthy, but may be found in any trigonometry textbook.)

In a twelfth grade high school mathematics class the Euler relationship

$$e^{i\theta} = \cos \theta + i \sin \theta$$

may be used to derive the same formula in this manner:

For any x, y:

$$e^{ix} = \cos x + i \sin x$$

$$e^{iy} = \cos y + i \sin y$$

(I) $e^{i(x + y)} = \cos (x + y) + i \sin (x + y)$

But also

$e^{i(x + y)} = e^{ix}e^{iy}$

(II) $\quad = (\cos x + i \sin x)(\cos y + i \sin y)$

$\quad = (\cos x \cos y - \sin x \sin y)$
$\qquad + i(\sin x \cos y + \cos x \sin y)$

Comparing the real and imaginary parts of (I) and (II), we get two formulas, one of which is

$$\sin (x + y) = \sin x \cos y + \cos x \sin y$$

Thus we see that if the same set of problems were presented to a freshman class and to an advanced mathematics senior class, the solutions suggested by the more mathematically mature group might readily reflect their additional knowledge, training and experience. At least, the teacher can direct his lesson so that this is the likely outcome.

Students will learn to be critical of and analytical with the problems presented to them. Standard type problems "with a twist" may be made to contain either insufficient or excessive information, or may be made to have no solution at all. Students should always be alerted to anticipate these possibilities.

Consider these three problems "with a twist".

1. The sum of 3 consecutive even integers is 26. What are the integers?
2. Find the area of a right triangle whose sides are 8, 15, and 17.
3. Two trains start from the same point at the same time. The first train travels 60 mph and the second 80 mph. In how many hours will they be 500 miles apart?

Each of these problems has something "wrong" with it. After students attempt to solve them, they should be analyzed for their specific pitfalls. This will inevitably lead to productive discussions and generalizations which should significantly improve the students' problem-solving skills by alerting them to be more critical. Thus in problem 1, the attempted solution might produce:

For $x =$ first even integer
$x + 2 =$ second consecutive even integer
$x + 4 =$ third consecutive even integer

Then $3x + 6 = 26$
$$3x = 20$$
$$x = 6\frac{2}{3}$$

x turns out to be non-integral, which is impossible.

An analysis and discussion would lead to the conclusion that the sum of three consecutive even integers must always be divisible by 3.

Problem 2 has a superfluous term, "right," since an 8-15-17 triangle is automatically right by virtue of the converse of the Pythagorean Theorem. However, further investigation by the class might lead to the possibility of encountering a similar problem type in which the sides have dimensions 8, 15, and 18, for example (a non-right triangle). Under proper guidance by the teacher, this could lead to a derivation of the general area formula of a triangle in terms of the length of the three given sides, a, b, c (this is known as Heron's formula).

$$\text{Area} = \sqrt{s(s - a)(s - b)(s - c)}$$

$$\text{for } s = \frac{1}{2}(a + b + c)$$

Problem 3 contains insufficient data. There is no indication of the paths taken by the trains. Thus, if the two trains travel in opposite directions, we get

For x = number of hours the trains travel

$$60x + 80x = 500$$

However, if the trains travel at right angles to each other, we conclude that

so that $100x = 500$ (Pythagorean Theorem). The paths of the trains may in fact make any other angle with each other, in which case the law of cosines would be needed to obtain a solution.

It therefore seems to be clear that problems that have "something wrong" with them may lead to challenging situations with fruitful results. A skilled teacher can use this technique to develop exciting mathematics.

Non-academically oriented students will learn to solve problems, though of a more elementary nature. Simple games of strategy are uniquely suited to develop problem-solving skills among general students. Most students are familiar with and enjoy participating in games of all types. They have been exposed to them regularly from early childhood. They know that there are rules to be followed, that there is usually a winner, and they know, furthermore, that if they develop a proper strategy for a particular game they could become a consistent winner. Checkers, chess, tic-tac-toe, backgammon, and electronic games are some of the more obvious ones. Although general mathematics students do not always have the verbal ability to deal with word problems, they can nevertheless learn subconsciously how to develop winning strategies. These turn out to be similar to the strategies needed to solve verbal problems:

ANALOGY	
GAME STRATEGY	**PROBLEM STRATEGY**
1. Read the rules	1. Read the problem.
2. Understand the rules	2. What is given and what are we looking for?
3. Develop a plan.	3. Write an equation.
4. Carry out the plan.	4. Solve the equation.
5. If you win, smile. Otherwise, figure out why you lost.	5. Check your answer.

Games alone might not be sufficient to develop the problem-solving skills of general mathematics students. In fact, many students may not be interested in "playing" games of strategy at all. Other activities that could develop analytical and critical skills in such students at their level might include:

1. Ask the students, in a motivating manner (and that is possible!) to state the characteristics of objects. For example: How long is a line? Say everything you can about a cube. Will a three-legged stool ever wobble?
2. Have the youngsters list (in a challenging way) similarities and differences between squares, and rectangles, circles and spheres, points and lines.

While general mathematics students have difficulty functioning at the level of problem solving which academically oriented students can handle with relative ease, exposure to some of the ideas just mentioned will prove beneficial to them and can improve their facility with many of the skills involved in problem solving.

STRATEGIES FOR SOLVING PROBLEMS

Planning to Solve a Problem

The number of strategies that can be developed to solve problems are probably as many and varied as the problems themselves. Some of the more common strategies may be described as

1. Making a picture
2. Working backward
3. Guessing and testing
4. Finding a pattern
5. Making a table
6. Collecting data
7. Using a computer
8. Deductive reasoning
9. Solving a simpler analogous problem

10. Approximating
11. Determining necessary and sufficient conditions
12. Determining characteristics of objects

We now pose some problems together with some sample suggested strategies for their solution. The reader may find other and better strategies and should indeed be encouraged to do so.

Making a Picture. Pictures, or diagrams, are a "must" in most geometric problems, but they are also useful in motion problems, mixture problems, and many others that have no "type" classification. Here is an example of a well-known problem, which clearly demonstrates why "a picture is worth a thousand words."

PROBLEM: A frog is at the bottom of a ten foot well. Each day it crawls up 3 feet and at night it slips back 2 feet. In how many days will the frog get out of the well?

SOLUTION: Make the following picture of a well and mark the position of the frog at the end of each day, and again at the end of each night. The frog will reach the top of the well on the eighth day, at which time it escapes and does not fall back.

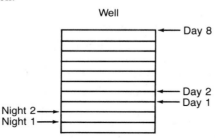

Working Backward.[1] Many proofs in geometry can be written by first assuming the conclusion and then determining which step must have preceded the last. Use the same reasoning for the penultimate step. Continue in this manner until the proof begins to unravel. One illustration of where this technique may be used in a non-geometric setting is after a student has learned to solve a quadratic equation by factoring.

PROBLEM: Write a quadratic equation whose roots are 2 and -3.

SOLUTION: Proceed in reverse order as follows:

roots: $x = 2$ and $x = -3$

---

[1]See "The Analytic Method" page 117.

previous line must have been: $x - 2 = 0$ and $x + 3 = 0$

previous line must have been: $(x - 2)(x + 3) = 0$

the answer must therefore be: $x^2 + x - 6 = 0$

Finding a Pattern. Finding a pattern among a sequence of numbers may be quite challenging. No single rule can be applied to all cases.

We will present several sequences of six numbers and in each case "discover" a pattern among them that will then yield the next three numbers in the sequence. Patterns in sequences are often not unique. It is highly recommended that students make up their own sequences of six numbers and suggest different patterns that might be used to generate the next three terms.

PROBLEM: Find the next three terms in the sequence 2,4,6,8,10,12.

SOLUTION: The pattern is

$$2 + 2 = 4$$
$$4 + 2 = 6$$
$$6 + 2 = 8$$
$$\cdot \quad \cdot \quad \cdot \quad \cdot \quad \cdot$$

So that the answer would be

$$12 + 2 = 14$$
$$14 + 2 = 16$$
$$16 + 2 = 18$$

PROBLEM: Find the next three terms in the sequence 3,6,12,24,48,96.

SOLUTION: The pattern is

$$3(2) = 6$$
$$6(2) = 12$$
$$12(2) = 24$$
$$\cdot \quad \cdot \quad \cdot \quad \cdot \quad \cdot$$

So that the answer would be

$$96(2) = 192$$
$$192(2) = 384$$
$$384(2) = 768$$

PROBLEM: Find the next three terms in the sequence 3,7,15,31,63,127.

SOLUTION: The pattern is

$$2(3) + 1 = 7$$
$$2(7) + 1 = 15$$
$$2(15) + 1 = 31$$
$$\cdot \quad \cdot \quad \cdot \quad \cdot \quad \cdot \quad \cdot$$

So that the answer would be

$$2(127) + 1 = 255$$
$$2(255) + 1 = 511$$
$$2(511) + 1 = 1023$$

PROBLEM: Find the next three terms in the sequence 2,4,8,24,72,144,288.

SOLUTION: The pattern is

$$2(2) = 4$$
$$2(4) = 8$$
$$3(8) = 24$$
$$3(24) = 72$$
$$2(72) = 144$$
$$2(144) = 288$$

So that the answer would be

$$3(288) = 864$$
$$3(864) = 2592$$
$$2(2592) = 5184$$

PROBLEM: Find the next number in the sequence: 2,4,8,16,31,___, (there is no misprint here; the last given number *is* 31.)

SOLUTION: Set up a table of successive differences:

```
2   4   8   16   31   57
  2   4   8   15  (26) ←
    2   4   7  (11) ←
      2   3  (4) ←── this must be 4.
              then this must be 11.──
              then 26, and on to 57.──
```

Determining Characteristics of Objects. Activities requiring seventh or eighth grade students to create geometric shapes enable them to understand the properties of polygons.

PROBLEM: Here are two triangles:

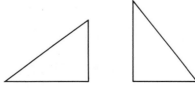

How many figures can be formed by arranging these triangles in different ways? Do these figures share any common properties, such as shape, area, perimeter, number of vertices, and number of sides?

SOLUTION:

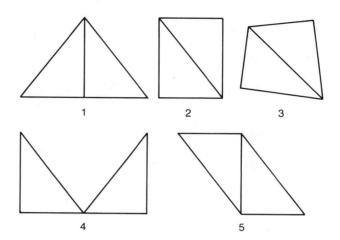

Organizing Data. While it is often desirable to approximate answers, there are occasions when exact answers are required. We will see here some strategies of organizing data that may be used when exact sums are requested.

PROBLEM: A $20.00 bill may not go very far in a variety store where you may see items with the following prices:

A: $ .38
B: $ 8.57
C: $ 3.00
D: $ .62
E: $ 11.43
F: $ 8.64
G: $ 16.00
H: $ 8.05
I: $ 18.68
J: $ 15.33
K: $ 7.95
L: $ 1.32

What combinations of items would cost exactly $20.00? Assume no tax is added.

SOLUTION: The strategy to solve this type of problem is to discover the proper combination of items. For example, first try to combine items whose units digits add up to 10. However, you must also try to find combinations of cents that have a sum of $1.00. Several correct answers are:

1. B,E
2. A,B,C,H
3. A,C,D,G
4. A,C,D,H,K

Using Computers to Solve Problems. Computers may often be used as a tool to assist pupils in solving problems whose solution might be suggested by the results of time-consuming calculations. These calculations would be of a repetitive nature, which is perfect for computer solution.

PROBLEM: A rectangular piece of cardboard measures 36 in. × 44 in. Suppose a box is to be made by cutting equal size squares from each corner and folding up the sides. (See the figure.) What is the maximum volume of the boxes formed when

   a. 1 in. squares are cut out?
   b. 2 in. squares are cut out?
   c. 3 in. squares are cut out?

   .
   .
   .

   q. 17 in. squares are cut out?

44″

36 ″

SOLUTION: RUN this program to compute the dimensions corresponding to the 17 volumes.

```
10 PRINT "HEIGHT", "VOLUME"
20 FOR H = 1 TO 17
30 LET L = 44 − 2 * H
40 LET W = 36 − 2 * H
50 LET V = L * W * H
60 PRINT H, V
70 NEXT H
80 END
```

Next, study the following data to determine the box of largest volume.

Height	Volume
1	1428
2	1560
3	3420
4	4032
5	4420
6	4608
7	4620
8	4480
9	4212
10	3840
11	3388
12	2880
13	2340
14	1792
15	1260
16	768
17	340

Trial and Error. No matter how clever your strategy for solving a problem, you may still have to resort to a "trial and error" scheme as part of a solution. This can at times be quite subtle.

PROBLEM: Find the replacement numerals that will make this addition correct:

$$\begin{array}{r} XY \\ YZ \\ \hline YZY \end{array}$$

SOLUTION: We begin with an inspection of the unit's digit addition. Which number when added to Y will leave it unchanged? Only zero has this property! Therefore, $Z = 0$. We have the following so far:

$$\begin{array}{r} XY \\ Y0 \\ \hline Y0Y \end{array}$$

We must now find numbers whose sum is a number with a unit's digit of 0. Since the sum of two single-digit numbers cannot be 20, the sum we seek for $X + Y$ must be 10. Let us "try" some of the possible combinations:

$$5 + 5$$
$$4 + 6$$
$$3 + 7$$
$$2 + 8$$
$$1 + 9$$

Each trial will give us a different value for Y. However, Y must be 1 (in the sum) therefore, $X = 9$. The correct addition problem is:

$$\begin{array}{r} 91 \\ 10 \\ \hline 101 \end{array}$$

STANDARD ALGEBRAIC PROBLEMS

Before a pupil can be expected to develop facility in solving verbal problems algebraically, a certain amount of preparatory work is needed. She must have considerable practice expressing English phrases and sentences in terms of their algebraic counterparts. (Newton compared the setting up of an equation in problem solving to ''translating'' from one language to another, and in fact we now use the word ''translate'' to direct pupils to rewrite the English ''longhand'' into its equivalent algebraic ''shorthand.'')

While many students find problem solving painful no matter how much assistance they get from the teacher, a set of strategies developed over the course of time can ease the pain of problem solving. For the simpler problems, one strategy is to start by selecting key phrases and sentences, determining the variables and algebraic expressions that would represent them, and finally formulating a relationship of equality that would make an equation (called the ''key'' equation) emerge. The solution to this ''key'' equation should yield a solution to the problem.

In more complicated problems, the teacher may resort to charts, diagrams and tables. Estimates, guesses, demonstrations and models all have a value in helping students see the problem more clearly. Underlying all these schemes is a relationship formula which will ultimately be used in the formulation of the key equation. It may be helpful for youngsters to know that even with the large variety of standard type problems such as uniform-motion, investment, coin, mixture and others, there is a unifying form for each formula:

$$A \times B = C$$

Thus

for motion problems:
RATE × TIME = DISTANCE

for investment problems:
PRINCIPAL × RATE = INTEREST

for coin problems:
NUMBER OF COINS × VALUE OF EACH COIN = TOTAL VALUE

for mixture problems:
NUMBER OF POUNDS × PRICE PER POUND = TOTAL COST

Whatever the strategy used, whether selecting key phrases, drawing boxes, diagrams or any other aid, the pupil should use the appropriate formula as a guide to setting up the key equation. Key equations can occasionally be elusive, however, for certain useful facts in verbal problems are sometimes obscure or implied and not explicitly stated. In many situations ''subtle'' equalities that are not explicitly stated lead to the key equation. For example, consider the following from a typical uniform motion problem.

PROBLEM: If two trains start from the same station, one earlier and the other later, and travel in the same direction along parallel tracks, the faster (second) train overtakes the slower train, then. . . .

The students should be led to realize that the key equation will emerge from the implied fact that the distances which the two trains travel are equal at the instant the second train overtakes the first.

A similar situation exists in the following mixture problem.

PROBLEM: How many liters of water must be added to 8 liters of pure alcohol to make a mixture which has 35% alcohol?

Here the point which needs to be highlighted is that by adding water to pure alcohol no change in the *amount* of alcohol was made during this process. Therefore, the key equation can be obtained from this equality of the amount of alcohol before and after the mixture with water.

We shall now demonstrate some specific methods of solving verbal problems, using techniques discussed above.

PROBLEM: Part of $10,000 is invested at 12% per year and the remainder at 8% per year. The total income from both investments is $920.00 per year. Find the amount invested at each rate.

SOLUTION 1: (Selecting and translating key phrases)

Let x = number of dollars invested at 12%
(*This comes from the phrase ''part of the $10,000 is invested at 12%.''*)

$10,000 - x$ = the number of dollars invested at 8%
(*This comes from the phrase, ''The remainder is invested at 8%.''*)

$.12x$ = amount of yearly income from the 12% investment
$.08 (10,000 - x)$ = amount of yearly income from the 8% investment
(*These came from the formula PRINCIPAL × RATE = INTEREST.*)

Sentence leading to the key equation:

The total income from both investments is $920.00 per year.
Key equation:

$$.12x + .08(10,000 - x) = 920$$

SOLUTION 2:   (Using a table or boxes)

	PRINCIPAL	× RATE	= INTEREST *
FIRST Investment	x	.12	$.12x$
SECOND Investment	$10,000 - x$	.08	$.08(10,000 - x)$

* (Income from each investment)

The key equation is usually obtained from the column whose boxes are filled in by multiplication (or, in some cases, division). Here the key equation (obtained from the third column) is:

$$.12x + .08(10,000 - x) = 920$$

The value of x would then be found and checked in the *statement* of the problem. The solution may be written and labeled as:

ANSWER: $3,000 was invested at 12%
$7,000 was invested at 8%

PROBLEM: Yolanda has $1.35 in nickels and dimes. She has a total of 15 coins. How many of each kind of coin are there?

SOLUTION 1:   Most students can guess the answer to this question with little difficulty before even attempting to use a formal approach. They should be encouraged to do so where possible; as every mathematician knows, intelligent guessing is a skill worth developing (provided teacher guidance is used at the outset, since students generally need instruction in guessing).

SOLUTION 2:   (Selecting and translating phrases and sentences)

Let y = number of dimes
$15 - y$ = number of nickels
$.10y$ = total value of dimes
$.05(15 - y)$ = total value of nickels

Total value of all coins is $1.35.

Therefore the key equation is

$$.10y + .05 (15 - y) = 1.35$$

SOLUTION 3:   (Using a table or boxes)

	NUMBER OF COINS	× VALUE OF EACH COIN	= TOTAL VALUE
DIMES	y	.10	$.10y$
NICKELS	$15 - y$	.05	$.05(15 - y)$

The key equation is usually obtained from the column whose boxes are filled in by multiplication (or, in some cases division). Here the key equation is:

$$.10y + .05(15 - y) = 1.35$$

SOLUTION 4:   This method of solution would be similar to 2 but would involve using two variables and then solving the resulting simultaneous equations.

ANSWER: There are 12 dimes and 3 nickels. (Note: The answer should be checked in the *statement* of the problem.)

As a general rule, we suggest that students be trained to take the following steps in the solution of verbal problems.

1. Read the problem carefully. If you are able to restate it in your own words, no matter how simply, you are well on your way towards understanding the problem.
2. Determine the formula (if any) for the type of problem under consideration.
3. If possible, estimate your answer and jot it down somewhere on your paper. If the solution to your key equation is not reasonably similar to your estimate, check your work.
4. Select a variable that can be used, such as, "Let $x = \ldots$" and express key phrases in terms of that variable.
5. Determine the subtle or explicit statement and write the key equation.
6. Solve the key equation.
7. Label answers correctly, in terms of the units stated in the problem.
8. Reread the problem and see if your answer makes sense. This is called, "checking your answer."

A word of advice to the teacher: *Do not do* the problem for your students. Once you have given them initial guidelines in solving problems, the most you ought to do is provide hints, clues or leading questions. And remind students that "neatness counts." Neat work can be helpful in developing a solution to a given problem, while sloppy work can be a hindrance.

STANDARD GEOMETRIC PROBLEMS

Problems in geometry usually include:

Proving theorems synthetically (using methods of Euclidean geometry).

Solving construction exercises with compasses and straightedge.

Proving geometric theorems using algebra, arithmetic, coordinate geometry or vectors.

Determining the measure of some part of a given geometric figure.

One aspect of geometric problem solving that is different from algebraic problem solving is that each problem requiring a proof, *with few exceptions,* is an "original" in the sense that there are no types one can follow to virtually guarantee a solution every time as in algebra. This is not to say that there are no similar approaches among such geometric proofs.

We offer three general suggestions to be considered in the process of proving theorems in geometry:

1. *Analyze the hypothesis:* Draw a neat, relatively accurate diagram and mark it, indicating segments, angles, etc. that are known to be congruent. Mark all parallel lines. A well-drawn figure frequently suggests a productive line of reasoning.
2. *Analyze the conclusion.* Consider the conclusion and how it may be reached. It is often wise to consider how similar conclusions have been reached in the past. Be certain that you clearly understand the desired conclusion before proceeding.
3. *Find the connection between hypothesis and conclusion.* In order to do this you must have, at your fingertips, all appropriate postulates, definitions, previously proved theorems, and common techniques. In addition, the experience you have acquired in solving other problems, your intuition and your imagination must all be synthesized in an effort to prove a theorem or perform a construction.

Finally, subscribe to the motto, "If at first you don't succeed, try again." But, give the problem time to "ferment." Often, not thinking about a problem for a while provides the needed mental rest to spark the creative fires.

The Analytic Method

Some have found a technique, known as the *analytic method,* helpful in bridging the gap between hypothesis and conclusion in geometry. This method consists of a series of retrogressive steps which start with the conclusion and end with the hypothesis. In other words, the entire proof may be constructed by starting with the conclusion and asking yourself, "What step must have immediately preceded this step?" After deciding on the answer, the same question is again asked about that answer, until the entire logical sequence is uncovered in reverse. After the hypothesis is reached, the proof is written by simply reversing these steps. This method of working backwards was discussed earlier in this chapter

as one of Polya's suggested techniques of problem solving. (For a detailed discussion of this technique see Enrichment Unit 93, "Problem Solving—A Reverse Strategy.")

Following is an illustration of how the analytic method may be used in proving a geometric theorem.

PROBLEM:

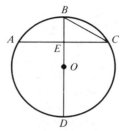

Given: O is the center of the circle; $\overline{AC} \perp \overline{BD}$

Prove: $BE \times BD = (BC)^2$

Analysis:

1. $BE \times BD = (BC)^2$ can be proved if we can show that
$$\frac{BE}{BC} = \frac{BC}{BD}$$
2. $\dfrac{BE}{BC} = \dfrac{BC}{BD}$ can be proved if we can show that $\triangle BEC \sim \triangle BCD$ (an auxiliary line segment, $\overline{CD}$, must be drawn).
3. $\triangle BEC$ can be proved similar to $\triangle BCD$ if we can show that two angles of one are congruent to two angles of the other (or possibly one of the other similarity theorems).
4. $\angle B$ is common to both triangles.
5. $\angle BEC$ and $\angle BCD$ are right angles ($\angle BCD$ is inscribed in a semicircle). Therefore, $\triangle BEC \sim \triangle BCD$.

A synthetic proof now can be written by reversing the arguments in the analysis.

The analytic approach also may be used to solve construction problems. Following are two illustrations of this procedure:

PROBLEM: Construct a triangle, given the lengths of a side and the altitude and median to that side.

Analysis:

1. Sketch the picture of the final step of the construction. where the given segments were

altitude $\overline{AH}$: A _____ H

median $\overline{AM}$: A _____ M

side $\overline{BC}$: B _____ C

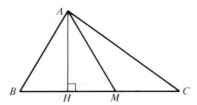

2. Construct right triangle *AHM*, using the lengths of given leg $\overline{AH}$ and the hypotenuse $\overline{AM}$. (This can be done in a number of ways.)

3. Draw $\overleftrightarrow{HM}$. Locate the midpoint *M* of $\overline{BC}$. On $\overleftrightarrow{HM}$, mark off $\overline{BM}$ and $\overline{MC}$ as shown in the diagram.

4. Complete the triangle *ABC* by drawing $\overline{AB}$ and $\overline{AC}$. This construction problem was solved by working in reverse. An inspection of the end product showed a need to establish some "structure," here in the form of a triangle ($\triangle AHM$). Once this structure provided rigidity to the figure, the rest was completed simply.

Another illustration of the analytic approach can be seen in the following more difficult problem.

PROBLEM: Construct a $\triangle ABC$ given only the lengths of the three medians, $\overline{AM}$, $\overline{BN}$, and $\overline{CK}$.

Analysis:
Begin by drawing the completed figure.

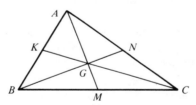

There is a need to establish some rigidity to the figure (by construction). With only the lengths of the medians given and no angles established we must seek out a way of constructing either an angle or a triangle.

Consider extending $\overline{GM}$ to *P* so that $GM = MP$.

Drawing $\triangle BGP$ gives us a triangle which is fully determined, since the lengths of its sides are each two-thirds the length of a median of $\triangle ABC$.

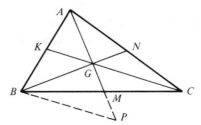

Since the point of intersection of the medians (the centroid) trisects each median, $GM = \frac{1}{3}AM$. Therefore

$GP = \frac{2}{3}AM$. Also $BG = \frac{2}{3}BN$. Since $\overline{GK}$ is a midline of $\triangle ABP$, it is half the length of $\overline{BP}$. But $GK = \frac{1}{3}CK$. Therefore $BP = \frac{2}{3}CK$.

Now having determined the lengths of the sides of $\triangle BGP$, we can construct it (with straightedge and compasses).

The remainder of the construction problem continues in the same reverse procedure. That is, we now ask how *C* may be found. This can be done by locating the midpoint, *M*, of $\overline{GP}$ and extending $\overline{BM}$ to *C* so that $BM = MC$. In a similar way *N* can be located. Then the intersection of $\overline{CN}$ and $\overline{PG}$ will determine point *A*.

The analysis is complete and all that remains is the actual construction which follows these designated steps.

Using "Brute Force"

Some problems are best solved by "brute force" methods. The example that follows illustrates such a problem. There are no shortcuts, and the analytic method does not properly apply. What does apply is some powerful geometric thinking.

A second solution of the same problem, this time using coordinate geometry, follows the first solution. The beauty of the second proof is that it illustrates how coordinate geometry techniques get about as close as one can to a methodical approach in the solution of geometric problems, as opposed to the often hit-or-miss synthetic method.

PROBLEM. In a parallelogram, the sum of the squares of the lengths of the diagonals is equal to twice the sum of the squares of the lengths of any two adjacent sides.

Proof 1:

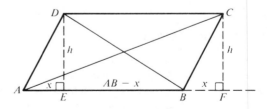

Given: $\square ABCD$
Prove: $(AC)^2 + (BD)^2 = 2[(AB)^2 + (AD)^2]$

1. Draw perpendiculars $\overleftrightarrow{DE}$ and $\overleftrightarrow{CF}$ as in the diagram.

2. $AE = BF = x$ and $DE = CF = h$
   (since $\angle ADE = \angle BCF$)

3. In right triangles *BDE* and *ADE*,
   $(BD)^2 = h^2 + (AB - x)^2 = h^2 + x^2 + (AB)^2 - 2x(AB)$
   and $h^2 + x^2 = (AD)^2$

4. ∴ $(BD)^2 = (AD)^2 + (AB)^2 - 2x(AB)$
5. In right △ *ACF*,
$(AC)^2 = h^2 + (AB + x)^2 = h^2 + x^2 + (AB)^2 + 2x(AB)$
6. ∴ $(AC)^2 = (AD)^2 + (AB)^2 + 2x(AB)$
7. From Steps 4 and 6,
$(AC)^2 + (BD)^2 = 2[(AB)^2 + (AD)^2]$

Proof 2:

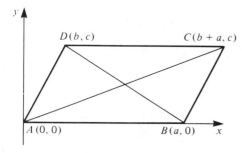

Given: ▱*ABCD*
Prove: $(AC)^2 + (BD)^2 = 2[(AB)^2 + (AD)^2]$

1. $(AC)^2 = (c - 0)^2 + (b + a - 0)^2 = c^2 + b^2 + 2ba + a^2$
2. $(BD)^2 = (b - a)^2 + (c - 0)^2 = b^2 - 2ab + a^2 + c^2$
3. ∴ $(AC)^2 + (BD)^2 = 2(a^2 + b^2 + c^2)$
4. $AB = a$, so that $(AB)^2 = a^2$
5. $(AD)^2 = (b - 0)^2 + (c - 0)^2 = b^2 + c^2$
6. ∴ $(AB)^2 + (AD)^2 = a^2 + b^2 + c^2$
7. ∴ From Steps 3 and 6, $(AC)^2 + (BD)^2 = 2[(AB)^2 + (AD)^2]$

The Algebraic Method

Algebraic methods are often used when solving geometric problems, especially when synthetic techniques become cumbersome. A prime example of this is the synthetic proof of the Pythagorean Theorem which the average geometry student usually finds somewhat difficult to follow. Compare this with a considerably simpler algebraic proof (of which there are many variations). You can appreciate the contrast if you study the outlines of these two proofs.

PROBLEM: Prove the Pythagorean Theorem

SOLUTION:
Version 1 (Synthetic method):
The area of the square on the hypotenuse of a right triangle is equal to the sum of the areas of the squares on the legs.

Given: Right △*ABC*;
Squares *ACHK*,
BCGF and *BAED*

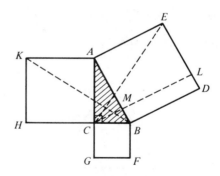

1. Construct $\overline{CL}$ perpendicular to $\overline{DE}$; draw the other lines as shown.
2. △*CAE* ≅ △*BAK*
3. Area △*CAE* = $\frac{1}{2}$(Area *MLEA*)
4. Area △*BAK* = $\frac{1}{2}$(Area *ACHK*)
5. Area *ACHK* = Area *MLEA*
6. In a similar manner, show that Area *BCGF* = Area *MLDB*
7. Area *ACHK* + Area *BCGF* = Area *BAED*

Version 2 (Algebraic method):
The square of the hypotenuse of a right triangle is equal to the sum of the squares of the legs.

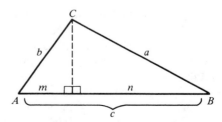

1. Since similar triangles are formed by constructing the altitude, then

$$\frac{c}{a} = \frac{a}{n} \quad \text{and} \quad \frac{c}{b} = \frac{b}{m}$$

or $a^2 = cn$ and $b^2 = cm$

2. Therefore $a^2 + b^2 = cn + cm$
$$= c(n + m)$$
$$= c \cdot c = c^2.$$

We cannot conclude a discussion on geometric proofs without mentioning the indirect method of reasoning (*reductio ad absurdum*) which is used extensively in higher mathematics.

PROBLEM: Prove by indirect reasoning that if two angles of a triangle are congruent, the sides opposite them are congruent.

A sketch of the proof follows. Incidentally, this is the proof found in Euclid's *Elements*. Current textbooks usually prove this theorem directly.

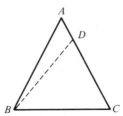

SOLUTION:

Given $\triangle ABC$, where $\angle B \cong \angle C$. If $\overline{AB} \ncong \overline{AC}$, then assume $AC > AB$. Mark off point D in $\overline{AC}$ such that $\overline{DC} \cong \overline{AB}$. Then $\triangle DCB \cong \triangle ABC$. This is impossible, so $\overline{AB} \cong \overline{AC}$.

NON-ROUTINE PROBLEMS

Solving a problem is like inventing something new, and there are no set rules that inventors follow. The best way to learn to solve mathematical problems is by solving more problems. Experience is often the best teacher. There is simply no substitute for building up a reservoir of experience, "tricks," or strategies (such as the analytic method, indirect proofs, estimating results, guessing, etc.).

For some, many of the problems described earlier would be "child's play." For them, the challenge comes with problems where non-routine, or novel, approaches are needed. We shall present several such problems together with their solutions, which, incidentally, you can best appreciate only after you attempt the problems yourself. These problems are not arranged in any special order; however, the first three appear in many forms, and knowledge of the basic versions should enable you to handle variations.

The problems illustrated here all exhibit some use of an unusual approach. A keen awareness might be developed by reading these and others similar to them.

PROBLEM: If the sum of two numbers is 12 and their product is 4, find the sum of their reciprocals.

The following solutions demonstrate the power of intuition, insight and some experience in problem solving—compare solution 1 with solution 2. You can easily see which is more elegant!

SOLUTION 1: Let x = first number
y = second number

Key equations: $x + y = 12$
$xy = 4$

By substitution:

$$x(12 - x) = 4$$
$$x^2 - 12x + 4 = 0$$

Using the quadratic formula we get:

$$x = 6 \pm 4\sqrt{2}$$

By substituting for x we get values for y:

x	$6 + 4\sqrt{2}$	$6 - 4\sqrt{2}$
y	$6 - 4\sqrt{2}$	$6 + 4\sqrt{2}$

By rationalizing denominators and simplifying:

$$\frac{1}{x} = \frac{1}{6 + 4\sqrt{2}} = \frac{3 - 2\sqrt{2}}{2}$$

$$\frac{1}{y} = \frac{1}{6 - 4\sqrt{2}} = \frac{3 + 2\sqrt{2}}{2}$$

so that

$$\frac{1}{x} + \frac{1}{y} = \frac{3 - 2\sqrt{2}}{2} + \frac{3 + 2\sqrt{2}}{2} = \frac{6}{2} = 3 \quad \text{(Answer)}$$

SOLUTION 2:

$$\frac{1}{x} + \frac{1}{y} = \frac{x + y}{xy} = \frac{12}{4} = 3 \quad \text{(Answer)}$$

This solution illustrates the value of using a "reverse strategy." For more on this strategy in problem solving, see Enrichment Unit 93.

PROBLEM: Find the sum of the coefficients in the binomial expansion of $(x + y)^8$.

(The solutions of this problem also demonstrate the power of intuition, insight, and experience.)

SOLUTION 1:
$$(x + y)^8 = \binom{8}{0}x^8 + \binom{8}{1}x^7y + \binom{8}{2}x^6y^2 + \binom{8}{3}x^5y^3 +$$
$$\binom{8}{4}x^4y^4 + \binom{8}{5}x^3y^5 + \binom{8}{6}x^2y^6 + \binom{8}{7}xy^7 + \binom{8}{8}y^8$$

$$\begin{aligned} \text{Sum of the} \atop \text{coefficients} &= \binom{8}{0} + \binom{8}{1} + \binom{8}{2} + \binom{8}{3} + \binom{8}{4} + \binom{8}{5} + \\ &\quad \binom{8}{6} + \binom{8}{7} + \binom{8}{8} \\ &= 1 + 8 + 28 + 56 + 70 + 56 + 28 + 8 \\ &\quad + 1 \\ &= 256 \quad \text{(Answer)} \end{aligned}$$

SOLUTION 2:
Let $x = y = 1$ in the first equation of solution 1.

Then

$$(x+y)^8 = (1+1)^8 = \binom{8}{0} + \binom{8}{1} + \binom{8}{2} + \binom{8}{3} + \binom{8}{4} +$$
$$\binom{8}{5} + \binom{8}{6} + \binom{8}{7} + \binom{8}{8}$$

So that the sum of the coefficient is
$$(1+1)^8 = 2^8 = 256$$

PROBLEM: A bug perched on corner B of a solid box chooses to reach the diagonally opposite corner H by the shortest route. What path does it take?

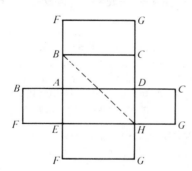

(The solution to this problem demonstrates the role that imagination as well as insight plays in problem solving)

SOLUTION: Open the box along several edges to flatten it out. The illustration below is one possibility. $\overline{BH}$ is the shortest path between B and H.

PROBLEM: As shown in the following figure, E is on $\overline{AB}$ and C is on $\overline{FG}$. Prove that parallelogram $ABCD$ is equal in area to parallelogram $EFGD$.

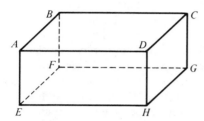

Although the solution is an easy one (once one knows it), the solution is invariably evasive, even for bright high school students who have some experience in solving difficult mathematics problems.

SOLUTION: Draw $\overline{EC}$ (see next figure). Since $\triangle EDC$ and $\square ABCD$ share the same

base ($\overline{DC}$) and a common altitude (from E to $\overleftrightarrow{DC}$ the area of $\triangle EDC$ is equal to one-half the area of $\square ABCD$.

Similarly, $\triangle EDC$ and $\square EFGD$ share the same base ($\overline{ED}$), and the same altitude to that base; thus, the area of $\triangle EDC$ is equal to one-half the area of $\square EFGD$.

Since the area of $\triangle EDC$ is equal to one-half the area of each parallelogram, the parallelograms are equal in area.

Sometimes the obvious solution is just overlooked because of prior training. That is, students often react to a problem in the manner in which similar problems have been done (this is not necessarily a bad idea). This oversight could lead the student to go awry, as illustrated with the preceding problems. Sometimes an alternate solution, albeit long and cumbersome, may not be possible or may be vastly out of a student's reach. The following will illustrate this.

PROBLEM: Two trains, each traveling uniformly, start towards each other at the same time along a straight track. One train is traveling at 60 mph and the other at 90 mph. At the start, with the trains 150 miles apart, a bee travels from one train to the other at the rate of 200 mph. When the bee reaches the second train, it immediately returns to the first train. This continues until the trains meet (and the bee is crushed by the impact). How many miles did the bee travel?

SOLUTION: Don't be distracted by trying to track the path of the bee! Instead, simply calculate the bee's distance by multiplying its rate of speed by the time it traveled. The latter is obtained from calculating the time it took the trains to meet.

> Let t = the number of hours
> the trains traveled
> before meeting.

$$60t + 90t = 150$$
$$150t = 150$$
$$t = 1$$

In one hour the bee traveled a total of 200 miles.

PROBLEM: *Monkey on a rope*
Suppose there was a rope hanging over a pulley with a weight on one end of the rope. Suppose also that at the other end was a monkey who weighed

the same as the weight. Assume that the rope weighed four ounces for every foot, and the age of the monkey and the monkey's mother was four years, and the weight of the monkey was as many pounds as the mother was years old. The monkey's mother is twice as old as the monkey was when the monkey's mother was half as old as the monkey will be when the monkey's mother was three times as old as the monkey, and the weight of the weight and the weight of the rope was half as much again as the difference between the weight of the weight and the weight of the weight and the weight of the monkey. What is the length of the rope?

SOLUTION:

Let L = length of rope, in feet

W = weight of rope, in ounces

A = age of mother, in years

a = age of monkey, in years

m = weight of monkey, in ounces

w = weight of weight, in ounces

x = number of years ago when monkey was . . .

y = number of years later when monkey will be . . .

z = number of years ago when mother was . . .

Solve these nine equations simultaneously.

1. $m = w$
2. $W = 4L$
3. $a + A = 4$
4. $\dfrac{m}{16} = A$
5. $A = 2(a - x)$
6. $A - x = \dfrac{(a + y)}{2}$
7. $a + y = 3(A - z)$
8. $A - z = 3(a - z)$
9. $w + W = \dfrac{3}{2}\left| w - (w + m) \right|$

Answer: Length of rope is 5 feet.

Naturally, there are many other non-routine problems, each with a different "message." Some books where these can be found are listed at the end of this chapter, but you may wish to be adventurous and create your own problems.

CREATING MATHEMATICAL PROBLEMS

The changes made in two of Euclid's five postulates (the Parallel Postulate and the Infinitude of a Line) led to a revolution in mathematics—the development of non-Euclidean geometries. The technique of making minor or major adjustments in the given conditions of a mathematics problem "just for the fun of it" has a long tradition among mathematicians and students of mathematics. The results have, on occasion, proved startling to say the least—as evidenced by the example just cited. Another example is an extension of the fact that there exist Pythagorean triplets (x, y, z), which satisfy $x^2 + y^2 = z^2$. However, one would not have such an easy time trying to find integers x, y and z that satisfy $x^n + y^n = z^n$ for integral $n > 2$. In fact this leads to the well known "Fermat's Last Theorem."

Students can be trained to develop and solve their own, self-made, problems by making changes in existing ones, even simple changes. When students are developing their own problems they may occasionally create problems which are beyond their ability or capacity to solve, however. Some may even be unsolvable.

Every problem that is posed can have some conditions changed to produce a new problem or variation of the original problem. Thus the teacher should determine some scheme for giving credit to students not only for solving problems correctly, as is traditionally the case, but also for creating problems. Through this creative effort students begin to really understand what problems are all about.

As an aid to teachers and prospective teachers, we shall offer some suggestions on how specific problems might be changed to produce new ones. These could be used to demonstrate to students the types of variations that might be made. The real creativity, however, will come from students' own variations of problems.

PROBLEM: David has 45 coins, consisting of nickels and dimes. The total value is $3.50. How many coins of each kind does he have?

POSSIBLE VARIATIONS:
1. What is the largest number of nickels and dimes he could have that would total $3.50?
2. What is the smallest number?
3. How would the problem change if it included quarters as well as nickels and dimes?
4. Is it possible to have only dimes and quarters instead of nickels and dimes?
5. In how many ways could $3.50 be represented in nickels and dimes?

PROBLEM: By construction (using straightedge and compasses), locate the midpoint of segment AB:

A ———————————————— B

POSSIBLE VARIATIONS:
1. Are there any other ways of locating the midpoint of a segment?

2. Suppose a pupil forgot to bring his straightedge to school. Is it possible to locate the midpoint with compasses alone?
3. With straightedge alone?
4. Suppose a student had a pair of compasses which were rusted and could not be adjusted; can the segment $\overline{AB}$ be bisected with unadjustable compasses?

PROBLEM: At a point on level ground 100 feet from the foot of a flagpole, the angle of elevation of the top of the pole is 31°. Find the height of the flagpole to the nearest foot.

POSSIBLE VARIATIONS:
1. Suppose the same pole had a 15° tilt. How would you then compute the length of the pole?
2. Suppose the original flagpole is standing vertically on a hill that has a 15° rise. How would you compute the height of the pole?

PROBLEM: Prove that in a circle, chords are congruent if they are equidistant from the center.

POSSIBLE VARIATIONS:
1. State and prove the inverse of the problem.
2. State and prove the converse of the problem.
3. State and prove the contrapositive of the problem.
4. Are there any other variations?

CREATIVITY IN PROBLEM SOLVING

If there is difficulty in teaching effective ways of using the techniques of problem solving, there is, perhaps, greater difficulty in teaching for "creativity." One of the major difficulties is in defining the term itself. At one time, it was thought that creativity was a genetic capacity granted to the fortunate few, but now a number of psychologists have attempted to demonstrate that processes associated with creativity are teachable (or, at least, encourageable). For our purposes, we may define creativity as the ability to evolve unusual, highly useful or unique solutions to problems. (Remember that such solutions do not necessarily occur quickly. It took Johannes Kepler almost twenty years to develop his three laws of planetary motion—one of the most creative performances in scientific history.)

While there is continuing investigation into the relationship between creativity and intelligence, preliminary findings indicate that the domains are not identical. Highly creative students are not, necessarily, those with the highest I.Q. Different tests of creativity may, of course, be responsible for some of the differences in findings, but some psychologists seem to agree that intelligence tests do not measure the same operations as found in creativity.

Following are some suggestions for encouraging creativity in the classroom.

1. Provide a classroom atmosphere that encourages freedom of expression.
2. Respect unusual questions, and set an example by your own inquiry and creativity.
3. Respect and reward unusual ideas.
4. Provide opportunities for learning that involve searching for students' own solutions without being graded.
5. Do not discourage controversy.
6. Encourage students to value their own ideas and to record them in concrete form whenever possible.
7. Share examples of the efforts of famous creative people—and their difficulties.
8. Encourage the acquisition of knowledge in a variety of fields.
9. When assignments are given, provide opportunities for originality and exploration.

SUMMARY

The one statement that best summarizes this chapter is, "We learn best how to solve problems by solving them." This is the case whether the problems are of the standard textbook varieties found in algebra or geometry textbooks, or any of the challenging types one finds in some textbooks as well as special puzzle or problem books. (See list on p. 115.) It is impossible to include in any chapter on the subject a sampling of every solution type. Rather, we have tried to impart a feeling or sensitivity towards the whole area of problem solving that establishes it as an interesting, challenging, and fruitful branch of mathematics.

Problem solving, perhaps more than any other branch of mathematics, sharpens a student's analytical and critical powers. At the same time, it may help develop a sense of accomplishment and achievement in students. As a matter of fact, the discovery (or development) of many areas of mathematics is a direct result of problem solving. Much of probability theory results from posed problems and challenges being solved.

Whatever one can say about the positive effects of problem solving on more gifted students can also be said to a different (perhaps lesser) degree about slower students. Whether we are engaged in efforts to train college-bound or general mathematics students in the fine art of problem solving, the challenge is not only theirs—it is ours as well.

EXERCISES

1. Write a lesson plan for each of the following topics:
  a. Introduction to uniform motion problems
  b. Introduction to coin problems
  c. Introduction to mixture problems
  d. Introduction to investment problems

2. Prepare a lesson on how you would teach students to create new problems by changing part of the hypothesis or given conditions for
  a. algebraic problems.
  b. geometric problems.

3. Write any two verbal problems in algebra and one geometric "proof" which have
  a. insufficient data.
  b. excessive data.
  Write a lesson plan indicating how you would introduce this type of problem to an algebra (or geometry) class.

4. Look in some of the books listed in the bibliography (see below) and select five challenging problems and their solutions that are appropriate for a high school mathematics class (you select the level). Indicate how you would use these problems in your classes.

5. List five activities that can be described as problem solving for a general mathematics class.

6. Consider the following challenging problems. In which types of classes would you present them? Indicate the benefits you think your pupils could derive from these problems.
  a. One method of obtaining the product of two numbers, say 43 and 75, is illustrated by the following:

43	75
21	150
(10)	(300)
5	600
(2)	(1200)
1	2400

  from which

  $$43 \times 75 = 75 + 150 + 600 + 2400 = 3225$$

  (1) Use this method to multiply 73×120.
  (2) Explain why the method is valid.

  b. Find to the nearest hundredth, the value of:

  $$1 + \cfrac{1}{1 + \cfrac{1}{1 + \cfrac{1}{1 + \cfrac{1}{1 + \ldots}}}}$$

  c. Solve: $x + y = 5xy$
  $\qquad\quad y + z = 7yz$
  $\qquad\quad z + x = 6xz$

  d. If $3^{2x} + 9 = 10(3^x)$, solve for x.

  e. Determine which is larger: $\sqrt[9]{9!}$ or $\sqrt[10]{10!}$

  f. How many integers less than or equal to one million are squares or cubes of integers?

7. Read *How To Solve It* by George Polya (Princeton University Press), then discuss how some of Polya's heuristic strategies can be applied to the secondary school mathematics curriculum. At least three strategies should be considered in your response to this exercise.

8. Read *How To Solve Problems* by Wayne A. Wickelgren (W.H. Freeman & Co., San Francisco, 1974), then discuss how Wickelgren's heuristic strategies can be applied to the secondary school mathematics curriculum. At least three strategies should be considered in your response to this exercise.

SOURCES FOR PROBLEMS

Aref, M.N. and Wernick, W. *Problems and Solutions in Euclidean Geometry.* New York: Dover, 1968.

Barbeau, E., Klamkin, M., and Moser, W. *1001 Problems in High School Mathematics.* Montreal: Canadian Mathematical Congress, 1976, 1978.

Brousseau, Bro. A., *Saint Mary's College Mathematics Contest Problems.* Palo Alto, Calif.: Creative Publications, 1972.

Bryant, S.J., Graham, G.E., and Wiley, K.G. *Nonroutine Problems in Algebra, Geometry, and Trigonometry.* New York: McGraw-Hill, 1965.

Burkill, J.C., and Kundy, H.M. *Mathematical Scholarship Problems.* London: Cambridge University Press, 1961.

Butts, T. *Problem Solving in Mathematics.* Glenview, Ill.: Scott, Foresman, 1973.

CEMREL, *Elements of Mathematics. Book B, Problem Book,* Vol. I and II. St. Louis, Mo.: CEMREL, 1975.

Charosh, M. *Mathematical Challenges.* Washington, D.C.: National Council of Teachers of Mathematics, 1965.

Dörrie, H. *100 Great Problems of Elementary Mathematics.* New York: Dover, 1965.

Dunn, A. *Mathematical Bafflers.* New York: McGraw-Hill, 1964.

Filipiak, A.S. *Mathematical Puzzles.* New York: Bell Publishing, 1942.

Garvin, A.D. *Discovery Problems for Better Students.* Portland, Maine: J. Weston Walch, 1975.

Graham, L.A. *Ingenious Mathematical Problems and Methods.* New York: Dover, 1959.

————. *The Surprise Attack in Mathematical Problems.* New York: Dover, 1968.

Grietzer, S.L. *International Mathematical Olympiads 1959-1977.* Washington, D.C.: Mathematical Association of America, 1978.

Higgins, A.M. *Geometry Problems.* Portland, Maine: J. Weston Walch, 1971.

Hill, T.J. *Mathematical Challenges II—Plus Six.* Washington, D.C.: National Council of Teachers of Mathematics, 1974.

Honsberger, R. *Mathematical Morsels.* Washington, D.C.: Mathematical Association of America, 1978.

Krechmer, V.A. *A Problem Book in Algebra.* Trans. V. Shiffer. Moscow: Mir Publishers, 1974.

Krulick, S., and Rudnjck, J.A. *Problem Solving: A Handbook for Teachers.* Boston: Allyn and Bacon, 1980.

Kutepov, A., and Rubanov, A. *Problems in Geometry.* Trans. O. Meshkov. Moscow: Mir Publisher, 1975.

————. *Problem Book: Algebra and Elementary Function.* Trans. L. Levant. Moscow: Mir Publisher, 1978.

Moser, W., and Barbeau, E. *The Canadian Mathematics Olympiads 1969, 1975.* Montreal: Canadian Mathematical Congress, 1976.

Mott-Smith, G. *Mathematical Puzzles for Beginners and Enthusiasts.* New York: Dover, 1954.

Newton, D.E. *One Hundred Quickies for Math Classes.* Portland, Maine: J. Weston Walch, 1972.

Phillips, H., Shovelton, S.T., and Marshal, G.S. *Caliban's Problem Book.* New York: Dover 1961.

Polya, G., and Kilpatrick, J. *The Stanford Mathematics Book.* New York: Teachers College Press, 1974.

Posamentier, A.S. *A Study Guide for the Mathematics Section of the Scholastic Aptitude Test.* Boston: Allyn and Bacon, 1983.

Posamentier, A.S., and Salkind, C.T. *Challenging Problems in Algebra,* Vol. I and II. New York: Macmillan, 1970.

————. *Challenging Problems in Geometry,* Vol. I and II. New York: Macmillan, 1970.

————. *Uncommon Problems for Common Topics in Algebra.* Portland, Maine: J. Weston Walch, 1981.

————. *Unusual Problems for Usual Topics in Algebra.* Portland, Maine: J. Weston Walch, 1981.

Ransom, W.R. *One Hundred Mathematical Curiosities.* Portland, Maine: J. Weston Walch, 1955.

Rapaport, E. *Hungarian Problem Book,* Vol. I and II. New York: Random House, 1963.

Salkind, C.T. *The Contest Problem Book.* New York: Random House, 1961.

————. *The MAA Problem Book II.* New York: Random House, 1966.

Salkind, C.T., and Earl, J.M. *The MAA Problem Book III.* New York: Random House, 1973.

Shklarsky, D.O., Chentzov, N.N., and Yaglom, I.M. *The USSR Olympiad Problem Book.* San Francisco: W.H. Freeman, 1962.

————. *Selected Problems and Theorems in Elementary Mathematics.* Trans. V.M. Volosov, and I.G. Volosova. Moscow: Mir Publisher, 1979.

Sitomer, H. *The New Mathlete Problems Book.* Valley Stream, N.Y.: Nassau County Interscholastic Mathematics League, 1974.

Steinhaus, H. *One Hundred Problems in Elementary Mathematics.* New York: Pergamon Press, 1963.

Straszewicz, S. *Mathematical Problems and Puzzles from the Polish Mathematical Olypiads.* Trans. J. Smslska. New York: Pergamon Press, 1965.

Trigg, C.W. *Mathematical Quickies.* New York: McGraw-Hill, 1967.

Ulam, S.M. *Problems in Modern Mathematics*. New York: John Wiley, 1960.

Yaglom, A.M., and Yaglom, I.M. *Challenging Mathematical Problems with Elementary Solutions,* Vol. I and II. San Francisco: Holden-Day, 1964, 1967.

SUGGESTED READINGS

Arnold, William R. "Students Can Pose and Solve Original Problems." *The Mathematics Teacher* 64 (1971): 325.

Skemp, Richard R. *The Psychology of Learning Mathematics*. Baltimore: Penguin Books, 1971.

The Mathematics Teacher 76 (1983). Special Issue—Gifted Students.

Topoly, William. "An Introduction to Solving Problems." *The Mathematics Teacher* 58 (1965): 48.

Troutman, Andrea, and Lichtenberg, Betty P. "Problem Solving in the General Mathematics Classroom." *The Mathematics Teacher* 67 (1974): 590.

Walter, Marion I., and Brown, Stephen I. "Problem Posing and Problem Solving." *The Mathematics Teacher* 70 (1977): 4.

Whirl, Robert J. "Problem Solving—Solution or Technique?" *The Mathematics Teacher* 66 (1973): 551.

CHAPTER 10
USING CALCULATORS AND COMPUTERS IN THE CLASSROOM

Following a dramatic period of development and improvement of electronic calculators, there appears, in the late 1970s, to have been a leveling-off of the innovations involving the use of calculators in the classroom. At the same time the price decline of these minicalculators also seems to have stabilized. We will therefore discuss the role of the calculator as we see it with an eye to the future.

On the other hand, discussion of the role of minicomputers, microcomputers and regular full size computers in the classroom will be a bit less stable. Since the prices for microcomputers are still declining, allowing more units to enter schools which earlier could not afford to buy them, the role of these microcomputers is still being assessed and new procedures for their use still being tried. We hope our assessments and suggestions will stand up to the test of time. With both calculators and computers, our discussion will be based on first-hand experience.

CALCULATORS

The low cost and convenience of hand-held calculators have made their application in the classroom a controversial topic in mathematics education. More studies on the effects of calculators on mathematics education have been conducted in the past five years than on any other single aspect of mathematics education during this century. The calculator industry began its sharp advances in 1958, when the invention of the integrated circuit eliminated the need for many separate transistors and mechanical connections in the design of calculators. In 1971, Texas Instruments' "calculator-on-a-chip" paved the way for the minicalculator of the 1970s.

It has not always been smooth sailing for the minicalculator in the classroom. In 1978, the National Council of Teachers of Mathematics stated their position as

> encouraging the use of calculators in the classroom as instructional aids and computational tools. Calculators give mathematics educators new opportunities to help their students learn mathematics and solve contemporary problems. The use of calculators, however, will not replace the necessity for learning computational skills.[1]

At about the same time, other factions of society voiced their disapproval for the use of calculators in the classroom as an unnecessary intrusion into the learning process. Some felt that the minicalculator presented an obtrusive crutch for students learning the basic skills of arithmetic. Some parents resented having their children use calculators for fear that they would not learn the basic computational algorithms. The controversy over the effectiveness of the calculator as a learning aid continues, and professional conferences are often held to discuss the effectiveness of this revolutionary tool. As somewhat of a compromise statement, the National Council of Teachers of Mathematics stated among its eight recommendations for the 1980s the following:

> Recommendation 3
>
> MATHEMATICS PROGRAMS MUST TAKE FULL ADVANTAGE OF THE POWER OF CALCULATORS AND COMPUTERS AT ALL GRADE LEVELS
>
> Beyond an acquaintance with the role of computers and calculators in society, most students must obtain a working knowledge of how to use them, including the ways in which one communicates with each and commands their services in problem solving.
>
> The availability of computing aids, including computers and calculators, requires a reexamination of the computational skills needed by every citizen. Some of these computational skills will no longer retain their same importance, whereas others will become more important.

> It is recognized that a significant portion of instruction in the early grades must be devoted to the direct acquisition of number concepts and skills without the use of calculators. However, when the burden of lengthy computations outweighs the educational contribution of the process, the calculator should become readily available.
>
> With the increasing availability of microcomputers at decreasing costs, it is imperative that schools play an active part in preparing students of the 1980s to live in a world in which more and more functions are being performed by computers.[2]

Studies of the effects of the minicalculator on mathematics education continue.

Although there is no concrete proof that the minicalculator is, or is not, an effective tool for mathematics instruction, an increasing number of mathematics teachers are using it in various ways. We shall explore some of these methods here.

A Check for Arithmetic

In classes in which arithmetic is being taught or reviewed, the use of minicalculators to check answers can often be a motivating experience. This can be particularly true in a remedial arithmetic class in high school, where students have continuously met with failure, and where this use of minicalculators provides them with a different experience and thereby attracts and hopefully sustains their interest. A typical example of how the minicalculator may be used in this way is to have students use either their own, or one of a class set of calculators, to check arithmetic drill exercises after they have been completed manually. Naturally, if this use of the minicalculator is not varied, it soon loses its effectiveness. The novelty of the minicalculator must be nurtured if this use is to remain effective. Special care must be taken to insure that this tool is not misused by students, in which case it would become counterproductive to the learning process.

The operation of a calculator is a skill that most people can pick up on their own. However, slower students, such as those often found in a remedial arithmetic class, might require training in its use. Before a teacher can expect his pupils to use the calculator for purposes such as checking arithmetic drill exercises, the teacher will need to demonstrate how to use the calculator and must also provide ample time for a drill lesson on its uses.

A typical introductory lesson on the use of a calculator might involve

---

[1]NCTM, *A Position Statement*, September, 1978.

[2]NCTM, *An Agenda for Action*, Recommendations for School Mathematics of the 1980s (National Council of Teachers of Mathematics, 1980).

1. Having enough calculators for at least half the class
2. Pairing students to share a calculator and to assist each other as they watch the teacher's demonstration
3. Having one pupil of the pair work on an arithmetic drill example manually while the other does it on the machine (after they compare results, they would switch roles).

Only when the class is trained in the use of a calculator can the teacher expect pupils to adequately check their own work. There is then also less likelihood that the machine will then be misused.

One popular way of making young people feel comfortable using a calculator, as well as improving their skill, speed and accuracy in its use, is a speed and accuracy contest. Students may be set against each other individually or in teams to answer a series of arithmetic questions that could get as complicated as:

$$\text{evaluate } \frac{23.4 \times 17.6}{50 \times 8} \text{ to the nearest tenth}$$

or even

$$\text{evaluate } \frac{2}{\sqrt{2} - 1} \text{ to the nearest hundredth}$$

When preparing the class for such contests, much excitement can be generated while good arithmetic is being taught.

Calculator Assisted Instruction

Many calculators on the market today can provide pre-programmed drill of arithmetic exercises to students. These units range from small hand-held calculators to larger desk-top models which provide a printout record. Each generates randomly selected exercises within a pre-selected skill area and reacts to a correct student response by offering another exercise while informing the student of an error if an incorrect response is given to the calculator. Generally the desk-top models allow the teacher to select more specifically the program on which a student will work than would be possible with the hand-held calculator models. For example, on the Monroe *Classmate-88*, the teacher can select the range of numbers used in any part of an arithmetic exercise chosen. Thus, if a student is having difficulty multiplying by 7, 8, and 9, exercises easily can be selected which will drill this type of skill. Very often the printout provided by the desk-top calculator will be particularly useful to the teacher who has to monitor numerous students working at different skills.

A Device for Better Understanding Mathematics Concepts

By experimenting with calculators, students can see various relationships between numbers evolve. For example, they can discover what type of divisors will generate repeating or terminating decimals. They can discover ways of detecting prime numbers. They may discover unusual number patterns. They can dissect the common arithmetic computational algorithms and perhaps devise others. All these activities can lead to creative work. Yet, most important is proper teacher guidance, for without this the student could end up losing the educational benefits of this attractive and potentially useful device.

An Aid to Learning Problem Solving

A common complaint among teachers of secondary school remedial classes is that "students have great difficulty with computation and, what is worse, they are very weak in problem solving." This is unfortunately a self-perpetuating ill. Students who cannot succeed with arithmetic computation are constantly told to drill these skills and rarely allowed to practice any problem-solving skills. Those who do go on to working on some elementary problems often do not get near an answer because of computational deficiencies. Their only exposure to problem solving is one of frustration, never realizing success because of computational obstacles. Here the calculator can be of significant assistance. Selective use of the calculator to bypass potential computational barriers will allow students to concentrate on problem-solving skills without fear of meeting frustration previously caused by their computational difficulties. Such activities should be carefully designed and monitored to be effective. After realizing success in problem solving, students should then be intrinsically motivated to conquer their computational deficiencies, since this would be their only remaining requirement to complete their remediation programs.

Making Mathematics Problem Solving More Realistic

Although continuously nurtured on the typical textbook problems, students usually find them boring and unrealistic. Traditionally, textbook authors design the problems in a way which will make the arithmetic computations as simple as possible so as not to detract from the problem. "Real life" situations frequently are quite different. The numbers used are generally not simple. With the aid of a calculator, a teacher can provide realistic situations for problem solving and not worry about computational distractions. A uniform motion problem, for example, can involve fractional quantities and yield an answer which is not an integer and cause no displeasure for the student if she has a calculator available. Furthermore, students using a calculator can be encouraged to create problems based on their own experiences (e.g., calculating their average speed walking to school). New vistas are opened up when a calculator is used to assist in problem solving.

Investigating Unusual Curiosities

With the aid of a calculator, many interesting (and often unquestioned) mathematical curiosities which appear in the average citizen's everyday experiences can serve as excellent applications of high school mathematics. For example, bank advertisements highlight the *effective annual yield* after stating their annual interest rate. A recent inspection turned up the following effective annual yields for a 5¼% annual interest rate compounded daily: 5.35%, 5.38%, 5.39%, and 5.46%. By legally inserting a varying number of days (in a year), n, at different parts of the formula $I = \left(1 + \frac{r}{n}\right)^n - 1$, a variety of answers will result. Availability of a calculator encourages this sort of investigation. Another possible investigation might involve determining the effect of tax-exempt income to individuals in various income tax brackets.

Lots of other real-life problems (such as loans, taxes, installment purchases, etc.) can be investigated with the aid of a calculator. Such investigations can serve as excellent sources of applications for the regular secondary school curriculum. You can gather ideas for projects from the National Council of Teachers of Mathematics' 1979 Yearbook, *Applications in School Mathematics*.

An Aid in Advanced Mathematics Courses

Problems in advanced secondary school mathematics courses can often involve extensive calculations. In earlier years either a slide rule or logarithms were used for such problems. Today the logical method of computation at this level is a calculator. A scientific calculator (i.e., one which among other features includes trigonometric functions) would be most helpful. Teacher judgment should determine the times when calculators may be used.

COMPUTERS

The advances of the electronic computer, since the development of ENIAC in 1946, have been dramatic. The ever-growing technology has made today's computers spectacular. As with the minicalculators, the decreasing costs and reduced size of today's computers make them increasingly more attractive for use as an aid in mathematics education.

Currently three types of computers are being used in schools: full-size computers located at a central location, with terminals for student use at various schools; minicomputers which consist of a smaller computer located in the school with a small number of terminals near the computer for student use; and the very popular microcomputer, which is a small self-contained computer and terminal in one unit. Although the selection of a computer is often a function of the funds available, other factors should be considered regardless of which type of computer is purchased.

The terminal at which a student works is commonly equipped with a *CRT* (Cathode Ray Tube or television screen) and a typewriter-like keyboard. Some units have printers instead of a CRT; however, a CRT is generally more desirable since it produces the program faster and is more versatile. Yet the addition of a printer can enhance the usability of a computer in a school tenfold, since a printer could provide a more cost-effective student/computer ratio. With the exception of specialized situations, such as providing for advanced programming applications (where a considerably large memory is required) or extensive use by the school or district administration for attendance, student programs, or business applications, any of the three types of computers cited earlier would suffice. Where a computer is required for these special applications, in addition to instructional uses, a larger computer or a more elaborate minicomputer would be necessary.

Computers can be used in numerous ways. We shall consider some of them here.

An Aid in Remediation

In a manner similar to that of the *Monroe Classmate-88* (described earlier in this chapter), computer programs can be developed or purchased which provide students with selected drill in most topics in the secondary school curriculum. Unlike the *Classmate-88*, which is limited to arithmetic drill, the computer can be made to provide drill in algebra, geometry, and trigonometry, as well as arithmetic. Moreover, the computer can do more than just acknowledge a correct answer and generate another problem (or indicate "error" and repeat the same problem). It can be programmed to indicate where an error was made or it can offer suggestions for reaching a correct answer based specifically on the student's incorrect answer.

Computer Assisted Instruction

Although not intended as a replacement for a teacher, the computer can be programmed to guide a student through the development of a mathematics topic. This sort of activity, often called Computer Assisted Instruction (CAI) must be carefully worked into the school curriculum. It may supplement, not supplant, the regular instruction. Using specially prepared programs, a teacher may have a student who missed a lesson (or topic) because of absence make up this missed work individually on the computer. This program would gently guide the student through the development and applications of the topic. Often such programs are written by the teacher to meet her specific needs. A similar arrangement can be used to accelerate a gifted student. This sort of instruction should be done in moderation, under the close monitoring of the teacher.

Some commercially prepared programs are quite appropriate for the purposes just described. Here are but a few examples of such types of software that are readily available from software dealers:

> how to solve linear equations—drill and practice
> solving quadratic equations—drill and practice
> arithmetic operations—drill and practice
> algebra tutorial disks—all of first year algebra
> selected areas in geometry
> graphing linear equations
> graphing trigonometric functions
> selected topics in calculus
> Scholastic Aptitude Test preparation

Many of these programs have built-in management systems that maintain records of student progress and achievement for the teacher's information. The management system is often arranged in such a way as to maintain the privacy of each pupil's records. Only the teacher will know the code and password needed to retrieve the information.

Computer Literacy

Virtually every school that has microcomputers for classroom use or has access to larger computer systems has instituted some type of computer literacy course. While not necessarily under the aegis of the mathematics department, it often is. A reasonable computer literacy course need not last for a full semester. Among the topics that might be included if the computers are micros, are:

> hands-on familiarity with the computer, including editing, DOS commands, and the keyboard. Using challenging computer games is a good way to begin.
> improving typing skills via computer typing programs.
> introduction to word processing. Select a word

processor program that is not too difficult to use and that will enable creating and saving documents.
> introduction to spreadsheet. Students can create a budget, copy formulas, do an income tax report, and so forth.
> database storage and retrieval.
> introduction to BASIC.

Management of a computer classroom will present new problems and challenges for you. You may or may not have a computer laboratory assistant in the room with you. Without such assistance you will have to select, distribute, and load the disks or tapes by yourself or with student monitors. Ideally, you will have one pupil per computer station, though you may be required to accommodate two or three students per computer station. Some disks may not load properly and you will have to solve the problem. Students may simply forget loading instructions. Some may secretly bring their own games to play while you are not looking. Pupils may attempt to copy programs legally or illegally. There is a temptation to "play" with the machine while the teacher is addressing the class. Students may forget to turn off the machines when they leave, etc., etc., etc. There are simply too many problems to even attempt to list them all, but be assured that you will be challenged!

A Source for Recreational Mathematics

Many programs are available which allow students to play games with the computer. Carefully selected games can be effective in furthering the development of a student's skills in logic. The level and sophistication of the game must be selected by the teacher with the specific student user clearly in mind. A game which is not challenging enough may either bore the student or make for a silly experience. On the other hand, a program which generates a game beyond the level of the intended student user may frustrate the student and eventually turn him away from computers. Computer games can provide a fine source for developing logic skills, as well as motivating students to study programming.

Programming—An Integrated Part of the School Curriculum

The proliferation of microcomputers has lowered their cost so that it is now feasible for all schools to purchase a considerable number of computers for classroom use. However, what role should the computer play in the general education of students? One interesting possibility is that students be taught how to use the computer as a tool for problem solving. This can be accomplished by infusing a computer component into various traditional mathematics courses (algebra, geometry and trigonometry), and/or offering elective courses in computer mathematics. In this section, we will describe three types of approaches to programs in computer mathematics, the relationship between the hardware available and the approach, and a set of expanded lesson ideas on how a topic in computer mathematics could unfold.

A computer mathematics curriculum should be designed to reinforce, enrich and extend concepts that are taught in the school's regular program. With this in mind, students should be challenged to solve various mathematical problems and then analyze them with an eye towards a computer solution. How to proceed from this point is dependent upon the computer equipment available.

Computer Equipment

Microcomputers generally have a central processing unit (CPU), keyboard, video display (CRT), and a cassette tape recorder or disk drive (disk operating system, DOS) for storing programs. This setup will certainly be satisfactory for students to run their programs. However, it has several drawbacks, including the following:

1. The cassette recorder is comparatively slow in saving and loading programs. If a student forgets how she named a program, she will have great difficulty locating it on a cassette. When someone has a computer at home, speed at which an item is found on the tape is relatively insignificant. Yet, in a school setting where the school day is sectioned into 40–50 minute intervals, the approximately five minutes spent saving and loading programs *is* significant. On the other hand, one can obtain a disk operating system to decrease the time needed to save or load programs. Instead of programs being stored on a cassette tape, they are stored on disks (magnetic objects similar to a 45 rpm record.) A DOS is fast and can quickly catalogue the names of the program being stored on the disk. Using a simple language command, the computer would display these names on the CRT. The speed of the system would save precious minutes which, in turn, would allow for more computer time per pupil. Unfortunately, the cost of a DOS is approximately ten times the cost for a cassette recorder.

2. If a pupil's program does not run properly after repeated attempts to correct it, he must get assistance from his teacher. If the teacher is not available at that time, the student must save the program on tape or disk for a future time. If the student cannot get a copy of the program,

he will be unable to work on it at home or during a free period in school. This problem can be overcome with the purchase of a printer. Unfortunately, a good printer may cost nearly as much as the remainder of the entire computer system.

When developing a program in computer mathematics, is it cost-effective to purchase a disk operating system and a printer? The answer is a resounding *yes*. By adding these two pieces of equipment to your system you will be able to conduct your class program with fewer microprocessors.

Students should have access to the computers all day. This means that a room or an office housing the equipment must be available for student use. The school might have a laboratory or a supervisor's office used for this purpose. Once you increase the amount of time the computer is available for student use, you, in effect, decrease the need for more equipment. The computer should rarely be used for demonstration purposes during class time since this will prevent students from other computer classes having access to the machine. Laboratory periods should also be discouraged unless you have a computer for every two students.

With a computer system including a DOS and a printer, the course should become project oriented. That is, students are given a choice of several problems to solve, of varying difficulty, every two weeks. A completed project should include a description of the solution, including the algorithm used, a flowchart, program listing and sample output showing that the program handles all special cases associated with the problem. This is all possible because the printer will enable the student to spend more time debugging his program, so that each time he sits at the computer he has already spent a considerable amount of time correcting his previous errors. This, coupled with the speed of the DOS, will permit approximately 70 students to complete a project every two weeks on one complete system (i.e., microprocessor with DOS and printer).

What Should Be Taught?

Computer problems should be designed to reinforce, enrich, or extend ideas taught in the regular program. This section contains several expanded lesson ideas around a topic which appears in the junior high school curriculum or in algebra or geometry. It is designed to give you a feeling for how a course in computer mathematics could unfold.

On the Junior High School Level.

LESSON A   To develop a formula for finding the area of a triangle.

LESSON B To develop a computer solution to find the area of a triangle.

1. **PROBLEM:** Find the area, *A*, of a triangle given the lengths of the base, *b*, and height, *h*.

2. Elicit from the class the following analysis:

   ANALYSIS: In this problem we are to find the area of a triangle. We use the formula $A = \dfrac{b \cdot h}{2}$

3. Have class develop a plan. Review that developing a plan is to list the steps taken to use the formula $A = \dfrac{b \cdot h}{2}$ to find the area of a triangle.

   Plan: 1. Enter B,H

   2. $A = \dfrac{B*H}{2}$

   3. Print A

   4. End

4. Elicit from the class the following planned output:

   a. | FINDING THE AREA OF A TRIANGLE
   b. | ENTER THE BASE
      | ?10
   c. | ENTER THE HEIGHT
      | ?6
   d. | THE AREA IS 30

   a. stress the need for a title
   b. instructions to user
   c. instructions to user
   d. explanation of the result

5. Have class code the program.

THE PROGRAM

```
10 PRINT "FINDING THE AREA OF A
   TRIANGLE"
20 PRINT "ENTER THE BASE"
30 INPUT B
40 PRINT "ENTER THE HEIGHT"
50 INPUT H
60 A = B * H/2
70 PRINT "THE AREA IS", A
80 END
```

On the High School Level.

LESSON A: To review solving systems of equations in two variables. Students could be asked to solve equations such as

$$3x + 2y = 10$$
$$2x + 3y = 10$$

LESSON B: To develop a formula for the solution of a system of equations. Students could be led through the solution of

$$ax + by = c$$
$$dx + ey = f$$

Several systems that were solved in Lesson A could be solved using the new formula.

With a more gifted class, one might introduce a 2 x 2 determinant and then show Cramer's Rule.

LESSON C: To develop a flowchart and code a program for the solution of a system of equations.

1. The flowchart might look like the following:

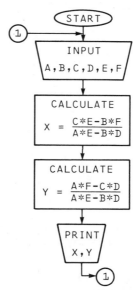

2. The program in BASIC (without any fancy print statements) would be:

```
10 INPUT A, B, C, D, E, F,
20 X = (C*E−B*F)/(A*E−B*D)
30 Y = (A*F−C*D)/(A*E−B*D)
40 PRINT X, Y
50 GOTO 10
60 END
```

LESSON D: To solve systems of equations graphically.

LESSON E: To discuss the possible intersections of linear graphs (intersect, parallel, and coincident).

LESSON F: To revise the flowchart and program to allow for coincident, parallel, and intersecting lines.

Students will see that if A*E − B*D = 0, then the lines will be parallel. If, in addition, C*E − B*F = 0 or A*F − C*D = 0, then the lines are coincident.

REVISED FLOWCHART

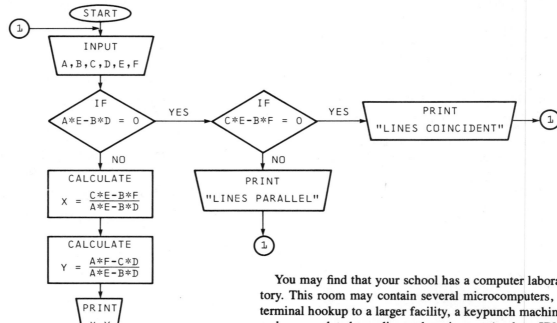

REVISED PROGRAM
```
10 INPUT A, B, C, D, E, F
20 If A*E−B*D=0 THEN GOTO 70
30 X = (C*E−B*F)/(A*E−B*D)
40 Y = (A*F−C*D)/(A*E−B*D)
50 PRINT X, Y
60 GOTO 10
70 IF C*E−B*F=0 THEN PRINT
     "LINES COINCIDENT": GOTO 10
80 PRINT "LINES PARALLEL": GOTO 10
90 END
```

Since computer programming is a necessary component of a modern mathematics curriculum, you may very likely find yourself teaching the subject early in your career. While BASIC is in common use because it is both a powerful language as well as a relatively simple one, some schools may have terminals or minicomputers that use other languages. PASCAL and BASIC are programming languages widely used in schools. FORTRAN, COBOL, RPG, and SPASM are other languages you may be asked to teach. Since many new teachers have at least some background in programming, they will probably not find it too difficult to use a standard text and brush up on the language their school uses. Fortunately, computer manufacturers usually supply reference manuals that explain any differences betweeen their version of the language and the standard version.

You may find that your school has a computer laboratory. This room may contain several microcomputers, a terminal hookup to a larger facility, a keypunch machine and some related supplies and equipment (such as IBM cards, cassettes, diskettes, card reader, and so on). You may even be asked to supervise this room at some time during the day in order to assist pupils who are using the facilities at that time.

Your teaching assignment may include an advanced computer techniques class where pupils will be involved with special computer projects. Typical projects might include:

Generating a Fibonacci sequence
Generating relatively prime pairs
Finding the prime factors of a number
Evaluating factorial n
Finding the area under a curve
Sum of series
Computing sales tax, discount, etc.

With a little creativity on your part, you can develop dozens of other projects.

There is a great deal of work involved in teaching such a course, such as checking each youngster's programs, helping them debug their programs and preparing lesson plans that will involve your own writing of programs—all very time-consuming tasks. But the satisfaction can be immense.

Remember, most of the classroom lessons will be developing mathematical ideas. The instructor must incorporate into the lessons the necessary programming concepts to enable the students to work on their projects and understand the lesson.

If you set up a project-oriented program, students may more readily accept having several classroom lessons to develop a mathematical topic that seems to be unrelated to programming, since *they* are always working on a computer project.

Usually at the beginning of a project-oriented course, students tend to wait for the last day to begin working on a project. This should not come as a surprise, since many of us may have been guilty of this same procrastination. Thus, the teacher must continually remind students to begin a new project the day they complete an earlier one. What can easily happen is that the day before a due date there can be long lines of students waiting to run projects on the computer. Students may ask to "skip a class" in order to run their programs. This should *not* be allowed since every class session is important, as it is the only time new material is presented. Students simply must learn to better organize their time. Most students follow the teacher's advice and have no trouble completing projects. However, if there are several classes using the same equipment, the teachers might stagger the due dates for a more balanced use of "hands-on-time" on the equipment. It might also be helpful to impose a "log-on-sheet" two days before projects are due. Students can be given fifteen minutes each on the computer to provide "hands-on" time for more students.

A Computer Component in a Regular Mathematics Class

Students who have taken an elective course in computer mathematics are ready to transfer this learning to their mathematics classes. Teachers of most mathematics courses could assign computer projects for extra-credit assignments. This might encourage other students to take advantage of the elective course offerings, so they too can work on computer projects. But it is possible to make the computer an integral part of a regular secondary school mathematics course.

The Computer as a Part of an Academic Mathematics Class

To incorporate the computer into an academic mathematics class, it would be necessary to either accelerate or delete approximately one week of the regular course material. This would provide enough time to teach the introductory skills necessary for writing programs in BASIC. The time taken for this would not be too harmful to the regular course work since the computer language would be developed relative to mathematics topics from the particular curriculum being studied.

Only a few programming concepts are needed to begin solving problems in mathematics. The INPUT, PRINT, IF-THEN and GOTO statements of the BASIC language are sufficient to solve many mathematics problems. But how could these statements be introduced in the secondary school mathematics curriculum? Use as an illustration the following method of introducing the concept of flowcharting and the computer statements above in the context of an elementary algebra class.

EXAMPLE: After solving equations of the form $ax + b = c$, students can be taught how to generalize the solution. Such generalizations are part of the curriculum and usually come under the title of *literal equations*. Once a student has solved the equations for x in terms of a, b and c, an algorithm has been developed for a computer solution to all linear equations of this form. Here we have a vehicle to introduce students to computer programming. Follow these five steps:

1. Flowcharting is shown as a means for planning computer solutions.

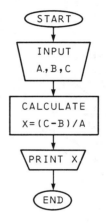

2. The program in BASIC is:
   10 INPUT A, B, C
   20 X = (C-B)/A
   30 PRINT X
   40 END

3. Instead of having the program end we can have it start again, which introduces the GOTO statement.

FLOWCHART (First Revision)

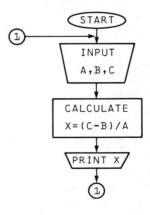

PROGRAM (First Revision)
10 INPUT A, B, C

```
20 X = (C-B)/A
30 PRINT X
40 GOTO 10
50 END
```

4. What happens if $A = 0$? Students should realize that we cannot divide by zero. Therefore an error would result. The IF-THEN statement could be introduced to avoid this problem.

FLOWCHART (Second Revision)

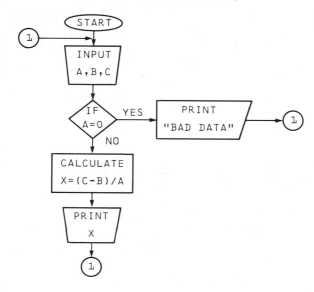

PROGRAM (Second Revision)

```
10 INPUT A, B, C
20 IF A = 0 THEN PRINT "BAD DATA":
   GOTO 10
30 X = (C-B)/A
40 PRINT X
50 GOTO 10
60 END
```

5. Time can be spent on how to make the output more readable by using the Print Statement with quotation marks.

This same procedure could be used in other courses, such as geometry or second year algebra.

If you are going to introduce a computer component in all mathematics classes, you must consider the availability of equipment. It might be wise to introduce the computer in each class at a different point in the curriculum. This will help alleviate the overcrowding that might occur around the computers.

This scheme for introducing programming as an integrated part of the school curriculum allows students to develop a better understanding of mathematics. This usually results from the special analysis required in writing a computer program. Whether through part of regular mathematics courses or as elective courses, programming concepts should be developed within the context of secondary school mathematics. Although you may not be specifically training computer programmers, students will be knowledgeable about developing algorithms for computer solutions, which is one of the highest levels in the computer programming process.

A Source for Boundless Creativity

Once the more gifted (or the more motivated) students become reasonably familiar with computer programming, the computer can serve as a source for boundless creativity. There are almost no limits to what students will do with a computer. They may develop games (which they will certainly use), try to continuously improve earlier programs, derive numerical relationships, generate special numbers (such as amicable numbers, or Pythagorean triples), or simply attempt to solve problems (some teacher-generated, some self-composed, and even some classical problems). Remember, the famous Four-Color Map Problem was recently "solved" by computer!

Computers should be available for use by students who are not part of a special course without infringing on the time set aside for students assigned to the computer as part of their coursework. With the constant decrease in microcomputer prices, schools should increasingly be more able to provide an adequate supply of computers for student use.

SUMMARY

Both technologically and educationally, the minicalculator has come a long way. As valuable a resource as it can be, it also can be harmful. Judgment must always be used when introducing a calculator in the classroom. It should not be used by a student to avoid learning computational algorithms, but on the other hand, the novelty of this device can greatly motivate a student struggling to improve his computational skills by giving him an immediate (and private) check of his work.

Computers are an increasingly valuable aid in mathematics education. Whether they are used for remediation, recreation, or as an integral part of the curriculum, they can greatly expand a student's knowledge of and perspective on mathematics. Teachers will probably find them increasingly more available. Therefore, they will need more knowledge of computer workings and uses in order to make the mathematics of the future relevant to their students.

EXERCISES

1. Develop a plan for using a class set of minicalculators in a high school remedial arithmetic class of 25 students.

2. Suppose you were assigned to teach a tenth grade remedial mathematics class and you are told you will have 20 students and will have available 10 minicalculators and 5 Monroe *Classmate-88* machines. Devise a plan for conducting this class, making full use of the equipment provided.

3. Provide four illustrations of how you would assign calculator-oriented projects to each of the following:
   a. An average seventh grade class
   b. A gifted eighth grade class (this may or may not be an elementary algebra class—you specify)
   c. An average-ability ninth grade algebra class
   d. A gifted second year algebra class

4. Give two examples of how a minicalculator might be used to improve a student's understanding of a mathematical concept. (Choose any secondary school grade for your response.)

5. Prepare three applications of the secondary school mathematics curriculum for which the calculator can be used to an appreciable advantage.

6. Develop three activities for the calculator which will enable the student to discover some mathematical phenomenon (or curiosity).

7. Identify five topics in the secondary school mathematics curriculum whose study can be significantly enhanced by the incorporation of minicalculators in the classroom.

8. Suppose you were asked by your supervisor to prepare a plan (and a budget) for incorporating computers into your regular high school instruction. Write a plan and provide a budget indicating *specific* equipment to be purchased.

9. Explain how you might use a computer to establish a mathematics remediation center in your school. Give specifics about equipment and software to be purchased and/or developed. Staffing considerations also should be addressed. (Specify the grade level used in your response.)

10. Suppose your supervisor informs you that the school has acquired a microcomputer for your classroom. Assume it has a DOS and printer. Explain how you would use this new equipment to supplement (or perhaps reinforce) your regular instruction. (Select any secondary school mathematics course for your response.)

11. Explain how you might use a microcomputer to provide recreational mathematics for your classes. Assume one such unit with DOS and printer is available.

12. Select five topics in the secondary school mathematics curriculum which would be greatly enhanced by having a computer available to the students. Specify in your response *how* the computer would be used for these topics.

SUGGESTED READINGS

Elgarten, G., and Posamentier, A.S. *Using Computers: Programming and Problem Solving.* Menlo Park, Ca.: Addison-Wesley Publishing Co., 1984.

Elgarten, G.; Posamentier, A.S.; and Moresh, S. *Using Computers in Mathematics.* 2nd ed. Menlo Park, Ca.: Addison-Wesley Publishing Co., 1986.

ADDITIONAL READINGS

Bitter, Gary G., and Mikesell, Jerald L. *Activities Handbook for Teaching with the Hand-held Calculator.* Boston: Allyn and Bacon, 1980.

Chin, William G.; Dean, Richard A.; and Tracewell, Theodore N. *Arithmetic and Calculators.* San Francisco: W.H. Freeman, 1978.

Kieren, Thomas E. "Computer Programming for The Mathematics Laboratory." *The Mathematics Teacher* 66 (1973): 9.

Maor, Eli. "The Pocket Calculator as a Teaching Aid." *The Mathematics Teacher* 69 (1976): 471.

The Mathematics Teacher 71 (May 1978). Special Issue—Computers and Calculators.

The Mathematics Teacher 74 (November 1981). Special Issue—Microcomputers.

CHAPTER 11
ENRICHING MATHEMATICS INSTRUCTION

A quick review of many of the books on methods of teaching mathematics in secondary school reveals that almost all consider enrichment as an activity reserved only for gifted students. We shall make a radical departure from this point of view: It is our strong belief that enrichment activities in mathematics should be provided for students at *all* levels of ability. Naturally, the activities will differ for the various ability levels. Careful selection and proper presentation are paramount in the ultimate success of such activities.

Enrichment is generally defined as "that which provides greater value or importance to something." Mathematics can be enriched in numerous ways, each applicable at the various grade levels and with many forms of presentation. In this chapter we shall explore briefly how the enrichment of mathematics can be carried out for each of the three basic levels of ability generally found in the secondary schools.

Before discussing enrichment at the various levels of ability, we shall consider the role of the history of mathematics in putting some "life" into the overall mathematics instructional process.

ENRICHING MATHEMATICS INSTRUCTION WITH AN HISTORICAL APPROACH

It is a popular myth that a mathematics class is lifeless and dull. Unfortunately, that myth is too often true—though it need not be so! We frequently find ourselves concentrating on the teaching of mathematics in order to reach a deadline such as giving a test or completing a course of study. The luxury of teaching what mathematics is all about seems to be beyond our grasp. But is it really? We can easily teach where mathematics comes from, who first thought of it, and who later developed and refined it. In short, we can use the history of the subject, including the lives, loves, successes, and failures of the people who created it to breathe life into what might otherwise be a golem. There are times when history should be integrated into the subject matter in a light and lively way.

The sections that follow provide a small sample of how such integration might be accomplished for certain topics in secondary school mathematics. A carefully selected bibliography appears at the end of the chapter and it is through the study of these materials that you will develop the background needed to use the "historical" approach when teaching mathematics.

Geometry: In the Beginning

The original development of geometry in Egypt and Babylonia was a result of the desire of priests to construct temples and of kings to survey land for tax purposes. The techniques were crude and intuitive, but sufficiently accurate for the needs. We have evidence of some of these techniques in the Ahmes Papyrus, which was written about 1650 B.C. and discovered in the nineteenth century. Portions of it are preserved in museums in London and New York. The papyrus contains formulas to calculate areas of rectangles, right triangles, trapezoids that have one leg perpendicular to the bases, and to approximate the area of a circle. The Egyptians apparently developed these formulas from their experience with area of land.

The first mathematician who appeared to be dissatisfied with methods based solely on experience was Thales (c.640–546 B.C.). We honor him today as the man who always said, "Prove it!" And he frequently did. Among the better known theorems first proved by Thales are:

> the base angles of an isosceles triangle are
> congruent
> vertical angles are congruent
> an angle inscribed in a semi-circle is a right angle

Pythagoras (c.582–507 B.C.) and his followers, the Order of the Pythagoreans, followed in the footsteps of Thales. They used his method of proof to develop not only the Pythagorean Theorem, but also theorems con-

cerning the sum of the angles of a polygon, the properties of parallel lines, the five regular solids, and incommensurable quantities.

It was Thales' work, however, that marked the beginning of an era of mathematical development in which deductive proof became the accepted method of logical reasoning. This method is used to derive theorems from postulates and, in this way, to develop a system of logically arranged statements. This era had its apex with Euclid's *Elements*, three hundred years after Thales.

In the *Elements*, Euclid unified the work of the scholars who had preceded him by presenting all the mathematics known in his day in a systematic manner—a truly stupendous achievement. Much of his work was also original, for by means of the deductive method he demonstrated the vast amount of knowledge that can be acquired through reasoning alone. Euclid included algebra and number theory as well as geometry in his writings.

The *Elements* turned out to be a work of major importance in the history of the civilized world. In later years it was translated from Greek to Arabic (c.800) and from Arabic to Latin (c.1120). The first printed edition appeared in Latin (1482) and many other editions followed. Next to the Bible, the *Elements* has been in more editions and in more languages than any other book.

The original work was written in thirteen separate parchment scrolls, or "books." The fifth theorem in Book I is the familiar: Base angles of an isosceles triangle are congruent. ("Isosceles" is derived from the Greek words "isos," meaning equal, and "skelos," meaning legs.) The method now most frequently used to prove this theorem requires the construction of an angle bisector through the vertex angle. This process has been disputed by "purists," since it prematurely introduced the angle bisector. Euclid, however, demonstrated it differently. A sketch of his proof follows:

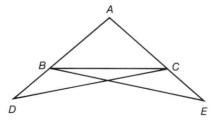

Given $\triangle ABC$ with $\overline{AB} \cong \overline{AC}$. Extend $\overline{AB}$ and $\overline{AC}$ through B and C, respectively, to points D and E, so that $\overline{BD} \cong \overline{CE}$. Therefore, $\triangle ADC \cong \triangle ABE$ so that $\angle D \cong \angle E$ and $\overline{DC} \cong \overline{BE}$. Then $\triangle BDC \cong \triangle BCE$, so that $\angle DBC \cong \angle ECB$. Therefore, $\angle ABC \cong \angle ACB$.   Q.E.D.[1]

---

[1]Q.E.D. is an abbreviation for "quod erat demonstrandum," which means "that which was to be demonstrated." It is sometimes written after the conclusion of a proof in mathematics.

The theorem just proved was known as the "pons asinorum," or "bridge of asses (fools)" in the Middle Ages. The implication was that certain students had difficulty "crossing" this bridge in order to proceed further in their study of geometry. Euclid proved the converse of this theorem by the indirect method (reductio ad absurdum.):

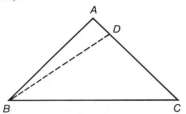

Given $\triangle ABC$, where $\angle B \cong \angle C$. If $\overline{AB} \not\cong \overline{AC}$, then assume $AC > AB$. Mark off point D in $\overline{AC}$ such that $\overline{DC} \cong \overline{AB}$. Then $\triangle DCB \cong \triangle ABC$. This is impossible, so $\overline{AB} \cong \overline{AC}$.

Throughout the course of history, but especially during the last four centuries, Euclid's *Elements* has endured unimaginable "torture." It has been simplified, complicated, projected, distorted, deformed, and sometimes changed beyond recognition. The result?—analytic geometry, projective geometry, topology, non-Euclidean geometry, logic, and even calculus and modern theoretical physics. The end is not yet in sight!

Constructions: Compasses and Straightedge

Whenever constructions are required in geometry, the tools to be used, unless otherwise noted, consist of the ordinary compasses[1] and an unmarked straightedge only. The justification for the employment of these instruments rests on the following three postulates mentioned at the beginning of Euclid's *Elements:*

"Let it be granted

1. That a straight line may be drawn from any one point to any other point; [straightedge]
2. That a line segment may be extended to any length along a straight line; [straightedge]
3. That a circle may be drawn from any center at any distance from that center; [compasses]."

Euclid worked with rather crude collapsible compasses. The ones we use today can only be used with the preceding postulates, and they have the advantage of making the constructions somewhat simpler than they were for Euclid.

Is it possible to perform the familiar constructions of Euclidean geometry with compasses alone? In 1797,

---

[1]The word "compasses" is a plural noun, as are the words "pants" and "scissors," because each has two branches. Although the word "compass" is often used to denote "compasses," a compass is, strictly speaking, an instrument for determining direction.

Lorenzo Mascheroni, an Italian mathematician, wrote *The Geometry of Compasses,* in which he proved that all construction problems that can be solved by the use of straightedge and compasses can be solved by compasses alone.[1] These are known as *Mascheroni Constructions.*

Here is an example of a simple Mascheroni construction:

Given a line segment $\overline{AB}$. Determine with compasses alone the midpoint, M, of $\overline{AB}$.

The following sequence of diagrams utilizes the popular compasses of today and demonstrates the solution to the problem just posed.

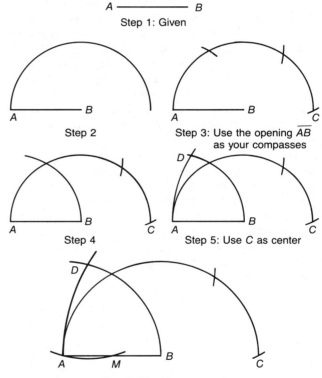

Step 1: Given

Step 2

Step 3: Use the opening $\overline{AB}$ as your compasses

Step 4

Step 5: Use C as center

Step 6: Use D as center; M is the midpoint

Here is an outline of the proof that the construction is correct.

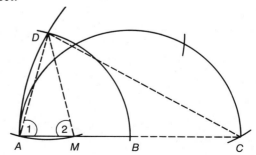

---

[1]For a proof that the straightedge alone can replace the straightedge and compasses see *Geometric Constructions,*by A.S. Posamentier and W. Wernick. (Portland, Maine: J. Weston Walch, 1973.)

Draw the construction lines as indicated. Note that $\overleftrightarrow{ABC}$ is a straight line.

1. Since $\triangle ACD$ is isosceles, $\angle CDA \cong \angle 1$
2. Since $\triangle DAM$ is isosceles, $\angle 1 \cong \angle 2$
3. Therefore, $\triangle ACD \sim \triangle DAM$
4. Therefore, $\dfrac{AM}{AD} = \dfrac{AD}{AC}$ or $AM = \dfrac{(AD)^2}{AC}$
5. But $AD = AB$ and $AC = 2(AB)$
6. Therefore, $AM = \dfrac{(AB)^2}{2(AB)}$ or $AM = \dfrac{AB}{2}$

Bisecting a line segment or an angle with compasses and straightedge is a simple matter. Trisecting a line segment is a bit more complicated but clearly possible. Early Greek geometers must have been quite puzzled when they were unsuccessful in all attempts to trisect an angle with straightedge and compasses alone. (We are speaking here of a general angle, not the special ones like right angles, which can be trisected by constructing a 60 degree angle and then a 30 degree angle.)

One of the most productive techniques in mathematics is that of changing the regulations under which you operate, if these regulations tie your hands. Thus, if the restriction to use traditional construction tools leads to failure in seeking a solution for the trisection problem, perhaps other tools will do the trick. This means, of course, that Euclid's construction postulates must be altered.

Archimedes suggested that he could trisect an angle with compasses and a straightedge that had only two marks on it. Here is a description of Archimedes' construction. The proof follows.

Let the distance between the markings be d

Step 1: Given

Step 2

Step 3

Step 4

Step 5:
$x = \dfrac{1}{3}\, m \angle m$ can be copied by ordinary construction methods into $\angle m$

PROOF:

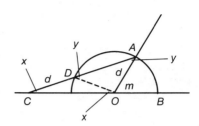

1. $\overline{OD}$ is drawn. $OD = d$.
2. Isosceles $\triangle DCO$ has congruent base angles. Isosceles $\triangle ADO$ has congruent base angles.
3. In $\triangle DCO$, $y = x + x = 2x$
4. In $\triangle ACO$, $m = y + x$.
5. Therefore, $m = 2x + x$ or $x = \dfrac{m}{3}$

This construction was made possible because the rules of the game (the postulates) were changed. Other mathematicians in ancient as well as modern times have changed the rules even more dramatically and have produced ingenious and elegant procedures for trisecting an angle.

The French mathematician Blaise Pascal invented an unusual instrument to trisect an angle. Here the rods represented by $\overline{PQ}$, $\overline{QO}$, and $\overline{OR}$ are equal in length. Q and O are moveable pivots, and R moves along the slot.

You can easily prove that:

$$x = \frac{1}{3}\, m \,\angle AOB$$

Still other constructions baffled the Greeks and later mathematicians for more than 2000 years. One of these, "squaring the circle," requires the construction of a square whose area is equal to that of a given circle. Another, "duplication of the cube" (doubling the volume), requires the construction of a cube whose volume is to be twice that of a given cube. These, like the trisection problem, were proved only in modern times to be capable of construction with compasses and straightedge alone.[1]

Other construction also eluded the capabilities of the best mathematicians for centuries. While certain polygons could be constructed with ease, using the traditional tools of geometry, others such as the regular seven-sided polygon (heptagon, or 7-gon) or regular 17-gon seemed to be beyond their reach. In 1796, a nineteen-year-old youth, Carl Friedrich Gauss, proved that it was possible to construct a regular seventeen-sided polygon with compasses and straightedge only and that certain others, such as the regular 7-gon, could not.

What Gauss proved is that a regular polygon with an odd number of sides can be constructed, if either of the following two conditions is satisfied:

CONDITION 1 The number of sides is equal to $2^{2^n} + 1$, where n is a whole number and $2^{2^n} + 1$, is a prime number; an example can be found in the following chart.

n	$2^{2^n} + 1$	Can a Polygon be Constructed?	Number of Sides
0	3	Yes	3
1	5	Yes	5
2	17	Yes	17
3	257	Yes	257
4	65537	Yes	65537
5	Not prime	No	—

CONDITION 2 The number of sides is the product of two or more different numbers obtained in Condition 1. (You can construct a regular polygon of, say, fifteen sides, because 15 = 5 × 3, and 5 and 3 are numbers derived from the rule in Condition 1.)

The discovery of this remarkable theorem convinced Gauss to enter into the field of mathematics for his life's work, instead of linguistics, in which he also excelled. A monument erected to him in Brunswick, Germany, at the place of his birth consists merely of a regular 17-gon, the symbol of his great achievement.

[1] For a proof of the impossibility of the angle trisection see *Geometry: Its Elements and Structure* by A.S. Posamentier, J.H. Banks, and R. Bannister. (New York: McGraw-Hill, 1977)

Practical Trigonometry: The Original Sin

Although Euclid showed in his *Elements* that two triangles which agree with respect to two sides and an included angle are congruent (*SAS*), in other words, that the size of the triangle is fixed when the measures, *S*, *A*, and *S* are given in that order, he did not indicate any particular concern about finding the specific measures of the remaining three parts of the triangles. Similarly for *ASA* and *SSS*. The Greek mathematician-philosophers of Euclid's day did not consider "practical" or "applied" geometry to be worthy of any serious consideration. This view slowed the development of that branch of mathematics known as trigonometry.[1]

Regardless of popular opinion against any serious study of the subject, trigonometry managed to get itself born among the Greeks. Its inventor, Hipparchus (c.140 B.C.), developed the need for triangle measurements in connection with his work in astronomy, and he developed techniques for determining the measures of the dimensions of a fixed triangle. Menelaus (c.100 A.D.) also contributed knowledge to this field by developing "spherical trigonometry," the measurement of triangles on a spherical surface, which he needed in connection with his work in astronomy. However, it remained for Ptolemy (c.150 A.D.), the great astronomer and mathematician who lived in Alexandria, to produce the first major contribution in the field of trigonometry (also in connection with astronomy) in his book *The Almagest*. In this work, whose title means "the greatest," the first extensive trigonometry tables appeared.

Trigonometry remained a servant of astronomy until 1464 when the German mathematician Johann Müller (also known as Regiomontanus) wrote a book that treated trigonometry as a purely mathematical subject, an outgrowth of geometry, which stood on its own merits. Today it is an important tool in mathematics because the nature of the trigonometry functions is such that it is appropriate for use in analyzing physical phenomena which occur with periodic regularity, such as electricity, music, and light.

We say that "a triangle is solved," when the measures of its six dimensions (three angles and three sides) have been determined. The four major tools used to solve triangles are

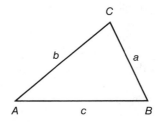

[1] Trigonometry is derived from the Greek words "trigonon," meaning triangle, and "metria," meaning measurement.

1. The Pythagorean Theorem
2. The sum of the angles of a triangle is 180 degrees
3. The law of sines:
   For any triangle ABC,
   $$\frac{a}{\sin A} = \frac{b}{\sin B} = \frac{c}{\sin C}$$
4. The law of cosines:
   For any triangle ABC,
   $$c^2 = a^2 + b^2 - 2ab \cos C$$
   or $\quad b^2 = a^2 + c^2 - 2ac \cos B$
   or $\quad a^2 = b^2 + c^2 - 2bc \cos A$

The trigonometry tables we now use to solve triangles had, as their forerunner, a table invented by Ptolemy. We now present a general idea of how the trigonometry table was developed by Ptolemy, except that we will use modern notation and symbols. (Ptolemy used the sexigesimal, base 60, number system.) First, some background material.

I Trig functions may be represented as line segments:

In a unit circle, O,

$$\sin x = \frac{AD}{OD}, \cos x = \frac{OA}{OD}, \tan x = \frac{BC}{OB}$$

Since $OD = OB = 1$, then
$$AD = \sin x$$
$$OA = \cos x$$
$$BC = \tan x$$

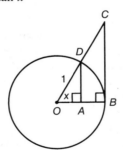

II Derivation of the word "sine": The segment AD in the diagram is a "half-chord" known as a "jiva" in Sanskrit. This word was first found in Hindu writings in the year 510. Translators mistakenly wrote this as "jaiv" in Arabic, meaning "pocket" or "cavity." This was eventually translated into the Latin word for "cavity"—"sinus." Thus the half-chord, "jiva," became "sine," or "sin" in abbreviated form.

III Certain formulas used to develop the trigonometry table appeared in the *Almagest*. Several of these are listed as follows

1. $\sin^2 x + \cos^2 x = 1$
2. $\sin (x - y) = \sin x \cos y - \cos x \sin y$
3. $\sin (x + y) = \sin x \cos y + \cos x \sin y$
4. $\sin 2x = 2\sin x \cos x$
5. $\sin \frac{1}{2} x = \sqrt{\dfrac{1 - \cos x}{2}}$
6. $\tan x = \dfrac{\sin x}{\cos x}$

The sixth formula, for tan x, was used by the Arab mathematician el-Hasib in the year 860 to produce the first table of tangents. (Derivations of these formulas can be found in any standard trigonometry textbook.)

IV Ptolemy computed a table of lengths of chords for arcs from 0° to 180° in steps of one-half degree, in a circle whose radius equals 60 units. Thus, his table gives the value of chord $\overline{ED}$, which cuts off an arc of $x°$, for $0 < x° < 180°$.

Part of the table, translated into notation we can follow easily, is reproduced below. The lengths of the chords are stated in sexigesimal notation. For example, 2, 5, 40 in sexigesimal become

$$2 + \frac{5}{60} + \frac{40}{60^2} = .0350 \text{ in decimal.}$$

Arcs	Chords
½°	0, 31, 25
1°	1, 21, 50
1½°	1, 34, 15
2°	2, 5, 40
2½°	2, 37, 4
3°	3, 8, 28
3½°	3, 39, 52

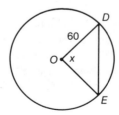

Modern trigonometry tables give the length of the half-chord AD ($= \sin y$) for the corresponding angle $2y$ in the circle of unit radius.

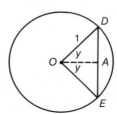

Thus, if you look up the value of sin 45° in your trigonometry table, you will find it to be .7071, whereas the corresponding notation in Ptolemy's table, after appropriate conversions, will tell you that an arc of 90° cuts off a chord of length 1.4142. In this way one can convert from Ptolemy's table of chords to the "modern" sine function.

The cosine and tangent can then be computed from the formulas

$$\sin^2 x + \cos^2 x = 1 \quad \text{and} \quad \tan x = \frac{\sin x}{\cos x}$$

The following is an outline of a proof known as Ptolemy's Theorem, from which he derived many of the formulas he needed to construct tables such as sin $(x - y)$ and sin $(x + y)$.

> **THEOREM:** If *ABCD* is a quadrilateral inscribed in a circle, then the sum of the products of the opposite sides equals the product of the diagonals.

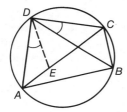

GIVEN: Quad. *ABCD* inscribed in a circle; diagonals $\overline{AC}$ and $\overline{BD}$.

PROVE: $AB \times CD + BC \times AD = DB \times AC$

1. Construct $\angle ADE \cong \angle BDC$
2. $\angle CDE \cong \angle ADB$
3. $\angle ACD \cong \angle ABD$
4. $\therefore \triangle ADB \sim \triangle CDE$
5. $\therefore \dfrac{CD}{DB} = \dfrac{CE}{AB}$ or $AB \times CD = CE \times DB$
6. Show that $\triangle ADE \sim \triangle CDB$
7. $\therefore \dfrac{AD}{DB} = \dfrac{AE}{BC}$ or $BC \times AD = DB \times AE$
8. From steps 5 and 7:

$$AB \times CD + BC \times AD = CE \times DB + DB \times AE$$
$$= DB(CE + AE)$$
$$= DB \times AC \qquad \text{Q.E.D.}$$

EXERCISE: Use Ptolemy's Theorem to derive the formula

$$\sin (x - y) = \sin x \cos y - \cos x \sin y$$

An outline of the proof is as follows

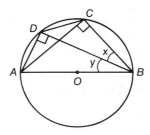

In a circle of unit diameter *AB*,
1. $AB \times CD + BC \times AD = DB \times AC$
2. In right $\triangle BDA$, $AD = \sin y$ and $DB = \cos y$
3. In right $\triangle BCA$, $BC = \cos x$ and $AC = \sin x$
4. In $\triangle DCB$, $\dfrac{CD}{\sin (x-y)} = \dfrac{BC}{\sin \angle CDB}$
5. But since $\angle CDB = \angle CAB$, then

$$\sin \angle CDB = \sin \angle CAB = \frac{BC}{AB} = \frac{BC}{1} = BC$$

6. From steps 4 and 5, $\dfrac{CD}{\sin (x - y)} = \dfrac{BC}{BC} = 1$
   or $CD = \sin (x - y)$
7. Now verify, by substituting the results of steps 2–6 into step 1, that sin $(x - y) = \sin x \cos y - \cos x \sin y$. \qquad Q.E.D.

EXERCISE: Use this diagram and Ptolemy's Theorem to derive the formula

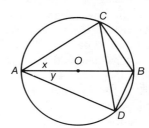

$$\sin (x + y) = \sin x \cos y + \cos x \sin y$$

Most of the material needed to solve a triangle was developed prior to the year 1600. Further refinements came about as a result of work with logarithms and calculus.

DeMoivre's Theorem (c.1722) demonstrated a relationship between the trig functions and the imaginary *i* in the formula

$$(\cos A + i \sin A)^n = \cos nA + i \sin nA$$

By the end of the 17th century the infinite series for sin *x* and cos *x* were known.

$$\sin x = x - \frac{x^3}{3!} + \frac{x^5}{5!} - \frac{x^7}{7!} + \ldots$$

$$\cos x = 1 - \frac{x^2}{2!} + \frac{x^4}{4!} - \frac{x^6}{6!} + \ldots$$

So, while trigonometry began as a tool to solve triangles in geometry, it is thought of today as a periodic relationship of complex numbers—quite different from its "practical" beginnings.

Algebra: Mathematical Shorthand

The algebra that is traditionally taught to our secondary school pupils came about as a result of independent developments by mathematicians of ancient Greece as well as those of the Hindu and Arab worlds.

The treatment of algebra by the Greeks was geometric. A large portion of Euclid's *Elements* is in fact devoted to finding solutions, geometrically, to what we call today "algebraic" equations. An illustration of this is shown on the bottom of this page.

Thus, what we write as

$$(a + b)^2 = a^2 + 2ab + b^2$$

was thought of by the Greeks in terms of this diagram:

$$a + b$$

ab	b²
a²	ab

$$a + b$$

Much of the algebraic knowledge of the Greeks was brought together by Diophantus (c.275), a prominent mathematician whose work on integral solutions to certain types of equations is still studied today. Incidentally, the first woman mathematician we hear of in ancient times is Hypatia (c.410), who wrote commentaries on the work of Diophantus.

In another part of the world, Hindu mathematicians were also concerned with methods for solving equations, especially the quadratic. One of their more interesting contributions to the subject is that they enjoyed posing problems in a colorful way. Here is one example: (Many more can be found in books on the history of algebra that are listed in the bibliography at the end of this section.) "Of a collection of mango fruits, the king took ⅙, the queen took ⅕ of the remainder, and the three chief princes took ¼, ⅓, and ½ of that same remainder, and the youngest child took the remaining 3 mangoes. Oh, you who are clever in problems on fractions, give out the number of mangoes in that collection."

Arab writers dominated the scene of algebraists in ancient times for many centuries. The greatest Arab writer on algebra was Mohammed ibn Musa al-Khowarizmi (c.825) from whose book *Al-Jabr W'al Mukabala* the name "algebra" is derived. His major contribution was the introduction of the use of algorithms as a mathematical tool. Incidentally, the word "algorithm" is derived from the name "al-Khowarizmi."

Al-Khowarizmi's work became known in Europe in the twelfth century. By the sixteenth century, the symbols we now use in algebra had already been, for the most part, slowly and painstakingly developed. Here are two examples of how equations were written in the years indicated. Just imagine how cumbersome they were to work with. (The modern notation is given in parentheses.)

1545: cubus p 6 rebus aequalis 20. ($x^3 + 6x = 20$)
1631: $xxx - 3bbx = 2ccc$. ($x^3 + 3b^2x = 2c^3$)

The "=" sign was first introduced by Robert Recorde in his book *The Whetstone of Witte* in 1557.

In 1637, Renee Descartes introduced the exponent notation that we take for granted today.

Quadratic equations and their solutions played a special role in the history of algebra. The Babylonians first solved certain forms of quadratic equations 3600 years ago, as found in tablets that are now in a collection, YBC 6967, at Yale University. A translation of the problem on these tablets is equivalent to "Find the dimensions of a rectangle whose length exceeds its width by 7, and whose area is 60." The Babylonian solution uses no algebraic notation but serves as a prototype for similar problems. Thus, the solution to the Babylonian quadratic

$$x^2 + px = q, \, q > 0$$

is shown in the tablet to be

$$x = \sqrt{\left(\frac{f}{2}\right)^2 + q} - \frac{p}{2}$$

So that for y = length and x = width, the equations $y = x + 7$ and $xy = 60$ reduce, after appropriate substitution, to the Babylonian type $x^2 + 7x = 60$. Thus the solution to the problem posed is

$$x = \sqrt{\left(\frac{7}{2}\right)^2 + 60} - \frac{7}{2} = 5$$

Compare this solution with the quadratic formula solution used today.

Another famous quadratic is solved geometrically by Euclid in propostion 11, Book 2 of *Elements*:

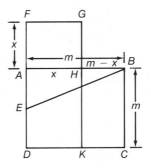

PROPOSITION: To divide a given straight line into two segments such that the rectangle contained by the whole line and one of its segments is equal to the square on the remaining segment; [i.e., to divide a line ($AB = m$) into two parts x and $m - x$, such that $m(m - x) = x^2$.]

SOLUTION:

1. On $\overline{AB}$ construct a square $ABCD$
2. Bisect $\overline{AD}$ at E and draw $\overline{EB}$
3. Extend $\overline{AD}$ through A to F so that $\overline{EF} \cong \overline{EB}$
4. On $\overline{AF}$ construct a square, $AFGH$
5. Extend $\overline{GH}$ to intersect $\overline{DC}$ at K
6. Therefore rectangle $HBCK$ equals, in area, the square $AHGF$

Here is the proof:

1. $\overline{AE} \cong \overline{ED}$ (because E is a midpoint)
2. Area of rectangle $FGKD =$ $(EF + ED) (EF - ED)$
3. Area of rectangle $FGKD = EF^2 - ED^2$
4. Area of rectangle $FGKD = EF^2 - AE^2$
5. $\therefore FGKD + AE^2 = EF^2$
6. $AB^2 + AE^2 = EB^2 = EF^2$ (because $EF = EB$ and AEB is a right triangle)
7. $\therefore AB^2 + AE^2 = FGKD + AE^2$ or $AB^2 = FGKD$
8. $\therefore AH^2 = HBCK$ (by subtracting $AHKD$ from both sides) Q.E.D.

What Euclid did here, translated into algebraic symbolism, is show how to divide the given line segment AB into segments x and $m - x$ such that $m (m - x) = x^2$, and segment AH, or x, is the required number. We now know by the quadratic formula that

$$x = \frac{m (\sqrt{5} - 1)}{2}$$

Those who delve beyond secondary school mathematics know of the powerful tool that algebra has become to solve problems of immense proportions via group theory and linear algebra.

We shall now consider the role of enrichment at each of the various ability levels.

ENRICHMENT TECHNIQUES FOR ALL ABILITY LEVELS

THE SLOW LEARNER

Relevant Applications of Mathematics

Whether or not the slow learner is in a remedial program, an opportunity always exists for the teacher to enrich the instruction. This enrichment is usually seen as a brief departure from the prescribed curriculum. Realistic and relevant *applications* of the mathematics being studied generally can provide an excellent source for enrichment. The following are some examples of enrichment at this level:

TOPIC: Addition and multiplication of fractions
ENRICHMENT: Computing simple probabilities after developing some class-made probability games (e.g., selecting cards from a deck, tossing a coin or die). The teacher's creativity is very important in making this a success.

TOPIC: Percents
ENRICHMENT: Computation of and verification of newspaper advertisements involving percents (e.g., sales, bank advertisements). Handled properly, these investigations can be both motivating and revealing. Some astonishing results often can appear.

TOPIC: Using formulas
ENRICHMENT: Have students compute the areas of real floor plans, or compute bank interest, or compute the volume of real, but irregular, shapes. When possible, these computations should take place in a realistic setting so as to take on more meaning for the students.

TOPIC: Reading tables
ENRICHMENT: Provide students with realistic problems using mileage charts, postal rate schedules, telephone rate schedules, bus schedules, income tax schedules, etc. Where possible, these should relate to local situations.

TOPIC: Basic concepts of geometry
ENRICHMENT: Direct and indirect measurement of local structures. Students should then be asked to compute areas, volume, etc. from the data gathered.

The examples above are by no means exhaustive, but are merely selected as representative of the kind of enrichment through applications which might be used with a class of slow learners (often found in a remedial setting).

Recreational Mathematics

Another form of enrichment for the weaker mathematics student is *recreational mathematics*. Anything "recreational" is generally of interest to students. Therefore, mathematics topics being studied can be reinforced enthusiastically under the guise of recreation.

TOPIC: Reducing fractions

ENRICHMENT: Introduce some divisibility rules for easier recognition of common factors. (see Enrichment Unit 84).

TOPIC: Practice with addition
ENRICHMENT: Magic squares of various kinds (see Enrichment Units 1 and 2) can be used to reinforce addition facts through an unusual drill.

TOPIC: Miscellaneous computational drill
ENRICHMENT: Various games and puzzles which require students to do computations as part of the activity can enrich an otherwise boring topic. These may be competitive games or puzzles which are individual activities. Here the enrichment activity can be very instrumental in the class's ultimate success with the regular work, since a motivated student should perform better than a student "turned-off" to mathematics.

TOPIC: Miscellaneous calculator activities
ENRICHMENT: Games and puzzles with a hand-held calculator (see Enrichment Unit 11) These must be carefully selected (and planned); otherwise the calculator activity could become a distraction.

It is easy to fall into a trap of letting the recreational aspects of a lesson dominate the session. When taken to this extreme, the introduction of recreational topics can become counterproductive so that any attempt to return to the intended curriculum will be viewed by the students with displeasure. Remember, the recreational aspect of a lesson is merely designed to enrich, not replace, the regular curriculum.

Historical Notes

The embellishment resulting from the inclusion of historical notes in a mathematics lesson may be considered enrichment. Students usually get a more complete appreciation of a topic if they can relate to its origin. Any book on the history of mathematics can provide useful ideas for enriching your instruction by the inclusion of short anecdotes from the history of mathematics. The following references are of particular value for this use.

Beckmann, Petr. *A History of* π. New York: St. Martin's Press, 1971.
Bell, E.T. *Men of Mathematics*. New York: Simon and Schuster, 1937.
Eves, Howard W. *The Other Side of the Equation.* Boston: Prindle, Weber, and Schmidt, 1971.
_____ . *In Mathematical Circles*. Vols. 1 and 2. Boston: Prindle, Weber, and Schmidt, 1969.
_____ . *Mathematical Circles Revisited*. Boston: Prindle, Weber, and Schmidt, 1971.

Gamon, George. *One, Two, Three . . . Infinity.* New York: Viking Press, 1947.
National Council of Teachers of Mathematics, *Historical Topics for the Mathematics Classroom,* 31st Yearbook. Reston, Virginia: NCTM, 1969.
Kasner, E., and J. Newman. *Mathematics and the Imagination.* New York: Simon and Schuster, 1940.
Moritz, R. E. *On Mathematics: A Collection of Witty, Profound, Amusing Passages about Mathematics and Mathematicians.* New York: Dover, 1958.
Schaaf, William L., ed. *Our Mathematical Heritage.* New York: Macmillan, 1963.
Turnbull, H.W. *The Great Mathematicians.* New York: New York University Press, 1961.
Willerding, Margaret. *Mathematical Concepts, A Historical Approach.* Boston: Prindle, Weber, and Schmidt, 1967.

Some of these books will lend themselves better to quick extraction of anecdotes for classroom use, while others will require a somewhat more thorough reading. These books, together with those listed on pages 125 and 126, should provide you with ample resources for enrichment through historical anecdotes.

Field Trips

Although perhaps less directly, some class trips can be used fruitfully to enrich the instruction of lower ability mathematics students. Similarly, films are available which, if properly introduced and later carefully reviewed, also can be effective in enriching the teaching of mathematics.

The imaginative teacher will certainly add much to our suggestions for enriching the mathematics instruction of the slow learner. Concerned teachers are constantly seeking new ways of enriching their teaching.

THE AVERAGE-ABILITY STUDENT

Many of the suggestions offered for enrichment of mathematics instruction for the slow learner, when adjusted, can be used effectively with students of average mathematical ability. This adjustment must take into account the interests, abilities and aspirations of this somewhat more capable group of students. That is, the applications selected might be more sophisticated, the recreational topics might be more challenging, and the historical anecdotes might be more involved and possibly go a bit beyond the "story" stage.

Enrichment for this average-ability group may also involve special courses. For example, students in this ability range may take a course in computer programming. With the decreasing prices of microcomputers, setting up a course of this kind should be increasingly more feasible. Such a course will go far in enriching the average-ability student's mathematical knowledge, since it will introduce him to a highly organized way of reasoning. It will also give him an opportunity to revisit previously learned topics and concepts in a different context.

Another special course which can enrich the mathematics education of average-ability students is one on the history of mathematics. The level to which this course will delve into the mathematics content considered will be determined by the intended audience's interests and capabilities. For the student, of particular interest (and importance) is a consideration of how various mathematical concepts, previously studied, were discovered and developed. The rewards from this sort of experience can be many for this middle-ability group of students.

On occasion some "sleepers" among these students, with the proper stimulus, usually in the form of enrichment activities, emerge and begin to demonstrate much higher abilities, and consequently greater achievement, than previously shown. Observing these few students take on a new academic posture is a truly rewarding experience for the teacher.

THE GIFTED STUDENT

Gifted students in mathematics are usually described as exhibiting ingenuity, intellectual curiosity, creative talent, an ability to assimilate and generalize, and a high level of mathematical achievement. Gifted students usually will participate in many extracurricular activities in mathematics (see Chapter 12). They are also more apt to read mathematics books, periodicals, and pamphlets. These independent activities may lead the more motivated among them to pursue a study of topics in mathematics which are either "off the beaten path" or are a part of some more advanced course (likely to be studied at a later date). Perhaps one of the more rewarding experiences for a teacher of gifted students is to observe a student making a discovery or developing an unusual approach to a topic or problem. This rare insight possessed by the gifted should be nurtured by the teacher through appropriately selected enrichment activities.

Enrichment activities for gifted students can be categorized into three types: *acceleration, expansion,* and *digression.*

Acceleration

Acceleration usually involves moving gifted students along at a faster than usual pace. This may mean starting a student's study of elementary algebra earlier and then enabling her to reach calculus (and sometimes beyond)

while still in high school. It could also mean that full-year courses would be covered in less time, making room for a study of more advanced topics earlier. Perhaps the main advantage of this practice is that it allows the gifted student to remain appropriately challenged, and thereby avoid loss of interest resulting from an otherwise lock-step curriculum geared to the average-ability student.

But there are also possible dangers to watch for when accelerating gifted students. If the acceleration is too rapid, the student may be asked to work with too much abstraction too quickly or too soon, that is, before he is actually "ready" for it. This sort of experience could be counterproductive, with long lasting after effects. Not only must the teacher look for student readiness, but he must also never lose sight of the motivation which any student needs, regardless of ability. A student, after having been identified as gifted, should not merely be *pushed* along a predetermined track. If a proper balance between interest and ability is not achieved, there exists a likelihood that this gifted student could be "turned-off" to mathematics.

Regardless of the form and degree of the acceleration, careful monitoring of the student both academically and socially is of paramount importance. The teacher must be sensitive to signs which may indicate that a student is perhaps mathematically overextended, generally overworked, or improperly placed socially. With this prescribed care, the acceleration process can be worthwhile; without such care it could be irreparably harmful.

Expansion

Expansion refers to that form of enrichment which allows students to delve more deeply into the topics being studied. Such expansion of the regular mathematics curriculum would take place primarily as part of the same classroom setting as the usual mathematics instruction. Yet this expansion of the curriculum topics might be a part of an extracurricular program as well (see Chapter 12). Let us look at some examples to get a better understanding of the sort of enrichment activity suggested here.

TOPIC: The Pythagorean Theorem (high school geometry course)
ENRICHMENT: Expansion would allow the students to study any or all of the following:

1. Investigate a variety of proofs of the Pythagorean Theorem.
2. Investigate the expansion of the Pythagorean Theorem to acute and obtuse triangles (i.e., for acute triangles: $a^2 + b^2 > c^2$ and for obtuse triangles $a^2 + b^2 < c^2$).
3. Study some of the properties of Pythagorean

Triples beginning with the formulas for generating these triples:

$$a = m^2 - n^2$$
$$b = 2mn$$
$$c = m^2 + n^2, \text{ where } m > n$$

4. Classify various types of Pythagorean Triples, such as discovering the generating values of m and n which produce triples where $|a - b| = 1$ or where $|b - c| = 1$, and so on.

5. Consider the relationship which the Pythagorean Theorem has with other topics in mathematics (e.g., trigonometry, Ptolemy's Theorem).

6. Generalize the Pythagorean Theorem to the Law of Cosines.

TOPIC: Factoring (elementary algebra course)
ENRICHMENT: From the usual factoring techniques (such as factoring the difference of two squares) taught in the elementary algebra course, an expansion might have students consider some "special factorings" such as:

$$a^3 - b^3 = (a - b)(a^2 + ab + b^2)$$
$$a^3 + b^3 = (a + b)(a^2 - ab + b^2)$$

For very gifted students the general case might be very rewarding:

1. For *odd n:* $x^n + y^n = (x + y)(x^{n-1} - x^{n-2}y + x^{n-3}y^2 + \ldots + y^{n-1})$

2. For *all n:* $x^n - y^n = (x - y)(x^{n-1} + x^{n-2}y + x^{n-3}y^2 + \ldots + y^{n-1})$

3. For *even n:* $x^n - y^n = (x^{\frac{n}{2}} + y^{\frac{n}{2}})(x^{\frac{n}{2}} - y^{\frac{n}{2}})$

In addition, some more intricate factoring examples might be provided for students to work on, such as:

$$y(y - 1)x^2 + (2y^2 - 1)x + y(y + 1)$$

which can be factored as:

$$(xy + y + 1)(xy - x + y)$$

A good source for some of these more unusual factoring examples is

Hall, H.S., and Knight, S.R. Revised by F.L. Sevenoak. *Algebra for Colleges and Schools.* New York: Macmillan, 1941.

Other older algebra texts generally have similar material.

TOPIC: Trigonometry (high school level)
ENRICHMENT: Here the teacher might lead students to expand the law of sines to the law of tangents and then develop Mollweide's equations.

After the law of cosines has been developed, some more complicated triangle solution problems might be presented as an expansion of the usual problems found in current textbooks.

Once again, older textbooks provide an excellent source for expansion of a topic. One such book on trigonometry is

Kells, L.M., Willis, F.K., Bland, J.R., and Orleans, J.B. *Elements of Trigonometry.* New York: McGraw-Hill, 1943.

TOPIC: The geometry of the circle
ENRICHMENT: One possible expansion of this topic might involve a discussion of the definition and history of π, beginning with its reference in the Bible (I Kings 7:23)[1] and tracing its development to the modern computer methods of computation. A discussion of the computation of π can lead to some very interesting investigations. If computers are available to students, many additional activities can be considered. (e.g., see "Constructing π," Enrichment Unit 59.)

TOPIC: Probability (grade 11 or 12)
ENRICHMENT: As easy as it is to state the Birthday Problem, that is how difficult it is to comprehend this unusual phenomenon. The development of the various probabilities makes a nice expansion of elementary probability and can lead the student to other related investigations (see "The Birthday Problem," Enrichment Unit 31).

TOPIC: Triangle Constructions (high school geometry course)
ENRICHMENT: Usually the only geometric constructions (using straightedge and compasses) of triangles in the high school geometry course are those made from given measures of sides and angles. The expansion of the data base to include the measures of any three of angle bisectors, medians, altitudes, or other triangle-related parts, should lead the student to a more genuine understanding of triangle properties. You can begin to acquaint yourself with this topic by reading "Triangle Constructions," Enrichment Unit 38. A far more extensive treatment of this very rich topic can be found in *Geometric Constructions* by A.S. Posamentier and W. Wernick (Portland, Maine: J. Weston Walch, Publisher, 1973).

---

[1] For an interesting interpretation of this reference see "An Astounding Revelation on the History of π" by A.S. Posamentier and N. Gordon. *The Mathematics Teacher.* (Reston, Virginia: January 1984.) National Council of Teachers of Mathematics.

In each of the examples of enrichment through the expansion of a topic in the regular curriculum above, you will notice that the discussion was always confined to an embellishment of the original topic and not a digression to another topic. This latter situation is our last form of enrichment to be discussed.

Digression

A popular form of enrichment generally results when the teacher digresses from a topic in the regular curriculum to consider another topic, which is related to and generally an outgrowth of the first topic. Since a gifted class can usually master a topic more quickly than an average class, more time is available for discussion of another related topic before resuming with the regular prescribed curriculum. These digressions are usually rewarding and can last from a portion of a class session to several sessions. As with other enrichment activities discussed, these digressions should be used to enrich the regular curriculum, not detract from it. Often these enrichment activities can be glamorous, which by contrast can make the regular curriculum appear somewhat less appealing. Therefore the teacher, conscious of this possibility, should try to continuously relate this digression to the regular curriculum, so that instead of detracting from it, the enrichment topic will in fact embellish it. The following examples should help provide a better understanding of what we mean by an enrichment activity which represents a digression from the regular curriculum.

TOPIC: Geometry (seventh grade course)
ENRICHMENT: Treated appropriately, the topic of networks can be a worthwhile digression from the study of informal geometry. With the possible goal of investigating the Konigsberg Bridge Problem, the study of networks can be exciting and can lead to other related topological investigations (see ''Networks,'' Enrichment Unit 96).

TOPIC: Trigonometry (high school level)
ENRICHMENT: After a student has a good working knowledge of the trigonometry included in the regular curriculum, an interesting digression might be one which allows the student to study spherical trigonometry. Of course, this presupposes a prior knowledge of some spherical geometry. Yet, this sort of digression can lead to a more complete understanding of trigonometry.

TOPIC: Concurrency (high school geometry)
ENRICHMENT: Perhaps because the topics of concurrency and collinearity are often slighted in the high school geometry course, a digression to study these topics more fully might be worthwhile. Specifically, the development of the theorems of Giovanni Ceva (1647–1736) and Menelaus of Alexandria (ca. 100 A.D.) can lead to many other interesting geometric phenomena. To begin to acquaint yourself with these topics, see ''Proving Lines Concurrent,'' Enrichment Unit 53, and ''Proving Points Collinear,'' Enrichment Unit 55. For futher ideas you may wish to consult *Excursions in Advanced Euclidean Geometry* by A.S. Posamentier (Portland, Maine: J. Weston Walch, Publisher, 1979).

TOPIC: Quadratic equations (second year algebra course)
ENRICHMENT: After studying the various ways to solve quadratic equations, students may wish to learn how to solve other higher degree equations. A consideration of some methods of solving cubic equations might be enlightening to gifted students. This sort of investigation will lead them to appreciate some of the work of the early mathematicians (e.g., Nicolo Tartaglia, 1506-1557).

TOPIC: Conic sections (advanced high school level)
ENRICHMENT: The resourceful teacher certainly will discuss some of the many physical applications of conic sections. Yet, rarely will a teacher digress to discuss how conics can be constructed. This discussion should lead to envelopes of the conic curves. An enjoyable off-shoot of this investigation is the topic of curve stitching (see ''Constructing Ellipses,'' Enrichment Unit 106, and ''Constructing the Parabola,'' Enrichment Unit 107).

The only restriction on the topics which make appropriate digressions for enrichment is the teacher's judgment. There are many possible topics from which to choose. The selected digression should be related to the topic which is to serve as the take-off point in the curriculum, and should be properly planned so as to have a clear beginning, a logical conclusion, and above all, a specific purpose.

SUMMARY

Teachers should be encouraged to constantly gather materials and ideas for enriching their teaching of mathematics. Regardless of the ability level of the students, appropriate enrichment activities can always be found. In some cases these enrichment activities may be harder to secure than in others, yet the process of searching for an appropriate topic can, in and of itself, prove to be of great benefit to the teacher.

Every teacher should make a genuine effort to enrich his instruction. Very often these motivating enrichment experiences go a long way to developing a new appreciation for mathematics among the weaker or average students, while among the above average and gifted students, enrichment activities can be instrumental in encouraging further study in mathematics.

The units offered in Part 2 of this book should provide you with many ideas for enriching your teaching of mathematics. Another fine source of ideas is *A Bibliography of Recreational Mathematics,* Vols. 1–4, by W. L. Schaaf (Washington, D.C.: National Council of Teachers of Mathematics, 1970, 1973, 1978). With these tools at your disposal, you are ready to enrich your students' knowledge and appreciation of mathematics.

EXERCISES

1. Select a topic for enriching your instruction of
   a. an average-ability eighth grade mathematics class.
   b. a gifted tenth grade class.
   c. a remedial ninth grade class.
   d. an average-ability eleventh grade class.
   e. a gifted seventh grade class.
   f. a gifted twelfth grade class (currently studying calculus).
   Explain how you would treat each of the topics listed above. Specify how much material you would plan to cover.

2. For each of the following, select a grade level and ability level and provide an example of an enrichment topic which represents
   a. expansion.
   b. digression.

3. Suppose you were approached by the parents of one of your better-achieving students and asked to accelerate their son's mathematics instruction because they feel he is not being adequately challenged. Explain how you would deal with this request. Discuss your response to the parents and actions before and after this response.

4. The parents of one of your remedial ninth grade students have come to ask why you occasionally spend time with the class on ''peripheral matters'' (i.e., enrichment) instead of spending all your instructional time with remedial work. Explain how you would answer these parents.

5. For a gifted class, prepare an outline for an enrichment unit for each of the following curriculum topics (specify whether it is an expansion or digression):
   a. Quadrilaterals (high school geometry course)
   b. Progressions (second year algebra course)
   c. Percents (seventh grade mathematics class)
   d. Binomial Theorem (eleventh or twelfth grade mathematics class)
   e. Angle measurement with a circle (high school geometry course)
   f. Simultaneous equations (elementary algebra course)
   g. Quadratic equations (elementary algebra course)

6. Locate a secondary school mathematics textbook whose copyright date is earlier than 1950, then list the various types of enrichment activities which this book provides. Repeat this for a textbook whose copyright date is later than 1970. Compare the two books with regard to their enrichment activities. How can you explain the differences in enrichment philosophies between the two books?

7. Choose a topic appropriate for the secondary school mathematics student that is not listed among the 119 enrichment units in Part 2 of this book. Develop an enrichment activity based on your chosen topic in a style similar to that used in Part 2 of this book. This unit should be aimed at a gifted audience.

8. Choose a topic appropriate for the secondary school mathematics student that is not listed among the 119 enrichment units in Part 2 of this book. Develop an enrichment activity based on your chosen topic in a style similar to that used in Part 2 of this book. This unit should be aimed at an average audience.

9. Choose a topic appropriate for the secondary school mathematics student that is not listed among the 119 enrichment units in Part 2 of this book. Develop an enrichment activity based on your chosen topic in a style similar to that used in Part 2 of this book. This unit should be aimed at a lower ability student.

REFERENCES

The following are National Council of Teachers of Mathematics Yearbooks published by the NCTM, Reston, Virginia:

Enrichment Mathematics for the Grades. Twenty-seventh Yearbook, 1963.

Enrichment Mathematics for High School. Twenty-eighth Yearbook, 1963.

Topics in Mathematics for Elementary School Teachers. Twenty-ninth Yearbook, 1964.

Historical Topics for the Mathematics Classroom. Thirty-first Yearbook, 1969.

Geometry in the Mathematics Curriculum. Thirty-sixth Yearbook, 1973.

Applications in School Mathematics. 1979 Yearbook.

Problem Solving in School Mathematics. 1980 Yearbook.

Teaching Statistics and Probability. 1981 Yearbook.

Computers in Mathematics Education. 1984 Yearbook.

Secondary School Mathematics Curriculum. 1985 Yearbook.

Chrystal, G. *Algebra and Elementary Textbook*. Two volumes. New York: Chelsea Publishing Co., 1964.

Court, N.A. *College Geometry*. New York: Barnes & Noble, 1952.

Hall, H.S., and Knight, S. R. *Higher Algebra*. London: Macmillan Co., 1960.

Lockwood, E.H. *A Book of Curves*. London: Cambridge University Press, 1971.

Loomis, E.S. *The Pythagorean Proposition*. Reston, Virginia: NCTM, 1968.

Posamentier, A.S. *Excursions In Advanced Euclidean Geometry*. Menlo Park, Ca.: Addison-Wesley, 1984.

Posamentier, A.S., and Sheridan, G. *Math Motivators: Investigations in Pre-Algebra*. Menlo Park, Ca.: Addison-Wesley, 1982.

————. *Math Motivators: Investigations in Geometry*. Menlo Park, Ca.: Addison-Wesley, 1982.

————. *Math Motivators: Investigations in Algebra*. Menlo Park, Ca.: Addison-Wesley, 1983.

Runion, G.E. *The Golden Section and Related Curiosa*. Glenview, Ill.: Scott, Foresman & Co., 1972.

Space Mathematics, A Resource for Teachers. National Aeronautics and Space Administration. Washington, D.C.: January 1972.

New Mathematical Library

Mathematical Association of America, New Mathematics Library. Over thirty titles on topics designed to enrich the mathematics curriculum. These can be ordered from the Mathematical Association of America, 1529 Eighteenth Street, N.W., Washington, D.C. 20036. A list of the first thirty titles follows:

1. *Numbers: Rational and Irrational* by Ivan Niven.
2. *What is Calculus About?* by W.W. Sawyer.
3. *An Introduction to Inequalities* by E.F. Beckenbach and R. Bellman.
4. *Geometric Inequalities* by N.D. Kazarinoff.
5. *The Contest Problem Book I*. Annual High School Mathematics Examinations 1950–1960. Compiled and with solutions by Charles T. Salkind.
6. *The Lore of Large Numbers* by P.J. Davis.
7. *Uses of Infinity* by Leo Zippin.
8. *Geometric Transformations I* by I.M. Yaglom, translated by A. Shields.
9. *Continued Fractions* by Carl D. Olds.
10. *Graphs and Their Uses* by Oystein Ore.
11. } *Hungarian Problem Books I and II*. Based on the Eötvös.
12. } Competitions 1894–1905 and 1906–1928, translated by E. Rapaport.

13.   *Episodes from the Early History of Mathematics* by A. Aaboe.
14.   *Groups and Their Graphs* by I. Grossman and W. Magnus.
15.   *The Mathematics of Choice* by Ivan Niven.
16.   *From Pythagoras to Einstein* by K.O. Friedrichs.
17.   *The Contest Problem Book II*. Annual High School Mathematics Examinations 1961–1965. Compiled and with solutions by Charles T. Salkind.
18.   *First Concepts of Topology* by W.G. Chinn and N.E. Steenrod.
19.   *Geometry Revisited* by H.S.M. Coxeter and S.L. Greitzer.
20.   *Invitation to Number Theory* by Oystein Ore.
21.   *Geometric Transformations II* by I.M. Yaglom, translated by A. Shields.
22.   *Elementary Cryptanalysis—A Mathematical Approach* by A. Sinkov.
23.   *Ingenuity in Mathematics* by Ross Honsberger.
24.   *Geometric Transformations III* by I.M. Yaglom, translated by A. Shenitzer.
25.   *The Contest Problem Book III*. Annual High School Mathematics Examinations 1966–1972. Compiled and with solutions by C.T. Salkind and J.M. Earl.
26.   *Mathematical Methods in Science* by George Polya.
27.   *International Mathematical Olympiads—1959–1977*. Compiled and with solutions by S.L. Greitzer.
28.   *The Mathematics of Games and Gambling* by Edward W. Packel.
29.   *The Contest Problem Book IV*. Annual High School Mathematics Examinations 1973–1982. Compiled and with solutions by R.A. Artino, A.M. Gaglione, and N. Shell.
30.   *The Role of Mathematics in Science* by M.M. Schiffer and L. Bowden.

Other titles in preparation.

Many additional ideas can be obtained from Part 2 of this book.

Bibliography for the History of Mathematics

Aaboe, Asger. *Episodes from the Early History of Mathematics*. New York: Random House, 1964.
Ball, W.W. Rouse. *A Short Account of the History of Mathematics*. 4th ed. New York: Dover Publications, 1960.
Bell, Eric Temple. *Men of Mathematics*. 6th paperback ed. New York: Simon & Schuster, 1937.
Boyer, Carl B. *A History of Mathematics*. New York: John Wiley & Sons, 1968.
Cajori, Florian. *A History of Mathematical Notations*, 2 Vols. LaSalle, Ill.: Open Court, 1928.
Eves, Howard. *An Introduction to the History of Mathematics*. 5th ed. New York: W.B. Saunders College Publishing, 1983.
Gittleman, Arthur. *History of Mathematics*. Columbus, Ohio: Charles E. Merrill Publishing Co., 1975.
The National Council of Teachers of Mathematics. *Historical Topics for the Mathematical Classroom*. Thirty-first Yearbook. Reston, Va.: The Council, 1969.
Newman, James Roy, ed. *The World of Mathematics*. 4 Vols. New York: Simon & Schuster, 1956; paperback, 1962.
Smith, David E. *History of Mathematics*. 2 Vols. New York: Dover, 1953.
Struik, Dirk J. *A Concise History of Mathematics*. 3rd revised ed. New York: Dover, 1967.

CHAPTER 12
EXTRA-
CURRICULAR
ACTIVITIES IN
MATHEMATICS

With the crowded mathematics curriculum at every level of the secondary school, teachers find extensive digressions from the sequential development of the mathematics course a hardship. Yet, there is great benefit to be derived from a consideration of mathematics outside the regular curriculum. One must therefore seek ways of providing students with mathematics which is extracurricular. Many extracurricular activities in mathematics can be conducted through the structure of a mathematics club.

THE MATHEMATICS CLUB

Although the mathematics club structure can facilitate many of the activities to be discussed in this chapter, it is not necessary to form a club in order to conduct any of these activities. Forming a mathematics club requires substantial planning, ranging from a selection of participants (both a faculty sponsor and student members) to a determination of an organization and purpose. The germination of a mathematics club can come from an administrator or an interested teacher, as well as from a group of students interested in participating in such a club. Whatever the origin of the mathematics club, the teacher who is chosen as faculty sponsor should realize that a sizable investment of time, work and effort will be required to make the venture successful. Naturally, the rewards for this investment usually make it all worthwhile. Club activities frequently allow the faculty sponsor to grow both mathematically and experientially. By permitting unlimited investigation of mathematical topics and applications beyond the scope of the secondary school curriculum, all involved can feel a sense of fulfillment which comes from a genuine appreciation of mathematics, its development and its role in society.

Establishing a Mathematics Club

Once the faculty sponsor has been chosen, she should begin to familiarize herself with the task by discussing the problem of getting started with colleagues, administrators and a select group of interested students. It would be of particular help to seek out a mathematics club faculty sponsor in another school who may have had to undergo similar experiences at some earlier date. Suggestions based on first-hand experiences and materials which have proved successful would be helpful to the new mathematics club sponsor, who would probably grapple for workable ideas. (See references listed at the end of this chapter.)

After having received advice and suggestions from colleagues both in and outside her school, and having gained the support of both the administration and a group of interested students, the teacher must tackle the job of recruiting. All paths of communication with the student body should be used. Announcements over the public address system, flyers sent to all homeroom sections, and student newspaper coverage of the new club should be included in the initial publicity. Especially important in the recruitment process is direct contact with mathematics classes which contain potential club members. This can be done by the class's teacher or by the faculty sponsor directly. The approach should be carefully planned so that the presentation about the club to these special classes is particularly attractive.

Part of the recruitment drive should involve inviting eligible students to an organizational meeting. It is important that this first meeting have a carefully planned and well-thought-out agenda. Student input should be welcomed, yet the faculty sponsor might present the plans which she prepared in consultation with the administration and colleagues, and have the group of interested students react. Although this prepared plan should be flexible and open for student suggestions, for the faculty advisor to come to the first meeting unprepared, without some sort of plan, would be ill-advised. The first meeting might also be used for the selection of club officers, which would in turn form a steering committee. Together with the faculty sponsor, this committee would decide on time and frequency of meetings, membership eligibility and, perhaps most important, the activities in which the club will engage. The rest of this chapter will present various extracurricular activities in mathematics which can be used with a mathematics club. However, a school may provide any of the activities without the structure of a mathematics club.

MATHEMATICS TEAMS

Most regions of the country have mathematics leagues organized for the competition of local secondary schools. These competitions are usually organized on three levels: junior high school students; senior high school students in grades nine, ten, and eleven; and seniors in high school. The competition questions for each level are intended to be appropriately challenging yet within the scope of the student's knowledge of mathematics. Some mathematics leagues are organized so that schools compete directly against each other on a rotating basis; however, most leagues simply make an award to the team with the highest total score (i.e., number of correctly solved problems) at the end of the school year (or semester). Information about the mathematics leagues in your area can be obtained easily through local professional organizations or colleges.

It is likely that students comprising the school's mathematics team are also members of the mathematics club. But recruiting should not by any means be limited to students in the mathematics club. There are likely to be some talented students in the school who, because of other commitments, were unable to join the mathematics club but might well join the mathematics team. In addition to teacher recommendation, the mathematics team coach should construct an entrance examination for all prospective candidates for the mathematics team. Such an examination should cover as wide a range of topics as possible, using the type of questions likely to come up at a mathematics team meet. In addition, a successful kind of item for this examination is one in which a new topic (or concept) is succinctly introduced and then a question about this new topic is asked. For such an examination for geometry students, one example of this might be to introduce Ptolemy's Theorem and then ask a question which could be solved using that theorem.

EXAMPLE: *Ptolemy's Theorem:* In an inscribed quadrilateral, the product of the lengths of the diagonals equals the sum of the products of the lengths of the opposite sides.

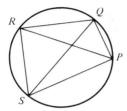

For the inscribed quadrilateral *PQRS*, Ptolemy's Theorem gives us:

$$(RP)(SQ) = (PQ)(RS) + (PS)(RQ)$$

Use Ptolemy's Theorem to find the length of side $\overline{BC}$ of $\triangle ABC$, which is inscribed in a circle of radius of length 5. The lengths of $\overline{AB}$ and $\overline{AC}$ are 5 and 6, respectively.

The above-average mathematics student should correctly solve this problem with either answer: $3\sqrt{3} - 4$ or $3\sqrt{3} + 4$. The truly gifted mathematics student, however, will realize that there are *two* possible solutions, depending on whether $\angle A$ is acute or obtuse. A sample solution follows.

SOLUTION:

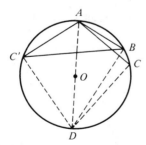

We notice that there are two possibilities to consider in this problem. Both $\triangle ABC$ and $\triangle ABC'$ are inscribed in circle O, with $AB = 5$ and $AC = AC' = 6$. We are to find BC and BC'.

Draw diameter $\overline{AOD}$, which measures 10, and draw $\overline{DC}$, $\overline{DB}$, and $\overline{DC'}$. $m\angle AC'D = m\angle ACD = m\angle ABD = 90°$.

Consider the case in which $\angle A$ in $\triangle ABC$ is acute. In right $\triangle ACD$, $DC = 8$, and in right $\triangle ABD$, $BD = 5\sqrt{3}$. By Ptolemy's Theorem applied to quadrilateral $ABCD$,

$$(AC)(BD) = (AB)(DC) + (AD)(BC)$$

or $(6)(5\sqrt{3}) = (5)(8) + (10)(BC)$, and
$$BC = 3\sqrt{3} - 4.$$

Now consider the case in which $\angle A$ is obtuse, as in $\triangle ABC'$. In right $\triangle AC'D$, $DC' = 8$. By Ptolemy's Theorem applied to quadrilateral $ABDC'$,

$$(AC')(BD) + (AB)(DC') = (AD)(BC')$$
$$(6)(5\sqrt{3}) + (5)(8) = (10)(BC'), \text{ and}$$
$$BC' = 3\sqrt{3} + 4$$

In addition to testing a student's ability to use a newly learned fact, this type of question permits the more able student to shine. She will discover the ambiguity in the question posed and offer a complete solution. Each question on this entrance test should serve a clearly defined function.

Once the mathematics team members have been selected, a time must be set for them to be trained. Mathematics teams have been known to meet before the school day begins, during the lunch hour (students would eat their lunch while working on mathematics team activities), during the regular school day, or after the last period of the day. In some instances, the mathematics team might meet as a class. Some schools have chosen to give students course credit for a course on problem solving and special topics in mathematics which are not part of the secondary school curriculum. A course of this kind also serves to train members of a mathematics team. In addition to the mathematics team materials listed at the end of this chapter, the mathematics team coach would be wise to try to obtain questions used at previous mathematics team meets. This will give students an excellent idea as to what to expect at future mathematics team meets, and how to prepare for them.

George Polya's classic book, *How To Solve It* (Princeton, N.J.: Princeton University Press, 1945) should serve as a good initial source for the mathematics team coach in her preparation for training the mathematics team in problem-solving skills (also see Chapter 9). Mathematics team training sessions provide an excellent opportunity to present topics normally not taught in the secondary school but useful for solving typical problems encountered at mathematics team meets.

To give you an idea of the sort of topics which might be useful to a mathematics team, we offer the following list as a sample.

Diophantine equations
Means: arithmetic, geometric, and harmonic
Modular arithmetic-algebraic applications
Divisibility tests
Geometry theorems of Ceva, Menelaus, Ptolemy, Stewart, Heron, etc.
Techniques in problem solving

SAMPLE MATHEMATICS CONTEST QUESTIONS

1. If $1 - \dfrac{4}{x} + \dfrac{4}{x^2} = 0$, then $\dfrac{2}{x}$ equals

   (a) -1 (b) 1 (c) 2 (d) -1 or 2 (e) -1 or -2

2. If four times the reciprocal of the circumference of a circle equals the diameter of the circle, then the area of the circle is

   (a) $\dfrac{1}{\pi^2}$ (b) $\dfrac{1}{\pi}$ (c) 1 (d) π (d) π^2

3. For all non-zero numbers x and y such that $x = \dfrac{1}{y}$, $\left(x - \dfrac{1}{x}\right)\left(y + \dfrac{1}{y}\right)$ equals

   (a) $2x^2$ (b) $2y^2$ (c) $x^2 + y^2$ (d) $x^2 - y^2$ (e) $y^2 - x^2$

4. If $a = 1$, $b = 10$, $c = 100$ and $d = 1000$, then $(a + b + c - d) + (a + b - c + d) +$ $(a - b + c + d) + (-a + b + c + d)$ is equal to

   (a) 1111 (b) 2222 (c) 3333 (d) 1212 (e) 4242

5. Four boys bought a boat for $60. The first boy paid one half of the sum of the amounts paid by the other boys; the second boy paid one third of the sum of the amounts paid by the other boys; and the third boy paid one fourth of the sum of the amounts paid by the other boys. How much did the fourth boy pay?

   (a) $10   (b) $12   (c) $13   (d) $14   (e) $15

6. The number of distinct pairs (x,y) of real numbers satisfying both of the following equations:
   $$x = x^2 + y^2$$
   $$y = 2xy$$
   is

   (a) 0 (b) 1 (c) 2 (d) 3 (e) 4

7. Opposite sides of a regular hexagon are 12 inches apart. The length of each side, in inches, is

   (a) 7.5 (b) $6\sqrt{2}$ (c) $5\sqrt{2}$ (d) $\dfrac{9}{2}\sqrt{3}$ (e) $4\sqrt{3}$

8. Al's age is 16 more than the sum of Bob's age and Carl's age, and the square of Al's age is 1632 more than the square of the sum of Bob's age and Carl's age. The sum of the ages of Al, Bob and Carl is

   (a) 64 (b) 94 (c) 96 (d) 102 (e) 140

9. How many pairs (m, n) of integers satisfy the equation $m + n = mn$?

   (a) 1 (b) 2 (c) 3 (d) 4 (e) more than 4

10. Each of the three circles in the adjoining figure is externally tangent to the other two, and each side of the triangle is tangent to two of the circles. If each circle has radius three, then the perimeter of the triangle is

    (a) $36 + 9\sqrt{2}$ (b) $36 + 6\sqrt{3}$
    (c) $36 + 9\sqrt{3}$ (d) $18 + 18\sqrt{3}$
    (e) 45

11. Three fair dice are tossed at random (i.e., all faces have the same probability of coming up). What is the probability that the three numbers turned up can be arranged to form an arithmetic progression with common difference one?

    (a) $\dfrac{1}{6}$ (b) $\dfrac{1}{9}$ (c) $\dfrac{1}{27}$ (d) $\dfrac{1}{54}$ (e) $\dfrac{7}{36}$

12. If $y = (\log_2 3)(\log_3 4) \ldots (\log_n [n+1]) \ldots (\log_{31} 32)$ then

    (a) $4 < y < 5$ (b) $y = 5$ (c) $5 < y < 6$ (d) $y = 6$
    (e) $6 < y < 7$

13. Let E be the point of intersection of the diagonals of convex quadrilateral $ABCD$, and let P, Q, R and S be the centers of the circles circumscribing triangles ABE, BCE, CDE and ADE, respectively. Then

    (a) $PQRS$ is a parallelogram
    (b) $PQRS$ is a parallelogram if and only if $ABCD$ is a rhombus
    (c) $PQRS$ is a parallelogram if and only if $ABCD$ is a rectangle
    (d) $PQRS$ is a parallelogram if and only if $ABCD$ is a parallelogram
    (e) none of the above are true

14. For how many paths consisting of a sequence of horizontal and/or vertical line segments, with each segment connecting a pair of adjacent letters in the diagram below, is the word CONTEST spelled out as the path is traversed from beginning to end?

    (a) 63 (b) 128 (c) 129
    (d) 255 (e) none of these

                          C
                        COC
                      CONOC
                    CONTNOC
                  CONTETNOC
                CONTESETNOC
              CONTESTSETNOC

Reprinted from the 1977 and 1978 Annual High School Mathematics Examinations with permission of the Mathematical Association of America, Committee on High School Contests.

Various algebraic relationships
Topics in number theory
Sequences and series
Probability
Inequalities
Systems of equations
Topics from theory of equations
Maxima-minima problems in geometry and algebra

As an outgrowth of a discussion of these and many other appropriate mathematics topics, useful facts and relationships should be separately recorded by each student and kept available for ready reference. A student's collection of facts and relationships might include those listed at the end of this chapter.

Mathematics team coaching requires a total commitment from the faculty sponsor. In addition to extensive preparation and gathering previously used mathematics team questions (and other related materials), the faculty sponsor must be available for after-school mathematics team meets. This could likely involve traveling with the team to other schools. The work of the mathematics team coach requires much dedication, but the rewards are gratifying.

MATHEMATICS CONTESTS

Closely aligned with the activities of a mathematics team is the administration of various national, statewide, or local mathematics contests. These contests, the Mathematical Association of America Annual High School Mathematics Contest chief among them, are usually open to all students (not just those on the mathematics team). Extensive publicity in the school is required to attract as large a group for the contest as possible. Here students who may not be among the ten strongest mathematics students in the school can enter a contest for purely recreational reasons. Many of the questions on these mathematics contests are within reach of average mathematics students. Naturally, these contests also contain challenging questions to help select the superior students. Often, school-wide awards are given as well as region-wide, statewide and sometimes national awards. As they are usually set up, the mathematics contests can offer entertainment and enrichment to a reasonably large portion of the school's population. This is particularly so when the mathematics team coach reviews the contest questions with students after the contest has ended.

High school mathematics contests generally go far toward promoting an interest in mathematics throughout the school. The National Council of Teachers of Mathematics as well as local mathematics teacher or-

ganizations are excellent sources of information about which mathematics leagues or which mathematics contests are available to your students. More information can be found in the bibliography at the end of this chapter.

MATHEMATICS PROJECTS

One rarely thinks of writing a term paper or doing a term project in a mathematics class. Yet this activity has proved to be successful with groups of varying levels of ability. A mathematics project may take the form of a construction project such as curve stitching, special tool constructions, and construction of linkages. The term paper might involve an original investigation of some mathematics topic; it might report on an experiment which the student has conducted (e.g., probability); it might be an exposition on some previously unfamiliar mathematics topic (this is best when not too broad in scope); or it may offer a discussion of a topic from the history of mathematics (i.e., involving the historical development of a topic or concept). We offer on page 140 a list of some possible topics which students might use for a term paper (or project). (This list is merely intended as a guide for generating additional topics.)

The topic for a mathematics project should be selected by the student. The teacher may serve as a facilitator by stimulating interest in various topics and then allowing the student to make an independent selection. Once a topic has been selected, the student should read as much about the topic as is available. Keeping accurate notes throughout this study period is essential for a successful project. Periodic conferences with the teacher will insure that the student is kept properly on track. Careful notes taken during these sessions along with complete and accurate notes obtained from readings will make work on the written report simpler.

Sometime during the early stages of the project, the teacher should specifically indicate what the written product should include. It is important that the teacher not fix the format and content so rigidly as to stifle creativity. The teacher might suggest individual conferences with students who find the suggested format inappropriate for their particular project. Such features as a bibliography would probably be a part of all papers.

THE MATHEMATICS FAIR

In many regions of the country, regular (annual, semiannual, etc.) exhibitions of student mathematics projects are held. These range from school-wide to national in

TOPICS FOR MATHEMATICS PROJECTS

Advanced Euclidean Geometry
Algebraic Fallacies
Algebraic Models
Algebraic Recreations
Analog Computer
Ancient Number Systems and Algorithms
Arithmetic Fallacies
Arithmetic Recreations
Bases Other than Ten
Binary Computer
Boolean Algebra
Brocard Points
Calculating Shortcuts
Cavalieri's Theorem
Checking Arithmetic Operations
Conic Sections
Continued Fractions
Crypotography
Crystallography
Curves of Constant Breadth
Cylindrical Projections
Desargues' Theorem
Determinants
Diophantine Equations
Divisibility of Numbers
Duality
Dynamic Symmetry
Elementary Number Theory Applications
The Euler Line
Extension of Euler's Formula to N-Dimensions
Extension of Pappus's Theorem
Fermat's Last Theorem
Fibonacci Numbers
Fields
Finite Differences
Finite Geometry
The Five Regular Polyhedra
Flexagons
The Four-Color Problem
The Fourth Dimension
Game Theory
Gaussian Primes
Geodesics
Geometry Constructions (Euclid)
Geometric Dissections—Tangrams
Geometric Fallacies
Geometric Models
Geometric Stereograms
Geometric Transformations
Geometry of Bubbles and Liquid Film
Geometry of Catenary
Gergonne's Problem
The Golden Section
Graphical Representation of Complex
   Roots of Quadratic and Cubic Equations
Groups
Higher Algebra
Higher Order Curves
Hyperbolic Functions

The Hyperbolic Paraboloid
Hypercomplex Numbers
Intuitive Geometric Recreations
Investigating the Cycloid
The Law of Growth
Linear Programming
Linkages
Lissajou's Figures
Lobachevskian Geometry
Logarithms of Negative and Complex Numbers
Logic
Magic Square Construction
Map Projections
Mascheroni's Constructions
Mathematics and Music
Mathematics of Life Insurance
Matrices
Maximum-Minimum in Geometry
Means
Methods of Least Squares
The Metric System
Minimal Surfaces
Modulo Arithmetic in Algebra
Monte Carlo Method of Number Approximation
Multinomial Theorem
Napier's Rods
Networks
The Nine Point Circle
Nomographs
The Number Pi, Phi or e
Number Theory Proofs
Paper Folding
Partial Fractions
Pascal's Theorem
Polygonal Numbers
Perfect Numbers
Prime Numbers
Probability
Problem Solving in Algebra
Projective Geometry
Proofs of Algebraic Theorems
Properties of Pascal's Triangle
Pythagorean Theorem—Triples
Regular Polygons
The Regular Seventeen-sided Polygon
Relativity and Mathematics
Riemannian Geometry
Special Factoring
Steiner Constructions
Solving Cubics and Quartics
Spherical Triangles
The Spiral
Tesselations
Theory of Braids
Theory of Equations
Theory of Perspectives
Three-Dimensional Curves
The Three Famous Problems of Antiquity
Topology
Unsolved Problems
Vectors

scope. Some are locally sponsored while others may be sponsored by national organizations. Such information should be readily available from school administrators or local mathematics teacher organizations. The prospect of eventual exhibit at a mathematics fair could serve as additional motivation for students.

Naturally, when a student's project involves some physical model such as a linkage, or a geometric construction, the mere exhibition may be meaningful; however, when a student's project is a mathematical development or a study of some concept, then a presentation is necessary. Most mathematics fairs are organized to allow students to present their papers (orally) before a group of judges. In progressive stages, winners are selected, usually from each grade level entered. Community members are often attracted to such events.

The learning experience involved in the process of preparing a project or writing a paper, and then presenting or even defending it, is very valuable. Whether a student wins this fair competition is not as important as the recognition offered for his work.

THE SCHOOL MATHEMATICS MAGAZINE

A common activity in which a mathematics club is often engaged is the publication of a school mathematics magazine. A school mathematics journal could consist of some of the better student term papers (or projects). Students' work (with some editorial refinements) could be easily disseminated by such a mathematics magazine. Typically such magazines are distributed (or sold) throughout the school and sent to other nearby schools, either to the students there or to the mathematics department head.

A project of this kind usually finds a productive place for every member of the club. The more motivated mathematics students and the more advanced mathematics students might undertake writing the content of the prospective mathematics magazine, while the more artistic students might become involved in designing the layout, cover, and art work. Others might be in charge of the "business" aspects of the project, such as publicity, circulation, costs, etc.

The role of the faculty sponsor is essentially that of a facilitator. He should define the job as he sees it and then allow students to adjust it to their needs and desires. As with any well-organized project, at least one person must be in charge of the entire project. Careful consideration to such things as organizational ability and leadership traits should be given before the student editor-in-chief is selected. The selection is most effective if it can come (at least in part) from the student group.

In addition to providing an outlet for exhibit of individual mathematics projects, a mathematics magazine will be a source of genuine pride on the part of all involved. Such an activity goes far in promoting an increased interest in mathematics while at the same time providing a good source for mathematics enrichment.

MATHEMATICS ASSEMBLY PROGRAM

Although less popular than a mathematics magazine, the mathematics program assembly may be an oral analogue of the magazine. Students are provided an opportunity to exhibit some individual or group work to a larger audience. Most teachers' first reaction to the prospect of a mathematics assembly program is one of incredulity! The thought of presenting a program to a large heterogeneous group is overwhelming.

There are a variety of possibilities for such an assembly program. For example, a series of short skits could be used to dramatize some of the major breakthroughs in the history of mathematics. These might also include some lighthearted (yet instructive) skits such as the story of young Gauss, described in Chapter 3 (page 41). Some of the books listed on pages 170–172 would be among those which would provide some interesting ideas for other topics and stories. A skit could be written which would dramatize a useful application of a topic in secondary school mathematics. Here caution must be exercised so that topics selected are appropriate to the majority of the intended audience.

Successful mathematics assembly programs have been produced which involved having individual or small groups of students present short and highly stimulating topics to a general audience. For example, short arithmetic tricks are usually simple enough to generate interest among students of all abilities in the audience. The presenter may show the audience a method of multiplying by 11 mentally. Multiplying 62 by 11 would simply involve adding $6 + 2$ and inserting this sum between the 6 and the 2 to get 682. For a number like 75, the mental multiplication, 75×11, would involve adding the tens digit of the sum $7 + 5$ to the 7 after inserting the units digit between the 7 and 5; that is $75 \times 11 = 825$. For numbers of three or more digits, the rule involves adding every pair of digits starting from the right and each time successively inserting the units digit of the sum (carrying the tens digit) between the end digits. An example of this can be seen when multiplying $3,542 \times 11 = 3(3 + 5)(5 + 4)(4 + 2)2$ which is the number 38,962.

Another exciting number "trick" might be the first example on page 37 in Chapter 3. Here the whole audience could become actively involved. Simply have each student select his own three-digit number and follow the specified steps to attain 1089. The unusual result that everyone, regardless of the number selected (within the guidelines), gets the same answer should certainly arouse student interest.

In part because of its visual nature, geometry offers many topics which might be appropriate for this type of mathematics assembly program. Cutting a very large Möbius strip first half the width from the edge and then one-third the width from the edge should produce some excitement in the audience. To avoid a lull in the presentation, it would be advisable to perforate (i.e., partially cut) the Möbius strip before the program.

Many other topological concepts can intrigue a general audience. Such topics might include removing a vest without removing a covering jacket, untying two people joined by ropes tied to their wrists without removing the rope, and others. A perusal of the second part of this book should enable you to come up with lots of additional ideas for a mathematics assembly program. Another fine source for such ideas is *Riddles in Mathematics* by E.P. Northrop (Princeton, N.J.: D. Van Nostrand, 1944).

It is sometimes educational as well as entertaining for an audience to watch a mathematics quiz show on stage. Two teams might be selected to compete before a general audience. As long as the questions are presented clearly for all to hear and see, this experience might be stimulating to the audience, who would likely work along with the contestants on stage. Where possible, the questions selected for use should be within the realm of understanding of most students in the audience. A large screen should be used to present the questions to the audience.

It should be noted that the suggestions offered for a mathematics assembly program could also be used as a television production, either taped for viewing by individual classes or presented live through a closed circuit television system (if available) within a school or district. The ideas for possible programs presented are merely intended to stimulate, and eventually generate, others which will be, perhaps, more appropriate to the intended audience.

GUEST SPEAKERS PROGRAM

In many areas throughout the country there are mathematics speakers bureaus available to secondary schools. They are often sponsored by local universities or professional organizations. Generally, a listing of speakers, their addresses and a list of topics on which they are prepared to speak is made available to all local schools. There is usually no cost to the host schools for this service. A usual activity for a mathematics club is to arrange the invitations for selected speakers and then to publicize each talk. Depending on the topic selected, the audience might be large or small, and it may be heterogeneous or homogeneous. It is probably most advisable to have students select the speaker

rather than have the selection made by a teacher. Students will likely turn to the teacher for guidance, at which time the teacher can offer her input. The teacher should be careful not to impose her biases onto the speaker selection process, but merely provide guidance. The teacher might contact other secondary schools to find out which speakers were well-received there and which were not. If properly planned, this activity should prove to be quite worthwhile.

CLASS TRIPS OF MATHEMATICAL SIGNIFICANCE

Large metropolitan areas offer many exciting examples of applications of mathematics. Occasionally, teachers in these areas should avail themselves of these resources. For example, an engineering or research laboratory (such as Bell Laboratories or IBM Laboratory) might be of interest to students. Others may find a visit to a race track parimutual installation interesting. There they can observe how betting odds are computed, a direct application of probability. There are occasionally special exhibits presented to motivate students towards further study in mathematics. These can also be used for an interesting mathematics class trip. A resourceful teacher will discover many other ideas for worthwhile mathematics class trips.

Proximity to a major metropolitan area is by no means necessary for a successful mathematics class trip. In every area there is industry which relies heavily on mathematics. For example, if a road is being constructed, a class can benefit from observing engineers and surveyors preparing maps and other plans. Even a police helicopter automobile speed surveillance would offer some interesting mathematics applications. In some localities a teacher's initiative and creativity would be more necessary than in others. This is part of the fun of being a mathematics teacher!

Perhaps most important in preparing a successful class trip is the careful planning which must be done before the trip. This refers to more than merely planning the logistics of the trip. Certainly the travel and other arrangements are necessary; however, perhaps even more important is planning a proper class preparation for the trip. This implies that the teacher should provide the class with the necessary mathematical and experiential background about a planned trip well before the departure dates. This may mean presenting a topic which may otherwise not be taught, presenting a topic sooner than it otherwise would be reached, or perhaps embellishing on a topic to make the trip more appropriate. Under certain circumstances, it may be possible to bring a representative from the place to be visited to the school to motivate and prepare the students for the impending class trip. This extra dimension may help to get the most out of the planned trip. Preplanning a trip can be indispensible if the trip involves visiting a nearby museum with the purpose of seeking out only items of mathematical significance. These can range from paintings and architecture to ancient tools. Whatever is involved, prior planning (including a preliminary visit by the teacher to the destination of the class trip) is an essential step in making a mathematics class trip a success.

PEER TEACHING PROGRAM

A program of peer teaching can be conducted for all three levels of teaching: on-grade teaching, remediation, and enrichment. Perhaps it will be an activity which the mathematics club chooses to undertake or simply an activity initiated by a group of students along with a faculty advisor. Peer teaching can benefit the student doing the teaching as well as the student being taught. By teaching a concept or topic, one gains a much more comprehensive understanding of the topic. This is, in part, the result of having to organize the presentation in an intelligible manner, which in turn causes the teacher to crystalize his thoughts on the topic. Therefore, although this is usually not the primary reason for establishing a peer teaching program, it is an added benefit.

Before any peer teaching begins, time must be provided to train the students involved in teaching their peers. These students must be familiarized with basic teaching techniques and the resources available to them. It is natural to focus on the content when preparing peer teachers; however, a significant amount of time must be devoted to the actual teaching process.

Peer teaching can take various forms. It can be individualized tutoring, it can involve small groups of students, or it can involve regular class instruction. Whichever format is used, substantial preparation must precede any peer teaching. Special skills are required for each type of instruction. If the peer teaching is to be for remedial purposes, then the peer teachers should be made aware of diagnostic procedures and trained to be sensitive to the needs of the slow learner. It is equally important for a peer teacher to know how to interest students considered average-ability learners. To insure success with this activity, methods of instruction should be carefully developed.

When peer teaching is done by gifted students for the purpose of enriching others, a model can be established for involving a majority of the school population. For example, the faculty advisor may present enrichment topics to this select group of gifted peer teachers or she may set up a schedule of outside speakers to present various enrichment topics to these students. Once this has been done and the peer teachers feel reasonably comfortable with the new topic learned, they would convene under the guidance of a faculty member to set up a strategy for presenting this topic to various types of classes. The level of the intended audience should be considered carefully in the preparation

of peer teaching. To the extent appropriate for varying ability levels, a majority of the students in the school can be offered enrichment in mathematics using this model.

Although we use the term "peer teaching" in the literal sense, one may easily extend the ideas presented here by having the "peer teachers" present material to younger students, either in the same school or in nearby lower schools. Under any circumstances, careful preparation and planning must be undertaken in both content and methodology before any peer teaching is attempted. Done properly, peer teaching can be rewarding for both the peer teachers as well as the students being taught.

THE COMPUTER

Largely because of their relatively low cost and their convenient size, the newer mini- and microcomputers are being used in various ways in many secondary schools. Once students have become reasonably proficient at programming, they should be encouraged to work with the computer during their unassigned time during the school day or after classes have ended. The computer has boundless potential for enrichment, both extracurricular and as a part of the regular curriculum (see Chapter 10).

THE BULLETIN BOARD

Every school should have at least one large bulletin board exclusively for mathematics and placed near the mathematics department office or near the mathematics classrooms. This bulletin board can tie together all the extracurricular activities described in this chapter. Both as an aid in providing these activities and as a means for publicity, the mathematics bulletin board can become indispensible in any secondary school. Often the bulletin board sets the tone for the mathematics department.

Some of the uses for the mathematics bulletin board are as follows:

1. The bulletin board can be used to stimulate interest in a mathematical topic or process. Similarly it can be used to motivate students to further study in mathematics by providing only enough material on a certain topic or concept to get students interested enough to do some individual research. Such motivation might well be in the form of a challenge as well as an open-ended question.

2. The results (including questions and model answers) of mathematics team meets can be exhibited on the bulletin board.

3. Mathematics contests (open to all students) can be publicized on the bulletin board.

4. The bulletin board can be the focus for an ongoing weekly intraschool mathematics contest. A "Problem of the Week" would be posted weekly. Every week the preceding week's problem would be shown along with a model solution and a list of successful solvers. Properly publicized by an enthusiastic teacher, this activity can set a very healthy mathematics atmosphere.

5. Mathematics club activities, including special events for non-members (e.g., guest speakers), could be publicized on the bulletin board.

6. Various appealing mathematics projects could be exhibited on the bulletin board. In addition, such events as mathematics fairs might also be publicized there.

7. The bulletin board also can be used to facilitate a peer teaching program by offering publicity and helping with the organization of the program.

8. Career guidance in mathematics, often sought after by stronger mathematics students, might well be given a place on the mathematics bulletin board.

9. The bulletin board might also be used to coordinate computer activities as well as display some more exceptional student programs. Done attractively, this can help to expand the use of the computer to other students.

10. By setting up seasonal displays as they relate to mathematics, students could be enticed to investigate some unusual applications of mathematics (e.g., a spring display might relate phyllotaxis to the Fibonacci numbers).

11. Announcements by colleges and universities concerning special mathematics programs which they offer should be posted on this bulletin board.

SUMMARY

We have discussed many types of extracurricular activities in secondary school mathematics. Some of these activities are carried on outside of the mathematics class (such as clubs, teams, and contests) while others can supplement the regular instruction (such as mathematics projects, guest speakers, and class trips).

It is highly unlikely that a single school will offer all these activities. Yet an awareness of some options for extracurricular activities in mathematics is essential in designing an extracurricular program in mathematics suitable for a particular school. A good program of extracurricular activities in mathematics can go a long way in strengthening the regular mathematics program in the school.

EXERCISES

1. Assume that you have volunteered to serve as faculty advisor to your school's mathematics club, which has been a department activity for some time. Your predecessor, who has just retired, was not very dynamic, and during his tenure the club membership declined sharply while activities involving the club became few and far between. Explain the steps you would take to rejuvenate the club, increase its membership, and develop an attractive program of activities.

2. Assume that you have been coaching your school's mathematics team, which has been trained on a rather informal basis until now, mostly meeting during your spare time to work a few practice problems before each meet. Your supervisor advises you that next term the school is willing to make provision for scheduling the mathematics team as a formal class on your program. Indicate your plans for improving the training program for members of the team and the topics you would plan to teach during the regularly scheduled class period, and justify your decisions.

3. In what type of mathematics class do you feel that a term paper or other project might be appropriately assigned as a requirement of the course? How would you respond to a student who feels that such a "chore" is a waste of time?

4. What would you do to encourage students to enter papers in a mathematics fair if they do not object to doing the research and writing the paper, but they fear giving an oral presentation of their findings before a group of their peers and the judges?

5. Assume that you are the faculty advisor to the school's mathematics magazine. Address the following problems and propose tentative solutions for each.
   a. Very few students are willing to expend the effort needed to write quality papers worthy of inclusion in the magazine.
   b. Too many articles are submitted for inclusion in the magazine. The student editorial staff fears rejecting any material submitted, lest the authors be offended and never submit material again.
   c. The magazine sells poorly and you are unable to meet the expenses of its production.
   d. Conflict develops among the members of the student editorial board and the editor-in-chief resigns two weeks before the due date of publication.

6. Plan a forty-minute mathematics assembly whose primary purpose is to fascinate a general audience of students and attract as many of them as possible to elect mathematics courses next term.

7. As faculty advisor to the mathematics club, you arrange for a speaker to be invited to address a meeting of the club. How would you deal with each of the following situations?
   a. The speaker's presentation is far over the heads of his audience and students begin to leave before the talk is completed.
   b. The speaker is boring, talks down to the students, discusses trivia to a great extent, and begins to lose his audience.
   c. The speaker's presentation degenerates into a sales pitch to have students apply for admission to the college at which he is a faculty member.
   d. The speaker does not appear as scheduled.

8. The chapter discussed planning class trips and preparing students in advance for the experiences they might have during the trip. What follow-up activities would be appropriate *after* the class has returned from a trip to make the trip a complete educational experience?

9. Assume that you are assigned to supervise a peer tutoring program operated by the mathematics department. Most of the tutors are members of the school's honor society and are in the highest mathematics classes in the department. However, students being tutored often complain that their tutors are haughty, impatient with their "slowness" in learning, and sometimes confusing. Peer tutoring is a compulsory activity of honor society members in order to maintain their standing therein. How would you handle this situation?

10. As a professional assignment, your supervisor asks you to maintain the department bulletin board in an attractive manner. You find it cluttered with class honor rolls, announcements of coming activities, team scores, computer schedules, the "Problem of the Week," and many other items. What steps would you take to bring order out of a chaotic arrangement and develop a bulletin board of which the mathematics department can be proud?

NOTES FOR THE MATHEMATICS TEAM

TRIANGLE PROPERTIES

Stewart's Theorem:

$$pb^2 + qc^2 = a(d^2 + pq)$$

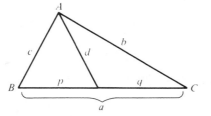

Angle Bisector Relationships:

1. $a : b = m : n$
2. $ab - mn = t_c^2$
3. $t_c = \dfrac{2\sqrt{abs(s - c)}}{a + b}$

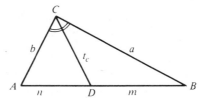

4. The point of intersection of the angle bisectors is the center of the inscribed circle of the triangle.

Triangle Median Relationships:

1. $m_a = \frac{1}{2}\sqrt{2b^2 + 2c^2 - a^2}$

2. $m_a^2 + m_b^2 + m_c^2 = \dfrac{3}{4}(a^2 + b^2 + c^2)$

3. $(a + b + c) > (m_a + m_b + m_c) > \dfrac{3}{4}(a + b + c)$

4. The medians of a triangle are concurrent at a point which trisects each median.

5. The median partitions a triangle into two triangles of equal area.
6. In a right triangle, the median to the hypotenuse: (a) divides the triangle into two isosceles triangles; (b) is one-half the length of the hypotenuse.

Triangle Altitude Relationships:

1. $ah_a = bh_b = ch_c = 2\mathcal{A}$ (Where $\mathcal{A}$ represents the area)

2. $a : \dfrac{1}{h_a} = b : \dfrac{1}{h_b} = c : \dfrac{1}{h_c} = 2$ or $h_a : h_b : h_c = \dfrac{1}{a} : \dfrac{1}{b} : \dfrac{1}{c} = bc : ac : ab$

3. $h_c = \dfrac{ab}{2R}$

Area of a Triangle:

1. $\mathcal{A} = \frac{1}{2}ah_a$

2. $\mathcal{A} = \frac{1}{2}ab \cdot \sin C$

3. $\mathcal{A} = \dfrac{abc}{4R}$

4. $\mathcal{A} = rs$

5. $\mathcal{A} = \sqrt{s(s-a)(s-b)(s-c)}$ *(Heron's Formula)*

6. $\mathcal{A} = \dfrac{b^2\sin A \cdot \sin C}{2 \sin (A+C)}$

7. For an equilateral triangle: $\mathcal{A} = \dfrac{S^2\sqrt{3}}{4} = \dfrac{h^2\sqrt{3}}{3}$

8. The ratio of the areas of two triangles having an angle of equal measure equals the ratio of the products of the lengths of the pairs of sides including the congruent angles.

Inscribed and Circumscribed Circles of a Triangle:

1. $r = \dfrac{a}{s} \sqrt{\dfrac{(s-a)(s-b)(s-c)}{s}}$

2. $R = \dfrac{abc}{4\mathcal{A}}$

3. $\dfrac{a}{\sin A} = \dfrac{b}{\sin B} = \dfrac{c}{\sin C} = 2R$

4. Radius of an *escribed circle:* $r_a = \sqrt{\dfrac{s(s-b)(s-c)}{s-a}}$

To Find the Measure of an Angle of a Triangle:

$\text{Cos } A = \dfrac{b^2 + c^2 - a^2}{2bc}$ *(Law of Cosines)*

Pythagorean Triples:

$a^2 + b^2 = c^2$ where $a = u^2 - v^2$; $b = 2uv$; $c = u^2 + v^2$ and $u > v$ for integers u and v.

Transversal Theorem:

1. In Figure 1, $\overline{AL}$, $\overline{BM}$, and $\overline{CN}$ are concurrent. Therefore: $AN \cdot BL \cdot CM = AM \cdot BN \cdot CL$

Figure 1

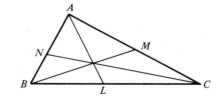

2. In Figure 2, points P, Q and R are collinear. Therefore: $AP \cdot BR \cdot CQ = AQ \cdot BP \cdot CR$

Figure 2

3. In Figure 3, lines a, b, and c are parallel. Therefore:

$$\frac{1}{a} + \frac{1}{b} = \frac{1}{c} \; ; \; \frac{a}{x} = \frac{b}{y}$$

Figure 3

PROPERTIES OF POLYGONS

1. The sum of the measures of the interior angles $= (n - 2)180°$ where $n = $ *number of sides*.
2. The sum of the measures of the exterior angles $= 360°$.
3. In an *equiangular polygon:*   (a) the measure of each interior angle $= 180° - $ (measure of exterior angle)

$$\text{(b) the measure of each interior angle} = \frac{(n-2)180°}{n}$$

$$\text{(c) each exterior angle has measure} = \frac{360°}{n}$$

Regular Polygons:

1. Triangle: $\mathcal{A} = \dfrac{S^2 \sqrt{3}}{4} = \dfrac{h^2 \sqrt{3}}{3} = \dfrac{3R^2 \sqrt{3}}{4} = 3r^2\sqrt{3}$

2. Pentagon: $S = \sqrt{2r} \sqrt{5 - 2\sqrt{5}} = \dfrac{1}{2}R\sqrt{10 - 2\sqrt{5}}$

3. Hexagon: $S = R$, and $\mathcal{A} = \dfrac{3}{2}R^2\sqrt{3} = 2r^2\sqrt{3}$

4. Octagon: $S = 2r(\sqrt{2} - 1) = R\sqrt{2 - \sqrt{2}}$

5. Decagon: $S = \dfrac{2}{5}(r\sqrt{25 - 10\sqrt{5}} = \dfrac{1}{2}R(\sqrt{5} - 1)$

6. Dodecagon: $\mathcal{A} = 3R^2$

7. General: $\mathcal{A} = \dfrac{1}{2}ap = \dfrac{1}{2}rp$ ($a = $ apothem; $p = $ perimeter)

Areas of Quadrilaterals:

1. Rectangle: $\mathcal{A} = bh$

2. Square: $\mathcal{A} = S^2 = \frac{1}{2}d^2 = 2R^2 = 4r^2$

3. Parallelogram: $\mathcal{A} = bh = ab \cdot \sin C$

4. Rhombus: $\mathcal{A} = bh = \frac{1}{2}d_1 d_2 = ab \cdot \sin C$

5. Trapezoid: $\mathcal{A} = \frac{1}{2}h(b_1 + b_2)$

Miscellaneous Triangle and Quadrilateral Theorems:

1. The sum of the lengths of the perpendiculars on the legs of an isosceles triangle from any point on the base is equal to the length of an altitude on one of the legs.

2. In an equilateral triangle, the sum of the lengths of the perpendiculars from any point to the three sides is equal to the lengths of an altitude.

3. In a circumscribed quadrilateral, the sum of the lengths of the opposite sides are equal.

4. In an inscribed quadrilateral, the sum of the products of the lengths of the opposite sides equals the product of the lengths of the diagonals (*Ptolemy's Theorem*).

5. The area of a *cyclic quadrilateral* (i.e., an inscribed quadrilateral) $= \sqrt{(s-a)(s-b)(s-c)(s-d)}$ (*Brahmagupta's Formula*).

6. In any parallelogram the sum of the squares of the lengths of the diagonals equals the sum of the squares of all the lengths of the sides.

7. In a triangle whose sides are 13, 14, 15, h_{14} divides side 14 into segments 5 and 9, and h_{14} is 12.

8. In any triangle, the square of the length of a side opposite an acute angle is equal to the sum of the squares of the other lengths of the other two sides diminished by twice the product of the length of one of those sides and the length of the projection of the other side upon it.

$$(\text{For } \triangle ABC: a^2 = b^2 + c^2 - 2cp)$$

9. In any obtuse triangle, the square of the length of the side opposite the obtuse angle is equal to the sum of the squares of the length of the other two sides, increased by twice the product of the length of one of these sides and the length of the projection of the other side upon it.

$$(\text{For obtuse } \triangle ABC: a^2 = b^2 + c^2 + 2cp)$$

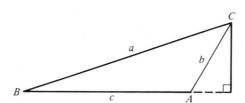

MISCELLANEOUS THEOREMS ON PERIMETER AND AREA

1. Of all triangles having the same base and equal areas, the isosceles triangle has the minimum perimeter.

2. Of all triangles having the same base and equal perimeters, the triangle whose other two sides are congruent has the greatest area.

3. Of all polygons constructed with the same given sides in a given order, that which can be inscribed in a circle has the greatest area.

4. Of two regular polygons with equal perimeters, that which has the greater number of sides has the greater area.

5. If similar polygons are constructed on the three sides of a right triangle, the sum of the areas of the polygons on the legs is equal to the area of the polygon on the hypotenuse. (This is an extension of the Pythagorean Theorem.)

PAPPUS' THEOREM

A *volume* which is generated by the motion of a plane section through space equals the product of the area of the plane section and the length of the path of the center of gravity of the plane section.

SOME NUMBER THEORY FACTS

1. Divisibility by 2: last digit of number is even (or "0").
2. Divisibility by 3: sum of the digits is divisible by 3.
3. Divisibility by 4: last two digits divisible by 4 (e.g., 7812).
4. Divisibility by 5: last digit 5 or 0.
5. Divisibility by 6: rules for divisibility by 2 and 3.
6. Divisibility by 8: last three digits when considered as a number is divisible by 8 (e.g., 57256).
7. Divisibility by 9: sum of the digits is divisible by 9.
8. Divisibility by 10: last digit is 0.
9. Divisibility by 11: the difference of the sums of alternate digits is divisible by 11.
10. Divisibility by 12: rules for divisibility by 3 and 4.
11. *Fermat's Theorem:* $N^{p-1} - 1$ = multiple of p, where p is prime and N is prime relative to p (e.g., $3^{7-1} - 1$ is a multiple of 7).

FACTORING

1. For *odd e:* $x^e + y^e = (x + y)(x^{e-1} - x^{e-2} y + x^{e-3}y^2 - \ldots + y^{e-1})$
2. For *all e:* $x^e - y^e = (x - y)(x^{e-1} + x^{e-2}y + x^{e-3}y^2 + \ldots + y^{e-1})$
3. For *even e:* $x^e - y^e = (x^{e/2} + y^{e/2})(x^{e/2} - y^{e/2})$

BINOMIAL THEOREM

$$(a + b)^n = a^n + na^{n-1}b + \frac{n(n - 1)}{1 \cdot 2} a^{n-2} b^2 = \frac{n(n - 1)(n - 2)}{1 \cdot 2 \cdot 3} a^{n-3}b^3 + \ldots + b^n$$

LOGARITHMS

1. $\text{Log}_a b = x$ means $a^x = b$
2. $(\text{Log}_a b)(\text{Log}_b c) = \text{Log}_a c$

INEQUALITIES

1. $a + \dfrac{1}{a} \geq 2$

2. $\dfrac{a}{b} + \dfrac{b}{a} \geq 2$

3. $\dfrac{a + b}{2b} \geq \dfrac{2ab}{a + b}$

MEANS

Arithmetic Mean: $(AM) = \dfrac{a + b}{2}$

Geometric Mean: $(GM) = \sqrt{ab}$

Harmonic Mean: $(HM) = \dfrac{2ab}{a + b}$

1. $AM \geq GM \geq HM$
2. $(AM)(HM) = (GM)^2$

RESOURCES FOR EXTRACURRICULAR ACTIVITIES

History of Mathematics

Ball, W.W. Rouse. *A Short Account of the History of Mathematics*. New York: Dover, 1960.

Bell, E.T. *Men of Mathematics*. New York: Simon & Schuster, 1937.

Boyer, Carl B. *A History of Mathematics*. New York: Wiley, 1968.

Bunt, Lucas N.H., Jones, Philip S., and Bedient, Jack D. *The Historical Roots of Elementary Mathematics*. Englewood Cliffs, N.J.: Prentice Hall, 1976.

Cajori, Florian. *A History of Mathematic Notations*. 2 Vols. LaSalle, Ill.: Open Court, 1928.

Eves, Howard. *An Introduction to the History of Mathematics,* 4th ed. New York: Holt, Rinehart & Winston, 1976.

Heath, Thomas L. *Greek Mathematics*. New York: Dover, 1963.

Smith, David E. *A Source Book in Mathematics*. New York: McGraw-Hill, 1929.

Smith, David E. *History of Mathematics*. 2 Vols. New York: Dover, 1953.

van der Waerden, B.L. *Science Awakening*. New York: Wiley, 1963.

Mathematical Recreations

Ball, W.W. Rouse, and Coxeter, H.S.M. *Mathematical Recreations and Essays*. New York: Macmillan, 1960.

Benson, William, and Jacoby, Oswald. *New Recreations with Magic Squares*. New York: Dover, 1976.

Caldwell, J.H. *Topics in Recreational Mathematics*. London: Cambridge University Press, 1966.

Cundy, H. Martyn, and Rollett, A.P. *Mathematical Models*. New York: Oxford University Press, 1961.

Honsberger, Ross. *Mathematical Morsels*. Washington, D.C.: Mathematics Association of America, 1978.

Kraitchik, Maurice. *Mathematical Recreations*. New York: Dover, 1942.

Madachy, Joseph. *Mathematics on Vacation*. New York: Charles Scribner's Sons, 1966.

Northrop, Eugene. *Riddles in Mathematics*. Princeton, N.J.: D. Van Nostrand, 1944.

Ogilvy, C. Stanley. *Through the Mathescope*. New York: Oxford University Press, 1956.

Posamentier, Alfred S. *Excursions in Advanced Euclidean Geometry*. Menlo Park, Ca.: Addison-Wesley, 1984.

Posamentier, Alfred S. *Geometric Constructions*. Portland, Maine: J. Weston Walch, 1973.

Posamentier, Alfred S., and Sheridan, Gordon. *Mathematics Motivators, Investigations in Pre-Algebra*. Menlo Park, Ca.: Addison-Wesley, 1982.

————. *Math Motivators, Investigations in Geometry*. Menlo Park, Ca.: Addison-Wesley, 1982.

————. *Math Motivators, Investigations in Algebra*. Menlo Park, Ca.: Addison-Wesley, 1983.

Schuh, Fred. *The Master Book of Mathematical Recreations*. New York: Dover, 1968.

Mathematics Clubs

Carnahan, Walter H., ed. *Mathematics Clubs in High Schools*. Washington, D.C.: National Council of Teachers of Mathematics, 1958.

Gruver, Howell L. *School Mathematics Contests: A Report*. Washington, D.C.: National Council of Teachers of Mathematics, 1968.

Hess, Adrien L. *Mathematics Projects Handbook*. Washington, D.C.: National Council of Teachers of Mathematics, 1977.

Mu Alpha Theta. *Handbook for Sponsors*. Norman, Oklahoma: University of Oklahoma, 1970.

Ransom, William R. *Thirty Projects for Mathematical Clubs and Exhibitions*. Portland, Maine: J. Weston Walch, Publisher, 1961.

Problem Solving

The Conference Board of Mathematical Sciences. *The Role of Axiomatics and Problem Solving in Mathematics*. Boston: Ginn, 1966.

Hudgins, Bryce B. *Problem Solving in the Classroom*. New York: Macmillan, 1966.

Krulik, Stephen, and Rudnick, Jesse A. *Problem Solving, a Handbook for Teachers*. Boston: Allyn and Bacon, 1980.

Polya, George. *How to Solve It*. Princeton, N.J.: Princeton University Press, 1945.

————. *Mathematics and Plausible Reasoning*. 2 Vols. Princeton, N.J.: Princeton University Press, 1954.

_____ . *Mathematical Discovery*. 2 Vols. New York: Wiley, 1962.

Whimbey, Arthur, and Lochhead, Jack. *Problem Solving and Comprehension, A Short Course in Analytical Reasoning*, 2d ed. Philadelphia: Franklin Institute Press, 1980.

Wickelgren, Wayne A. *How To Solve Problems*. San Francisco: W.H. Freeman, 1974.

Sources for Mathematics Team Problems

Aref, M.N., and Wernick, William. *Problems and Solutions in Euclidean Geometry*. New York: Dover, 1968.

Barbeau, E., Klamkin M., and Moser, W. *1001 Problems in High School Mathematics*. Montreal, Canada: Canadian Mathematics Congress, 1978.

Brousseau, Brother Alfred, ed. *Mathematics Contest Problems*. Palo Alto, Calif.: Creative Publications, 1972.

Bryant, Steven J., Graham, George E., and Wiley, Kenneth G. *Nonroutine Problems in Algebra, Geometry and Trigonometry*. New York: McGraw-Hill, 1965.

Butts, Thomas. *Problem Solving in Mathematics*. Glenview, Ill.: Scott, Foresman, 1973.

Charosh, Mannis, ed. *Mathematical Challenges*. Washington D.C.: National Council of Teachers of Mathematics, 1965.

Comprehensive School Mathematics Program. *E.M. Problem Book*. 2 Vols. St. Louis: CEMREL, 1975.

Dunn, Angela, ed. *Mathematical Bafflers*. New York: McGraw-Hill, 1964.

_____ . *Second Book of Mathematical Bafflers*. New York: Dover, 1983.

Greitzer, Samuel L. *International Mathematical Olympiads*. Washington, D.C. Mathematical Association of America, 1978.

Hill, Thomas J., ed. *Mathematical Challenges II—Plus Six*. Washington, D.C.: National Council of Teachers of Mathematics, 1974.

Polya, George, and Kilpatrick, Jeremy. *The Stanford Mathematics Book*. New York: Teachers College Press, 1974.

Posamentier, Alfred S., and Salkind, Charles T. *Challenging Problems in Algebra*. 2 Vols. New York: Macmillan, 1970.

_____ . *Challenging Problems in Geometry*. 2 Vols. New York: Macmillan, 1970.

_____ . *Uncommon Problems for Common Topics in Algebra*. Portland, Me.: J. Weston Walch, 1981.

_____ . *Unusual Problems for Usual Topics in Algebra*. Portland, Me.: J. Weston Walch, 1981.

Rapaport, Elvira, trans. *Hungarian Problem Book*. 2 Vols. New York: Random House, 1963.

Salkind, Charles T., ed. *The Contest Problem Book*. New York: Random House, 1961.

_____ . *The MAA Problem Book II*. New York: Random House, 1966.

Salkind, Charles T., and Earl, James M., eds. *The MAA Problem Book III*. New York: Random House, 1973.

Shklarsky, D.O., Chentzov, N.N., and Yaglom, I.M. *The U.S.S.R. Olympiad Problem Book*. San Francisco: W.H. Freeman, 1962.

Sitomer, Harry. *The New Mathlete Problem Book*. Nassau County, N.Y.: Interscholastic Mathematics League, 1974.

Steinhaus, Hugo. *One Hundred Problems in Elementary Mathematics*. New York: Pergamon Press, 1963.

Straszewicz, S. *Mathematical Problems and Puzzles from the Polish Mathematical Olympiads*. New York: Pergamon Press, 1965.

Trigg, Charles W. *Mathematical Quickies*. New York: McGraw-Hill, 1967.

Basic References

Altshiller-Court, Nathan A. *College Geometry*. New York: Barnes & Noble, 1952.

Barnett, I.A. *Elements of Number Theory*. Boston: Prindle, Weber & Schmidt, 1972.

Chrystal, G. *Textbook of Algebra*. 2 Vols. New York: Chelsea, 1964.

Courant, Richard, and Robbins, Herbert. *What Is Mathematics?* New York: Oxford University Press, 1941.

Coxeter, H.S.M., and Greitzer, S.L. *Geometry Revisited*. New York: Random House, 1967.

Davis, David R. *Modern College Geometry*. Reading, Mass.: Addison-Wesley, 1949.

Hall, H.S., and Knight, S.R. *Higher Algebra*. London: Macmillan, 1960

James, Robert C., and James, Glenn, eds. *Mathematics Dictionary*, 4th ed. New York: Van Nostrand Reinhold, 1976.

Johnson, Roger A. *Modern Geometry*. Boston: Houghton Mifflin, 1929.

Karush, William. *The Crescent Dictionary of Mathematics*. New York: Macmillan, 1962.

Newman, James R. *The World of Mathematics*. 4 Vols. New York: Simon & Schuster, 1956.

Olds, C.D. *Continued Fractions*. New York: Random House, 1963.

Posamentier, Alfred S. *Excursions in Advanced Euclidean Geometry*. Menlo Park, Ca.: Addison-Wesley, 1984.

Schaaf, William L., ed. *A Bibliography of Recreational Mathematics*. 4 Vols. Washington, D.C.: National Council of Teachers of Mathematics, 1978.

Smith, David E., ed. *Source Book in Mathematics*. New York: McGraw-Hill, 1929.

SUGGESTED READINGS

Bruckheimer, Maxim, and Hirshkowitz, Rina. "Mathematics Projects in Junior High School." *The Mathematics Teacher* 70 (1977): 573.

Elgarten, Gerald H. "A Mathematics Intramurals Contest." *The Mathematics Teacher* 69 (1976): 477.

Holmes, Joseph E. "Enrichment or Acceleration?" *The Mathematics Teacher* 63 (1970): 471.

Jones, Mary H. "Mathcounts: A New Junior High School Mathematics Competition." *The Mathematics Teacher,* 76 (1983): 482.

Lichtenberg, Betty K. "Some Excellent Sources of Material for Mathematics Clubs." *The Mathematics Teacher* 74 (1981): 284.

Wright, Frank. "Motivating Students With Projects and Teaching Aids." *The Mathematics Teacher* 58 (1965): 47.

CHAPTER 13 CLASSROOM MANAGEMENT

Paper planes? Spitballs? Tacks on the teacher's seat? All quaint relics of the past. What could you really expect to see today if you walked into any class at a random high school? Anything imaginable! The little red schoolhouse has yielded to the assembly-line secondary school whose population often numbers in the thousands and which must, therefore, be a microcosm of society and all that is good and bad in it.

Many classrooms are managed well, and you would see an orderly, business-like atmosphere where students are learning while teachers are teaching. Yet, the identical group of students could very well be raising havoc in another room while the teacher is wringing his hands in despair. Wherein lies the difference?

In this chapter we will present three aspects of classroom management that affect, both directly and indirectly, the teaching-learning process: classroom practices, discipline, and administrative details.

CLASSROOM PRACTICES

The development of proper habits and attitudes concerning classroom practices, for pupils as well as the teacher, ought to begin from the first day that the class meets. From the moment the starting bell of the class sounds until the end of the class period, students should see in you an efficient, well-organized teacher who is aware of everyone and everything that is happening in the classroom. If this atmosphere is maintained in the succeeding days, the result will ultimately be a class where every minute of learning time is considered precious and where wasted moments are unacceptable. Following are some suggestions you may find helpful in the classroom.

Establish Routine

Accustom the pupils to sit down to work as soon as they enter the room. Loitering in the halls in the vicinity of the classroom while waiting for the starting bell to ring should not be permitted, for it is a distraction to those who do begin promptly or even early. You need only stand at the door for a moment to check outside the room and move students in. Students should be accustomed to then look for the homework and do-now exercise, or whatever activity you want them to work on, on the same corner of the board every day. As school policy, latecomers are usually expected to present a late pass, and you will find that if you adhere strictly to this policy, pupils will tend to arrive promptly to your class. Students should realize that their mathematics class *always* starts on time and with meaningful work. Remember that teachers have no right to expect of students what they do not demand of themselves. Arrive in class on time yourself, and always be prepared!

Start Out Strict!

As a new teacher you will find it helpful to be a bit more stern at the beginning of the term than you might generally like to be. Try not to engage in frivolous remarks or behavior; avoid smiling too much until you are certain that you are master of the situation. By starting off as a strict disciplinarian, you capture control. Then when appropriate you can relax this strictness. The reverse, that is, starting off in a relaxed fashion and then becoming stricter, is difficult, if not almost impossible! You will also find the initial strictness to be helpful in "nipping in the bud" the tendency of some students to call out answers and thus distract you as well as other students.

Learn Names

Learn students' names quickly. Most teachers prefer using first names but others prefer the more formal Mr. or Ms. Choose whichever you are more comfortable with and remain consistent. If your room has fixed furniture, you will find it helpful to keep a seating plan on your desk while you teach, so you can learn the names quickly at the beginning of the term. If you have movable seats, try to have the students return to the same location (or as close to it as possible) daily, at least until you have learned their names.

Distribute and Collect Materials Efficiently

Avoid wasting time when passing out or collecting papers, books, supplies, folders, etc. If your furniture is fixed in a "column" and "row" formation, this can be done most efficiently by passing and collecting either by column or row. The advantage of row passing is that this requires only a hand motion from side to side and avoids the confusion caused by pupils turning around and rising from their seats when papers are passed by column. When seats are not fixed, they may be arranged in semicircular formation, by ability grouping, in various parts of the room, column-row formation or many other possibilities. The teacher ought to make a conscious effort to determine the most efficient collection-distribution scheme for the prevailing conditions.

Keep the Classroom Tidy

Make yourself conscious of the physical condition of the room, such as ventilation, lighting, condition of floors, bulletin boards and teacher's desk. Remind the class to treat school property, such as loaned textbooks, properly. When you erase boardwork from the previous class, be sure that you do it completely. Any stray marks left on the board can interfere with later boardwork. For example, a stray vertical line can later on be interpreted as a "one" for a future problem. If the floor is littered with paper from the previous period, pupils can help you place the litter in wastebaskets. You are thereby training them in the virtue of cleanliness in a public area. Gum chewing disturbs many youngsters as well as the teacher and should be curtailed.

Have Supplies on Hand

Plan to have all necessary supplies in the room before the lesson begins. Some of the items you may need might include overhead projectors, graph charts, calculators, colored chalk, etc. To send for them during the period, when the supply room might be locked, would cause a needless interruption in the lesson.

Insist on Neatness

Insist on neat written work both on the board and on paper. The students should understand that work written on the board is not only for themselves but for the entire class. It should be legible so that all may be able to read it easily.

Use Correct English

Pay particular attention to your own use of English and to the accuracy of the oral responses of your students, although, generally, students "understand" each other's careless and inaccurate responses to teacher questions. Yet there may be a few students who may be confused or misled by such careless responses. Thus, it is the teacher's responsibility to insure accuracy. Not all answers need to be given in complete sentence form, but whenever a response requires it, insist upon correct English. In mathematics, more so than in other subjects, every word uttered is important and the pupils must say exactly what they mean and not leave it to the teacher to remedy the deficiencies.

Omit Reasons in Chalkboard Proofs

When teaching geometry classes, some teachers feel that once the class has learned to write proofs, theorems and proof exercises written on the board should show only the diagram, hypothesis, conclusion and the statements of the proof. Reasons need not appear on the board except in those instances when the teacher wants to demonstrate a model solution. They feel that there is little value in having pupils read aloud reasons from the board, for they can be done orally. Furthermore, the omission of the reasons will tend to avoid crowded, illegible handwriting. You will, of course, eventually make your own judgment.

Keep Homework Relevant

Even though the homework assignment may have been put on the board at the beginning of the period, or presented early in the week, reference should be made to it during the period so that the pupils will see its relation to the work being done. It is not necessary to review every single homework exercise in class every day, since the purpose of the assignment is to enable the pupil to determine whether or not he has mastered the work that has been taught, and this can sometimes be done after reviewing only a few exercises. See Chapter 4 on homework for a detailed analysis on the many methods of handling homework.

Prevent Cheating on Tests

Be vigilant while proctoring a test or quiz. Walk about the room constantly. Students can be very creative in devising schemes to obtain answers improperly. Proctor-ing is a full-time job and should not be shared with marking other tests or reading a newspaper.

Work the Entire Period

Give the classroom the atmosphere of a well-managed team. Be especially efficient by planning what you will be doing every moment of the period. Work up to the bell at the end of the period. Insist that youngsters not stop working until you tell them that the lesson is over. If it should happen that there are a few minutes remaining, do *not* dismiss the class early, for they may disturb other classes. Keep them in their seats either working on more "if time" exercises in your lesson plan or beginning their homework for the next day.

Don't Sit Down!

Some experienced, competent teachers believe that the purpose of the chair at the teacher's desk is to remind him of the one spot in the room where he should *never* be. Youngsters can be best taught and supervised by a teacher who is constantly up and around the room. The teacher should teach from different parts of the room. When a teacher is at the side of the room, the adjacent column of students is at the new "front of the room," and when a teacher is standing in the middle, the students around him for that moment feel a sense of being "up front."

Check Attendance Daily

Attendance and lateness to class should be recorded daily, usually during a moment of the lesson when students are working on their own at their seats. It is best done quietly and quickly by looking about the room, spotting the empty seats, checking the seating plan or class list, and recording the date of absence on either the list, the seating plan or other document provided by the school. In order to avoid forgetting to check attendance, the procedure should be routinized to occur at the same moment of the lesson every day if possible, usually during the do-now exercise. Some teachers allow students to assist them in this task, and if you do, remember that you are still responsible for errors.

Grouping Students by Ability

Some teachers find it helpful to arrange the class into ability groups so that special assignments can be made to meet the needs of each particular group of students. Also, the teacher can work with each group as the need arises, during the course of the lesson. Slow students might receive special remedial work and bright pupils could get enrichment. Grouping is especially valuable if a paraprofessional assistant to the teacher is available in the room.

Call on Every Student

Volunteers as well as non-volunteers should be called upon during the course of every lesson—whether it is to answer a question directed by the teacher or to write an exercise or homework example on the board. You must make every effort to call on every student at least once during the day, and be especially careful not to let the loud, aggressive student monopolize the responses.

Work that has been put on the chalkboard by one student could occasionally be explained by another student. To be able to explain what another student has written, or to locate his error, is almost as important as being able to do the exercise oneself. This method of classwork (or homework review) tends to hold the attention of the class and as a result obviates the need for special concern with class discipline.

Adjust the Lesson Plan

Keep an eye on your lesson plan as well as on your watch throughout the period. There will be times when you will find it necessary to adjust your plans during the lesson in order to be able to end it on time and in a logical spot.

Develop Bulletin Boards

Well-maintained, informative, colorful bulletin boards are often a useful way to disseminate information as well as to provide a vehicle for displaying unusual student work—whether special projects or examinations. You may assign a pupil to be in charge of the care of the bulletin board, or you may prefer to maintain it entirely yourself (see Chapter 12).

Encourage Active Involvement

The ability to develop a teacher-pupil-pupil–pupil-teacher dialogue is one requiring skill and practice. This type of socialization can be the outgrowth of a skillfully placed question. For example, consider this conversation in a high school geometry class:

> Teacher: What is the locus of points 3 inches from a given line?
> Student 1: The locus consists of two lines parallel to the given line, on either side of it and 3 inches away.
> Student 2: Isn't it really a circular cylinder of radius 3 with the given line as an axis?
> Student 3: Student 1 is right because the course we're studying is called Plane Geometry.
> Teacher: The fault is really mine. What should my original question have been?
> Student 4: What is the locus of points in a plane, that are 3 inches from a given line?

DISCIPLINE

Discipline problems, like accidents, may often be avoided with keen awareness and if proper precautions are taken. Poor classroom practices tend to promote an atmosphere which is ripe for potential troublemakers to fill the vacuum in class control with undesirable actions. Every dean of discipline and guidance counselor knows that there are some teachers who rarely if ever have discipline problems in their classroom while others have frequent flare-ups, often serious, with students. It would be foolish to say that, in general, discipline problems are caused by the teacher. No teacher seeks them. Yet there are days when a teacher may not be feeling well, or is particularly irritable for some personal reason, or has a real bias towards a student. The sensitive teacher may be able to understand and control these feelings while some may not be capable of doing so. Thus, confrontations with students that might occur one day, might not come about on the next.

What are some disciplinary problems a teacher may encounter in the classroom? Different teachers have differing notions of what constitutes a breach of discipline, so the list below is by no means exhaustive. It is merely suggestive, to get you thinking in the right direction. Also, it is impossible to arrange the items in any order of seriousness, for out of context many of the items appear to be not worth fussing over. But in the setting of a classroom where effective control over a large number of students is needed, the teacher must often respond (either actively or passively) to save face. However, pupils must also save face before their peers. Thus a confrontation over a seemingly insignificant matter may arise and may be blown entirely out of proportion. Some examples of breaches of class discipline by students include the following.

> Getting out of seat and walking around during the lesson
> Leaving the room without permission
> Excessive talking to neighbors
> Calling out answers in spite of the teacher's request not to do so
> Not doing his homework
> Coming to class unprepared—no text, no notebook, etc.
> Cheating on a test
> Using improper language in class
> Often arriving late to class
> Chewing and cracking gum
> Tossing paper across the room
> Throwing paper on the floor
> Doing work for another subject in the mathematics class
> Laughing aloud, wisecracking
> Fighting with another pupil

Excessive absence or cutting

Reading a newspaper in class

Daydreaming, staring out the window and not paying attention to the lesson

Speaking to another pupil across the room in a foreign language

Threatening the teacher verbally or physically

Handling Discipline Problems

Now suppose you are in your classroom and, for whatever reason, a disciplinary problem arises with a student. Will you feel intimidated by his aggressive behavior into doing nothing, waiting for the "storm" to pass, hoping that it will "go away by itself" soon? Or will you resolve the situation quickly? Instinct sometimes plays an uncontrollable role in a situation where tempers flare, but perhaps even certain instinctive behavior can be channeled into the proper direction. We therefore offer the following thoughts, as well as do's and don'ts, which might prove helpful in various situations.

Speak to the student involved in a loud, clear, firm voice. Do not shriek, or become hysterical. Remain calm. Do not show evidence of timidity or fear or uncertainty. Be polite!

Merely tell the student, "Please stop doing that" or "Cut it out!" or "Please see me after class" (this can be said to the pupil publicly or privately). Do not insult, embarrass or curse at the pupil. More students will respond to a polite request than you might believe. It is often said, "You can catch more flies with honey than with vinegar."

Try to avoid making public demands that you cannot enforce and that might cause a confrontation. Thus, if a pupil is misbehaving and you tell her, "Change your seat," she may refuse to do so. At this point, you must weigh the effect on the class if you either call in a supervisor to assist you or merely back off for the moment and ignore her refusal to obey. The situation might have been avoided if you had approached the youngster quietly and asked her to behave and/or change her seat. In fact, quiet, "behind-the-scenes diplomacy" is often an effective discipline tool in every area of misbehavior.

Remember that there may be times when you will have to swallow your pride if you feel this will defuse the situation. Keep in mind that this is only a temporary action that may be the most expedient one for that moment.

You might, of course, try to speak to the student in an attempt to resolve the issue on a one-to-one level later.

In every case in which you want to pursue action against the student who has created a problem in class, *referral* could be made after class to the dean of discipline, guidance counselor, or other appropriate school official. They have several courses of action they might take, such as removal of a student from the class (permanently or temporarily), a class discussion led by the dean or a counselor (not necessarily in the presence of the teacher) on behavior in school, automatic failure in the subject, etc. The proper person to notify will vary with each school. A new teacher would be wise to familiarize herself with the organizational structure in the school.

The dean might notify the parents as a matter of course. However, you might also want to discuss the matter with them. A telephone call, rather than a parental visit, might be all that's needed. Just remember to make no threats. Simply inform them of their child's misconduct and the *possible* consequences of such behavior.

If you prefer to send a note, one that follows this format might be recommended:

Dear Mrs. Smith,

Suzanne has been disrupting her mathematics class with her behavior. Such behavior may adversely effect her course work and ultimately result in lower grades.

I would very much like to discuss this matter with you as soon as possible. Please call me at 567-7879 so that we may set up a conference to discuss ways in which we can solve this problem together.

Sincerely,

More Serious Problems

In most cases, discipline problems do *not* involve physical danger to anyone. However, if the discipline problem in question appears to be a direct or imminent threat to the physical well-being of one or more students, or yourself, such as when a fight breaks out between two students, you may (if you are capable of doing so) attempt to physically separate them to prevent the pupils from harming each other or you. Often, students themselves will break up fights among other students. In any event, aid must be summoned to keep the youngsters apart even if the fight has already been stopped, in order to escort the students involved in the fracas to the dean of discipline (if he has not already appeared on the scene). Similarly, the dean or a supervisor should be summoned if there is an immediate threat against you. A student in the class, or a neighboring teacher, can help in the situation by calling for additional help. After matters have calmed down in the classroom, continue the lesson. You will handle the necessary disciplinary details after class.

If you suspect a youngster in your class of using drugs, notify the guidance counselor or dean. You may be wrong, but allow experts to make that determination. If you are right, you may be instrumental in preventing the student from committing further harm to himself. In any event, the problem is out of your hands once you've reported it.

Student Responsibilities

Students ought to be reminded by you early in the term of their duties and obligations in a classroom, and that infractions will inevitably lead to disciplinary action. In order to avoid problems in class, they will be expected to:

> Arrive in class before the late bell sounds
> Take their seats quickly and quietly
> Get started on the do-now exercise immediately
> Remain in their seats throughout the period
> Leave the room only with permission of the teacher
> Do homework regularly
> Come to class fully prepared to do work—with pencil, notebook, textbook, etc.
> Speak courteously
> Keep a civil tongue
> Refrain from shouting out answers or calling across the room
> Keep the room clean
> Refrain from fighting
> Refrain from cutting class
> Refrain from doing other than mathematics work in class

Unacceptable Teacher Practices

Below are some situations in which the teacher may have failed to use ordinary common sense or acceptable classroom practices, and which may have provoked either direct disciplinary eruptions or behavior leading to such eruptions:

> Often arriving late to class
> Walking out of the room during a lesson to talk to a colleague
> Turning pages to look for suitable exercises while the class waits
> Leaving the classroom to pick up supplies
> Talking to a colleague who comes to the classroom
> Giving examples that are too complicated, too trivial, or too repetitious
> Teaching in a monotonous, dull manner
> Offering no motivation for pupils to learn
> Always embarrassing students
> Often making mathematical errors

> Not knowing students' names, and not looking at them when teaching the class
> Making direct or indirect racial slurs
> Showing no enthusiasm for teaching
> Never praising pupils when it might be deserved
> Spending excessive time discussing matters of little general interest or unrelated to the topic
> Ignoring minor infractions
> Erasing the chalkboard too early
> Rarely asking or answering questions
> Irritating mannerisms—constantly looking at watch, pacing back and forth, etc.
> Talking too quickly or too slowly
> Carrying on private discussions or helping one or two students with classwork while ignoring the rest of the class

Common sense dictates that the teacher will make every effort to avoid the situations above. Sometimes it will require a supervisor's assistance. Other times it will require a greater awareness by the teacher in order to avoid them. Thus, while improved pupil motivation techniques can be suggested by the supervisor, *you* are the one who must implement the program of improvement. Do it eagerly and enthusiastically for you will be the ultimate beneficiary with classes which are manageable and functioning properly.

Other causes of disciplinary eruptions in a classroom that are beyond the control of the teacher may be:

> Flare-up of a disagreement between two students (perhaps carried over from another class)
> Family or other personal problems affecting a student
> Racial attitude of student
> Aggressive behavior towards peers and/or adults
> Mental or emotional problems resulting in antisocial behavior.

These problems are best left for the dean to handle.

ADMINISTRATIVE DETAILS

Most administrative aspects of classroom management (called "clerical work") affect the teaching process peripherally. They may be required for legal reasons, disciplinary purposes or organizational needs. Most professionals who have secretarial services available need not be personally involved in them. However, teachers, generally, do not have such services available, or if they do, the services are only minimal. Thus, some consider these chores onerous, performing them only perfunctorily, yet they are necessary for the smooth functioning of the classroom as well as the entire school. Some of these tasks are the following:

Writing a test on a spirit master and making copies on the duplicator machine

Maintaining records of grades, attendance, lateness

Calling or writing parents personally

Distributing notices, announcements, information to pupils

Completing governmental or board-of-education-mandated surveys

Recording end-of-term grades and recommendations to counselors

Maintaining records and files of absence notes from parents, book receipts, supervisors' notices, etc.

Recording minutes of departmental meetings

Who has not seen the absent-minded-professor type walking down the hallway with books, papers, folders, supplies, etc. flying about in disorganized disarray? Teachers are often inundated with paperwork, but if you have to do it, you might learn to at least do it well. Plan a schedule and stick to it!

If you make an effort to perform your clerical tasks well early in your teaching career, it will be to your advantage in the years to come, for it will become habit-forming. Those who don't will find them to be a constant burden, and it need not be so!

SUMMARY

Proper classroom practices are most important in maintaining a refreshing teaching-learning atmosphere. These involve not only training students to respond positively to the teacher's efforts, but having the teacher perform and behave in a responsible, professional manner. The teacher must always be fully prepared and knowledgeable in the lesson for the day, and he must at the same time maintain effective discipline as well as perform his clerical chores satisfactorily.

A well-managed classroom is a pleasure to behold. To the uninformed it seems the "natural" way for a class to be conducted. The informed observer, however, is well aware of the effort and skill required to establish and maintain a viable classroom situation with a wholesome setting, where genuine and enthusiastic learning takes place.

Some consider the classroom to be the teacher's private castle. Others reject this description of the teacher's role in the classroom as implying a sort of dictatorial approach towards classroom management. Whatever your feelings, it is every teacher's desire to teach a class that is well behaved, attentive and receptive. It is up to you to make that possible.

EXERCISES

1. Comment on the following note by a teacher to the dean of discipline: "I found Frank cheating on a test, so I tore up his paper. He cursed at me and threatened to 'get me,' then he ran out of the room in the middle of the period. I think he should be suspended from school."

2. A student receives his report card indicating 23 days' absence in his mathematics class, resulting in a failing mark since a school rule mandates failure for pupils absent over 21 days. The student vehemently denies being absent that many days and claims that no other teacher recorded that many absences. How would you handle the situation?

3. A school guidance counselor informs you that three girls want to drop your class because there is too much noise in the room and they can't concentrate. What would be your reaction?

4. A note from the assistant principal summons you to her office to explain why your attendance records are often submitted late and why students from your home room class are often found wandering the hallways. What are some explanations that might be tenable?

5. A supervisor admonishes a teacher for regularly coming to class a little late. The teacher's response is, "The homework assignment and do-now are always up on the board (from my earlier class) before the period begins, the class knows which row is to put the homework up on the back chalkboard, and I have an excellent student monitor taking attendance, so it makes no difference whether or not I come in one or two minutes late." What is your reaction?

6. One of your students asks permission to leave the room. For some reason, you refuse his request. He insists he "must go" and, after an ensuing verbal battle, gets up and walks out. How would you handle the situation upon his return?

7. Several different teachers have, upon occasion, found one of their students repeatedly doing work for another subject during that mathematics class, despite warnings not to do so. Following are the ways the situation was handled by the various teachers:
   a. Material was confiscated and destroyed.

   b. Situation was discussed with the teacher of the other subject.
   c. Parent was notified.
   d. Dean was notified.
   e. Student was sent out of the room.
   What are your reactions to these "solutions"?

8. A teacher has a preparation period immediately preceding his two consecutive elementary algebra classes. Therefore, he always constructs and duplicates the tests and quizzes for these classes during this period. He feels that this increases the security of these exams. What are some arguments for and against this procedure?

9. Comment on the following solution to a discipline problem. If a student persists in disturbing your class, send him out of the room and into a nearby mathematics class functioning on a much lower level (with the other teacher's permission, of course).

10. Suppose a student in a ninth grade mathematics class is constantly inattentive and intentionally disturbs other students nearby. Frequent requests to curb this disruptive activity go unheeded. Explain some steps you may take to seek relief of this situation. Justify your responses.

11. Ask a mathematics department supervisor to discuss classroom management during a portion of a department conference. At this conference you would serve as a recorder. Following this conference, write a report to summarize the conference highlights and contrast the different styles of classroom management as voiced by the teachers at the conference.

12. Arrange to have a videotape made of the mathematics lesson you would teach. Invite several teachers, both experienced and inexperienced, to view the videotape and comment on your classroom management techniques. Summarize the comments rendered during this videotape viewing.

SUGGESTED READINGS

Gnagey, William J. *Motivating Classroom Discipline*. New York: Macmillan, 1981.

Wolfgang, Charles H., and Glickman, Carl D. *Solving Discipline Problems: Strategies for Classroom Teachers*. Boston: Allyn and Bacon, 1980.

CHAPTER 14 PREPARING FOR A NEW COURSE

To teach geometry for the first time is to repeat the experience of every teacher of mathematics from the time of Euclid. Whether it is geometry, algebra or computer mathematics, unless you are being asked to create a new course *ex nihilo*, it is wise to use the experience of others so you will not flounder, or even worse, sink.

We shall offer a procedure on how to go about preparing to teach any course for the first time. Whether you have six months to prepare or only a few hours, a plan of action will be presented that will enable you to move in the direction of teaching that course.

When and how can you expect to learn that you will be teaching a particular course? Your immediate supervisor (department chairman, assistant principal or principal) may inform you about it six months, perhaps a year or perhaps only two days beforehand. Advanced high school courses such as calculus, computer programming, statistics or linear algebra will require longer periods of preparation, whereas the traditional courses of algebra, geometry, trigonometry, general and remedial mathematics require less time. This should not imply that the advanced courses are better or more noble. For the beginning teacher any course is a challenge and needs ample time. Unfortunately, the new teacher, who needs the greatest amount of preparation time, usually gets the least advance notice.

After you are told what you will be teaching, what next? Expect that your supervisor will arrange to meet you for a discussion of steps you will be advised to follow. The course of study will be presented. Available texts will be recommended or perhaps mandated. Names of experienced teachers to whom you may turn for assistance will be offered. You will be told of any supplementary materials that are available at the school.

After the meeting with your supervisor, the matter rests solely in your hands, for at this point it becomes your obligation to prepare yourself fully and honestly. Only then will you be able to meet your youngsters with the confidence of a master rather than with the insecurity of a novice.

LONG-RANGE PREPARATION

If you become aware as much as a year or a full semester in advance that you will be teaching a particular course, some or all of the steps listed below are recommended as procedures to help you begin preparing yourself. If, on the other hand, you are aware of the situation for only a few days to a few hours, modifications of the listed suggestions must be made. These modifications will vary, depending upon the amount of time available as well as your own "drive" and ambition towards a goal of excellence in your classroom.

Observe an Experienced Teacher

There is no step you can take that is more useful, practical or helpful than your daily observation of an experienced, competent teacher who is presently teaching the course you expect to teach. First obtain the teacher's consent, then if agreeable, observe regularly and take careful notes on what you see and hear. Copy the questions, the remarks, even the jokes for possible future use. Note the handling of homework, testing procedures and classroom management. Especially note motivational techniques and clever ways of developing a topic. Even if you ultimately decide to "improve" upon her style, now you at least have a basis upon which your judgment is grounded.

It will be helpful if the teacher you are observing can meet with you regularly to discuss the course and reasons why certain teaching techniques were used.

Obtain Several Course Outlines

Your supervisor may have given you the official school outline or course of study or the appropriate state curriculum. You can and should secure similar outlines from other schools or state education departments simply by sending away for them. In addition to providing you with a suggested order of topics in the course, a good course outline will also provide you with guidance regarding the approximate amount of time to be devoted to each topic in the course.

Some state or local curriculum guides even offer a series of lesson plans for use in regular (standard) courses. These should be consulted and used sparingly so that your style is not "cramped" by these plans, written by someone else and not necessarily designed for your needs. What is important is that you gather as much curriculum information about the course you are about to teach as you can.

Examine Various Textbooks

Texts are a rich source of information and enrichment you can bring with you to the classroom. You will discover new approaches to certain topics and you will have a large source of problems from which to draw. Publishers are often pleased to send copies of their books to teachers for possible classroom adoption. You might even convince the school authorities to purchase a text you believe particularly suitable.

It is useful to obtain teachers' manuals or teacher editions of textbooks you will be using. Also, read the preface of each of your textbooks to determine the author's approach and viewpoint. Since the order in which topics are presented in a course often depends heavily on the order in which they appear in the textbook, caution must be exercised in using supplementary books in which the order differs from that of the textbook. Naturally, there are some topics whose development is independent of the order, yet caution should still be used.

Prepare Lessons in Advance

Based on the knowledge you are beginning to accumulate, do some advance planning of specific lessons, especially the early ones. But first, plan outlines for broad, larger units of work. You will be happy you did. Perhaps you can map out the entire course and then prepare some unit plans. This will give you some idea about properly anticipating the time factor involved. (Refer to lesson planning in Chapter 1.)

As part of advanced lesson planning, prepare solutions to as many exercises as possible prior to their consideration in class. This will provide many valuable insights into difficulties your students may encounter, and it will make you much more comfortable standing before the class with the full knowledge that you have complete mastery of the subject matter. This is especially important in such subjects as geometry, where proofs may often be done in a variety of ways.

Observe Additional Teachers

Observe several teachers if you have the time, mainly to get different perspectives. You may be very surprised at the differences you see. Follow similar procedures with each observation. Your supervisor can make valuable suggestions about which teachers it would be most valuable to observe.

Read Professional Literature

The major journal in the United States published for secondary school mathematics teachers is *The Mathematics Teacher. The Arithmetic Teacher* is also a useful journal even though it is often of greater interest to elementary school teachers of mathematics. For information on both magazines, write to: National Council of Teachers of Mathematics, 1906 Association Drive, Reston, Virginia 22091.

The NCTM also publishes yearbooks that ought to become part of every teacher's library. For example, the 1978 yearbook on "Developing Computational Skills" offers a wealth of ideas you can use even if you never teach a specific course in basic skills. The 1979 and 1980 yearbooks on applications in mathematics and problem solving, respectively, are important reading for teachers at all levels of secondary school mathematics. Information on all the yearbooks is available at the address above.

School Science and Mathematics is another journal of interest to mathematics teachers. It can be obtained from School Science and Mathematics Association, Stright Hall, P.O. Box 1614, Indiana University of Pennsylvania, Indiana, Pennsylvania 15705.

Other professional journals are often published by local mathematics teacher associations. Magazines such as *Scientific American* are available in most libraries or by subscription. Your school supervisor can probably provide specific additional information on appropriate literature and local organizations.

Familiarize Yourself with the Library or Media Center

The school and/or department library may have many books you will find useful for yourself as well as your more talented students. While becoming familiar with the school library, begin to build your own personal collection. In addition to *The Mathematics Teacher* and yearbooks of the NCTM, refer to the bibliographies in Chapter 3 and Chapter 11 for a useful list of books with which to start. Many of these books can be obtained used in bookstores, or from the book publishers. You can also obtain free and inexpensive materials. Publications of such lists is yet another service of the NCTM.

Learn Pupils' Backgrounds

What types of youngsters will you be teaching? Try to obtain information from guidance counselors about your pupils' backgrounds before walking into the classroom, for it will be helpful to know in advance who is a weak student and who is strong. Although this is generally helpful, try not to prejudice your assessments before giving students a chance to prove themselves. You may also be alerted to potential discipline problems and you will be aware of who is repeating the course because of past failure or poor attendance.

On the other hand, some teachers prefer not to investigate the backgrounds of new students first so that they can form their own judgments without prejudice.

If it happens that your class will consist of youngsters from a particular ethnic background, you might find it helpful to learn about their language, culture, habits and behavior patterns.

Obtain Supplies

Besides the usual "tools of the teaching trade," you might need board compasses, protractor, graph chart, geometric models, "flexible" quadrilaterals and other polygons, overhead projector, graph paper or a myriad of other supplies. Try to secure these well before they will actually be needed.

Enroll in a Course

Whether you expect to teach a remedial mathematics class or one in advanced geometry, there may be a college or in-service course that will be of value to you. Most professionals seek constantly to improve their skills and knowledge. A teacher of mathematics should do the same to remain current and avoid getting stale.

SHORT-RANGE PREPARATION

If you are made aware a few weeks, a few days, or even a few hours in advance that you will be teaching a particular course which you have never taught before, read the steps listed above for the long-range preparation program, but take the following preliminary actions so you can begin in an orderly manner. However, as the term progresses, begin to implement as many of the long-range steps as possible.

1. *Study the course outline.* Your supervisor will provide you with this so you can at least begin with something tangible.
2. *Get the textbook.* Take it home and read it, always keeping the course outline in mind.
3. *Prepare initial lesson plans.* Specific plans for the opening days should be prepared in advance, both daily plans and longer-range unit plans.
4. *Arrange to observe a teacher.* Try to observe an experienced teacher who is teaching the same subject during the same term as you are. This is perhaps the most valuable action you can take.
5. *Pray for the best!*

SELECTING A TEXTBOOK

Although some schools will provide you with the textbook for your new teaching assignment, other schools will offer you a choice of available books or ask you to select a book (or in some states, those on approved texbook lists).

If you are told that there is only one book available for your new teaching assignment, you ought to get the teacher's edition as well as the various supportive materials. These might include:

> a solutions book
> a booklet with teacher commentary
> a booklet of tests for the course (these are often in the form of spirit masters or simply in reproducible form)
> overhead transparencies (or transparency masters, from which you can make your own transparencies)
> coordinated computer software to supplement the text
> other assorted enrichment material

You will then be in a better position to make the most of the textbook you have been told to use.

It is far more challenging (and interesting) to have an opportunity to select a textbook to suit your needs, rather than to merely accept the book that just happens to be available in your school. Therefore you ought to opt for the former case where possible. Whether you have been asked to select a textbook individually, or as a member of a textbook selection committee, you might want to use a system such as follows.

Surveying the Textbook Market

One of the best ways of surveying the textbook market is to attend a professional convention, such as the National Council of Teachers of Mathematics annual convention, or regional meeting, and examine the books at the many commercial exhibits. Ask the company representative whatever questions you may have and make sure you request an examination copy of those texts that may have potential for your classroom.

If you are unable to attend a professional conference, or the time such a conference is held in your region is too late to be helpful in selecting a textbook, you could contact companies which have books available on the subject you are to teach and ask them to send you an examination copy, along with any available peripheral material. These items are usually sent to you without cost. You can identify these companies by:

1. Reading advertisements in professional journals.
2. Visiting nearby schools to determine what textbooks they are using for similar courses.
3. Calling nearby curriculum specialists or mathematics education professors at local colleges to find out which books they recommend.
4. Inspecting the appropriate sections in your school or community library.

The Selection Process

As you accumulate textbooks for possible adoption in your classroom, you would be well advised to make a list of the order of topics your ideal textbook would have. You should also list the features you would like to see in the textbook you finally select. If you are a member of a textbook selection committee, each member of the committee should go through this exercise and then a consolidated list should be developed, incorporating as much common input from the members as possible. There may be some discussion necessary to resolve any points of disagreement, but this is a healthy academic exercise. It encourages a careful inspection of a point of view and can generate a productive professional exchange of ideas.

Once you secure all the textbooks you are considering for adoption and you have a check list of items which would comprise your ideal section, review each book and rate it on each of these categories. Sometimes a numerical rating scale can be helpful in making a decision. One possible checklist used by several schools follows.

Textbook Rating Checklist

Directions: Rate each book for the following criteria. Use numbers from 1–10, where 1 is very poor and 10 is ideal.

Criterion	Book		
	1	2	3
Order of topics			
Expository style			
Clarity of developments			
Clarity of explanation of concepts			
Comprehensiveness of treatment			

Appropriateness for intended population			
Readability level			
Ease of use (clear diagrams)			
Overall design of book (page layouts)			
Mathematical accuracy			
Number of exercises			
Quality of exercises			
Provision for different ability levels in exercises			
Extra features (usefulness)			
Enrichment topics			
Timeliness			
Cost			
Recency of copyright date			
Peripheral materials			
Consistency with books used in other courses in the school			
TOTAL RATINGS			

Unless there are unusual circumstances, the book with the highest rating should be the one selected. Once the selection has been completed, you must work diligently to adapt the book to your needs.

SUMMARY

Although careful, long-range preparation is most desirable when planning to teach a new course, events and circumstances do not always make this possible. Whenever the situation does arise, however, where long-range preparation is not possible, to whom and to what should you turn? You turn to the experienced teacher who is willing to help, to the course of study that you must follow, to the textbook that will guide you, and perhaps most important of all, you call upon your own strength and determination to succeed. These are the ingredients that will enable you to stay afloat, properly teach and challenge your students, and even chart new courses at the appropriate time.

EXERCISES

1. Suppose you are informed that you will be teaching Algebra 2 (second year algebra) for the first time next semester. Study three textbooks that are used in this course and determine:
   a. any differences in approach.
   b. which books have graded exercises (i.e. exercises that are arranged from simple to more complex).
   c. differences in sequence of topics.
   d. which book you would prefer to use and why.

2. Do the same as in question 1 for geometry.

3. Do the same as in question 1 for seventh grade mathematics.

4. Which of the steps that one should take for long-range preparation of a new course would you expect the most difficulty in implementing? Why? How would you overcome this difficulty?

5. Suppose you were told of a new course you would be teaching beginning the next day. How serious a disadvantage would you have over the teacher who has had ample opportunity for long-range planning? How would you prepare overnight for your new assignment?

6. Select five textbooks from your school or community library and rate the books on the checklist found on page 184. Be sure that the books are all for the same subject area (e.g., elementary algebra, geometry, etc.).

7. Write a short report justifying your selection of a textbook based on the results of the ratings in Exercise 6.

CHAPTER 15
USING PERFORMANCE OBJECTIVES

As we discussed in previous chapters, part of your planning to teach a unit of work may involve assembling courses of study, reviewing textbooks and other relevant material and then eventually developing a sequence of logically arranged lessons that cover the appropriate topics. You then get more specific and prepare daily lesson plans. Because of your efforts and careful planning, you expect to be able to teach successful developmental, review, drill or other types of lessons.

But now we raise the question, "How do you measure a successful lesson?" One way is by observing the performance of the teacher. Another is by judging the performance exhibited by students after the lesson has been presented.

Some time ago during a snow storm when few teachers and students arrived at school, one teacher, who apparently did not want to feel that his difficult trip was in vain, was seen presenting an elaborately prepared introductory lesson on drawing graphs of the trigonometric functions. The boardwork was well done and colorful and the presentation was energetic and lively. The sight of all this was humorous, however, because only one pupil was in the room.

Had the aim of the lesson, so carefully planned by the teacher, been fulfilled? Was the lesson a successful one? If we answer these questions from the point of view of teacher performance, then we might have to answer "yes." If, however, we consider the skills that students were expected to learn and perform as a result of this lesson, then the success of the lesson, at least for the one youngster involved, will be known only when that youngster is tested. Furthermore, one must determine what percent of a class must show mastery of a topic in order for the lesson to be judged successful.

Some teachers believe that a properly planned lesson *must* include a set of student objectives, in addition to the traditional "aim." In other words, with every lesson the teacher would focus her attention on the students and state objectives *they* will achieve by the end of the lesson. Furthermore, these objectives should be clearly stated at the beginning of the lesson in terms of expected student performance at the end of the lesson. Some argue rather forcefully that this sort of thing ought *not* to be done. We shall not resolve this controversy here; however, the pros and cons of this argument will be presented later in this chapter. We shall begin our discussion of student objectives by considering how these objectives should be formulated and when they should be used, if the teacher chooses to use them.

PERFORMANCE OBJECTIVES

A statement specifying the particular capabilities of a learner (known as "observable student behavior") when he has reached the end of a specific learning activity, together with any given conditions or restrictions, as well as a statement of the evaluation process (known as "minimum level of acceptable performance") is known as a "performance objective" (or "behavioral objective"). To paraphrase the definition above, the statement of a performance objective must actually name the type of act a student will be observed performing successfully, under specific given conditions, at the completion of the activity.

Let us suppose, for example, that at the completion of a unit on conic sections in a second year algebra class you might expect that students will have acquired not only an appreciation of the practical applications and aesthetic aspects of the conic sections but also specific skills related to second degree equations. With this in mind, we shall now formulate some typical performance objectives for this topic (see Sample 1). We shall analyze each from the point of view of given conditions, observable student behavior, and minimum level of acceptable performance. The reader should realize that these performance objectives are written in an ideal form. An individual teacher's objectives may likely vary with his needs and personality.

Performance Verbs

Let us now consider this statement of a performance objective written for the unit on conic sections just discussed:

The student will appreciate the practical applications of conics.

Sample 1. Performance Objectives for a Unit on Conic Sections

---

1. *Given eight equations of the form $Ax^2 + By^2 + Cx + Dy + Exy + F = O$, the student will correctly name the described conic (or one of its special or degenerate cases) and state the coordinates of the center for at least six of them within a forty-minute period.*

   a. Given Conditions: eight equations of the form $Ax^2 + By^2 + Cx + Dy + Exy + F = O$

   b. Observable Student Behavior:
   Student will
   1. Name the conic
   2. State the coordinates of the center

   c. Minimum Level of Acceptable Performance: Students will correctly answer at least six questions within a forty-minute period.

2. *The student will use the coordinates of the center and major and minor axes to sketch the graph represented by an equation of the form $Ax^2 + By^2 = C$.*

   a. Given Conditions: An equation of the form $Ax^2 + By^2 = C$

   b. Observable Student Behavior: Students will determine coordinates of the center, major and minor axes. They will then sketch the curve using that information.

   c. Minimum Level of Acceptable Performance: the same as *b*.

3. *Given two second-degree equations, the student will estimate (correct to the nearest tenth) their intersection points, if any, graphically.*
   a. Given Conditions: Two second degree equations
   b. Observable Student Behavior: Students will draw the graphs and estimate the coordinates at their intersection points
   c. Minimum Level of Acceptable Performance: Same as *b* and answer correct to the nearest tenth.

4. *The student will be able to state how a conical solid ought to be "sliced" in order to obtain each of the regular conic sections. The special cases of these may be demonstrated for extra credit.*
   a. Given Conditions: A conical solid
   b. Observable Student Behavior: Students will describe how to "slice" the conic so that parabolic, elliptic and hyperbolic sections will be formed; also they will show how to form two intersecting lines and one point.
   c. Minimum Level of Acceptable Performance: Students will be able to show the regular conics as described in *b*.

While some practical applications of conics might have been discussed in class, the verb "will appreciate" is so vague that the observable student behavior cannot be clearly determined in terms of it. How will the student show his appreciation? By presenting the teacher with a gift in appreciation of the knowledge imparted? By writing an essay on the subject? By thinking or dreaming about it? The answer here is obvious: the desired student behavior must be not only observable but also *measureable* to be useful in assessing the success of an instructional experience.

Similarly, consider this statement of a "performance objective":

The student will know what conic sections are.

If the observable student behavior is to be determined, what will be observed? Does knowing the names of the conics indicate knowledge of the corresponding graphs? Does knowing how to draw the graphs indicate a knowledge of their names as well as their properties? Certainly "knowing" can take on a host of definitions, some of which are easily measurable while others are not. At any rate more specificity is required, so you now see that the *key* to stating well-defined performance objectives is the verb. Verbs such as *understand, appreciate,* and *know* are open to a very wide range of interpretations and are therefore poor verb choices to use in formulating statements of performance objectives. On the other hand, the other verbs used in the previously stated performance objectives, such as *name, state, sketch, slice* and *estimate* are clearer and certainly less ambiguous.

Since certain words are open to less interpretation than others, the formulation of performance objectives should be stated so there is some understanding and agreement concerning any observable student behavior associated with the verb used in the objective. As a matter of fact, the main criteria of a satisfactory performance objective is that it communicate clearly without any ambiguity the intent of its writer. One test of the clarity of a performance objective is whether another competent person can use that objective to write a question which will test a student on the achievement of that objective in such a way that the original writer will find that test question acceptable.

HOW TO WRITE PERFORMANCE OBJECTIVES

A unit plan on radicals was presented in Chapter 1. We shall now consider how a set of performance objectives may be developed using that unit as a model. But first,

when preparing a unit of work or a daily lesson plan, we suggest the following initial steps to be taken before actually writing the objectives:

1. Select the unit (or topic) to be taught.
2. Study relevant syllabi and texts, and speak to experienced colleagues.
3. List the major formulas, theorems, concepts, etc.
4. Write a performance objective for each of the "skills" to be taught.
5. After the objective has been written, check it against the ability of your students. That is, are you requiring too much of them, or too little? Are your objectives realistic for the type of students you have? (We may indicate these as "high-" or "low-level" objectives.) Remember to write realistic objectives, but don't keep your expectations of pupil achievement too low just to be sure that the objectives will be met. Also remember that the objectives should be written appropriately for students at various levels.

Sample 2 contains some possible performance objectives for the unit on radicals. These are written in a practical rather than an ideal form, for if a teacher were to prepare each objective in its ideal form, they would become too lengthy and cumbersome to write for each lesson plan.

USING PERFORMANCE OBJECTIVES

Now that you have seen examples of performance objectives, you can decide whether you would like to use them some of the time, all of the time or none of the time. The objections to their use are mainly that the teacher will select those objectives that are relatively low-level, such as simple skills that lend themselves easily to direct observation and that more youngsters are likely to attain. Furthermore, higher-level skills that are not so easily observed and tested, but which may be even more important because they involve "power" thinking, may be neglected. Also, it may not be possible to state in advance all objectives of a lesson because of frequently unanticipated events that may occur during the lesson. These events may lead to the attainment of an objective which the teacher never even considered. There is also the danger that the teacher may use performance objectives as a "show" for a supervisor to indicate that mastery in a certain area had been attained as the teacher planned.

The performance objectives should appear in the lesson plan. They are often written immediately after the aim of the lesson, although some teachers have found it

Sample 2.   Performance Objectives for a Unit on Radicals

---

1. *Powers and roots; square root table*

   Students will name the base, exponent and power of any expression of the form A^b (low level).

   Students will evaluate four expressions such as 5^3; 16^2; $\sqrt{9}$; $\sqrt[3]{8}$.

   Students will determine the values of four expressions such as $\sqrt{12}$ using a square root table, correct to tenths.

   Students will use a standard secondary school square root table to determine the values of four expressions such as $\sqrt{576}$ (high level).

2. *Pythagorean theorem and quadratic equations of the form $x^2 = 9$ and $x^2 = 3$*

   Students will recite the Pythagorean theorem (low level).

   Students will find one side of a right triangle given the other two sides, correct to the nearest tenth. They will have the square root table available.

   Students will find the positive integral root of two equations such as $x^2 = 9$.

   Students will find the positive root of three equations such as $x^2 = 12$, leaving answers either in radical form or expressing them to nearest tenth. The square root table may be used.

3. *Square root algorithm*

   Students will find values of four numbers such as $\sqrt{576}$, $\sqrt{27}$, $\sqrt{3}$ correct to the nearest tenth by using the square root algorithm.

4. *Simplifying radicals*

   Students will write three expressions such as $\sqrt{9x^2}$, $\sqrt{27a^4}$ in simplest radical form.

   Students will write three expressions such as $\sqrt{27a^4}$, $\sqrt{20y^5}$ in simplest radical form.

5. *Adding and subtracting radicals*

   Students will combine radicals in three expressions such as $2\sqrt{3} + \sqrt{27}$ and present the answer in simplest radical form.

   Students will combine radicals in three expressions such as $3\sqrt{18c^3} - 5c\sqrt{2c}$ and write answers in simplest radical form (high level).

6. *Multiplying radicals*

   Students will find the value of two examples such as $\sqrt{3} \cdot \sqrt{12}$ without using the table or algorithm.

   Students will find the value, correct to the nearest tenth, of two expressions such as $\sqrt{5} \cdot \sqrt{6}$ by using the square root table only once.

7. *Dividing radicals*

   Students will find the value of three expressions such as $\dfrac{\sqrt{12}}{\sqrt{3}}$ without using the square root table or the the square root algorithm.

8. *Rationalizing denominators*

   Students will express two examples such as $\dfrac{2}{\sqrt{5}}$ as an equivalent fraction with a rational denominator.

   Students will express two examples such as $\dfrac{\sqrt{3} + \sqrt{2}}{\sqrt{3}}$ as a equivalent fraction with a rational denominator.

   Students will express two examples such as $\dfrac{2}{\sqrt{3} - 2}$ as an equivalent fraction with a rational denominator.

9. *Solving radical equations*

   Students will two solve equations such as $\sqrt{x} = 3$ and $\sqrt{x - 1} = 2$ and check answers by substitution.

   Students will two solve equations such as $\sqrt{x - 1} - 1 = 3$ and check answers by substitution.

10. *Review*

Students will correctly answer at least eleven of the following fourteen questions within forty minutes:

a. Evaluate 3^3; 14^2; $\sqrt{25}$; $3\sqrt{27}$.

b. Use the square root table to evaluate $\sqrt{13}$ and $\sqrt{27}$ correct to tenths.

c. Use the square root table to evaluate $\sqrt{121}$ and $\sqrt{324}$.

d. Use the square root table to find the positive root of $x^2 = 21$ correct to the nearest tenth.

e. Given a right triangle with a leg of length of 8 and the hypotenuse of length 17, find the length of the other leg.

f. Use the square root table to find the positive root of $2x^2 = 10$ correct to the nearest hundredth.

g. Solve for x in terms of a: $x^2 = 9a^4$.

h. Solve for x and leave answer in simplest radical form: $x^2 = 24$.

i. Express in simplest radical form: $\sqrt{8y^4}$; $\sqrt{18a^5}$. Check by multiplication.

j. Combine and express in simplest radical form: $5\sqrt{2} + \sqrt{8}$.

k. Combine and express in simplest radical form: $3a\sqrt{2a} - \sqrt{8a^3}$.

l. Without any tables, find the value of $\dfrac{\sqrt{12}}{\sqrt{3}}$; $\sqrt{12} \cdot \sqrt{3}$.

m. Express $\dfrac{3}{\sqrt{2}+1}$ as an equivalent fraction with a rational denominator.

n. Solve and check by substitution: $\sqrt{x-2} + 1 = 3$.

11. *Test*

This will reflect the review objectives stated above.

---

convenient to list these objectives at the end of the plan, as the culmination or summary of the lesson. This does not preclude their use at the beginning of the lesson as well.

It would appear advisable that if you choose to use performance objectives in your daily lessons and if in spite of the most careful planning on your part you find the lesson not progressing as planned, be prepared to adjust your lesson or your objectives on the spot! Remember, be flexible. If in fact the objectives are carefully thought out and well stated, they should be able to withstand most unexpected events. Your lesson should always be tailored to your audience, even if this "tailoring" must be done during the lesson.

SUMMARY

Whenever you prepare a unit of work, or a daily lesson plan, you are in effect writing a "script" for the teacher to follow so that certain information, concepts, thought processes and skills will be acquired by the pupils. Thus the type of lesson selected, whether developmental, review, drill or any other, is the one that is determined to be best suited for the particular purpose selected. Some professionals, however, feel that no unit or daily plan is complete until a set of performance objectives has been developed alongside it. Furthermore, students should be made well aware of these objectives so they will understand how the work being done is tied to the expected outcome. Some teachers believe that a student learns better knowing what his learning goal for a particular lesson is.

Those who disagree with this opinion feel that no set of objectives can ever be fully complete because they cannot all be anticipated in advance. Furthermore, the limitations imposed by predetermined objectives might tend to restrict the teacher's freedom to develop objectives that do not have clearly measurable outcomes, such as "the student will be inspired by the teacher," or "the student will learn to love the subject." Some teachers simply do not feel they need to use objectives. They may feel that a student's prior knowledge of the intent of the lesson diminishes the suspense the teacher would like to generate as a possible motivational device.

Once a teacher has decided to use performance objectives, she must formulate them well—using clear, unambiguous verbs. Well-formulated objectives contain three major parts:

1. Given conditions
2. Observable student behavior
3. Minimum level at acceptable performance

Finally, the teacher will know that the objectives have been attained by observing the written or oral behavior exhibited by the students at the conclusion of the lesson.

We note that although some teachers do not use performance objectives specifically, they still need to use the same *idea* in another form in such places, for example, as testing and drill work.

EXERCISES

1. Here is a poorly stated performance objective:
   The student must be able to understand the law of cosines.
   Indicate whether the following test questions are appropriate for testing whether the objective has been attained or not.
   a. Derive the formula for the law of cosines, for an acute or obtuse triangle.
   b. Given a triangle *ABC* and the measures of *a*, *b* and $\angle C$, solve for *c* correct to the nearest tenth.

2. Suppose a supervisor came to your class and asked to see the performance objectives your students were expected to attain during the past week. She then randomly selected pupils to test them according to the objectives.
   a. Is this a fair way to examine your effectiveness?
   b. Would you choose low-level objectives from now on to insure a better chance of demonstrating student success?
   c. Do you think that knowing that your supervisor will do this periodically will make you a more effective teacher? Justify your responses!

3. Write a list of twelve verbs that are too vague and unclear to be used in a performance objective statement. Write another twelve verbs that are unambiguous and which may be used to clearly state performance objectives.

4. Below are five performance objectives (not necessarily good ones). Write two questions that would test each objective to determine whether or not it had been attained. Also state whether the objective is well formulated.
   a. The pupils will state the domain and range of a function given the graph of the function.
   b. The pupils will understand how to solve a quadratic equation by "completing the square."
   c. The student will define parallelogram, rectangle, square, rhombus.
   d. The student will appreciate "indirect reasoning" in geometry.
   e. The student will punch his own cards on the "keypunch."

5. a. In Chapter 1, "Planning a Lesson," you wrote a developmental lesson in response to Exercise 3. Now write a set of performance objectives for that lesson.
   b. Do the same for Exercise 7 in Chapter 1.
   c. Do the same for Exercise 8 in Chapter 1.
   d. Do the same for Exercise 9 in Chapter 1.

6. Survey at least twelve high school or junior high school mathematics teachers to determine how they use performance objectives in their teaching and in their lesson planning. If a respondent claims not to use performance objectives, try to elicit whether similar structures are used in teaching or in planning to teach their mathematics lessons. Write a report to summarize your findings.

SUGGESTED READINGS

Flanagan, John C.; Shanner, William M.; and Mager, Robert F. *Mathematics Behavioral Objectives, A Guide to Individualizing Learning.* Palo Alto, Ca.: Westinghouse Learning Press, 1971.

Mager, Robert F. *Preparing Instructional Objectives.* Palo Alto, Ca.: Fearon Publishers, 1962.

CHAPTER 16 OVERCOMING MATHEMATICS ANXIETY

Skill in mathematics is the key to success in a great many of the most powerful and prestigious jobs in our highly technical society. Without mathematics, it is impossible to get into medicine, science, engineering, computing, and most of the jobs requiring technical expertise. Mathematics is also useful around the home and in pursuits like music, art, dance, and business. Clearly, it is to an individual's advantage to be conversant with mathematics. Unfortunately, many individuals are afraid of mathematics and will go to great lengths to avoid numbers and number operations. *Mathematics anxiety*, as this fear is called, is finally being recognized as a major obstacle in the development of the well-educated individual.

Those who suffer from mathematics anxiety report a range of emotional responses when confronted with numbers: increased heart rate, increased perspiration, a feeling of light-headedness, a dry mouth, a mind that "goes blank," etc. In short, mathematics anxiety is not some sort of silly hysteria or a tactic used to get out of doing school work. Mathematics anxiety is a real physiological response set off by the thought of doing mathematics. Individuals with this anxiety become extremely nervous and go to great lengths to get away from the sources of their fear. These persons learn about mathematics only under duress, which further increases their fear and anxiety, and, as can be imagined, they immediately forget whatever facts they were forced to learn. Thus, mathematics anxiety plays a major role in preventing people from learning and using mathematics skills. Math anxiety is a problem today because, as any mathematics teacher will attest, many students in mathematics classes suffer from it as do many of the non-mathematics teachers in today's schools.

The impact of mathematics anxiety on our society is both indirect and subtle: It has been suggested that mathematics anxiety may be at the root of the widespread anti-technological pressures in our society. Others have noted that mathematics anxiety may be responsible for the dramatic decline in SAT scores over the past two decades. Mathematics anxiety has also been accused of playing a role in keeping women and minorities out of the technical curricula and therefore out of the boardrooms of the major corporations.

It is time, therefore, that teachers recognize that mathematics anxiety is a real problem and that it is a problem that must be dealt with from the very first years of schooling. The purpose of this chapter is to help you, the mathematics teacher, to recognize and understand the origins and consequences of mathematics anxiety so that you will be in a position to help your students overcome their fear. In addition, suggestions and techniques will be offered that have proven successful in turning students on to mathematics.

SOURCES OF MATHEMATICS ANXIETY

Mathematics anxiety is a phobia. A phobia is an unreasonable fear response to particular events and situations. Like all phobias, mathematics anxiety is learned. Phobias are learned as the consequence of either a traumatic event associated with a particular situation or object, as in a fear of dentists, or because an important individual shows the fear. As an example of this second type of learning, if a mother always has an emotional response around spiders and moths, and the child sees that response, chances are very good that the child will also experience fear and anxiety around spiders and moths. Both of these learning processes contribute to the development of mathematics anxiety.

The difference between mathematics anxiety and the more well-known phobias is that the fear-inducing event is a threat to the individual's self-concept rather than a threat to physical well-being. Mathematics is seen as a situation that makes an individual appear dumb, stupid, and clumsy. It becomes a threat, therefore, to an individuals image of himself as a bright and competent person (which we all believe of ourselves).

The notion that mathematics is something to be dreaded begins in the child's first years in school. Teachers and other significant adults indicate that mathematics is difficult and something to fear, while at the same time indicating that mathematical skills are very important for future success. In addition, mathematics is presented as something that only the very bright can really do, children are forced to reproduce mathematics "facts" (e.g., the multiplication tables) under timed pressure, and they are constantly exhorted to do better. Under these conditions, failure is guaranteed and feelings of incompetence are inevitable. It is important to remember, too, that the first exposure children have to do mathematics will be by primary teachers who, more than likely, are not trained in mathematics and who are also anxious around mathematics.

Consider the signals projected by a teacher who is forced to teach mathematics but who would rather not: It will be presented in somewhat strained tone of voice; it will be presented as an onerous task for both the teacher and the students which must be completed in the shortest time possible; it will be presented as a drill/memorization exercise rather than a thinking/problem-solving tool; and it will be readily used as a punishment (e.g., "You are out of your seat, Ronnie, so stay after class and do 50 math problems"). Any of these would be enough to scare a young child and, in concert, it is not too hard to understand how and why so many young adolescents begin their first junior high mathematics class in a cold sweat.

In addition, these children's parents will also probably have had negative experiences with mathematics and will therefore, consciously or otherwise, support the child's developing dread of things mathematical.

In short, the first encounter many children have with mathematics is that it is something that makes them feel stupid, it is presented by teachers who clearly do not like it, and, when they get home, they find that mom and dad do not like it either.

Unfortunately, most junior and senior high mathematics teachers are not prepared to deal with this psychological fear, nor are they prepared to deal with the defense mechanisms and strategies their students use to protect themselves from appearing to fail in mathematics.

STRATEGIES FOR PREVENTING FAILURE

Given that students see mathematics as a threat to their image of themselves as competent individuals, it is understandable that those same individuals will develop means for protecting that image. The means they use are often indirect and subtle because while they want to protect themselves from looking stupid, and the easiest way to do that would be to avoid mathematics altogether, teachers punish students who just refuse to participate. Accordingly, we see a variety of subtle strategies, all pursued with the same purpose of projecting an image of participation while reducing the threat of forcing the student to admit that he is dumb.

In general, these strategies come in two types: (1) those used to get the student out of the threatening situation as quickly as possible with the minimum effort and pain, and (2) those used by students to reduce the uncertainty of the mathematics situation. The most familiar example of the first category of strategies is the impulsive responder, while cheating and memorization are the most common ways of reducing the uncertainty of mathematics.

As a strategy, impulsive responding is straightforward: "Since I'm going to get it wrong anyway, there is no use thinking about it and trying to solve it. I'll just guess and get the teacher off my back." The usefulness of this strategy is that it gets the pupil out of the anxiety-producing situation quickly and, since he did not invest any effort into the problem, the fact that he failed is not taken as a negative reflection on his basic ability. A variation of this avoidance strategy is that used by the student who sets goals that are clearly beyond her present achievement levels and which, therefore, guarantee failure. The student knows this and is not hurt by the inevitable failure, but many teachers praise the student for her "high level of expectation" on the mistaken assumption that high expectations translate directly into high levels of motivation. The strategy works nicely for the student. The impact of failure is moderated by both the expectation of failure and by the teacher's praise for having set such "admirable goals." Furthermore, the teacher's praise guarantees that the student will continue setting unrealistic goals and, accordingly, continue failing.

The second category of strategies is also tied together by a common theme. In these strategies the goal is to reduce the threat of mathematics by reducing the uncertainty associated with testing. One variety of strategy is displayed by the compulsive overachiever. By studying the material two or three times more than is necessary to master the material, this student overpowers the material so that there will be no question of failure. The motivation, however, is fear and the compulsive overstriving does nothing to reduce that fear. As a consequence, when that person is removed from the fear-provoking situation, he will forget most of what he learned under those fear conditions and he most likely will have nothing to do with mathematics whatsoever. In other words, even though the overachiever appears to do well in mathematics, the fact that he is afraid of mathematics will mean that he will avoid using mathematics in his day-to-day experience. In short, this person will behave no differently from the child who learned no mathematics.

A second general tactic for reducing uncertainty is persuading the teacher to use only those types of problems in which the solution procedures are known or are obvious. Pressure is put on the teacher to reduce mathematical problem solving to a formula or procedure that can be memorized and applied with minimum uncertainty. From the point of view of the anxious student, something that can be memorized is much less threatening to the self-image than an ambiguous problem situation. If a memorized problem is missed, it is only because one didn't memorize the right information or the teacher was "tricky," rather than because one was "stupid." This distinction may seem contrived but to the fragile ego of the adolescent it can be an important and face-saving distinction.

Finally, the most common strategy of this second category is cheating. Contrary to the popular notion, it is usually the better student who cheats. This student has an image to protect and, given a fear of mathematics, will resort to cheating to maintain that image of competence. Unfortunately, cheating is a short-sighted strategy that often backfires on the student. Once she does well by cheating, the cheater is obligated to continue to do well. Since the initial material was not learned, the pressure to continue cheating increases, as does the general anxiety associated with mathematics. In an effort to resolve the conflicting images of competence and cheating, the student will blame mathematics. With that, the anxiety and fear associated with mathematics increases as does the motivation to avoid mathematics. The key process

motivating these avoidance strategies is the fear generated by mathematics. Any attempt to deal with mathematics anxiety and the avoidance strategies must first deal with that fear and the sources of that fear, a perceived threat to the student's self-image.

OVERCOMING MATHEMATICS ANXIETY

What Should a Teacher Do?

© 1979 United Feature Syndicate, Inc.

High anxiety levels are detrimental to anyone's being able to function effectively. This does not mean that the teacher's goal should be to eliminate anxiety completely. Problem solving, by its very nature, is anxiety-producing, and that is not necessarily a bad thing, for it provides the motivation to continue working until the problem is solved. However, the teacher must see to it that no pupil becomes too incapacitated and immobilized with fear.

No simple formula exists to help your youngsters overcome excessive math anxiety. Yet, you will want to make sure that your pupils are provided with a positive experience in your classroom every day. Here are some simple, practical suggestions:

1. Relax and Enjoy. Teachers should be comfortable with the mathematics they are teaching as well as with their classes. Youngsters are perceptive about the likes and dislikes of their teachers, and their own behavior and attitudes will reflect what they perceive as their teacher's attitude.

2. Curb Excessive Competitiveness. Provide opportunities for pupils to work together in small groups so that they may discuss and explore problem-solving techniques. They will learn to focus on the process rather than, or in addition to, the product. They will learn to experiment, take risks, and try new methods—all critical abilities in achieving mathematical understanding. Slower students face frustration and anxiety when they are in a class of thirty-five youngsters all competing to get the correct answer first! They may even know the correct process for getting the answer, but are a bit too slow to verbalize it. Give these youngsters a chance in a small group setting.

3. No Speed Tests. Speed tests, timed tests, and deadlines interfere with those curiosity, question-asking behaviors that lead to in-depth exploration of a problem. Speed tests force a teacher into selecting problems that require a single correct solution. Once again, anxiety levels among students are raised—an undesirable effect, whereas the dynamic process of working through second alternatives is neither tested nor learned—another undesirable effect.

4. Praise a Pupil's Efforts. Do not focus only on answers, but on *how* the solution was gotten. All reasonable attempts and efforts should be recognized and praised. Even unreasonable attempts might have some redeeming qualities that you could point out. This will boost a student's self confidence and self image.

5. Never Humiliate. Often one of the strongest memories of math-anxious adults is remembering that they had been humiliated in front of the class. The humiliation might take the form of a verbal assault by an insensitive teacher, a comment by a fellow pupil, or even just standing helplessly in front of the room not being able to answer any questions.

6. Develop a Sense of Humor. Laughter and a sense of humor can probably cure more ailments than we imagine. Try it! It will have a positive effect on you, on your youngsters and, in fact, on everyone you meet.

7. Be a Positive Role Model. Develop a reputation for being an excellent teacher, fair marker, reasonable and consistent disciplinarian and one whom pupils can turn to when they have problems (either mathematical or personal). Go out of your way to show your concern for them. In other words, make the youngsters want to be around you. Furthermore, make occasional "mistakes" on the board while at the front of the room and show them how you react and what you do about it. They will see that you are "only human," that we each sometimes make mistakes, and that when you do make a mis-

take you do something about it. In effect, show them how one should founder constructively.

8. Do Not Use Mathematics as a Punishment. Never assign a large number of exercises for homework as a punishment for misbehavior. This is clearly self defeating.

9. Teach How to Read Mathematics. A mathematics textbook cannot be read as if one were skimming a novel. Compare the language in a mathematics text to that of a recipe or the instructions in a do-it-yourself kit. Students will then realize that they cannot move to the next statement until they have understood the previous ones. Pupils who learn to read a mathematics textbook with confidence will have acquired the most valuable skill a math teacher can impart.

10. Treat Girls and Boys Equally. The differences between males' and females' achievement in mathematics tends to become acute towards the end of their high school career. Studies have shown that this is because more women than men tend to avoid mathematics, lack confidence in their mathematical ability, and do not see any great need for mathematics in their future. The positive, non-sexist attitudes you exhibit in your classroom may be just one small step in countering these feelings. But it is at least a beginning.

11. Develop Spatial Relations. Encourage pupils to participate in activities that develop good spatial sense. The best activities are probably sports related: Where will the ball meet the bat? Where is the best place to stand to catch the ball? How do you get the ball through the hoop? Spatial skills are not explicitly taught in school even though they are necessary and useful in some fields of mathematics. Youngsters who somehow develop them do have a clear advantage and encounter considerably less frustration in certain areas of mathematics, for example geometry and calculus.

12. Have Pupils Make up Problems. (See Chapter 9—Problem Solving, pages 105–26.) This is a great confidence building technique designed to take the mystery out of mathematics.

13. "Humanize" Mathematics. Provide a bibliography of men and women who developed mathematics over the ages. Let your students see that mathematicians are people whose problems and lives are sometimes unusual and fascinating and at other times not too different from their own. Not all pupils may be interested in this, but for those who are, it is just one more avenue through which they might be reached.

SUMMARY

Mathematics anxiety is a serious problem which is not amenable to easy solutions. Because of the avoidance strategies which develop because of the fear and anxiety associated with mathematics, students with mathematics anxiety learn little mathematics; what they do learn they memorize without understanding, and they forget that little bit as soon as they can. A single student with a negative attitude can be disruptive to the development of positive attitudes for all the others in a classroom. That student can make teaching mathematics an onerous and unpleasant task. It is to the teacher's advantage, then, to do everything possible to reduce the level of mathematics anxiety in the classroom. Anything that reduces the level of anxiety while increasing the interest in problem solving and mathematics, and a few such methods were described above, will contribute to both the emotional and educational growth of the child.

EXERCISES

1. Describe three different ways in which mathematics phobia can affect the learning of mathematics.

2. Describe two different ways in which the teacher can unintentionally teach a fear of mathematics.

3. Explain the consequences of mathematics assignments as a punishment when a child misbehaves or upsets the teacher.

4. Describe two different types of strategies a child who hates mathematics might use to avoid having to appear incompetent in mathematics. Give an example of each.

5. Give two reasons for not using the "speed" test when evaluating a child's ability to use mathematics.

6. Describe two general tactics that you as a teacher could use in exploiting your potential as a positive role model.

7. Explain why it is generally inadequate to simply provide "positive reinforcement" when you are attempting to motivate a child.

8. Explain why it is important that you provide your students success experiences.

9. Locate cartoons, and cite anecdotes and jokes that might provide a light touch in your math class at appropriate moments during the lesson.

10. Develop a questionnaire (informal and open-ended) to determine how people who are not in fields related to mathematics feel about mathematics. Administer this questionnaire to at least 24 adults that you know who are not in any way working in fields related to mathematics. Write a report to summarize their responses. What conclusions can you draw regarding any mathematics anxieties that may be imbedded in the respondents' answers to your questionnaire?

SUGGESTED READINGS

Burton, Grace M. "Regardless of Sex." *The Mathematics Teacher* 72 (1979): 261.

Fennema, Elizabeth. "Women and Girls in Mathematics—Equity in Math Education." *Educational Studies in Math* 10 (1979): 389–401.

Fennema, Elizabeth, et al. "Increasing Women's Participation in Mathematics." *Journal for Research in Mathematics Education* 12 (1981): 3–14.

Oberlin, L. "How to Teach Children to Hate Math." *School Science and Math* 82 (1982): 261.

Tobias, Sheila. "Math Anxiety." *Today's Education* (1980): 26.

————. "Stress in The Math Classroom." *Learning* (1981): 34.

PART 2 ENRICHMENT UNITS FOR THE SECONDARY SCHOOL CLASSROOM

A wide variety of mathematics topics are well suited as enrichment for secondary school mathematics courses. We can draw such topics from all branches of mathematics. Numerical curiosities, algebraic investigations of number relationships, geometric phenomena not usually available to this audience, as well as many other topics generally not found in the secondary school or college curricula are among the units found in this part of the book.

A very common topic viewed from a not-so-common viewpoint would certainly provide enrichment for the appropriate audience. The trick to providing students with enrichment activities is to present the material in a highly motivating and intelligible manner. This rather challenging objective will guide us through the many units presented here. It should be remembered from the outset that enrichment activities are *not* limited only to gifted students. As you will see throughout this part of the book, many enrichment activities can be successfully used with students of average mathematical ability as well as in remedial classes, provided proper adjustments are made. Naturally these modifications in the presentation (both in content and in method of presentation) can be made only by the classroom teacher using the material. With this in mind let us consider the format in which these enrichment units are presented.

Each enrichment unit treats a separate topic. With few exceptions, the topics can be considered in almost any order. Following a brief introduction, *Performance Objectives* for that unit are stated. Not only do these objectives succinctly foreshadow the content of the unit, but they provide you with a good indication of the scope of the material which follows. So that you can better determine the suitability of the unit for your particular class, a *Preassessment* section is offered. In addition to assisting you to ascertain your students' readiness for the unit, this section often also serves as a source for motivation which you may wish to use in presenting the topic to your class.

In the next section, *Teaching Strategies,* the enrichment topic is presented in a manner which you may use to introduce it to your class. Here the topic is carefully developed with an eye towards anticipating possible pitfalls and hurdles students may encounter along the way. The style is conversational throughout, making the reading more relaxed. Occasionally suggestions for extensions are offered so that the units do not appear to be terminal. Perhaps an underlying goal throughout these enrichment units is to allow them to serve as springboards for further investigation. Where appropriate, additional references are offered for further study.

One efficient way to ascertain whether the objectives for a particular unit have been met is to question the students on the topic presented. Sample questions are provided in the *Postassessment* section at the end of the unit. You are invited to augment these questions with some of your own where needed.

Since many of these enrichment units can be used in a variety of different mathematics classes and with students of different levels of mathematical ability, a cross-cataloguing chart is provided. This chart will enable you to select enrichment units according to subject, grade level, and student ability level. Naturally, you will need to make some modifications in the form to make the unit properly suited for the intended audience.

On the whole, you ought to make every effort to inject enrichment activities into all your mathematics instruction, regardless of the students' mathematical ability. Such activities can be just as rewarding in a remedial class as in one comprised of gifted students. The benefit, although manifested differently, should be about the same for all classes.

CROSS-CATALOGUE OF ENRICHMENT UNITS

To facilitate using the enrichment units found in this section, a cross-catalogue is provided. The units are listed in the order which they are presented in this section. In addition to providing page numbers for each unit, the grade level, the ability level and branch of mathematics to which each unit is related are also provided. These assessments are simply the opinion of the authors and some secondary school teachers. You may, however, try these units with audiences other than those specified.

You will notice that each ability level—Remedial, Average and Gifted—has been partitioned into four grade level divisions: 7–8, 9, 10, 11–12.

For the remedial student, grades 7–8 are usually the junior high school low level mathematics courses, while at grades 9 and 10 a general mathematics or introductory algebra is assumed. At grades 11–12 there is usually a continuation of the earlier courses, but with a greater degree of sophistication.

The average student partition refers to the junior high school pre-algebra program for grades 7–8, the elementary algebra course for grade 9, the high school geometry course for grade 10, and the second-year algebra (with trigonometry) course and beyond for grades 11–12.

Although very often the gifted student begins the study of elementary algebra in the eighth grade (or earlier), for the sake of simplicity we shall use the same course determination for the gifted students as for the average students (above). A greater ability in mathematics is assumed here, however.

The numbers 1 and 2 indicate the primary and secondary audiences for each unit. This implies that variations of these units can (and should) be used at all levels as you deem appropriate. Naturally, some modifications will have to be made. Some units may have to be "watered down" for weaker mathematics students, while for more gifted youngsters some units may serve as springboards for further investigation.

Ratings:
1—Primary use
  (specifically intended for that audience)
2—Secondary use
  (may be used for that audience with some modifications)

Another important consideration when selecting an enrichment unit is the branch of mathematics to which it is related. For many units this is difficult to isolate, since these units relate to many branches of mathematics. Using the code listed below, the *Subject* column indicates the related branches of mathematics. Although very often the order could easily be changed with no loss of accuracy, every attempt has been made to list the branches of mathematics in descending order of relevance to each unit, as judged by a group of mathematics teachers.

Subject Code:
1—Arithmetic
2—Number Theory
3—Probability
4—Logic
5—Algebra
6—Geometry
7—Analytic Geometry
8—Topology
9—Statistics
10—Problem Solving
11—Applications
12—Mathematical Curiosities

	Topic	Subject	Remedial Classes				Average Classes				Gifted Classes				Page Number
			7–8	9	10	11–12	7–8	9	10	11–12	7–8	9	10	11–12	
1	Constructing Odd Order Magic Squares	1,4,12	1	1	1	2	1	2							206
2	Constructing Even Order Magic Squares	1,12	1	1	1	2	1	2							208
3	Introduction to Alphametics	1,4	2	2	1	1	1	1			1	2			210
4	A Checkerboard Calculator	1,12	1	1	1	2	1	2			2	2			212
5	The Game of Nim	4,1,12	2	1	1	1	1	2			2	2			214
6	The Tower of Hanoi	4,1,12	2	1	1	1	1	2			2	2			216
7	What Day of the Week Was It?	4,1,12	2	2	1	1	1	1			1	2		2	218
8	Palindromic Numbers	2,1,12	1	1	2	2	1	1		2	1	1		2	223
9	The Fascinating Number Nine	1,2,12	2	1	1	1	1	2			1	2			224
10	Unusual Number Properties	1,2,12	2	1	1	1	1	2			1	2			226
11	Enrichment with a Hand-Held Calculator	1,2,12	1	1	1	1	1	2			1	2			228
12	Symmetric Multiplication	1,2,12	2	1	1	1	1	2		2	1	2			230
13	Variations on a Theme—Multiplication	1,2,12	2	1	1	1	1	2		2	1	2		2	232
14	Ancient Egyptian Arithmetic	2,1		2	2	1	1	2		2	1	1		2	234
15	Napier's Rods	1,2,11	1	1	1	1	1	2		2	2				236
16	Unit Pricing	1,11	1	1	1	1	1	2							237
17	Successive Discounts and Increases	1,11,12	2	2	1	1	1	1		2	1	2			238
18	Prime and Composite Factors of a Whole Number	1,2	1	1	1	2	2	2							240
19	Prime Numeration System	2,1,12		2	1	1	2	1		2	1				241
20	Repeating Decimal Expansions	2,1				2	2	1		2	2				243
21	Peculiarities of Perfect Repeating Decimals	2,1,12	1				1	1		2	1	2			245
22	Patterns in Mathematics	4,5	1	1	2	2	1	1			2	2			246
23	Googol and Googolplex	1,12	2	1	1	2	1	2			2	2			248
24	Mathematics of Life Insurance	3,9,5			2	2	2	2	1	1	2	1		2	250
25	Geometric Dissections	6,4,10			2	2	1	1			1	1	2		252

			Remedial Classes				Average Classes				Gifted Classes				Page Number
#	Topic	Subject	7–8	9	10	11–12	7–8	9	10	11–12	7–8	9	10	11–12	
26	The Klein Bottle	8						2		2	1	1	1	2	254
27	The Four Color Map Problem	8,4					1	1	1	2	1	2		2	255
28	Mathematics on a Bicycle	6,4,1		2	1	1	1	2	2	2	2				257
29	Mathematics and Music	11,1						2	2	2	1	1		2	260
30	Mathematics in Nature	11,12,2		2	2	2	1	1	1	2	1	1	2	2	262
31	The Birthday Problem	3,12,11			2	2	2	1	2	1	1	1	1	1	264
32	The Structure of the Number System	1,5					2	1		1	1	1			265
33	Excursions in Number Bases	2,1,5		2	2	2	1	1	2	2	1	2		2	267
34	Raising Interest	5,11			2	2		1	2	1	1	1		2	269
35	Reflexive, Symmetric and Transitive Relations	4,2					1	1	1		1	1	2		271
36	Bypassing an Inaccessible Region	6,10						2	1	1	1	1	1		273
37	The Inaccessible Angle	6,10						2	1	1		1	1		274
38	Triangle Constructions	6,10						2	1	1		2	1	1	276
39	The Criterion of Constructibility	6,5						2		1				1	278
40	Constructing Radical Lengths	6,5						1	1	1		1		1	280
41	Constructing a Pentagon	6,5						2	1			1	1	2	281
42	Investigating the Isosceles Triangle Fallacy	6,12						1	1	1		2	1	1	282
43	The Equiangular Point	6							1			2	1	1	284
44	The Minimum Distance Point of a Triangle	6							1	1		2	1	2	285
45	The Isosceles Triangle Revisited	6,10							1			2		2	287
46	Reflective Properties of the Plane	6,11						2	1	1		1	1	2	289
47	Finding the Length of a Cevian of a Triangle	6,5						2	1	1		2	1	2	291
48	A Surprising Challenge	6,10							1	2		2	1		293
49	Making Discoveries in Mathematics	6					2	1	1	1	1	1	2		295
50	Tessellations	6,5					2	2	1	1	2	1	1	2	296

#	Topic	Subject	Remedial Classes 7–8	Remedial 9	Remedial 10	Remedial 11–12	Average Classes 7–8	Average 9	Average 10	Average 11–12	Gifted Classes 7–8	Gifted 9	Gifted 10	Gifted 11–12	Page Number
51	Introducing the Pythagorean Theorem	6,2,5						1	1	2		1	1	2	298
52	Trisection Revisited	6,5,12						1	1	1		1	1	2	300
53	Proving Lines Concurrent	6,10					2		2	2	2	2	1	2	302
54	Squares	6,10							1	2		1	1	2	304
55	Proving Points Collinear	6,10							2	2		2	1	1	305
56	Angle Measurement with a Circle	6						1	1			2	1		307
57	Trisecting a Circle	6 12						1	1	1		1	1	2	309
58	Ptolemy's Theorem	6,10						2	1	1		1	1	2	310
59	Constructing π	6,1						2	1	1		1	1	2	312
60	The Arbelos	6,5						2	1	1		1	1	1	314
61	The Nine Point Circle	6					2	2	1	2	2	1	1	2	316
62	The Euler Line	6					2	2	1	2	2	1	1	2	317
63	The Simson Line	6					2	2	1	2	2	1	1	2	319
64	The Butterfly Problem	6,10					2	2	1	2	2	1	1	1	320
65	Equicircles	6,5						2	1	2		2	1	1	322
66	The Inscribed Circle and the Right Triangle	6,5					1		2	2		2	1	1	324
67	The Golden Rectangle	6,5,2					1	2	1	1		1	1	2	326
68	The Golden Triangle	6,5,2					1		1	1		1	1	1	328
69	Geometric Faliacies	6,5					1		1	1		1	1	2	330
70	Regular Polyhedra	6,5				2		2	2	1	2	1	1	1	332
71	An Introduction to Topology	8,4	1	2	2	1	1	1	1	2		1		2	334
72	Angles on a Clock	1,5		1	1	1	1	1	1	2		1	2	2	335
73	Averaging Rates—The Harmonic Mean	5,1			2	2	1	1	2	1		1	2	2	337
74	Howlers	1,5		1	1	1	1	1	1	1		1	1	1	339
75	Digit Problems Revisited	5,1		1	1	1	1	1	1	1		1	1	1	341
76	Algebraic Identities	5,6						1	1	2		1	2		342
77	A Method for Factoring Trinomials of the Form: $ax^2 + bx + c$							1	2	1		1			344
78	Solving Quadratic Equations	5						1	2	1		1		2	345
79	The Euclidean Algorithm	5,10						1		1		1		1	347
80	Prime Numbers	2,5						2		2		1		1	349

No.	Topic	Subject	Remedial Classes				Average Classes				Gifted Classes				Page Number
			7–8	9	10	11–12	7–8	9	10	11–12	7–8	9	10	11–12	
81	Algebraic Fallacies	5,12						1	2	1		1	2	1	351
82	Sum Derivations with Arrays	5,6,12				2	2	1	2	1		1		1	353
83	Pythagorean Triples	2,5,6	2			2		2	1	1	1	1	1	1	355
84	Divisibility	2,1,5		1	1	1		1	2	1	2	1	2	1	357
85	Fibonacci Sequence	5,2,12	2		2	2	2	1	2	1	1	1	2	1	359
86	Diophantine Equations	5,2						2			2	1	2	1	361
87	Continued Fractions and Diophantine Equations	5,2						2		1	2	1	2	1	362
88	Simplifying Expressions Involving Infinity	5,2						2			2	1	2	1	364
89	Continued Fraction Expansions of Irrational Numbers	5						2		1	2	1	2	1	366
90	The Farey Sequence	1,5	2	2	2	2	2	2		1	1	1	2	1	368
91	The Parabolic Envelope	6,7	2		2	2	2	1	2	1	1	1	2	2	370
92	Application of Congruence to Divisibility	2,5						2	1	2	2	1	2	1	372
93	Problem Solving—A Reverse Strategy	10,6,5						1	1	2	2	1		1	374
94	Decimals and Fractions in Other Bases	1,5						2	2	1	2	1	1	2	377
95	Polygonal Numbers	2,5				2		1	1	1	2	1	2	1	378
96	Networks	4,5,11,8	2		2	1	2	1	1	1	2	1	1	1	381
97	Angle Trisection—Possible or Impossible?	5,6,2							2	1		2	1	1	383
98	Comparing Means	5,2,6						1	1	1		1	1	1	384
99	Pascal's Pyramid	5								1	2	1		1	386
100	The Multinomial Theorem	5,1,4						2		1	1	1	2	1	388
101	Algebraic Solution of Cubic Equations	5								2		1		1	390
102	Solving Cubic Equations	5						2		2		1		1	392
103	Calculating Sums of Finite Series	5						2		1	1	1		1	394
104	A General Formula for the Sum of a Series of the Form $\sum_{i=1}^{n} r.$	5						2		2	2	2		1	396

	Topic	Subject	Remedial Classes				Average Classes				Gifted Classes				Page Number
			7–8	9	10	11–12	7–8	9	10	11–12	7–8	9	10	11–12	
105	A Parabolic Calculator	7,5						2	2	1		1	1	1	399
106	Constructing Ellipses	6,5,12,7				2		2	2	1		1	1	1	401
107	Constructing the Parabola	6,7,5	2		2	2		2	1	1		1	1	2	403
108	Using Higher Plane Curves to Trisect an Angle	7,5,6							2	1		1	1	1	405
109	Constructing Hypocycloid and Epicycloid Circular Envelopes	6,5,7							2	1		1	1	1	407
110	The Harmonic Sequence	5,6						2	1	1		1	1	1	409
111	Transformations and Matrices	5,7								2		2	2	1	410
112	The Method of Differences	1,5								1		2	2	1	413
113	Probability Applied to Baseball	3,5,4				2	2	1	1	1		1	1	1	414
114	Introduction to Geometric Transformations	6,5							1	1		2	1	1	416
115	The Circle and the Cardioid	6,5,11						2	1	1		1	1	1	418
116	Complex Number Applications	6,5,11						2		1		2	1	1	421
117	Hindu Arithmetic	2, 1	1	2	2	1		2		2	1	1	1	2	423
118	Proving Numbers Irrational	5							2	1		1	2	1	425
119	How to Use a Computer Spreadsheet to Generate Solutions to Certain Mathematics Problems	1,2,10	1				1	2	1	1	1	1	2	2	426

1 Constructing Odd Order Magic Squares

This unit is intended for enrichment of students who have already mastered the fundamentals of elementary algebra. Carefully chosen parts of this unit may also prove effective in remedial classes, where students would appreciate some "recreational" mathematics.

Performance Objectives

1. *Students will construct magic squares of any odd order required.*

2. *Students will discover properties of given odd order magic squares.*

3. *Students will determine the sum of the elements of any row (or column, or diagonal) of any magic square, given only its order.*

Preassessment

Challenge students to form a 3×3 matrix with the numbers 1-9 so that the sum of the elements in each row, column or diagonal is the same. Indicate to them that such a matrix is called a *magic square* (of order 3).

Teaching Strategies

After students have had enough time to be either successful with, or thoroughly frustrated by, the challenge (usually less than 15 minutes), you may begin to attack the problem with them. Have them realize the advantage of knowing beforehand the sum of each row (or column, or diagonal).

In order to develop a formula for the sum of the elements in any row, column, or diagonal of a magic square[*], students must be familiar with the formula for the sum of an arithmetic series, $S = \frac{n}{2}(a_1 + a_n)$. If they are not familiar with this formula it can be very easily related to them by telling the story of young Karl Friedrich Gauss (1777-1855) who, at the age of 10, successfully responded to his teacher's challenge.

His teacher had a habit of providing rather lengthy chores for the students to complete (while he knew of a shortcut formula). One day this teacher told the class to add a series of numbers of the sort: $1+2+3+4+\ldots+97+98+99+100$. As the teacher finished stating the problem, young Gauss submitted the answer. In amazement the teacher asked Gauss to explain his rapid solution. Gauss explained that rather than merely adding the 100 numbers in the order presented, he considered the following pairs $1+100=101$; $2+99=101$; $3+98=$

[*]Unless stated otherwise this **unit** will be concerned with magic squares of consecutive natural numbers beginning with 1.

101; $4+97=101$; ...; $50+51=101$. Since there were 50 pairs of numbers whose sum was 101, his answer was $50\times101=5,050$. In effect, he multiplied one-half the number of numbers to be added ($\frac{n}{2}$) by the sum of the first and last numbers in the series (a_1+a_n) in order to obtain the sum of the entire series.

From this formula, the sum of natural numbers from 1 to n^2 (the numbers used in an $n\times n$ magic square) is $S = \frac{n^2}{2}(1+n^2)$. However, if it is required that each row must have the same sum, then the sum is $\frac{S}{n}$. (From here on the expression "the sum of a row" will actually refer to "the sum of the numbers in a row.") Therefore the sum of any row is $\frac{n}{2}(n^2+1)$. You might want to have students consider why the sum of a diagonal is also $\frac{n}{2}(n^2+1)$.

Students are now ready to begin to systematically consider the original problem. Have them consider the following matrix of letters representing the numbers 1-9.

	c_1	c_2	c_3	
d_1				d_2
r_1	a	b	c	
r_2	d	e	f	
r_3	g	h	i	

Using the formula developed earlier, $S = \frac{n}{2}\times(n^2+1)$, we find that the sum of a row of a third order (3×3) magic square is $\frac{3}{2}(3^2+1) = 15$. Therefore $r_2 + c_2 + d_1 + d_2 = 4\cdot15 = 60$. However $r_2 + c_2 + d_1 + d_2 = (d+e+f) + (b+e+h) + (a+e+i) + (c+e+g) = 3e + (a+b+c+d+e+f+g+h+i) = 3e + 45$ (since the sum of $1+2+3+\ldots+9 = \frac{9}{2}(1+9) = 45$). Therefore $3e + 45 = 60$ and $e = 5$.

Thus it is established that the center position of a third order magic square must be occupied by 5.

Since the sum of each row, column, and diagonal in this magic square is 15, $a + i = g + c = b + h = d + f = 15 - 5 = 10$. (Note: two numbers of an nth order magic square are said to be complementary if their sum is n^2+1; thus a and i are complementary.) Now lead your students through the following argument.

The number 1 cannot occupy a corner position. Suppose $a=1$; then $i=9$. However 2, 3, and 4 cannot be in the same row (or column) as 1, since there is no natural number less than 10 which would be large enough to occupy the third position of such a row (or column). This would leave only two positions (the non-shaded squares below) to accommodate these three numbers (2, 3, and 4). Since this cannot be the case, the numbers 1 and 9 may occupy only the middle positions of a row (or column).

1		
	5	
		9

The number 3 cannot be in the same row (or column) as 9, for the third number in such a row (or column) would then have to be 3, to obtain the required sum of 15. This is not possible because a number can be used only once in the magic square.

Now have students realize that neither 3 nor 7 may occupy corner positions. They should then use the above criteria to construct a magic square of order 3. Students should get any of the following magic squares.

2	7	6
9	5	1
4	3	8

4	3	8
9	5	1
2	7	6

8	1	6
3	5	7
4	9	2

6	1	8
7	5	3
2	9	4

2	9	4
7	5	3
6	1	8

4	9	2
3	5	7
8	1	6

8	3	4
1	5	9
6	7	2

6	7	2
1	5	9
8	3	4

Students might now want to extend this technique to constructing other odd order magic squares. However this scheme becomes somewhat tedious. Following is a rather mechanical method for constructing an odd order magic square.

Begin by placing a 1 in the first position of the middle column. Continue by placing the next consecutive numbers successively in the cells of the (positive slope) diagonal. This, of course, is impossible since there are no cells "above" the square.

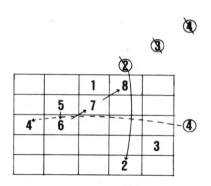

When a number must be placed in a position "above" the square, it should instead be placed in the last cell of the next column to the right. Then the next numbers are placed consecutively in this new (positive slope) diagonal. When (as in the figure above) a number falls outside the square to the right, it should be placed in the first (to the left) cell of the next row above the row whose last (to the right) cell was just filled (as illustrated). The process then continues by filling consecutively on the new cell until an already occupied cell is reached (as is the case with 6, above). Rather than placing a second number in the occupied cell, the number is placed below the previous number. The process continues until the last number is reached.

After enough practice students will begin to recognize certain patterns, e.g., the last number always occupies the middle position of the bottom row.

It should be noted that this is just one of many ways of constructing odd order magic squares. More adept students should be urged to justify this rather mechanical technique.

Postassessment

Have students do the following exercises:

1. Find the sum of a row of a magic square of order (a) 4; (b) 7; (c) 8.

2. Construct a magic square of order 11.

3. State some properties common to magic squares of odd order less than 13.

2 Constructing Even Order Magic Squares

This topic can be used with a remedial class in high school as well as with a more advanced class at any secondary school grade level. In the former case, only magic squares of doubly-even order should be considered, while in the latter case, singly-even order magic squares may be included. When used with a remedial class, the development of doubly-even order magic squares may serve as motivation for drill of arithmetic fundamentals.

Performance Objectives

1. *Students will construct magic squares of any even order required.*

2. *Students will discover properties of given even order magic squares.*

Preassessment

Begin your introduction with a historical note. Mention the German artist (and mathematician) Albrecht Dürer (1471-1528), who did considerable work with mathematics related to his art work. One of the more curious aspects of his work was the appearance of a magic square in an engraving of 1514 entitled "Melancholia" (Figure 1).

Figure 1

Figure 2

At the upper right hand corner of the engraving is the magic square (Figure 2). It is believed that this was one of the first appearances of magic squares in Western civilization. Of particular interest are the many unusual properties of this magic square. For example, the two center positions of the bottom row indicate the year the engraving was made, 1514. Offer your students some time to find other unusual properties (other than merely a constant sum of rows, columns, and diagonals).

Teaching Strategies

Students will probably enjoy discussing the many properties of this magic square, some of which are:

1. The four corner positions have a sum of 34.

2. The four corner 2×2 squares each has a sum of 34.

3. The center 2×2 square has a sum of 34.

4. The sum of the numbers in a diagonal equals the sum of those not in a diagonal.

5. The sum of the squares of the numbers in the diagonals (748) equals the sum of the squares of the numbers not in the diagonals.

6. The sum of the cubes of the numbers in diagonals (9,248) equals the sum of the cubes of the numbers not in the diagonals.

7. The sum of the squares of the numbers in both diagonals equals the sum of the squares of the numbers in the first and third rows (or columns), which equals the sum of the squares of the numbers in the second and fourth rows (or columns.)

8. Note the following symmetries:
$$2+8+9+15 = 3+5+12+14 = 34$$
$$2^2+8^2+9^2+15^2 = 3^2+5^2+12^2+14^2 = 374$$
$$2^3+8^3+9^3+15^3 = 3^3+5^3+12^3+14^3 = 4,624$$

9. The sum of each upper and lower pair of numbers vertically or horizontally produces an interesting symmetry (see below).

vertically:	21	13	13	21
	13	21	21	13

horizontally:	19	15
	15	19
	15	19
	19	15

Consider first constructions of magic squares whose *order is a multiple of 4,* (sometimes referred to as *doubly-even order.*) Have students construct the square below with the diagonals as shown.

Figure 3

1	2	3	4
5	6	7	8
9	10	11	12
13	14	15	16

Then have them replace each number in a diagonal with its complement (i.e. that number which will give a sum of $n^2+1 = 16+1 = 17$.) This will yield a 4×4 magic square (Figure 4.) (Note: Durer simply interchanged columns 2 and 3 to obtain his magic square.)

A similar process is used to construct larger doubly-even order magic squares. To construct an 8×8 magic square, divide the square into 4×4

16	2	3	13
5	11	10	8
9	7	6	12
4	14	15	1

Figure 4

magic squares (Figure 5) and then replace the numbers in the diagonals of each of the 4×4 squares with their complements.

1	2	3	4	5	6	7	8
9	10	11	12	13	14	15	16
17	18	19	20	21	22	23	24
25	26	27	28	29	30	31	32
33	34	35	36	37	38	39	40
41	42	43	44	45	46	47	48
49	50	51	52	53	54	55	56
57	58	59	60	61	62	63	64

Figure 5

64	2	3	61	60	6	7	57
9	55	54	12	13	51	50	16
17	47	46	20	21	43	42	24
40	26	27	37	36	30	31	33
32	34	35	29	28	38	39	25
41	23	22	44	45	19	18	48
49	15	14	52	53	11	10	56
8	58	59	5	4	62	63	1

Figure 6

The resulting magic square is shown as Figure 6. Now have students construct a magic square of order 12.

A different scheme is used to construct magic squares of singly-even order, i.e., those whose order is even but *not* a multiple of 4. Any singly-even order (say, of order *n*) magic square may be separated into quadrants (Figure 7). For convenience label them A, B, C, and D.

Figure 7

A	C
D	B

Students should now be instructed to construct four *odd order* magic squares in the order A, B, C, and D (refer to the accompanying Model "Constructing Odd Order Magic Squares". That is, square A will be odd order magic square using the first $\frac{n^2}{4}$ natural numbers: square B will be an odd order magic square beginning with $\frac{n^2}{4}+1$; and ending with $\frac{n^2}{2}$; square C will be an odd order magic square beginning with $\frac{n^2}{2}+1$; and ending with $\frac{3n^2}{4}$; square D will be an odd order magic square beginning with $\frac{3n^2}{4}+1$ and ending with n^2. (Figure 8 illustrates the case where n=6.)

8	1	6	26	19	24
3	5	7	21	23	25
4	9	2	22	27	20
35	28	33	17	10	15
30	32	34	12	14	16
31	36	29	13	18	11

Figure 8

0 + 8	0 + 1	0 + 6	18 + 8	18 + 1	18 + 6
0 + 3	0 + 5	0 + 7	18 + 3	18 + 5	18 + 7
0 + 4	0 + 9	0 + 2	18 + 4	18 + 9	18 + 2
27 + 8	27 + 1	27 + 6	9 + 8	9 + 1	9 + 6
27 + 3	27 + 5	27 + 7	9 + 3	9 + 5	9 + 7
27 + 4	27 + 9	27 + 2	9 + 4	9 + 9	9 + 2

Figure 9

Have students notice the relation of the four magic squares of Figure 8 to the first magic square in the upper left position, A (Figure 9).

Now only some minor adjustments need be made to complete the construction of the magic squares. Let $n = 2(2m+1)$. Take the numbers in the first *m* positions in each row of A (except the middle row, where you skip the first position and take the next *m* positions) and interchange them with the numbers in the corresponding positions of square D. Then take the numbers in the last *m*-1 positions of square C and interchange them with the number in the corresponding posi-

35	1	6	26	19	24
3	32	7	21	23	25
31	9	2	22	27	20
8	28	33	17	10	15
30	5	34	12	14	16
4	36	29	13	18	11

Figure 10

tions of square B. Notice that for $n=6$ (Figure 10) $m-1=0$, hence squares B and C remain unaltered.

Have students apply this technique to the construction of a magic square of order 10 ($n=10$ and $m=2$; see Figures 11 and 12).

Figure 11

17	24	1	8	15	67	74	51	58	65
23	5	7	14	16	73	55	57	64	66
4	6	13	20	22	54	56	63	70	72
10	12	19	21	3	60	62	69	71	53
11	18	25	2	9	61	68	75	52	59
92	99	76	83	90	42	49	26	33	40
98	80	82	89	91	48	30	32	39	41
79	81	88	95	97	29	31	38	45	47
85	87	94	96	78	35	37	44	46	28
86	93	100	77	84	36	43	50	27	34

Figure 12

92	99	1	8	15	67	74	51	58	40
98	80	7	14	16	73	55	57	64	41
4	81	88	20	22	54	56	63	70	47
85	87	19	21	3	60	62	69	71	28
86	93	25	2	9	61	68	75	52	34
17	24	76	83	90	42	49	26	33	65
23	5	82	89	91	48	30	32	39	66
79	6	13	95	97	29	31	38	45	72
10	12	94	96	78	35	37	44	46	53
11	18	100	77	84	36	43	50	27	59

Postassessment

As a formal postassessment, have students

1. construct a magic square of order (a) 12; (b) 16;

2. construct a magic square of order (a) 14; (b) 18;

3. find additional properties of magic squares of order (a) 8; (b) 12.

3   Introduction to Alphametics

This unit can be used to reinforce the concept of addition.

Performance Objective

Given alphametic problems, students will solve them in a systematic fashion.

Preassessment

Have students solve the following addition problems, either by simple addition in (a) and by filling in the missing digits in (b).

```
a)   562          b)  5 6 7 __
    3943              __ 8 __ 9
    8807             _____
                      3 __ 3 3
```

Teaching Strategies

The preceding problems should serve as a motivation for this lesson. Alphametics are math-ematical puzzles which appear in several disguises. Sometimes the problem is associated with the restoration of digits in a computational problem, while at other times, the problem is associated with decoding the complete arithmetical problem where letters of the alphabet represent all the digits. Basically, construction of this type of puzzle is not difficult, but the solution requires a thorough investigation of all elements. Every clue must be tested in all phases of the problem and carefully followed up. For example, suppose we were to eliminate certain digits in problem (*a*) above and supply the answer with some digits missing. Let us also assume that we do not know what these digits are. We may then be left with the following skeleton problem:

①②③④⑤
```
      _  6  2
   3  9  4  _
   _  8  _  7
   _  3  3  1  2
```

Have students analyze the problem. Lead them through the reconstruction as follows. From column five, $2 + \_ + 7 = 12$. Therefore the missing digit in the fifth column must be 3. In the fourth column, we have $1 + 6 + 4 + \_ = 1$, or $11 + \_ = 1$, therefore the digit must be zero. In the third column, we have $1 + \_ + 9 + 8 = 23$, and the missing digit must be 5. Now, from the second column, we have now $2 + 3 + \_ = 13$. This implies that the digit must be 8, and therefore, the digit to the left of 3 in the first column, botton row must be 1. Thus, we have reconstructed the problem. Students should now be able to find the missing digits in the second problem of the preassessment (if they haven't already solved it). The completed solution is

```
     5  6  7  ④
     ⑦  8  ⑤  9
   ①  3  ⑤  3  3
```

Have students make up their own problems and then interchange them with other students. We have considered problems that had exactly one solution. The following example will show a problem that has more than one solution.

①②③④
```
      _  8  7
   3  _  1
   5  6  _
   _  3  _  0
```

In $7 + 1 + \_ = 10$, the missing digit must be 2. In the third column, $1 + 8 + \_ + 6 = \_\_\_$, or $15 + \_ = \_\_\_$. An inspection must now be made of column two, so that all possible outcomes are considered. In the second column we have $\_ + 3 + 5 = 13$. Thus, if we assigned the digits 5, 6, 7, 8, 9, for the value of the missing number in the third column, second row, we would have $15 + 5 = 20$, $15 + 6 = 21$, $15 + 7 = 22$, $15 + 8 = 23$, $15 + 9 = 24$. This will then make the digit in column two equal to 3, since a 2 is being carried. Hence, we have as possible solutions:

387		387		387		387		387
351		361		371		381		391
562	or	562	or	562	or	562	or	562
1300		1310		1320		1330		1340

On the other hand, if we assigned values for the missing digit in the second row, third column, to be 0, 1, 2, 3, 4, then the digit in the first row, first column will be a 4, since a 1 was now carried. Therefore, there are ten different solutions which result from having two missing digits in the same column. Students should determine if this is true in all cases. Have students make up a similar problem where more than two digits are missing in the same column, and see what conclusion they can discover.

In the second type of problem, where all digits are represented by letters (hence the name alphametics), the problem is quite different from the preceding ones. Here, the clues from the "puzzle" must be analyzed for all different possible values to be assigned to the letters. No general rule can be given for the solution of alphametic problems. What is required is an understanding of basic arithmetic, logical reasoning, and plenty of patience.

One fine example of this type is the following addition problem:

①②③④⑤
```
   F  O  R  T  Y
      T  E  N
      T  E  N
   S  I  X  T  Y
```

Since the first line and the fourth line have **T Y** repeated, this would imply that the sum of both the **E**'s and the **N**'s in columns four and five must end in zero. If we let **N** = 0, then **E** must equal 5, and 1 is carried over to column three. We now have

```
   F  O  R  T  Y
      T  5  0
      T  5  0
   S  I  X  T  Y
```

Since there are two spaces before each **T E N,** the 0 in **F O R T Y** must be 9, and with 2 carried over from the hundred's place (column three), the **I** must be one. And a 1 is carried to column one, making **F + 1 = S**. Ask the students why 2 and not 1 was carried over to the second column. The reason 2 must be carried from column three is that if a 1 were carried, the digits **I** and **N** would both be zero. We are now left with the following numbers 2, 3, 4, 6, 7, 8 unassigned.

```
   F  9  R  T  Y
      T  5  0
      T  5  0
   S  I  X  T  Y
```

In the hundreds column, we have $2T + R + 1$ (the 1 being carried over from column four), whose sum must be equal to or greater than 22; which implies **T** and **R** must be greater than 5. Therefore, **F** and **S** will be either 2, 3, or 4. Now **X** cannot be equal to 3, otherwise **F** and **S** would not be consecutive numbers. Then **X** equals 2 or 4, which is impossible if **T** is equal to or less than 7. Hence **T** must be 8, with **R** equal to 7 and **X** equal to 4. Then **F** = 2, **S** = 3, leaving **Y** = 6. Hence the solution to the problem is

$$
\begin{array}{r}
2\,9,7\,8\,6 \\
8\,5\,0 \\
8\,5\,0 \\
\hline
3\,1,4\,8\,6
\end{array}
$$

Postassessment

Have students solve the following alphametic problems.

1)   4 __ __ 3
    __ __ 1 4 __
  __ __ 3 7 4 6

Answer
4603
99143
103746

2)   5 __ 4 __
   __ 4 5 __ 8
   6 __ 2 5 9
   ─────────
   9 4 1 9 6

Answer
5349
24588
64259
94196

3) T R I E D
   D R I V E
   ─────────
   R I V E T

Answer
17,465
57,496
74,961

4) S E N D
    M O R E
   ────────
   M O N E Y

Answer
9,567
1,085
10,652

5) A L L S
    W E L L
    T H A T
    E N D S
   ────────
   S W E L L

Answer
9,332
8,433
6,596
4,072
28,433

4 **A Checkerboard Calculator**

This enrichment unit will give students an easy, enjoyable method of operation with binary numerals.

Performance Objective
Students will be able to use a checkerboard calculator to do addition, subtraction, multiplication, and division with binary numerals.

Preassessment
Have students find:
a) $1100_2 + 110_2 = $ __   b) $12 + 6 = $ __
c) $111_2 \times 10_2 = $ __   d) $7 \times 2 = $ __

Teaching Strategies
John Napier, the 16th century mathematician who developed logarithms and Napier's Bones (the calculating rods), also described in his work *Rabdologia* a method for calculating by moving counters across a chessboard. Besides being the world's first binary computer, it is also a valuable teaching aid. Although use of checkered boards was common in the Middle Ages and Renaissance period, by adopting a binary system and basing algorithms on old methods of multiplying by "doubling", Napier's Counting Board became much more efficient than any previous device.

Have students bring to school a standard chessboard or checkerboard. Begin by having students label rows and columns with the doubling series: 1, 2, 4, 8, 16, 32, 64, 128.

Now show how the board can be used for addition and subtraction. Every number is expressed by placing counters on a row. Each counter has the value of its column. For example, ask the students to add 89+41+52+14. The fourth row (89) will show 64+16+8+1(Figure 1).

Figure 1

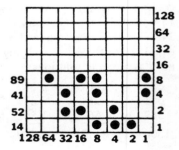

If the students think of each counter as a 1 and each empty space as a 0, 89 is represented in binary notation as 1011001_2.

The counters are positioned by starting at the left and putting a counter on the column of the largest number less than the number the student is representing. Place subsequent counters on the next largest number that when added to the previous number will not exceed the desired total, and so on.

To add, have students move all counters straight down (Figure 2).

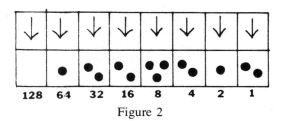

Figure 2

Adding the values of these counters will give the correct sum, but to use the board for binary notation, we must first "clear" the row of multiple counters on one cell. Have students start at the right, taking each cell in turn. Remove every PAIR of counters on a cell and replace them with a single counter on the next cell to the left. Assure students that this will not affect the sum as every two counters having value n, are replaced by one counter having value $2n$. In our example, the final result is the binary number 11000100_2 (Figure 3).

Figure 3

Subtraction is almost as simple. Suppose students want to take 83 from 108. Have them represent the larger number on the second row and the smaller number on the bottom row (Figure 4).

Figure 4

Students can now do subtraction in the usual manner, starting at the right and borrowing from cell to cell. Or instead, students can alter the entire second row until each counter on the bottom row has one or two counters above it, and no empty cell on the bottom row has more than one counter above it. This can be done by "doubling down" on

the second row; removing a counter and replacing it with two counters on the next cell to the right (Figure 5).

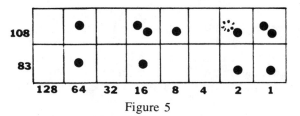

Figure 5

After this, "king" each counter in the bottom row by moving a counter on top of it from the cell directly above (Figure 6).

Figure 6

The top row now shows the difference of the two numbers in binary notation ($11001_2 = 25_{10}$).

Multiplication is also very simple. As an example use $19 \times 13 = 247$. Have students indicate one number, say 19, by marking below the board under the proper *columns* and the other number, 13, by marking the proper *rows*. Place a counter on every intersection of a marked column and marked row. (Figure 7A). Every counter not on the extreme right-hand column is next moved diagonally up and to the right as a bishop in chess (Figure 7B).

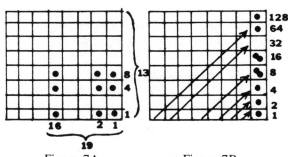

Figure 7A   Figure 7B

Clear the column by halving up as in addition, and the desired product is expressed in binary notation as 11110111_2 or 247_{10}, which students can quickly confirm.

Students will want to know how this works. Counters on the first row keep their values when moved to the right; counters on the second row double in value; counters on the third row quadruple in value; and so on. The procedure can be shown to be equivalent to multiplying with powers of the base 2. Nineteen is expressed in our example as $2^4 + 2^1 + 2^0$ and 13 as $2^3 + 2^2 + 2^0$. Multiplying the two trinomials gives us $2^7 +$

$2^6 + 2 \cdot 2^4 + 2 \cdot 2^3 + 2^2 + 2^1 + 2^0 = 247$. Moving the counters is equivalent to multiplying. We are, in effect, *multiplying* powers by *adding* exponents.

As an example of division, use $250 \div 13$. The procedure, as students may be expecting, is the reverse of multiplication. The divisor, in this case, 13, is marked at the bottom of the board and the dividend by counters on the column at the extreme right (Figure 8A). The dividend counters now move down and to the left, again like chess bishops, but in the opposite direction to multiplication. This procedure produces a pattern that has counters (one to a cell) only on marked columns, and each marked column must have its counters on the same rows. Only one such pattern can be formed. To do so it is necessary at times to double down on the right column; that is, remove single counters, replacing each with a pair of counters on the next lower cell. Have students start with the top counter and move it diagonally to the leftmost marked column. If the counter cannot proceed, have students return it to the original cell, double down, and try again. Have them continue in this way, gradually filling in the pattern until the unique solution is achieved (Figure 8B).

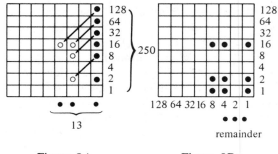

Figure 8A   Figure 8B

After the final counter is in place students should note that three counters are left over. This represents the remainder (3 or 11_2). The value of the right margin is now 10011_2 or 19_{10}, with $\frac{3}{13}$ left over.

Postassessment
Have students solve the following problems by using the checkerboard methods:

a) $27 \cdot 64 =$ b) $194 - 63 =$
c) $54 + 43 =$ d) $361 \div 57 =$

5 The Game of Nim

This unit will present an application of the binary system through the playing of a simple game called Nim.

Performance Objective
Students will play the game of Nim using binary notation system strategy to win.

Preassessment
Have students represent in binary notation:
(a) 14   (b) 7   (c) 13

Teaching Strategies
Nim, although sometimes played for money, can hardly be classified as a gambling game. This is because a player who knows the "secret" of the game can virtually always win.

The game of Nim may be played with sticks, pebbles, coins or any other small objects. Describe the game to students as played with toothpicks. Have students arrange the toothpicks in three piles (other numbers of piles may be used, also) with any number of toothpicks in each pile. Have two students be players. The two players take turns

making their moves. A move consists of taking away toothpicks according to certain rules. The rules are:

1. In each move a student may take away toothpicks from only one pile.

2. Each player may take any number of toothpicks, but must take at least one, and may take an entire pile at one time.

3. The player who takes away the last toothpick wins.

The "secret" of winning is quite simple, but practice is necessary to accurately perform mentally the arithmetic involved. Therefore, it is probably easier to start with a small number of toothpicks. The winning technique is based on choosing a move so that your opponent must draw from an *even set*.

First, it is necessary to learn how to identify an even set and an odd set. Suppose, for example, that the toothpicks are divided into three piles of (14), (7), and (13) toothpicks. Have students express each of these numbers in binary notation, and add the digits in each column in the same manner as when the decimal base is used. If at least one of the individual sums or digits is an odd number, the distribution is called an odd set. This example is an odd set because one sum is an odd number.

```
Fourteen  = 1 1 1 0
Seven     =   1 1 1
Thirteen  = 1 1 0 1
            ─────────
            2 3 2 2        (odd set)
```

If the toothpicks are divided into the piles (9), (13) and (4) toothpicks, each individual sum is even and so it is considered an even set.

```
Nine      = 1 0 0 1
Thirteen  = 1 1 0 1
Four      =   1 0 0
            ─────────
            2 2 0 2        (even set)
```

If a student draws from any even set, he necessarily must leave an odd set, for, considering the representation of the set in the binary scale, any draw will remove a one from at least one column, and the sum of the column will no longer be even.

On the other hand, if a player draws from an odd set, he can leave either an odd set or an even set. There are, however, usually only a few moves that can be made which will change an odd set into an even set. Therefore, a drawing at random from an odd set will very likely result in leaving an odd set.

Explain to the students that the object of the game is to try to force your opponent to draw from an even set, and his drawing will then leave an odd set. There are two winning end distributions that are even sets:

(a) Two piles of two toothpicks each, designated symbolically (2), (2).

(b) Four piles of one toothpick each, designated (1), (1), (1), (1).

If the student can leave an even set each time he plays, he is eventually able to force his opponent to draw from one of the above even sets, and the game is won. If at the start of the game the student has an even set before him, the best procedure is to draw a single toothpick from the largest pile leaving an odd set. If the opponent does not know the "secret" of the game, he or she will probably draw, leaving an odd set and you will then be able to force a win.

Have students follow moves in a sample game. Put toothpicks in piles of (7), (6) and (3) toothpicks each. /////// ////// ////

```
Seven     = 1 1 1
Six       = 1 1 0
Three     =   1 1
            ───────
            2 3 2         (odd set)
```

To leave an even set, the first student must draw two toothpicks from any one pile. Drawing from the first pile would give:

///// ////// ///
```
Five      = 1 0 1
Six       = 1 1 0
Three     =   1 1
            ───────
            2 2 2         (even set)
```

No matter how the second student moves, he is forced to leave an odd set. For instance, let him remove three toothpicks from the second pile.

///// /// ///
```
Five      = 1 0 1
Three     =   1 1
Three     =   1 1
            ───────
            1 2 3         (odd set)
```

At this point the first student should draw all five toothpicks from the first pile.

/// ///
```
Three     = 1 1
Three     = 1 1
            ─────
            2 2           (even set)
```

Now, regardless of how the second student chooses the first will win. Students should now be permitted to play each other. This will provide reinforcement of the binary numeration system. After they have mastered the game as presented above, have them reverse the objective. (That is, let the loser be the player who must pick the last toothpick).

Postassessment

Have a student, who has been taught the strategy, play Nim against a student who only knows the rules. Use any (or all) of the following choices of piles of toothpicks:

(a) 17), (15), (4) (b) (18), (15), (4) (c) (18), (15), (3)

The student who has been taught the strategy of the game should always win.

6   The Tower of Hanoi

This unit provides students with an opportunity to construct and solve an ancient puzzle using the binary system of numeration. The puzzle, known as the Tower of Hanoi, was invented in 1883 by the French mathematician Edward Lucas.

Performance Objective

Each student will build and solve his own Tower of Hanoi puzzle using the binary system, and making use of knowledge required in this lesson.

Preassessment

Prior to this lesson students should be able to convert base 10 numerals to base 2 numerals. Administer the following quiz, instructing students to convert the given numerals (base 10) to base 2: a) 4 b) 8 c) 16 d) 60 e) 125.

Teaching Strategies

Begin the lesson by relating the "history" of the puzzle to the class:

W.W. Rouse Ball in his book *Mathematical Recreations and Essays,* relates an interesting legend of the origin of a puzzle called the Tower of Hanoi. In the great temple at Benares, beneath the dome that marks the center of the world, rests a brass plate in which are fixed three diamond needles, each a cubit high and as thick as the body of a bee. During creation, God placed 64 gold disks of diminishing size on one of these needles, the largest disk at the base resting on the brass plate. This is the tower of Bramah.

According to the legend the priests work day and night transferring the disks from one diamond needle to another according to the fixed laws of Bramah, which require that the priest on duty must *not* move *more than one disk at a time* and that he must place each disk on a needle so that *there is no smaller disk beneath it.* When the 64 disks have been transferred from the needle on which God placed them at creation to one of the other needles, tower, temple and Brahmins alike will crumble into dust, and with a thunderclap the world will vanish.

The puzzle, which is sold commercially, can easily be made by each member of the class. Instruct students to cut out eight cardboard circles, each of different size. Have them punch three holes into a piece of thick cardboard so that the distance between the holes is greater than the outside radius of the largest disk. Next have them glue a dowel or pencil upright into each hole. In each disk, they should cut a hole at the center, wide enough for the dowel to fit through. Now they can place each disk

on one of the dowels in order of size, with the largest one at the bottom. The arrangement of disks is called a *tower.*

If you do not want to trouble yourself with cutting circles and gluing dowels into a board, you can make a simplified set by cutting eight squares of different sizes, and resting them on three plates instead of on dowels. In any case be sure to observe the rules:

At the start all the disks are placed on one post in order of size, the largest disk on the bottom. The puzzle involves shifting the disks, one at a time, from this post to another in such a way that a disk shall never rest on one smaller than itself. This should be done in the least possible number of moves. Remind students of the basic rules:

1) *Move only one disk at a time.*
2) *Never put a disk on top of a smaller disk.*

To familiarize students with the way the game works, demonstrate it first with only three disks. They should be able to transfer a tower of three disks in seven moves.

Now have them try it with four disks. To do this, seven moves are required to transfer the three top disks to one of the other two dowels. This frees the fourth disk which can then be moved to the vacant dowel. Seven more moves are now required to transfer the other three disks back on top the fourth. Thus, the total number of moves required is 15.

When students consider the game with five disks they must move the top four disks twice, once to free the bottom disk, and once to get them back on the bottom disk, after the bottom disk has been moved. Thus, moving five disks takes 31 moves; six disks, 63 moves. Ask the class how many moves are required to transfer seven disks. Eight disks?

As students begin to comprehend the challenge of the puzzle, an interesting mathematical problem will emerge: *What is the minimum number of moves required to shift a specific number of disks from one post to another?* To solve this problem, suggest that students denote the number of disks by n; the least number of moves required by $2^n - 1$. Therefore, if there are eight disks, the least number of moves is $2^8 - 1 = 256 - 1 = 255$.

Have students consider the Brahmins with their 64 disks of gold. How many moves will it take them? $2^{64} - 1 = 18,446,744,073,709,551,615$.

If the priests were to make one transfer every second and work 24 hours a day, 365 days a year, they would need more than *580 billion years* to perform the feat, assuming that they never made a mistake. How long would it take the priests to transfer half (or 32) of the disks? ($4,294,967,296$ sec. = 136 years.)

Now have the class consider the problem of moving eight disks, the Tower of Hanoi. Suggest that students number the disks, one to eight according to size, from the smallest to the largest. Also, have them number the moves from 1 to 225 ($2^8 - 1$ = 225). As a class (or independent) project they should write the number of each move in the binary scale. To discover which disk to transfer at each move, and where to place it, they can refer to the binary scale numeral that corresponds to that move. Then have them count the digits from the right until the first unit digit is reached. The number of digits counted tells which disk to move. For example, if the first 1 from the right is the third digit, then the third disk is moved. Now its placement must be determined. If there are no other digits to the left of the first 1, then the disk is

placed on the dowel that has no disks on it. If there *are* other digits to the left of the first 1, students should count digits from the right again until they reach the second 1. The number of digits counted this time identifies a larger disk that was previously moved. Students must decide whether to place the disk they are moving on top of this larger disk or on the "empty" dowel. To decide which strategy to take, they should count the number of zeros between the first 1 from the right and the second 1 from the right. If there are no zeros between them, or if there is an even number of zeros between them, they should put the disk that they are moving onto the disk that the second 1 refers to. If the number of zeros between them is odd, they put the disk on the empty dowel.

The numbers 1 to 15, written in the binary scale are presented here, along with the instructions for the first fifteen moves.

1	Move disk 1.
10	Move disk 2.
11	Place disk 1 on disk 2.
100	Move disk 3.
101	Place disk 1 not on disk 3.
110	Place disk 2 on disk 3.
111	Place disk 1 on disk 2.
1000	Move disk 4.
1001	Place disk 1 on disk 4.
1010	Place disk 2 not on disk 4.
1011	Place disk 1 on disk 2.
1100	Place disk 3 on disk 4.
1101	Place disk 1 not on disk 3.
1110	Place disk 2 on disk 3.
1111	Place disk 1 on disk 2.

Postassessment

To assess student progress have them complete the above table. Then have them make the first 25 moves on their model of the Tower of Hanoi.

7   What Day of the Week Was It?

This topic may be used for enrichment in a recreational spirit, as well as an interesting application of mathematics. Students will also enjoy seeing the relationship between astronomy and mod 7. In addition, students will be surprised to see how many factors have to be considered in this seemingly simple problem.

Performance Objectives

1. Given any date, the student will determine the day of the week corresponding to this date.

2. Given any year, the student will determine the date of the Easter Sunday that year.

Preassessment

The students must be familiar with the construction of the calendar.

Give the students a date in this year and ask them to indicate the day corresponding to this date. After they try this, ask them to do this for a date in the past. The students will be anxious to develop a rapid and accurate method for doing this.

Teaching Strategy

Start with a brief history of the calendar. The students will be most interested in knowing the development of the present day Gregorian Calendar and fascinated by how it was changed.

Discuss the relationship of the calendar to astronomy. Time can be measured only by observing the motions of bodies that move in unchanging cycles. The only motions of this nature are those of the celestial bodies. Hence we owe to astronomy the establishment of a secure basis for the measurement of time by determining the lengths of the day, the month, and the year. A year is defined as the interval of time between two passages of the earth through the same point in its orbit in relation to the sun. This is the solar year. It is approximately 365.242216 mean solar days. The length of the year is not commensurable with the length of the day; the history of the calendar is the history of the attempts to adjust these incommensurable units in such a way as to obtain a simple and practical system.

The calendar story goes back to Romulus, the legendary founder of Rome, who introduced a year of 300 days divided into 10 months. His successor, Numa, added two months. This calendar was used for the following six and a half centuries until Julius Caesar introduced the Julian Calendar. If the year were indeed 365.25 days, the introduction of an additional day to 365 days once every four years, making

the fourth year a leap year, would completely compensate for the discrepancy. The Julian Calendar spread abroad with other features of Roman culture, and was generally used until 1582.

The difficulty with this method of reckoning was that 365.25 was not 365.242216, and although it may seem an insignificant quantity, in hundreds of years it accumulates to a discrepancy of a considerable number of days. The Julian Year was somewhat too long and by 1582 the accumulated error amounted to ten days.

Pope Gregory XII tried to compensate for the error. Because the Vernal Equinox occurred on March 11 in 1582, he ordered that ten days be suppressed from the calendar dates in that year so that the Vernal Equinox would fall on March 21 as it should. When he proclaimed the calendar reform, he formulated the rules regarding the leap years. The Gregorian Calendar has years (based on approximately 365.2425 days) divisible by four as leap years, unless they are divisible by 100 and not 400. Thus 1700, 1800, 1900, 2100, . . . are not leap years, but 2000 is.

In Great Britain and its colonies the change of the Julian to the Gregorian Calendar was not made until 1752. In September of that year, eleven days were omitted. The day after September 2 was September 14. It is interesting to see a copy of the calendar for Sept. 1752 taken from the almanac of Richard Saunders, Gent., published in London (Figure A).

Mathematicians have pondered the question of the calendar and tried to develop ways of determining the days of any given date or holiday.

To develop a method for determining the day, the student should be aware that a calendar year (except for a leap year) is 52 weeks and one day long. If New Year's day in some year following a leap year occurs on a Sunday, the next New Year's will occur on Monday. The following New Year's day will occur on a Tuesday. The New Year's day of the leap year will occur on a Wednesday. Since there are 366 days in a leap year, the next New Year's day will occur on a Friday, and not on a Thursday. The regular sequence is interrupted every four years (except during years where numbers are evenly divisible by 100 but not evenly divisible by 400).

First develop a method to find the weekday for dates in the same year.

Suppose February 4 falls on Monday. On what day of the week will September 15 fall? Assuming that this calendar year is not a leap year, one need only: (1) Find the number of days between Feb. 4 and Sept. 15.

| 2752 | | September hath XIX Days this Year. | | | | |

First Quarter, the 15th day at 2 afternoon.
Full Moon, the 23rd day at 1 afternoon.
Last Quarter, the 30th day at 2 afternoon.

M D	W D	Saints' Days Terms, &c.	Moon South	Moon Sets	Full Sea at Lond.	Aspects and Weather
1	f	Day br. 3.35	3 A 27	8 A 29	5 A 1	♉ ♃ ☿
2	g	London burn.	4 26	9 11	5 38	Lofty winds

According to an act of Parliament passed in the 24th year of his Majesty's reign and in the year of our Lord 1751, the Old Style ceases here and the New takes its place; and consequently the next Day, which in the old account would have been the 3d is now to be called the 14th; so that all the intermediate nominal days from the 2d to the 14th are omitted or rather annihilated this Year; and the Month contains no more than 19 days, as the title at the head expresses.

M D	W D	Saints' Days Terms, &c.	Moon South	Moon Sets	Full Sea at Lond.	Aspects and Weather
14	e	Clock slo. 5 m.	5 15	9 47	6 27	HOLY ROOD D.
15	f	Day 12 h. 30 m.	6 3	10 31	7 18	and hasty
16	g		6 57	11 23	8 16	showers
17	A	15 S. AFT. TRIN.	7 37	12 19	9 7	
18	b		8 26	Morn.	10 22	More warm
19	c	Nat. V. Mary	9 12	1 22	11 21	and dry
20	d	EMBER WEEK	9 59	2 24	Morn.	weather
21	e	ST. MATTHEW	10 43	3 37	0 17	☌ ♀ ☿
22	f	Burchan	11 28	☾ rise	1 6	♉ ♃ ♀ ☿
23	g	EQUAL D. & N.	Morn.	6 A 13	1 52	☌ ☉ ☿
24	A	16 S. AFT. TRIN.	0 16	6 37	2 39	☌ ☉ ☿
25	b		1 5	7 39	3 14	
26	c	Day 11 h. 52 m.	1 57	8 39	3 48	Rain or hail
27	d	EMBER WEEK	2 56	8 18	4 23	☌ ♂ ☿
28	e	Lambert bp.	3 47	9 3	5 6	now abouts
29	f	ST. MICHAEL	4 44	9 59	5 55	✳ ♄ ☿
30	g		5 43	11 2	6 58	

Figure A

First find that Feb. 4 is the 35th day of the year and that Sept. 15 is the 258th day of the year. (The table Figure B expedites this). The difference of 258 and 35 is the number of days, namely, 223. (2) Since there are seven days in a week, divide 223 by 7. [223/7 = 31 + remainder 6.] (3) The 6 indicates that the day on which Sept. 15 falls is the sixth day after Monday, thus Sunday. In the case of a leap year, one day must be added after February 28 to account for February 29.

A similar method for finding the weekday of the dates in the same year can be discussed thusly.

Because January has 31 days, the same date in the subsequent month will be 3 days after that day in January; the same date in March will also be 3 days later than in January; in April, it will be 6 days later than in January. We can then construct a table of Index Numbers for the months which will adjust all dates to the corresponding dates in January:

Jan.	0	Apr.	6	July	6	Oct.	0
Feb.	3	May	1	Aug.	2	Nov.	3
Mar.	3	June	4	Sept.	5	Dec.	5

(The Index Numbers are actually giving you the days between the months divided by 7 to get the excess days as in the previous method.)

Now you need only add the date to the Index Number of the month, divide by 7 and the remainder will indicate the day of the week.

Example: Consider the year 1925. January 1 was on a Thursday. Find March 12.

To do this, add 12 + 3 = 15; divide 15/7 = 2 remainder 1. This indicates Thursday. In leap years an extra 1 has to be added for dates after February 29.

Students will now want to find the day for a date for any given year. Point out that first one need know what day January 1 of the Year 1 fell and also make adjustments for leap years.

The day of the week on which January 1 of Year 1 fell can be determined as follows. Using a known day and date, we find the number of days which have elapsed since January 1 of the Year 1. Thus, since January 1, 1952, was Wednesday, in terms of the value of the solar year, the number of days since January 1 is $1951 \times 365.2425 = 712588.1175$. Dividing by 7, we get 101,798 with a remainder of 2. The remainder indicates that 2 days should be counted from Wednesday. Since calculations refer to the past, the counting is done backwards, indicating that January 1 (in the Gregorian Calendar) fell on Monday.

One method for determining the day for any year suggests that dates in each century be treated separately. Knowing the weekday of the first day of that period, one could, in the same fashion as before, determine the excess days after that weekday (thus the day of the week that a given day would fall on for that century). For the years 1900–1999, the information needed is:

1. The Index Numbers of the months (see earlier discussion).

2. January 1 of 1900 was Monday.

3. The number of years (thus giving the number of

days over the 52 week cycles) that have elapsed since the 1st of the century.

4. The number of leap years (i.e., additional days) that have occurred since the beginning of the century. Knowing this, we can ascertain how many days in that Monday-week cycle we need count.

Examples:

1. *May 9, 1914.* Add 9 (days into the month), 1 (Index Number of the month), 14 (Number of years since the beginning of the century), and 3 (number of leap years in that century thus far). 9 + 1 + 14 + 3 = 27. Divide by 7, leaves 6, which is Saturday.

2. *Aug. 16, 1937.* Add 16 + 2 + 37 + 9 = 64. Divide by 7, leaves 1, which is Monday.

For the period, 1800–1899, the same procedure is followed except that January 1, 1800, was on Wednesday. For the period September 14, 1752, through 1799, the same procedure is followed except that the

first day of that period would be Friday. For the period up to and including September 2, 1752, the same procedure is followed except that the whole year would be added and the number of the days would start with Friday.

Example: May 13, 1240. Add 13 + 1 + 1240 + 10 = 1264/7, leaves 4, Monday.

There is another method for determining the day without having to consider separate periods.

Again we start by knowing the day of Jan. 1 of the Year 1. We will not count the actual number of days which have elapsed since Jan. 1 of Year 1, but count the number of excess days over weeks which have elapsed and to this number, add the number of days which have elapsed since January 1 of the given year. This total must be divided by 7, the remainder will indicate the number of days which must be counted for that week, thus the formula is, 1 (Monday) + the remainder of the division by 7 of (the number of years

DATE	1	2	3	4	5	6	7	8	9	10	11	12	13	14	15	16
JANUARY	1	2	3	4	5	6	7	8	9	10	11	12	13	14	15	16
FEBRUARY	32	33	34	35	36	37	38	39	40	41	42	43	44	45	46	47
MARCH	60	61	62	63	64	65	66	67	68	69	70	71	72	73	74	75
APRIL	91	92	93	94	95	96	97	98	99	100	101	102	103	104	105	106
MAY	121	122	123	124	125	126	127	128	129	130	131	132	133	134	135	136
JUNE	152	153	154	155	156	157	158	159	160	161	162	163	164	165	166	167
JULY	182	183	184	185	186	187	188	189	190	191	192	193	194	195	196	197
AUGUST	213	214	215	216	217	218	219	220	221	222	223	224	225	226	227	228
SEPTEMBER	244	245	246	247	248	249	250	251	252	253	254	255	256	257	258	259
OCTOBER	274	275	276	277	278	279	280	281	282	283	284	285	286	287	288	289
NOVEMBER	305	306	307	308	309	310	311	312	313	314	315	316	317	318	319	320
DECEMBER	335	336	337	338	339	340	341	342	343	344	345	346	347	348	349	350

Figure B

DATE	17	18	19	20	21	22	23	24	25	26	27	28	29	30	31
JANUARY	17	18	19	20	21	22	23	24	25	26	27	28	29	30	31
FEBRUARY	48	49	50	51	52	53	54	55	56	57	58	59			
MARCH	76	77	78	79	80	81	82	83	84	85	86	87	88	89	90
APRIL	107	108	109	110	111	112	113	114	115	116	117	118	119	120	
MAY	137	138	139	140	141	142	143	144	145	146	147	148	149	150	151
JUNE	168	169	170	171	172	173	174	175	176	177	178	179	180	181	
JULY	198	199	200	201	202	203	204	205	206	207	208	209	210	211	212
AUGUST	229	230	231	232	233	234	235	236	237	238	239	240	241	242	243
SEPTEMBER	260	261	262	263	264	265	266	267	268	269	270	271	272	273	
OCTOBER	290	291	292	293	294	295	296	297	298	299	300	301	302	303	304
NOVEMBER	321	322	323	324	325	326	327	328	329	330	331	332	333	334	
DECEMBER	351	352	353	354	355	356	357	358	359	360	361	362	363	364	365

Figure B (Continued)

which have elapsed thus far + the number of days which have elapsed since Jan. 1 of the given year + the number of leap years which have occurred since year 1) = the number of days of the week. The calculation of the number of leap years must take into account the fact that those years whose number ends with two zeros, which are not divisible by 400, are not leap years. Thus from the total number of leap years, a certain number of leap years must be subtracted.

Example: Dec. 25, 1954. 1 + 1953 + 488 (leap years) − 15 (century leap years 19 − 4) + 358 (number of days between Jan. 1, 1954, and Dec. 25, 1954) = 2785 Dividing by 7 gives remainder 6. Thus Dec. 25, 1954, fell on the sixth day of the week, Saturday.

Many other tables and mechanisms have been devised to solve the problem of determining days. The following are two nomograms devised for this.

The first (see Figure C) consists of four scales and is to be used as follows:

1. With a straightedge, join the point on the first scale indicating the date with the proper month on the third scale. Mark the point of intersection with the second scale.

2. Join this point on the second scale with the point on the fourth scale indicating the proper century. Mark the point of intersection with the third scale.

3. Join this point with the point indicating the appropriate year on the first scale. The point of intersection with the second scale gives the desired day of the week. (N.B. For the months of January and February use the year diminished by 1.)

Figure C. *Perpetual Calendar.*

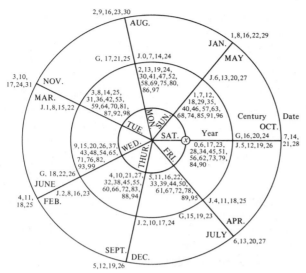

Figure D. *Perpetual Calendar, Radius-ring Type.*

The second arrangement (see Figure D) consists of three concentric rings intersected by seven radii. The procedure is: 1) Locate the date and the month on the outer ring; if they are two points, draw a line between them; if they coincide, draw a tangent. 2) Locate the century on the intermediate ring. Through this point draw a line parallel to the line drawn, until it intersects the intermediate ring at another point. The point found will be a ring-radius intersection. 3) From the point just found, follow the radius to the inner ring, then locate the year. (If the month is Jan. or Feb. use the preceding year.) Draw a line between these two points on the inner ring. (If they coincide on Saturday, then Saturday is the weekday sought.) 4) Now find the point where the Saturday radius cuts the inner ring, and through this Saturday point draw a line parallel to the line just drawn. The line will meet the inner ring at some radius-ring intersection. The weekday on this latter radius is the weekday of the date with which we began.

The problem of a perpetual calendar occupied the attention of many mathematicians and many of them devoted considerable attention to calculating the date of Easter Sunday. All church holidays fall on a definite date. The ecclesiastical rule regarding Easter is, however, rather complicated. Easter must fall on the Sunday after the first full moon which occurs after the Vernal (Spring) Equinox. Easter Sunday, therefore, is a movable Feast which may fall as early as March 22 or as late as April 25. The following procedure to find Easter Sunday in any year from 1900–1999 is based on a method developed by Gauss.

1. Find the remainder when the year is divided by 4. Call this remainder a.

2. Find the remainder when the year is divided by 7. Call this remainder b.

3. Find the remainder when the year is divided by 19. Multiply this remainder by 19, add 24, and again find the remainder when the total is divided by 30. Call this remainder c.

4. Now add $2a + 4b + 6c + 3$. Divide this total by 7 and call the remainder d.

The sum of c and d will give the number of days after March 22 on which Easter Sunday will fall.

Example: Easter 1921
(1) 21/4 leaves 1
(2) 21/7 leaves 0
(3) 21/19 leaves 2; $[2(19) + 24]/30$ leaves 2
(4) $[2 + 0 + 12 + 3]/7$ leaves 3
$2 + 3 = 5$ days after March 22 = March 27

(The method above gives the date accurately except for the years 1954 and 1981. These years it gives a date exactly 1 week late, the correct Easters being April 18 and 19 respectively.)

Postassessment

1. Have the students determine the day of the week of their birth.

2. Have the students work out several given dates.

Oct. 12, 1492   May 30, 1920   Christmas 1978
April 1, 1945   Oct. 21, 1805   August 14, 1898
                                                        July 4, 1776

3. Have the students find the dates of several Easter Sundays.

    1944, 1969, 1950, 1978, 1930, 1977, 1929

4. George Washington was born February 11, 1732. Why do we celebrate it February 22?

8 Palindromic Numbers

This unit will define palindromic numbers and introduce some of their properties. The study of palindromic numbers is suited for any class: while it provides all students an approach for analyzing numbers and their relationships, certain aspects of this topic can be selected for the slow students (e.g., the reverse addition property) while more advanced properties can be investigated by the more adept students (e.g., modular palindromes).

Performance Objectives

1. Students will state and analyze properties of palindromic numbers.

2. Students will construct new palindromes from any specified integer.

Preassessment

Have students analyze the expression "Madam I'm Adam" and the words "rotator" and "reviver" and point out their peculiarity (they spell the same backward and forward). Indicate to them that such an expression is called a palindrome and that in mathematics, numbers having the same property like 343 and 59695 are called palindromic numbers. Students can be asked to give their own examples of palindromic numbers and make a short list.

Teaching Strategies

After the students have compiled their lists, an analysis can be made of these numbers. Questions such as the following can be put to them to get a discussion going: Does a palindrome have an odd or even number of digits, or both? Are palindromic numbers prime, composite, or both? Is the square or cube of a palindromic number still a palindrome? Given a positive integer can a palindrome be constructed from some sort of operation on this integer? Students can attempt to answer these questions by testing their validity on the numbers from their lists or by seeking some new ones.

The students are ready at this point to study some of the following palindromic properties:

1. Palindromic numbers contain both prime and composite numbers (e.g., 181 is a palindromic prime while 575 is a composite palindrome); however, a palindromic prime, with the exception of 11, must have an odd number of digits.

Proof of the latter: (by contradiction)

Let p be a palindromic prime having an even number of digits. Let r be the sum of all digits in the even positions of the prime p and s be the sum of all the digits in the odd positions of the prime p. Since p is a palindrome with an even number of digits, the digits in odd positions duplicate the digits in even positions; therefore $s - r = 0$. But the test for divisibility by 11 states that a number is divisible by 11 if the difference between the sum of all digits in even positions and the sum of all digits in odd positions is 0 or a multiple of 11. Therefore, p has 11 as a factor and cannot be prime, a contradiction.

2. All integers N which yield palindromic squares are not necessarily palindromes. While there are infinitely many palindromes yielding palindromic squares (e.g., $22^2 = 484$ and $212^2 = 44944$), there exist some non-palindromic integers whose squares are palindromes (e.g., $26^2 = 676$ and $836^2 = 698896$) as well as some palindromic integers yielding non-palindromic squares (e.g., $131^2 = 17161$ and $232^2 = 53824$).

Repunits, numbers consisting entirely of 1's (by notation, R_k where k is the number of 1's) are palindromic numbers and produce palindromic squares when $1 \leq k \leq 9 : R_2^2 = 121 : R_3^2 = 12321$ and in general $R_k^2 = 12 \ldots k \ldots 21$, where $k = 9$. However, when $k > 9$ the carrying in addition would lose the palindromic product (e.g., $R_{10}^2 = 12 \ldots 6790098 \ldots 21$).

It has been found that square numbers are much richer in palindromes than randomly chosen integers.

3. In general, numbers which yield palindromic cubes (some of which are prime and some composite) are palindromic in themselves. The numbers N which yield palindromic cubes are as follows:

a) $N = 1,7,11$ ($1^3 = 1$, $7^3 = 343$, $11^3 = 1331$)

b) $N = 10^k + 1$ has a palindromic cube consisting of $k - 1$ zeros between each consecutive pair of 1,3,3,1: e.g., when $k = 1$, $N = 11$ and $N^3 = 1331$; when $k = 2$, $N = 101$ and $N^3 = 1030301$; when $k = 3$, $N = 1001$ and $N^3 = 1003003001$, etc. Notice that when $k = 2m + 1$, $m > 0$, then N is divisible by 11 and hence is composite.

c) N consisting of 3 1's and any desired number (which must be even) of zeros is divisible by 3 and has palindromic cubes: e.g., $(111)^3 = 1367631$, $(10101)^3 = 1030607060301$.

d) $N = $ any palindromic arrangement of zeros and four 1's is a non-prime and has a palindromic cube, except when the same number of zeros appears in the three spaces between the 1's: e.g., $(11011)^3 = 1334996994331$, $(10100101)^3 = 1003033091390931903303001$, whereas $(1010101)^3$ is not a palindrome.

The only $N < 2.8 \times 10^{14}$ which is not a palindrome yet yields a palindromic cube is $2201^3 = 10662526601$.

4. *Given any integer N we can often reach a palindrome by adding the number to its reversal (the number obtained by reversing the digits) and continuing the process until the palindrome is achieved.* For example, if $N = 798$, then $798 + 897 = 1695$, $1695 + 5961 = 7656$, $7656 + 6567 = 14223$, $14223 + 32241 = 46464$ (a palindrome). Whereas some numbers can reach a palindrome in only two steps (e.g., 75 and 48), there are others that reach it in 6 steps like 97, and still others like 89 and 98 that reach a palindrome in 24 steps. It has been found, however, that certain numbers like 196 when carried out to over 1000 steps still do not achieve palindromes so that this rule cannot be taken to hold for all integers but certainly for most since these cases are very rare. It has been proven that the rule does not hold in base two: the smallest counterexample is 10110 which after 4 steps reaches the sum 10_11_01_00_, after 8 steps it is 10_111_01_000_, after 12 steps it is 10_1111_01_0000_. Every fourth step increases by one digit each of the two sequences underlined and it is seen that each of these increasing sums is not a palindrome. There are some generalities found in this process of reverse addition:

(a) Different integers when subjected to this technique produce the same palindrome. For example, 554, 752, and 653 all produce the palindrome 11011 in 3 steps. In general, all integers in which the corresponding digit pairs symmetrical to the middle have the same sum will produce the same palindrome in the same number of steps. (In this case, all the digit pairs add up to 9.) There are however different integers which produce the same palindrome in different numbers of steps. For example, 99 reaches 79497 in 6 steps whereas 7299 reaches it in 2 steps.

(b) Two digit numbers can be categorized according to the total sum of the two digits to ascertain the number of steps needed to produce a palindrome. It is obvious that if the sum of the digits is 9, only 1 step is needed; if their digit sum is 10 (e.g., 64 and 73), 2 steps are needed. Similar analyses will lead the students to conclude that if their digit sum is 11, 12, 13, 14, 15, 16, 17, or 18, a palindrome results after 1, 2, 2, 3, 4, 6, 24, and 1 respectively. The students can be asked to perform an analysis of this type and put their results in table form.

This topic of palindromes can be investigated further by more adept students. Further investigation lies in the areas of multigrades with palindromic numbers as elements, special palindromic prime numbers such as primes with prime digits as elements, modular palindromes, and triangular and pentagonal numbers that are also palindromes.

Postassessment

1. Do the following numbers yield palindromic cubes: (a) 1001001 (b) 1001001001 (c) 10100101 (d) 100101

2. Given the following 2 digit numbers, indicate the number of steps required in reversal addition to reach a palindrome: (a) 56 (b) 26 (c) 91 (d) 96

3. Perform the reverse addition technique on these integers and find other integers that will yield the same palindrome as these: (a) 174 (b) 8699

9   The Fascinating Number Nine

This unit is intended to offer a recreational presentation of the many interesting properties of the number 9. A long range goal of presenting these amusing number topics is to motivate further student investigation and insight into the properties of numbers.

Performance Objectives

1. Students will demonstrate at least three properties of the number nine.

2. Students will provide an example of a short-cut calculation involving the number nine.

Preassessment

Students should be familiar with the various field postulates and be reasonably adept with the operations of addition, subtraction, multiplication, and division. A knowledge of algebra is helpful but not essential.

Teaching Strategies

In presenting new ideas to a class it is always best to build on what they already know. For example, ask students to multiply 53×99. Unsuspecting students will perform the calculation in the usual way. After their work has been completed, suggest the following:

$$\begin{aligned} \text{Since} \quad 99 &= 100 - 1 \\ 53 \times 99 &= 53(100 - 1) \\ &= 53(100) - 53(1) \\ &= 5300 - 53 \\ &= 5247 \end{aligned}$$

Now have them use this technique to multiply 42×999.

"Casting Out Nines" is a popular technique for checking calculations. For example, if students wish to check the addition $29+57+85+35+6 = 212$, they simply divide each number in the addition by 9 and retain only the remainder. Thus they have 2, 3, 4, 8, and 6, the sum of which is 23. (See below)

$$
\begin{array}{rr}
29 \rightarrow & 2 \\
57 \rightarrow & 3 \\
85 \rightarrow & 4 \\
35 \rightarrow & 8 \\
+\ 6 \rightarrow + & 6 \\
\hline
212 & 23
\end{array}
$$

The remainder of $212 \div 9$ is 5. If the remainder of $212 \div 9$ is the same as the remainder of $23 \div 9$, then 212 could be the correct answer. In this case, where 5 is the remainder of both divisions by 9; 212 *could* be the correct answer. Students cannot be sure from this checking method whether in fact this answer is correct since a rearrangement of the digits, to say 221, would also yield the same remainder when divided by 9.

It is interesting to note that division by 9 is not necessary to find the remainder. All one has to do is add the digits of the number (to be divided by 9) and, if the result is not a single digit number, repeatedly add the digits until a single digit remains. In the above example the remainders are:

for 29: $2 + 9 = 11; 1 + 1 = 2$
for 57: $5 + 7 = 12; 1 + 2 = 3$
for 85: $8 + 5 = 13; 1 + 1 = 4$
for 35: $3 + 5 = 8$
for 6: 6
for the sum of $2 + 3 + 4 + 8 + 6 = 23: 2 + 3 = 5$
for 212: $2 + 1 + 2 = 5$

Students can use a similar procedure for other operations. For example, to check a multiplication operation: $239 \times 872 = 208,408$, they will find the remainders (when divided by 9) of each of the above numbers.

for 239: $2 + 3 + 9 = 14; 1 + 4 = 5$
for 872: $8 + 7 + 2 = 17; 1 + 7 = 8$
for the product $5 \times 8 = 40; 4 + 0 = 4$
for 208,408: $2 + 0 + 8 + 4 + 0 + 8 = 22; 2 + 2 = 4$

Stress to your classes that this is not a fool-proof check of a calculation, but simply one indication of possible correctness. Present this topic in a way which will have them begin to marvel at the interesting properties of the number 9.

Another unusual property of 9 occurs in the multiplication of 9 and any other number of 2 or more digits. Consider the example $65,437 \times 9$. An alternative to the usual algorithm is as follows:

1. Subtract the units digit of the multiplicand from 10. $\quad 10 - 7 = \boxed{3}$
2. Subtract each of the remaining digits from 9 and add the rest to the preceding number of the multiplicand (at right). For any two-digit sums carry the tens digit to the next sum.

$9 - 3 = 6 + 7 = 1\boxed{3}$
$9 - 4 = 5 + 3 + 1 = \boxed{9}$
$9 - 5 = 4 + 4 = \boxed{8}$
$9 - 6 = 3 + 5 = \boxed{8}$

3. Subtract 1 from the left-most digit of the multiplicand. $\quad 6 - 1 = \boxed{5}$
4. Now list the results in reverse order to get the desired product. $\boxed{588,933}$

Although this method is somewhat cumbersome, it can set the groundwork for some rather interesting investigations into number theory.

To further intrigue your students with other fascinating properties of the number 9, have them multiply 12,345,679 by the first nine multiples of 9, and record their results:

12345679	$\times$	9	=	111,111,111
12345679	$\times$	18	=	222,222,222
12345679	$\times$	27	=	333,333,333
12345679	$\times$	36	=	444,444,444
12345679	$\times$	45	=	555,555,555
12345679	$\times$	54	=	666,666,666
12345679	$\times$	63	=	777,777,777
12345679	$\times$	72	=	888,888,888
12345679	$\times$	81	=	999,999,999

Students should realize that in the sequence of natural numbers (making up the above multiplicands) the number 8 was omitted. In other words, the number that is two less than the base, 10, is missing. Ask students how to extend this scheme to bases other than 10.

Now have them reverse the sequence of natural numbers including the 8, and multiply each by the first nine multiples of 9. The results will be astonishing:

987654321	$\times$	9	=	8 888 888 889
987654321	$\times$	18	=	17 777 777 778
987654321	$\times$	27	=	26 666 666 667
987654321	$\times$	36	=	35 555 555 556
987654321	$\times$	45	=	44 444 444 445
987654321	$\times$	54	=	53 333 333 334
987654321	$\times$	63	=	62 222 222 223
987654321	$\times$	72	=	71 111 111 112
987654321	$\times$	81	=	80 000 000 001

Some other interesting properties of the number 9 are exhibited below. Have students discover them by carefully guiding them to the desired result. Stronger students should be encouraged to investigate these relationships and discover *why* they "work."

1.
$$9 \times 9 = 81$$
$$99 \times 99 = 9801$$
$$999 \times 999 = 998001$$
$$9999 \times 9999 = 99980001$$
$$99999 \times 99999 = 9999800001$$
$$999999 \times 999999 = 999998000001$$
$$9999999 \times 9999999 = 99999980000001$$

2.
$$999999 \times 2 = 1999998$$
$$999999 \times 3 = 2999997$$
$$999999 \times 4 = 3999996$$
$$999999 \times 5 = 4999995$$
$$999999 \times 6 = 5999994$$
$$999999 \times 7 = 6999993$$
$$999999 \times 8 = 7999992$$
$$999999 \times 9 = 8999991$$

3.
$$1 \times 9 + 2 = 11$$
$$12 \times 9 + 3 = 111$$
$$123 \times 9 + 4 = 1111$$
$$1234 \times 9 + 5 = 11111$$
$$12345 \times 9 + 6 = 111111$$
$$123456 \times 9 + 7 = 1111111$$
$$1234567 \times 9 + 8 = 11111111$$
$$12345678 \times 9 + 9 = 111111111$$

4.
$$9 \times 9 + 7 = 88$$
$$98 \times 9 + 6 = 888$$
$$987 \times 9 + 5 = 8888$$
$$9876 \times 9 + 4 = 88888$$
$$98765 \times 9 + 3 = 888888$$
$$987654 \times 9 + 2 = 8888888$$
$$9876543 \times 9 + 1 = 88888888$$
$$98765432 \times 9 + 0 = 888888888$$

An interesting way to conclude this Model would be to offer your students a seemingly harmless challenge. That is, ask them to find an eight-digit number in which no digit appears more than once, and which, when multiplied by 9, yields a nine-digit number in which no digit appears more than once. Most of their attempts will fail. For example, $76541238 \times 9 = 688,871,142$, which has repeated 8's and 1's. Here are several correct numbers:

$$81274365 \times 9 = 731469285$$
$$72645831 \times 9 = 653812479$$
$$58132764 \times 9 = 523194876$$
$$76125483 \times 9 = 685129347$$

Postassessment

Ask students to:

1. Demonstrate three unusual properties of 9.

2. Show a short cut for multiplying 547×99.

3. Explain now to "check" a multiplication calculation by "casting out nines."

10   Unusual Number Properties

(Author's Note: This unit should be used after the unit entitled "Enrichment with a Hand-Held Calculator.")

The intention of this unit is to present a good supply of interesting number properties that can be best exhibited on a calculator.

Performance Objective

Students will investigate mathematical problems with the help of a hand calculator and then draw appropriate conclusions.

Preassessment

Students should be familiar with the basic functions of a calculator. The instrument required for this unit need only have the four basic operations.

Teaching Strategies

Perhaps one of the best ways to stimulate genuine excitement in mathematics is to demonstrate some short, simple and dramatic mathematical phenomena. The following are some examples that should provide you with ample material with which to motivate your students toward some independent investigations.

Example 1

When 37 is multiplied by each of the first nine multiples of 3 an interesting result occurs. Let students discover this using their calculators.

$$37 \times 3 = 111$$
$$37 \times 6 = 222$$
$$37 \times 9 = 333$$
$$37 \times 12 = 444$$
$$37 \times 15 = 555$$
$$37 \times 18 = 666$$
$$37 \times 21 = 777$$
$$37 \times 24 = 888$$
$$37 \times 27 = 999$$

Example 2

When 142,857 is multiplied by 2, 3, 4, 5, and 6, the products all use the same digits in the same order as in the original numbers, but each starting at a different point.

$$142,857 \times 2 = 285,714$$
$$142,857 \times 3 = 428,571$$
$$142,857 \times 4 = 571,428$$
$$142,857 \times 5 = 714,285$$
$$142,857 \times 6 = 857,142$$

When 142,857 is multiplied by 7, the product is 999,999. When 142,857 is multiplied by 8, the product is 1,142,856. If the millions digit is removed and added to the units digit (142,856 + 1) the original number is formed. Have students investigate the product 142,857 × 9. What other patterns can be found involving products of 142,857?

A similar pattern occurs with the following products of 76,923: 1, 10, 9, 12, 3, and 4; also 2, 5, 7, 11, 6, and 8. Ask students to inspect the sum of the digits of each of the products obtained. They should discover a truly fascinating result! Ask if they can find other such relationships.

Example 3

The number 1089 has many interesting properties. Have students consider the products of 1089 and each of the first nine natural numbers.

$$1089 \times 1 = 1089$$
$$1089 \times 2 = 2178$$
$$1089 \times 3 = 3267$$
$$1089 \times 4 = 4356$$
$$1089 \times 5 = 5445$$
$$1089 \times 6 = 6534$$
$$1089 \times 7 = 7623$$
$$1089 \times 8 = 8712$$
$$1089 \times 9 = 9801$$

Tell students to notice the symmetry of the first two and last two columns of the products. Each column lists consecutive integers. Encourage students not just to establish and explain this unusual occurrence, but also to build on it. What makes 1089 so unusual? What are the factors of 1089? Why does 1089 × 9 reverse the number 1089? Does a similar scheme work for other numbers? These questions and others should begin to set the tone for further investigation. Naturally students' calculators will be an indispensable tool in their work. The calculators will permit students to see patterns rapidly and without the side-tracking often caused by cumbersome calculations.

Example 4

Some other interesting number patterns for students to generate are given below. Be sure to encourage students to extend the patterns produced and to try to discover why they exist.

$$1 \times 8 + 1 = 9$$
$$12 \times 8 + 2 = 98$$
$$123 \times 8 + 3 = 987$$
$$1,234 \times 8 + 4 = 9,876$$
$$12,345 \times 8 + 5 = 98,765$$
$$123,456 \times 8 + 6 = 987,654$$
$$1,234,567 \times 8 + 7 = 9,876,543$$
$$12,345,678 \times 8 + 8 = 98,765,432$$
$$123,456,789 \times 8 + 9 = 987,654,321$$

$$11 \times 11 = 121$$
$$111 \times 111 = 12,321$$
$$1,111 \times 1,111 = 1,234,321$$
$$11,111 \times 11,111 = 123,454,321$$
$$111,111 \times 111,111 = 12,345,654,321$$
$$1,111,111 \times 1,111,111 = 1,234,567,654,321$$
$$11,111,111 \times 11,111,111 = 123,456,787,654,321$$
$$111,111,111 \times 111,111,111 = 12,345,678,987,654,321$$

Example 5

Have your students compute the divisions indicated by each of the following fractions. Tell them to record their results.

$$\frac{1}{7} = .\overline{142857} = \frac{142857}{999999}$$

$$\frac{2}{7} = .\overline{285714} = \frac{285714}{999999}$$

$$\frac{3}{7} = .\overline{428571} = \frac{428571}{999999}$$

$$\frac{4}{7} = .\overline{571428} = \frac{571428}{999999}$$

$$\frac{5}{7} = .\overline{714285} = \frac{714285}{999999}$$

$$\frac{6}{7} = .\overline{857142} = \frac{857142}{999999}$$

Students will notice the similar order of the repeating part along with the different starting points. Point out that the product of 7 × .142857 = .999999 (which is *close* to $7 \times \frac{1}{7} = 1$). Remind students that this is not the same as $7 \times .\overline{142857}$.

Some students may want to inspect this product in a nondecimal form:

$$7 \times 142,857 = 999,999$$
$$= 999,000 + 999$$
$$= 1,000(142 + 857) + (142 + 857)$$
$$= (142 + 857)(1000 + 1)$$
$$= 1001(142 + 857)$$
$$= 142,142 + 857,857$$

A better insight into an investigation of these fractions would come after students have already calculated the following quotients:

$$\frac{1}{13} = .\overline{076923} = \frac{076923}{999999}$$

$$\frac{3}{13} = .\overline{230769} = \frac{230769}{999999}$$

$$\frac{4}{13} = .\overline{307692} = \frac{307692}{999999}$$

$$\frac{9}{13} = .\overline{692307} = \frac{692307}{999999}$$

$$\frac{10}{13} = .\overline{769230} = \frac{769230}{999999}$$

$$\frac{12}{13} = .\overline{923076} = \frac{923076}{999999}$$

Once these have been fully discussed, students may wish to consider the remaining proper fractions with a denominator of 13. They should discover similar patterns and relationships.

The positive impact of the above *Examples* will be lost if students are not immediately guided to investigate and extend their discoveries. While the calculator is the guiding tool for discovering new relationships, students' logical conjectures will come from a deeper investigation of the properties of numbers.

Postassessment

Have students complete the following exercises.

1. Multiply and add each of the following pairs of numbers:

$$9,9$$
$$24,3$$
$$47,2$$
$$497,2$$

How do their sums compare with their products? (reverses) ·

2. Perform the indicated operations and justify the resulting patterns. Then extend the pattern and see if it holds true.

$$12321 = \frac{333 \times 333}{1+2+3+2+1} = \frac{110889}{9}$$
$$= 12321$$

$$1234321 = \frac{4444 \times 4444}{1+2+3+4+3+2+1} = \frac{19749136}{16}$$
$$= 1234321$$

11 Enrichment With A Hand-Held Calculator

In recent years, with the increased accessibility of the hand-held calculator, mathematics teachers have had the responsibility of finding (or developing) a place for this useful tool in the current curriculum. One of the most frequently observed uses of the calculator is that of providing some excitement to remedial drill work. Here the calculator is merely used to check a student's drill calculation. Experience shows that this novelty seems to wear off soon and then loses its effectiveness as a motivational device.

A longer range and more effective use of the calculator is as a problem-solving facilitator. Students who have difficulty solving problems are often faced with a double dilemma. They are unable to interpret the given problem into a solvable form, and they are unable to do the calculations necessary to compute an answer. Normally they cannot concentrate on problem solving until they can do the necessary calculations. However, by using the calculator, they can temporarily avoid the calculations pitfall and thereby concentrate on the key to successful problem solving: interpretation. When this aspect has been learned a student can concentrate on mastering calculations as an essential ingredient in problem solving.

The calculator also has a very definite place in mathematics enrichment. This unit presents some enrichment activities involving the calculator. In most cases the calculator will provide ideas which will serve as a springboard for further student investigation. In effect, the instrument will be a discovery and motivational device.

Performance Objective

Students will investigate mathematical problems with the help of a hand calculator and then draw appropriate conclusions.

Preassessment

Students should be familiar with the basic function of a calculator. The instrument required for this unit need have only the four basic operations.

For both practice and amusement, have students do the following on their calculators.

1. Compute:

   $2[60 - .243 + (12)(2400)] - 1$. To find what every man must pay read your answer upside down.

2. Compute:

   $4590.5864 + (568.3)(.007) - 1379.26$. Then turn your calculator upside down and after reading your answer, look inside your shoe.

These two exercises should give your students a relaxed feeling about working with calculators.

Teaching Strategies

Begin the lesson with a simple but intriguing oddity. Have students consider the calendar for the month of May 1977. Tell them to make a square around *any* nine dates; one way to do so is shown in the figure below.

Next, students should add 8 to the smallest number in the square and multiply it by 9. In the above example, we have $(11 + 8) \times 9 = 171$. Then students can use their calculators to multiply the sum of the numbers in the middle row (or column) by 3 and find the same result, 171. Have your students try this for other selections of 9 numbers. You should have them realize that the sum of the numbers in the middle row or column multiplied by 3 is in fact the sum of the 9 numbers. Students can verify this easily with their calculators.

From this point, you have an excellent opportunity to investigate properties of the arithmetic mean, as such study will shed more light on this cute "calendar trick." Students should realize that the *middle number* of the square of 9 numbers is in fact the arithmetic mean of the selected numbers. The use of the calculator will relieve them of burdensome computations and permit them to focus all their attention on the mathematical concepts being discovered.

For their next number investigation, have your students select any 3-digit number, say 538. Then have them enter it twice into their calculators, without pressing any operation buttons. Their display should show 538538. Now have them divide by 7, then divide by 11, then divide by 13. Much to their surprise they will find their original number displayed. Immediately, student curiosity will arise. Ask them what single operation can be used to replace the 3 divisions. They should realize that a single division by $7 \times 11 \times 13 = 1001$ was actually performed. Since $538 \times 1001 = 538538$, the puzzle is essentially solved; yet students may wish to try this scheme on their calculators using other numbers. This should strengthen their knowledge about numbers, especially 1001, a rather significant number.

Students should now be motivated to try the following multiplications so that they can begin to appreciate (and predict) number patterns:

(a) $3 \times 11 = 33$
    $3 \times 111 = 333$
    $3 \times 1111 = 3333$
    $3 \times 11111 = 33333$

(b) $4 \times 101 = 404$
    $4 \times 10101 = 40404$
    $4 \times 1010101 = 4040404$
    $4 \times 101010101 = 404040404$

(c) $5 \times 1001 = 5005$
    $5 \times 110011 = 550055$
    $5 \times 11100111 = 55500555$

(d) $65 \times 101 = 6565$
    $65 \times 10101 = 656565$
    $65 \times 1010101 = 65656565$

(e) $65 \times 1001 = 65065$
    $65 \times 10001 = 650065$
    $65 \times 100001 = 6500065$
    $65 \times 1001001 = 65065065$

(f) $7 \times 11 = 77$
    $7 \times 11 \times 101 = 7777$
    $7 \times 11 \times 10101 = 777777$
    $7 \times 111 \times 1001 = 777777$

Now have students discover other ways of generating by multiplication: 777777, 7777777, and 77777777. At this point students ought to be interested enough to establish other number patterns from products.

Most of your students should now be ready to consider somewhat more sophisticated problems.

A *palindrome* is defined as "a word or verse reading the same backward or forward, e.g. *madam, I'm Adam.*" In mathematics a number which reads the same in either direction is a palindrome. For example, have your students select any 2-digit number and add to it the number whose digits are the reverse order of the original one. Now have them take the sum and add it to the number whose digits are in the reverse order. They should continue this process until a palindrome is formed. For example:

$75 + 57 = 132$
$132 + 231 = 363$, a *palindrome*

$79 + 97 = 176$
$176 + 671 = 847$
$847 + 748 = 1595$
$1595 + 5951 = 7546$
$7546 + 6457 = 14003$
$14003 + 30041 = 44044$, a *palindrome*

No matter which original 2-digit number is selected, a palindrome will eventually be formed. Using a calculator the students will see various patterns arising, which should lead them to discover why this actually "works."

Encourage your students to carefully conjecture about other possible number relationships and then verify them using a calculator.

Postassessment

Tell your students to use their calculators to verify the following phenomenon for 6 different numbers. Then they should try to prove it.

Select any 3-digit number in which the hundreds digit and the units digit are unequal. Then write the number whose digits are in the reverse order from the selected number. Now subtract the smaller of these 2 numbers from the larger. Take the difference, reverse its digits, and add the "new" number to the original difference. What number do you always end up with? Why?

12   Symmetric Multiplication

This unit shows how some numbers, because of their symmetry, can be multiplied easily through the use of "form multiplication."

Performance Objective

Given a form multiplication example, students will perform the multiplication using the technique described in this unit.

Preassessment

Have students multiply each of the following by conventional means:
(a) 66666×66666 (b) 2222×2222 (c) 333×777

Teaching Strategies

After students have completed the above computations, they will probably welcome a more novel approach to these problems. Have them consider the following rhombic form approach.

```
        66666
     ×  66666
     ─────────
           36
         3636
       363636
     36363636
   3636363636
     36363636
       363636
         3636
           36
   ───────────
   44443555556
```

Students might wonder if this scheme works for other numbers of this type. Have them square 88888 first by conventional method and then by rhombic form multiplication. To do the latter, students should replace the "36's" in the previous example with "64's." Soon students will wonder how to extend this multiplication technique to squaring a repeated-digit number where the square of a digit is a *one-digit* number.

In squaring a number such as 2222, students must write each partial product as 04.

```
        2222
     ×  2222
     ─────────
          04
        0404
      040404
    04040404
      040404
        0404
          04
    ─────────
     4937284
```

At this juncture students may be convinced that this will be true for all numbers of this type. Have them consider squaring an n-digit number $uuu\ldots uuu$, where $u^2 = 10s + t$ (or written in base 10 as st). This multiplication would require an nth order rhombic form (i.e. one which increases the number of st's by one in each of the first n rows, and then decreases by one st in each of the remaining n - 1 rows). The case where $n = 5$ is shown below.

```
          uuuuu
       ×  uuuuu
       ──────────
             st
           stst
         ststst
       stststst
     ststststst
       stststst
         ststst
           stst
             st
       ──────────
```

Students will be interested to notice that this multiplication technique can be further extended to finding the product of two *different* repeated-digit numbers. That is, if the product of *uuu...u* and *vvvv...v* is sought, then the rhombic form of *st*'s is formed, where $uv = 10s + t$. For example, the product of 8888 × 3333 = 29623704 or:

$$
\begin{array}{r}
8888 \\
\times\ 3333 \\
\hline
24 \\
2424 \\
242424 \\
24242424 \\
242424 \\
2424 \\
24 \\
\hline
29623704
\end{array}
$$

When students have mastered the rhombic form of multiplying repeated-digit numbers, you might want to show them another form of repeated-digit multiplication. A *triangular* form of multiplication is shown below. Notice that after students sum the triangular array, they must multiply by 6.

$$
\begin{array}{r}
66666 \\
\times\ 66666 \\
\hline
6 \\
666 \\
66666 \\
6666666 \\
666666666 \\
\hline
740725926 \\
\times\ 6 \\
\hline
4444355556
\end{array}
$$

In general, to square an *n* digit repeated-digit number, sum the columns of the triangular array of the repeated digit (where there are *n* rows beginning with a single digit and increasing succeeding rows by two digits), and then multiply this sum by the repeated digit.

This multiplication technique may be extended to finding the product of two different repeated digit numbers. Have students form their own rule after considering the following example.

$$
\begin{array}{r}
8888 \\
\times\ 3333 \\
\hline
8 \\
888 \\
88888 \\
8888888 \\
\hline
9874568 \\
\times\ 3 \\
\hline
29623704
\end{array}
$$

$$
\begin{array}{r}
3333 \\
\times\ 8888 \\
\hline
3 \\
333 \\
33333 \\
3333333 \\
\hline
3702963 \\
\times\ 8 \\
\hline
29623704
\end{array}
$$

Notice that the number of lines of the triangular form equals the number of digits in each number being multiplied. The rest of the rule can be easily elicited from the students.

The only other variation in the multiplication of repeated-digit numbers is when the number of digits of each number being multiplied is not the same. Suppose an *n* digit number is being multiplied by an *m* digit number. Set up the triangular form as if both numbers had *n* digits (as was done earlier). Then draw a diagonal to the right of the *m*th row and delete all the digits below the diagonal. The sum of the remaining digits is the desired product. The following example illustrates this procedure.

$$
\begin{array}{r}
44444 \\
\times\ 666 \\
\hline
24 \\
2424 \\
242424 \\
24242424 \\
2424242424 \\
242424242424 \\
242424242424 \\
2424242424 \\
24 \\
\hline
29599704
\end{array}
$$

Now have students multiply 66666 × 444. They should get the same array of numbers to be summed as above. This implies that 44444 × 666 = 66666 × 444. After factoring, students should have no trouble justifying this equality.

Students should be encouraged to explain mathematically why the various form multiplications actually "work."

Postassessment

Have students compute each of the following using rhombic form multiplication:

a. 22222 × 77777   b. 9999 × 9999   c. 444 × 333

Have students compute each of the following using triangular form multiplication:

a. 555555 × 555555   b. 7777 × 4444

13 Variations on a Theme—Multiplication

This unit will present unconventional methods for determining the product of two integers.

Performance Objective
Given two integers and a method of multiplication, students will compute the product.

Preassessment
Have students compute the product of 43 and 92 by *more than one method.*

Teaching Strategies
The preceding problem should serve as excellent motivation for this unit. Most students will probably multiply the numbers correctly using the "conventional" method of multiplication shown below.

$$
\begin{array}{r}
92 \\
\times\ 43 \\
\hline
276 \\
368 \\
\hline
3956
\end{array}
$$

Before discussing other methods of multiplication, the teacher should show why the "conventional" multiplication algorithm works. It may be easily seen that

$$
\begin{aligned}
43 \times 92 &= (40+3) \times 92 \\
&= 40 \times 92 + 3 \times 92 \\
&= 3680 + 276 \\
&= 3956
\end{aligned}
$$

which is exactly what is done, although mechanically.

The Doubling Method
To multiply 43 by 92 construct the following columns of numbers, starting with 1 and 92, and double each number.

$$
\begin{array}{rr}
\bullet\ 1 & 92 \\
\bullet\ 2 & 184 \\
4 & 368 \\
\bullet\ 8 & 736 \\
16 & 1472 \\
\bullet\ 32 & 2944
\end{array}
$$

We stop at 32 because twice 32 is 64 which is larger than 43. We start with the last number in the first column and add the appropriate numbers such that the sum is 43. Hence we choose (32, 8, 2, 1). Now we add the corresponding numbers in the second column.

$$
\begin{array}{r}
92 \\
184 \\
736 \\
2944 \\
\hline
3956
\end{array}
$$

Therefore $43 \times 92 = 3956$. The reason this method works is illustrated below.

$$
\begin{aligned}
43 \times 92 &= (32 + 8 + 2 + 1) \times 92 \\
&= (32 \times 92) + (8 \times 92) + (2 \times 92) + (1 \times 92) \\
&= 2944 + 736 + 184 + 92 \\
&= 3956
\end{aligned}
$$

Russian Peasant Method
Again suppose we wish to multiply 43 and 92. Construct the following columns of numbers, starting with 43 and 92. In successive rows, halve the entries in the first column, rejecting the remainder of 1 when it occurs. In the second column, double each successive entry. This process continues until 1 appears in the first column.

$$
\begin{array}{rr}
{}^*43 & 92 \\
{}^*21 & 184 \\
10 & 368 \\
{}^*\ 5 & 736 \\
2 & 1472 \\
{}^*\ 1 & 2944
\end{array}
$$

Choose the numbers in the second column that corresponds to the "odd numbers" of the first column (those starred). Add those corresponding numbers of the second column and the result is the product of 43 and 92. That is, $92 + 184 + 736 + 2944 = 3956$. The proof that the Russian Peasant Method is always correct follows.

Assume "a" even: $a \cdot b = c$, where c is the desired result.

Assume "$\frac{1}{2}a$" odd: $\frac{1}{2}a - 2b = c$

The next step in the method is:

$$
\left[\frac{1}{2}\left(\frac{1}{2}a\right) - \frac{1}{2}\right] \cdot 4b = y
$$

Then using the distributive property:

$$
\left[\frac{1}{4}a \cdot 4b\right] - \left[\frac{1}{2} \cdot 4b\right] = y
$$

Since $\frac{1}{4}a \cdot 4b = c$, then $c - 2b = y$

Therefore the new product, y, will be short of the correct answer, c, by $2b$ (which is the first desired number to be added since it is paired with an odd number, $\frac{1}{2}a$).

As the process continues, the "new products" will remain the same if ka (an entry in the first column) is even. If ka is odd and $ka \cdot mb = w$, the next product will decrease by *mb* (the number matches with the odd number). For example, $\left(\dfrac{1}{2}ka - \dfrac{1}{2}\right) \cdot 2mb =$

$$\left(\dfrac{1}{2}ka \cdot 2mb\right) - \left(\dfrac{1}{2} \cdot 2mb\right) = w - mb$$

Finally when 1 appears in the first column:

$1 \cdot pb = Z$, with $pb = Z$

$Z = c -$ all deductions (numbers referred to above matched with odd *ka*'s)

c (desired result) $= Z +$ all deductions

A further consideration of the Russian Peasant Method for multiplication can be seen from the following illustration:

```
*43•92    = (21•2+1)(92)   = 21•184  +   92   = 3956
*21•184   = (10•2+1)(184)  = 10•368  +  184   = 3864
 10•368   = (5•2+0)(368)   =  5•736  +    0   = 3680
* 5•736   = (2•2+1)(736)   =  2•1472 +  736   = 3680
  2•1472  = (1•2+0)(1472)  =  1•2944 +    0   = 2944
* 1•2944  = (0•2+1)(2944)  =      0  + 2944   = 2944
                                        ─────
                                         3956
```

Notice that summing only those numbers in the second column whose corresponding entries in the first column are odd, is justified by the above representation.

The teacher may wish to shed further light on this curiosity by presenting the binary nature of this multiplication.

$(43)(92)$

$= (1 \cdot 2^5 + 0 \cdot 2^4 + 1 \cdot 2^3 + 0 \cdot 2^2 + 1 \cdot 2^1 + 1 \cdot 2^0)(92)$

$= 2^0 \cdot 92 + 2^1 \cdot 92 + 2^3 \cdot 92 + 2^5 \cdot 92$

$= 92 + 184 + 736 + 2944$

$= 3956$

Other investigations should be encouraged by the students.

Lattice Multiplication

Once again consider the multiplication $43 \cdot 92$. To perform this method, a 2 by 2 array is constructed and diagonals are drawn as shown.

First multiply $3 \cdot 9 = 27$, the 2 is placed above the 7 as shown below.

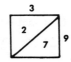

The next step is to multiply $4 \cdot 9 = 36$. Again, the 3 is placed above the 6 in the appropriate box.

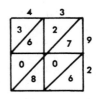

This process is continued, filling in the remainder of the square. Notice that $3 \cdot 2 = 6$ is recorded as $0/6$.

Now that there are entries in all cells, add the numbers in the diagonal directions indicated, beginning at the lower right. The sums are circled.

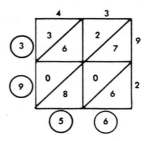

Notice that in the second addition, $8 + 0 + 7 = 15$, the 5 is recorded and the 1 is carried to the next diagonal addition. The correct answer (the product of $43 \cdot 92$) is then merely read from the circled numbers. That is, the answer is 3,956.

Trachtenberg System

The Trachtenberg System is a method for high-speed multiplication, division, addition, subtraction, and square root. There are numerous rules for these operations. Concern here will only be focused on the multiplication of two 2-digit numbers.

Again, suppose the product of 43 and 92 is desired.

Step 1. Multiply the two units digits
$$[3 \cdot 2 = 6]$$
$$\begin{array}{r} 43 \\ \times 92 \\ \hline 6 \end{array}$$

Step 2. Cross-multiply and add mentally
$$[(9 \cdot 3) + (2 \cdot 4) = 27 + 8 = 35]$$
Place the 5 as shown and carry the 3 (as an addend to the next step)
$$\begin{array}{r} 43 \\ \times 92 \\ \hline 56 \end{array}$$

Step 3. Multiply the two tens digits and then add any number carried over from the previous step.
$$[9 \cdot 4 = 36 \text{ and } 36 + 3 = 39]$$
$$\begin{array}{r} 43 \\ \times\ 92 \\ \hline 3956 \end{array}$$

The algebraic justification of this method is shown below:

Consider the two 2-digit numbers ab and mn (written in place-value form)

$$(10a + b) \cdot (10m + n)$$
$$= 10a \cdot 10m + 10a \cdot n + 10b \cdot m + bn$$
$$= \underbrace{100am}_{} + \underbrace{10an + bm}_{} + \underbrace{bn}_{}$$

$$\text{Step 3} \qquad \text{Step 2} \qquad \text{Step 1}$$

Another Method

A multiple of ten "squared" is an easy mental computation. This method of multiplication incorporates this idea. Have students consider the product of $M \cdot N$. They then choose X such that $X = 10p$ and $M < X < N$ with $X - M = a$ and $N - X = b$. Then $M \cdot N = (X-a)(X+b) = X^2 - aX + bX - ab$.

Consider the multiplication of $43 \cdot 92$.

Let $X = 60$.

Then $43 \cdot 92 = (60 - 17)(60 + 32)$
$$= 3600 + (-17 \cdot 60 + 60 \cdot 32) + (-17 \cdot 32)$$
$$= 3600 + (-1020 + 1920) + (-544)$$
$$= 3600 + 900 - 544$$
$$= 3956$$

However, if the numbers are the same distance from the multiple of ten, the method is much faster. The middle term will be eliminated!

Suppose students wish to multiply $57 \cdot 63$. Then $57 \cdot 63 = (60-3)(60+3) = 60^2 - 3^2 = 3600 - 9 = 3591$.

Part of the skill in working with different multiplication methods involves selection of the most efficient method for the particular problem. This should be stressed with the class.

Other Methods

Now that students have been exposed to several methods for multiplication, the teacher should suggest that students do research and explore other methods for multiplication. These could then be presented to the class.

Postassessment

1. Multiply 52 by 76 using any four different methods.

14   Ancient Egyptian Arithmetic

The study of a number system and its arithmetic is valuable to students on many levels. A student on a high level can delve into the mechanics of the system through an intricate comparison between that system and our own, and perhaps go off on a suitable tangent from there, such as an inspection of bases and still other number systems. For other students it can serve as a reinforcement of basic arithmetic (multiplication and division) both of integers and of fractions since the students will want to check if this system really works. This unit introduces students to the ancient Egyptian numerical notation and to their system of multiplying and dividing.

Performance Objectives

1) Given a multiplication problem, students will find the answer using an Egyptian method.

2) Given a division problem, students will find the answer using an Egyptian method.

3) Given a non-unit fraction, students will obtain its unit fraction decomposition.

Preassessment

Students should be familiar with addition and multiplication of fractions, as well as with the distributive property of real numbers. A knowledge of bases may also be useful.

Teaching Strategies

An example of a simple grouping system can be seen in the Egyptian hieroglyphics. This numeral system is based on the number 10. The symbols used when representing their numbers on stone, papyrus, wood and pottery were:

$$| \qquad \text{for } 1$$

$$\cap \qquad \text{for } 10$$

$$9 \qquad \text{for } 10^2$$

$$\text{\textogonekcentered} \qquad \text{for } 10^3$$

$$\Gamma \qquad \text{for } 10^4$$

Therefore, 13,521 would be represented as:

$$| \; \cap \cap \quad \begin{matrix} 9 \, 9 \, 9 \\ 9 \, 9 \end{matrix} \quad \text{\textbardbl} \, \text{\textbardbl} \, \text{\textbardbl} \, \Gamma$$

(Have students notice that the Egyptians wrote numbers from right to left.)

The Egyptians avoided a difficult multiplication or division method by using an easier (although at times longer) method. To multiply 14 by 27, they would have done the following:

1	27
* 2	54
* 4	108
* 8	216
16	432

To advance from any line to the next line, all the Egyptians had to do was double the number. Then, they picked out the numbers in the left-hand column that added up to 14 (the numbers with a *). By adding up the corresponding numbers in the right-hand column they arrived at the answer: $54 + 108 + 216 = 378$. This is an application of the distributive property of multiplication over addition, for what the Egyptians did is equivalent to:

$27(14) = 27(2 + 4 + 8) = 54 + 108 + 216 = 378$.

Further justification for the method lies in the fact that any number can be expressed as the sum of powers of two. Investigate this process with your students to the extent you feel necessary.

The Egyptians performed division in a similar way. They viewed the problem $114 \div 6$ as 6 times whatever number equals 114.

1	6 *
2	12 *
4	24
8	48
16	96 *

Now since $114 = 6 + 12 + 96$, the Egyptians would have found that $114 = 6(1 + 2 + 16)$ or $6 \times 19 = 114$. The answer is 19.

While no problems could arise in the Egyptian method of multiplication, a slight one occurs with respect to their method of division. To call attention to this problem, ask your class to use the above method to solve $83 \div 16$.

1	16 *
2	32
4	64 *
8	128

Using $16 + 64 = 80$, the Egyptians were still missing 3. Since $1 \times 16 = 16$, they found that they needed fractions to complete this problem.

In the Egyptian number system, every fraction except $\frac{2}{3}$ was represented as the sum of "unit fractions," fractions whose numerators are 1. In this way, the Egyptians avoided some of the computational problems one encounters when working with fractions. Since their arithmetic was based on doubling,

the only problem they had to deal with was how to change a fraction of the form $\frac{2}{n}$ to one of the form $\frac{1}{a} + \frac{1}{b} + \ldots$. They handled this problem with a table (found in the Rhind papyrus, dated approximately 1650 B.C.) which gives the decomposition of all fractions of the form $\frac{2}{n}$ for all odd n from 5 to 101. (Your class should be able to see why they considered only *odd n*.) A fraction such as $\frac{2}{37}$ was written as $\frac{1}{19} + \frac{1}{703}$ or, using the common notation for unit fractions, $\overline{19} + \overline{703}$. (This notation survives from the Egyptians who wrote a fraction such as $\frac{1}{4}$ as 𝍱 and $\frac{1}{14}$ as 𝍱 in hieroglyphics.) $\frac{2}{3}$ had its own symbol and sometimes $\frac{1}{2}$ appeared as ⌐.

The need now arises to consider a rule which can be used to decompose a fraction of the form $\frac{2}{pq}$ (where p or q may be 1). Have the class consider $\frac{2}{pq} = \frac{1}{\frac{p(p+q)}{2}} + \frac{1}{\frac{q(p+q)}{2}}$. They can add the fractions on the right side of the equation together to prove this is true. Also have them notice that since pq is odd (since we only need a rule to decompose $\frac{2}{n}$ where n is odd) p and q are odd, so $p + q$ will be even, and therefore $\frac{p+q}{2}$ will be an integer.

Students can decompose $\frac{2}{15}$ at least two ways. If they set $p = 3$ and $q = 5$ they will have $\frac{2}{15} = \frac{1}{\frac{3(8)}{2}} + \frac{1}{\frac{5(8)}{2}} = \frac{1}{12} + \frac{1}{20}$, or $\overline{12} + \overline{20}$. If they let $p = 1$ and $q = 15$ they will have $\frac{2}{15} = \frac{1}{\frac{1(16)}{2}} + \frac{1}{\frac{15(16)}{2}} = \frac{1}{8} + \frac{1}{120}$ or $\overline{8} + \overline{120}$.

It seems the Egyptians had other ways to decompose fractions so as to make the new denominator less complicated. For instance, we could also view $\frac{2}{15}$ as $\frac{4}{30}$.

Then we have $\frac{4}{30} = \frac{3}{30} + \frac{1}{30} = \frac{1}{10} + \frac{1}{30}$. Have students check these conversions.

Now, have students reconsider the earlier division problem 83 ÷ 16.

1	16 *
2	32
4	64 *
8	128
$\overline{2}$	8
$\overline{4}$	4
$\overline{8}$	2 *
$\overline{16}$	1 *

By selecting a sum of 83 from the right column, they

will arrive at the following answer: $1 + 4 + \overline{8} + \overline{16}$

$= 5 + \overline{8} + \overline{16} = 5\frac{3}{16}$. Students should now be able to solve their arithmetic problems using methods developed by the ancient Egyptians.

Postassessment

A. Have students write each of the following numbers in hieroglyphics.

1) 5,280   2) 23,057   3) $\frac{2}{25}$ 4) $\frac{2}{35}$

B. Have students change each of the following fractions into 2 different unit fraction decompositions.

1) $\frac{2}{27}$ 2) $\frac{2}{45}$ 3) $\frac{2}{99}$

C. Have students solve the following problems using Egyptian methods.

1) 30×41 2) 25×137 3) $132 \div 11$ 4) $101 \div 16$

15   Napier's Rods

Performance Objectives

1. Students will construct a cardboard set of Napier's Rods.

2. Students will successfully perform multiplication examples using Napier's Rods.

Preassessment

The only essential skill for this activity is the ability to do multiplication.

Teaching Strategies

Begin your presentation with a brief historical note about Napier's Rods. This multiplication "machine"

was developed by John Napier (1550–1617), a Scotch mathematician, who was principally responsible for the development of logarithms. The device he developed consisted of flat wooden sticks with successive multiples of numbers 1–9. (See fig. 1)

Each student should be given an opportunity to construct his own set of Napier's Rods. Perhaps the best way to explain how to use Napier's Rods is to illustrate with an example using this device.

Consider the multiplication 523×467. Have students select the rods for 5, 2, and 3, and line them up adjacent to the Index Rod. (See fig. 2)
Students must then select the appropriate rows from the index corresponding to the digits in the multiplier.

Figure 1

Figure 2

In a diagonal direction addition is done for each row (see fig. 2). The numbers thus obtained:

$$2092 = 4 \times 523$$
$$3138 = 6 \times 523$$
$$3661 = 7 \times 523$$

are added after considering the appropriate place values of the digits from which they were generated.

$$467 = 400 + 60 + 7$$
$$(467)(523) = (400)(523) + (60)(523) + (7)(523)$$

$$
\begin{aligned}
(467)(523) = \quad &209200 \\
&31380 \\
&\underline{3661} \\
&244241
\end{aligned}
$$

A careful discussion of this last step will not only insure a working knowledge of the computing "machine" by your students, but also should give them a thorough understanding as to *why* this technique "works."

1. 561×49
2. 308×275
3. 4932×7655

Postassessment

Have students use a set of Napier's Rods (which they have constructed) to multiply each of the following:

16   Unit Pricing

Performance Objectives

1. Students will determine which of two given fractions is greater using the technique described on this card.

2. Students will determine which of two quantities of the same product has the more favorable price, given the quantity and the price for that quantity.

Preassessment

The only skill students need for this activity is multiplication of whole numbers.

Teaching Strategies

Ask your students if they would rather buy a 32 oz. jar of applesauce costing 30¢ or a 27 oz. jar costing 25¢. An organized thinker might translate the problem to one which asks which is larger, $\dfrac{30}{32}$ or $\dfrac{25}{27}$.

Students should realize that the fractions come from "price *per* ounce". The word "per" indicates

division so a fraction $\dfrac{\text{price}}{\text{ounces}}$ can be attained.

There are many ways in which two fractions can be compared: dividing the numerator by the denominator and comparing the resulting decimal, changing both fractions to equivalent fractions with the same denominator, and so on.

We shall now consider another method, which could easily be the most efficient method. Draw two arrows as indicated below. Then multiply as the arrows show, writing the product under the arrowheads.

$$
810 \;\nwarrow\; \frac{30}{32} \times \frac{25}{27} \;\nearrow\; 800
$$

Simple inspection of these products indicates that 810 is the larger of the two; hence the fraction above the 810 (i.e., $\dfrac{30}{32}$) is the larger of the two fractions. Therefore, the unit price of the 27 ounce jar is lower and thus the better buy.

Before giving students problems involving comparison of unit prices, offer them some drill problems involving only comparison of fractions.

Postassessment

Select the larger of each for the following pairs of fractions.

1. $\dfrac{5}{6}, \dfrac{7}{8}$

2. $\dfrac{8}{11}, \dfrac{17}{23}$

3. $\dfrac{7}{9}, \dfrac{4}{5}$

4. $\dfrac{13}{17}, \dfrac{19}{25}$

5. $\dfrac{11}{19}, \dfrac{5}{9}$

6. $\dfrac{7}{12}, \dfrac{18}{31}$

7. Which quantity has the lower unit price: a 7 oz. jar of mustard costing 11¢ or a 9 oz. jar of mustard costing 13¢?

17 Successive Discounts and Increases

This unit provides students with a simple technique for expressing various successive discounts and/or increases as one equivalent discount or increase. They may be rather fascinated by the ease of solution which this method brings to a usually complicated consumer situation.

Performance Objectives

1. Students will convert two or more successive discounts to one equivalent discount.

2. Students will convert two or more successive discounts and increases to one equivalent discount or increase.

Preassessment

Use the following problem for diagnostic purposes as well as to motivate discussion.

Ernie is deciding where to buy a shirt. Barry's Bargain Store offers the shirt at a 30% discount off the list price. Cheap Charlie's Store usually offers the same shirt at a 20% discount off the same list price. However, today Cheap Charlie's Store is offering the shirt at a 10% discount off the already discounted (20%) price. At which store will Ernie get a greater discount on the shirt today?

Teaching Strategies

Students may not immediately realize the difference in the discounts of the two stores mentioned in the problem above. Some students may feel that both stores offer the same discount. With your help they should begin to notice that, whereas Barry's Bargain Store offers a 30% discount off the original list price, Cheap Charlie's Store only offers a 20% discount off the original list price, while the 10% discount is taken off the lower, already discounted price. Hence, Ernie gets a greater discount with the 30% discount.

At this juncture your students may begin to wonder how large the actual difference is between the discounts offered by the two stores. You might then elicit from them that this quantitative comparison calls for finding a single discount equivalent to the two *successive discounts* of 20% and 10%.

Some students may suggest finding the required discounts by starting with a list price such as $10.00. This would work well as 100 is the basis of percents. That is, a discount of 20% off $10.00 yields a price of $8.00. Then a 10% discount off $8.00 yields a new price of $7.20. Since $7.20 may be obtained by a single discount of 28% off the original $10.00, *successive discounts* of 20% and 10% are equivalent to a single discount of 28%. It is simple to compare this with the 30% discount from the original problem.

Students should consider a general method of converting any number of successive discounts to a single discount. Illustrate with two successive discounts percents of d_1 and d_2 operating on a price p.

Use the same procedure as before:

$p - \dfrac{pd_1}{100} = p(1 - \dfrac{d_1}{100})$ represents the price after one discount has been computed; $[p(1 - \dfrac{d_1}{100})] - [p(1 - \dfrac{d_1}{100})] (\dfrac{d_2}{100}) = p(1 - \dfrac{d_1}{100})(1 - \dfrac{d_2}{100})$ represents the price after the second discount has been computed; $(1 - \dfrac{d_1}{100})(1 - \dfrac{d_2}{100})$ represents the percent that the new price is of the original price.

Therefore $1 - (1 - \dfrac{d_1}{100})(1 - \dfrac{d_2}{100})$ represents the discount taken off the original price in order to obtain the new price.

Hence, successive discounts of d_1% and d_2% are equivalent to a single discount percent of:

$1 - (1 - \frac{d_1}{100})(1 - \frac{d_2}{100})$. By translating this final algebraic expression into verbal form the students should be able to establish the following simple technique for converting two successive discounts to a single equivalent discount:

1) Change each of the successive discounts to decimal fractions.
2) Subtract each of these decimal fractions from the whole (i.e., 1.00).
3) Multiply the results of Step 2.
4) Subtract the results of Step 3 from the whole (i.e., 1.00).
5) Change the result of Step 4 to percent form.

Applying this to the successive discounts of 20% and 10% the students should show the following work:

1) 20% = .20 and 10% = .10
2) 1.00 − .20 = .80, and 1.00 − .10 = .90
3) (.80)(.90) = .72
4) 1.00 − .72 = .28
5) .28 = 28% (discount)

Students will notice that the rules above do not specify the number of successive discounts considered. This may prompt them to investigate the case where more than two successive discounts are to be converted to a single equivalent discount. Students should proceed in a manner similar to the one used above for two successive discounts. They should find that these same rules do in fact hold true in converting any number of successive discounts to a single equivalent discount.

A natural question to be expected at this juncture would probe the nature of *successive increases* or *successive decreases* and *increase*. Since an increase requires adding a percent of the price to the original price, while a discount requires subtracting a percent of the price from the original price, the students could be expected to guess that the technique for converting successive increases or combinations of successive increases and discounts to a single increase or discount will be similar to the conversion technique used for successive discounts. Suggest they work out this technique.

Broadening the scope of this conversion technique to include increases as well as discounts will allow students to consider problems such as the following:

When the entrance price to a basketball game was decreased by 25%, the attendance at the game increased by 35%. What was the effect of these changes on the daily receipts?

In solving this problem the student's work should resemble the following:

1) 25% = .25, and 35% = .35
2) 1.00 − .25 = .75 and 1.00 + .35 = 1.35
3) (.75)(1.35) = 1.0125
4) 1.0125 − 1.0000 = .0125
5) .0125 = 1.25% (increase)

You might wish to ask your students what they feel would be the net effect of a successive discount of 10% and increase of 10%. Students generally feel that these two changes counteract one another, leaving the original price unaltered. However they should be encouraged to apply the conversion technique. The net effect of these two changes is in fact a discount of 1%.

The following chart of successive discounts and increases of the same percent should lead students to making an intelligent conjecture about the "break even" point.

Successive Changes							
% Discount	20	15	10	5	1	.5	.1
% Increase	20	15	10	5	1	.5	.1
Equivalent % Discount Change	4	2.25	1	.25	.01	.0025	.0001

It might be satisfying for students to discover what combinations of successive discount and increase will leave the original price unaltered. One possible approach would be to use the conversion technique for a successive discount of d% and increase of i%:

$1 - (1 - d/100)(1 + i/100) = 0$; $1 - (1 - d/100 + i/100 - di/100^2) = 0$; $100d - 100i + di = 0$;

$$d = \frac{100i}{100 + i} \text{ or } i = \frac{100d}{100 - d}$$

The chart below lists possible values for d and i.

d	0	$9.09\overline{09}$	$16.66\overline{6}$	20	50	75	10	25
i	0	10	20	25	100	300	$11.11\overline{1}$	$33.33\overline{3}$

By now the students should have some insight into the topic of *successive percents*. The conversion technique introduced in this model is rather easy to remember as the basic steps merely call for: subtraction (and/or addition), multiplication, and subtraction (and/or addition).

Postassessment

Have students try to solve several problems such as the following.

1. Alice wants to buy a dress whose list price is $20. One store which generally discounts its dresses 12½% is offering an additional 20% on its already discounted price. A nearby store offers the same dress at a single 32% discount. Which store offers the lower price?

2. When the price of a magazine was decreased by 15% the sales increased by 20%. How were the receipts affected by these changes?

References

Posamentier, Alfred S. *A Study Guide for the Scho-* *lastic Aptitude Test, Mathematics Section.* Boston: Allyn and Bacon, 1983.

Posamentier, Alfred S., and Charles T. Salkind, *Uncommon Topics for Common Topics in Algebra.* Portland, Maine: J. Weston Walch, 1981.

18 Prime and Composite Factors of a Whole Number

This unit presents a different approach to the process of factoring a number. It allows students to find the complete set of all different factors of a composite whole number. At the same time, this unit helps students better understand the factorization process.

Performance Objectives

1. Students will determine the total number of factors, prime and composite, of a given composite whole number.

2. Students will determine each of the elements of the set of prime and composite factors of this number.

3. Students will find the sum of all the elements of this set.

Preassessment

Students should be familiar with the basic rules of divisibility and able to find the prime factorization of a number.

Teaching Strategies

To find the set of prime and composite factors of the given number, you should first find the prime factorization of the number and then determine all possible products of these factors.

To find the prime factorization of the number, the "peeling" technique may be used. For example, to find the prime factorization of 3960, you should proceed as follows:

$$
\begin{array}{ll}
2)\ \underline{3960} & 3960 = 2 \times 1980 \\
2)\ \underline{1980} & = 2 \times 2 \times 990 \\
2)\ \underline{990} & = 2 \times 2 \times 2 \times 495 \\
3)\ \underline{495} & = 2 \times 2 \times 2 \times 3 \times 165 \\
3)\ \underline{165} & = 2 \times 2 \times 2 \times 3 \times 3 \times 55 \\
5)\ \underline{55} & = 2 \times 2 \times 2 \times 3 \times 3 \times 5 \times 11 \\
\ \ \ 11 &
\end{array}
$$

The prime factorization of 3960 is:
$2 \times 2 \times 2 \times 3 \times 3 \times 5 \times 11 = 2^3 \times 3^2 \times 5 \times 11$

The total number of factors of a given number is determined by the product of the exponents (*each in-* creased by one) of the different factors in the prime factorization of the number expressed in exponential form.

Therefore, the total number of factors of 3960 will be given by the product:
$(3 + 1)(2 + 1)(1 + 1)(1 + 1) = 4 \times 3 \times 2 \times 2 = 48$

To find each of the 48 factors, prepare the following self-explanatory table:

$$
\begin{array}{cccc}
1 & 2 & 2^2 & 2^3 \\
1 & 3 & 3^2 & \\
1 & 5 & & \\
1 & 11 & &
\end{array}
$$

Now have students multiply each number in the first row by each number in the second row:

$$
\begin{array}{cccc}
1 \times 1 & 1 \times 2 & 1 \times 2^2 & 1 \times 2^3 \\
1 \times 3 & 2 \times 3 & 2^2 \times 3 & 2^3 \times 3 \\
1 \times 3^2 & 2 \times 3^2 & 2^2 \times 3^2 & 2^3 \times 3^2
\end{array}
$$

Then each resulting product would be multiplied by each number in the third row:

$$
\begin{array}{cccc}
1 \times 1 \times 1 & 1 \times 1 \times 2 & 1 \times 1 \times 2^2 & 1 \times 1 \times 2^3 \\
1 \times 1 \times 3 & 1 \times 2 \times 3 & 1 \times 2^2 \times 3 & 1 \times 2^3 \times 3 \\
1 \times 1 \times 3^2 & 1 \times 2 \times 3^2 & 1 \times 2^2 \times 3^2 & 1 \times 2^3 \times 3^2 \\
1 \times 1 \times 5 & 1 \times 2 \times 5 & 1 \times 2^2 \times 5 & 1 \times 2^3 \times 5 \\
1 \times 3 \times 5 & 2 \times 3 \times 5 & 2^2 \times 3 \times 5 & 2^3 \times 3 \times 5 \\
1 \times 3^2 \times 5 & 2 \times 3^2 \times 5 & 2^2 \times 3^2 \times 5 & 2^3 \times 3^2 \times 5
\end{array}
$$

You should continue this same process until all rows are exhausted. In the case of our example, 3960, we finally have:

$$
\begin{array}{cccc}
1 \times 1 \times 1 \times 1 & 1 \times 1 \times 1 \times 2 & 1 \times 1 \times 1 \times 2^2 & 1 \times 1 \times 1 \times 2^3 \\
1 \times 1 \times 1 \times 3 & 1 \times 1 \times 2 \times 3 & 1 \times 1 \times 2^2 \times 3 & 1 \times 1 \times 2^3 \times 3 \\
1 \times 1 \times 1 \times 3^2 & 1 \times 1 \times 2 \times 3^2 & 1 \times 1 \times 2^2 \times 3^2 & 1 \times 1 \times 2^3 \times 3^2 \\
1 \times 1 \times 1 \times 5 & 1 \times 1 \times 2 \times 5 & 1 \times 1 \times 2^2 \times 5 & 1 \times 1 \times 2^3 \times 5 \\
1 \times 1 \times 3 \times 5 & 1 \times 2 \times 3 \times 5 & 1 \times 2^2 \times 3 \times 5 & 1 \times 2^3 \times 3 \times 5 \\
1 \times 1 \times 3^2 \times 5 & 1 \times 2 \times 3^2 \times 5 & 1 \times 2^2 \times 3^2 \times 5 & 1 \times 2^3 \times 3^2 \times 5 \\
1 \times 1 \times 1 \times 11 & 1 \times 1 \times 2 \times 11 & 1 \times 1 \times 2^2 \times 11 & 1 \times 1 \times 2^3 \times 11 \\
1 \times 1 \times 3 \times 11 & 1 \times 2 \times 3 \times 11 & 1 \times 2^2 \times 3 \times 11 & 1 \times 2^3 \times 3 \times 11 \\
1 \times 1 \times 3^2 \times 11 & 1 \times 2 \times 3^2 \times 11 & 1 \times 2^2 \times 3^2 \times 11 & 1 \times 2^3 \times 3^2 \times 11 \\
1 \times 1 \times 5 \times 11 & 1 \times 2 \times 5 \times 11 & 1 \times 2^2 \times 5 \times 11 & 1 \times 2^3 \times 5 \times 11 \\
1 \times 3 \times 5 \times 11 & 2 \times 3 \times 5 \times 11 & 2^2 \times 3 \times 5 \times 11 & 2^3 \times 3 \times 5 \times 11 \\
1 \times 3^2 \times 5 \times 11 & 2 \times 3^2 \times 5 \times 11 & 2^2 \times 3^2 \times 5 \times 11 & 2^3 \times 3^2 \times 5 \times 11
\end{array}
$$

However, students can obtain the same results in a

simpler and quicker way: Find the divisors of each of the factors in the number's prime factorization when written in exponential form. In our example:

$$2^3 \begin{cases} 2^1 = 2 \\ 2^2 = 4 \\ 2^3 = 8 \end{cases} \quad 3^2 \begin{cases} 3^1 = 3 \\ 3^2 = 9 \end{cases} \quad 5^1 \{5^1 = 5 \quad 11^1 \{11^1 = 11$$
$$\qquad a \qquad\qquad b \qquad\quad c \qquad\qquad d$$

Have students prepare a table in which the first row is formed by number one and the numbers in *a* (see below). Have pupils draw a line and multiply each number in *b* by each number above this line. Students will draw a new line and multiply the element in *c* by all the numbers above the second line. The process will continue until all divisors of each of the factors in the number's prime factorization are multiplied.

1	2	4	8	I
3	6	12	24	
9	18	36	72	II
5	10	20	40	
15	30	60	120	III
45	90	180	360	
11	22	44	88	
33	66	132	264	
99	198	396	792	
55	110	220	440	IV
165	330	660	1320	
495	990	1980	3960	

The table which contains the 48 factors we are looking for starts with number 1 and ends with our given number 3960.

Part I is formed by number 1 and the factors in *a*. Part II is constituted by the products of each of the numbers in *b* and each of the numbers in I. Part III is made up by the products obtained when multiplying each of the numbers of *c* by each of the numbers in I and II. And finally, part IV is formed by multiplying each number of *d* by each of the numbers in I, II, and III. The table has 4 × 12 = 48 factors. All of the factors of 3960 appear in this table: The prime as well as the composite factors of 3960.

To find the sum of the factors of a number N, let us represent the prime factorization of N by $a^\alpha \cdot b^\beta \cdot c^\rho \cdot d^\theta$, such that, $N = a^\alpha \cdot b^\beta \cdot c^\rho \cdot d^\theta$. The sum of all the factors of N will be given by the formula:

$$s = \frac{a^{\alpha+1} - 1}{a - 1} \cdot \frac{b^{\beta+1} - 1}{b - 1} \cdot \frac{c^{\rho+1} - 1}{c - 1} \cdot \frac{d^{\theta+1} - 1}{d - 1}.$$

In our example: N = 3960, $a = 2$, $b = 3$, $c = 5$, $d = 11$, $\alpha = 3$, $\beta = 2$, $\rho = 1$, $\theta = 1$ as $3960 = 2^3 \times 3^2 \times 5 \times 11$ Therefore:

$$s = \frac{2^4 - 1}{2 - 1} \cdot \frac{3^3 - 1}{3 - 1} \cdot \frac{5^2 - 1}{5 - 1} \cdot \frac{11^2 - 1}{11 - 1}$$
$$= \frac{15}{1} \cdot \frac{26}{2} \cdot \frac{24}{4} \cdot \frac{120}{10}$$
$$= 15 \times 13 \times 6 \times 12$$
$$= 14{,}040$$

Postassessment

Have students calculate the total number of factors and then find each of them (either prime or composite), for each of the following:

a) 3600 b) 540 c) 1680 d) 25725

Find the sum of all the factors in each of the cases above.

19 Prime Numeration System

This unit will present an unusual way to express numbers. Consideration of this "strange" numeration system should strengthen student understanding of a place value system as well as appreciation of prime factorization.

Performance Objectives

1. *Students will convert numbers from the prime numeration system into base-ten numerals.*

2. *Students will convert numbers from base-ten into the prime numeration system.*

Preassessment

Students should know what a prime number is. Students should also be able to factor a base-ten numeral into its prime factors.

Teaching Strategies

To familiarize students with the prime numeration system, have students consider the following problems: a) 5·4 = 9, b) 12·24 = 36 c) 8÷2 = 6. Initially students will be quite puzzled. After further inspection those familiar with exponents will begin to conjecture along those lines. Yet, this system is probably quite different from any numeration system studied before.

In the prime numeration system, there is no base. The value of each place is a prime number. The first place (starting at the right) is the first prime, 2; the next place (to the left) is the next prime, 3. This continues with the consecutive prime numbers with each succeeding place (moving left) corresponding to the next consecutive prime. This can be shown by using a dash for each place and indicating its value below it.

$$\overline{29}\ \overline{23}\ \overline{19}\ \overline{17}\ \overline{13}\ \overline{11}\ \overline{7}\ \overline{5}\ \overline{3}\ \overline{2}$$

As with our base-ten system, this prime system continues indefinitely to the left.

In order to find the value of a number in base-ten, digits occupying each place are multiplied by their place value and then added. However, in this prime numeration system, the value of a number is obtained by taking each place value to the *power* of the number occupying that place and then *multiplying*. For example, the number 145_p (the subscript p will be used to indicate that the number is in the prime numeration system) equals $5^1 \cdot 3^4 \cdot 2^5$ $= 5 \cdot 81 \cdot 32 = 12960$. Notice the exponents of the prime numbers 5, 3, and 2 are 1, 4, and 5, respectively. Have students practice converting from the prime numeration system to base-ten numeration. When they begin to feel somewhat comfortable with this work, have them consider the representation of 0 and 1. Have students express 0_p and 10_p as a base-ten numeral. Indicate to the students that by definition $2^0 = 1$. Elicit from students that representation of zero will be impossible in the prime numeration system.

In order to convert a base-ten numeral into the prime numeration system, a review of prime factorization is necessary. Explain to students that any whole number greater than one can be expressed as the product of prime factors in precisely one way (The Fundamental Theorem of Arithmetic). For example, 420 can be factored as follows: $7^1 \cdot 5^1 \cdot 3^1 \cdot 2^2$. Therefore $420 = 1112_p$. Have students factor a) 144, b) 600, c) 1960, into their prime factors and represent their equivalents in the prime numeration system. Emphasize that exponents of the prime factors are the digits of the prime numeral.

When students have mastered this numeration system challenge them with multiplication; $5_p \cdot 4_p$ $5_p \cdot 4_p$ may be rewritten as $2^5 \cdot 2^4 = 2^9 = 512$. Therefore, $5_p \cdot 4_p = 9_p$. Now have them consider $25_p \cdot 4_p = 3^2 \cdot 2^5 \cdot 2^4 = 3^2 \cdot 2^9 = 29_p$ (or 4608). Other related exercises should be presented (e.g. $8_p \div 2_p$). It should be indicated that the operations of addition and subtraction would require conversion to base-ten numeration before actually adding or subtracting. These problems allow students to practice working with exponents in a new and unusual way.

The prime numeration system can be implemented to review the greatest common divisor and least common multiple of two numbers.

Suppose students were required to find the greatest common divisor of 18,720 and 3,150. They should change these two base-ten numerals to the prime numeration system to get: 100125_p and 1221_p. By listing the *smallest value of each place* to form a new number, they will obtain 121_p, which is the greatest common divisor of the two numbers.

Now suppose students were faced with the problem of finding the least common multiple of 18,720 and 3,150. Having changed these two base-ten numerals to the prime numeration system to get 100125_p and 1221_p, they must merely list the *largest value of each place* to get 101225_p, which is the least common multiple of the two numbers.

Students will enjoy applying the prime numeration system methods to other problems which require finding the greatest common divisor or the least common multiple of given numbers (more than two numbers may be considered at one time). The true value of these methods rests in the justification of these methods. Teachers should present these justifications as soon as students have mastered the techniques involved.

Now have students convert 0_p through 29_p into base-ten numerals and record their answers. Students will begin to see the base-ten numerals being generated in an unusual way.

Prime System	Base-Ten	
0_p	$2^0 =$	1
1_p	$2^1 =$	2
2_p	$2^2 =$	4
3_p	$2^3 =$	8
4_p	$2^4 =$	16
5_p	$2^5 =$	32
6_p	$2^6 =$	64
7_p	$2^7 =$	128
8_p	$2^8 =$	256
9_p	$2^9 =$	512
10_p	$3^1 \cdot 2^0 =$	3
11_p	$3^1 \cdot 2^1 =$	6
12_p	$3^1 \cdot 2^2 =$	12
13_p	$3^1 \cdot 2^3 =$	24
14_p	$3^1 \cdot 2^4 =$	48
15_p	$3^1 \cdot 2^5 =$	96
16_p	$3^1 \cdot 2^6 =$	192
17_p	$3^1 \cdot 2^7 =$	384
18_p	$3^1 \cdot 2^8 =$	768
19_p	$3^1 \cdot 2^9 =$	1536
20_p	$3^2 \cdot 2^0 =$	9
21_p	$3^2 \cdot 2^1 =$	18
22_p	$3^2 \cdot 2^2 =$	36
23_p	$3^2 \cdot 2^3 =$	72
24_p	$3^2 \cdot 2^4 =$	144
25_p	$3^2 \cdot 2^5 =$	288
26_p	$3^2 \cdot 2^6 =$	576
27_p	$3^2 \cdot 2^7 =$	1152
28_p	$3^2 \cdot 2^8 =$	2304
29_p	$3^2 \cdot 2^9 =$	4608

Elicit from students other possible applications of the prime numeration system.

Postassessment

Students should:

1. Express each of the following numbers in the base-ten numeration system.

a) 31_p b) 24_p c) 15_p d) 41_p e) 221_p f) 1234_p

2. Express each of the following base-ten numerals as a product of primes, and then in the prime numeration system.

a) 50 b) 100 c) 125 d) 400 e) 1000 f) 260 g) 350

3. Solve the following problems:

a) $3_p \cdot 6_p$ b) $12_p \cdot 13_p$ c) $6_p \div 3_p$

20 Repeating Decimal Expansions

The terms "never-ending" and "infinite" are often confusing to students. One of the first places they really come into contact with the concept is in the junior high school where they confront non-terminating decimal expansions. Students themselves realize the need for specific notation when they encounter the repeating decimals certain fractional forms produce. In this unit students discover the patterns and seemingly inconsistent arithmetic procedures that occur with repeating decimals.

Performance Objectives

1. Students will be able to determine which rational numbers will yield repeating decimal expansions and which will terminate.

2. Students will determine maximum length of a repeating cycle.

3. Students will be able to use decimal equivalents to find other repeating decimals.

4. Students will examine an alternate method to determine decimal expansions.

Preassessment

Students should know how to change from the fractional form $(\frac{a}{b})$ of a rational number to its decimal equivalent. They should be familiar with prime factorization.

Have students guess which of the following fractions would become repeating decimals: $\frac{1}{2}$, $\frac{1}{3}$, $\frac{1}{4}$, $\frac{1}{5}$, $\frac{1}{6}$. Have them work out these fraction-to-decimal conversions to check the accuracy of their guesses. Note also that a terminating decimal can be considered a repeating decimal with an infinite repetition of zeroes.

Teaching Strategies

Begin by having students work with fractions of the form $\frac{1}{n}$. This will force them to focus their attention (and guesswork) on the denominator. If they have difficulty figuring out how to determine repeating decimals without actually performing the expansion, suggest they factor into primes each of the denominators to see if any patterns become apparent. They will quickly see that the decimal terminates if, and only if, the prime factors of the denominator are 2's and/or 5's. They can easily justify that when the numerator takes on a decimal point and a series of zeroes, it becomes a multiple of 10 (for division purposes only); since the only prime factors of 10 are 5 and 2, it is only division by these factors that will terminate the division process.

Challenge students to determine to how many decimal places they must proceed before a pattern becomes evident. In some cases, as in $\frac{1}{3}$, it will take two decimal places before the pattern is clear. In others, it will not be so simple. Ask students to find the repeating pattern of $\frac{1}{17}$. This decimal expansion has 16 places before any pattern establishes itself $\frac{1}{17}$ = $.0588235294117647\overline{0588235294117647}$.

Some students may want to generalize and assume $\frac{1}{n}$ will have $(n-1)$ repeating digits. However, $\frac{1}{3} = .\overline{3}$, one repeating digit, which quickly disproves their theory. However, by examining each of the expansions of $\frac{1}{n}$, students will see that each expansion has at most $(n-1)$ repeating digits. They should realize that each of the expansion digits comes from the remainder after the division process of the previous step. For each of the remainders there are only $(n-1)$ choices. (The remainder cannot equal zero because then the process would terminate; it cannot equal n because then it would have been divisible once again.) If the remainder is the same as any previous remainder, students have found the repeating digits; if not they must continue until a remainder repeats. This will have to happen in, at most, $(n-1)$ steps. Therefore $\frac{1}{n}$, if repeating, will have at most $(n-1)$ repeating digits.

Students will also find it interesting to note that the repeating expansion for a number such as $\frac{1}{7}$ also yields the expansions for $\frac{2}{7}$, $\frac{3}{7}$, $\frac{4}{7}$, $\frac{5}{7}$, and $\frac{6}{7}$. The fraction $\frac{2}{7}$ can be rewritten in terms of $\frac{1}{7}$. Thus,

$$\frac{2}{7} = 2 \times \frac{1}{7} = 2 \times .\overline{142857} = .\overline{285714}.$$

By adding different repeating decimals, students will be able to find new repeating decimals. For example,

$$\begin{array}{r} \frac{1}{3} = .\overline{333333} \\ + \\ \frac{1}{7} = + .\overline{142857} \\ \hline \frac{10}{21} = .\overline{476190} \end{array}$$

To find the general repeating digits for $\frac{1}{n}$ when $n = 21$, have students divide $.\overline{476190}$ by the numerator, 10, to get $.\overline{047619}$.

In working with repeating decimals and in performing arithmetic operations, students may come upon the fact that $1 = .\overline{9}$. This is a difficult concept for a junior high school student to grasp. The following proof, which they can perform for themselves, should clarify the situation.

$$\begin{array}{r} \frac{1}{3} = .\overline{3} \\ + \\ \frac{2}{3} = .\overline{6} \\ \hline 1 = .\overline{9} \end{array}$$

Similarly, since

$$\frac{1}{9} \times 9 = .\overline{1} \times 9$$
$$\frac{9}{9} = .\overline{9}$$
$$1 = .\overline{9}$$

Students often concentrate and comprehend more thoroughly when they feel they are learning something new. The following method, which basically outlines the division process used to change from fractional to decimal form, gives students another means of finding the repeating decimal.

To find the decimal expansion of $\frac{3}{7}$, let $r_0 = \frac{3}{7}$, and multiply by 10 (comparable to bringing down the 0).

1. $\frac{3}{7} \times 10 = \frac{30}{7} = 4\frac{2}{7}$

Now let the 4 occupy the tenths place of the decimal and use $\frac{2}{7}$ as the new remainder, r_1. Repeat the process, using the fraction as the new remainder and retaining the whole as the decimal digit for the next place.

2. $\frac{2}{7} \times 10 = \frac{20}{7} = 2\frac{6}{7} \quad r_2 = \frac{6}{7}$
   hundredths place = 2

3. $\frac{6}{7} \times 10 = \frac{60}{7} = 8\frac{4}{7} \quad r_3 = \frac{4}{7}$
   thousandths place = 8

4. $\frac{4}{7} \times 10 = \frac{40}{7} = 5\frac{5}{7} \quad r_4 = \frac{5}{7}$
   ten thousandths place = 5

5. $\frac{5}{7} \times 10 = \frac{50}{7} = 7\frac{1}{7} \quad r_5 = \frac{1}{7}$
   hundred thousandths place = 7

6. $\frac{1}{7} \times 10 = \frac{10}{7} = 1\frac{3}{7} \quad r_6 = \frac{3}{7}$
   millionths place = 1

Tell students to repeat the process until the remainder is the same as the one with which they began. In this case $r_6 = r_0 = \frac{3}{7}$, and the decimal expansion is $\frac{3}{7} = .\overline{428571}$

A clear demonstration of this method is an excellent tool to help students better understand what is involved in the division process and why remainders are such a big factor in determining the length of the repetition.

Postassessment

Have students do the following:
1. Determine which of the following will terminate, without actually finding their decimal expansions: $\frac{2}{9}$, $\frac{1}{8}$, $\frac{3}{13}$, $\frac{19}{20}$
2. Determine the maximum number of digits in the repeating cycle of each: $\frac{1}{37}$, $\frac{4}{9}$, $\frac{3}{7}$
3. Knowing that $\frac{1}{14} = .0\overline{714285}$, find the decimal expansion for $\frac{3}{14}$ without dividing.
4. Show that $.5 = .4\overline{9}$. (Hint: think about the fractions $\frac{1}{3}$ and $\frac{1}{6}$).
5. Using the alternate method described, evaluate $\frac{2}{9}$ as a repeating decimal.

21 Peculiarities Of Perfect Repeating Decimals

This unit can be used as an interesting sidelight to the subject of decimals and fractions by showing "magical" properties of a certain class of numbers. These numbers are reciprocals of prime numbers whose decimal equivalents repeat after no less than P−1 places, where P is the prime number. Such numbers are said to have *perfect repetends*. In any repeating decimal, the sequence that repeats is called the repetend. It would be advisable to use this unit after the preceding one.

Performance Objectives
1. *Students will test various examples of perfect repetends to verify specific principles.*
2. *Students will discover and reinforce important ideas about division, remainders, and decimal equivalents of fractions.*

Preassessment
Students should know that the decimal equivalents of some fractions have 0 remainders, while others have repeating periods of various lengths.

They should begin by converting $\frac{1}{7}$ to a decimal.

Teaching Strategies
It should be noted that in converting A/P to a decimal, the repetend can have no more than P−1 places, because in dividing A by P there can be at most P−1 different remainders, and as soon as a remainder appears for the second time, the same sequence will be repeated. Perfect repetends, as well as the sequence of P−1 remainders that accompanies each one, have several interesting properties. Only the simplest of these will be discussed here, but a more thorough listing of the principles of repeating decimals appears in *Philosophy of Arithmetic* by Edward Brooks, (Norwood Editions) pp. 460-485.

One of the simpler properties to explain is that multiples 1 to P−1 of 1/P are cyclic variations of the repetend of 1/P. After students find $\frac{1}{7} = .\overline{142857}$, students can multiply the decimal by 2, 3, 4, 5, or 6, and get answers of $.\overline{285714}$, $.\overline{428571}$, $.\overline{571428}$, $.\overline{714285}$, $.\overline{857142}$, which are also decimal equivalents of $\frac{2}{7}$, $\frac{3}{7}$, $\frac{4}{7}$, $\frac{5}{7}$, $\frac{6}{7}$, respectively. Once this is understood, an easy way to find the multiples of $\frac{1}{7}$ is to find the last place first. For example, $4 \times .\overline{142857}$ ends in 8, so it must be $.\overline{571428}$. Where the period is longer, or where any digit appears more than once in the repetend, it may be necessary to find the last two or three digits

first. An explanation of this cyclic variation is that in dividing P into 1, at the point where the remainder is A, the same sequence will begin as occurs when dividing P into A. Remember also that every possible A (1<A<P) occurs as a remainder. Incidentally, when the repetend of 1/P is multiplied by P the result is .999999. Some other perfect repetends are:

$$\frac{1}{17} = .0588235294117647$$

$$\frac{1}{19} = .052631578947368421$$

$$\frac{1}{23} = .0434782608695652173913$$

The only others for $P < 100$ are: $\frac{1}{29}$, $\frac{1}{47}$, $\frac{1}{59}$, $\frac{1}{61}$, $\frac{1}{97}$

Another curiosity of these numbers is that if the repetend is divided into two equal shorter sequences, their sum is $.\overline{99999}$. A graphic illustration of this is shown below. The inner circle is the repetend of $\frac{1}{29}$, and the outer circle is the sequence of remainders occurring after each number on the inner circle. The figure has the following properties (as do similar figures for all perfect repetends).

1) Any two diametrically opposite terms of the repetend add up to 9.

2) Any two opposite remainders add up to 29.

3) To multiply the repetend by a ($1<a<29$), find a in the circle of remainders and begin the new repetend with the decimal term following the one associated with a (clockwise).

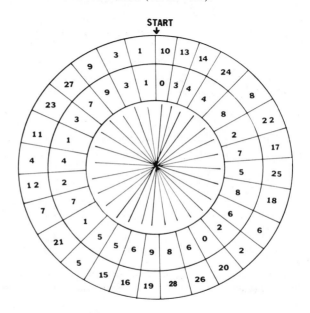

Some students may not have the patience to test out these generalizations on this figure, but of course a similar figure can be made for any of the perfect repetends. Students may construct their own figures, starting only with the information that $\frac{1}{17}$ is such a number.

Here is one alternative to plowing straight ahead with division when generating a repetend: after dividing 19 into 1 to five places, we get a remainder of 3. $\frac{1}{19} = .05263 \frac{3}{19}$. But from this we know that $\frac{3}{19} = 3(.05263 \frac{3}{19}) = .15789 \frac{9}{19}$. So $\frac{1}{19} = .0526315789 \frac{9}{19}$.

But since we know that $\frac{1}{19}$ is a perfect repetend, 9 = first + tenth digit = second + eleventh = third + twelfth, etc., and we have generated all 18 digits.

This leads into a special property of the repetend of $\frac{1}{97}$. $\frac{1}{97} = .01 \frac{3}{97} = .0103 \frac{9}{97} = .010309 \frac{27}{97} =$

$.01030927 \frac{81}{97}$. Unfortunately, 243 has 3 places, so this neat pattern changes, but we can still add powers of three in the following way to generate the repetend;
.0103092781
           243
             729
             2187
              6561 etc.
Students should be encouraged to discover other patterns of repetends.

Postassessment
Have students generate any of the perfect repetends by using the rules shown here, then find multiples of the repetend. Explore with the class for reasons why only primes have this peculiarity. For example, if $\frac{1}{14}$ had a perfect repetend, what happens to $\frac{2}{14}$ or $\frac{4}{14}$?

22 Patterns in Mathematics

This unit is designed for ninth year students of mathematics. Parts of this unit could be used for enrichment of remedial classes in finding the patterns by observation alone.

Performance Objectives
1. *Students will find patterns by observation.*
2. *Students will find formulas for the patterns by trial and error.*
3. *Students will find the formulas for the patterns by discovering the rules for finding the constant and the coefficients of x and x^2.*

Preassessment
Challenge students to find succeeding numbers in the following patterns and formulas for the patterns:

a) x	y		b) x	y		c) x	y		d) x	y
0	1		0	1		0	1		0	3
1	3		1	4		1	5		1	5
2	5		2	7		2	9		2	7
3	7		3	10		3	13		3	9
4	?		4	?		4	?		4	?
5	?		5	?		5	?		5	?

Most students will be able to find the patterns and the formulas by trial and error. Have students fill in

missing numbers, formulas, and note the differences between the successive y's. The completed charts will look like this. D denotes difference between successive y's:

a) x	y	D	b) x	y	D	c) x	y	D	d) x	y	D
0	1		0	1		0	1		0	3	
1	3	2	1	4	3	1	5	4	1	5	2
2	5	2	2	7	3	2	9	4	2	7	2
3	7	2	3	10	3	3	13	4	3	9	2
4	9	2	4	13	3	4	17	4	4	11	2
5	11	2	5	16	3	5	21	4	5	13	2

$y = 2x + 1$ $\quad$ $y = 3x + 1$ $\quad$ $y = 4x + 1$ $\quad$ $y = 2x + 3$

Have students notice constants in each case. Do they observe any pattern? Perhaps they will notice that the constant is the value of y when x is zero. Draw their attention to the difference between the successive y's. Do they observe anything? Yes, the difference between the y's is the coefficient of x. Do several patterns of this type until students can quickly find the patterns and the formulas for the patterns.

Teaching Strategies
Give your students the following exercise and have them find the pattern and the formula if they can.

How many rectangles in all?   Complete the table

x No. of small rectangles	y Total no. of rectangles
0	
1	
2	
3	
4	
5	
6	

By observation of the rectangles, many will be able to find the pattern and fill in the table. Have them record the first difference. They will notice that it is not constant. Have them record the second difference. They will notice it is constant. Have them summarize their findings in a table. Perhaps some will find the formula also.

x No. of small rectangles	y Total no. of rectangles	D_1	D_2
0	0		
1	1	1	
2	3	2	1
3	6	3	1
4	10	4	1
5	15	5	1
6	21	6	1

$$y = \frac{x^2}{2} + \frac{x}{2}$$

Have them do the same with the following pattern: What is the largest number of pieces you can make with x cuts?

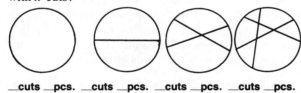

__cuts __pcs. __cuts __pcs. __cuts __pcs. __cuts __pcs.

Have them fill out the following:

x No. of cuts	y No. of pcs.	D_1	D_2
0	1		
1	2	1	
2	4	2	1
3	7	3	1
4	11	4	1
5	16	5	1

Notice the first difference. It is not constant. Notice the second difference. It is constant. Perhaps someone will be able to come up with the formula—

$$y = \frac{x^2}{2} + \frac{x}{2} + 1.$$

Are there any patterns one can see for the values of the constants or the coefficients in the two preceding problems? Yes, the constant is the value of y when x is zero.

Let us examine the formula $ax^2 + bx + c = y$ and find the values of y for various values of x.

x	y	D_1	D_2
0	c		
1	$a+b+c$	$a+b$	
2	$4a+2b+c$	$3a+b$	2a
3	$9a+3b+c$	$5a+b$	2a
4	$16a+3b+c$	$7a+b$	2a

Let us examine the pattern. As we found in the formulas, y is the constant when x is zero. The first difference is $a+b$, the sum of the coefficients of x^2 and x. The second difference is 2a, twice the value of the coefficient of x^2. The value of the first difference when $x=1$ is $a+b$. Since we know the value of a (it is one-half of the second difference), we can find the value of b by subtracting a from the first difference $(a+b)$. So if we reexamine the earlier pattern, we can derive the formula.

The constant is the value of y when x is zero. Therefore the constant is 1. D_2 is 2a. Since D_2 is 1, the value of a is ½. D_1 is $a+b$. Since D_1 is 1, and a is ½, the value of b is ½. The formula therefore is

$$y = \frac{1}{2}x^2 + \frac{1}{2}x + 1.$$

Postassessment

Finish the tables and find the formulas for the following patterns by finding the first and second differences:

x	y
0	3
1	6
2	13
3	24
4	
5	

x	y
0	0
1	5
2	14
3	27
4	
5	

x	y
0	0
1	13
2	34
3	63
4	
5	

x	y
0	2
1	3
2	6
3	11
4	
5	

23 Googol and Googolplex

This unit presents a discussion of large numbers. It introduces students to the finite world of large numbers and the ease of expressing large numbers using scientific notation.

Performance Objectives
1. *Students will give examples of scientific notation as used in science and mathematics.*
2. *Given any number, students will convert it into scientific notation.*

Preassessment
Students should be able to solve the following problems:
1. Compute the following products: Find the solution without using a pencil: *a*) 10 × 63 *b*) 100 × .05 *c*) 1000 × 951.
2. Compute the following quotients: *a*) 470 ÷ 10 *b*) 4,862 ÷ 1000 *c*) 46,000 ÷ 1000
3. What is the largest number you can think of?

Teaching Strategies
You might want to tell the old story of two children engaged in a violent argument in the street. The argument stems from the fact that each child is trying to state a larger number than the other. Finally, they realize each one can state a larger number than the other.

Numbers are fun to play with and many interesting things can be done with them. However, all too often we forget what a number really is. The students should be asked, how large is one million? Can we visualize the sum of the first billion natural numbers? Why should we care about numbers of great magnitude, we never use them—or do we?

At this point the teacher should state that scientists who use very large or very small numbers usually express these numbers in scientific notation. To learn how to use this system of numeration, we will recall some patterns in mathematics. It is up to the teacher at this point to introduce scientific notation. You may wish to refer to any standard textbook for an appropriate development.
1. When a number is expressed as the product of a power of 10 and a number that is less than ten but greater than or equal to one ($1 \leq n < 10$), the number is said to be written in scientific notation.
2. A science teacher may be able to suggest very large or very small numbers that students have used or read about in their science classes. These can then be converted into scientific notation.

A general discussion should ensue on when large numbers are used (for example, grains of sand on a beach, stars in the sky, or in economics, science, etc). Current newspaper and magazine articles abound with references to millions and billions, etc. How many people have seen a million of anything? Most people do not have a clear idea of the size of a million.

To earn a million dollars how long would you have to work at $100 a week? (almost 200 years). How many stars can you see with the naked eye on a clear night? No, not millions, but only about 3,500 (3.5×10^3 in scientific notation). A hundred sheets of paper make a stack about 5 millimetres thick or $\frac{1}{5}$ of an inch (25.4 millimetres equal an inch). A million sheets of paper would make a pile about 55 yards high, or roughly the height of a 12 story building. Suppose you are riding in a car at 65 mph. How long would it take you going constantly to travel one million miles? ($1\frac{3}{4}$ years).

Just how big is a billion? The 1981 federal budget calls for more tax dollars than there have been seconds since the birth of Christ. (Note: according to the ability of a particular class and allotted time all large numbers should be converted to scientific notation by the student.) Students should be led to the fact that it is virtually impossible for the human mind to comprehend the enormity of a billion. Remember how high a pile of a million sheets of paper would be—a hundred sheets of paper make a stack about 5 millimetres thick (about $\frac{1}{5}$ of an inch). A billion sheets of paper would make a pile 31 miles high.

A car traveling nonstop at 100 mph would take 1,140 years to travel a billion miles. If you earn $100 a week, you would have to work 192,307 years to earn a billion dollars. (Some of these illustrations may be calculated on an electronic calculator.)

You should pose the following problem. "John did me a favor the other day and I asked him what reward he would like. John, being very wise said, "Give me one penny for the first day, two pennies for the second day, four pennies for the third day, and likewise for sixty-four days, doubling the number of pennies for each successive day." How much money would I have to pay John?"

Making a table gives students an opportunity to see numbers growing and the magnitude they can reach.

Number of Days	Number of Pennies
1	1
2	2
3	4
4	8
5	16
etc.	etc.
64	9,223,372,036.854,775,808

Now the sum of all the numbers in the second column is the number of pennies needed to pay John:

$$18,446,744,073,709,551,615$$

It is read: Eighteen quintillion, four hundred forty-six quadrillion, seven hundred forty-four trillion, seventy-three billion, seven hundred nine million, five hundred fifty-one thousand, six hundred fifteen. Students should be able to see that even though it is an enormous number it is not infinite, but finite. Have them express it approximately in scientific notation.

The next question that may arise at this point concerns the largest number that can be expressed by three digits. In ordinary notation the answer is 999. What about 99^9? (review of exponents reveals the fact that this means 99 multiplied by itself 8 times.) But if exponents are permitted, the answer is 9^{9^9}, that is, 9 with the exponent 9^9, or simply 9 with the exponent 387,420,489. (the product of 387,420,489 nines). If printed with 16 figures to an inch, it has been estimated, this huge number would fill 33 volumes of 800 pages each, printing 14,000 figures on a page. It has been estimated that this number is more than four million times as large as the number of electrons in the universe, but a *finite* number. (Ask students to find the largest three digit number that can be written with fours.)

Say the number of grains of sand at Coney Island is about 10^{20}. Students could be asked to devise a method for establishing this estimate. The number of electrons which pass through the filament of an ordinary light-bulb in a minute equals the number of drops of water that flow over Niagara Falls in a hundred years. The reason for giving such examples of very large numbers to students is to emphasize that the elements of even very large sets can be counted.

Students may now ask what the largest number that has a name is. The term *googol* was coined to describe the figure 1 followed by a hundred zeros. Another term, *googolplex*, was invented for a still larger, but still finite, number consisting of a 1 followed by a googol of zeros. Thus, a googol times a googol would be a 1 with 200 zeros. Students who try to write a googolplex on the chalkboard or a sheet of paper will get some idea of the size of this very large but finite number (there would not be enough room to write it if you travelled to the farthest visible star, writing zeros all the way).

Astronomers find the light-year a very convenient unit of length in measuring great astromical distances. The North Star is 47 light years away. What does this mean? Light travels at the rate of 186,000 miles per-second. In one year light travels 6,000,000,000,000 (6×10^{12}) miles. This tremendous distance is called a light year. The nearest star is 4.4 light-years away, and the farthest known star is 1.4×10^9 light years away. Have students consider this: It takes 47 light-years for light from Earth to reach the North Star. What would a person looking at the Earth from the North Star see today? (Events happening around 1934.)

Postassessment

Have students complete the following:

1. The distance of the planet Pluto from the earth is approximately 4,700,000,000,000 miles, Express this answer in scientific notation. (4.7×10^{12})

2. The circumference of the earth at the equator is approximately 25,000 miles. Express this in scientific notation. (2.5×10^4)

24 Mathematics of Life Insurance

This unit describes to students how insurance companies take into account probability and compound interest in calculating the net premium of life insurance.

Performance Objective
1. *Students will use a compound interest formula to compute the value of money left in a bank for a given period at a given rate.*
2. *Students will compute the present value of money that increases to a given amount when left in a bank for a given period at a given rate.*
3. *Students will use appropriate probabilities and interest rate to calculate the net premium a life insurance policy holder must pay.*

Preassessment
Use the following problem for diagnostic purposes as well as to motivate the lesson. Out of 200,000 men alive at age 40, 199,100 lived at age 41. What is the probability that an insured man of age 40 will live at least one year? What is the probability that he will die within one year?

Teaching Strategies
By posing the above problem, students become aware of the applicability of probability theory to life insurance. It is important for these companies to be able to measure the risks against which people are buying the life insurance. In order to decide on the premiums, a life insurance company must know how many people are expected to die in any group. They do this by collecting data about the number of people who died in the past from each age group. Since the data is collected from a large number of events, the law of large numbers applies. This law states that *with a large number of experiments, the ratio of the number of successes to the number of trials gets very close to the theoretical probability.*

Life insurance companies construct mortality tables based on past deaths in order to predict the number of people who will die in each age group. Below is a portion of the Commissioners 1958 Standard Ordinary Mortality Table. To construct this table a sample of ten million people was used. Their life span was recorded from birth till age 99. At each age level the table records the number of people alive at the start of the year and the number of deaths that occurred during the year. Then the following ratio is computed:

$$\frac{\text{Number of deaths during year}}{\text{Number of people alive at start of year}}$$

This ratio is then converted to deaths per 1000. The number of deaths per 1000 is called the *death rate*. This death rate, as students will see, is crucial in computing the premium that policyholders will pay.

Age	Number Living	Deaths Each Year	Deaths Per 1,000
0	10,000,000	70,800	7.08
1	9,929,200	17,475	1.76
2	9,911,725	15,066	1.52
3	9,896,659	14,449	1.46
4	9,882,210	13,835	1.40
10	9,805,870	11,865	1.21
11	9,794,005	12,047	1.23
12	9,781,958	12,325	1.26
13	9,769,633	12,896	1.32
18	9,698,230	16,390	1.69
25	9,575,636	18,481	1.93
30	9,480,358	20,193	2.13
42	9,173,375	38,253	4.17
43	9,135,122	41,382	4.53
44	9,093,740	44,741	4.92

Figure 1

After this introduction, the teacher should ask the class: What is the probability that an 18-year-old will die if out of 6,509 18-year-olds alive at the beginning of the year, 11 died? The probability is 11/6509. However, life insurance companies prefer to transform this ratio into death rate per 1000. The teacher should have the class change 11/6509 into $x/1000$ by setting up the following proportion:

$$\frac{x}{1000} = \frac{\text{Number of dying during the year}}{\text{Number alive at start of year}}$$

x = death rate per 1000

The answer to the above problem is:

$$\frac{11}{6509} = \frac{x}{1000} \text{ or } x = 1.69$$

This means that 1.69 people out of the original 1000 will have died by the end of the eighteenth year. The insurance company uses this information to calculate the premium it will charge a group of 18-year-olds. Suppose there were 1000 people age 18 who insured themselves for $1000 each for one year. How much would the company have to pay out at the end of the year? If 1.69 people die, the company will pay out $1690 (1.69 × 1000 = 1690). Thus, how much must the company charge each of the 1000 policyholders? (This does not take into account profit or operating expenses). The $1690 divided evenly among 1000 people equals $1.69 per person.

In the previous discussion, students did not take into consideration the fact that money paid to the company earns interest during the year. So besides considering the death rate, the interest rate must also be taken into account when calculating the premium.

The teacher must now develop the concepts of compound interest. The teacher should ask the class how much money will be on deposit in a bank at the end of the year if one deposits $100 at 5 percent interest. The answer is $100 plus .05 (100) or 100×1.05 which is $105. If the $105 is kept in the bank another year, what will it amount to? $105 + .05(105)$ or $100 \times 1.05 \times 1.05$ or $100 \times (1.05)^2$ which amounts to $110.25. Have the students write the general formula using P = original principal, i = rate of interest per period, A = the amount of money at the end of the specified time and n = the number of years the principal is on deposit. The formula is $A = P(1 + i)^n$.

The teacher should now ask the students how much money they would have to deposit now in a bank whose rate of interest is 5 percent, if they wanted $100 accumulated in one year from now. In the previous example, the students saw that $100 grew to $105 in one year's time. This information is used to set up a proportion: $x/100 = 100/105 = .9524$. $x = 100(.9524) = 95.24.

How much would have to be deposited now in order to accumulate $100 at the end of two years from now? $x/100 = 100/110.25 = .9070$. $x = 90.70.

The students should now be able to derive a formula for calculating the present value from the formula for compound interest ($A = P(1 + i)^n$).

This formula is: $P = \dfrac{A}{(1 + i)^n}$.

Your students will now return to the original problem of the life insurance company that has to pay out $1690 at the end of the year to the deceased 18-year-olds. What is the present value of $1690? In other words, how much must the insurance company collect at the beginning of the year so that it can pay out $1690 at the end of the year? By using the present value formula, the students computed that for every $1 the company has to pay, it must collect $.9524 at the beginning of the year. If the company has to pay $1690, then it has to collect $1609.56 in total from its 1000 18-year-olds ($1690 \times .9524 = 1609.56). Thus each policyholder must contribute a premium of $1609.56/1000 = 1.60956$ or about $1.61.

You may now pose another problem. Suppose another group of 1000 people aged 25 bought policies for one year worth $1000 apiece (the death benefit is $1000). According to the mortality table their death rate is 1.93, or 1.93 out of 1000 25-year-olds die during their twenty-fifth year. What will the net premium be if the interest rate is 5 percent? Death rate per 1000 at age 25 = 1.93. Amount needed to pay claims = $(1.93 \times 1000) = 1930. Interest factor = $.9524. Present value of claims due in 1 year ($1930 \times .9524$) = $1838.13. Number of persons paying premium = 1000. Net premium $1838.13/1000 = 1.83813$ of $1.84. This process may be continued for additional years of insurance.

Postassessment

Calculate the net premium for a two-year policy for a group of 1000 all age 30, with interest at 5 percent. Death rate at 30 is 2.13, death rate at 31 is 2.19.

25 Geometric Dissections

Unlike Humpty Dumpty, dissected geometric figures can be put back together again. In fact, the primary purpose of dissections is to cut a plane rectilinear figure with straight lines in such a way that the resulting pieces can be reassembled into a desired figure. This unit will introduce the wide range of geometric dissections by emphasizing their mathematical as well as recreational value.

Performance Objectives

1. Students will see familiar polygonal area formulas in a concrete and interrelated manner.

2. Students will transform certain polygonal figures into other polygonal figures of equal area through dissections.

Preassessment

Present your students with the following problem: Given an equilateral triangle, dissect the triangle into four pieces, which can be put together to form a rectangle. One possible solution: construct the perpendicular bisector from C to point D on side $\overline{AB}$; from D draw a line segment to the midpoint of $\overline{BC}$; bisect $\angle A$ extending the bisecting ray to point F on $\overline{CD}$. These four pieces will form a rectangle.;

Figure 1

Teaching Strategies

Begin discussion of dissections by demonstrating the area equality between a rectangle and a parallelogram with the same base. The dissection proceeds as follows. Using heavy paper or cardboard, construct a rectangle ABCD. Make a straight cut from vertex A to a point E on side $\overline{DC}$. Remove $\triangle$ ADE placing side $\overline{AD}$ along side $\overline{BC}$ to form parallelogram ABE'E.

Figure 2

In a similar manner, you can also demonstrate that a parallelogram and a trapezoid with the same base have equal areas. Consider any trapezoid; find the midpoint E of side $\overline{BC}$, and through E draw a line parallel to $\overline{AD}$ which intersects $\overline{AB}$ at X and $\overline{DC}$ at Y. Since $\triangle$CEY and $\triangle$BEX are congruent, the areas of trapezoid ABCD and parallelogram AXYD are equal.

Figure 3

The range of possible transformations of polygons into other polygons by means of dissections is vast. Janos Bolyai, one of the founders of non-Euclidean geometry, was the first to suggest that given any two polygons with equal area, either figure could be dissected a finite number of times such that upon rearrangement it would be congruent to the other. However, we are concerned with specific transformations that require a minimum number of dissections.

For example, you could consider the problem of dissecting a given acute triangle to form a rectangle. In Figure 4, first find the midpoints of sides $\overline{AC}$ and $\overline{BC}$ and connect these points to form $\overline{DE}$. From C construct a perpendicular to $\overline{DE}$ at X. Take $\triangle$DXC and place it so that X is now at X' and $\angle$DCX is adjacent to $\angle$CAB. Similarly move $\triangle$EXC so that X is now at X'' and $\angle$ECX is adjacent to $\angle$CBA.

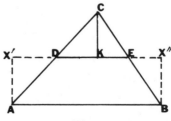

Figure 4

To encourage students to begin solving dissection problems on their own, suggest that they carefully construct a 10cm. by 10 cm. square as follows: Let AL=BG=7, CT_1=3.1, AR$_1$=2.9, DN=4.2; draw $\overline{AG}$ and $\overline{LN}$; on $\overline{LN}$ let LS$_1$=1.6; on $\overline{AG}$ locate points R,S,K, and T such that AR=2.4, RS=3.3, SK=2.4 and KT=3.3; draw $\overline{RR_1}$, $\overline{SS_1}$, $\overline{KB}$, and $\overline{TT_1}$.

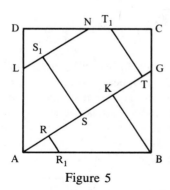

Figure 5

After cutting the student should have seven pieces. Using all of these pieces, students should attempt to form: (1) three squares of the same size, and (2) an isoceles trapezoid.

A beautiful dissection is possible with three regular hexagons. Leaving the first hexagon uncut, dissect the second and third as shown below in Figure 6. These 13 pieces can be combined to form a single hexagon.

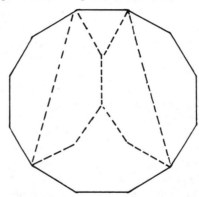

Figure 6

It should be noted that this transformation can be considered in terms of rotations, and others in terms of reflections, translations, as well as rotations. You can then determine that a side of the larger hexagon is $\sqrt{3}$ times a side of the smaller hexagons. Since the area of the new hexagon is three times the area of each of the smaller hexagons, we have verified a significant relationship which holds between similar figures: that the ratio of their areas is the square of the ratio between any two corresponding sides.

Postassessment

Students should complete the following exercises.

1. Demonstrate by dissection that a rectangle can be divided into two congruent trapezoids which each have one-half the area of the rectangle.

2. With the pieces from the dissected 10cm by 10cm square, form: (1) a rectangle, and (2) a parallelogram.

3. Dissect the regular dodecagon which appears below into a square (cut along indicated lines).

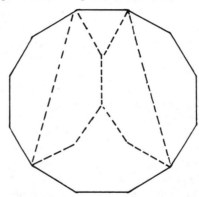

26   The Klein Bottle

This unit will provide students with an insight into one of the very fascinating topics of topology, the Klein bottle. They will be surprised to see a solid figure whose inside cannot be distinguished from its outside.

Performance Objectives

1. *Students will create a Klein bottle from a flat piece of paper.*

2. *Students will characterize a surface by certain topological properties.*

3. *Students will determine the Betti of topological surfaces.*

Teaching Strategies

Before demonstrating how the above situation can be created, briefly discuss the one-sided topological figure, the Klein bottle. The Klein bottle was invented by Felix Klein, a German mathematician, in 1882. If we were to compare the Klein bottle to something realistic, we would use a flexible object, such as a cylinder with a hole cut through the surface. We would then stretch one end to make a wide base and the other end narrowed like the neck of a bottle. But we would have to bring these two-end circles together with their arrows running in opposite directions (see diagram below). Imagine the narrow end of the cylinder bent up, and plunged through the hole on the cylinder and joined to the wide base as in the figure below.

DIAGRAM 1

The hole on the surface of the cylinder should not be actually thought of as a hole but rather an intersection of surfaces covered by a continuation of the surface of the bottle.

Let us now return to the original problem. The situation can easily be visualized if we compare the sleeves of the jacket to the ends of the cylinder and one of the armholes to the hole in the cylinder. We have now created a figure that is topologically equivalent to the Klein bottle.

Once the students have a clear understanding as to what a Klein bottle appears to be, demonstrate how it can be created from a piece of paper. In order to construct a Klein bottle, what we are supposed to do with the flat piece of paper is to join the respective corners of the edges AB to A′B′, but we are also to join the remaining edges AB′ to A′B.

DIAGRAM 2

First create a cylinder by folding the sheet of paper in half and joining the open edges with a strip of tape. Cut a slot through the thickness of the paper nearest you about a quarter of the distance from the top. This will correspond to the "hole" in the surface of the cylinder. Fold the model in half and push the lower end through the slot. Join the edges as indicated by the arrows in the diagram. It is easily seen that this paper model is topologically identical to the Klein bottle created from the cylinder.

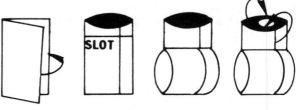

DIAGRAM 3

If we were now to examine the Klein bottle and try to distinguish the outside from the inside, and vice versa, we would find it impossible to do so. It would be evident that the surface is one-sided and edgeless, a notion very unusual to geometric figures.

Since it may be difficult to recognize a Klein bottle or any surface whose shape has been extremely distorted, it is necessary to be able to characterize each surface by simpler topological properties. Two of the properties have already been mentioned: number of edges and number of sides. A Klein bottle was found to be one-sided and have no edges. A third distinguishing feature of these surfaces is the *Betti number*. The Betti number is the maximum number of cross cuts (a simple cut with a pair of scissors which begins and ends on the edge) that can be made on a surface without dividing it into more than one piece. This means that a figure in the shape of a disk has a Betti number zero, since any cross cut will divide it into two pieces. On the other hand a cylinder has a Betti number of one.

Ask students why it would be difficult to determine the Betti number of a doughnut shaped figure or a Klein bottle using the cross cut method. Most students should realize that the problem here is that both of these topological figures contain no edges. Therefore, an alternate method using a *loop-cut* (it starts at any point on the surface, and returns to it without crossing itself, avoiding the edge entirely) provides another way of determining the Betti number. When using the loop-cut to determine the Betti number, we count the number of edges and say that the Betti number equals the number of loop-cuts we can make in a surface without dividing it into more pieces than there were edges. A doughnut shaped figure requires two loop-cuts: one horizontally and the other vertically so the Betti number is two. The Klein bottle also requires two loop-cuts as shown in the diagram below.

DIAGRAM 4

Postassessment

1. Have students determine the Betti number of the following surfaces:
   a. a tube
   b. a punctured tube
   c. a punctured sphere

2. Have students determine which figures would be created if you cut a Klein bottle in half.

27 The Four Color Map Problem

Topology is a branch of mathematics related to geometry. Figures discussed may appear on plane surfaces or on three-dimensional surfaces. The topologist studies those properties of a figure that remain *after* the figure has been distorted or stretched according to a set of rules. A piece of string with its ends connected may take on the shape of a circle, or a square. In going through this transformation, the order of the "points" along the string does not change. This retention of ordering has survived the distortion of shape, and is a property that attracts the interest of topologists.

Performance Objectives

1. Students will state the Four Color Map Problem.

2. Given a geographical map on a plane surface, the student will show, by example, that four colors are sufficient to successfully color the entire map.

Preassessment

Students should know the meaning of common boundaries and common vertices as applied to geographical maps on a plane surface.

Teaching Strategies

Begin by indicating that this problem was only recently solved with the extensive aid of computers. Previously it was considered one of the famous unsolved problems of mathematics.

Figure 1

Have students analyze this fictional, geographic map of eight different countries, and list all countries that have a common boundary with country H and countries that share a common vertex with region H. A map will be considered correctly colored when each country is completely colored and two countries that share a common boundary have different colors. Two countries sharing a common vertex may also share the same color. Have students color in several maps according to the rules for coloring as stated above. (*b*/blue; *r*/red; *y*/yellow; *g*/green)

Figure 2

This map consists of two regions with one common boundary and therefore requires two colors to color correctly.

This map consists of three different regions and the students should conclude that three different colors are required to color it correctly. It seems as though a map with two regions requires two colors and a map with three regions requires three colors.

Ask the students if they can devise a map that has three different countries that will require less than three colors to color it. As an example see Figure 4.

Figure 4

Since the innermost country and the outermost country share no common boundary, they may share the color red and still retain their separate identity.

It seems reasonable to conclude that if a three-country map can be colored with less than three colors, a four-region map can be colored with less than four colors. Have the students create such a map.

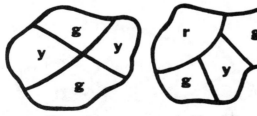

Figure 5   Figure 6

Figure 5 has four regions and requires only two colors for correct coloring. Figure 6 also consists of four regions and requires three colors for correct coloring.

Challenge students to devise a map that consists of four countries and requires exactly four colors for correct coloring. Before undertaking such a task students should now realize that this map calls for each of the four countries to share a common boundary with the other three. Figure 7 is an example of this map.

Figure 7

Ask students to take the next logical step in this series of map-coloring problems. They should come up with the idea of coloring maps involving five distinct regions. It will be possible to draw maps that have five regions and require two, three, or four colors to be colored correctly. The task of drawing a five-country map that *requires* five colors for correct coloring will be impossible. This curiosity can be generalized through further investigation and students should arrive at the idea that any map, on a plane surface, with any number of regions, can be successfully colored with four or fewer colors.

It is more satisfying to present the problem as a direct challenge in the following form: "Can you draw a geographic map, on a plane surface, with any number of regions, that requires five colors to be correctly colored?" This is the statement of the Four Color Problem. It should be noted that whereas the Three Famous Problems of antiquity have been proved to be impossible many years ago, this problem was only solved recently.

Postassessment

1. In a paragraph, using diagrams, describe what is meant by The Four Color Problem of Topology.

2. Using the colors *g*/green, *r*/red, *b*/blue, *y*/yellow, show that it is possible to correctly color each of the following maps with four or fewer colors.

(a)

(b)

(c)

3. Draw a map that has an infinite number of regions but requires only two colors for correct coloring.

Reference
Appel, K. and Haken, W. "The Solution of the Four-Color-Map Problem." *Scientific American* 237, no. 4 (December 1977): 108–21.

28 Mathematics on a Bicycle

With the many variations of gears on the traditional ten speed bicycle, there are lots of applications of mathematics. These ought to help students better understand their bicycles while at the same time reinforce their mathematics.

Performance Objectives
1. Given the number of teeth (or sprockets) in the front and rear sprocket wheels, and diameter of the wheel, students will find gear ratios and distance traveled with each turn of the pedals. (New vocabulary will be developed.)

2. Students will be able to explain why pitch is important.

Preassessment
Students should have the basic skills of algebra, and be somewhat familiar with a bicycle.

Teaching Strategies
The adult bicycles which we shall consider have two wheels, front and rear cable brakes, gears—either three, five or ten, and are made of steel in its various alloys.

Let's examine first the differences in gearing between the three and ten speed bicycles, and in particular the mechanism of the ten speed bicycle.

In a three speed bicycle the gearing mechanism is located within the rear hub (or axle). It is a clutch type

Cross section

mechanism with pieces that interlock within the hub. It has constraints in that no ratio greater than the inside diameter of the rear hub can exist.

On a ten speed bicycle the back wheel has five sprocket wheels called a cluster, with the largest sprocket wheel closest to the spokes and then the rest gradually getting smaller. The gearing (i.e., the connection of sprocket wheels by a chain) is obtained by moving the chain from one sprocket to the other by means of a derailleur.

Let's examine closely the basic set-up.

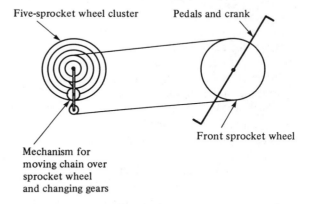

Five-sprocket wheel cluster   Pedals and crank

Mechanism for moving chain over sprocket wheel and changing gears

Front sprocket wheel

There exists a front and rear sprocket wheel with teeth set in gear by a connecting chain. The numbers of teeth on the front and rear sprocket wheels are important. Suppose the front sprocket wheel has 40 teeth and the rear sprocket wheel has 20 teeth; the ratio would then be 40/20 or 2. This means that the rear sprocket wheel turns twice every time the front sprocket wheel turns once. But the rear sprocket wheel is attached to the bicycle wheel and a translation of energy again occurs depending on the diameter of the wheel. On a ten speed bicycle the diameter of the wheel (including the tire) is 27 inches. This arrangement is shown in the diagram below.

The relationship (when the bicycle wheel is included in the consideration is: gear ratio = ratio × diameter = $\frac{2}{1} = 27'' = 54$. The number generated here is usually between 36 and 108. It gives a comparison between gears and is useful for relating gear ratios to work performed.

For example, a rider using a sprocket wheel with 46 teeth in the front and a 16 tooth wheel in the rear along with a 27″ wheel gets a rear ratio of $77.625 \approx 78$. Another rider using a 50 tooth front sprocket wheel and 16 tooth sprocket wheel in the rear gets a gear ratio of $84.375 \approx 84$, which would be harder to pedal than a 78 gear ratio.

Where does this extra difficulty in pedaling benefit the rider? If one multiplies the gear ratio obtained in the formula above by π, one gets the distance traveled forward with each turn of the pedals. Students should recall that Circumference = π × Diameter.

For example, the rider with the 78 gear ratio goes approximately 245 inches forward for each turn of the pedals, while the rider with the 84 gear ratio goes approximately 264 inches forward for each complete turn of the pedals. Hence the increase in work (increased difficulty in pedaling) is returned in greater distance per pedal revolution.

Now let us examine applications of various gearing ratio to the average rider.

Suppose Mr. Carter was riding comfortably on level ground in a 78 gear ratio and then he came to a rather steep hill. Should he switch to a higher or lower gear ratio?

Your reasoning should be as follows: If Mr. Carter switches to an 84 gear ratio, he will go 264 inches forward for each turn of the pedals. This requires a certain amount of work. To overcome the effects of gravity to get up the hill requires additional energy. So Mr. Carter would probably end up walking his bicycle. If Mr. Carter had switched to a lower gear he would use less energy to turn the pedals and the additional energy required to climb the hill would make his gearing feel about the same as the 78 gear ratio. So the answer is to switch to a lower number gear ratio.

Mr. Carter will have to turn the pedal more revolutions to scale the hill; more than if he had chosen the 84 gear ratio and more than if he stayed in the 78 gear

ratio. Remember, his gearing only feels like 78 because of the hill. This is the "trade-off" Mr. Carter made: more revolutions at a constant torque (angular force) instead of the same number of revolutions per distance with varying force.

The benefit of this "trade-off" is understood by comparing the human body to the engine. An engine works most effectively at a constant torque than a varying torque and compensates by changing gear ratios with changing speed and revolutions per minute.

A more concise description is given below. A car uses gears to overcome static friction and accelerate to operating speed while providing constant torque or less torque than overload to the engine. This is not similar to the bicycle because the human machine can overcome an increase in torque for the short period of time to accelerate the bicycle. When a bicycle is in motion, the only force needed to keep it in motion at constant speed on level ground is that required to overcome internal friction and wind resistance. This is the same for a car. Should a rider wish to accelerate quickly, he would want to turn the pedals as fast as possible. All machines (including the human machine) have optimum torque capacity for this. There are two things that can happen to prevent the machine from reaching its maximum possible speed. First, if the torque is too high, it prevents rapid spin. This corresponds to a car in third gear trying to pass without a "downshift". The engine doesn't have the power for rapid acceleration and can only accelerate slowly. The same is true for a rider trying to accelerate quickly in the "harder gears"; he is without the necessary power. Second is "spin-out". This corresponds to when your car reaches 30 m.p.h. in first gear and cannot turn any faster even though there exists power for greater distance with each turn. An example is a manual shift car accelerating from a light in first without shifting. This compares on a bicycle to the rider turning the pedals as fast as possible but not at maximum force.

If the rider reaches maximum spin at maximum torque, he will reach maximum speed.

At this point you might want to have your students try some applications.

Model Problem: Mr. Bannister can turn a 68 gear ratio at 100 r.p.m. or a 72 gear ratio at 84 r.p.m. For maximum speed which should Mr. Bannister choose? (These are the very considerations bicycle racers use in determining which gear to use for the final sprint). Assume these speeds are constant for the duration of the sprint.

Solution: A 68 gear ratio times $\pi = 214$ inches per revolution (approximately). If Mr. Bannister spins 100 r.p.m., he is traveling at 21,400 inches/min. or 20.27 m.p.h.

A 72 gear ratio times $\pi = 226$ inches per revolution (approximately) at a rate of 84 r.p.m. would produce a speed of 18,984 inches/min. or 17.98 m.p.h. Therefore Mr. Bannister would be better off sprinting in the 68 gear ratio.

As mentioned earlier, these torque and spin performance items are given careful attention by racers. A racer will carefully select his back sprocket wheel cluster depending on the course. A relatively flat course would necessitate a 13–18 tooth range in the rear sprocket wheel cluster with a 47 tooth inner front sprocket wheel and 50 tooth outer front sprocket wheel.

This is where the ten speeds come from. When the chain is on the 47 tooth sprocket wheel, there are 5 different gear ratios as the rear derailleur moves the chain through the 5 rear sprocket wheels. When the chain is on the 50 tooth sprocket wheel, there are again 5 different gear ratios.

— Front Derailler

— 50 Teeth

— 47 Teeth

There is one other consideration a racer will make in selecting his gears and that is inertia. You will notice that a 54 front sprocket wheel and 18 tooth rear sprocket wheel gives the same gear ratio as would a 48 tooth front sprocket wheel and a 16 tooth rear sprocket wheel; that is, 48/16 = 3. The rider will choose the 48/16 because work is expended without return to accelerate through an angular acceleration a sprocket wheel of larger radius than a sprocket wheel of smaller radius due to inertia considerations. Since a 10″ radius sprocket wheel is the smallest to take the heavy shear forces, a 34 tooth sprocket wheel is the smallest available. We are currently using ½ pitch (distance between teeth), an improvement over 1″ pitch to increase the number of ratios without letting sprocket wheels get too large. A well-made sprocket wheel would look like the diagram below, where most of the unnecessary mass is cut out.

Inertia = M × distance from the axle of rotation squared. The smaller the distance, the smaller the inertia.

Thus in selecting a ten speed bicycle remember that with each difference in price goes a difference in thought toward design, performance, and work required for riding.

As a final example many inexpensive bicycles really only have 6–8 speeds because of duplication. Consider our previous example on inertia, where the choice was between a 48 tooth and 54 tooth front sprocket wheel. We saw duplication of the same gear ratio with a 16 and 18 rear sprocket wheel. This case occurs on many less expensive bicycles.

Postassessment

1. Lisa approaches a hill which raises whatever gear ratio she is in by 10. Lisa cannot pedal anything harder than a 62 gear ratio. If her 3 speed bicycle has 48, 58, and 78 gear ratio, which should she use?

2. How far forward with each revolution of the pedals will a 78 gear ratio move a bicycle whose wheel radius is 27″?

3. Josh can spin a 72 gear ratio 80 r.p.m. and a 96 gear ratio 48 r.p.m. Which gives a greater velocity?

29   Mathematics and Music

Students who are acquainted with operations on fractions but whose knowledge of music theory is limited will find a correlation between these fields.

Performance Objectives
1) *Students will demonstrate knowledge of certain formulas relating pitch of a note to properties of a string or an air column.*

2) *Students will know how to create Pythagoras' diatonic scale.*

3) *Students will show how Euclid proved that an octave is less than six whole tones.*

Preassessment
Obtain a stringed instrument such as a banjo, violin or a guitar. If these are unavailable the science department can probably lend you a sonometer, which is a scientific instrument with strings used in experimentation.

Perform the following three demonstrations. In each case, have students determine whether the pitch becomes higher or lower.

1) Pluck a string, tighten it, then pluck it again.

2) Pluck a string. Then by pressing down on the middle of the string (fretting) cause only half the string to vibrate.

3) Using two strings of different diameters (thickness), pluck each one.

Teaching Strategies
Elicit from the students the following three facts:

1) As tension increases, pitch becomes higher.

2) As length decreases, pitch becomes higher.

3) As diameter decreases, pitch becomes higher.

At this point explain that the above is grounded in mathematical formulas. However, these formulas use frequency, which is the number of vibrations of the string per second, rather than pitch. Since the pitch of a tone gets higher whenever the frequency increases, it will not really alter the formulas. They are:

$$\frac{F_1{}^2}{F_2{}^2} = \frac{T_1}{T_2}; \quad \frac{F_1}{F_2} = \frac{L_2}{L_1}; \quad \frac{F_1}{F_2} = \sqrt{\frac{D_2}{D_1}}$$

$$\left(\begin{array}{c}\text{strings are} \\ \text{same type}\end{array}\right) \quad \left(\begin{array}{c}\text{tension} \\ \text{constant}\end{array}\right) \quad \left(\begin{array}{c}\text{length and ten-} \\ \text{sion constant}\end{array}\right)$$

where F = frequency
      T = tension
      D = diameter
          of string

Have students try numerical examples: A string which vibrates at a frequency of 400 vps (vibra-tions per second) is 20 inches long. A second string of the same type is plucked in a similar manner. (The tension being the same as in the first case.) If its frequency is 800 vps, how long is it? Have them solve $\frac{400}{800} = \frac{L_2}{20}$, concluding that the length of the second string is 10 inches. Another example could be the effect on the tension if the frequency of a string doubles. Elicit that the tension quadruples. $\left(\frac{1^2}{2^2} = \frac{1}{4}\right)$

Music and mathematics are also related to the creation of a scale. Pythagoras, familiar to most students for his work with the right triangle, produced a scale that could make beautiful melodies, but limited the combination of tones possible and the use of harmony.

Pythagoras felt that those tones which were particularly pleasing, or *consonant,* were related to the numbers 1, 2, 3 and 4. He took several strings of the same length, letting the note C be the fundamental tone. If the sonometer is used, the teacher can demonstrate the basics of what Pythagoras did. This means that the string vibrates as a whole (See Diagram 1). To obtain the note C an octave higher, the string must vibrate in two parts, i.e., have twice the frequency (See Diagram 2). One can also accomplish the same thing by dividing a string into two parts of the ratio 1:2 (See Diagram 3).

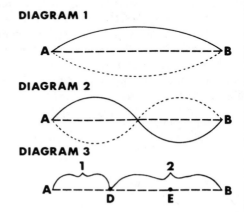

DIAGRAM 1

DIAGRAM 2

DIAGRAM 3

In Diagram 3, vibrating $\overline{AD}$ and $\overline{DB}$ separately will have the same effect of producing 2 notes an octave apart. Thus, if C corresponds to the number 1, then C an octave higher would correspond to the number $\frac{2}{1}$ or 2. Pythagoras also added notes F and G corresponding to $\frac{4}{3}$ and $\frac{3}{2}$ respectively. Ask the students how the string can be divided into the ratio 3:2. Elicit that the string can be divided into five parts to obtain the result.

This is one reason why this note can be called a perfect fifth. To obtain a note corresponding to $\frac{4}{3}$ the string should be divided into seven parts as shown.

However, this note is called a fourth and not a seventh.

Pythagoras added to his scale $\frac{3}{2}$G or $\frac{3}{2} \cdot \frac{3}{2}$C $= \frac{9}{4}$C. Since C = 1 and the octave C = 2, $\frac{9}{4}$C $= 2\frac{1}{4}$C would not fit between these notes. Chal lenge the students to find a tone "basically" the same that would fit between C and its octave. Have them recall that doubling or halving a frequency only changes a tone by an octave. Thus, instead of $\frac{9}{4}$, Pythagoras used $\frac{1}{2}$ of $\frac{9}{4}$ or $\frac{9}{8}$. By adding the third harmonic of each successive tone (i.e. multiplying by $\frac{3}{2}$), students will be able to obtain tones whose relative frequencies are $1, \frac{3}{2}, \frac{9}{8}, \frac{27}{16}, \frac{81}{64}, \frac{243}{128}$. Of course, some additional "halving" was done when needed as in the case of $\frac{9}{8}$. Pythagoras' diatonic scale is thus obtained.

C	D	E	F	G	A	B	C	
1	$\frac{9}{8}$	$\frac{81}{64}$	$\frac{4}{3}$	$\frac{3}{2}$	$\frac{27}{16}$	$\frac{243}{128}$	2	$\left(\begin{array}{c}\text{Relative} \\ \text{Frequencies}\end{array}\right)$

G, which occupies the fifth position, is considered a perfect fifth. This occurs whenever the ratio of the fifth to the first is $\frac{3}{2}$. Throughout the discussion, the fact that frequencies are in the same ratio as their lengths should be stressed.

Have students study the scale in its new form. Elicit that there is a constant ratio of $\frac{9}{8}$ between notes (except between E and F and between B and C where the ratio is $\frac{256}{243}$). It should also be noted that $\frac{9}{8}$ corresponds to a whole tone (W) while the other is called a semitone (S). Thus, the pattern obtained is as follows:

	C	D	E	F	G	A	B	C
1		$\frac{9}{8}$	$\frac{81}{64}$	$\frac{4}{3}$	$\frac{3}{2}$	$\frac{27}{16}$	$\frac{243}{128}$	2
	W	W	S	W	W	W	S	

This is called a major scale.

However, there is some difficulty with harmony. When one sounds a tone on a musical instrument it not only vibrates in one piece making the fundamental tone, but also in parts creating tones called overtones. The overtones have 2, 3, 4 and 5 times the frequency of the fundamental. The fifth overtone corresponds to 5 or $\frac{5}{4}$ if it is to be placed between 1 and 2 (recall continuous halving like $\frac{1}{2} \cdot \frac{1}{2}$ creates a similar tone). The closest tone on the Pythagorean scale is E of frequency $\frac{81}{64}$. When a C is played and then followed by an E, the ear expects to hear the same E just heard as an overtone of C. However, to the individual the Pythagorean E can be quite disturbing. This disturbance is due to the fact that the two E's involved have only slightly different frequencies, one being $\frac{81}{64}$ and the other $\frac{5}{4}$ or $\frac{80}{64}$.

Postassessment

1) If the tension is constant and the length is increased, how is a string's pitch affected?

2) How does string tightening affect pitch?

3) Suppose C corresponds to $\frac{4}{5}$ instead of 1 in Pythagoras' scale. Find the relative frequencies of the next 8 notes of this major scale.

30   Mathematics In Nature

Performance Objective
Students will identify and explain where mathematics is found in nature in at least one situation.

Preassessment
A famous sequence of numbers (*The Fibonacci Numbers*) was the direct result of a problem posed by Leonardo of Pisa in his book *Liber Abaci* (1202) regarding the regeneration of rabbits. A brief review of this problem indicates that the total number of pairs of rabbits existing each month determined the sequence: 1,1,2,3,5,8,13,21,34,55, 89,. . . .

Fibonacci Numbers have many interesting properties and have been found to occur in nature.

Teaching Strategies
Have students divide each number in the Fibonacci sequence by its right hand partner to see what sequence develops. They will get a series of fractions:

$$\frac{1}{1}, \frac{1}{2}, \frac{2}{3}, \frac{3}{5}, \frac{5}{8}, \frac{8}{13}, \frac{13}{21}, \frac{21}{34}, \frac{34}{55}, \frac{55}{89}, \cdots$$

Ask students if they can determine a relationship between these numbers and the leaves of a plant (have a plant on hand). From the standpoint of Fibonacci Numbers, one may observe two items: (1) the number of leaves it takes to go (rotating about the stem) from any given leaf to the next one 'similarly placed' (i.e., above it and in the same direction) on the stem; and (2) the number of revolutions as one follows the leaves in going from one leaf to another one 'similarly placed'. In both cases, these numbers turn out to be the Fibonacci numbers.

In the case of leaf arrangement, the following notation is used: $\frac{3}{8}$ means that it takes three revolutions and eight leaves to arrive at the next leaf 'similarly placed'. In general, if we let r equal the number of revolutions, and s equal the number of leaves it takes to go from any given leaf to one 'similarly placed', then $\frac{r}{s}$ will be the *phyllotaxis* (the arrangement of leaves in plants). Have students look at Figure 1 and try to find the plant ratio. Draw a diagram on the board, and if possible, provide a live plant.

In this figure, the, plant ratio is $\frac{5}{8}$.

Figure 1

The pine cone, also presents a Fibonacci application. The bracts on the cone are considered to be modified leaves compressed into smaller space. Upon observation of the cone, one can notice two spirals, one to the left (clockwise) and the other to the right (counterclockwise). One spiral increases at a sharp angle, while the other spiral increases more gradually. Have students consider the steep spirals and count them as well as the spirals that increase gradually. Both numbers should be Fibonacci numbers. For example, a white pine cone has five clockwise spirals and eight counterclockwise spirals. Other pine cones may have different Fibonacci ratios. Later, have students examine the daisy to see where the Fibonacci ratios apply to it.

If we look closely at the ratios of consecutive Fibonacci numbers, we can approximate their decimal equivalents. Some are:

(1) $\frac{2}{3} = .666667$ (2) $\frac{3}{5} = .600000$

(3) $\frac{89}{144} = .618056$ (4) $\frac{144}{233} = .618026$

Continuing in this manner, we approach what is known as the *golden ratio*. Point B in Figure 2 divides line $\overleftrightarrow{AC}$ into the golden ratio, $\frac{AB}{BC} = \frac{BC}{AC} \approx .618034$.

Figure 2

Now consider the series of golden rectangles (Fig. 3a and 3b), those whose dimensions are chosen so that the ratio of $\frac{width}{length}$ is the golden ratio (i.e., $\frac{w}{1} = \frac{1}{w+1}$)

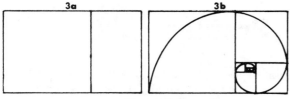

Figure 3

If the rectangle (Fig. 3a) is divided by a line into a square and a golden rectangle, and if we keep partitioning each new golden rectangle in the same way, we can construct a 'logarithmic spiral' in the successive squares (Fig. 3b). This type of curve is frequently found in the arrangements of seeds in flowers or in the shapes of seashells and snails. Bring in illustrations to show these spirals. (Fig. 4)

Figure 4

For another example of mathematics in nature, students should consider the pineapple. Here there are three distinct spirals of hexagons: a group of *five* spirals winding gradually in one direction, a second group of *13* spirals winding more steeply in the same direction, and a third group of *eight* spirals winding in the opposite direction. Each group of spirals consists of a Fibonacci number. Each pair of spirals interacts to give Fibonacci numbers. Figure 5 shows a representation of the pineapple with the scales numbered in order. This order is determined by the distance (relative) each hexagon is from the bottom. That is, the lowest is numbered 0, the next higher one is numbered 1. Note hexagon 42 is slightly higher than hexagon 37.

Figure 5

See if students can note three distinct sets of spirals in Figure 5 which cross each other, starting at the bottom. One spiral is the 0,5,10, etc., sequence, which increases at a slight angle. The second spiral is the 0,13,26, etc., sequence, which increases at a steeper angle. The third spiral has the 0,8,16, etc., sequence, which lies in the opposite direction from the other two. Have students figure out the common difference between the numbers in each sequence. In this case, the differences are 5,8,13, all of which are Fibonacci numbers. Different pineapples may have different sequences.

In concluding this topic, consider briefly the regeneration of male bees. Male bees hatch from unfertilized eggs; female bees from fertilized eggs. The teacher should guide students in tracing the regeneration of the male bees. The following pattern develops:

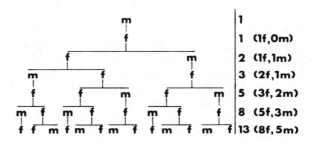

It should be obvious by now that this pattern is the Fibonacci sequence.

Postassessment

1) Ask students to explain two distinct ways mathematics manifests itself in nature.
2) Have students find examples of Fibonacci numbers in nature (other than those presented in this unit) and have them explain the manner in which the sequence is used.

References

Brother U. Alfred, *An Introduction to Fibonacci Discovery.* San Jose, Calif.: The Fibonacci Association, 1965.

Bicknell, M. and Verner E. Hoggatt, Jr., *A Primer for the Fibonacci Numbers.* San Jose, Calif.: The Fibonacci Association, 1972.

Hoggatt, Verner E., Jr. *Fibonacci and Lucas Numbers.* Boston: Houghton Mifflin, 1969.

31 The Birthday Problem

Students are fascinated by problems that involve surprise or unpredictable outcomes. The "birthday problem" will engage them in the study of mathematical probability.

Performance Objective

In problems involving sequences of successive events, such as indications of birthdays, tossing of coins, drawing of cards, throwing of dice, students will calculate the probability that a specified outcome (a) occurs at least once, (b) fails to occur at all.

Preassessment

Ask the class what they think the probability is of two students in the class sharing the same birthday. The students will respond that the chances of this being true are remote. Surprise them by telling them that, in a class of 30 students, the probability of at least two students having the same birthday is approximately 0.68 (a probability of 1.00 indicates an absolute certainty). In a class of 35 students, this probability rises to about 0.80. Restate these probabilities in the language of "odds." Point out that the odds in favor of the desired outcome in the first instance are better than two to one and in the second about four to one. Ditto and distribute a list of the 40 Presidents of the U.S.A. with the dates of their birth and death next to their names. Give students time to look for any dates the Presidents had in common. (Two, Polk and Harding, were born on November 2; two, Fillmore and Taft, died on March 8; and three, Adams, Jefferson, and Monroe, died on July 4.) Now take a class survey to determine if any students share the same birthday. If they do, this fact will reinforce the probability figures and will help convince them of the statistical plausibility. If they do not, indicate that no claim of absolute certainty was made.

Teaching Strategies

Review the following fundamental principles the students will need to know. Mathematical probabilities are stated as decimals (or equivalent fractions) between 0.00 and 1.00, and a probability of 0 (zero) means that a particular outcome is impossible while a probability of 1 (one) means that a particular outcome is a certainty.

Each of the principles enumerated here may be illustrated by simple examples in the tossing of coins, the throwing of dice, the drawing of cards, etc. For example, the probability of throwing a total of 13 with a pair of ordinary dice is equal to zero, while the probability of throwing some number between two and 12 inclusive is equal to one. The probability of a desired outcome occurring can be calculated by forming a fraction whose numerator represents the number of "acceptable" or "successful" outcomes and whose denominator represents the sum of the "successful" outcomes and the "unsuccessful" outcomes or "failures." Symbolically, $P = \dfrac{S}{S + F}$ or $P = \dfrac{S}{T}$. P represents the probability of a particular event occurring, S the number of successful outcomes, F the number of failures, and T the total number of outcomes possible. Either form of this fraction may be converted to a decimal between zero and one, since the numerator may never exceed the denominator.

The students should also note that the probability of a desired outcome <u>failing</u> to occur would be equal to $\dfrac{F}{S + F}$. Since $\dfrac{S}{S + F} + \dfrac{F}{S + F} = \dfrac{S + F}{S + F} = 1$, it follows that $\dfrac{S}{S + F} = 1 - \dfrac{F}{S + F}$.

The students should now state in words that the probability of a desired outcome <u>occurring</u> is equal numerically to 1.00 minus the probability of this outcome failing to occur. This statement enables them to complete the lesson.

Students should be familiar with a fundamental theorem of probability and it is presented here without proof: If the probability of an event is P_1, and if, after it has happened, the probability of a second event is P_2, then the probability that both events will happen is $P_1 P_2$. Point out that this principle may be generalized to calculate the probability that a sequence of n events will occur, given that each preceding event has occurred, and that the result would be $P_1 P_2 P_3 P_4 \ldots P_n$. For example, the students, by performing the following activities, will realize that the probability of drawing a spade from an ordinary deck of 52 cards is 13/52 or 0.25 and the probability of <u>not</u> drawing a spade is 39/52 or 0.75; where both probabilities refer to the drawing of a single card from the deck; they should note that 0.25 = 1.00 − 0.75. The probability of tossing a head, followed by a tail, followed by another tail, where a "true" coin is tossed three times in succession, is $1/2 \cdot 1/2 \cdot 1/2$ or 1/8, illustrating the use of the fundamental principle for dealing with successive events.

Back to the birthday problem. You might point

out that it will be simpler to calculate the probability that *no* students in the class share the same birthday and then to subtract this result from 1.00, than to directly calculate the probability that at least two students in the class have the same birthday. Help the students to formulate the following representation of the probability that *no* students in the class share the same birthday:

$$\frac{365}{365} \cdot \frac{364}{365} \cdot \frac{363}{365} \cdot \frac{362}{365} \cdot \frac{361}{365} \cdot \frac{360}{365} \cdot \frac{359}{365} \cdot \frac{358}{365} \cdot \frac{357}{365} \cdot \frac{356}{365} \cdot \cdot \cdot \cdot$$

There will be as many fractions in this product as there are students in the class. Note that this formulation is based on an ordinary year of 365 days. If any of your students has a February 29 birthday, use denominators of 366 and have the first fraction read 366/366.

Explain that these fractions represent the probabilities that students questioned in sequence as to their birthdays would *not* name a day already mentioned by a preceding student. Point out the fundamental principle for calculating the probability of successive events—sequential questioning. They will be interested in learning how they can best perform the sequence of multiplications and divisions—the simplest approach is through the use of calculators.

The students will discover that the value of their product has decreased to about 0.32 when the number of factors has reached 30, and to about 0.20 when the number of factors has reached 35. Since these figures represent the probabilities that no students in the class shared the same birthday, they represent "failures," in the terminology of this problem. Using the principle of subtraction from 1.00, already mentioned, to arrive at the probabilities of "successes"—the probabilities that at least two students in the class share the same birthday—we arrive at 0.68 or 0.80 or some other high decimal, depending on the size of the class. When the number of people in a group reaches just 55, the probability of finding at least two with the same birthday reaches the astonishing value of 0.99!

Evaluation

Students who have met the performance objective will be able to answer these or similar probabilities correctly:

1. Represent the probability that, given a group of 15 people, at least 2 share the same birthday.

2. If a coin is tossed into the air five times, what is the probability that (a) none of the tosses will turn up "heads" and (b) at least one of the tosses will turn up "heads"?

3. If a card is drawn from an ordinary deck of 52 cards, examined and replaced, and if this is repeated four times, what is the probability that (a) at least one of the cards drawn is a spade, and (b) none of the cards drawn is an ace?

32 The Structure of the Number System

Performance Objectives

Given any number, the student will identify it as belonging to the set of natural numbers, integers, rational numbers, real numbers, or complex numbers. The student will also convert any decimal representing a rational number to its equivalent fractional form and vice versa.

Preassessment

Assess students' ability with the following pretest, assuring them, of course, that this is a trial test and they will not be graded on it:

1. Identify the following numbers as belonging to the set of natural numbers, integers, rational numbers, real numbers, or complex numbers (name the "smallest" possible set in each case): -3, 5/3, 17, $\sqrt{2}$, 3.14, 22/7, $\sqrt{-9}$, $.\overline{4}$, 0.2133333 . . . , 2.71828 . . . , 0.121121112 . . . , $.\overline{15}$, $.1\overline{5}$, $-1/4$, $-\sqrt{16}$, etc.

2. Convert each of the following fractions to decimals: 3/8, 7/5, 2/3, 7/9, 5/11, 5/12.

3. Convert each of the following decimals to fractions: 0.875, $.\overline{8}$, .272727 . . . , 0.8333333 . . . .

Students who do well on the pretest have already attained the performance objective. Give them a different assignment while you present this lesson to the rest of the class.

Teaching Strategies

Ask your students to solve a simple linear equation such as $3x + 5 = 11$. When the correct solution, $x = 2$, is offered, ask what kind of number this is. Students may use such terms as "whole number" or "positive number" in their responses. Explain that 2 is a *counting* number and that the set of counting numbers is known mathematically as the set of natural numbers. Elicit other illustrations of natural numbers and have the students describe the set by roster: N =

{1, 2, 3, . . . }. They should note that the elements of this set are ordered and infinite in number, and that the set possesses a first or smallest element, the member 1.

Proceed in a similar fashion to develop the concept of the set of integers. Modify the equation just explored by reversing the two constants: $3x + 11 = 5$. When they obtain $x = -2$ as the solution, the students will volunteer that this is a negative whole number or some other similar description. Introduce the term "integer" if it is not mentioned by the class. They will readily understand that this term is synonymous with the term "whole number" and that the natural numbers just studied are a subset of the set of integers. This can be illustrated by a Venn diagram which, at this stage of the lesson, consists of an inner circle labeled "N" to represent the set of natural numbers and an outer circle labeled "I" to represent the set of integers. This diagram will be built up as the lesson develops by the addition of three more circles, each completely encircling all of the preceding circles. Elicit several illustrations of integers and help your students to describe this set by roster: $I = \{ . . . , -3, -2, -1, 0, 1, 2, 3 . . . \}$. They will note that this set is also an infinite one and that it is ordered, but that it possesses *no* first element.

Now offer the equation $2x + 1 = 6$. When the answer, 5/2, is forthcoming, students will recognize that this number is *not* a member of the set of natural numbers or the set of integers since it is not a whole number but, rather, a fraction. Point out that such numbers are formed by setting up the ratio of two integers, a/b, where the denominator, b, is not equal to zero (ask your students why not!). The term "rational number" derives naturally from the word "ratio." Add the third circle to your Venn diagram, completely enclosing the previous two circles. Label the new circle "Q" for quotient.

Elicit numerous illustrations of rational numbers, including proper and improper fractions, both positive and negative. Students should be aware that the set of rational numbers is infinite and ordered, but that no roster can be prepared for this set. You might explain that the rational numbers are "everywhere dense" and that an infinitude of rationals exists between any two rational numbers.

We are now ready to examine the decimals. Students will generally exhibit some uncertainty as to which of these represent rational numbers. We must consider terminating decimals, nonterminating but repeating decimals, and nonterminating and non-repeating decimals. Your students can obtain some clues by converting a few fractions such as 1/8, 5/9, and 1/6 to decimals by dividing their numerators by their denominators. They will observe that the result

in every case is either a terminating decimal or a nonterminating but repeating decimal. Students can show easily that every terminating decimal represents a rational number by simply writing each one as a decimal fraction.

Next, introduce nonterminating decimals. Students who believe that $0.\overline{3}$ represents a rational number can be challenged to write it in fractional form. Some may recognize this decimal as being equal to 1/3. If so, challenge them with the decimal $0.\overline{5}$ which they obtained earlier themselves by converting 5/9 to a decimal, or with $0.16666 . . .$ which they also obtained themselves by converting 1/6 to a decimal. Ask them whether they could convert these decimals to fractions if they did *not* know the answers! Or, challenge them with the decimal $0.\overline{13}$, for which it is unlikely that they will know the result. If they need your help to convert such decimals to fractions, two illustrations will make the technique clear.

$$N = 0.131313 . . .$$
Multiply by 100:
$$100N = 13.131313 . . .$$
$$N = 0.131313 . . .$$
$$99N = 13 \text{ by subtraction}$$
$$N = \frac{13}{99}$$

$$N = .1666666 . . .$$
Multiply by 10:
$$10N = 1.666666 . . .$$
$$N = 0.166666 . . .$$
$$9N = 1.5 \text{ by subtraction}$$
$$90N = 15$$
$$N = \frac{15}{90} = \frac{1}{6}$$

Provide several illustrations for your students, including some with nonrepeating portions in the decimal before the repetand appears, as in the second example above. Help them to grasp the fact that such decimals represent rational numbers, even though their non-repeating portions may be lengthy, as long as they are finite in length *and* they are followed by repetands of one or more digits.

Your students are now ready to consider the non-terminating, nonrepeating decimals. They are already familiar with some of these, notably $\pi = 3.14159$ . . . and perhaps the square roots of some of the non-perfect squares. (Be certain they understand that such numbers as 22/7 and 3.14 or 3.1416 are only *rational approximations* to the *irrational* number π.) Propose the equation $x^2 + 2 = 7$. Those who are familiar with the square root algorithm may be asked to work out $\sqrt{5}$ to a few decimal places to determine whether a pattern of repetition appears. They will discover, of course, that it does not, since $\sqrt{5} = 2.236\ldots$ and is irrational.

Students unfamiliar with the algorithm may refer to a table of square roots. They will discover that the only square roots which contain a repetand in their decimal representations are those of perfect squares. All other square roots are irrational numbers, since they are nonterminating, nonrepeating decimals. You may also wish to generalize this result to the *n*th roots of nonperfect *n*th powers.

Explain to your students that the set of the rational numbers together with the set of irrational numbers form the set of real numbers. Add a fourth circle to your Venn diagram, labeling it "R," and have it completely enclose the three circles previously drawn. The students should realize that the sets of natural numbers, integers, and rational numbers are each proper subsets of the set of real numbers.

This development of the structure of the number system may be concluded with a brief treatment of the complex numbers. Ask your students to try to solve the equation $x^2 + 4 = 0$. Help them to see why answers such as $+2$ and -2 are incorrect. They should soon realize that no real number squared can equal -4, or any other negative number, for that matter. Explain that numbers which are not real are called "imaginary" and that the imaginary numbers and the real numbers together form the set known as the "complex numbers." You may wish to introduce the symbol $i = \sqrt{-1}$ so they can write a solution for their equation as $+2i$ and $-2i$. Complete the Venn diagram with the fifth and last circle, completely enclosing the other four circles, and showing the real numbers as a proper subset of the complex numbers, "C."

Evaluation

Give students a test similar to the pretest. Compare each student's pre- and posttest answers to measure progress.

33 Excursions in Number Bases

Students learn early in their school careers that the base used in our everyday number system (the "decimal system") is the number 10. Later, they discover that other numbers can serve as bases for number systems. For example, numbers written in base 2 (the "binary system") are used extensively in computer work. This lesson will explore a variety of problems involving numbers written in many different positive integral bases.

Performance Objective

Students will solve a variety of numerical and algebraic problems involving numbers expressed as numerals in any positive integral base b, b ≥ 2.

Preassessment

How far you go in this lesson will depend somewhat on the algebraic background of the class. Question students or evaluate their previous work to determine how well they understand the idea of place value in writing numerals, the meaning of zero and negative exponents, and the techniques for solving quadratic and higher degree equations.

Teaching Strategies

Review briefly the fact that decimal numerals are written by using a system of place values. Point out, for example, that in the numeral *356* the digit *3* represents

300 rather than merely a *3*, the digit *5* represents *50* rather than merely a *5*, while the digit *6* is a units digit and really does represent a *6*. Briefly, $356 = 300 + 50 + 6 = 3(100) + 5(10) + 6 = 3(10)^2 + 5(10)^1 + 6(10)^0$. Likewise, $3,107 = 3(10)^3 + 1(10)^2 + 0(10)^1 + 7(10)^0$. Ask students for further illustrations. If necessary, review or teach at this point the meaning of the zero exponent and also of negative exponents, since these will be used later.

Explain that the use of the number 10 as a base is somewhat arbitrary, and students should note that other numbers can be used as bases. If the number 2 is used as a base, numbers are expressed as sums of powers of 2 rather than as sums of positive integral multiples of powers of 10, and the only digits used to represent numerals are 0 and 1. For example, the number 356 considered above is equal to $256 + 64 + 32 + 4 = 2^8 + 2^6 + 2^5 + 2^2 = 1(2)^8 + 0(2)^7 + 1(2)^6 + 1(2)^5 + 0(2)^4 + 0(2)^3 + 1(2)^2 + 0(2)^1 + 0(2)^0 = 101100100_{\text{two}}$, the subscript indicating the base. In base 3 (where the digits used to represent the numerals are 0, 1, and 2) $356 = 243 + 81 + 27 + 3 + 2(1) = 1(3)^5 + 1(3)^4 + 1(3)^3 + 0(3)^2 + 1(3)^1 + 2(3)^0 = 111012_{\text{three}}$. In base 5 (where the digits used are 0, 1, 2, 3, and 4) $356 = 2(125) + 4(25) + 1(5) + 1(1) = 2(5)^3 + 4(5)^2 + 1(5)^1 + 1(5)^0 = 2411_{\text{five}}$. Subscripts should be written in words rather than in numerals to avoid any possible confusion.

The class should note that when numerals are in base b, the only digits available for such representations are those from zero to $b - 1$, and that if the value of b is greater than 10, new digits must be created to represent the numerals 10, 11, 12, etc. Remind the class that numerals such as 2411_{five} should be read "two, four, one, one, base 5." Provide practice in writing and reading whole numbers in the numerals of bases other than base 10, according to class needs.

Next consider numbers other than integers. Help your students to see that 12.2_{ten} means $1(10)^1 + 2(10)^0 + 2(10)^{-1}$, since $10^0 = 1$ and $10^{-1} = 1/10$, and that this number can be represented in the numerals of other bases just as integers can. For example, in base 5 we have $12.2_{\text{ten}} = 2(5)^1 + 2(5)^0 + 1(5)^{-1}$, since $1/5 = 2/10$, so $12.2_{\text{ten}} = 22.1_{\text{five}}$. Illustrate further with such problems as the conversion of 7.5_{ten} to base 2: $7.5_{\text{ten}} = 1(2)^2 + 1(2)^1 + 1(2)^0 + 1(2)^{-1} = 111.1_{\text{two}}$. Decimal numerals whose decimal parts are $.5(1/2), .25(1/4), .75 (3/4), .125 (1/8)$, etc., can be easily converted to base 2 numerals. For example, $8.75_{\text{ten}} = 1(2)^3 + 1(2)^{-1} + 1(2)^{-2}$, since $.75 = 3/4 = 1/2 + 1/4 = 1/2^1 + 1/2^2 = 2^{-1} + 2^{-2}$, so $8.75_{\text{ten}} = 1000.11_{\text{two}}$. Numbers can also be converted from numeral representations in one base to equivalent numeral representations in another base, where neither base is equal to 10. For example, 12.2_{four} can be represented in base 6 numerals as follows: $12.2_{\text{four}} = 1(4)^1 + 2(4)^0 + 2(4)^{-1} = 4 + 2 + 2/4 = 6 + 3/6 = 1(6)^1 + 0(6)^0 + 3(6)^{-1} = 10.3_{\text{six}}$. In base 10, this is the numeral 6.5. Provide practice with these types of numerical problems according to the interests and abilities of your students.

The class is ready to consider algebraic problems next. Offer the following challenge: "In a certain base b, the number 52 is double the number 25. Find the value of b." The students should note that 52 (read "five, two") really represents the expression $5b + 2$, since $52_b = 5(b)^1 + 2(b)^0$. Accordingly, the problem states that $5b + 2 = 2(2b + 5)$. Solve for b to get $b = 8$. Checking shows that $52_{\text{eight}} = 5(8) + 2 = 42_{\text{ten}}$ and $25_{\text{eight}} = 2(8) + 5 = 21_{\text{ten}}$ and $42 = 2(21)$. The above equation is only a linear one, but the following problem requires the use of a quadratic equation: "In what base b is the number represented by 132 twice the number represented by 33?" You have $132b = 1(b)^2 + 3(b)^1 + 2(b)^0$ and $33_b = 3(b)^1 + 3(b)^0$, so our equation becomes $b^2 + 3b + 2 = 2(3b + 3)$ or $b^2 - 3b - 4 = 0$. Solve for b in the usual fashion to obtain $b = -1$, (which must be rejected since the domain of b is positive), and $b = 4$, the only acceptable solution. Check: $132_{\text{four}} = 1(4)^2 + 3(4)^1 + 2(4)^0 = 1(16) + 3(4) + 2 = 30_{\text{ten}}$ and $33_{\text{four}} = 3(4)^1 + 3(4)^0 = 3(4) + 3 = 15_{\text{ten}}$; and 30 is twice 15. Offer students similar problems. If they have studied the solution of equations of degree higher than two, by synthetic division (since all results will be integral),

include numbers whose representations in the bases being used involve more than three digits. For example: "In what base b is the number represented by the numeral 1213 triple the number represented by the numeral 221?" You have $1(b)^3 + 2(b)^2 + 1(b)^1 + 3(b)^0 = 3[2(b)^2 + 2(b)^1 + 1(b)^0]$ or $b^3 + 2b^2 + b + 3 = 3(2b^2 + 2b + 1)$, which simplifies to $b^3 - 4b^2 - 5b = 0$. Since this equation can be factored without resorting to synthetic division, solve it as follows: $b(b - 5)(b + 1) = 0$ and $b = 0, 5, -1$. As before, the only acceptable solution is the positive one, $b = 5$. Ask the class to check this result.

A final interesting algebraic application of number base problems is suggested by the following: "In base 10, the numeral 121 represents a number that is a perfect square. Does the numeral represent a perfect square in any other positive integral base?" Help your students investigate this problem as follows: $121_b = 1(b)^2 + 2(b)^1 + 1(b)^0 = b^2 + 2b + 1 = (b + 1)^2$. Surprise! The numeral 121 represents a perfect square in *any* positive integral base $b \geq 3$, and is the square of one more than the base number! Are there any other such numerals? Students may discover others by squaring such expressions as $b + 2$ and $b + 3$ to obtain the numerals 144 and 169. These perfect squares in base 10 are also perfect squares in any positive integral base containing the digits used in them ($b \geq 5$ and $b \geq 10$, respectively). It's not necessary for the coefficient of b to equal 1. If you square $2b + 1$, for example, you obtain $4b^2 + 4b + 1 = 441_b$, which will be a perfect square in any positive integral base $b \geq 5$. Invite your students to try to square expressions such as $3b + 1, 2b + 2, 4b + 1$, etc., to obtain other perfect squares. Some may wish to continue this investigation into a search for perfect cubes, perfect fourth powers, etc. Help them to cube $b + 1$, for example, to obtain $b^3 + 3b^2 + 3b + 1$, indicating that the numeral 1331 is a perfect cube in any positive integral base $b \geq 4$ (in base 10, $1331 = 11^3$). As a matter of fact, 1331 is the cube of one more than the base number in each case! This study can be carried as far as the interest and ability of your class permits. Students familiar with the binomial theorem will find it convenient to use in expanding higher powers of such expressions as $b + 1, 2b + 1$, etc.

Evaluation

Students who have met the performance objective will be able to solve problems such as the following:

1. Represent the decimal numeral 78 as a numeral in base 5.

2. The number represented by the numeral 1000.1 in base 2 is represented by what numeral in base 8?

3. In a certain base b, the number represented by the numeral 54 is three times the number represented by the numeral 16. Find the value of b.

4. In a certain base b, the number represented by the numeral 231 is double the number represented by the numeral 113. Find the value of b.

5. In what bases would the numeral 100 represent a

perfect square? In what bases would the numeral 1000 represent a perfect cube? Can you make a generalization of these results?

34   Raising Interest

Students are often confronted with advertisements by savings institutions offering attractive interest rates and frequent compounding of interest on deposits. Since most banks have a variety of programs, it's valuable for potential depositors to understand how interest is calculated under each of the available options.

Performance Objective
Students will use the formula for compound interest to calculate the return on investments at any rate of interest, for any period of time, and for any commonly used frequency of compounding, including instantaneous (continuous) compounding. They will also determine which of two or more alternatives gives the best return over the same time period.

Preassessment
Since this lesson requires the ability to apply the laws of logarithms, question students to be certain they're familiar with these laws. You should also determine the extent to which they are familiar with limits, since the class' background will help you determine how deeply you treat the concept of instantaneous compounding.

Teaching Strategies
Propose the following interesting problem: "In the year 1626, Peter Minuit bought Manhattan Island for the Dutch West India Company from the Indians for trinkets costing 60 Dutch guilders, or about $24. Suppose Indians had been able to invest this $24 at that time at an annual interest rate of 6%, and suppose further that this same interest rate had continued in effect all these years. How much money could the present-day descendants of these Indians collect if (1) only simple interest were calculated, and (2) interest were compounded (a) annually, (b) quarterly and (c) continuously?" The answers to a, b and c should surprise everyone!

Review briefly the formula for simple interest, studied in earlier lessons. The class will recall that simple interest is calculated by taking the product of the principle P, the annual interest rate r, and the

time in years t. Accordingly, you have the formula $I = Prt$, and in the above problem $I = (24)(.06)(354) = \$509.76$ simple interest. Add this to the principle of $24.00 to obtain the amount A of $533.76 available at present. You have just used the formula for "amount," $A = P + Prt$.

With this relatively small sum in mind (for a return after 354 years!) turn to investigate the extent to which this return would have been improved if interest had been compounded annually instead of being calculated on only a simple basis. With a principle P, an annual rate of interest r, and a time $t = 1$, the amount A at the end of the first year is given by the formula $A_1 = P + Pr = P(1 + r)$. (The subscript indicates the year at the end of which interest is calculated.) Now $A_1 = P(1 + r)$ becomes the principle at the beginning of the second year, upon which interest will be credited during the second year. Therefore, $A_2 = P(1 + r) + P(1 + r)r = P(1 + r)(1 + r) = P(1 + r)^2$. Since the last expression represents the principle at the beginning of the third year, you have $A_3 = P(1 + r)^2 + P(1 + r)^2 r = P(1 + r)^2(1 + r) = P(1 + r)^3$. By now, your students will see the emerging pattern and should be able to suggest the generalization for the amount after t years, $A_t = P(1 + r)^t$.

Now try this formula on the $24 investment made in 1626! Assuming annual compounding at 6% per annum, you have $A_{354} = 24(1 + .06)^{354} = 21,801,558,740$. This means that the original $24 is now worth almost $22 billion! Most students are truly surprised by the huge difference between this figure and the figure $533.76 obtained by computing simple interest.

Most banks now compound not annually, but quarterly, monthly, daily, or continuously, so next generalize the formula $A = P(1 + r)^t$ to take into account compounding at more frequent intervals. Help your students observe that if interest is compounded semi-annually, the *periodic rate* would be only *one-half* the annual rate, but the number of periods would be *twice* the number of years: so

$$A = P\left(1 + \frac{r}{2}\right)^{2t}.$$ Likewise, if interest is com-

pounded quarterly $A = P\left(1 + \frac{r}{4}\right)^{2t}$. In general, if interest is compounded n times per year, you have $A = P\left(1 + \frac{r}{n}\right)^{nt}$. This formula may be used for any finite value of n. Letting $n = 4$ in the problem yields $A = 24\left(1 + \frac{.06}{4}\right)^{4(354)} = 24(1.015)^{1416} = 34,365,848,150$. The $24 has now risen to about $34 billion.

Students should note that changing the compounding from annually to quarterly increased the yield by about $12 billion.

Students may now ask whether the yield can be increased indefinitely by simply increasing the frequency of compounding. A complete treatment of this question requires a thorough development of the concept of limits, but an informal, intuitive approach will suffice here. Have students first explore the simpler problem of an investment of $1 at a nominal annual interest rate of 100% for a period of one year. This will give $A = 1\left(1 + \frac{1.00}{n}\right)^{n} = \left(1 + \frac{1.00}{n}\right)^{n}$ Ask the students to prepare a table of values for A for various common values of n, such as $n = 1$ (annual compounding), $n = 2$ (semiannual), $n = 4$ (quarterly), $n = 12$ (monthly). They should note that the amount A does *not* rise astronomically as n increases, but rather rises slowly from $2.00 ($n = 1$) to about $2.60 ($n = 12$). Explain that the amount A would approach, but not quite reach, the value $2.72. (The extent to which you may wish to discuss the fact that $\lim_{n \to \infty}\left(1 + \frac{1}{n}\right)^{n} = e = 2.71828 \ldots$ will depend on the backgrounds and abilities of your math students.)

Since investments generally don't draw 100% interest, you must next convert to a general interest rate or r. Setting $\frac{r}{n} = \frac{1}{k}$, you have $n = kr$, and $A = P\left(1 + \frac{r}{n}\right)^{nt}$ becomes $A = P\left(1 + \frac{1}{k}\right)^{krt} = P\left[\left(1 + \frac{1}{k}\right)^{k}\right]^{rt}$. Clearly, as n approaches infinity so does k, since r is finite, so the expression in brackets approaches the value e as a limit. You then have the formula $A = Pe^{rt}$ *for instantaneous compounding,*

where r is the nominal annual rate of interest and t is the time in years.

Students might be interested in knowing that this formula is a special representation of the general "Law of Growth," which is usually written in the $N = N_0 e^{rt}$ form, where N represents the final amount of a material whose initial amount was N_0. This law has applications in many other areas such as population growth (people, bacteria in a culture, etc.) and radioactive decay of elements (in which case it becomes the "Law of Decay," $N = N_0 e^{-rt}$).

Completing the investment problem, using 2.72 as an approximation to e, you have $A = 24(2.72)^{.06(354)} = 40,780,708,190$.

Students can see that the "ultimate" return on a $24 investment (at a nominal annual interest rate of 6% for 354 years) is about $41 billion.

Students may now apply the formulas developed. Banks currently offer interest rates ranging from 5% to as much as 12% (usually for time deposits of two years or more) and compounding is commonly done quarterly, monthly, daily or continuously. Students can work problems with varying principles, periodic rates, frequencies of compounding and time periods, and compare yields. They'll probably be surprised by what they learn!

Evaluation

Students who have met the performance objective will be able to answer questions such as these:

1. Banks offering 5% annual interest compounded quarterly claim that money doubles in 14 years. Is this claim accurate?

2. If you had $1,000 to invest for two years, would you get a greater return from a savings bank offering a 5% annual rate compounded quarterly or from a commercial bank offering a 4½% annual rate compounded continuously?

3. Banks offering a 6% nominal annual rate compounded continuously on term savings of two years or longer claim that this rate is equivalent to an "effective annual rate" (the rate under annual compounding) of 6.27%. Prove that this is true, assuming a deposit of $500 (the usual minimum) for a period of two years.

35 Reflexive, Symmetric and Transitive Relations

In this lesson students will have the opportunity to explore some properties of mathematical relations between numbers, geometric figures, sets, propositions, persons, places and things.

Performance Objective
Students will identify a given relation as reflexive, symmetric, transitive, or as an equivalence relation.

Preassessment
Ask students to describe what the mathematical term "relation" refers to. If you are not satisfied they understand the term, present some examples before beginning the lesson. You may wish to vary the relations you present students, according to their grade level and background in such areas as algebra, geometry, set theory, number theory, and logic.

Teaching Strategies
Begin with a consideration of a very simple relation such as "is equal to" for real numbers. From their previous math experience, students will recognize that any quantity a is equal to itself; that if a quantity a is equal to another quantity b, then b is also equal to a; and that if a quantity a is equal to another quantity b, and b is in turn equal to a third quantity c, then a is equal to c. Symbolically, we have $a = a$, $a = b \rightarrow b = a$, and $a = b$ and $b = c \rightarrow a = c$. The arrow is read "implies" as in ordinary symbolic logic. (Replace the arrow with the word if the class is unfamiliar with this notation.) Explain that when a quantity a has a given relation to itself (as in $a = a$) that relation is called *reflexive*. Further, when a quantity a has a given relation to another quantity b and this results in b having the same relation to a (as in $a = b \rightarrow b = a$) that relation is called *symmetric*. Add that when a quantity a has a given relation to another quantity b and b has the *same* relation to a third quantity c, and this results in a having that *same* relation to c (as in $a = b$ and $b = c \rightarrow a = c$) that relation is called *transitive*. A relation possessing all three of these properties is an *equivalence relation*.

Now invite students to examine some of the relations with which they are familiar from earlier work in mathematics. You've just established that "is equal to" is an equivalence relation. Follow up by considering the relations "is greater than" and "is less than" for real numbers. Your class will quickly discover that these relations are neither reflexive nor symmetric, but that they *are* transi-

tive. An interesting variation is the relation "is not equal to" for real numbers. Although this relation is not reflexive, it *is* symmetric. Students may also think that this relation is transitive, but a simple counterexample will prove that it is not: $9 + 6 \neq 7 + 2$ and $7 + 2 \neq 11 + 4$, but $9 + 6 = 11 + 4$. So the relation "is not equal to" is not transitive.

Of course, none of the relations just considered is an equivalence relation. Have the class consider other relations, for example: "is a multiple of" (or "is divisible by") and "is a factor of" for integers. Both of these relations are reflexive and transitive, but neither is symmetric. Ask students to prove these facts algebraically. For the first relation, for example, they may write $a = kb$ and $b = mc$, where k and m are integers. Clearly, $a = 1a$ so a is divisible by a (reflexivity); $a/b = k$ since a is divisible by b but $b/a = 1/k$, which is *not* an integer, so b is not divisible by a (no symmetry); $a = kb$ and $b = mc \rightarrow a = k(mc)$ or $a/c = km$, which *is* an integer, since the product of two integers is an integer (the set of integers being closed under multiplication), so a is divisible by c (transitivity).

Consider next some relations in geometry. First explore the relations "is congruent to" and "is similar to" for geometric figures. Students will have little difficulty recognizing that both of these are equivalence relations. Ask the class to examine each of these relations when it is negated. Each will then possess only the symmetric property.

The relations "is parallel to" and "is perpendicular to" are very interesting when applied to lines in a plane and to planes themselves. For example, for lines in a plane, "is parallel to" is symmetric *and* transitive but "is perpendicular to" is *only* symmetric. Ask your students why! They should recall such ideas from geometry as "lines parallel to the same line are parallel to each other" and "lines perpendicular to the same line are parallel to each other." These relations may also be negated as exercises.

Students who have some familiarity with set theory may explore the relations "is equal to" and "is equivalent to" as applied to sets. Since *equal* sets are sets containing identical elements, it's obvious that "is equal to" is an equivalence relation. *Equivalent* sets have the same number of elements (their elements can be placed into one-to-one correspondence with each other), but not necessarily identical ones. A little reflection reveals that "is equivalent to" is also an equivalence relation. Another interesting relation is "is the complement of" as applied to sets. The class should discover that this relation is symmetric, but that it is neither reflexive nor transitive. (If a is the complement of b and b is the complement of c, then a is *not* the complement of c, but rather $a = c$.)

An interesting relation from number theory is "is congruent to, modulo m" for integers. Students familiar with this concept should be able to prove easily that this is an equivalence relation, using simple algebra: $a \equiv a \pmod{m}$ since $a - a = 0m$ (proving the reflexive property); $a \equiv b \pmod{m} \rightarrow b \equiv a \pmod{m}$ since $b - a = -(a - b) = -km$ (proving the symmetric property); $a \equiv b \pmod{m}$ and $b \equiv c \pmod{m} \rightarrow a \equiv c \pmod{m}$ since $a - c = (a - b) + (b - c) = km + pm = (k + p)m$ (proving the transitive property).

Students familiar with symbolic logic may be invited to consider the relation "implies" for propositions (e.g., as designated by p, q, r). The alert student will recognize that this relation is reflexive, $p \rightarrow p$ (since any proposition implies itself) and transitive, $(p \rightarrow q) \wedge (q \rightarrow r) \rightarrow (p \rightarrow r)$ (since this can be proved to be a tautology by using a truth table) but that it is *not* symmetric, $(p \rightarrow q) \rightarrow (q \rightarrow p)$ is *false*, (since the truth of a proposition does *not* guarantee the truth of its converse).

Now broaden the concept of relations from strictly mathematical settings to involve relations between persons, places and things. Your class should find this amusing as well as instructive. Suggest a relation such as "is the father of." A little reflection reveals that this relation is not reflexive, not symmetric and not transitive! It is obvious that a cannot be his own father (not reflexive); that if a is the father of b, then b is the son or daughter and not the father of a (not symmetric); and that if a is the father of b and b is the father of c, then a is the grandfather of c, not the father (not transitive)! Many similar relations may be considered, including "is the mother of," "is the brother of" (caution: *only* transitive, *not* symmetric, since b may be the sister of a), "is

the sister of," "is the sibling of" (this one *is* symmetric), "is the spouse of," "is the ancestor of," "is the descendent of," "is taller than" and "weighs more than." Any of these relations may be explored in the negative sense as well as in the positive one. With respect to places, students may consider relations such as: "is north of," "is west of" (caution: transitivity here is *not* necessarily true if places may be selected from anywhere on the globe rather than from merely a small area or only one country), "is at a higher altitude than," "is exactly one mile from" (symmetric only) and "is less than one mile from" (reflexive *and* symmetric). Relations among things may include "is above," "is older than," "costs as much as" and "costs more than," among others.

Evaluation

Students who have met the performance objective will be able to answer questions such as the following:

1. Identify each of the following relations as reflexive, symmetric, transitive or as an equivalence relation:

(a) "is supplementary to" for angles
(b) "is congruent to" for line segments
(c) "is a subset of" for sets
(d) "is a proper subset of" for sets
(e) "is equivalent to" for propositions
(f) "is wealthier than" for nations
(g) "is smaller than" for objects
(h) "is colder than" for places

2. Prove algebraically that the relation "is complementary to" for acute angles is symmetric but neither reflexive nor transitive.

3. Which of the following relations is reflexive and transitive but not symmetric?

(a) "is a positive integral power of" for real numbers
(b) "has the same area as" for triangles
(c) "is the converse of" for propositions
(d) "is younger than" for people

36 Bypassing An Inaccessible Region

This unit will present the problem of constructing a straight line through an inaccessible region using only straightedge and compasses, and without using the tools in or over this inaccessible region. This activity will provide an opportunity for students to exhibit creativity.

Performance Objectives

1. Given a straight line segment with an endpoint on the boundary of an inaccessible region, students, using straightedge and compasses, will construct another straight line segment collinear with the given one and on the other side of the inaccessible region (an endpoint will be on the boundary of this region).

2. Given one point on either side of an inaccessible region, students, using only straightedge and compasses, will construct two collinear straight line segments, each having one given point as an endpoint and neither intersecting the inaccessible region.

Preassessment

Students should be familiar with the basic geometric constructions using straightedge and compasses.

Teaching Strategies

To generate initial interest, begin this topic by developing a story about two countries which are separated by a mountain, and each of which wants to construct a straight road and tunnel through the mountain. Since neither country can decide how to dig the tunnel, they both decide to construct a road on one side of the mountain at the point where the anticipated tunnel (the continuation of a straight road on the other side of the mountain) will emerge from the mountain. Using only straightedge and compasses they seek to plot the path for this new road.

Once students understand the problem, have them draw a diagram (maps) of this situation.

Figure 1

Students must construct the collinear "continuation of $\overline{SR}$" at point P (using straightedge and compasses) and never touch or go over the inaccessible region.

There are various ways to construct the collinear continuation of $\overline{SR}$ at P. One method is to erect a per-

pendicular (line ℓ) to $\overline{SR}$ at a convenient point N of $\overline{SR}$. Then at a convenient point M of line ℓ a perpendicular (line k) to ℓ is constructed (see Figure 2).

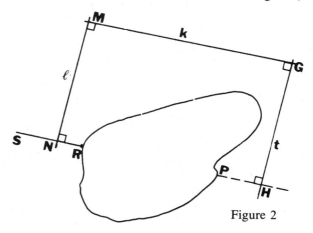

Figure 2

At a convenient point G of line k a perpendicular (line t) to line k is constructed. Point H is then obtained on line t, so that GH = MN. The line constructed perpendicular to line t at point H will be the required line through P and collinear with $\overline{SR}$. (It should be noted that although P was collinear with $\overline{SR}$ it was virtually not needed for the construction.) The justification for this method is that a rectangle (minus part of a side) was actually constructed.

Another method for solving this problem involves replacing the above rectangle with an equilateral triangle, since angles of measure 60° are rather simple to construct. Figure 3 presents this method and ought to be rather self-explanatory.

Figure 3

The problem of constructing a straight line "through" an inaccessible region, when only the two endpoints (at either side of the region) are given, is a much more challenging problem. Naturally an appropriate story can be built around this situation.

To construct two collinear straight line segments at each of two points (P and Q) situated at opposite sides of an inaccessible region, begin by drawing any convenient line segment from point P and construct a perpendicular line to it at a convenient point R. This perpendicular should not intersect the inaccessible region. See Figure 4.

Figure 4

Now construct a perpendicular from Q, to this last line drawn, intersecting it at S. Locate T on $\overleftrightarrow{QS}$ so that PR = QS. Draw $\overline{RT}$. At P construct $\angle RPN \cong \angle PRT$, and at Q construct $\angle TQM \cong \angle QTR$. This completes the required construction, since $\overline{NP}$ and $\overline{QM}$ are extensions of side $\overline{PQ}$ of "parallelogram" PRTQ, and therefore are collinear.

There are many other methods of solving this problem. Many involve constructing similar triangles in order to then construct the two required lines. However students select to approach this problem, they are apt to be led to a creative activity.

Postassessment

1. Have students construct a "continuation" of $\overline{SP}$ on the other side of the inaccessible region

(using only straightedge and compass and not touching or going over the inaccessible region).

Figure 5

2. Have students construct two collinear segments at opposite ends (P and Q) of an inaccessible region (using only straightedge and compasses and not touching or going over the inaccessible region). These postassessment items become more challenging if original methods are sought.

Figure 6

This decision depends upon the ability level of the class.

37 The Inaccessible Angle

Through a recreational application, this unit will provide the students the opportunity to use in novel ways various geometrical relationships they have learned. It also opens the door to a host of creative activities.

Performance Objective
Given an angle whose vertex is in an inaccessible region (hereafter referred to as an inaccessible angle), students will construct its angle bisector using straightedge and compasses.

Preassessment
Students should be familiar with the basic geometric constructions using straightedge and compasses.

See that students can properly bisect a given angle using only straightedge and compasses.

Teaching Strategies
After students have reviewed the basic geometric constructions present them with the following situation:

Problem: Given an angle whose vertex is inaccessible (i.e. tell students that the vertex of the angle is in a region in which, and over which, a straightedge and compasses cannot be used), construct the angle bisector using only straightedge and compasses.

Figure 1

Most students' first attempts will probably be incorrect. However, careful consideration of students' responses should serve as a guide to a correct solution. Students will eventually present some rather strange (and creative) solutions. All should be given careful attention.

To best exhibit the true source of creativity that this problem provides, three different solutions are presented.

Solution I:

Draw any line ℓ intersecting the rays of the inaccessible angle at points A and B. Label the inaccessible vertex P.

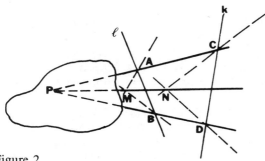

Figure 2

Construct the bisectors of ∠PAB and ∠PBA, which then intersect at M. Remind students that since the angle bisectors of a triangle (here △APB) are concurrent, the bisector of ∠P, which we are trying to construct must contain point M.

In a similar way, draw any line k, intersecting the rays of the inaccessible angle at points C and D. Construct the bisectors of ∠PCD and ∠PDC, which intersect at N. Once again students should realize that, since the bisectors of a triangle (in this case △CPD) are concurrent, the bisector of ∠P must contain point N. Thus it has been established that the required line must contain points M and N, and therefore by drawing $\overleftrightarrow{MN}$ the construction is completed.

Solution II:

Begin this method by constructing a line parallel to one of the rays of the inaccessible angle. See Figure 3. This can be done in any one of various ways.

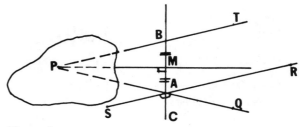

Figure 3

In Figure 3, $\overleftrightarrow{RS}$ is parallel to $\overrightarrow{PT}$ (a ray of the inaccessible ∠P), and intersects $\overrightarrow{PQ}$ at point A. Construct the bisector of ∠SAQ which will intersect $\overrightarrow{PT}$ at B. Since $\overleftrightarrow{SR}//\overrightarrow{PT}$, ∠SAC ≅ ∠PBA. However ∠SAC ≅ ∠CAQ ≅ ∠PAB. Therefore ∠PBA ≅ ∠PAB, thereby making △PAB isosceles. Since the perpendicular bisector of the base of an isosceles triangle also bisects the vertex angle, the perpendicular bisector of $\overline{AB}$ is the required angle bisector of the inaccessible angle (∠P).

Solution III:

Start by constructing a line ($\overline{MN}$) parallel to one of the rays ($\overrightarrow{PT}$) of the inaccessible angle (∠P), and intersecting the other ray at point A. See Figure 4.

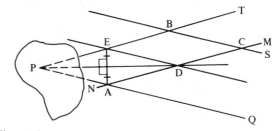

Figure 4

Then construct a line ($\overleftrightarrow{RS}$) parallel to the other ray ($\overrightarrow{PQ}$) of the inaccessible angle intersecting $\overrightarrow{PT}$ and $\overleftrightarrow{MN}$ at points B and C, respectively. With a pair of compasses, mark off a segment, $\overline{AD}$, on $\overrightarrow{AC}$ of the same length as $\overline{BC}$. Through D, construct $\overleftrightarrow{DE}//\overrightarrow{PQ}$, where E is on $\overrightarrow{PT}$. It can now be easily shown that ED = AD (since EBCD is a parallelogram and ED = BC. Since PEDA is a parallelogram with two adjacent sides congruent ($\overline{ED} \cong \overline{AD}$), it is a rhombus. Thus, the diagonal $\overline{PD}$ *is* the bisector of the inaccessible angle. $\overline{PD}$ can be constructed simply by bisecting ∠EDA or constructing the perpendicular bisector of $\overline{EA}$.

After presenting these solutions to your students, other solutions created by the students should follow directly. Free thinking should be encouraged to promote greater creativity.

Postassessment

Present students with an inaccessible angle and ask them to bisect it.

38 Triangle Constructions

Often teachers will justify the basic triangle congruence postulates by showing that unique triangles can be constructed with such given data as the lengths of three sides of a triangle or perhaps the lengths of two sides and the measure of the included angle. This unit will extend this usually elementary discussion of triangle constructions to some rather interesting problems.

Performance Objective

Given the measures of three parts of a triangle (which determine a triangle) students will analyze and construct the required triangle with straightedge and compasses.

Preassessment

Students should be familiar with the basic geometric constructions normally taught in the high school geometry course.

Teaching Strategies

To begin to familiarize students with this topic have them construct the triangle, where the measures of two angles and the length of the included side are given.

Figure 1

Students will draw a line and mark off the length of $\overline{AB}$ (sometimes referred to by c, the length of the side opposite $\angle C$). By constructing angles A and B at either end of $\overline{AB}$, they eventually find that they have constructed a *unique* $\triangle ABC$.

Surely, if the students were given the measures of the three angles of a triangle, each student would probably construct a triangle of different size (although all should be the same shape). Yet if the students were given the lengths of the three sides of a triangle they would all construct triangles congruent to one another. At this point students should realize that certain data will determine a *unique* triangle while other data will not. A student is thus limited in investigating such cases where the measures of only sides and angles are provided. Students will want to consider other parts of triangles as well. Present the following problem:

Construct a triangle given the lengths of two sides and the length of an altitude to one of these sides.

We shall write this problem as $[a, b, h_a]$, where h_a is the length of the altitude to side a.

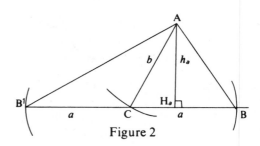

Figure 2

To do this construction, take the point H_a on any line and erect a perpendicular $H_a A$ (using the usual straightedge and compasses method) of length h_a. With arc (A,b) (Note: This ordered pair symbol is merely a short way of referring to the circle with center A and radius b) intersect the base line at C, then with arc (C,a), intersect this base line again at B and B'. The *two* solutions are $\triangle ABC$ and $\triangle AB'C$, each of which has the given $\{a, b, h_a\}$. Further inspection of this solution will indicate that $b > h_a$ was a necessary condition, and that if $b = h_a$ there would have only been *one* solution.

A much simpler problem is to construct a triangle given $\{a, b, h_c\}$. Here students begin in much the same way. On any line, erect at H_c a perpendicular length h_c. At C, the other extremity of h_c, draw (C,a) and (C,b). Their points of intersection with the original base line will determine points B and A, respectively. Once again a discussion of uniqueness should follow.

Figure 3

The figure above should help in this discussion.

Some triangle constructions require a good deal more analysis before actually beginning the construction. An example of such a problem is to construct the triangle given the lengths of its three medians $\{m_a, m_b, m_c\}$.

One approach for analyzing this problem is to consider the finished product, $\triangle ABC$.

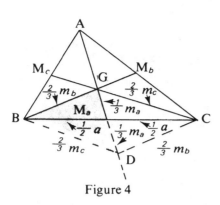

Figure 4

The objective here is to be able to construct one of the many triangles shown in the above figure by various elementary methods. By extending m_a (the median to side a), one third of its length to a point D and then drawing $\overline{BD}$ and $\overline{CD}$, we have created a triangle, $\triangle BGD$, which is easily constructible. Since the medians of a triangle trisect each other, we know that $BG = \frac{2}{3} m_b$. Since $GM_a = DM_a = \frac{1}{3} m_a$, (by construction) and $BM_? = CM_a$, we may conclude that BGCD is a parallelogram. Therefore $BD = GC = \frac{2}{3} m_c$. It is then rather simple to construct $\triangle BGD$, since its sides are each two thirds the length of one of the given medians (lengths easily obtained). After constructing $\triangle BGD$, the students should be able to complete the required construction by (1) extending BG one half its length to point M_b, (2) extending $\overline{DG}$ its own length to A, and (3) extending $\overline{BM_a}$ its own length to C (where M_a is the midpoint of $\overline{DG}$). The required triangle is then obtained by drawing $\overrightarrow{AM_b}$ to intersect $\overrightarrow{BM_a}$ at point C, and drawing $\overline{AB}$.

Not only does this problem review for the students many important concepts from elementary geometry, but it also provides an excellent opportunity for students to practice "reverse" reasoning in analyzing the problem.

For additional practice have students construct $\triangle ABC$ given $\{a, h_b, m_c\}$.

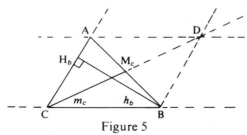

Figure 5

Once again have students first inspect the desired triangle. They should notice that $\triangle CBH_b$ can be easily constructed by erecting at H_c a perpendicular to $\overleftrightarrow{AC}$ of length h_b. At its extremity, B, draw (B,a) to intersect $\overleftrightarrow{AC}$ at C, to complete $\triangle CBH_b$. Further inspection of the above figure suggests that $\triangle CDB$ may also be constructed. Construct a line $(\overleftrightarrow{DB})$ parallel to $\overleftrightarrow{AC}$ and intersecting arc $(C, 2m_c)$ at D. To find A, construct a line $(\overleftrightarrow{AD})$ parallel to $\overleftrightarrow{CB}$ and intersecting $\overleftrightarrow{CH_b}$ at A. Since ADBC is a parallelogram, $\overleftrightarrow{CD}$ bisects $\overleftrightarrow{AB}$ at M_c, and $CM_c = \frac{1}{2}CD = m_c$. Thus the problem is analyzed in a rather reverse fashion, and then the required triangle is constructed.

When you consider the measures of other parts of a triangle such as angle bisectors, radius of the inscribed circle, radius of the circumscribed circle, and the semi-perimeter (as well as the measures of parts considered earlier in this Model), then there exist 179 possible triangle construction problems, where each consists of measures of three of these parts of a triangle. While some may be rather simple (e.g., $\{a,b,c\}$) others are somewhat more difficult (e.g., $\{h_a, h_b, h_c\}$).

This type of construction problem may very well serve as a springboard for a more careful study of this topic as well as various other geometric construction problems. A recently published book which contains much more on this topic (including the *complete* list of the 179 triangle constructions!) as well as a variety of other stimulating geometric construction topics (e.g., a review of the basic constructions, a variety of applications, circle constructions, restricted-tool constructions, etc.) is available from:

J. Weston Walch, Publisher
Portland, Maine 04104
and is entitled:
Geometric Constructions
by: Alfred S. Posamentier and William Wernick

Postassessment
Have students construct triangles given:

1. $\{a,b,m_a\}$ 3. $\{a,h_b,h_c\}$ 5. $\{h_a,h_b,h_c\}$
2. $\{a,h_b,t_c\}$ 4. $\{h_a,m_a,t_a\}$

N.B. t_a is the length of the angle bisector of $\angle A$.

39 The Criterion of Constructibility

This unit will develop a criterion of constructibility for the Euclidean tools, straightedge and compasses.

Performance Objectives

1. Students will state the criterion of constructibility.

2. Students will represent algebraic expressions geometrically (in terms of given lengths).

Preassessment

Ask students to represent geometrically AB + CD and AB − CD, given AB and CD.

Teaching Strategies

Most students should have been able to successfully do the above problem. Now let AB = *a* and CD = *b*.

A $\underline{\qquad a \qquad}$ B   C $\underline{\qquad b \qquad}$ D

The next logical concern would be to represent the *product* of two given line segments. Here, however, a segment of unit length must be introduced.

To construct *ab*, two cases should be considered: (I) where $a > 1$ and $b > 1$, and (II) where $a < 1$ and $b < 1$.

In the first case (I), students would construct the figure below. Note $\overline{MN} \parallel \overline{AB}$, and $\angle C$ is any convenient angle.

Since $\overline{MN} \parallel \overline{AB}$, $\frac{x}{a} = \frac{b}{1}$, and $x = ab$; thus $\overline{NB}$ is the segment of desired length (i.e. *ab*). It should be noted that $ab > a$, and $ab > b$, which is expected if $a > 1$ and $b > 1$.

In the second case (II), students would proceed in the same way as in case I, however since $a < 1$ and $b < 1$, it should be made clear that geometrically $ab < a$, and $ab < b$.

Students should now be challenged to discover a similar scheme for constructing a line segment which

can represent the quotient of two given line segments, *a* and *b*. Again two cases should be considered:

Case I: $a < b < 1$. Once again have students construct the figure above, where $\overline{MN} \parallel \overline{AB}$.

In this case either $a < \frac{a}{b} < b < 1$ or $a < b < \frac{a}{b} < 1$. Students should be encouraged to verify this.

Case II: $b < a \leq 1$. Proceed as above to construct the figure below.

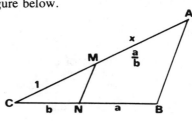

Here $b < a < \frac{a}{b}$

Until now all segments considered were of positive length. Students will now become curious about using segments of negative length to represent products and quotients.

In order to consider segments of negative length, we must introduce number line axes, horizontal and oblique. To find *ab*, locate A on the horizontal axis so that OA = *a*, and locate B on the oblique axis so that OB = *b*. Draw the line through the 1 on the oblique axis and A. Through B draw a line parallel to the first line, intersecting the horizontal axis in a point C. Thus OC = *ab*.

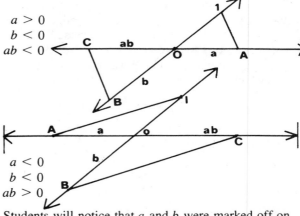

Students will notice that *a* and *b* were marked off on different axes and that in each case the product, *ab*, was appropriately less than or greater than zero.

As before, we shall find a quotient by considering division as the inverse of multiplication. To find

$\frac{a}{b}$, we find x such that $bx = a$. $a > 0$, and $b > 0$,

then $\frac{a}{b} > 0$.

$OB = b$
$OA = a$
$OC = 1$
$OD = \frac{a}{b}$

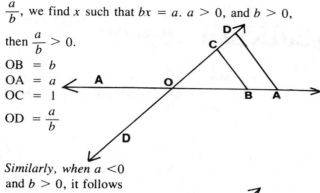

*Similarly, when $a < 0$
and $b > 0$, it follows
that $\frac{a}{b} < 0$*

$OB = b$
$OA = a$
$OC = 1$
$OD = \frac{a}{b}$

Have students consider division by zero. That is, where is B if $b = 0$? What happens to OD?

The only remaining operation for which a geometric representation is needed is square root extraction. Here students merely construct a semicircle on $1 + a$ (where $\sqrt{a}$ is sought). Then at the common endpoint, B, of segment 1 and a erect a perpendicular to intersect the semicircle at D. Thus $BD = \sqrt{a}$. Students should be able to apply mean proportional theorems to prove this.

The solution to a construction problem may be expressed as a root of an equation. For example, consider the problem of duplication of a cube. We must find the edge of a cube whose volume is twice that of a given cube. That is, we must find x, when $x^3 = 2$.

If we can obtain the solution by a finite number of applications of the operations $+$, $-$, $\times$, $\div$, and $\sqrt{\ }$, using given segments and a unit length, then the construction is possible.

Conversely, if the construction is possible, then we can obtain it by a finite number of applications of addition, subtraction, multiplication, division and extractions of square root, using the given segments and an arbitrary unit of length. We know that the straight lines and circles that we construct are deter-

mined either by given segments or those obtained from the intersections of two straight lines, a straight line and a circle, or two circles. To show the converse above, we must show that these intersections can be obtained from the coefficients of the equations by a finite number of applications of the operations of addition, subtraction, multiplication, division, and extraction of square root.

Two straight lines

$$y = mx + b$$
$$y = m'x + b' \qquad m \neq m'$$

have as their point of intersection the point (x, y) with

$$x = \frac{b - b'}{m - m'} \qquad\qquad y = \frac{mb' - m'b}{m - m'}$$

These relationships are obtained from the equations by applying the above operations. An equation for a circle with radius r and center (c, d) is $(x - c)^2 + (y - d)^2 = r^2$. To find the intersection of the circle with the line $y = mx + b$, we can substitute for y in the equation for the circle

$$(x - c)^2 + (mx + b - d)^2 = r^2$$

This forms a quadratic equation in x. Since the solution of the quadratic $ax^2 + bx + c = 0$ is

$$x = \frac{-b \pm \sqrt{b^2 - 4ac}}{2a}$$

we know that the quadratic $(x - c)^2 + (mx + b - d)^2 = r^2$ has a root that can be obtained from the known constants by applying the above five operations.

The intersection of two circles is the same as the intersection of one circle with the common chord. Thus, this case can be reduced to finding the intersection of a circle and a line.

Criterion of Constructibility   A proposed geometric construction is possible with straightedge and compass alone if and only if the numbers that define algebraically the required geometric elements can be derived from those defining the given elements by a finite number of rational operations and extractions of square root.

Postassessment

1. Restate and explain the Criterion of Constructibility.

2. Given lengths a, b, 1 construct a line segment of length $\sqrt{\dfrac{ab}{a + b}}$

Reference

Posamentier, Alfred S. and William Wernick, *Geometric Constructions*. Portland, Maine: J. Weston Walch, Publisher, 1973.

40 Constructing Radical Lengths

Often students ask how a line of length $\sqrt{2}$ can be constructed. This activity will address itself to this question as well as find the length of other radical segments.

Performance Objective
Students will construct a segment of a given radical length after being given a unit length.

Preassessment
Students should be able to apply the Pythagorean Theorem and be familiar with the basics of geometric constructions with straightedge and compasses.

Teaching Strategies
Ask students to construct a triangle with one side of length $\sqrt{2}$ (be sure to tell them to select a convenient unit length). In all likelihood they will draw an isosceles right triangle with a leg of length 1. By the Pythagorean Theorem they will find that the hypotenuse has length $\sqrt{2}$.

Now have them construct a right triangle using this hypotenuse and have the other leg be of unit length. This newly formed right triangle has a hypotenuse of length $\sqrt{3}$. Students should easily discover that fact using the Pythagorean Theorem.

By repeating this process, students will generate, in sequence, radicals of integers, i.e., $\sqrt{2}, \sqrt{3}, \sqrt{4}, \sqrt{5}$, . . . The figure, frequently referred to as a "radical spiral", shows this process.

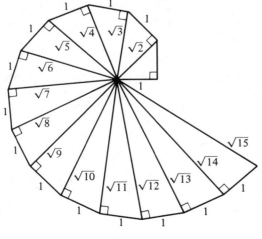

Figure 1

It could be expected that a student might ask if there is a more expedient method for constructing $\sqrt{15}$, rather than generating a radical spiral up to $\sqrt{15}$,

Lead students to recall one of the "mean proportional" theorems. In the figure below CD is the mean proportional between AD and BD.

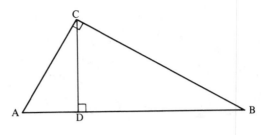

Figure 2

That is, $\dfrac{AD}{CD} = \dfrac{CD}{BD}$, or $(CD)^2 = (AD)(BD)$, which implies that $CD = \sqrt{(AD)(BD)}$

This relationship will help them construct a segment of length $\sqrt{15}$ in one construction. All they need do is to construct the above figure and let $AD = 1$ and $BD = 15$; then $CD = \sqrt{(1)(15)} = \sqrt{15}$.

What they should do is draw a segment of length 16 and partition it into two segments of lengths 1 and 15. At the partitioning point have them erect a perpendicular to this segment. The intersection of the perpendicular and the semicircle having the segment of length 16 as diameter determines the other endpoint of the perpendicular segment of length $\sqrt{15}$. See the figure below.

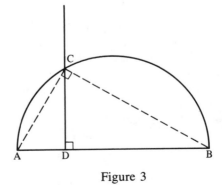

Figure 3

The dashed lines are merely needed to justify the construction.

Postassessment
1. Construct a radical spiral up to $\sqrt{18}$.
2. Construct a segment of length $\sqrt{18}$ using a given unit length. Do *not* construct a radical spiral here.

41   Constructing a Pentagon

Performance Objective
Students will construct a regular pentagon given the length of the radius of the circumscribed circle.

Preassessment
Students should be familiar with the properties of regular polygons.

Teaching Strategies
Begin your lesson by having the class consider a regular decagon whose radius is 1 (Figure 1).

Figure 1

With center O, draw $\overline{OA}$ and $\overline{OB}$ to form isosceles $\triangle AOB$. The class should easily see that $m\angle AOB = 36°$. (i.e. $\frac{360}{10} = 36$). Therefore $m\angle OAB = m\angle OBA = 72°$.

Isolate $\triangle AOB$ for clarity (Figure 2).

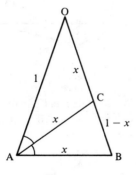

Figure 2

Draw angle bisector $\overline{AC}$. Therefore $m\angle OAC = 36°$, making $\triangle OCA$ isosceles. Similarly, $\triangle CAB$ is isosceles.

Moreover, $\triangle AOB \sim \triangle BAC$. If we let $x = OC$, then $CB = 1 - x$; also $CA = x = AB$. From the similarity students should obtain the proportion: $\frac{1}{x} = \frac{x}{1 - x}$, which leads to the equation $x^2 + x - 1 = 0$.

This equation has two roots, one of which has geometric significance: $x = \frac{\sqrt{5} - 1}{2}$.

Now have students consider the construction of this value of x. At any point A of a line, erect a perpendicular of length $1 = OA$, and construct the unit circle (i.e. the circle with radius of length 1) tangent to that line at A. On the line make $AP = 2$ and then draw $\overline{OP}$. By using the Pythagorean Theorem, students should establish that $OP = \sqrt{5}$ and $PQ = OP - OQ = \sqrt{5} - 1$. Finally the perpendicular bisector of $\overline{PQ}$ gives us $QR = \frac{\sqrt{5} - 1}{2} = x$.

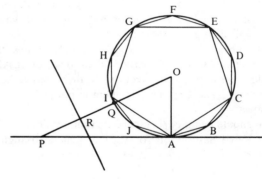

Figure 3

Students should now mark consecutive segments of x on the original unit circle. When done accurately, this value of x will give exactly 10 arcs on the circle. After students have constructed the decagon, they ought to realize that by joining the alternate vertices of the decagon, the desired pentagon is formed.

Postassessment
Have students construct a regular pentagon given a specific unit length.

42 Investigating the Isosceles Triangle Fallacy

This unit offers an opportunity to consider fully the Isosceles Triangle Fallacy. This fallacy can be used to reinforce the concept of betweeness.

Performance Objectives
1. *Students will exhibit the Isosceles Triangle Fallacy.*
2. *Students will indicate the "error" in the Isosceles Triangle Fallacy and prove their conjecture.*

Preassessment
Students should be familiar with the various methods for proving triangles congruent, as well as angle measurement in a circle.

Teaching Strategies
Begin the discussion by challenging your students to drawn any *scalene* triangle on the chalkboard which you will then prove isosceles.

To prove the scalene ΔABC isosceles, draw the bisector of ∠C and the perpendicular bisector of $\overline{AB}$. From their point of intersection, G, draw perpendiculars to $\overline{AC}$ and $\overline{CB}$, meeting them at points D and F, respectively.

It should be noted that there are four possibilities for the above description for various scalene triangles: figure 1, where $\overline{CG}$ and $\overline{GE}$ meet inside the triangle:

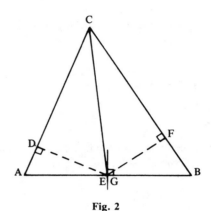

Fig. 2

figure 3, where $\overline{CG}$ and $\overline{GE}$ meet outside the triangle, but the perpendiculars $\overline{GD}$ and $\overline{GF}$ fall on $\overline{AC}$ and $\overline{CB}$;

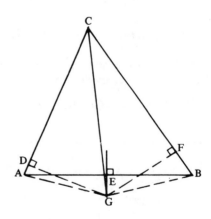

Fig. 3

figure 4, where $\overline{CG}$ and $\overline{GE}$ meet outside the triangle, but the perpendiculars $\overline{GD}$ and $\overline{GF}$ meet $\overrightarrow{CA}$ and $\overrightarrow{CG}$ outside the triangle.

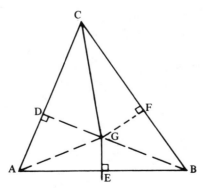

Fig. 1

figure 2, where $\overline{CG}$ and $\overline{GE}$ meet on $\overline{AB}$;

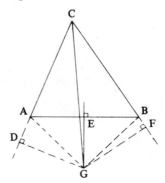

Fig. 4

The "proof" of the fallacy can be done with any of the above figures. Have students follow the "proof" on any (or all) of these figures.

Given:

ABC is scalene

Prove:

AC = BC (or ΔABC is isosceles)

"Proof": Since ∠ ACG ≅ ∠ BCG and *rt* ∠ CDG ≅ *rt* ∠ CFG, ΔCDG ≅ ΔCFG (SAA). Therefore DG = FG and CD = CF. Since AG = BG (a point on the perpendicular bisector of a line segment is equidistant from the endpoints of the line segment) and ∠ADG and ∠ BFG are right angles, ΔDAG ≅ ΔFBG (H.L.). Therefore DA = FB. It then follows that AC = BC (by addition in figures 1, 2, and 3; and by subtraction in figure 4).

At this point students will be quite disturbed. They will wonder where the error was committed which permitted this fallacy to occur. Some students will be clever enough to attack the figures. By rigorous construction students will find a subtle error in the figures:

a. The point G *must* be outside the triangle.

b. When perpendiculars meet the sides of the triangle, one will meet a side *between* the vertices, while the other will not.

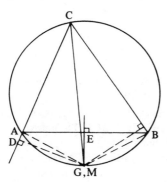

Fig. 5

Some discussion of Euclid's neglect of the concept of betweenness should follow. However, the beauty of this particular fallacy is the powerful proof of items *a* and *b* (above), which indicate the *error* of the fallacy.

Begin by considering the circumcircle of ΔABC The bisector of ∠ ACB must contain the midpoint, M, of $\widehat{AB}$ (since ∠ ACM and ∠ BCM are congruent inscribed angles). The perpendicular bisector of $\overline{AB}$ must bisect $\widehat{AB}$, and therefore pass through M. Thus, the bisector of ∠ ACB and the perpendicular bisector of $\overline{AB}$ intersect *outside* the triangle at M (or G). This eliminates the possibilities of figures 1 and 2.

Now have students consider inscribed quadrilateral ACBG. Since the opposite angles of an inscribed (or cyclic) quadrilateral are supplementary, *m∠*CAG + *m∠* CBG = 180. If ∠ CAG and ∠ CBG are right angles then $\overline{CG}$ would be a diameter and ΔABC would be isosceles. Therefore since ΔABC is scalene, ∠CAG and ∠CBG are not right angles. In this case one must be acute and the other obtuse. Suppose ∠CBG is acute and ∠CAG is obtuse. Then in ΔCGB the altitude on $\overline{CB}$ must be *inside* the triangle, while in obtuse ΔCAG, the altitude on $\overline{AC}$ must be *outside the triangle*. (*This is usually readily accepted by students but can be easily proved.*) The fact that one and *only* one of the perpendiculars intersects a side of the triangle *between* the vertices destroys the fallacious "proof." It is important that the teacher stress the importance of the concept of betweenness in geometry.

Postassessment

Have students:

1. "Prove" that any given scalene triangle is isosceles.

2. Indicate (and prove) where the "proof" in question 1 is fallacious.

3. Discuss the concept of betweenness in terms of its significance in geometry.

43   The Equiangular Point

This unit will develop interesting geometric relationships from an unusual geometric configuration. The topic is appropriate for any student who has mastered most of the high school geometry course.

Performance Objectives

1. Students will define the equiangular point of an acute triangle.

2. Students will locate the equiangular point of an acute triangle.

3. Students will state at least three properties of the figure used to locate the equiangular point of an acute triangle.

Preassessment

Before attempting to present this unit to your classes, review with them angle measurement of a circle and the basic properties of congruence and similarity.

Teaching Strategies

Begin your presentation by challenging students with the following problem:

Given: Acute $\triangle ABC$.
$\triangle ACD$ and $\triangle ABF$
are equilateral.
Prove: DB = CF

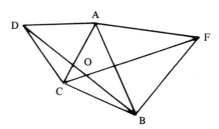

Figure 1

Although this problem uses only the most elementary concepts of the high school geometry course, students tend to find it somewhat challenging. What seems to be most perplexing is the selection of the proper pair of triangles to prove congruent. If, after a few minutes, students do not find these, tell them to name triangles that use the required segments $\overline{DB}$ and $\overline{CF}$ as sides. Soon they will realize that they must prove $\triangle CAF \cong \triangle DAB$.

Next arises the problem of *how* to prove these triangles congruent. Lead students to realize that overlapping triangles usually share a common element. Here the common element is $\angle CAB$. Since $\triangle ACD$ and

$\triangle ABF$ are equilateral, m$\angle DAC = 60°$, m$\angle FAB = 60°$, and m$\angle DAB = $ m$\angle FAC$ (addition). Since $\triangle ACD$ is equilateral, AD = AC, and since $\triangle ABF$ is equilateral, AB = AF. Therefore $\triangle CAF \cong \triangle DAB$ (S.A.S.), and thus DB = CF.

Once students have fully understood this proof, have them consider a third equilateral triangle, $\triangle BCE$, drawn on side $\overline{BC}$. Ask them to compare the length of $\overline{AE}$ to that of $\overline{DB}$ and $\overline{CF}$.

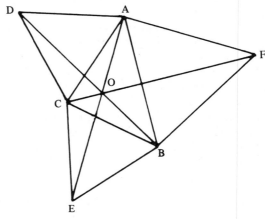

Figure 2

Most students will realize that all three segments have the same length. A proof of this is done in the same way as the previous one. That is, simply have them prove that $\triangle CAE \cong \triangle CDB$ to get AE = DB.

The fact that AE = DB = CF is quite astonishing when we bear in mind that $\triangle ABC$ was *any* acute triangle. A number of equally surprising results can now be established from this basis. Present each of these separately, but once each has been proved, carefully relate it to the previously established facts.

1. The line segments $\overline{AE}$, $\overline{DB}$, and $\overline{CF}$ are concurrent.

Proof: Consider the circumcircles of the three equilateral triangles, $\triangle ACD$, $\triangle ABF$, and $\triangle BCE$.

Let K, L, and M be the centers of these circles (see Figure 3).

Circles K and L meet at points O and A. Since m$\widehat{ADC} = 240°$, and we know that m$\angle AOC = \frac{1}{2}$(m$\widehat{ADC}$), m$\angle AOC = 120°$. Similarly, m$\angle AOB = \frac{1}{2}$(m$\widehat{AFB}$) = $120°$. Therefore m$\angle COB = 120°$, since a complete revolution = $360°$.

Since m$\widehat{CEB} = 240°$, $\angle COB$ is an inscribed angle and point O must lie on circle M. Therefore, we can see

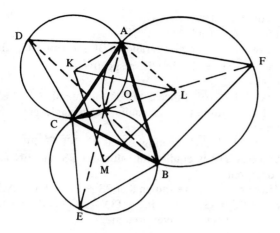

Figure 3

that the three circles are concurrent, intersecting at point O.

Now have students join point O with points A, B, C, D, E, and F. m∠DOA = m∠AOF = m∠FOB = 60°, and therefore $\overleftrightarrow{DOB}$. Similarly $\overleftrightarrow{COF}$ and $\overleftrightarrow{AOE}$.

Thus it has been proved that $\overline{AE}$, $\overline{CF}$, and $\overline{DB}$ are concurrent, intersecting at point O (which is also the point of intersection of circles K, L, and M).

Now ask the class to determine the point in ΔABC at which the three sides subtend congruent angles. They should quickly recall that we just proved that m∠AOB = m∠AOC = m∠BOC = 120°. Thus, the point—called the *equiangular point* of a triangle—at which the sides of ΔABC subtend congruent angles is point O.

2. *The circumcenters K, L, and M of the three equilateral triangles ΔACD, ΔABF, and ΔBCE, respectively, determine another equilateral triangle.*

Proof: Before beginning this proof, review briefly with students the relationship among the sides of a 30-60-90 triangle.

Have your students consider equilateral ΔDAC. Since AK is 2/3 of the altitude (or median), we obtain the proportion AC:AK = $\sqrt{3}$:1.
Similarly, in equilateral ΔAFB, AF:AL = $\sqrt{3}$:1.
Therefore, AC:AK = AF:AL.
m∠KAC = m∠LAF = 30°, m∠CAL = m∠CAL (reflexive) and m∠KAL = m∠CAF (addition).
Therefore, ΔKAL ~ ΔCAF.
Thus, CF:KL = CA:AK = $\sqrt{3}$:1.
Similarly, we may prove DB:KM = $\sqrt{3}$:1, and AE:ML = $\sqrt{3}$:1. Therefore, DB:KM = AE:ML = CF:KL. But since DB = AE = CF, as proved earlier, we obtain KM = ML = KL. Therefore, ΔKML is equilateral.

As a concluding challenge to your class, ask them to discover other relationships in Figure 3.

Postassessment

To test student comprehension of this lesson, give them the following exercises.

1. Define *the equiangular point* of an acute triangle.

2. Draw any acute triangle. Using straightedge and compasses, locate the equiangular point of the triangle.

3. State three properties found in Figure 3, above.

Reference

Posamentier, Alfred S., *Excursions in Advanced Euclidean Geometry.* Menlo Park, Ca.: Addison-Wesley, 1984.

44   The Minimum Distance Point of a Triangle

This unit will develop a search for the point in a triangle the sum of whose distances to the vertices is a minimum.

Performance Objectives

1. Students will prove that the sum of the distances to the sides of an equilateral triangle from an interior point is constant.

2. Students will locate the minimum distance point of a triangle with no angle of measure 120° or greater.

Preassessment

Students should be familiar with basic concepts of geometric inequalities.

Ask students to find the position of a point of a quadrilateral, the sum of whose distances to the vertices is a minimum.

Teaching Strategies

Begin the discussion by having students consider the location of the point in the interior of a given quadrilateral, the sum of whose distances from the vertices is the smallest possible (from here on we shall refer to such a point as the *minimum distance point*).

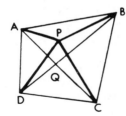

Figure 1

You can expect most students to guess that the point of intersection of the diagonals (point Q in Figure 1) would be this "minimum distance point." Although the conjecture is a clever one, try to elicit a justification (proof) for this point selection.

Let students select any point P (not at Q) in the interior of quadrilateral ABCD (Figure 1). PA + PC > QA + QC (since the sum of the lengths of two sides of a triangle is greater than the length of the third). Similarly, PB + PD > QB + QD. By addition, PA + PB + PC + PD > QA + QB + QC + QD, which shows that the sum of the distances from the point of intersection of the diagonals of a quadrilateral to the vertices is less than the sum of the distances from *any other* interior point of the quadrilateral to the vertices.

The next logical concern of students is usually, "What is the minimum distance point in a triangle?" Before tackling this question, it is useful to first consider another interesting theorem that will later help students develop the minimum distance point of a triangle.

Once again ask students to use their intuition and reason inductively. Have them construct a large equilateral triangle. Then have them select any interior point and carefully measure its distances from the three *sides* of the equilateral triangle. After students have recorded the sum of these three distances, ask them to repeat the procedure three times, each time with a different interior point. Accurate measurements should yield equal distance sums for each point selected. Consequently, students ought to be able to draw the following conclusion: *The sum of the distances from any point in the interior of an equilateral triangle to the sides of the triangle is constant.* Two proofs of this interesting finding are provided here:

Method I:

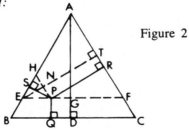

Figure 2

In equilateral $\triangle ABC$, $\overline{PR} \perp \overline{AC}$, $\overline{PQ} \perp \overline{BC}$, $\overline{PS} \perp \overline{AB}$, and $\overline{AD} \perp \overline{BC}$.
Draw a line through P parallel to $\overline{BC}$ meeting $\overline{AD}$, $\overline{AB}$, and $\overline{AC}$ at G, E, and F, respectively.
$PQ = GD$.
Draw $\overline{ET} \perp \overline{AC}$. Since $\triangle AEF$ is equilateral, $\overline{AG} \cong \overline{ET}$ (all the altitudes of an equilateral triangle are congruent).
Draw $\overline{PH} \parallel \overline{AC}$ meeting $\overline{ET}$ at N. $\overline{NT} \cong \overline{PR}$.
Since $\triangle EHP$ is equilateral, altitudes $\overline{PS}$ and $\overline{EN}$ are congruent.
Therefore, we have shown that PS + PR = ET = AG.
Since PQ = GD, PS + PR + PQ = AG + GD = AD, a constant for the given triangle.

Method II:

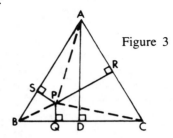

Figure 3

In equilateral $\triangle ABC$, $\overline{PR} \perp \overline{AC}$, $\overline{PQ} \perp \overline{BC}$, $\overline{PS} \perp \overline{AB}$, and $\overline{AD} \perp \overline{BC}$,
Draw $\overline{PA}$, $\overline{PB}$, and $\overline{PC}$.
The area of $\triangle ABC$
$= $ area of $\triangle APB$ + area of $\triangle BPC$ + area of $\triangle CPA$
$= \frac{1}{2}(AB)(PS) + \frac{1}{2}(BC)(PQ) + \frac{1}{2}(AC)(PR)$.

Since AB = BC = AC, the area of $\triangle ABC$ = $\frac{1}{2}(BC)[PS + PQ + PR]$. However, the area of $\triangle ABC$ = $\frac{1}{2}(BC)(AD)$ therefore, PS + PQ + PR = AD, a constant for the given triangle.

Students are now ready to consider the original problem: to find the minimum distance point of a triangle. We shall consider a scalene triangle with no angle having a measure greater than 120°.

Students, realizing the apparent need for symmetry in this problem, may suggest selecting the point at which the sides subtend congruent angles. If they are to accept this conjecture, they must prove it.

We shall therefore prove that: *the point in the interior of a triangle (with no angle greater than 120°), at which the sides subtend congruent angles, is the minimum distance point of the triangle.*

Proof:

In Figure 4, let M be the point in the interior of $\triangle ABC$, where m$\angle$AMB = m$\angle$BMC = m$\angle$AMC = 120°.

Draw lines through A, B, and C which are perpendicular to $\overline{AM}$, $\overline{BM}$, and $\overline{CM}$, respectively.

These lines meet to form equilateral $\triangle PQR$. (To prove $\triangle PQR$ is equilateral, notice that each angle has measure 60°. This can be shown by considering, for example, quadrilateral AMBR. Since $m\angle RAM = m\angle RBM = 90°$, and $m\angle AMB = 120°$, it follows that $m\angle ARB = 60°$.)

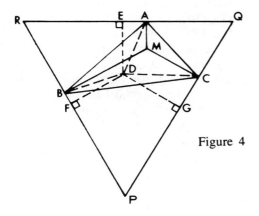

Figure 4

Let D be *any other* point in the interior of $\triangle ABC$. We must show that the sum of the distances from M to the vertices is less than the sum of the distances from D to the vertices.

From the theorem we proved above, $MA + MB + MC = DE + DF + DG$, (where $\overline{DE}$, $\overline{DF}$ and $\overline{DG}$ are the perpendiculars to $\overline{REQ}$, $\overline{RBP}$ and $\overline{QGP}$, respectively).

But $DE + DF + DG < DA + DB + DC$. (The shortest distance from an external point to a line is the length of the perpendicular segment from the point to the line.)

By substitution:

$MA + MB + MC < DA + DB + DC$.

Now having proved the theorem, students may wonder why we chose to restrict our discussion to triangles with angles of measure less than 120°. Let them try to construct the point M in an obtuse triangle with one angle of measure 150°. The reason for our restriction should become obvious.

Postassessment

To test student comprehension of the above exercises, ask them to:

1. Prove that the sum of the distances to the sides of an equilateral triangle from an interior point is constant.
2. Locate the minimum distance point of a triangle with no angle of measure greater than 120°.
3. Locate the minimum distance point of a quadrilateral.

Reference

Posamentier, Alfred S. *Excursions in Advanced Euclidean Geometry*. Menlo Park, Ca.: Addison-Wesley, 1984.

45　The Isosceles Triangle Revisited

Early in the high school geometry course, students perform many practice proofs using isosceles triangles. One such proof involves proving that the angle bisectors of the base angles of an isosceles triangle are congruent. Although this is a rather simple proof, its converse is exceedingly difficult; perhaps among the most difficult statements to prove in Euclidean geometry. This unit presents several methods by which students can prove the statement.

Performance Objectives

Students will prove that if two angle bisectors of a triangle are congruent, then the triangle is isosceles.

Preassessment

Students should have had practice with geometric proofs, including indirect proofs.

Teaching Strategies

Begin your presentation by asking students to prove:
The angle bisectors of the base angles of an isosceles triangle are congruent.

You may wish to start them uniformly:

Given: Isosceles $\triangle ABC$, with AB = AC, $\overline{BF}$ and $\overline{CE}$ are angle bisectors

Prove: $\overline{BF} \cong \overline{CE}$

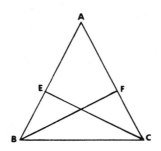

Proof: $m\angle FBC = \frac{1}{2}m\angle ABC$, and $m\angle ECB = \frac{1}{2}m\angle ACB$.

Since $m\angle ABC = m\angle ACB$ (base angles of an isosceles triangle), $m\angle FBC = m\angle ECB$.
Since $\overline{BC} \cong \overline{BC}$, $\triangle FBC \cong \triangle ECB$ (ASA).
Therefore $\overline{BF} \cong \overline{CE}$.

When students have completed this proof, ask them to state the converse of the statement just proved:

If two angle bisectors of a triangle are congruent, then the triangle is isosceles.

Challenge students to prove this new statement. Since it is highly unlikely that your students will be able to prove this statement in a short time, you may wish to show them some of the following proofs. They will be quite astonished that the converse of a rather simply proved statement is so difficult to prove. Each of the following proofs is quite instructional and merits special attention.

Given: $\overline{AE}$ and $\overline{BD}$ are angle bisectors of $\triangle ABC$.
$\overline{AE} \cong \overline{BD}$.

Prove: $\triangle ABC$ is isosceles.

Proof: Draw $\angle DBF \cong \angle AEB$ so that $\overline{BF} \cong \overline{BE}$
Draw $\overline{DF}$.
Also draw $\overline{FG} \perp \overline{AC}$ and $\overline{AH} \perp \overline{FH}$.
By hypothesis, $\overline{AE} \cong \overline{DB}$, $\overline{FB} \cong \overline{EB}$.
And $\angle 8 \cong \angle 7$.
Therefore $\triangle AEB \cong \triangle DBF$ (SAS) $DF = AB$
and $m\angle 1 = m\angle 4$.

$m\angle x = m\angle 2 + m\angle 3$ (exterior angles) of a triangle)
$m\angle x = m\angle 1 + m\angle 3$ (substitution)
$m\angle x = m\angle 4 + m\angle 3$ (substitution)
$m\angle x = m\angle 7 + m\angle 6$ (exterior angles of a triangle)
$m\angle x = m\angle 7 + m\angle 5$ (substitution)
$m\angle x = m\angle 8 + m\angle 5$ (substitution)
Therefore, $m\angle 4 + m\angle 3 = m\angle 8 + m\angle 5$ (transitivity).

Thus $m\angle z = m\angle y$.
Right $\triangle FDG \cong$ right $\triangle ABH$(SAA), DG = BH, and FG = AH.
Right $\triangle AFG \cong$ right $\triangle FAH$ (HL) and AG = FH
Therefore, GFHA is a parallelogram.
Also, $m\angle 9 = m\angle 10$ (from $\triangle ABH$ and $\triangle FDG$)
$m\angle DAB = m\angle DFB$ (subtraction)
$m\angle DFB = m\angle EBA$ (from $\triangle DBF$ and $\triangle AEB$)
Therefore, $m\triangle DAB = m\triangle EBA$ (transitivity), and $\triangle ABC$ is isosceles.

The following proofs of this theorem are *indirect proofs* and may deserve special introduction.

Given: $\overline{BF}$ and $\overline{CE}$ are angle bisectors of $\triangle ABC$.
$\overline{BF} \cong \overline{CE}$

Prove: $\triangle ABC$ is isosceles

Indirect proof I:
Assume $\triangle ABC$ is *not* isosceles.
Let $m\angle ABC > m\angle ACB$
$\overline{BF} \cong \overline{CE}$ (hypothesis)
$\overline{BC} \cong \overline{BC}$
$m\angle ABC > m\angle ACB$ (assumption)
$\overline{CF} > \overline{BE}$.
Through F, construct $\overline{GF}$ parallel to $\overline{EB}$.
Through E, construct $\overline{GE}$ parallel to $\overline{BF}$.
BFGE is a parallelogram.
$\overline{BF} \cong \overline{EG}$, $\overline{EG} \cong \overline{CE}$, $\triangle GEC$ is isosceles.
$m\angle(g + g') = m\angle(c + c')$
but $m\angle g = m\angle b$
$m\angle(b + g') = m\angle(c + c')$
Therefore, $m\angle g' < m\angle c'$, since $m\angle b > m\angle c$.
In $\triangle GFC$, we have CF < GF
But GF = BE
Thus CF < BE.

The assumption of the inequality of $m\angle ABC$ and $m\angle ACB$ leads to two contradictory results, CF < BE and CF > BE. Therefore $\triangle ABC$ is isosceles.

A second indirect proof follows:

Given: $\overline{BE}$ and $\overline{DC}$ are angle bisectors of $\triangle ABC$.
$\overline{BE} \cong \overline{DC}$

Prove: $\triangle ABC$ is isosceles.

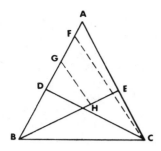

Indirect Proof II:

In ΔABC, the bisectors of angles ABC and ACB have equal measures (i.e., BE = DC). Assume that $m\angle ABC < m\angle ACB$; Then $m\angle ABE < m\angle ACD$.

We then draw ∠FCD congruent to ∠ABE. Note that we may take F between B and A without loss of generality. In ΔFBC, FB > FC. (If the measures of two angles of a triangle are not equal, then the measures of the sides opposite these angles are also unequal, the side with the greater measure being opposite the angle with the greater measure.)

Choose a point G so that $\overline{BG} \cong \overline{FC}$.

Then draw $\overline{GH} \parallel \overline{FC}$

Therefore, ∠ BGH ≅ ∠ BFC (corresponding angles), and ΔBGH ≅ ΔCFD (ASA)

Then it follows that BH = DC.

Since BH < BE, this contradicts the hypothesis that the angle bisectors are equal. A similar argument will show that it is impossible to have $m\angle ACB < m\angle ABC$.

It then follows that $m\angle ACB = m\angle ABC$ and that ΔABC is isosceles.

Postassessment

Have students prove that if two angle bisectors of a triangle are congruent then the triangle is isosceles.

Reference

Posamentier, Alfred S. and Charles T. Salkind, *Challenging Problems in Geometry, Volume II*. New York: Macmillan, 1970.

46 Reflective Properties of the Plane

Performance Objective

Given a line and two points on one side of a line, students will determine the shortest combined path from one point to the line and then to the second point.

Preassessment

Using the following illustration, ask students to locate the precise point on the cushion $\overline{PQ}$ of the "billiard table" which ball A must hit in order to then hit ball B (assume no "English" on the ball).

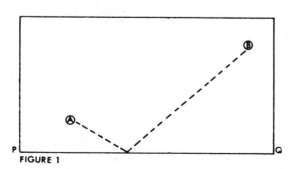

FIGURE 1

The disagreement as to where to hit the ball will develop enough interest to motivate the topic of the properties of reflection.

Teaching Strategies

Have the class try to prove the following property: "A ray of light will make equal angles with a mirror before and after reflecting off a mirror." (This theorem can be easily proved after considering the following proof.)

To find the *shortest path* from point A to line m then to point B in Figure 2, consider the perpendicular from A to line m (meeting line m at point C). Let D be the point on $\overrightarrow{AC}$ such that $\overline{AC} \cong \overline{CD}$. Point D is called the *reflected image* of point A in line m.

The point of intersection of $\overline{BD}$ and line m determines point P, the required point in the original problem. However, what must be shown now is

FIGURE 2

that AP + PB is less than *any other* path from A to line m (say at point Q), and then to B.

Students might be more comfortable stating this as a "formal proof":

Given: Points A and B are on the same side of line m $\overleftrightarrow{ACD} \perp \overleftrightarrow{CPQ}$, where Q is any point on $\overleftrightarrow{CP}$ (other than P)
$\overline{DPB}$
$\overline{AC} \cong \overline{CD}$

Prove: AP + PB < AQ + QB

Outline of proof: Because line m is the perpendicular bisector of $\overline{ACD}$, $\overline{AP} \cong \overline{DP}$ and $\overline{AQ} \cong \overline{QD}$. In △DQB, BD < BQ + QD (triangle inequality). Since BD = DP + PB, AP + PB < AQ + BQ.

You can now show the class that since ∠BPQ ≅ ∠CPD, and ∠APC ≅ ∠CPD, that ∠APC ≅ ∠BPQ. If $\overrightarrow{PN} \perp$ line m, then ∠APN, the angle of incidence, is congruent to ∠BPN, the angle of reflection.

Have students apply the properties of reflection to the billiard table problem. A billiard ball will rebound off a cushion as a ray of light "bounces" off a mirror. Thus if a ball is at position A (Figure 3) and the player desires to hit it off cushion $\overline{PQ}$ to position B, he can aim his shot at the point on $\overline{PQ}$ where he would see B (if a mirror were placed along $\overline{PQ}$).

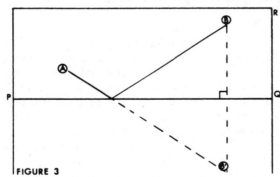

FIGURE 3

Now have students consider the problem of hitting two cushions ($\overline{PQ}$ then $\overline{QR}$) before hitting B.

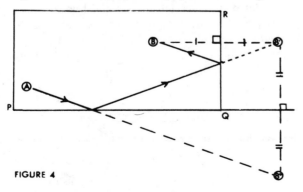

FIGURE 4

Consider the reflected image of B in $\overline{QR}$; call it B' (Figure 4). Now they merely have to consider

the problem of where to hit the ball from A off cushion $\overline{PQ}$ so that it will roll toward B'. To do this, have them take the reflected image of B' in $\overleftrightarrow{PQ}$, then the intersection of the line connecting A and the reflected image of B' (call it B'') and $\overleftrightarrow{PQ}$ is the point to aim for to make this two-cushion shot. Students may envision this point as the reflection of the ball at B in the mirror placed along $\overrightarrow{PQ}$ that they would see as the reflection in the mirror placed along $\overline{QR}$.

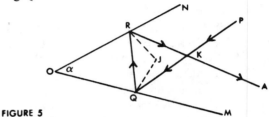

FIGURE 5

A motivated class may now wish to look beyond the double reflection to where the angle between the two planes is always fixed as a right angle.

Two mirrors with a fixed dihedral angle between them are called *angle mirrors*. Have the class prove that if an observer shines a light into the angle mirrors so that the ray reflects off one mirror, then the other, the final reflected ray will form an angle with the original ray which is double the dihedral angle between the two mirrors. In other words:

Given: Mirrors OM and ON, let ∠NOM = α also a light ray originating at point P aimed at point Q reflecting off OM onto $\overrightarrow{ON}$ then to A

Prove: m∠PKR = 2α (Figure 5)

Outline of proof: Draw the normals (the perpendiculars) to the planes (the mirrors) at the points of incidence in each plane, i.e., $\overleftrightarrow{QJ} \perp \overleftrightarrow{OM}$, at point Q, and draw $\overleftrightarrow{RJ} \perp \overleftrightarrow{ON}$, at point R (the point of incidence in mirror $\overline{ON}$). Then, by the property of reflection, $\overleftrightarrow{QJ}$ and $\overleftrightarrow{RJ}$ bisect ∠PQR and ∠QRA, respectively. Then m∠PKR = m∠KQR + m∠KRQ, (exterior angle of a triangle theorem). Then m∠PKR = 2(m∠JQR + m∠QRJ) and m∠PKR = 2(180 − m∠RJQ). But, since both ∠JRO and ∠JQO are right angles, m∠ROQ = 180 − m∠RJQ (the sum of the measures of the interior angles of a quadrilateral is 360). By substituting, m∠PKR = 2(m∠ROQ) = 2α.

One of the applications of angle mirrors is that when the dihedral angle is 45° the ray will be reflected 90°. Such a pair of mirrors is often called an "optical square", because it is used to determine perpendicular lines of sight.

To show how the optical square is used, station one student at each of the three points O, A, and B, so that the three points will define a triangle (Figure 6). Using the optical square they will be able to determine where the perpendicular from B to $\overrightarrow{AO}$ meèts $\overrightarrow{AO}$. Have the student standing at O look at the student standing at A. Have another student, P, holding the optical square move along

FIGURE 6

the line of sight from O to A until (at some point m) the student at O is able to see the student at B in the angle mirror. The point m is the foot of the altitude from B to $\overrightarrow{OA}$.

Postassessment

Using the property of reflection, have students prove that the height of a flagpole is

$$x = \frac{h \cdot AB}{AC - DB}$$

where x is the height of the flagpole and h is the height of an observer.

47 Finding The Length Of A Cevian Of A Triangle

This unit presents a method for finding the length of *any* line segment joining a vertex of a triangle with any point on the opposite side. Such a line segment is called a cevian, after Giovanni Ceva who developed a theorem about the concurrency of such line segments. This technique is particularly useful to students since it fills a void in many curricula. Students are usually taught methods for finding the lengths of special cevians such as altitudes and some medians. However, by using Stewart's Theorem (named after Matthew Stewart who published it in 1745), students will now be able to find the length of *any* cevian of a triangle.

Performance Objectives

1. Students will find the length of a specific cevian of a given triangle, all of whose side (and segment) lengths are known.

2. Students will use a special formula to find the length of an angle bisector of a triangle, given the lengths of its sides.

Preassessment

Students should have mastered most of the standard high school geometry course. For review purposes, have students work the following problem:

In a triangle whose sides have lengths 13, 14, and 15, what is the length of the altitude to the side of length 14?

Teaching Strategies

One of the major skills needed to develop Stewart's Theorem is a working knowledge of the Pythagorean

Theorem. The problem stated above requires this skill.

After students have drawn the diagram required by this problem, they will immediately see two right triangles.

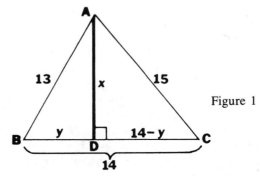

Figure 1

To this figure they will apply the Pythagorean Theorem twice, once to $\triangle ACD$ and a second time to $\triangle ABD$.

For $\triangle ACD$: $x^2 + (14 - y)^2 = 225$
For $\triangle ABD$: $x^2 + y^2 = 169$

By subtraction: $(14 - y)^2 - y^2 = 56$
                          $196 - 28y + y^2 - y^2 = 56$
                                                        $y = 5$
                  and then $x = 12$

Thus, students will see two right triangles with integral length sides: 5, 12, 13, and 9, 12, 15.

Now challenge your students to find the length of the angle bisector from vertex A of $\triangle ABC$. After a short time, their frustration will be evident. At this juncture, have the class stop working and discuss with them Stewart's Theorem:

Stewart's Theorem:

In Figure 2, the theorem states that:
$$a^2n + b^2m = c(d^2 + mn)$$

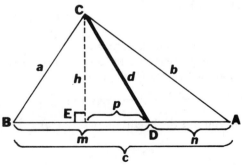

Figure 2

By this theorem, d may be found if a, b, m, and n are known. The proof of this most useful theorem follows.

Proof:

In $\triangle ABC$, let $BC = a$, $AC = b$, $AB = c$, $CD = d$. Point D divides $\overline{AB}$ into two segments; $BD = m$ and $DA = n$. Draw the altitude $CE = h$ and let $ED = p$.

In order to proceed with the proof of Stewart's Theorem, we first derive two necessary formulas. The first one is applicable to $\triangle CBD$. We apply the Pythagorean Theorem to $\triangle CEB$ to obtain
$$(CB)^2 = (CE)^2 + (BE)^2.$$
Since $BE = m - p$, $a^2 = h^2 + (m - p)^2$. (I)
However, by applying the Pythagorean Theorem to $\triangle CED$, we have $(CD)^2 = (CE)^2 + (ED)^2$, or $h^2 = d^2 - p^2$. Replacing h^2 in equation (I), we obtain
$$a^2 = d^2 - p^2 + (m - p)^2,$$
$$a^2 = d^2 - p^2 + m^2 - 2mp + p^2.$$
$$\text{Thus, } a^2 = d^2 + m^2 - 2mp. \quad \text{(II)}$$
A similar argument is applicable to $\triangle CDA$. Applying the Pythagorean Theorem to $\triangle CEA$, we find that
$$(CA)^2 = (CE)^2 + (EA)^2.$$
Since $EA = (n + p)$, $b^2 = h^2 + (n + p)^2$. (III)
However, $h^2 = d^2 - p^2$, substitute for h^2 in (III) as follows:
$$b^2 = d^2 - p^2 + (n + p)^2,$$
$$b^2 = d^2 - p^2 + n^2 + 2np + p^2.$$
$$\text{Thus, } b^2 = d^2 + n^2 + 2np. \quad \text{(IV)}$$
Equations (II) and (IV) give us the formulas we need. Now multiply equation (II) by n to get
$$a^2n = d^2n + m^2n - 2mnp, \quad \text{(V)}$$
and multiply equation (IV) by m to get
$$b^2m = d^2m + n^2m + 2mnp. \quad \text{(VI)}$$
Adding (V) and (VI), we have
$$a^2n + b^2m = d^2n + d^2m + m^2n + n^2m + 2mnp - 2mnp.$$
Therefore, $a^2n + b^2m = d^2(n + m) + mn(m + n)$.
Since $m + n = c$, we have $a^2n + b^2m = d^2c + mnc$, or
$$a^2n + b^2m = c(d^2 + mn).$$
Your students should now be ready to find the length of the median from vertex A of $\triangle ABC$, where

$AB = 13$, $BC = 14$, and $AC = 15$. All they need do is apply Stewart's Theorem as follows:
$$c^2n + b^2m = a(d^2 + mn)$$
However, since $\overline{AD}$ is a median $m = n$.

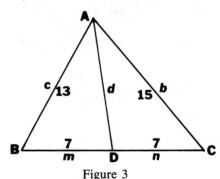

Figure 3

Substituting in the above formula:
$$13^2(7) + 15^2(7) = 14(d^2 + 49)$$
Therefore, $d = 2\sqrt{37}$.

To find the length of an angle bisector of a triangle, Stewart's Theorem leads to a very concise relationship, which students will find easy to use.

Have students consider $\triangle ABC$ with angle bisector $\overline{AD}$.

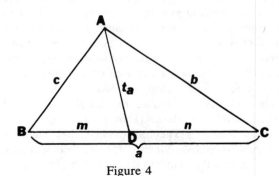

Figure 4

By Stewart's Theorem we obtain the following relationship: $c^2n + b^2m = a(t_a{}^2 + mn)$, or
$$t_a{}^2 + mn = \frac{c^2n + b^2m}{a}, \text{ or}$$
as illustrated by Figure 4.

But, $\dfrac{c}{b} = \dfrac{m}{n}$. (The bisector of an angle of a triangle divides the opposite side into segments whose measures are proportional to the measures of the other two sides of the triangle. The converse is also true.)
Therefore, $cn = bm$.
Substituting in the above equation,
$$t_a{}^2 + mn = \frac{cbm + cbn}{m + n} = \frac{cb(m + n)}{m + n} = cb.$$
Hence, $t_a{}^2 = cb - mn$.

At this juncture, your students should be able to find the length of *any* cevian of a triangle. For reinforcement, present problems involving angle bisectors and medians before going on to other types of cevians.

Postassessment

Have students complete the following exercises:

1. Find the length of an altitude drawn to the longest side of a triangle whose sides have lengths 10, 12, and 14.

2. Find the length of a median drawn to the longest side of a triangle whose sides have lengths 10, 12, and 14.

3. Find the length of an angle bisector drawn to the longest side of a triangle whose sides have lengths 10, 12, and 14.

4. In $\triangle PQR$, if $PR = 7$, $PQ = 8$, $RS = 4$, and $SQ = 5$, find PS when S is on $\overline{RQ}$.

48 A Surprising Challenge

This activity will alert geometry students to the fact that what may appear easy may actually be quite difficult.

Performance Objective
Given a geometric problem of the kind posed here, students will properly analyze it and solve it.

Preassessment
Students should be able to handle geometric proofs with relative ease before attempting this unit. The problem posed here is quite difficult to prove, yet easy to state. It ought to be within the reach of a slightly above average student of high school geometry.

Teaching Strategies
The geometric problem you are about to pose to your students appears to be quite simple and certainly innocent.

Problem: $\triangle ABC$ is isosceles ($CA = CB$). $m \angle ABD = 60°$, $m \angle BAE = 50°$, and $m \angle C = 20°$. Find the measure of $\angle EDB$.

Figure 2

Figure 1

Figure 3

Students should be given a fair amount of time to grapple with this problem. Immediately, they will find the measures of most of the angles in the diagram. However, they will soon realize that this problem was not as simple as they first imagined, since they will be most likely unable to solve the problem. At this point you can begin your discussion of a solution of this problem.

Students will be quick to realize that auxiliary lines are necessary in order to solve this problem. Suggest that they draw $\overline{DG} \parallel \overline{AB}$, where G is on $\overline{CB}$. Then draw $\overline{AG}$ intersecting $\overline{BD}$ at F. The last segment to be drawn is $\overline{EF}$. (See Fig. 2.)

Students should be able to prove that $\angle ABD \cong \angle BAG$. Then $m \angle AGD = m \angle BAG = 60°$ (alternate interior angles of parallel lines). Thus $m \angle AFB$ must be $60°$ and $\triangle AFB$ is equilateral, and $AB = FB$.

Since $m \angle EAB = 50°$, and $m \angle ABE = 80°$, $m \angle AEB = 50°$ making $\triangle ABE$ isosceles and $AB = EB$. Therefore $FB = EB$ (transitivity), and $\triangle EFB$ is isosceles.

Since $m \angle EBF = 20°$, $m \angle BEF = m \angle BFE = 80°$. As $m \angle DFG = 60°$, $m \angle GFE = 40°$. $GE = EF$ (equal length sides of an isosceles triangle), and $DF = DG$ (sides of an equilateral triangle). Thus $DGEF$ is a kite, i.e., two isosceles triangles externally sharing a common base. $\overline{DE}$ bisects $\angle GDF$ (property of a kite), therefore $m \angle EDB = 30°$.

Another possible method of solution follows:
In isosceles $\triangle ABC$, $m \angle ACB = 20°$, $m \angle CAB = 80°$, $m \angle ABD = 60°$, and $m \angle EAB = 50°$.
Draw $\overline{BF}$ so that $m \angle ABF = 20°$; then draw $\overline{FE}$ (Fig. 3).
In $\triangle ABE$, $m \angle AEB = 50°$ (sum of measures of the angles of a triangle is $180°$) therefore $\triangle ABE$ is isosceles and $AB = EB$.   (I)

Similarly, $\triangle FAB$ is isosceles, since $m \angle AFB = m \angle FAB = 80°$.
Thus $AB = FB$.   (II)

From (I) and (II), $EB = FB$. Since $m \angle FBE = 60°$, $\triangle FBE$ is equilateral and $EB = FB = FE$.   (III)

Now, in $\triangle DFB$, $m \angle FDB = 40°$, and $m \angle FBD = m \angle ABD - m \angle ABF = 60° - 20° = 40°$.
Thus $\triangle DFB$ is isosceles and $FD = FB$.   (IV)

It then follows from (III) and (IV) that $FE = FD$, making $\triangle FDE$ isosceles, and $m \angle FDE = m \angle FED$.
Since $m \angle AFB = 80°$ and $m \angle EFB = 60°$, then $m \angle AFE$, the exterior angle of isosceles $\triangle FDE$, equals $140°$, by addition. It follows that $m \angle ADE = 70°$. Therefore, $m \angle EDB = m \angle ADE - m \angle FDB = 70° - 40° = 30°$.

There are various other methods for solving this problem. One source for seven solutions of this problem is *Challenging Problems in Geometry, Volume 2,* by A.S. Posamentier and C.T. Salkind, pp. 34–39 (Macmillan, 1970).

Postassessment

Have students discover another solution for the above problem.

49 Making Discoveries in Mathematics

This activity is intended to permit the student to make discoveries based on observation, and then propose a conclusion.

Performance Objective
Faced with a mathematical pattern students will state their discoveries and propose a conclusion.

Teaching Strategies
This activity will be comprised of a series of mathematical mini-activities each of which will require the student to discover a pattern or relationship and then state his or her conclusion.

1. Select any two consecutive square numbers (e.g., 4 and 9). Give one prime between these two numbers. Repeat this for 10 other pairs of consecutive square numbers. Now try to find a pair of consecutive square numbers which do *not* have a prime number between them. What conclusion can you draw from this experiment?
2. Select any even integer greater than 2. Now express this even integer as the sum of exactly two prime numbers. For example, $8 = 3 + 5$, and $18 = 7 + 11$. Repeat this for at least 25 even integers before you draw any conclusions.
3. Draw *any* triangle. Using a protractor carefully trisect each of the angles of the triangle. Locate the points of intersection of the adjacent angle trisectors as illustrated below.

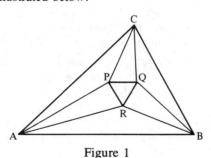

Figure 1

Join these three points and inspect the triangle formed. Repeat this construction for at least six different triangles before drawing any conclusion.
4. Draw *any* parallelogram. Construct an equilateral triangle externally on two adjacent sides as shown below. Then join the two remote vertices of the equilateral triangles to each other and to the farthest vertex of the parallelogram. What kind of triangle is formed? Before stating a conclusion repeat this experiment with at least six different parallelograms.

Students ought to be able to actually prove this last example. However, the other three examples should not be attempted; 1 and 2 have never been proved while 3 is extremely difficult to prove.*

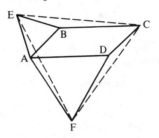

Figure 2

You might try to replicate these experiments with others similar to these. It is important for students to learn to trust their intuition in mathematics and be able to draw correct inductive conclusions.

Postassessment
Ask students to find the sum of the first 1,2,3,4,5,6, . . . 15 odd integers and list the 15 different sums. Then have the students state a logical conclusion.

*Two proofs of this theorem can be found in *Challenging Problems in Geometry, Volume 2*, by A.S. Posamentier, and C.T. Salkind. (New York: Macmillan, 1970) pp. 43–46.

50 Tessellations

Performance Objectives

1. *Given a regular polygon, each student will determine whether it will tessellate a plane.*

2. *Given a combination of various regular polygons, each student will determine whether they will tessellate a plane.*

Preassessment

Before beginning this lesson explain to students that when polygons are fitted together to cover a plane with no spaces between them and no overlapping, the pattern is called a *tessellation*. (Mention the pattern of tiles on bathroom floors as one of the more common tessellations.) A tessellation which is made up entirely of congruent regular polygons that meet so that no vertex of one polygon lies on a side of another is referred to as a regular tessellation. Explain further that a network of equilateral triangles, a checkerboard pattern of squares and a hexagonal pattern are the *only* tessellations of regular polygons that exist.

Teaching Strategies

To mathematically show why the previous three patterns are the only tessellations which fit the description, ask the class to suppose m regular polygons are required to fill the space around one point (where the vertex of the angles of the polygon is situated). If they assume that each regular polygon has n sides, each interior angle of the polygon is equal to $\frac{(n-2)\ 180°}{n}$. Therefore $\frac{m(n-2)\ 180°}{n} = 360°$ and $(m-2)(n-2) = 4$.

Considering the nature of the problem, both integers m and n are greater than 2. If $m=3$, then $n=6$. If $m>3$, then $n<6$ and since $n>2$ only the values $n=3$, $n=4$ and $n=5$ need be considered. If $n=3$, then $m=6$; if $n=4$, then $m=4$. If $n=5$, m is non-integral; therefore, the only solutions are $m=3$, $n=6$; $m=4$, $n=4$; $m=6$, $n=3$. Have students suggest more convenient ways of symbolizing these tessellations (6^3, 4^4, 3^6). Use the following diagrams to show that no other regular polygon has an interior angle that will divide 360°. (Fig. 1 & 2)

Through further investigation the range of tessellations may be expanded. Tessellations can also be formed by fitting together two or more kinds of regular polygons, vertex to vertex, in such a way that the same polygons, in the same cyclic order, surround each vertex. These are called *semi-regular* tessellations in which there can be no fewer than three and no more than six polygons at any vertex.

Ask students to consider a ternary arrangement

(three polygons share one point as vertex). Because the sum of the angles around any vertex must be 360°, a ternary arrangement of polygons of n_1, n_2 and n_3 sides respectively will be possible only if

$$(\frac{n_1-2}{n_1} + \frac{n_2-2}{n_2} + \frac{n_3-2}{n_3})\ 180° = 360°.$$

From this we obtain

$$(\frac{n_1}{n_1} - \frac{2}{n_1} + \frac{n_2}{n_2} - \frac{2}{n_2} + \frac{n_3}{n_3} - \frac{2}{n_3})\ 180° = 360°.$$

$$1 + 1 + 1 - 2(\frac{1}{n_1} + \frac{1}{n_2} + \frac{1}{n_3}) = 2.$$

Therefore, $\frac{1}{n_1} + \frac{1}{n_2} + \frac{1}{n_3} = \frac{1}{2}$.

In a similar way students can find the following conditions for other possible arrangements.

$$\frac{1}{n_1} + \frac{1}{n_2} + \frac{1}{n_3} + \frac{1}{n_4} = 1$$

$$\frac{1}{n_1} + \frac{1}{n_2} + \frac{1}{n_3} + \frac{1}{n_4} + \frac{1}{n_5} = \frac{3}{2}$$

$$\frac{1}{n_1} + \frac{1}{n_2} + \frac{1}{n_3} + \frac{1}{n_4} + \frac{1}{n_5} + \frac{1}{n_6} = 2$$

Following are the seventeen possible integer solutions that need be considered. (Table 1)

(Solutions 10, 14, and 17 have already been discussed. Solutions 1, 2, 3, 4, 6, and 9 each can be formed at a single vertex but they cannot be extended to cover the whole plane.) They are made up of different combinations of triangles, squares, hexagons, octagons, and dodecagons.

Any of the remaining solutions can be used as the only type of arrangement in a design covering a whole plane except #11, which must be used in conjunction with others, e.g. #5 or #15.

Have the class consider what happens in solution #5. Here two dodecagons and a triangle meet at a vertex. The extended figure can be formed by juxtaposing dodecagons as in figure 3. The remaining spaces form the triangles.

It may be noted that #7, composed of dodecagons, hexagons and squares, one at each vertex, gives a more complicated pattern (figure 4).

A juxtaposition of octagons (figure 5) forms #8. The empty spaces provide the areas needed for the squares.

Two different patterns can be obtained from #12 by the juxtaposition of hexagons. In one the hexagons have edges in common; in the other they have only vertices in common (figures 6 and 7). The empty spaces form triangles or diamond shapes composed of pairs of triangles.

Call on individual students to determine and draw the patterns for the remaining solutions.

Postassessment

1. Which of the following regular polygons will tessellate a plane: a) a square; b) a pentagon; c) an octagon; d) a hexagon.

2. Which of the following combinations of regular polygons will tessellate a plane: a) an octagon and a square; b) a pentagon and a decagon; c) a hexagon and triangle.

No.	n_1	n_2	n_3	n_4	n_5	n_6
1	3	7	42			
2	3	8	24			
3	3	9	18			
4	3	10	15			
5	3	12	12			
6	4	5	20			
7	4	6	12			
8	4	8	8			
9	5	5	10			
10	6	6	6			
11	3	3	4	12		
12	3	3	6	6		
13	3	4	4	6		
14	4	4	4	4		
15	3	3	3	3	4	
16	3	3	3	3	6	
17	3	3	3	3	3	3

Table 1

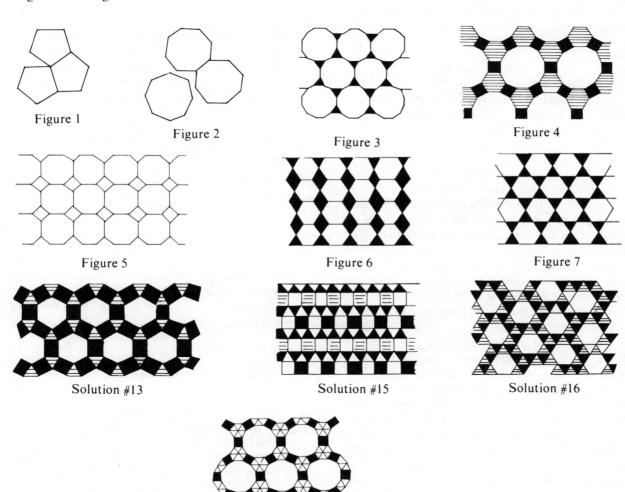

Figure 1

Figure 2

Figure 3

Figure 4

Figure 5

Figure 6

Figure 7

Solution #13

Solution #15

Solution #16

Solutions #11 & 17

51 Introducing the Pythagorean Theorem

This unit is intended for students taking the regular geometry course.

Performance Objective
Given appropriate measures, the student will use the Pythagorean Theorem to solve geometric problems.

In addition, it is expected that student appreciation for the Pythagorean Theorem will increase.

Preassessment
Have your students answer the following question:

Can a circular table top with a diameter of 9 feet fit through a rectangular door whose dimensions are 6 feet wide and 8 feet high?

Teaching Strategies
Students will immediately realize that the table top can possibly only fit through the door if it is tilted. Thereupon they will find a need for determining the length of the diagonal of this 6′ by 8′ rectangle. This is where you ought to introduce the Pythagorean Theorem. There are over 360 proofs of the Pythagorean Theorem available (see Elisha S. Loomis, *The Pythagorean Proposition,* National Council of Teachers of Mathematics, Washington, D.C., 1968.) A teacher may select the proof which he feels would be most interesting and intelligible for his particular class. Some proofs rely heavily on algebra while others are purely geometric.

Once the Pythagorean Theorem has been proved, the student is ready to apply his knowledge of the Theorem to some problems. Surely, he can now find that the length of the diagonal of the door (of the original problem) is 10 feet, and hence conclude that the table top would certainly fit through. There are many other "practical" problems which may be used to offer further application of the Pythagorean Theorem. For example, suppose your students wanted to find the diameter of a pipe. All they would have to do is place a carpenter's measuring square as shown in the figure. Then by measuring the length of x, the diameter would merely be $4.828x$. Students should of course be asked to analyze this. The broken lines in the diagram will help in the justification of this situation. Applying the Pythagorean Theorem to the right triangle shown:

$R^2 + R^2 = (R + x)^2$, or $R = x(1 + \sqrt{2})$.

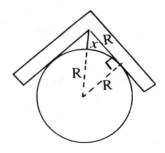

Another problem which you might have your students solve is that of finding the original diameter of broken plate where only a segment of the circle remains. Once again the diagram below depicts the situation: The lengths AB and CD

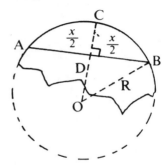

are measurable, and the broken lines are provided only for a discussion of the solution. Let $AB = x$, $CD = y$ and OB (the radius to be found) $= R$. Thus $OD = R - y$ and by the Pythagorean Theorem (in $\triangle ODB$) $(R - y)^2 + \frac{x^2}{2} = R^2$ and then $R = \frac{y}{2} + \frac{x^2}{8y}$ so that the diameter (in terms of the measurable lengths x and y) is $y + \frac{x^2}{4y}$.

From a strictly geometric point of view there are some rather interesting relationships which may be proved by applying the Pythagorean Theorem. You may wish to present some of these to your class as further application of this theorem.

1. If E is any point on altitude $\overline{AD}$, then $(AC)^2 - (CE)^2 = (AB)^2 - (EB)^2$.

2. If medians $\overline{AD}$ and $\overline{BE}$ of ΔABC are perpendicular then $AB = \sqrt{\dfrac{(AC)^2 + (BC)^2}{5}}$

3. If from any point inside a triangle, perpendiculars are drawn to the sides of the triangle, the sum of the squares of the measures of every other segment of the sides so formed equals the sum of the squares of the remaining three segments. That is in ΔABC below:

$$(BD)^2 + (CE)^2 + (AF)^2$$
$$= (DC)^2 + (EA)^2 + (FB)^2.$$

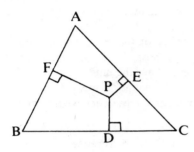

4. If $\overline{AD}$, $\overline{BE}$, and $\overline{CF}$ are medians of ΔABC,

   (I) then $\dfrac{3}{4}[(AB)^2 + (BC)^2 + (CA)^2]$

        $= (AD)^2 + (BE)^2 + (CF)^2.$

  (II) then $5(AB)^2 = 4(AE)^2 + (BE)^2$,
      if $m \angle C = 90$.

The complete solutions of these problems and many other more challenging problems can be found in: Posamentier, Alfred S., and Charles T. Salkind. *Challenging Problems in Geometry, Volume 1*. New York: Macmillan, 1970.

Once students have a fair command of this celebrated theorem, they are ready to consider a generalization of it.

To this juncture the students have considered the Pythagorean Theorem as $a^2 + b^2 = c^2$, where a and b represented the *lengths* of the legs of a right triangle and c represented the *length* of its hypotenuse. However this statement could also be interpreted to mean the following: "The sum of the *areas* of the squares on the legs of a right triangle equals the *area* of the square on the hypotenuse." For the right triangle below $\mathscr{A}\, S_a + \mathscr{A}\, S_b = \mathscr{A}\, S_c$ ($\mathscr{A}$ represents "area of").

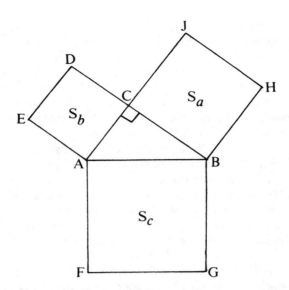

Now have students replace these squares with semicircles with diameters $\overline{BC}$, $\overline{AC}$, and $\overline{AB}$, or have them replace the squares with any similar polygons so that the corresponding sides are on the sides of ΔABC.

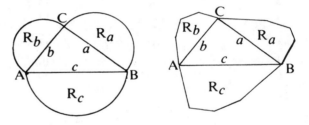

From a basic area relationship:

$$\frac{\mathscr{A}\, R_a}{\mathscr{A}\, R_c} = \frac{a^2}{c^2} \quad \text{and} \quad \frac{R_b}{R_c} = \frac{b^2}{c^2}$$

Then $\dfrac{\mathscr{A}\, R_a + \mathscr{A}\, R_b}{\mathscr{A}\, R_c} = \dfrac{a^2 + b^2}{c^2}$

However, by the Pythagorean Theorem:

$a^2 + b^2 = c^2$ so that $\dfrac{\mathscr{A}\, R_a + \mathscr{A}\, R_b}{\mathscr{A}\, R_c} = 1$, and $\mathscr{A}\, R_a$ $+ \mathscr{A}\, R_b = \mathscr{A}\, R_c$. The interesting significance of this extension of the Pythagorean Theorem ought to be highlighted. Then students pose other extensions.

Before leaving the geometric discussion of the Pythagorean Theorem, you might wish to show students how the converse of this theorem can be used to determine whether an angle of a triangle is acute, right or obtuse, given the lengths of the sides of the triangle.

That is,
  if $a^2 + b^2 = c^2$, $\angle C$ is a right angle;
  if $a^2 + b^2 > c^2$, $\angle C$ is acute;
  if $a^2 + b^2 < c^2$, $\angle C$ is obtuse.
These relationships should prove to be quite fascinating and useful to the students.

Having considered the Pythagorean Theorem from a geometric standpoint, it should be interesting to consider this theorem from a number theoretic point of view. A *Pythagorean Triple*, written as (a, b, c), is a set of three positive integers a, b, and c, where $a^2 + b^2 = c^2$. For any Pythagorean Triple (a, b, c) and any positive integer k, (ka, kb, kc) is also a triple. Your students should be able to prove this.

A *Primitive Pythagorean Triple* is a Pythagorean Triple whose first two members are *relatively prime*, one even and the other odd. Introduce this: where $a^2 + b^2 = c^2$ (and m and n are natural numbers, and $m > n$), $a = m^2 - n^2$, $b = 2mn$ and $c = m^2 + n^2$. (For a development of these relationships see: Sierpinski, W., *Pythagorean Triangles*. New York: Yeshiva University Press, 1962.) After setting up a table such as the following, students will begin to conjecture about properties of m and n which generate specific types of Pythagorean Triples. Students will also begin to group different types of Pythagorean Triples.

m	n	$m^2 - n^2$	$2mn$	$m^2 + n^2$
2	1	3	4	5
3	2	5	12	13
4	1	15	8	17
4	3	7	24	25
5	4	9	40	41
3	1	8	6	10
5	2	21	20	29

Some questions to anticipate are: What must be true about m and n in order for (a, b, c) to be a Primitive Pythagorean Triple? Can c of this triple ever be even? Why must the even member of a Primitive Pythagorean Triple be divisible by 4? What must be true about m and n in order that the third member of a Primitive Pythagorean Triple exceed one of the other members by 1? Why is one side of a Primitive Pythagorean Triple always divisible by 5? And why is the product of the three members of any Pythagorean Triple divisible by 60?

In a short while students will begin to probe the parity of numbers and the relationships of Pythagorean Triples. This genuine interest brought about by a rather elementary and superficial introduction to a topic in number theory may be the beginning of a student's investigation into a heretofore unfamiliar field.

Thus a study of the Pythagorean Theorem has a wide range of possibilities for interesting your students. *You* must take the initiative of introducing these variations on the theme. If this is properly done, your students will carry these endeavors further.

Reference

Posamentier, A.S., Banks, J.H., and Bannister, R.L. *Geometry, Its Elements and Structure,* 2d ed. New York: McGraw-Hill, 1977.

52 Trisection Revisited

Performance Objectives

1. Students will trisect a given angle using any of the four methods presented.

2. Students will prove the four methods of trisection.

Preassessment

Students should have a working knowledge of algebra. They should also have mastered constructions commonly taught in high school geometry and proofs of those constructions.

Teaching Strategies

After demonstrating and proving the following construction, discuss why it is not really a solution to the ancient problem of trisecting an angle using only Euclidean tools.

Given $\angle AOB_0$ with $m \angle AOB_0 = x$
Construct $\angle AOB_n$ such that $m \angle AOB_n = 2x/3$

Figure 1

Construction and Proof

1. Construct $\overline{OB_1}$, the bisector of $\angle AOB_0$ then
$$m\angle AOB_1 = x - \frac{1}{2}x$$

2. Construct $\overline{OB_2}$, the bisector of $\angle B_1OB_0$ then
$$m\angle AOB_2 = x - \frac{1}{2}x + \frac{1}{4}x$$

3. Construct $\overline{OB_3}$, the bisector of $\angle\ B_1OB_2$ then

$m\angle\ AOB_3 = x - \dfrac{1}{2}x + \dfrac{1}{4}x\quad -\dfrac{1}{8}\ x$

4. Construct $\overline{OB_4}$, the bisector of $\angle\ B_3OB_2$ then

$m\angle\ AOB_4 = x - \dfrac{1}{2}x + \dfrac{1}{4}x\quad -\dfrac{1}{8}\ x +\dfrac{1}{16}\ x$

5. Continuing in this fashion we will reach

$m\angle\ AOB_n= x - \dfrac{1}{2}x+ \dfrac{1}{4}x -\dfrac{1}{8}\ x + \ldots \pm (\dfrac{1}{2})^{n}x$

then we multiply by $(\dfrac{1}{2})$ to obtain $(\dfrac{1}{2})m\angle\ AOB_n$

$= \dfrac{1}{2}x - \dfrac{1}{4}x + \dfrac{1}{8}x - \dfrac{1}{16}x + \ldots \pm(\dfrac{1}{2})^{n+1}x.$ Now
we add the second equation to the first to get

$$(\dfrac{3}{2})m\angle\ AOB_n= x \pm (\dfrac{1}{2})^{n+1}\ x$$
$$m\angle\ AOB_n=\dfrac{2x}{3}\left[1\pm(\dfrac{1}{2})^{n+1}\right]$$

6. Now we observe that as n increases to infinity (which corresponds to carrying out an *infinite number* of construction operations) the term $(\dfrac{1}{2})^{n+1}$ approaches zero. Then $m\angle\ AOB_n$ approaches $\dfrac{2x}{3}$

The second construction adds to the Euclidean tools a strange looking device called a *tomahawk* (first published by Bergery in the third edition of *Geometrie Appliquee a l' Industrie*, Metz, 1835).

Figure 2

To construct a tomahawk, start with a line segment $\overline{RS}$ trisected at U and T. Draw a semicircle about U with radius $\overline{UT}$ and draw $\overline{TX}$ perpendicular to $\overline{RS}$. Complete the instrument as shown in the diagram.

To trisect any $\angle\ AOB$, simply place the implement on the angle so that S falls on $\overrightarrow{OB}$, TX passes through vertex O, and the semicircle is tangent to $\overrightarrow{AO}$ at some point, say D. Then, since we may easily show that $\triangle DOU \cong \triangle TOU \cong \triangle TOS$, we have $m\angle\ DOU=m\angle\ TOU=m\angle\ TOS$

$= \dfrac{1}{3}m\angle\ AOB$

The third construction is implied by a theorem given by Archimedes. In it we use a straightedge upon which a line segment has been marked. This extension of Euclidean tools makes possible an *insertion principle trisection*.

To demonstrate the insertion principle to students, have them try the following problem using Euclidean tools.

Given $\overline{MN}$ with curves q and n (such that the smallest distance between q and n is $\leq MN$) and point O not on q or n

Construct a line through O which intersects q and n at M_1 and N_1 respectively so that $M_1N_1 = MN$.

Except for certain special cases, this problem is impossible using only Euclidean tools. Now have students mark a line segment on their straightedges whose measure is equal to MN. It is now a

Figure 3

simple matter to adjust the marked straightedge until it describes a line through O with the distance between the two intersections equal to MN.

Now students are ready for the insertion principle trisection.

Given Circle O with central $\angle\ AOB$

Construct $\angle\ ADB$ so that $m\angle\ ADB = \dfrac{1}{3}m\angle\ AOB$

Figure 4

Construction

1. Draw $\overrightarrow{AO}$.
2. Mark AO on a straightedge.
3. Using the insertion principle draw $\overline{BD}$ such that D is on $\overrightarrow{AO}$ and $\overline{BD}$ intersects circle O at C with $\overline{AO} \cong \overline{CD}$. Then $m\angle\ ADB = \dfrac{1}{3}m\angle\ AOB$.

Proof

1. Draw $\overline{OC}$.
2. By construction $\overline{AO} \cong \overline{BO} \cong \overline{CO} \cong \overline{DC}$ (since the first three are radii of circle O and the last was constructed to be congruent to $\overline{AO}$).
3. $\triangle OCD$ and $\triangle BOC$ are isosceles.
4. Therefore $m \angle DOC = m\angle CDO = x$ and $m\angle OCB = m\angle OBC = y$
5. Since $\angle OCB$ is the exterior angle of $\triangle OCD$, $m\angle OCB = m\angle DOC + m\angle CDO = 2x$ or $y = 2x$.
6. Similarly since $\angle AOB$ is the exterior angle of $\triangle OBD$, $m\angle AOB = m\angle ADB + m\angle OBD = x + 2x = 3x$.
7. Thus, $m\angle ADB = \frac{1}{3} m\angle AOB$.

Ceva's method of trisection (the last of this unit) utilizes a device which consists of four hinged straightedges. In the diagram of Ceva's linkage, points C, D, E, and O are pivots such that the figure CDEO is a rhombus. To trisect a given angle A'O'B' one must first draw the circle about the vertex O' with radius equal to the length of a side of the rhombus CDEO. Ceva's instrument is then placed on the angle so that O and O' coincide. It is then adjusted until $\overrightarrow{DC}$ and $\overrightarrow{DE}$ go through the points where $\overrightarrow{OA'}$ and $\overrightarrow{OB'}$ intersect the circle,

points A and B respectively. Then $m\angle AOF = m\angle FOG = m\angle GOB = (\frac{1}{3})m\angle AOB$

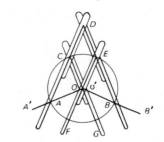

Figure 5

The proof uses the rhombus CDEO to obtain $m\angle ACG = m\angle COE = m\angle FEB = m\angle CDE = x$. Then $m\angle FOG = x$. Noting that points C and E are on the circle, we have $\angle ACG$ and $\angle FEB$ inscribed in the circle. Then $m\angle ACG = x = \frac{1}{2} m\angle AOG$ and $m\angle FEB = x = \frac{1}{2} m\angle FOB$ which gives us $2x = m\angle AOG$ and $2x = m\angle FOB$. Clearly then $m\angle AOF = m\angle FOG = m\angle GOB = \frac{1}{3} m\angle AOB$.

Postassessment

1. Prove the *tomahawk* trisection method valid.
2. Trisect any given arbitrary angle using any two of the methods presented in this unit.

53   Proving Lines Concurrent

This unit will present the student with a theorem which is quite useful in some cases when proving lines concurrent.

Performance Objective

Given appropriate problems, students will apply Ceva's Theorem to prove lines concurrent.

Preassessment

Have students try to prove any of the following:
1. Prove that the medians of a triangle are concurrent.
2. Prove that the angle bisectors of a triangle are concurrent.
3. Prove that the altitudes of a triangle are concurrent.

Teaching Strategies

An above average geometry student should, given enough time, be able to prove some of these theorems. It should be noted that the proofs they

would normally attempt (synthetically) are among the more difficult in the high school geometry course. Challenging students with these rather difficult problems sets the stage for the introduction of a theorem which will permit these problems to be done quite easily.

This theorem, first published in 1678 by the Italian mathematician Giovanni Ceva, is stated as follows:

Three lines drawn from the vertices A, B, and C of $\triangle ABC$ meeting the opposite sides in points L, M, and N, respectively, are concurrent if and only if

$$\frac{AN}{NB} \cdot \frac{BL}{LC} \cdot \frac{CM}{MA} = 1$$

Note: There are two cases: The three lines meeting inside or outside the given triangle.

Before applying this theorem to the problems posed earlier, it might be wise to prove the theorem.

Given: $\triangle ABC$, with N on $\overleftrightarrow{AB}$, M on $\overleftrightarrow{AC}$ and L on $\overleftrightarrow{BC}$; also $\overleftrightarrow{AL}$, $\overleftrightarrow{BM}$, and $\overleftrightarrow{CN}$ are concurrent at P.

Prove: $\dfrac{AN}{NB} \cdot \dfrac{BL}{LC} \cdot \dfrac{CM}{MA} = 1$

Proof: Draw a line through A, parallel to $\overleftrightarrow{BC}$ meeting $\overleftrightarrow{CP}$ at S and $\overleftrightarrow{BP}$ at R.

$$\triangle AMR \sim \triangle CMB$$

Therefore $\dfrac{AM}{MC} = \dfrac{AR}{CB}$ (I)

$$\triangle BNC \sim \triangle ANS$$

Therefore $\dfrac{BN}{NA} = \dfrac{CB}{SA}$ (II)

$$\triangle CLP \sim \triangle SAP$$

Therefore $\dfrac{CL}{SA} = \dfrac{LP}{AP}$ (III)

$$\triangle BLP \sim \triangle RAP$$

Therefore $\dfrac{BL}{RA} = \dfrac{LP}{AP}$ (IV)

From (III) and (IV) we get $\dfrac{CL}{SA} = \dfrac{BL}{RA}$, or

$\dfrac{CL}{BL} = \dfrac{SA}{RA}$ (V)

Now multiplying (I), (II), and (V) yields

$$\dfrac{AM}{MC} \cdot \dfrac{BN}{NA} \cdot \dfrac{CL}{BL} = \dfrac{AR}{CB} \cdot \dfrac{CB}{SA} \cdot \dfrac{SA}{RA} = 1$$

Since Ceva's Theorem is biconditional, it is necessary to prove the converse of the implication we have just proved.

Given: $\triangle ABC$ with N on $\overleftrightarrow{AB}$, M on $\overleftrightarrow{AC}$ and L on $\overleftrightarrow{BC}$; also $\dfrac{BL}{LC} \cdot \dfrac{CM}{MA} \cdot \dfrac{AN}{NB} = 1$.

Prove: $\overleftrightarrow{AL}$, $\overleftrightarrow{BM}$ and $\overleftrightarrow{CN}$ are concurrent.

Proof: Let $\overleftrightarrow{BM}$ and $\overleftrightarrow{AL}$ meet at P. Let $\overleftrightarrow{CP}$ meet AB at N'. Since $\overleftrightarrow{AL}$, $\overleftrightarrow{BM}$ and $\overleftrightarrow{CN'}$ are concurrent, by the part of Ceva's Theorem we have already proved we get:

$$\dfrac{BL}{LC} \cdot \dfrac{CM}{MA} \cdot \dfrac{AN'}{N'B} = 1.$$

However $\dfrac{BL}{LC} \cdot \dfrac{CM}{MA} \cdot \dfrac{AN}{NB} = 1$ (given)

Therefore $\dfrac{AN'}{N'B} = \dfrac{AN}{NB}$, so that N and N' must coincide. Thus the three lines are concurrent.

Students should now be ready to apply Ceva's Theorem to the three problems posed earlier.

1. Prove that the medians of a triangle are concurrent.

Proof: In $\triangle ABC$, $\overline{AL}$, $\overline{BM}$, and $\overline{CN}$ are medians (see figure below).

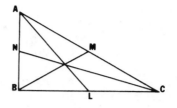

Therefore, AN = NB, BL = LC, and CM = MA. By multiplication (AN)(BL)(MC) = (NB)(LC)(MA), or $\dfrac{AN}{NB} \cdot \dfrac{BL}{LC} \cdot \dfrac{CM}{MA} = 1$.

Thus by Ceva's Theorem $\overleftrightarrow{AL}$, $\overleftrightarrow{BM}$, and $\overleftrightarrow{CN}$ are concurrent.

2. Prove that the angle bisectors of a triangle are concurrent.

Proof: In $\triangle ABC$, $\overline{AL}$, $\overline{BM}$, and $\overline{CN}$ are interior angle bisectors (see figure below).

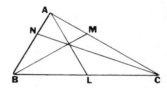

Since an angle bisector of a triangle partitions the opposite side into segments proportional to the two remaining sides of the triangle it follows that:

$\dfrac{AN}{NB} = \dfrac{AC}{BC}$, $\dfrac{BL}{LC} = \dfrac{AB}{AC}$ and $\dfrac{CM}{MA} = \dfrac{BC}{AB}$.

Then by multiplying

$$\dfrac{AN}{NB} \cdot \dfrac{BL}{LC} \cdot \dfrac{CM}{MA} = \dfrac{AC}{BC} \cdot \dfrac{AB}{AC} \cdot \dfrac{BC}{AB} = 1$$

Thus by Ceva's Theorem the three angle bisectors are concurrent.

3. Prove that the altitudes of a triangle are concurrent.

Proof: In $\triangle ABC$, $\overline{AL}$, $\overline{BM}$, and $\overline{CN}$ are altitudes (see figures below).

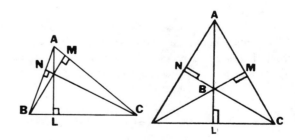

$\triangle ANC \sim \triangle AMB$, and $\dfrac{AN}{MA} = \dfrac{AC}{AB}$

$\triangle BLA \sim \triangle BNC$, and $\dfrac{BL}{NB} = \dfrac{AB}{BC}$

$\triangle CMB \sim \triangle CLA$, and $\dfrac{CM}{LC} = \dfrac{BC}{AC}$

By multiplying these three fractions we get:

$$\frac{AN}{MA} \cdot \frac{BL}{NB} \cdot \frac{CM}{LC} = \frac{AC}{AB} \cdot \frac{AB}{BC} \cdot \frac{BC}{AC} = 1$$

Thus by Ceva's Theorem the altitudes are concurrent.

These are some of the simpler applications of Ceva's Theorem. One source for finding more applications of Ceva's Theorem is *Challenging Problems in Geometry Vol. II*, by A.S. Posamentier and C.T. Salkind, Macmillan, 1970.

Postassessment

1. Have students use Ceva's Theorem to prove that when △ABC has points P, Q and R on sides $\overline{AB}$, $\overline{AC}$ and $\overline{BC}$, respectively, and when

$\dfrac{AQ}{QC} = \dfrac{BR}{RC} = 2$, and AP = PB, it follows that $\overline{AR}$, $\overline{BQ}$, and $\overline{CP}$ are concurrent.

2. △ABC cuts a circle at points E, E′, D, D′, F, F′ (see figure below). Prove that if $\overline{AD}$, $\overline{BF}$, and $\overline{CE}$ are concurrent, then $\overline{AD'}$, $\overline{BF'}$ and $\overline{CE'}$ are also concurrent.

54   Squares

This unit will strengthen students' skills at proving quadrilaterals to be squares in addition to revisiting the topic of concurrency.

Performance Objective

Students will explain a method for proving concurrency.

Preassessment

Students should be familiar with the various properties of a square and should have had some experience in proving quadrilaterals to be squares.

Teaching Strategies

Have students construct a square externally on each side of a given parallelogram (see figure below). Have them locate the center of each square by drawing the diagonals. Ask the class what figure they believe will result by joining the centers of consecutive squares. Natural curiosity should motivate them to try to prove that PQRS is a square.

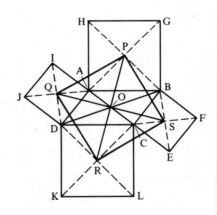

Proof:

ABCD is a parallelogram.

Points *P*, *Q*, *R*, and *S* are the centers of the four squares *ABGH*, *DAIJ*, *DCLK* and *CBFE*, respectively. *PA = DR* and *AQ = QD* (each is one-half a diagonal).

∠*ADC* is supplementary to ∠*DAB*, and ∠*IAH* is supplementary to ∠*DAB* (since ∠*IAD* and ∠*HAB* are right angles). Therefore ∠*ADC* ≅ ∠*IAH*.

Since m∠*RDC* = m∠*QDA* = m∠*HAP* = m∠*QAI* = 45°, ∠*RDQ* ≅ ∠*QAP*. Thus △*RDQ* ≅ △*PAQ* (SAS) and *QR = QP*.

In a similar fashion, it may be proved that *QP = PS* and *PS = RS*.

Therefore, *PQRS* is a rhombus.
Since $\triangle RDQ \cong \triangle PAQ$, $\angle DQR \cong \angle AQP$; therefore, $PQR \cong \angle DQA$ (by addition).
Since $\angle DQA \cong$ right angle, $\angle PQR \cong$ right angle, and *PQRS* is a square.

Careful drawing of the figure above should indicate that the diagonals of square *PQRS* and the diagonals of parallelogram *ABCD* are concurrent. This proof deserves special attention since it illustrates an all too often neglected skill; proving concurrency.

To prove that the diagonals of square *PQRS* are concurrent with the diagonals of parallelogram *ABCD*, we must prove that a diagonal of the square and a diagonal of the parallelogram bisect each other. In other words, we prove that the diagonals of the square and the diagonals of the parallelogram all share

the same midpoint, (i.e., point *O*).
$BAC \cong \angle ACD$, and $m\angle PAB = m\angle RCD = 45$, therefore $\angle PAC \cong \angle RCA$.
Since $\angle AOP \cong \angle COR$ and $AP = CR$, $\triangle AOP \cong \triangle COR$ (SAA)
Thus, $AO = CO$, and $PO = RO$.
Since $\overline{DB}$ passes through the midpoint of $\overline{AC}$, (diagonals bisect each other) and similarly, $\overline{QS}$ passes through the midpoint of $\overline{PR}$, and since $\overline{AC}$ and $\overline{PR}$ share the same midpoint (i.e., *O*) we have shown that $\overline{AC}$, $\overline{PR}$, $\overline{DB}$, and $\overline{QS}$ are concurrent (i.e., all pass through point *O*).

Postassessment

Ask students to explain a method for proving lines concurrent. It is expected that they will explain the method used in this lesson.

55 Proving Points Collinear

This unit will present the student with a theorem which is quite useful in certain cases, when proving points collinear.

Performance Objective
Given appropriate problems students will apply Menelaus' Theorem to prove points collinear.

Preassessment
Have students try to prove that the interior angle bisectors of two angles of a non-isosceles triangle and the exterior angle bisector of the third angle meet the opposite sides in three collinear points.

Teaching Strategies
The average student of high school geometry is not properly trained or equipped to prove points collinear. Thus, in most cases you will find the preassessment problem beyond student ability. However, this **unit** will provide you with sufficient student interest to introduce a theorem which will provide a simple solution.

This theorem, originally credited to Menelaus of Alexandria (about 100 A.D.) is particularly useful in proving points collinear. It states that:
Points P, Q, and R on sides $\overline{AC}$, $\overline{AB}$, and $\overline{BC}$ of $\triangle ABC$ are collinear if and only if

$$\frac{AQ}{QB} \cdot \frac{BR}{RC} \cdot \frac{CP}{PA} = 1$$

This is a two part (biconditional) proof.

Part I to prove $\dfrac{AQ}{QB} \cdot \dfrac{BR}{RC} \cdot \dfrac{CP}{PA} = 1$

Proof: Points P, Q, and R are collinear. Consider the line through C, parallel to $\overline{AB}$, and meeting $\overline{PQR}$ at D.

Since $\triangle DCR \sim \triangle QBR$, $\dfrac{DC}{QB} = \dfrac{RC}{BR}$ or

$$DC = \frac{(QB)(RC)}{BR} . \qquad (a)$$

Similarly, since $\triangle PDC \sim \triangle PQA$, $\dfrac{DC}{AQ} = \dfrac{CP}{PA}$, or

$$DC = \frac{(AQ)(CP)}{PA} \qquad (b)$$

From (a) and (b): $\dfrac{(QB)(RC)}{BR} = \dfrac{(AQ)(CP)}{PA}$.

Therefore $(QB)(RC)(PA) = (AQ)(CP)(BR)$ which indicates that $\dfrac{AQ}{QB} \cdot \dfrac{BR}{RC} \cdot \dfrac{CP}{PA} = 1$.

Part II involves proving the converse of the implication proved in Part I since this theorem is biconditional.

Proof: In the figures above let the line through R and Q meet $\overleftrightarrow{AC}$ at P'. Then by the theorem just proved $\dfrac{AQ}{QB} \cdot \dfrac{BR}{RC} \cdot \dfrac{CP'}{P'A} = 1$

However by hypothesis,

$\dfrac{AQ}{QB} \cdot \dfrac{BR}{RC} \cdot \dfrac{CP}{PA} = 1$

Therefore $\dfrac{CP'}{P'A} = \dfrac{CP}{PA}$ and P and P' must coincide.

At this point students should be ready to apply Menelaus' Theorem to the problem presented in the preassessment.

Given: $\triangle ABC$, where $\overline{BM}$ and $\overline{CN}$ are interior angle bisectors and $\overline{AL}$ bisects the exterior angle at A

Prove: N, M and L are collinear.

Have students recall the important proportionality theorem about the angle bisector of a triangle.

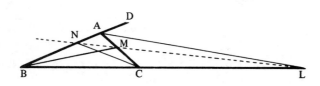

Proof: Since $\overline{BM}$ bisects $\angle ABC$, $\dfrac{AM}{MC} = \dfrac{AB}{BC}$

Since $\overline{CN}$ bisects $\angle ACB$, $\dfrac{BN}{NA} = \dfrac{BC}{AC}$.

Since $\overline{AL}$ bisects the exterior angle at A, $\dfrac{CL}{BL} = \dfrac{AC}{AB}$.

Therefore by multiplication:

$\dfrac{AM}{MC} \cdot \dfrac{BN}{NA} \cdot \dfrac{CL}{BL} = \dfrac{AB}{BC} \cdot \dfrac{BC}{AC} \cdot \dfrac{AC}{AB} = 1$

Thus, by Menelaus' Theorem N, M, and L must be collinear.

To provide further practice applying this useful theorem have students consider the following problem.

Prove that if tangents to the circumcircle of $\triangle ABC$, at A, B, and C, meet sides $\overline{BC}$, $\overleftrightarrow{AC}$ and $\overleftrightarrow{AB}$ at points P, Q, and R, respectively, then points P, Q, and R are collinear.

Proof: Since $m\angle BAC = \frac{1}{2}m\widehat{BC} = m\angle QBC$, $\triangle ABQ \sim \triangle BCQ$

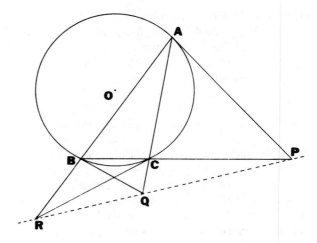

and $\dfrac{AQ}{BQ} = \dfrac{BA}{BC}$, or $\dfrac{(AQ)^2}{(BQ)^2} = \dfrac{(BA)^2}{(BC)^2}$.   (I)

However $(BQ)^2 = (AQ)(CQ)$ (II)

Substituting (II) into (I) yields $\dfrac{AQ}{CQ} = \dfrac{(BA)^2}{(BC)^2}$ (III)

Similarly, $m\angle BCR = \frac{1}{2}m\widehat{BC} = m\angle BAC$; therefore

$\triangle CRB \sim \triangle ARC$ and $\dfrac{CR}{AR} = \dfrac{BC}{AC}$, or

$\dfrac{(CR)^2}{(AR)^2} = \dfrac{(BC)^2}{(AC)^2}$.   (IV)

However, $(CR)^2 = (AR)(RB)$.   (V)

Substituting (V) into (IV) yields

$\dfrac{RB}{AR} = \dfrac{(BC)^2}{(AC)^2}$.   (VI)

Students should now be asked to use the same scheme to prove $\triangle CAP \sim \triangle ABP$ and in a similar manner obtain $\dfrac{PC}{BP} = \dfrac{(AC)^2}{(BA)^2}$ (VII)

Now multiplying these proportions (i.e. (III), (VI), and (VII)) yields:

$\dfrac{AQ}{CQ} \cdot \dfrac{RB}{AR} \cdot \dfrac{PC}{BP} = \dfrac{(BA)^2}{(BC)^2} \cdot \dfrac{(BC)^2}{(AC)^2} \cdot \dfrac{(AC)^2}{(BA)^2} = 1$

Thus, by Menelaus' Theorem, P, Q and R are collinear.

Postassessment

Have students use Menelaus' Theorem to prove that the exterior angle bisectors of any non-isosceles triangle meet the opposite sides in three collinear points. The figure below should be useful.

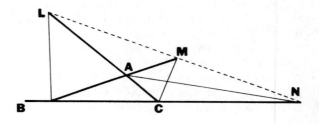

56 Angle Measurement with a Circle

This unit presents a rather unusual method for developing the theorems on angle measurement with a circle, normally considered in the tenth grade geometry course.

Performance Objectives

1. *Given appropriate materials, students will generate the various angle measurement theorems in the manner developed in this unit.*

2. *Given problems which require the use of the theorems discussed in this unit, students will be able to solve them successfully.*

Preassessment

Students should be familiar with an inscribed angle and the relationship of its measure to that of its intercepted arc.

Teaching Strategies

In addition to using the usual classroom materials, you should prepare the following:

a) A piece of cardboard with two dark colored pieces of string attached, forming an angle of convenient size.

b) A cardboard circle with an inscribed angle congruent to the "string angle."

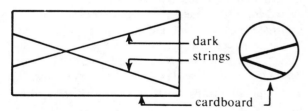

Naturally, it would be best if each student could prepare his own set of these materials in order to perform the following activities individually.

Refresh your students' memories about the relationship of an inscribed angle and its intercepted arc. Have them place the circle under the strings so that the two angles coincide:

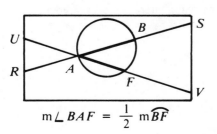

$$m\angle BAF = \frac{1}{2} m\widehat{BF}$$

Now have students slide the circle to the position illustrated below, where the rays of $\angle BAF$ are respectively parallel to the rays of the "string angle," $\angle NMQ$, and where the circle is tangent to $\overleftrightarrow{UQV}$ at M.

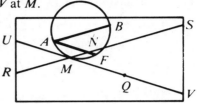

Students should realize that $m\widehat{FM} = m\widehat{AM}$, and $m\widehat{AM} = m\widehat{BN}$ (due to the parallel lines). Therefore $m\widehat{FM} = m\widehat{BN}$. Since $m\angle NMQ = m\angle BAF$, and $m\angle BAF = \frac{1}{2} m\widehat{BF} = \frac{1}{2}(m\widehat{BN} + m\widehat{NF}) = \frac{1}{2}(m\widehat{FM} + m\widehat{NF}) = \frac{1}{2}m\widehat{MN}$, $m\angle NMQ = \frac{1}{2}m\widehat{MN}$. This proves the theorem that *the measure of an angle formed by a tangent and a chord of a circle is one half the measure of its intercepted arc.*

Now have your students slide the circle to a position where the vertex of the string angle is on a $\overline{AF}$ and where $\overline{AB}//\overline{RS}$.

Once again because parallel lines exist here ($\overleftrightarrow{AB} // \overleftrightarrow{MN}$) $m\widehat{AM} = m\widehat{BN}$, and $m\angle BAF = m\angle NEF$. The students should now see that $m\angle BAF = \frac{1}{2}m\widehat{BF} = \frac{1}{2}(m\widehat{BN} + m\widehat{NF}) = \frac{1}{2}(m\widehat{AM} + m\widehat{NF})$. They may then conclude that $m\angle NEF = \frac{1}{2}(m\widehat{AM} + m\widehat{NF})$. This proves the theorem that *the measure of an angle formed by two chords intersecting in a point in the interior of a circle is one half the sum of the measures of the arcs intercepted by the angle and its vertical angle.*

To consider the next type of angle, have your students slide the circle to the position illustrated below, where the string angle now appears as an angle formed by two secants.

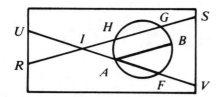

In this new position $\overrightarrow{AB}\,//\,\overrightarrow{GI}$ and $\overrightarrow{AF}$ is in $\overleftrightarrow{IF}$. Because $\overrightarrow{AB}\,//\,\overrightarrow{GI}$, $m\widehat{BG} = m\widehat{HA}$ and $m\angle BAF = m\angle GIF$. Have students once again follow the reasoning that $m\angle BAF = \frac{1}{2}m\widehat{BF} = \frac{1}{2}(m\widehat{BF} + m\widehat{BG} - m\widehat{BG}) = \frac{1}{2}(m\widehat{BF} + m\widehat{BG} - m\widehat{HA}) = \frac{1}{2}(m\widehat{GBF} - m\widehat{HA})$. They may then conclude that $m\angle GIF = \frac{1}{2}(m\widehat{GBF} - m\widehat{HA})$, which proves the theorem that *the measure of an angle formed by two secants intersecting in a point in the exterior of a circle is equal to one half the difference of the measures of the intercepted arcs.*

The next position of the circle will enable students to consider an angle formed by a tangent and a secant intersecting in the exterior of a circle. Have students slide the circle to the position as indicated in the following illustration.

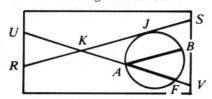

Here $\overrightarrow{AB}\,//\,\overrightarrow{KJS}$, $\overrightarrow{AF}$ is in $\overrightarrow{KV}$ and the circle is tangent to $\overleftrightarrow{KS}$ at J. Because $\overrightarrow{AB}\,//\,\overrightarrow{KJS}$, $m\widehat{JA} = m\widehat{JB}$ and $m\angle BAF = m\angle JKF$.

By now students should be able to produce the following without much difficulty:

$m\angle BAF = \frac{1}{2}m\widehat{BF} = \frac{1}{2}(m\widehat{BF} + m\widehat{JB} - m\widehat{JB})$
$= \frac{1}{2}(m\widehat{BF} + m\widehat{JB} - m\widehat{JA}) = \frac{1}{2}(m\widehat{JBF} - m\widehat{JA})$.

They should then conclude that $m\angle JKF = \frac{1}{2}(m\widehat{JBF} - m\widehat{JA})$, which proves the theorem that *the measure of an angle formed by a secant and a tangent to a circle intersecting in a point exterior to the circle is equal to one half the difference of the measures of the intercepted arcs.*

The last type of angle to be considered is an angle formed by two tangents. To form this angle the circle should be positioned tangent to each of the two strings so that each string is parallel to one of the rays of the angle in the circle.

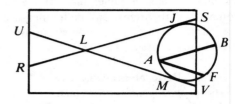

With the circle in the above position $\overrightarrow{AB}\,//\,\overrightarrow{LJS}$ and $\overrightarrow{AF}\,//\,\overrightarrow{LMV}$. Students should now be able to complete this proof independently. They should reason that $m\widehat{JB} = m\widehat{JA}$ and $m\widehat{MF} = m\widehat{MA}$; also $m\angle BAF = m\angle JLM$. Hence, $m\angle BAF = \frac{1}{2}m\widehat{BF}$
$= \frac{1}{2}(m\widehat{BF} + m\widehat{JB} + m\widehat{MF} - m\widehat{JB} - m\widehat{MF})$
$= \frac{1}{2}(m\widehat{BF} + m\widehat{JB} + m\widehat{MF} - m\widehat{JA} - m\widehat{MA}) = \frac{1}{2}(m\widehat{JBM} - m\widehat{JAM})$. Thus, $m\angle JLM = \frac{1}{2}(m\widehat{JBM} - m\widehat{JAM})$, which proves the theorem that *the measure of an angle formed by two tangents is equal to one half the difference of the measures of the intercepted arcs.*

To summarize this presentation have students realize that (1) the measure of an angle whose vertex is *on* the circle is one half the measure of the intercepted arc, (2) the measure of an angle whose vertex is *inside* the circle is one half the *sum* of the measures of the intercepted arcs, and (3) the measure of an angle whose vertex is *outside* the circle is one half *the difference* of the measures of the intercepted arcs.

As an alternative method for using this technique with your classes see *Geometry, Its Elements and Structure,* 2d ed., by A. S. Posamentier, J. H. Banks, and R. L. Bannister (McGraw-Hill, 1977), pp. 396–402.

Postassessment

Have students redevelop some of the above theorems using methods presented in this unit.

57 Trisecting a Circle

To partition a circle into two regions of equal area is a rather simple matter. However, to partition a circle into <u>three</u> regions of equal area is a more interesting problem. In this unit students will investigate various methods of accomplishing this.

Performance Objective
Students will be able to partition a circle into three regions of equal area.

Preassessment
Students should be able to perform some simple geometric constructions using a straightedge and compass. They should also be familiar with the Pythagorean Theorem and the formula for the area of a circle.

Teaching Strategies
Ask students to partition a circle into two regions of equal area. The obvious solution is for them merely to draw the diameter of the given circle. Now ask students to partition a circle into three regions of equal area (hereafter referred to as "trisecting a circle"). This too, should cause no problem as students will realize that they must merely construct (using straightedge and compasses) three adjacent angles of measure 120°.

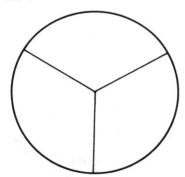

Figure 1

To construct this trisection they simply mark off six equal arcs along the circle with the compasses open to the radius of the circle. You may wish to justify this construction by referring to the inscribed hexagon, similarly constructed.

If you now ask students for another method of trisecting a circle, you will find them experimenting with another symmetry about the center. Ultimately this experimentation should lead to a consideration of two concentric circles, each concentric with the given circle. The problem then is to determine the lengths of the radii of the two circles.

Suppose students first find the radius, x, of a circle whose area is ⅓ that of a given circle of radius r. Then $\pi x^2 = \frac{1}{3}\pi r^2$, which yields $x = \frac{r}{\sqrt{3}} = \frac{r\sqrt{3}}{3}$. In a similar way they can find the radius, y, of a circle whose area is ⅔ that of a given circle of radius r. That is, $\pi y^2 = \frac{2}{3}\pi r^2$, which yields $y = \frac{r\sqrt{2}}{\sqrt{3}} = \frac{r\sqrt{6}}{3}$.

Now that the lengths have been established, the only problem remaining is to do the actual construction. Have students begin with a circle of radius r. To construct x, rewrite $x = \frac{r\sqrt{3}}{3}$ as $\frac{x}{\sqrt{3}} = \frac{r}{3}$. Then mark off the lengths r and 3 on a convenient line segment.

Figure 2

With any convenient angle, have students mark off a length $\sqrt{3}$ along this newly drawn ray. To construct a line segment of length $\sqrt{3}$ students may use any convenient method. For example, the radical spiral may be used (Figure 3).

Figure 3

Another method for constructing a line segment of length $\sqrt{3}$ would involve setting up a diagram as shown in Figure 4.

Figure 4

Once this length ($\sqrt{3}$) has been marked off along $\overline{DCB}$ (see Figure 2), students can construct a line through A parallel to $\overrightarrow{EC}$ to meet $\overrightarrow{DC}$ at B. Using proportions, they can establish that $x = BC = \dfrac{r\sqrt{3}}{3}$.

Thus, tell students to draw a circle of radius x concentric with the given circle. (Figure 5). The smaller circle has an area ⅓ that of the large circle. To complete the trisection students should construct a circle, radius y, concentric with the given circle.

The area of the circle of radius y must be ⅔ the area of the circle of radius r. Therefore, $\pi y^2 = \frac{2}{3}\pi r^2$, and $y = \dfrac{r\sqrt{2}}{\sqrt{3}} = \dfrac{r\sqrt{6}}{3}$. Have students construct y in a manner similar to the construction of x and then draw the circle concentric with the others (see the dotted-line circle in Figure 5).

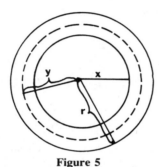

Figure 5

The resulting figure shows a trisected circle.

A more intriguing trisection of a circle involves a rather unusual partitioning.

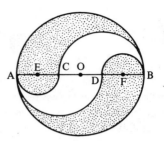

Figure 6

In Figure 6 the diameter of the given circle is trisected at points C and D. Four semicircles are then drawn as shown in the figure. Each of the two shaded regions is ⅓ the area of the given circle. Therefore the non-shaded region must also be ⅓ the area of the circle and thus the circle is trisected.

To prove this trisection valid, students need to show that one of the shaded regions has an area ⅓ that of the original circle. The area of the "upper" shaded region = area semicircle AB − area semicircle BC + area semicircle AC. If AE = r, AO = $3r$, and BD = $2r$. Therefore the area of the "upper" shaded region = $\frac{1}{2}\pi(3r)^2 - \frac{1}{2}\pi(2r)^2 + \frac{1}{2}\pi r^2 = \dfrac{9\pi r^2}{2} - \dfrac{4\pi r^2}{2} + \dfrac{\pi r^2}{2} = 3\pi r^2$. However the area of the original circle to be trisected = $\pi(3r)^2 = 9\pi r^2$. Thus, the area of each shaded region is ⅓ the area of the original circle, which is then trisected.

Postassessment

Give students a circle and ask them to partition it into three regions of equal area.

58 Ptolemy's Theorem

This unit will offer the student a very powerful theorem about cyclic (inscribed) quadrilaterals.

Performance Objective

Given appropriate problems, students will apply Ptolemy's Theorem to successfully solve the problem.

Preassessment

Present students with an isosceles trapezoid with bases of length 6 and 8 and legs of length 5.

Ask them to find the length of a diagonal of the trapezoid.

Teaching Strategies

Students who are familiar with the Pythagorean Theorem should be able to solve this problem with two applications of this theorem. However, most students, after being shown this method, will certainly welcome a less tedious method of solution. This is when you introduce Ptolemy's Theorem.

Ptolemy's Theorem: In a cyclic (inscribed) quadrilateral, the product of the lengths of the diagonals is equal to the sum of the products of the lengths of the pairs of opposite sides.

Before proving this theorem be sure students understand the statement of the theorem and understand what a cyclic quadrilateral is. Some of the more popular theorems about cyclic quadrilaterals ought to be reviewed here. Examples of non-cyclic quadrilaterals should also be given, so that students better appreciate cyclic quadrilaterals.

Proof: Consider quadrilateral ABCD inscribed in circle O. Draw a line through A to meet $\overrightarrow{CD}$ at P, so that $m\angle BAC = m\angle DAP$.

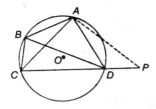

Since quadrilateral ABCD is cyclic, $\angle ABC$ is supplementary to $\angle ADC$. However, $\angle ADP$ is supplementary to $\angle ADC$. Therefore $m\angle ABC = m\angle ADP$. We can then prove $\triangle BAC \sim \triangle DAP$, and $\dfrac{AB}{AD} = \dfrac{BC}{DP}$, or $DP = \dfrac{(AD)(BC)}{AB}$.

Since $m\angle BAC = m\angle DAP$, $m\angle BAD = m\angle CAP$.

Since $\triangle BAC \sim \triangle DAP$, $\dfrac{AB}{AD} = \dfrac{AC}{AP}$. Therefore

$\triangle ABD \sim \triangle ACP$, then $\dfrac{BP}{CP} = \dfrac{AB}{AC}$, or $CP = \dfrac{(AC)(BD)}{AB}$.

But, $CP = CD + DP$.

By substitution $\dfrac{(AC)(BD)}{AB} = CD + \dfrac{(AD)(BC)}{AB}$.

Now simplifying this expression gives us the desired result:

$$(AC)(BD) = (AB)(CD) + (AD)(BC)$$

which is Ptolemy's Theorem.

Show students how Ptolemy's Theorem may be used to solve the preassessment problem. Since an isosceles trapezoid is a cyclic quadrilateral, Ptolemy's Theorem may be used to get $d^2 = (6)(8) + (5)(5) = 73$.

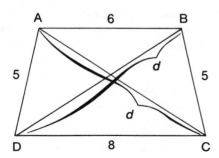

Therefore the length of a diagonal (d) is $\sqrt{73}$.

Students are often curious if a "new" theorem is consistent with theorems they learned earlier. Have students apply Ptolemy's Theorem to a rectangle (which is clearly a cyclic quadrilateral). For rectangle ABCD, Ptolemy's Theorem appears as: $(AC)(BD) = (AD)(BC + (AB)(DC)$.

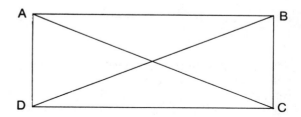

However, in the rectangle AB = DC, AD = BC, and AC = BD. Therefore by substitution $(AC)^2 = (AD)^2 + (DC)^2$, which is the Pythagorean Theorem.

Now have students consider a rather simple application of this celebrated theorem.

Problem: If point P is on arc AB of the circumscribed circle of equilateral $\triangle ABC$, and AP = 3 while BP = 4, find the length of $\overline{CP}$.

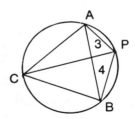

Solution: Let t represent the length of a side of equilateral $\triangle ABC$. Since quadrilateral APBC is cyclic, we may apply Ptolemy's Theorem, which yields:

$$(CP)(t) = (AP)(t) + (BP)(t).$$

Therefore CP = AP + BP = 3 + 4 = 7.

Students should be encouraged to investigate similar problems where the equilateral triangle is replaced with other regular polygons.

Often problems appear to be easier than they actually are. The next problem to be considered is one which seems to be easily solvable by simply using the Pythagorean Theorem. However, in solution it becomes useful to employ Ptolemy's Theorem.

Problem: On side $\overline{AB}$ of square ABCD, a right $\triangle ABF$, with hypotenuse $\overline{AB}$, is drawn externally to the square. If AF = 6 and BF = 8, find EF, where E is the point of intersection of the diagonals of the square.

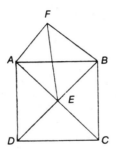

Solution: Applying the Pythagorean Theorem to right △AFB, we get AB = 10, and to right △AEB, we get AE = BE = $5\sqrt{2}$. Since $m\angle$AFB = $m\angle$AEB = 90, quadrilateral AFBE is cyclic. Now we may apply Ptolemy's Theorem to quadrilateral AFBE, to get (AB)(EF) = (AF)(BE) + (AE)(BF)

Substituting the appropriate values gives us: (10)(EF) = (6)$(5\sqrt{2})$ + $(5\sqrt{2})$(8), or EF = $7\sqrt{2}$.

Students should be encouraged to reconsider this problem with right △ABF drawn internally to the square. In that case EF = $\sqrt{2}$.

Postassessment

Have students solve each of the following problems:

1. E is a point on side $\overline{AD}$ of rectangle ABCD, so that DE = 6, while DA = 8, and DC = 6. If $\overline{CE}$ extended meets the circumcircle of the rectangle at F, find the measure of chord $\overline{DF}$.

2. Point P on side $\overline{AB}$ of right △ABC is placed so that BP = PA = 2. Point Q is on hypotenuse AC so that $\overline{PQ}$ is perpendicular to $\overline{AC}$. If CB = 3, find the measure of $\overline{BQ}$, using Ptolemy's Theorem.

 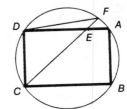

Reference

Posamentier, Alfred S. and Charles T. Salkind, *Challenging Problems in Geometry, Volume II*. New York: Macmillan, 1970.

59 Constructing π

Performance Objectives

1) *Students will demonstrate a clear knowledge of the π ratio and its relationship to the circle.*

2) *Students will construct π in more than one way.*

Preassessment

Before beginning a discussion of π, review with students the meaning of diameter and circumference. Have students measure the diameter and circumference of a 25-cent piece. Also ask them to obtain similar measurements of other circular objects. Stress the importance of accurate measurement.

Teaching Strategies

Begin the lesson by writing the following chart on the chalkboard:

Record some of the measurements that the students obtained. They should all have found that the diam-

eter of the quarter is *about* 2.4 mm long and that its circumference is *approximately* 7.8 mm. Have students then fill in the rest of the chart for the objects that they have measured. Ask them if any column seems to result in approximately the same value for each object measured and have them take the average of the numbers in that column. Their averages should be close to 3.14 (i.e. $\frac{C}{D}\approx 3.14$). It should be reemphasized that all the other columns produced varying results, whereas in the last column $\frac{C}{D}$ was the same regardless of the size of the object.

In 1737, this ratio was given the special name of "π" by Leonhard Euler, a famous Swiss mathematician. The exact value of π can never be determined; only approximations can be established. Here is the value of π correct to 50 decimal places:

$$\pi = 3.14159265358979323846264338327950288419716939937 51\ldots$$

Throughout the years, many attempts have been made to compute π, both algebraically and geometrically. This unit presents some of the geometric constructions involving π.

One of the first serious attempts to compute π to a certain degree of accuracy goes back to Archimedes, who tried to exactly determine π. His method was based on the fact that the perimeter of a regular polygon of n sides is smaller than the circumference of the circle circumscribed about it, while the perimeter of a similar polygon circumscribed about the circle is greater than the circle's circumference. By successively repeating this situation for larger values of n, the two perimeters will approach the circumference from both sides. Archimedes started with a regular hexagon and each time doubled the number of sides until he obtained a polygon of 96 sides. He was then able to determine that the ratio of the circumference of a circle to its diameter, or π, is less than $3\frac{10}{70}$ but greater than $3\frac{10}{71}$. We can write this in decimal notation as $3.14085 < \pi < 3.142857$. To aid in the students' understanding of this method, it might be beneficial if you illustrate with a few diagrams. The following chart might also aid in explaining this concept, as the students will see that as the number of sides increases, π is more accurately approximated.

Number of sides	Perimeter of circumscribed polygon	Perimeter of inscribed polygon
4	4.0000000	2.8284271
8	3.3137085	3.0614675
16	3.1825979	3.1214452
32	3.1517249	3.1365485
64	3.1441184	3.1403312
128	3.1422236	3.1412773
256	3.1417504	3.1415138
512	3.1416321	3.1415729
1024	3.1416025	3.1415877
2048	3.1415951	3.1415914

Figure A

Students will now see how they can actually construct a line segment whose length closely approximates π. This construction was developed in the mid 1800's and it involves the ratio $\frac{355}{113}$ (which had been previously discovered by a Chinese astronomer in the fifth century). $\frac{355}{113} = 3 + \frac{16}{113} = 3.1415929\ldots$ which is a correct approximation of π to six decimal places. The construction begins with a quadrant of unit radius. AO is $\frac{7}{8}$ of the radius, $\overline{AB}$ is drawn and a point C is marked off so that CB = $\frac{1}{2}$ of the radius. $\overline{CD}$ is drawn parallel to $\overline{AO}$ and $\overline{CE}$ is drawn parallel to $\overline{AD}$.

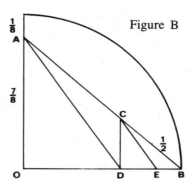

Figure B

Have students find AB: $(\frac{7}{8})^2 + 1^2 = (AB)^2$ $\therefore$ AB $= \frac{\sqrt{113}}{8}$.

Using similar triangles, the following relationships can easily be seen. (Have students explain why $\triangle CDB \sim \triangle AOB$ and $\triangle CEB \sim \triangle ADB$.)
$$\frac{DB}{OB} = \frac{CB}{AB} \text{ and } \frac{EB}{DB} = \frac{CB}{AB}$$
Multiplying these expressions we obtain
$$\frac{EB}{OB} = \frac{CB^2}{AB^2} = \frac{\frac{1}{4}}{\frac{113}{64}} = \frac{16}{113}$$
but since OB = 1, we get
$$\frac{EB}{1} = \frac{16}{113} \text{ or } EB \quad \frac{16}{113} \text{ or } \approx .1415929204\ldots$$
Since $\frac{355}{113} = 3 + \frac{16}{113}$, a line segment can now be drawn that is 3 times the radius extended by the distance EB. This will give us a line segment that differs from π by less than a millionth of a unit.

A slightly more difficult geometric approximation of π was developed in 1685 by Father Adam Kochansky, a librarian to King John III of Poland. A circle of unit radius is drawn. Then draw a tangent segment $\overline{QR}$, equal in length to 3 times the radius. Draw a diameter perpendicular to $\overline{QR}$ at Q, the point of tangency. Now draw a line, d, tangent at the other end of the diameter such that the measure of central angle $= 30°$. Connect points and extend line segments to form the figure pictured in the figure below. The students are now ready to calculate the value of π. (It will be shown that if the length of the radius is 1, line c approximates π.)

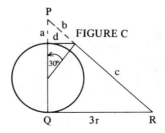

FIGURE C

If $r = 1$, in $\triangle PQR$, $(a + 2)^2 + (3)^2 = (b + c)^2$ (1)

Also, using similar triangles, we have $\dfrac{a}{a + 2} = \dfrac{d}{3}$ (2)

and $\dfrac{b}{b + c} = \dfrac{d}{3}$ (3)

From equation (2) we obtain $3a = ad + 2d$ or

$a = \dfrac{2d}{3 - d}$. But $\tan 30° = \dfrac{d}{1} = d = \dfrac{\sqrt{3}}{3}$

Therefore $a = \dfrac{2 \dfrac{\sqrt{3}}{3}}{3 - \dfrac{\sqrt{3}}{3}}$ or $a = \dfrac{2\sqrt{3}}{9 - \sqrt{3}}$ (4)

Similarly, from equation (3) we can obtain

$b = \dfrac{cd}{3 - d} = \dfrac{c\sqrt{3}}{9 - \sqrt{3}}$ (5)

Substituting equations (4) and (5) into equation (1) we now have $\left(\dfrac{2\sqrt{3}}{9 - \sqrt{3}} + 2\right)^2 + 9 = \left(\dfrac{c\sqrt{3}}{9 - \sqrt{3}} + c\right)^2$

Students should be able to solve this equation for c and obtain $c = \sqrt{\dfrac{40 - 2\sqrt{3}}{3}}$

Have students simplify this radical to obtain 3.141533 as an approximate value for c.

Throughout the lesson it should be emphasized that these are all *approximations* of the value π, since it is impossible to construct π with straightedge and compasses.

Postassessment

1) Find the diameter of a circle whose circumference is 471 feet.

2) Construct a geometric approximation of π in more than one way.

60   The Arbelos

The region bounded by three semicircles in a manner resembling a shoemaker's knife has some rather interesting properties. This region, often called an arbelos, is the topic of this unit. Here the student will be introduced to this geometric figure with the intention of pursuing its properties further.

Performance Objectives

1. *Students will identify the arbelos.*
2. *Students will solve problems involving the arbelos.*

Preassessment

This unit should be presented to students who have studied geometry (or are currently enrolled in the last term of a geometry course). They should be able to compute lengths of arcs, areas of triangles and areas of circles.

Teaching Strategies

Have students draw a semicircle with center O and diameter $\overline{AB}$. Let $AB = 2R$. Have them then mark off a point C, between A and B. Then have them let $\overline{AC}$ and $\overline{CB}$ be diameters of semicircles D and E respectively. (see Figure 1) Let $AC = 2r_1$ and BC

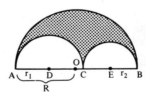

Figure 1

$= 2r_2$. The shaded portion of the figure is known as the *Arbelos* or *Shoemaker's Knife*. It has some very interesting properties which were considered by Archimedes, the famous Greek mathematician.

You should now direct student attention to the diagram. Try to elicit from your students the following property of the arbelos: that $\ell\widehat{AB} = \ell\widehat{AC} + \ell\widehat{CB}$. Once students understand this property, a proof should be established. In a circle, the length of an arc $= \dfrac{n}{360} \times 2\pi r$ (where n is the number of degrees of the arc and r is the length of the radius), we have

$$\ell\widehat{AB} = \frac{180}{360} \cdot 2\pi R = \pi R$$

$$\ell\widehat{AC} = \frac{1}{2} \cdot 2\pi r_1 = \pi r_1$$

$$\ell\widehat{CB} = \frac{1}{2} \cdot 2\pi r_2 = \pi r_2$$

Also $R = r_1 + r_2$, therefore multiplying by π we get $\pi R = \pi r_1 + \pi r_2$ or $\ell\widehat{AB} = \ell\widehat{AC} + \ell\widehat{CB}$. Have students consider the case where three semicircles (instead of two) are taken on $\overline{AB}$. Would a similar relationship hold true?

Students should now draw the perpendicular to $\overline{AB}$ at point C, which meets the circle at H. Also draw the common tangent to circles D and E and call the points of tangency F and G, respectively. Denote the point where these two segments intersect as S. (see Figure 2) Since a line segment drawn perpendicular to a diameter is the geometric mean

Figure 2

between the segments of the diameter, we have that $(HC)^2 = 2r_1 \cdot 2r_2 = 4r_1r_2$. Also FG = JE (have students explain why from the diagram). Since $JD = r_1 - r_2$ and $DE = r_1 + r_2$, then $(JE)^2 = (r_1 + r_2)^2 - (r_1 - r_2)^2 = r_1^2 + 2r_1r_2 + r_2^2 - r_1^2 + 2r_1r_2 - r_2^2 = 4r_1r_2$. Therefore $(FG)^2 = 4r_1r_2$ or $(HC)^2 = (FG)^2 = 4r_1r_2$.

Ask your students if they can suggest another relationship that exists between $\overline{HC}$ and $\overline{FG}$. Once someone gives the response that $\overline{HC}$ and $\overline{FG}$ bisect each other at S, have the students try to prove it by themselves. $\overline{SC}$ is a common internal tangent to both circles, therefore, FS = SC and SC = SG, which gives us FS = SG. But since HC = FG (have students explain why), we also know that HS = SC. Also since FS = SG = HS = SC, the points F, H, G, C determine a circle with center S.

A very interesting property of the arbelos is one that involves this circle which has $\overline{HC}$ and $\overline{FG}$ as diameters. Have students try to express the area of the arbelos in terms of r_1 and r_2. Area of the arbelos = Area of semicircle AHB − (Area of semicircle AFC + Area of semicircle CGB)

Since Area of a semicircle = $\dfrac{\pi r^2}{2}$, we have

Area of the arbelos = $\dfrac{\pi R^2}{2} - (\dfrac{\pi r_1^2}{2} + \dfrac{\pi r_2^2}{2})$

$$= \dfrac{\pi}{2}(R^2 - r_1^2 - r_2^2)$$

We know that $R = r_1 + r_2$ and substituting we get

Area of the arbelos = $\dfrac{\pi}{2}((r_1 + r_2)^2 - r_1^2 - r_2^2)$

$$= \dfrac{\pi}{2}(r_1^2 + 2r_1r_2 + r_2^2 - r_1^2 - r_2^2)$$

$$= \dfrac{\pi}{2}(2r_1r_2) = \pi r_1 r_2$$

Have the students now find the area of circle S. The diameter HC = $2\sqrt{r_1r_2}$, therefore the radius = $\sqrt{r_1r_2}$. The area of the circle then = $\pi(\sqrt{r_1r_2})^2 = \pi r_1 r_2$. It is now apparent that they have must proved that the area of the arbelos is equal to the area of circle S.

You may wish to introduce another interesting arbelos.

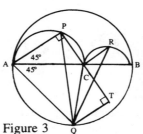

Figure 3

Let P and R be the midpoints of arcs $\widehat{AC}$ and $\widehat{CB}$ respectively. Let Q be the midpoint of the semicircle below $\overline{AB}$. Connect points P and R to C and to Q. A concave quadrilateral PQRC is formed (see Figure 3).

The area of this quadrilateral is equal to the sum of the squares of the radii, r_1 and r_2, of the two smaller semicircles.

A proof follows: The quadrilateral can be divided into two triangles by drawing $\overline{CQ}$. The area of $\triangle QCP$ can be shown to be equal to the area of right $\triangle APC$. The two triangles have a common base $\overline{CP}$, therefore their heights must be proved to be equal. To do this, draw $\overline{AP}$, $\overline{AQ}$ and draw $\overline{QT}$ perpendicular to $\overline{PC}$ extended. (see Figure 3) Since Q is the midpoint of semicircle AB, $m\widehat{QB} = 90°$. Therefore $m\angle QAB = 45°$. Also since $\triangle APC$ is an isosceles right triangle, $m\angle PAB = 45°$, which gives us that $m\angle PAQ = 90°$. But since $m\angle APC = 90°$ and $m\angle PTQ$ is also $= 90°$, quadrilateral APTQ is a rectangle and AP = QT.

Therefore, Area of $\triangle QCP = \dfrac{CP \cdot PA}{2}$

Since in isosceles right triangle APC, $(CP)^2 + (PA)^2 = (2r_1)^2$ or $2(CP)^2 = (2r_1)^2$

Therefore $(CP)^2 = 2r_1^2$ or $\dfrac{CP \cdot PA}{2} = r_1^2$

We therefore have that area of $\triangle QCP = r_1^2$
Similarly, it can be shown that area of $\triangle QCR = \dfrac{CR \cdot RB}{2} = r_2^2$. Therefore,

Area of the quadrilateral = $r_1^2 + r_2^2$.

Postassessment

1) If $r_1 = 16$ and $r_2 = 4$, show that $\widehat{AB} = \widehat{AC} + \widehat{CB}$; find the radius of circle S; find the area of the arbelos.

2) Describe semicircle D below $\overline{AB}$ (Figure 4). Let $\overline{AN}$ be tangent to circle E. Show that the area of the shaded region is equal to the area of the circle which has $\overline{AN}$ as its diameter.

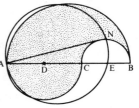

Figure 4

3) Find the area of quadrilateral PQRC (Figure 3), if $r_1 = 8$ and $r_2 = 5$.

4) What is the relationship between the arbelos in Figure 3 and Fibonacci numbers (see page 337)?

Reference

Gardner, Martin. "The Diverse Pleasures of Circles that Are Tangent to One Another." *Scientific American*, 240 (1), January, 1979.

61   The Nine-Point Circle

An often neglected concept in the high school geometry curriculum is that of establishing points concyclic (on the same circle). This unit presents one of the more famous sets of concyclic points.

Performance Objectives
1. Students will define and construct the nine-point circle.

2. Students will locate the center of the nine-point circle.

Preassessment
Students should be aware of elementary methods of proving four points concyclic. For example, they should be aware of at least the following two theorems:

1. If one side of a quadrilateral subtends congruent angles at the two nonadjacent vertices, then the quadrilateral is cyclic (may be inscribed in a circle).

2. If a pair of opposite angles of a quadrilateral are supplementary, then the quadrilateral is cyclic.

Teaching Strategies
Present students with a $\triangle$ ABC, with midpoints of its sides A′, B′, C′ (see Figure 1). Draw altitude $\overline{CF}$. Ask

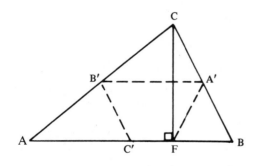

Figure 1

students to prove that quadrilateral A′B′C′F is an isosceles trapezoid. To do this they should realize that since $\overline{A'B'}$ is a segment joining the midpoints of two sides of a triangle, it is parallel to the third side of the triangle. Since $\overline{B'C'}$ joins the midpoints of $\overline{AC}$ and $\overline{AB}$, B′C′ = ½(BC). Since the median to the hypotenuse of a right triangle is half the length of the hypotenuse, A′F = ½(BC). Therefore, B′C′ = A′F, and trapezoid A′B′C′F is isosceles.

Now have students prove that an isosceles trapezoid is always cyclic (using Theorem 2, above).

To avoid confusion redraw $\triangle$ ABC with altitude $\overline{AD}$ as shown below.

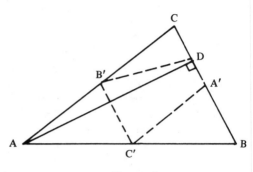

Figure 2

In the same way as for altitude $\overline{CF}$, have students independently prove that the points B′, C′, A′ and D are concyclic. This should be done with the above proof as a guide.

Students should now be prepared to generalize a statement about the points B′, C′, A′ and E, for altitude $\overline{BE}$. This will lead to the conclusion that the points D,F, and E each lie on the unique circle determined by points A′, B′, C′. Thus, students can summarize that the feet of the altitudes of a triangle are concyclic with the midpoints of the sides. So far they have established a "six-point circle."

By this time, students should have proved that the altitudes of a triangle are concurrent. This point is called the *orthocenter*. Have them consider the orthocenter, H, of $\triangle$ ABC, and the midpoint M of $\overline{CH}$.

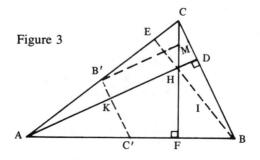

Figure 3

$\overline{B'M}$ is a segment joining the midpoints of two sides of $\angle$ ACH. Therefore $\overline{B'M}$ // $\overline{AH}$. Similarly in ∠ ABC, we have $\overline{B'C'}$ // $\overline{BC}$. Since altitude $\overline{AD} \perp \overline{BC}$, $\overline{B'M} \perp \overline{B'C'}$, or m ∠ MB'C' = 90°. Remember that m ∠ AFC = 90°. Therefore quadrilaterial MB'C'F is cyclic, since its opposite angles are supplementary. This is the same circle established above, since three vertices (B', C', and F) are common with the six concyclic points, and three points determine a unique circle. Thus, a "seven-point circle" has been established.

To reinforce this proof, students should now prove that K and L (the midpoints of $\overline{AH}$ and $\overline{BH}$, respectively), also lie on this circle. To do this they merely need to repeat the above procedure for points K, C',

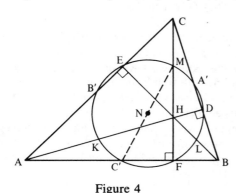

Figure 4

A', D and for points L, C', B', E. A brief review of the entire proof thus far will reveal a *nine-point circle*.

Have students consider $\overline{MC'}$ in Figure 4. Since it subtends right angles at points B' and F, it must be the diameter of the circle through B', C', F and M. To locate the center N, of this circle, simply tell students to find the midpoint of $\overline{MC'}$. This is the center of the nine-point circle.

Postassessment

To conclude the lesson ask students to do the following:

1. Define the nine-point circle.
2. Construct the nine-point circle using straightedge and compasses.
3. Locate the center of the nine-point circle.

Interesting relationships involving the nine-point circle can be found in the accompanying unit, The Euler Line.

Many other interesting relationships involving the nine point circle can be found in:

Posamentier, Alfred S. *Excursions in Advanced Euclidean Geometry*. Menlo Park, Ca.: Addison-Wesley, 1984.

62 The Euler Line

This unit should be presented to students *after* they have studied the unit on the nine-point circle. This unit uses some of the material developed in *The Nine-Point Circle* and relates it to other points of a triangle.

Performance Objectives

1. Students will locate the Euler line of a triangle.
2. Students will establish a relationship between the circumcenter, orthocenter, centroid and the center of the nine-point circle of a triangle.

Preassessment

Have students draw a scalene triangle and construct its nine-point circle as well as the circumcircle of the triangle.

Teaching Strategies

To facilitate the discussion, students should label their construction as in Figure 1 below.

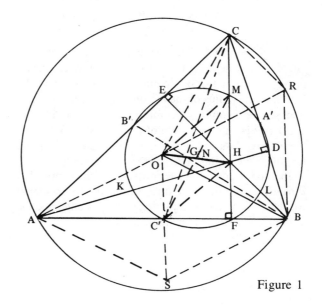

Figure 1

Students should now draw $\overline{OH}$, the segment joining the orthocenter (the point of intersection of the altitudes) and the circumcenter, (the point of intersection of the perpendicular bisectors of the sides of the triangle). This is the *Euler Line*.

Have students locate the center of the nine-point circle by finding the midpoint of $\overline{MC'}$, (this was proved in *The Nine-Point Circle*). An accurate construction should place this point on the midpoint of the Euler line $\overline{OH}$. Student curiosity should now request a proof of this astonishing occurrence.

1. Draw $\overleftrightarrow{OA}$ to intersect circle O at R.
2. $\overline{OC'} \perp \overline{AB}$ (since O is on the perpendicular bisector of $\overline{AB}$ and C' is the midpoint of $\overline{AB}$).
3. $m\angle ABR = 90°$ (an angle inscribed in a semicircle).
4. Therefore, $\overline{OC'} \mathbin{/\mkern-5mu/} \overline{RB}$ (both are perpendicular to $\overline{AB}$).
5. Similarly, $\overline{RB} \mathbin{/\mkern-5mu/} \overline{CF}$, and $\overline{RC} \mathbin{/\mkern-5mu/} \overline{BE}$.
6. $\triangle AOC' \sim \triangle ARB$ (with a ratio of similtude of $\frac{1}{2}$).
7. Therefore $OC' = \frac{1}{2}(RB)$.
8. Quadrilateral RBHC is a parallelogram (both pairs of opposite sides are parallel).
9. Therefore, RB = HC, and $OC' = \frac{1}{2}(HC) = HM$.
10. Quadrilateral OC'HM is a parallelogram (one pair of sides is both congruent and parallel).
11. Therefore, since the diagonals of a parallelogram bisect each other, N, (the midpoint of $\overline{MC'}$), is the midpoint of $\overline{OH}$.

So far we proved that the center of the nine-point circle bisects the Euler Line. At this point we can easily prove that the radius of the nine-point circle is half the length of the radius of the circumcircle. Since $\overline{MN}$ is a line segment joining the midpoints of two sides of $\triangle COH$, it is half the length of the third side $\overline{OC}$. Thus the radius, $\overline{MN}$, of the nine-point circle is half the length of the radius, $\overline{OC}$, of the circumcircle.

In 1765, Leonhard Euler proved that the centroid of a triangle (the point of intersection of the medians) trisects the line segment joining the orthocenter and circumcenter (the Euler line).

Since $\overline{OC'} \mathbin{/\mkern-5mu/} \overline{CH}$, $\triangle OGC' \sim \triangle HGC$.

Earlier we proved that $OC' = \frac{1}{2}(HC)$,

Therefore, $OG = \frac{1}{2}(GH)$,

or $OG = (\frac{1}{3})(OH)$.

The only thing remaining is to show that G is the centroid of the triangle.

Since $\overline{CC'}$ is a median and $\overline{GC'} = \frac{1}{2}(GC)$,

G must be the centroid since it appropriately trisects the median.

Thus G trisects $\overline{OH}$.

Ask students why the median $\overline{BB'}$ also trisects $\overline{OH}$ (because it contains G, the centroid).

To this point we have bisected and trisected the Euler line with significant triangle points. Before ending the discussion of the Euler line, an interesting vector application should be considered. Review the concept of a vector and a parallelogram of forces. We shall show that $\overline{OH}$ is the resultant of $\overline{OA}$, $\overline{OB}$, and $\overline{OC}$. This was first published by James Joseph Sylvester (1814 - 1897).

Consider the point S on $\overline{OC'}$,
  where OC' = SC'.
Since $\overline{OC'S}$ is the perpendicular bisector of $\overline{AB}$, quadrilateral AOBS is a parallelogram (rhombus).
Therefore, $\overrightarrow{OS} = \overrightarrow{OA} + \overrightarrow{OB}$, or $\overrightarrow{OC'} = \frac{1}{2}(\overrightarrow{OA} + \overrightarrow{OB})$.
Since $\triangle OGC' \sim \triangle HGC$, CH = 2(OC').
Thus $\overrightarrow{CH} = \overrightarrow{OA} + \overrightarrow{OB}$.
Since $\overrightarrow{HO}$ is the resultant of $\overrightarrow{OC}$ and $\overrightarrow{CH}$,
  $\overrightarrow{HO} = \overrightarrow{OC} + \overrightarrow{CH}$.
Therefore, $\overrightarrow{HO} = \overrightarrow{OC} + \overrightarrow{OA} + \overrightarrow{OB}$. (Substitution)

Postassessment

At the conclusion of this lesson ask students:
1. To construct the Euler line of a given scalene triangle, and
2. To state a relationship which exists between the circumcenter, orthocenter, centroid, and the center of the nine-point circle of a given scalene triangle.

63 The Simson Line

One of the more famous sets of collinear points is known as the *Simson Line*. Although this line was discovered by William Wallace in 1797, careless misquotes have, in time, attributed it to Robert Simson, (1687-1768). This unit will present, prove and apply the Simson Theorem.

Performance Objectives
1. Students will construct the Simson Line.
2. Students will prove that the three points which determine the Simson Line are, in fact, collinear.
3. Students will apply the properties of the Simson Line to given problems.

Preassessment
When students are presented with this unit, they should be well into the high school geometry course, having already studied angle measurement with a circle. Students should also review cyclic quadrilaterals (quadrilaterals which may be inscribed in a circle) before beginning this unit.

Teaching Strategies
Have each student construct a triangle inscribed in a circle. Then, from any convenient point on the circle (but not at a vertex of the triangle), have students construct perpendicular segments to each of the three sides of the triangle. Now, ask the class what relationship seems to be true about the three feet of the perpendiculars. If the constructions were done accurately, everyone should notice that these three points determine the *Simson Line*.

The obvious question should be quickly forthcoming: "Why are these three points collinear?" This is where you begin your proof.

Simson's Theorem: The feet of the perpendiculars drawn from any point on the circumcircle of a given triangle to the sides of the triangle are collinear.

Given: ∆ABC is inscribed in circle O.
P is on circle O.
$\overrightarrow{PY} \perp \overleftrightarrow{AC}$ at Y, $\overrightarrow{PZ} \perp \overleftrightarrow{AB}$ at Z, and $\overrightarrow{PX} \perp \overleftrightarrow{BC}$ at X.
Prove: Points X, Y, and Z are collinear.
Proof:

1. ∠PYA is supplementary to ∠PZA (both are right angles).
2. Quadrilateral PZAY is cyclic (opposite angles are supplementary).
3. Draw $\overline{PA}$, $\overline{PB}$, and $\overline{PC}$.

4. m ∠PYZ = m ∠PAZ (both are inscribed in the same arc).
5. ∠ PYC is supplementary to ∠ PXC (both are right angles).
6. Quadrilateral PXCY is cyclic (opposite angles are supplementary).
7. m∠ PYX = m∠ PCB (both are inscribed in the same arc).
8. m ∠ PAZ (m ∠ PAB) = m ∠ PCB (both are inscribed in the same arc of circle O).
9. m ∠PYZ = m ∠ PYX (transitivity with steps 4, 7, and 8).
10. Since both angles, ∠ PYZ and ∠ PYX, share the same ray $\overrightarrow{YP}$, and have the same measure, their other rays $\overrightarrow{YZ}$ and $\overrightarrow{YX}$ must coincide. Therefore, points X, Y, and Z are collinear.

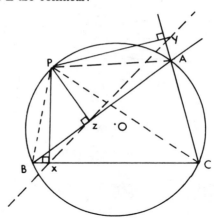

Figure 1

Present carefully to students this technique for proving collinearity. Although it is a somewhat unusual approach, it should prove quite useful to them in later work.

To strengthen the impact of the Simson Line, show students a proof of the converse of the above theorem.
Given: ∆ABC is inscribed in circle O.
Points X, Y, and Z are collinear.
$\overrightarrow{PY} \perp \overleftrightarrow{AC}$ at Y, $\overrightarrow{PZ} \perp \overleftrightarrow{AB}$ at Z, and $\overrightarrow{PX} \perp \overleftrightarrow{BC}$ at X.
Prove: P is on the circumcircle of ∆ ABC.
Proof:

1. Draw PA, PB, and PC. (see Figure 1)
2. m ∠ PZB = 90° = m ∠ PXB.
3. Quadrilateral PZXB is cyclic ($\overline{PB}$ subtends two congruent angles in the same half-plane).
4. ∠ PBX is supplementary to ∠ PZX (opposite angles of a cyclic quadrilateral).

5. ∠ PZX is supplementary to ∠ PZY (points X, Y, and Z are collinear).

6. Therefore, m ∠ PBX = m ∠ PZY (both are supplementary to ∠PZX).

7. Quadrilateral PZAY is cyclic (opposite angles, ∠ PYA and ∠ PZA, are supplementary).

8. m ∠ PZY = m ∠ PAY (both are inscribed in the same arc of the circumcircle of quadrilateral PZAY).

9. Therefore, m ∠ PBX = m ∠ PAY (transitivity of steps 6 and 8).

10. Thus, ∠ PBC is supplementary to ∠ PAC (since $\overleftrightarrow{YAC}$ is a line).

11. Quadrilateral PACB is cyclic (opposite angles are supplementary), and, therefore, P is on the circumcircle of △ABC.

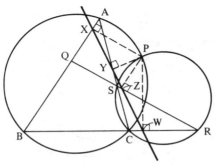

Figure 2

Students should now be ready to apply the Simson Line to a geometric problem.

Sides $\overleftrightarrow{AB}$, $\overleftrightarrow{BC}$, and $\overleftrightarrow{CA}$ of △ABC are cut by a transversal at points Q, R, and S, respectively. The circumcircles of △ABC and △SCR intersect at P. Prove that quadrilateral APSQ is cyclic.

Draw perpendiculars $\overline{PX}$, $\overline{PY}$, $\overline{PZ}$ and $\overline{PW}$ to $\overleftrightarrow{AB}$, $\overleftrightarrow{AC}$, $\overleftrightarrow{QR}$, and $\overleftrightarrow{BC}$, respectively, as in Figure 2. Since point P is on the circumcircle of △ABC, points X, Y, and W are collinear (Simson's Theorem). Similarly, since point P is on the circumcircle of △SCR, points Y, Z, and W are collinear. It then follows that points X, Y, and Z are collinear. Thus, P must lie on the circumcircle of △AQS (converse of Simson's Theorem), or quadrilateral APSQ is cyclic.

Postassessment
Have students complete the following exercises.
1. Construct a Simson Line of a given triangle.
2. How many Simson Lines does a triangle have?
3. Prove Simson's Theorem.
4. From a point P on the circumference of circle O, three chords are drawn meeting the circle in points A, B, and C. Prove that the three points of intersection of the three circles with $\overline{PA}$, $\overline{PB}$, and $\overline{PC}$ as diameters, are collinear.

64   The Butterfly Problem

One of the most intriguing geometric relationships involves a figure which resembles a butterfly. Most students will easily understand the problem and think it just as simple to prove. But this is where the problem begins to generate further interest since the proof is somewhat elusive. This unit will suggest ways of presenting the problem to your class and provide a number of different proofs of this celebrated theorem.

Performance Objective
1. Students will state the Butterfly Problem.
2. Students will prove the Butterfly Problem valid.

Preassessment
Students should have mastered most of the high school geometry course (especially the study of circles and similarity).

Teaching Strategies
Use a duplicating machine to prepare a sheet of paper for each student with a large circle containing a chord, $\overline{AB}$, (not the diameter), and its midpoint, M, clearly marked. Tell students to draw *any* two chords, $\overline{EF}$, and $\overline{CD}$, containing M. Now have them draw the chords $\overline{CE}$ and $\overline{FD}$ which intersect $\overline{AB}$ at points Q and P, respectively. Their diagrams should resemble the Figure below.

Figure 1

Ask your class to measure any segments that appear congruent in their diagrams, and to list the pairs. You should find that most students will have included on their lists the segments $\overline{AP} \cong \overline{BQ}$ and $\overline{MP} \cong \overline{MQ}$ Remind students that they all started their diagrams with *different* segments $\overline{CE}$ and $\overline{FD}$, and, although their diagrams resemble a butterfly in a circle, their art may differ substantially from their classmates'. This should dramatize the most astonishing result of this situation, that *everyone's* $\overline{MP} \cong \overline{MQ}$!

Students will now want to prove this remarkable result. Toward this end, a number of proofs of this celebrated theorem are presented here.

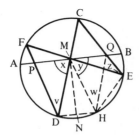

Figure 2

Proof I   With M the midpoint of $\overline{AB}$ and chords $\overline{FME}$ and $\overline{CMD}$ drawn, we now draw $\overline{DH}$ // $\overline{AB}$, $\overline{MN} \perp \overline{DH}$, and line segments $\overline{MH}$, $\overline{QH}$, and $\overline{EH}$. Since $\overline{MN} \perp \overline{DH}$ and $\overline{DH}$ // $\overline{AB}$, $MN \perp AB$.

$\overline{MN}$, the perpendicular bisector of $\overline{AB}$, must pass through the center of the circle. Therefore $\overline{MN}$ is the perpendicular bisector of $\overline{DH}$, since a line through the center of the circle and perpendicular to a chord, bisects it.

Thus $MD = MH$, and $\Delta MND \cong \Delta MNH$, (H.L.). $m\angle DMN = m\angle HMN$, so $m\angle x = m\angle y$ (they are the complements of congruent angles). Since $\overline{AB}$ // $\overline{DH}$, $m\widehat{AD} = m\widehat{BH}$, $m \angle x = \frac{1}{2}(m\widehat{AD} + m\widehat{CB})$ (angle formed by two chords) $m \angle x = \frac{1}{2}(m\widehat{BH} + m\widehat{CB})$ (substitution). Therefore, $m \angle y = \frac{1}{2}(m\widehat{BH} + m\widehat{CB})$. But $m \angle CEH = \frac{1}{2}(m\widehat{CAH})$ (inscribed angle). Thus, by addition, $m \angle y + m \angle CEH = \frac{1}{2}(m\widehat{BH} + m\widehat{CB} + m\widehat{CAH})$. Since $m\widehat{BH} + m\widehat{CB} + m\widehat{CAH} = 360°$, $m \angle y + m\angle CEH = 180°$. It then follows that quadrilateral MQEH is inscriptable, that is, a circle may be circumscribed about it. Imagine a drawing of this circle. $\angle$ w and $\angle$ z are measured by the same arc, $\widehat{MQ}$ (inscribed angle), and thus $m \angle w = m \angle z$.

Now consider our original circle $m\angle v = m\angle z$, since they are measured by the same arc, $\widehat{FC}$ (inscribed angle.) Therefore, by transitivity, $m\angle v = m\angle w$, and $\Delta MPD \cong \Delta MQH$ (A.S.A.). Thus, $MP = MQ$.

Figure 3

Proof II   Extend $\overline{EF}$ through F. Draw $\overline{KPL}$ // $\overline{CE}$.

$m\angle PLC = m\angle ECL$ (alternate interior angles),

therefore, $\Delta PML \sim \Delta QMC$ (A.A.), and $\dfrac{PL}{CQ} = \dfrac{MP}{MQ}$

$m\angle K = m\angle E$ (alternate interior angles),

therefore, $\Delta KMP \sim \Delta EMQ$ (A.A.), and $\dfrac{KP}{QE} = \dfrac{MP}{MQ}$

By multiplication,

$$\frac{(PL)\,(KP)}{(CQ,(QE)} = \frac{(MP)^2}{(MQ)^2}. \qquad (I)$$

Since $m\angle D = m\angle E$ (inscribed angle), and $m\angle K = m\angle E$ (alternate interior angles), $m\angle D = m\angle K$. Also, $m\angle KPF = m\angle DPL$ (vertical angles). Therefore, $\Delta KFP \sim \Delta DLP$ (A.A.), and $\dfrac{PL}{DP} = \dfrac{FP}{KP}$; and so

$$(PL)\,(KP) = (DP)\,(FP). \qquad (II)$$

In equation (I), $\dfrac{(MP)^2}{(MQ)^2} = \dfrac{(PL)\,(KP)}{(CQ)\,(QE)}$;

we substitute from equation (II) to get

$$\frac{(MP)^2}{(MQ)^2} = \frac{(DP)\,(FP)}{(CQ)\,(QE)}$$

Since $(DP)\,(FP) = (AP)\,(PB)$, and $(CQ)\,(QE) = (BQ)\,(QA)$, (product of segments lengths of intersecting chords), $\dfrac{(MP)^2}{(MQ)^2} = \dfrac{(AP)\,(PB)}{(BQ)\,(QA)} =$

$$\frac{(MA - MP)\,(MA + MP)}{(MB - MQ)\,(MB + MQ)} = \frac{(MA)^2 - (MP)^2}{(MB)^2 - (MQ)^2}$$

Then $(MP)^2\,(MB)^2 = (MQ)^2\,(MA)^2$. But $MB = MA$. Therefore, $(MP)^2 = (MQ)^2$, or $MP = MQ$.

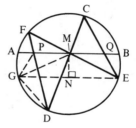

Figure 4

Proof III   Draw a line through E parallel to $\overline{AB}$ meeting the circle at G, and draw $\overline{MN} \perp \overline{GE}$. Then draw $\overline{PG}$, $\overline{MG}$ and $\overline{DG}$.

m∠ GDP (∠ GDF) = m∠ GEF (inscribed angles). (I)
m∠ PMG = m∠ MGE (alternate interior angles). (II)
Since the perpendicular bisector of $\overline{AB}$ is also the perpendicular bisector of $\overline{GE}$,
then GM = ME, and m∠ GEF = m∠ MGE (base angles).   (III)
From (I), (II), and (III), m∠ GDP = m∠ PMG. (IV)

Therefore, points P,M,D, and G are concyclic (A quadrilateral is cyclic if one side subtends congruent angles at the two opposite vertices). Hence, m∠PGM = m∠ PDM (inscribed angles, in a new circle).   (V)
However, m∠ CEF = m∠ PDM (∠ FDM) (inscribed angles).   (VI)
From (V) and (VI), M∠ PGM = m∠ QEM (∠ CEF).
From (II), we know that m∠ PMG = m∠ MGE.
Thus, m∠ QME = m∠ MEG (alternate interior angles), and m∠ MGE = m∠ MEG (base angles).

Therefore, m∠ PMG = m∠ QME and ΔPMG ≅ ΔQME (A.S.A.). It follows that PM = QM.

Although these proofs of the Butterfly Problem are not of the sort the average student is likely to discover independently, they do provide a very rich learning experience in a well motivated setting.

Postassessment

Ask students to:
1. State the Butterfly Problem.
2. Explain why the Butterfly Problem is true.
(Students should either present one of the above proofs or one of their own.)

Additional solutions can be found in:
Posamentier, Alfred S., *Challenging Problems in Geometry,* Volume II. New York: Macmillan, 1970.

65   Equicircles

Equicircles is a term used to refer to both the inscribed and escribed circles of a triangle. This unit will develop a number of fascinating relationships between these circles.

Performance Objectives

1. Students will define equicircles.
2. Students will state at least four properties involving equicircles.
3. Students will state and prove one property of equicircles.

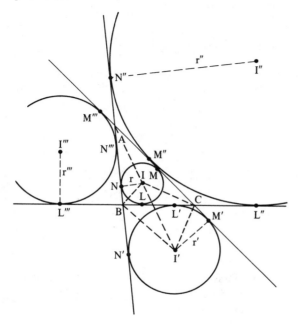

Preassessment

Students should have mastered the topic of circles in their high school geometry course.

Present the following figure to your students and ask them to find the length of $\overline{AN'}$, if the perimeter of ΔABC = 16. (Points M′, N′ and L′ are points of tangency.)

Teaching Strategies

Although the problem posed above is quite simple, its approach is rather unusual and therefore could cause your students some difficulty. The only theorem they need to recall is that two tangent segments from an external point to a circle are congruent. Applying this theorem to the above problem we get:
BN′ = BL′ and CM′ = CL′
The perimeter of ΔABC = AB + BC + AC
= AB + (BL′ + CL′) + AC
which by substitution yields:
AB + BN′ + CM′ + AC
or
AN′ + AM′
However, AN′ = AM′ (they too are tangent segments from the same external point to the same circle).

Therefore AN′ = $\frac{1}{2}$ (perimeter of ΔABC) = 8. By summarizing this rather fascinating fact, students will be motivated towards pursuing further relationships in this figure.

Next, let s = semiperimeter of ΔABC
a = BC; b = AC; c = AB

With your guidance, students should now be able to establish the following relationship:
$$BN' = BL' = AN' - AB = s - c$$
$$CM' = CL' = AM' - AC = s - b$$
At this point you ought to indicate to students that these are just a few of the segments that will be expressed in terms of the lengths of the sides of $\triangle ABC$. Here the relationship of the two circles to the triangle should be defined. Students will recognize circle I as the *inscribed* circle of $\triangle ABC$. Most likely they are not familiar with circle I'. This circle, which is also tangent to the lines of the three sides of $\triangle ABC$, yet contains no interior points of the triangle, is called an *escribed* circle. A triangle has four equicircles, one inscribed, and three escribed. The center of an escribed circle, called an *excenter,* is the point of intersection of two exterior angle bisectors and one interior angle bisector.

Students should gain further familiarity with these circles by expressing other segments in terms of the lengths of the sides of $\triangle ABC$. Once again provide guidance where necessary.
$$AN + AM = (AB - NB) + (AC - MC)$$
$$= (AB - LB) + (AC - LC)$$
$$= (AB + AC) - (LB + LC)$$
$$= c + b - a$$

Challenge your students to show that
$$c + b - a = 2(s - a).$$
Therefore $AN + AM = 2(s - a)$.
However $AN = AM$, thus $AN = s - a$.
Have your students conjecture how BN and CL can be expressed in terms of the lengths of the sides of $\triangle ABC$.
$$BN = s - b$$
$$CL = s - c$$
We are now ready to apply some of these expressions to establish two interesting relationships. These are: $BL = CL'$, and $LL' = b - c$, the difference between the lengths of the other two sides of $\triangle ABC$.

Since both BL and CL' were shown to be equal to $s - b$, $BL = CL'$.
Consider LL' which equals $BC - BL - CL'$
By substitution $LL' = a - 2(s - b) = b - c$.

We can now prove rather easily that the length of the common external tangent segment of an inscribed and escribed circle of a triangle equals the length of the side contained in the line which intersects the tangent segment.
The proof proceeds as follows: $NN' = AN' - AN$
Earlier we showed that $AN' = s$, and $AN = s - a$.
By substitution, $NN' = s - (s - a) = a$
The same argument holds true for MM'.

Another interesting theorem states that the length of the common external tangent segment of two escribed circles of a triangle equals the sum of the lengths of the two sides which intersect it.

To prove this theorem, have students recall that $BL'' = s$ and $CL''' = s$. This was proved when the *Preassessment* problem was solved. Therefore
$$L'''L'' = BL'' + CL''' - BC$$
$$= s + s - a$$
$$= b + c$$
We can also show that the length of each of the common internal tangent segments of two escribed circles of a triangle equals the length of the side opposite the vertex they determine. The proof is rather simple:
$$L'L'' = BL'' - BL' = BL'' - BN' = s - (s - c) = c$$
Encourage students to investigate the above figure and discover other relationships. A consideration of the radii of the equicircles will produce some interesting results. These radii are called *equiradii*.

A theorem states that the radius of the inscribed circle of a triangle equals the ratio of the area to the semiperimeter. That is:
$$ \measuredangle \triangle ABC = \measuredangle \triangle BCI + \measuredangle \triangle CAI + \measuredangle \triangle ABI(\text{note:} \measuredangle \text{ reads} $$
"area of")
$$ \measuredangle \triangle ABC = \frac{1}{2}\, ra + \frac{1}{2}\, rb + \frac{1}{2}\, rc $$
$$ = \frac{1}{2} r(a + b + c) = sr. $$
Therefore $r = \dfrac{\measuredangle \triangle ABC}{s}$

A natural extension of this theorem states that the radius of an escribed circle of a triangle equals the ratio of the area of the triangle to the difference between the semiperimeter and the length of the side to which the escribed circle is tangent.

To prove this have students consider:
$$ \measuredangle \triangle ABC = \measuredangle \triangle ABI' + \measuredangle \triangle ACI' - \measuredangle \triangle BCI' $$
$$ = \frac{1}{2}r'c + \frac{1}{2}r'b - \frac{1}{2}r'a $$
$$ = \frac{1}{2}r'(c + b - a) $$
$$ = r'(s - a) $$
Therefore $r' = \dfrac{\measuredangle \triangle ABC}{s - a}$

In a similar manner students should show that
$$ r'' = \frac{\measuredangle \triangle ABC}{s - b} $$
and
$$ r''' = \frac{\measuredangle \triangle ABC}{s - c} $$

To conclude this discussion, have students find the product of all the equiradii of a circle. All they need do is multiply the last few expressions:
$$ rr'r''r''' = \frac{(\measuredangle \triangle ABC)^4}{s(s - a)(s - b)(s - c)} $$

However by Heron's formula:
$$\measuredangle\triangle ABC = \sqrt{s(s-a)(s-b)(s-c)}$$
Therefore: $rr'r''r''' = (\measuredangle\triangle ABC)^2$.

At this point ask students to summarize the various theorems and relationships developed in this Model.

Postassessment

To conclude the lesson, have students complete the following exercises.

1. Define equicircles and equiradii.
2. State four properties of equicircles.
3. State and prove one property of equicircles.

Reference

Posamentier, Alfred S., *Excursions in Advanced Euclidean Geometry*. Menlo Park, Ca.: Addison-Wesley, 1984.

66 The Inscribed Circle and the Right Triangle

After having completed a unit on circles and a separate unit dealing with right triangles, students may enjoy seeing some relationships that integrate these units. This unit will deal with some interesting properties of the radius of an inscribed circle of a right triangle.

Performance Objectives

1. *Given a right triangle with integral length sides, students will be able to show that the inradius is an integer.*

2. *Students will be able to explain how the altitude drawn to the hypotenuse of a right triangle is related to the inradii of the triangles formed.*

3. *Students will know and be able to derive a formula relating the inradius to the area and perimeter of a right triangle.*

4. *Given a particular integral inradius, students will be able to determine the number of right triangles with integral relatively prime sides having this given inradius.*

5. *Students will be able to give one possible triple of the lengths of sides of a right triangle when given a positive integral value of the inradius.*

Preassessment

Have students try the following problems:

1. Find the radius of a circle inscribed in a right triangle whose sides have lengths 3, 4, 5.

2. Repeat this problem for a triangle whose sides have lengths 5, 12, 13.

Teaching Strategies

After having completed the above problems either individually or as a class, students will want to con-

sider the following question. "Given a right triangle of integral sides, will this guarantee that the radius of the inscribed circle is also an integer?" In order to prove that the answer is affirmative, consider the diagram below. Here, r is the inradius, (i.e., the radius of the inscribed circle) and $\triangle ABC$ has a right angle at

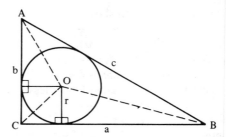

C and sides of lengths a, b, c. The proof involves finding a relationship between r, a, b and c. If the center of the circle is joined to each of the three vertices, three triangles are formed. The area of one triangle is $\frac{1}{2}ra$, the second triangle's area is $\frac{1}{2}rb$ and the third's is $\frac{1}{2}rc$. The area of $\triangle ABC$ is $\frac{1}{2}ab$. Challenge the students to set up a relationship between r and a, b, c. By adding areas one gets $\frac{1}{2}ra + \frac{1}{2}rb + \frac{1}{2}rc = \frac{1}{2}ab$ which is the area of $\triangle ABC$. Thus, $r = \frac{ab}{a+b+c}$. But this only seems to make r rational for integral a, b and c. At this point, remind students (or show them for the first time) how integral values of a, b and c are obtained from a formula. That is, show them this generating formula for sides of right triangles.

$$a = (m^2 - n^2)$$
$$b = 2mn$$
$$c = (m^2 + n^2),$$ where $m > n$ and m and n are relatively prime positive integers of different parity.

Using $r(a+b+c) = ab$, substitute a, b and c. Thus, $2r(m^2 + mn) = 2mn(m^2 - n^2)$ or $r = n(m-n)$.

Since m and n are integers, $m > n$, then r is also an integer. Therefore, *whenever a right triangle has integral sides it also has an integral inradius.*

As a result of the above, a concise formula can be established relating the inradius to the area and perimeter of a right triangle. Since $r = \dfrac{ab}{a+b+c}$, substitute p (perimeter) for $a+b+c$. Also note that the area of $\triangle ABC = \mathcal{A}\dfrac{ab}{2}$ or $2\,\mathcal{A}\triangle ABC = ab$ (where $\mathcal{A}$ represents "area of"). Thus $r = \dfrac{2\,\mathcal{A}\Delta}{p}$. For practice, have students find the inradius, given various values of $\mathcal{A}\Delta$ and p.

Students have probably worked for some time with right triangles whose altitude to the hypotenuse is drawn (see figure below). Now they can relate the inradius to this familiar diagram.

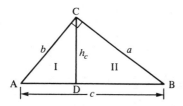

Let $\triangle ADC$ be called ΔI with inradius r_I. Similarly, $\triangle DCB$ (ΔII) has inradius r_{II} and $\triangle ABC$ (ΔIII) has inradius r_{III}. It can be shown that the sum of the inradii of ΔI, ΔII and ΔIII equals the length of the altitude from C, which will be called h_c. Note that $\triangle ADC \sim \triangle DCB \sim \triangle ABC$. Since the corresponding inradii of the similar triangles are in the same ratio as any pair of corresponding sides, $\dfrac{r_I}{r_{III}} = \dfrac{b}{c}$ or $r_I = \dfrac{b}{c} r_{III}$. In the same manner, $r_{II} = \dfrac{a}{c} r_{III}$. Therefore, $r_I + r_{II} + r_{III} = \dfrac{a+b+c}{c} r_{III}$.

Recalling that $r = \dfrac{2\,\mathcal{A}\Delta III}{p}$, $\dfrac{a+b+c}{c} r_{III} =$
$\left(\dfrac{a+b+c}{c}\right) \left(\dfrac{2\,\mathcal{A}\Delta III}{p}\right) = \dfrac{2\,\mathcal{A}\Delta III}{c}$. But

$\mathcal{A}\Delta III = \dfrac{1}{2} h_c c$. Thus $\dfrac{2\,\mathcal{A}\Delta III}{c} = h_c$ making $r_I + r_{II} + r_{III} = h_c$ which is what was to be proved.

One can also use the above to prove that the area of the inscribed circle in ΔI plus the area of the inscribed circle in ΔII equals the area of the inscribed circle in ΔIII. This can be seen by recalling

that it has been shown that $r_I = \dfrac{b}{c} r_{III}$ and $r_{II} = \dfrac{a}{c} r_{III}$. Thus $r_I^2 + r_{II}^2 = \dfrac{b^2}{c^2} r_{III}^2 + \dfrac{a^2}{c^2} r_{III}^2 = \dfrac{a^2+b^2}{c^2} r_{III}^2 = r_{III}^2$ (since $a^2 + b^2 = c^2$). Multiplying by π one gets $\pi r_I^2 + \pi r_{II}^2 = \pi r_{III}^2$ which is the theorem to be proved.

Another interesting relationship concerning the inradius is: "The number of primitive Pythagorean Triples is 2^{ℓ}, where ℓ is the number of odd prime divisions of r ($\ell \geq 0$), and r is the length of the corresponding inradius." The full meaning of this theorem should be clear to students before embarking on the proof. Show students that for every natural number r there exists at least one right triangle of sides $2r+1$, $2r^2+2r$ and $2r^2+2r+1$ where r is the inradius. Students should be able to check that this satisfies the Pythagorean Theorem. As an example, have them try various values for r. For $r = 1$, one gets a triangle of side lengths 3, 4 and 5.

Getting back to proving the above theorem, let a, b and c be sides of a right triangle with sides of integral length, where b is even, a, b and c are relatively prime. The inradius of this triangle is the positive integer r. Recall that $r = \dfrac{ab}{a+b+c}$ r can also be written as $\dfrac{1}{2}(a+b-c)$ by noting that $\dfrac{ab}{a+b+c} = \dfrac{a+b-c}{2}$ is an identity. Students should be urged to verify this identity remembering that $a^2 + b^2 = c^2$. From the original generating formula substitute for a, b and c. Students should obtain $r = (m-n)n$. Since m and n are relatively prime, then $(m-n)$ and n are also relatively prime. (Note: $(m-n)$ is odd since m and n are relatively prime and of opposite parity.) Thus, the inradius can be decomposed into a product of two positive integers which are relatively prime and where the factor $(m-n)$ is odd.

Now consider r as any positive integer where $r = xy$ is any decomposition of r into a product of two relatively prime positive integers where one is odd. Let $m = x+y$, $n = y$. Then m and n are also relatively prime. Also, since x is odd, if $n = y$ is odd, then $m = x+y$ is even. Similarly, if m is odd, n must be even. Thus, one of the numbers m and n is even.

Recall $m > n$. Letting $a = m^2 - n^2$, $b = 2mn$, $c = m^2 + c^2$ one obtains the type of triangle desired with inradius $r = (m-n)\,nab$. Therefore, every decomposition of the number r into a product of two relatively prime numbers where one is odd will determine the type of triangle desired of inradius r. It can be shown that if $\ell \geq 0$ where $r = 2p_1^{x_1} p_2^{x_2} p_3^{x_3} \ldots p_{\ell}^{x_{\ell}}$ with p_i being an odd prime integer (i a positive integer), then the number of decompositions of r is 2^{ℓ}. Thus

2_ℓ must be the number of decompositions or r into two relatively prime factors where one is odd.

Thus, for every positive integer r, there exists as many distinct right triangles whose sides have lengths which are relatively prime integers with inradius r as there are distinct decompositions of r into a product of two relatively prime factors of which one is odd. The numbers of such triangles are 2_ℓ. This completes the proof.

Students desiring to look into the matter further might try to prove that if r is a positive even integer, then the total number of right triangles with intregal length sides which are not necessarily relatively prime, having r as an inradius, is given by $(x + 1)(2x_1 + 1)(2x_2 + 1) \cdots (2x_\ell + 1)$ where x and ℓ are the numbers found by decomposing r into $2^x p_1^{x_1} p_2^{x_2} \ldots p_\ell^{x_\ell}, x \geq 0, \ell \geq 0$ and $p_\ell =$ odd prime, $x_1 \geq 1$ and $2 < p_1 < p_2 < \ldots < p_\ell$. Any positive integer can be so decomposed.

Other interesting relationships concerning the inradius might be researched by the students. For example, they might try to prove the formula (for any triangle) that the inradius r of $\triangle XYZ$ (sides x,y,z and $s = \frac{x + y + z}{2}$) is $r = \sqrt{\frac{(s - x)(s - y)(s - z)}{5}}$. Other investigations should prove to be challenging to the class.

Postassessment

1. If a right triangle has sides of 5, 12 and 13 does this guarantee r will also be an integer? If so, which integer is it? If not, explain why.

2. If an altitude drawn to the hypotenuse of a right triangle creates three similar triangles of inradii 2, 3 and 4 find the length of this altitude.

3. Find the number of distinct right triangles whose sides have lengths which are relatively prime integers having 70 as its inradii.

4. If the inradius equals 3, find the lengths of the sides of one right triangle with this inradius.

5. $\triangle XYZ$ has an area of 6 and a perimeter of 12. Find the length of its inradius.

67   The Golden Rectangle

In this unit, the concept of the Golden Ratio will be introduced together with some of its elementary algebraic and geometric ramifications.

Performance Objectives

1. Students will construct a golden rectangle.
2. Students will state the golden ratio.
3. Students will demonstrate certain properties of the golden rectangle and the golden ratio.

Preassessment

Some knowledge of geometry and intermediate algebra is necessary.

Teaching Strategies

Have your students draw a golden rectangle using the following construction. Given square ABCD, with each side one unit long, locate the midpoint, M, of $\overline{AD}$. Draw $\overline{MC}$. By the Pythagorean theorem, $MC = \frac{\sqrt{5}}{2}$. With center of compasses at M and radius $\overline{MC}$, have students describe an arc cutting $\overrightarrow{AD}$ at E. Then,

$$DE = ME - MD = \frac{\sqrt{5}}{2} - \frac{1}{2}, = \frac{\sqrt{5} - 1}{2}. \quad (1)$$

From this result, it follows that AE = AD + DE

$$= 1 + \frac{\sqrt{5} - 1}{2}, \text{ or } = \frac{\sqrt{5} + 1}{2} = 1.61803\cdots.$$

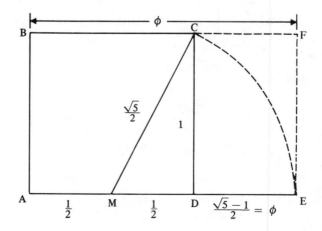

Figure 1

By erecting a perpendicular at E to meet $\overrightarrow{BC}$ at F, rectangle ABFE is constructed, where the ratio of length to width is

$$\frac{AE}{AB} = \frac{\dfrac{\sqrt{5}+1}{2}}{1} = \frac{\sqrt{5}+1}{2}. \tag{2}$$

The ratio (2) is called the *golden ratio* or *golden section*, denoted by the Greek letter phi (ϕ), and a rectangle having such a ratio of length to width is called a *Golden Rectangle*. Note that the value of (2), $\phi = 1.61803\cdots$, is an irrational number approximately equal to $\frac{8}{5}$. A rectangle with such a ratio of length to width was thought by the ancient Greeks, and corroborated experimentally by the psychologist Fechner in 1876, to be the most pleasing and harmoniously balanced rectangle to the eye.

Have your students solve the equation $x^2 - x - 1 = 0$, solutions for which are

$$r_1 = \frac{\sqrt{5}+1}{2} \text{ and } r_2 = \frac{-\sqrt{5}+1}{2}. \tag{3}$$

From (2), $r_1 = \phi$, and r_2, when evaluated, is equal to $-0.61803\cdots$.

A relation between ϕ and r_2 will become apparent if we first evaluate the reciprocal of ϕ, i.e., determine $\frac{1}{\phi}$. From (2),

$$\frac{1}{\phi} = \frac{1}{\dfrac{\sqrt{5}+1}{2}} = \frac{\sqrt{5}-1}{2} = 0.61803\cdots.$$

The ratio $\frac{\sqrt{5}-1}{2}$ is denoted by ϕ'. Thus, from (3), $r_2 = \frac{-\sqrt{5}+1}{2}$ is the additive inverse of ϕ' and is denoted by $-\phi'$. In summary, then,

$$\phi = \frac{\sqrt{5}+1}{2} = 1.61803\cdots, \tag{4}$$

$$-\phi = \frac{-\sqrt{5}-1}{2} = -1.61803\cdots, \tag{5}$$

$$\frac{1}{\phi} = \phi' = \frac{\sqrt{5}-1}{2} = 0.61803\cdots, \tag{6}$$

$$-\phi' = \frac{-\sqrt{5}+1}{2} = -0.61803\cdots. \tag{7}$$

In passing, it should be kept in mind that the ratio of width to length for a Golden Rectangle is ϕ', whereas the ratio of length to width is ϕ. Thus, in Figure 1, $\frac{DE}{DC} = \phi'$, so that CDEF is a golden rectangle.

Some rather unique relationships can be derived from (4) $-$ (7). For example, using (4) and (6),

$$\phi \cdot \phi' = 1, \tag{8}$$

and $\phi - \phi' = 1$. $\tag{9}$

ϕ and ϕ' are the only two numbers in mathematics which bear the distinction of having both their products and differences equal to one!

$$\phi^2 = \left(\frac{\sqrt{5}+1}{2}\right)^2 = \frac{5+2\sqrt{5}+1}{4} = \frac{3+\sqrt{5}}{2}. \tag{10}$$

But, $\phi + 1 = \frac{\sqrt{5}+1}{2} + 1 = \frac{3+\sqrt{5}}{2}. \tag{11}$

Thus, from (10) and (11),

$$\phi^2 = \phi + 1. \tag{12}$$

Furthermore, by using (6) and (12),

$$(\phi')^2 + \phi = \frac{1}{\phi^2} + \phi = \frac{1}{\phi+1} + \phi = \frac{1+\phi^2+\phi}{\phi+1}$$

$$= \frac{\phi^2+\phi^2}{\phi^2} = \frac{2\phi^2}{\phi^2} = 2. \tag{13}$$

Again, using (6) and (12),

$$\phi^2 - \phi' = \phi + 1 - \frac{1}{\phi} = \frac{\phi^2+\phi-1}{\phi} = \frac{\phi+1+\phi-1}{\phi} = 2. \tag{14}$$

Hence, from (13) and (14)

$$(\phi')^2 + \phi = \phi^2 - \phi' \tag{15}$$

Powers of ϕ: A fascinating occurrence of the Fibonacci series can be obtained if we derive powers of ϕ in terms of ϕ and take note of the co-efficients and constants that arise.

For example, using (12),

$$\phi^3 = \phi^2 \cdot \phi = (\phi + 1)\phi = \phi^2 + \phi =$$
$$\phi + 1 + \phi = 2\phi + 1, \tag{16}$$

$$\phi^4 = \phi^3 \cdot \phi = (2\phi + 1)\phi = 2\phi^2 + \phi =$$
$$2(\phi + 1) + \phi = 2\phi + 2 + \phi =$$
$$3\phi + 2, \tag{17}$$

and $\phi^5 = \phi^4 \cdot \phi = (3\phi + 2)\phi = 3\phi^2 + 2\phi =$
$$3(\phi + 1) + 2\phi = 3\phi + 3 + 2\phi =$$
$$5\phi + 3. \tag{18}$$

Have students generate further powers of ϕ.

$$
\begin{aligned}
\phi^1 &= 1\phi + 0 \\
\phi^2 &= 1\phi + 1 \\
\phi^3 &= 2\phi + 1 \\
\phi^4 &= 3\phi + 2 \\
\phi^5 &= 5\phi + 3 \\
\phi^6 &= 8\phi + 5 \\
\phi^7 &= 13\phi + 8 \\
\phi^8 &= 21\phi + 13 \\
&\vdots \qquad \vdots
\end{aligned}
\tag{19}
$$

Let us return to figure 1. If, along $\overline{CD}$, the length $DE = \phi'$ is marked off, we obtain square DEGH, each side equal in length to ϕ'.

Thus, $CH = 1 - \phi'$ (remember that originally CD = one unit). But $1 - \phi' = 1 - \frac{1}{\phi} = \frac{\phi-1}{\phi} = \frac{\dfrac{1}{\phi}}{\phi} =$

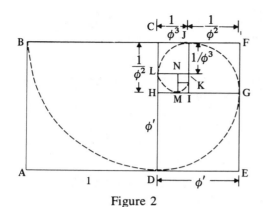

Figure 2

$\frac{1}{\phi^2} = (\phi')^2 = \frac{1}{\phi^2}$. With CF (or GH) $= \phi' = \frac{1}{\phi}$,

$\frac{CH''}{CF} = \frac{(\phi')^2}{\phi'} = \phi'$.

Thus, CFGH is also a golden rectangle.

In like fashion, a square, each of whose sides is $(\phi')^2$ units in length, can be partitioned along side CF of CFGH, whereby we obtain another golden rectangle CJIH. CJIH can similarly be partitioned to obtain square GJKL, leaving golden rectangle IKLH. This process of partitioning

squares from golden rectangles to obtain another golden rectangle can be indefinitely continued in the manner suggested in figure 2.

If points B,D,G,J,L,M are connected by a smooth curve (see figure 2), a spiral-shaped curve will result. This is part of an equiangular spiral, a detailed discussion of which is not possible at this time.

Postassessment

1. A line segment $\overline{AE}$ is said to be divided into *extreme and mean ratio* if a point D can be located on $\overline{AE}$ such that $\dfrac{\overline{AE}}{\overline{AD}} = \dfrac{\overline{AD}}{\overline{DE}}$ (20)

In figure 1, let AE = x and AD = 1. Then, from (20), derive the quadratic equation which was used to determine the value of ϕ in (3).

Reference

Posamentier, Alfred S., *Excursions in Advanced Euclidean Geometry*. Menlo Park, Ca.: Addison-Wesley, 1984.

68   The Golden Triangle

This unit will help to develop student understanding in areas of mathematics not usually dealt with.

Performance Objectives

1. Students will demonstrate understanding of various relationships between the pentagon, the pentagram and the golden ratio.

2. Students will construct a Golden Triangle.

3. Students will demonstrate certain properties of the Golden Triangle with trigonometric functions.

Preassessment

Some knowledge of geometry and intermediate algebra is necessary.

Teaching Strategies

Have your students construct a regular pentagon ABCDE by any method, after which they should draw pentagram ACEBD (see Figure 1.) Let each side of the pentagon be ϕ units in length. Review with your students the various angle measures and isosceles triangles formed by the pentagram and

pentagon. Particular note should be made of similar isosceles triangles BED and DEF since they

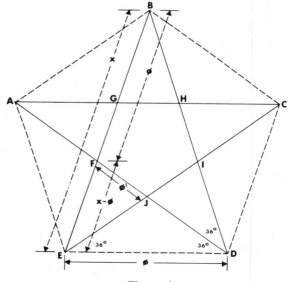

Figure 1

will be chosen, quite arbitrarily, from the many similar triangles in Figure 1, for the discussion that follows.

With $\overline{DF}$ the bisector of $\angle BDE$, triangles DEF and BDF are isosceles, so that

$$ED = DF = FB = \phi. \qquad (1)$$

Let $BE = BD = x$. Then $FE = x - \phi$, and

$$\frac{BF}{FE} = \frac{BD}{ED}, \frac{\phi}{x - \phi} = \frac{x}{\phi}, \qquad (2)$$

so that $x^2 - \phi x - \phi^2 = 0$. $\qquad (3)$

The positive root of (3), from the quadratic formula, is

$$x = \phi \left(\frac{1 + \sqrt{5}}{2}\right). \qquad (4)$$

But by definition, $\dfrac{1 + \sqrt{5}}{2} = \phi.$

Hence, from (4),

$$x = \phi \cdot \phi = \phi^2 = BE, \qquad (5)$$

and $\quad EF = x - \phi = \phi^2 - \phi = \phi + 1 - \phi = 1.$ $\quad (6)$

Thus, in $\triangle BED$, the ratio of leg to base, using

(5), is $\dfrac{BE}{ED} = \dfrac{\phi^2}{\phi} = \phi,$

and in $\triangle DEF$, the ratio of leg to base is again ϕ,

since $\dfrac{DE}{EF} = \dfrac{\phi}{1} = \phi,$

so that in any 72°-72°-36° isosceles triangle

(hereafter referred to as *The Golden Triangle*), the ratio of

$$\frac{\text{leg}}{\text{base}} = \phi \qquad (7)$$

This is the same ratio of length to width defined for the Golden Rectangle.

In isosceles $\triangle EFJ$, $FJ = \phi'$, since, using (6) and

(7), $\dfrac{EF}{FJ} = \dfrac{1}{FJ} = \phi$, implying that $FJ = \dfrac{1}{\phi} = \phi'$. (8)

Thus, regular pentagon FGHIJ has side length of ϕ'.

Returning to isosceles $\triangle DEF$, it is apparent that $\overline{EJ}$ is the bisector of $\angle DEF$. In figure 2, let $\overline{FK}$ be the bisector of $\angle EFJ$. Then $FJ = FK = \dfrac{1}{\phi}$ and

base $JK = \dfrac{1}{\phi^2}$. Moreover, $\overline{FK} \parallel \overline{BD}$, since $m \angle KFJ = m \angle JDB.$

In like fashion, the bisector of $\angle FJK$ is parallel to $\overline{ED}$ and meets $\overline{FK}$ at L, forming another golden triangle, $\triangle JKL$. This process of bisecting a base angle of a golden triangle can be continued indefinitely to produce a series of smaller and smaller golden triangles which converge to a limiting point, 0. This point, comparable to that obtained in the golden rectangle, is the pole of an equiangular spiral which passes through the vertices B,D,E,F,J,K,L, . . . of each of the golden triangles.

A number of additional properties of the golden triangle are worth mentioning:

1. In figure 2, let ML be of unit length. Then, from (7),

$$
\begin{aligned}
LK &= \phi &&= 1\phi + 0 \\
KJ &= \phi^2 &&= 1\phi + 1 \\
JF &= \phi^3 &&= 2\phi + 1 \\
FE &= \phi^4 &&= 3\phi + 2 \\
ED &= \phi^5 &&= 5\phi + 3 \\
DB &= \phi^6 &&= 8\phi + 5
\end{aligned} \qquad (9)
$$

forming a Fibonacci Series.

2. The bisector of the vertex angle of a golden triangle divides the bisectors of the base angles in the golden ratio (see Figure 1.) Since the angle bisectors of a triangle are concurrent, the bisector of $\angle EBD$ must pass through J. However, from

Figure 2

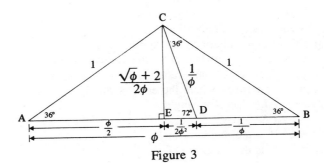

Figure 3

(6), EF = 1 = EJ = JD, and from (8), FJ = ϕ'.

Hence, $\dfrac{JD}{FJ} = \dfrac{1}{\phi'} = \phi$.

3. The golden triangle can be used to represent certain trigonometric functions in terms of ϕ (see Figure 3.) Let $\triangle ABC$ be a 36°-36°-108° isosceles triangle, with $AC = CB = 1$. Let one of the trisectors of angle C meet $\overline{AB}$ at D. Then $\triangle ACD$ is a golden triangle with $m\angle CDA = m\angle DCA = 72°$. Since $AC = 1$, then $AD = 1$, and from (7), $CD = \dfrac{1}{\phi}$. Furthermore, $\triangle BCD$ is isosceles with

$m\angle BCD = m\angle DBC = 36°$. Thus $CD = DB = \dfrac{1}{\phi}$, and $AB = AD + DB = 1 + \dfrac{1}{\phi} = \phi$.

From C, drop a perpendicular to meet $\overline{AB}$ at E. This makes $AE = EB = \dfrac{\phi}{2}$. Immediately, in right $\triangle ACE$ $\cos 36° = \dfrac{\phi}{2}$, implying that $\qquad$ (10)

$\sin 54° = \dfrac{\phi}{2}$. $\qquad$ (11)

Furthermore,

$ED = AD - AE = 1 - \dfrac{\phi}{2} = \dfrac{2-\phi}{2} = \dfrac{1}{2\phi^2}$. (12)

Now in right $\triangle CED$,

$$\cos 72° = \dfrac{ED}{CD} = \dfrac{\dfrac{1}{2\phi^2}}{\dfrac{1}{\phi}} = \dfrac{1}{2\phi} = \sin 18°. \qquad (13)$$

Postassessment

1. Using the reciprocal trigonometric identities, determine values in terms of ϕ for tan, cot, sec and csc for the angle measures indicated in (10), (11) and (13) above.

2. Using the half-angle formulas, determine trigonometric function values for 18° and 27° in terms of ϕ.

This unit should be used in conjunction with "The Golden Rectangle."

Reference

Huntley, H.E., *The Divine Proportion*. New York: Dover, 1970.

69 Geometric Fallacies

Geometry students studying proofs using auxillary sets often question the need for a rigorous reason for that set's existence. Often they don't appreciate the need for proving the existence and uniqueness of these sets. Students also develop a dependence upon a diagram without analyzing its correctness. This unit introduces fallacious proofs to students in the hope that they can better grasp the need for such rigor.

Performance Objective

Given a geometric fallacy, students will determine where the fallacy occurs.

Preassessment

Students should be well acquainted with geometric proofs of both congruent and similar triangles.

Present your students with the following proof. They will recognize that it contains a fallacy. Ask them to try to determine where the error occurs.
Given: $\underline{ABCD}$ is a rectangle
$\overline{FA} \cong \overline{BA}$
R is the midpoint of $\overline{BC}$
N is the midpoint of $\overline{CF}$

To Prove: A right angle is equal in measure to an obtuse angle ($\angle CDA \cong \angle FAD$)
Draw $\overleftrightarrow{RL}$ perpendicular to $\overline{CB}$.
Draw $\overleftrightarrow{NM}$ perpendicular to $\overline{CF}$.
$\overleftrightarrow{RL}$ and $\overleftrightarrow{NM}$ intersect at point O. If they didn't intersect, $\overleftrightarrow{RL}$ and $\overleftrightarrow{NM}$ would be parallel and this would mean $\overline{CB}$ is parallel to $\overline{CF}$ which is impossible.
Draw $\overline{DO}$, $\overline{CO}$, $\overline{FO}$ and $\overline{AO}$.
Since $\overline{RO}$ is the perpendicular bisector of $\overline{CB}$ and $\overline{DA}$, $\overline{DO} \cong \overline{AO}$.
Since $\overline{NO}$ is the perpendicular bisector of $\overline{CF}$, $\overline{CO} \cong \overline{FO}$.
And, since $\overline{FA} \cong \overline{BA}$ and $\overline{BA} \cong \overline{CD}$, we have $\overline{FA} \cong \overline{CD}$.
$\therefore \triangle CDO \cong \triangle FAO$ (SSS $\cong$ SSS), so $\angle ODC \cong \angle OAF$.
Since $\overline{OD} \cong \overline{OA}$ we have $\angle ODA \cong \angle OAD$.

Now, $m\angle ODC - m\angle ODA = m\angle OAF - m\angle OAD$ or $m\angle CDA = m\angle FAD$.

Teaching Strategies

When students have inspected the proof and have found nothing wrong with it, ask them to use rulers and compasses to reconstruct the diagram. The correct diagram looks like this:

Although the triangles are congruent, our ability to subtract the specific angles no longer exists. Thus, the difficulty with this proof lies in its dependence upon an incorrectly drawn diagram.

In order to show that $\angle OAF$ cannot be obtuse, we must show that when $\overline{OF}$ intersects $\overline{AB}$ and $\overline{AD}$, and point O is on the perpendicular bisector of $\overline{CF}$, then point O cannot be on the perpendicular bisector of $\overline{AD}$.

Suppose point O is the intersection of the two perpendicular bisectors. (As in the original diagram.) Since $\overline{CD}\,//\,\overline{AQ}$, $\angle DCF \cong \angle AQF$. In isosceles $\triangle ABF$, $\angle ABF \cong \angle AFB$. But $m\angle AFB > m\angle AFC$; by substitution $m\angle ABF > m\angle AFC$. Since $\angle AQF$ is an exterior angle of $\triangle BQF$, $m\angle AQF > m\angle ABF$. Therefore $m\angle AQF > m\angle ABF > m\angle AFC$, or $m\angle AQF > m\angle AFC$. By substitution $m\angle DCF > m\angle AFC$. Since $\angle OCF \cong \angle OFC$ by subtraction we have $m\angle DCO > m\angle OFA$. Thus, $DO > OA$. This is a contradiction since $DO = AO$ if O is bisector of $\overline{DA}$ on the perpendicular. Therefore point O cannot be on the perpendicular bisector of $\overline{DA}$ for any point O such that $\angle OAF$ is obtuse.

The above proof also holds true for the following diagram which shows that $\angle OAF$ cannot be acute.

Now present your students with the following proof that any point in the interior of a circle is also on the circle.

Given: Circle O, with radius r

Let A be any point in the interior of the circle distinct from O.

Prove: A is on the circle

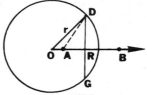

Let B be on the extension of $\overline{OA}$ through A such that $OA\cdot OB = r^2$. (Clearly OB is greater than r since OA is less than r.) Let the perpendicular bisector of $\overline{AB}$ meet the circle in Points D and G, where R is the midpoint of $\overline{AB}$.

We now have $OA = OR - RA$ and $OB = OR + RB = OR + RA$.

$\therefore r^2 = (OR - RA)(OR + RA)$

$r^2 = OR^2 - RA^2$

$r^2 = (r^2 - DR^2) - (AD^2 - DR^2)$ by the Pythagorean Theorem

$r^2 = r^2 - AD^2$

$\therefore AD^2 = 0$

$\therefore$ A coincides with D, and lies on the circle.

The fallacy in this proof lies in the fact that we drew an auxiliary line ($\overleftrightarrow{DRG}$) with *two* conditions— that $\overleftrightarrow{DRG}$ is the perpendicular bisector of $\overline{AB}$ and that it intersects the circle. Actually, all points on the perpendicular bisector of $\overline{AB}$ lie in the exterior of the circle and therefore cannot intersect the circle.

$r^2 = OA\,(OB)$

$r^2 = OA\,(OA + AB)$

$r^2 = OA^2 + (OA)\,(AB)$

now, the proof assumes $OA + \dfrac{AB}{2} < r$

$$2(OA) + AB < 2r$$
$$4(OA)^2 + 4(OA)(AB) + AB^2 < 4r^2$$

Since $r^2 = OA^2 + (OA)(AB)$

we have $4r^2 + AB^2 < 4r^2$

$AB^2 < 0$

which is impossible.

This proof points to the care we must take when drawing auxillary sets in using *one* condition only.

Here is a "triangle" consisting of four right triangles, four rectangles and a "hole."

1. Have your students calculate the area of the eight regions (not the hole) [416]

2. Now have them calculate the area of the entire figure. [Since PQ = 32 and height = 26, $\frac{1}{2}$PQ$\cdot h$ = 416] We are now faced with this problem: how did we arrive at the same area with and without the hole?

The fallacy occurs because of an error in 2. The figure is *not* a triangle, since points M, N and P are not collinear.

If points M, N and P were collinear,
since ∠RNO is a right angle, ∠PNR is the complement of ∠MNT
since ∠NRP is a right angle, ∠PNR is the complement of ∠ RPN
∴ ∠MNT ≅ ∠RPN
∴ΔMNT ∼ ΔNPR

But, this is not the case.
The same argument holds for points M, O and Q. Therefore the figure is a pentagon; thus the formula we used in 2 is incorrect.

Postassessment
Have students select a geometric fallacy from any of the following books and explain the "error" in the proof.

References
Maxwell, E. A., *Fallacies in Mathematics*, Cambridge University Press, 1963.

Northrop, E. P., *Riddles in Mathematics*, D. Van Nostrand Co., 1944.

Posamentier, A. S., J. H. Banks, and R. L. Bannister, *Geometry, Its Elements and Structure*, 2d ed., McGraw-Hill, 1977. pp 240–44, 270–71.

70   Regular Polyhedra

This unit will present a method which can be used to prove that there are not more than five regular polyhedra.

Performance Objective
Students will define a regular polyhedron, identify all regular polyhedra, and explain why no more than five regular polyhedra exist.

Preassessment
Display physical models of various polyhedra and have students count the number of vertices (V), the number of edges (E), and the number of faces (F) of each polyhedron. After tabulating their results they should notice the relationship:
$$V + F = E + 2$$

Teaching Strategies
Having empirically established Euler's Theorem, $(V + F = E + 2)$, students may wish to apply it to reach other conclusions about polyhedra. Depending upon class interest, proof of this theorem may be in order. One source for the proof is *Geometry, Its Elements and Structure* by A.S. Posamentier, J.H. Banks, and R.L. Bannister, pp. 574–576 (McGraw-Hill, 1977).

One interesting application of this theorem is the proof that more than five *regular* polyhedra cannot exist. You should begin by defining a regular polyhedron as *a solid figure bounded by portions of planes called faces, each of which is a regular polygon* (congruent sides and angles). The cube is a common example of a regular polyhedron.

To begin the proof that *there are only five regular polyhedra*, let s represent the number of sides of each face and let t represent the number of faces at each vertex.

Since there are t faces at each vertex students should realize that there are also t edges at each vertex. Suppose in counting the number of edges (E) of a given polyhedron, the number of edges at each vertex were counted and then multiplied by the number of vertices (V). This would produce *twice* the number of edges (2E) of the polyhedron, as each edge was counted twice, once at each of the two vertices it joins. Hence:

$$tV = 2E, \text{ or } \frac{V}{\frac{1}{t}} = \frac{E}{\frac{1}{2}}$$

Similarly, in counting the number of edges of the polyhedron, the number of sides (s) of each face were counted and then multiplied by the number of faces (F) of the polyhedron. This would also produce *twice* the number of edges of the polyhedron, as each side (edge) counted belongs to two faces. Hence, $sF = 2E$, or $\dfrac{F}{\frac{1}{s}} = \dfrac{E}{\frac{1}{2}}$

Therefore $\dfrac{V}{\frac{1}{t}} = \dfrac{E}{\frac{1}{2}} = \dfrac{F}{\frac{1}{s}}$

Students should recall the following theorem on proportions: $\dfrac{a}{b} = \dfrac{c}{d} = \dfrac{e}{f} = \dfrac{a+c+e}{b+d+f}$
Then have them apply it to the following:

$$\frac{V}{\frac{1}{t}} = \frac{-E}{-\frac{1}{2}} = \frac{F}{\frac{1}{s}} = \frac{V - E + F}{\frac{1}{t} - \frac{1}{2} + \frac{1}{s}}$$

However, by Euler's Theorem (V − E + F = 2),

$$\frac{V}{\frac{1}{t}} = \frac{E}{\frac{1}{2}} = \frac{F}{\frac{1}{s}} = \frac{2}{\frac{1}{t} - \frac{1}{2} + \frac{1}{s}}$$

Students may now solve for V, E, and F:

$$V = \frac{4s}{2s + 2t - st}$$

$$E = \frac{2st}{2s + 2t - st}$$

$$F = \frac{4t}{2s + 2t - st}$$

Students should be asked to inspect the nature of V, E, and F. Realizing that these numbers must be positive, elicit from students that the denominators must be positive (since s and t are positive, as well as the numerators). Thus,

$$2s + 2t - st > 0$$

To enable factoring add −4 to both members of the inequality to get:

$$2s + 2t - st - 4 > -4$$

Then multiply both sides by −1:

$$-2s - 2t + st + 4 < 4, \text{ or } (s-2)(t-2) < 4.$$

At this point have students place restrictions on s and t. They should be quick to state that no polygon may have less than three sides; hence $s \geq 3$. Also, they should realize that at each vertex of the polyhedron there must at least be three faces; hence $t \geq 3$.

These facts will indicate that $(s-2)$ and $(t-2)$ must be positive. Since their product must be less than four, students should be able to generate the following table:

(s−2)(t−2)	(s−2)	(t−2)	s	t	V	E	F	Name of Polyhedron
1	1	1	3	3	4	6	4	Tetrahedron
2	2	1	4	3	8	12	6	Hexahedron (cube)
2	1	2	3	4	6	12	8	Octahedron
3	3	1	5	3	20	30	12	Dodecahedron
3	1	3	3	5	12	30	20	Icosahedron

Since there are no other possible values for s and t the above table is complete, and hence there are only five regular polyhedra. More able students should be encouraged to investigate the existence of these five regular polyhedra. One source is Euclid's *Elements*, Book XIII.

Further inspection of the above table reveals an interesting symmetry between the hexahedron and the octahedron as well as the dodecahedron and the icosahedron. That is, if s and t are interchanged these symmetries will be highlighted. Furthermore, this table indicates that the faces of these regular polyhedra are either equilateral triangles, squares, or regular pentagons (see column s). Students should also be encouraged to

further verify Euler's Theorem (V + F = E + 2) with the data in the above table.

The figure shows the five regular polyhedra as well as "patterns" which can be used to construct (by cutting them out and appropriately folding them) these polyhedra.

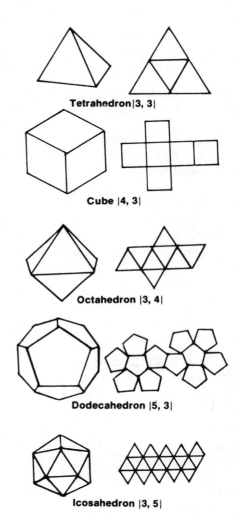

Tetrahedron ⦃3, 3⦄

Cube ⦃4, 3⦄

Octahedron ⦃3, 4⦄

Dodecahedron ⦃5, 3⦄

Icosahedron ⦃3, 5⦄

Although often referred to as the five Platonic Solids, it is believed that three (tetrahedron, hexahedron, and dodecahedron) of the five solids were due to Pythagoreans, while the remaining two solids (octahedron, and icosahedron) were due to the efforts of Theaetetus (414 − 369 B.C.). There is enough history about these solids to merit a brief report by one of the students.

Postassessment

1. Have students define and identify regular polyhedra.

2. Have students explain why more than five regular polyhdra cannot exist.

71   An Introduction to Topology

A lesson on topology can be taught immediately after teaching geometry. This unit will present some basic concepts of topology and their applications.

Performance Objectives

1. *Given two geometric drawings students will determine whether they are topologically equivalent.*

2. *Given a polyhedron or a plane figure students can show that V + F − E = 2 (space), and V + F − E = 1 (plane).*

Preassessment

A basic knowledge of seventh grade geometry is desirable preceding this unit.

Teaching Strategies

Have students draw several closed curves. Then have them distinguish between those that are simple closed curves and those that are not. Some possible student responses may be the following.

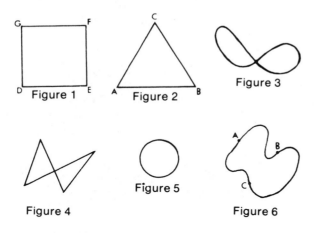

Figure 1   Figure 2   Figure 3

Figure 4   Figure 5   Figure 6

Ask students to redraw each of the figures without lifting their pencils off their paper. Students should realize that if Figure 1 were drawn on a rubber sheet they could twist and bend it into figures 2, 5, and 6.

Suppose they now consider some geometric figures in space. Have them draw a cube.

Figure 7

Ask students if this cube can be transformed into any of figures 8, 9, or 10 by twisting or bending it.

Figure 8   Figure 9   Figure 10

They should find that the only figure of these that the cube can be transformed into is a sphere.

It may therefore be said that a cube is topologically equivalent to a sphere. Tell students that studying figures in this way leads to a branch of mathematics called *topology* or "rubber sheet geometry."

One of the more fascinating relationships in geometry is directly taken from topology. This relationship involves the vertices (V), edges (E) and faces (F) of a polyhedron or polygon. It reads: V + F − E = 2 (in three-dimensional space) or V + F − E = 1 (in a plane). Have students consider a pentagon. A pentagon has five vertices, five edges and one face; hence V + F − E = 5 + 1 − 5 = 1. Students may now wish to consider a three-space figure. The cube (figure 7) has eight vertices, six faces and twelve edges. Therefore, V + F − E = 8 − 12 + 6 = 2. These relationships can be demonstrated to the class by using overhead projector transparencies or with physical models.

Suppose a plane were to cut all edges of one of the trihedral angles of a cube (a piece of clay in the form of a cube would be useful here). This plane would then separate one of the vertices from the cube. However, in the process, there would be added to the original polyhedron: 1 face, 3 vertices and 3 edges. Thus, for this new polyhedron, V is increased by 2, F is increased by 1 and E is increased by 3; yet, V + F − E remains unchanged. More such experiments should be encouraged.

Figures are topologically equivalent if one can be made to coincide with the other by distortion, shrinking, stretching, or bending. If one face of a polyhedron is removed the remaining figure is topologically equivalent to a region of a plane. This new figure (see figure 11) will not have the same shape or size, but its *boundaries* are preserved. The edges will become sides of polygonal regions, and there will be the same number of edges and vertices in the plane figure as in the polyhedron. Each polygon that is not a triangle can be cut into triangles, or triangular regions, by drawing diagonals. Each time a diagonal is drawn, we increase the number of edges by one but we also increase the number of faces by one. The value of V − E + F is preserved. Triangles on the outer edge of the region will have either one edge on the boundary of the region, as △ABC in the accompanying figure, or have two edges on the boundary, as △DEF. Triangles such as △ABC can be removed by removing the one boundary side (i.e., $\overline{AC}$). By doing this we decrease the number of faces by one and the number of edges by one. Still V − E + F is unchanged. Triangles such as DEF can be removed by removing two edges (i.e., $\overline{DF}$ and $\overline{EF}$). By doing this we decrease the number of edges by two, the number of faces by one, and the number of vertices by one. V − E + F is still preserved. We continue in this manner until we are left with one triangle. This triangle has three vertices, three edges, and one face. Hence, V − E + F = 1 in the plane. We conclude that when we replace the face we removed we have V − E + F = 2 for a polyhedron in space.

After students have had a chance to familiarize themselves with this theorem, they should be encouraged to test it empirically with student constructed polyhedra. Clay is a good medium for this activity. Students may want to record their results on a chart.

Figure 11

Figure 12a

Figure 12b

Figure 13a

Figure 13b

Figure 14a

Figure 14b

Postassessment

1. Have students decide if any of Figures 12, 13, or 14 can be bent into the other figures.

2. Show that V + F − E = 2 holds for a tetrahedron and an octahedron.

3. Show that V + F − E = 1 holds for a hexagon and a dodecagon.

72   **Angles On A Clock**

This unit can be used in earlier junior high school grades as a recreational activity where some interesting relationships can be discovered, or it can be used as an enrichment application for beginning algebra students studying the topic of uniform motion.

Performance Objectives

1. Students will determine the precise time that the hands of a clock form a given angle.

2. Students will solve problems related to the positions of the hands on a clock.

Preassessment

Ask students at what time (exactly) will the hands of a clock overlap after 4 o'clock.

Teaching Strategies

Your students' first reaction to the solution to this problem will be that the answer is simply 4:20. When you remind them that the hour hand moves uniformly, they will begin to estimate the answer to be between 4:21 and 4:22. They will realize that the hour hand moves through an interval between minute markers every 12 minutes. Therefore it will leave the interval 4:21-4:22 at 4:24. This however doesn't answer the original question about the exact time of this overlap.

In a beginning algebra class studying uniform motion problems, have students consider this problem in that light. The best way to have a student begin to understand the movement of the hands of a clock is by having him or her consider the hands traveling independently around the clock at uniform speeds. The minute markings on the clock (from now on referred to as "markers") will serve to denote distance as well as time. An analogy should be drawn here to the uniform motion of automobiles (a popular and overused topic for verbal problems in an elementary algebra course). A problem involving a fast automobile overtaking a slower one would be appropriate.

Experience has shown that the analogy should be drawn between specific cases rather than mere generalizations. It might be helpful to have the class find the distance necessary for a car traveling at 60 m.p.h. to overtake a car with a head start of 20 miles and traveling at 5 m.p.h.

Now have the class consider 4 o'clock as the initial time on the clock. Our problem will be to determine exactly when the minute hand will overtake the hour hand after 4 o'clock. Consider the speed of the hour hand to be r, then the speed of the minute hand must be $12r$. We seek the distance, measured by the number of markers traveled, that the minute hand must travel to overtake the hour hand.

Let us refer to this distance as d markers. Hence the distance that the hour hand travels is $d-20$ markers, since it has a $20-$marker head start over the minute hand. For this to take place, the times required for the minute hand, $\dfrac{d}{12r}$, and for the hour hand, $\dfrac{d-20}{r}$, are the same. Therefore, $\dfrac{d}{12r} = \dfrac{d-20}{r}$, and $d = \dfrac{12}{11} \cdot 20 = 21\dfrac{9}{11}$. Thus the minute hand will overtake the hour hand at exactly $4{:}21\dfrac{9}{11}$.

Consider the expression $d = \dfrac{12}{11} \cdot 20$. The quantity 20 is the number of markers that the minute hand had to travel to get to the desired position, assuming the hour hand remained stationary. However, quite obviously, the hour hand does not remain stationary. Hence, we must multiply this quantity by $\dfrac{12}{11}$ as the minute hand must travel $\dfrac{12}{11}$ as far. Let us refer to this fraction$(\dfrac{12}{11})$ as the correction factor. Have the class verify this correction factor both logically and algebraically.

To begin to familiarize the students with use of the correction factor, choose some short and simple problems. For example, you may ask them to find the exact time when the hands of a clock overlap between 7 and 8 o'clock. Here the students would first determine how far the minute hand would have to travel from the "12" position to the position of the hour hand, assuming again that the hour hand remains stationary. Then by multiplying the number of markers, 35, by the

correction factor, $\dfrac{12}{11}$, they will obtain the exact time $(7{:}38\dfrac{2}{11})$ that the hands will overlap.

To enhance students' understanding of this new procedure ask them to consider a person checking a wristwatch against an electric clock and noticing that the hands on the wristwatch overlap every 65 minutes (as measured by the electric clock). Ask the class if the wristwatch is fast, slow, or accurate.

You may wish to have them consider the problem in the following way. At 12 o'clock the hands of a clock overlap exactly. Using the previously described method we find that the hands will again overlap at exactly $1{:}05\dfrac{5}{11}$, and then again at exactly $2{:}10\dfrac{10}{11}$, and again at exactly $3{:}16\dfrac{4}{11}$ and so on. Each time there is an interval of $65\dfrac{5}{11}$ minutes between overlapping positions. Hence, the person's watch is inaccurate by $\dfrac{5}{11}$ of a minute. Have students now determine if the wristwatch is fast or slow.

There are many other interesting, and sometimes rather difficult, problems made simple by this correction factor. You may very easily pose your own problems. For example, you may ask your students to find the exact times when the hands of a clock will be perpendicular (or form a straight angle) between, say, 8 and 9 o'clock.

Again, you would have the students determine the number of markers that the minute hand would have to travel from the "12" position until it forms the desired angle with the stationary hour hand. Then have them multiply this number by the correction factor $(\dfrac{12}{11})$ to obtain the exact actual time. That is, to find the exact time that the hands of a clock are *first* perpendicular between 8 and 9 o'clock, determine the desired position of the minute hand when the hour hand remains stationary (here, on the 25 minute marker). Then, multiply 25 by $\dfrac{12}{11}$ to get $8{:}27\dfrac{3}{11}$, the exact time when the hands are *first* perpendicular after 8 o'clock.

For students who have not yet studied algebra, you might justify the $\dfrac{12}{11}$ correction factor for the interval between overlaps in the following way:

Think of the hands of a clock at noon. During the next 12 hours (i.e. until the hands reach the same position at midnight) the hour hand makes one revolution, the minute hand makes 12 revolutions, and the minute hand coincides with the hour hand 11 times (including midnight, but not noon, starting just after the hands separate at noon).

Since each hand rotates at a uniform rate, the hands overlap each $\frac{12}{11}$ of an hour, or $65\frac{5}{11}$ minutes.

This can be extended to other situations.

Your students should derive a great sense of achievement and enjoyment as a result of employing this simple procedure to solve what usually appears to be a very difficult clock problem.

Postassessment

1. At what time will the hands of a clock overlap after 2 o'clock?

2. At what time will the hands of a clock be perpendicular after 3 o'clock?

3. How would the "correction factor" change if our clock were a 24-hour cycle clock?

4. What would the "correction factor" be if we sought the exact time when the second hand and the minute hand were perpendicular after: (*fill in a specified time*)?

5. What angle is determined by the hands of a clock at: (*fill in a specified time*)?

6. What is the first time (exactly) when the second hand bisects the angle formed by the minute and hour hands of a clock after: (*fill in a specified time*)?

73 Averaging Rates—The Harmonic Mean

This unit will present a shortcut method for determining the average of two or more rates, (rates of speed, cost, production, etc.).

Performance Objectives

1. Given various rates for a common base, students will find the average of these rates.
2. Given a problem calling for the average of given rates, students will correctly apply the concept of a harmonic mean when applicable.

Preassessment

Have students solve the following problem:

Noreen drives from her home to work at the rate of 30 mph. Later she returns home from work over the same route at the rate of 60 mph. What is her average rate of speed for both trips?

Teaching Strategies

The preceding problem should serve as excellent motivation for this unit. Most students will probably incorrectly offer 45 mph as their answer to this problem. Their explanation will be that 45 is the average of 30 and 60. True! You must convince them that since the numbers 30 and 60 represent rates, they cannot be treated as simple quantities. Students will wonder what difference this should make.

The first task is to convince your students that their original answer, 45 mph, is incorrect. Have them realize that when Noreen drove from home to work she had to drive twice as much time than she did on her return trip. Hence, it would be incorrect to give both rates the same "weight." If this still

does not convince your students, ask them that if their test scores throughout the semester were 90, 90, 90, 90 and 40, which of the following methods would they use to find their average:

   90 (average of first four tests)
  +40 (their last test score)
  $\overline{130 \div 2 = 65}$
Or: $90 + 90 + 90 + 90 + 40 = 400; 400 \div 5 = 80$.

It would be expected that students would now suggest that the answer to the original problem could be obtained by: $\frac{30 + 30 + 60}{3} = 40$. This is perfectly correct; however, a simple solution as this would hardly be expected if one rate were not a multiple of the other. Most students would now welcome a more general method of solution. One such solution is based on the relationship: *Rate × Time = Distance.* Consider the following:

$$T_1 \text{ (time going to work)} = \frac{D}{30}$$
$$T_2 \text{ (time returning home)} = \frac{D}{60}$$
$$T \text{ (total time for both trips)} = T_1 + T_2 = \frac{D}{20}$$
$$R \text{ (rate for the entire trip)} = \frac{2D}{T} = \frac{2D}{\frac{D}{20}} = 40$$

R is actually the *average rate* for the entire trip, since problems of this nature deal with uniform motion.

Of particular interest are those problems where the rates to be averaged are for a common base (e.g., the same distance for various rates of speed). Have students consider the original problem in general terms, where the given rates of speed are R_1 and R_2 (instead of 30 and 60), each for a distance D. Therefore, $T_1 = \dfrac{D}{R_1}$ and $T_2 = \dfrac{D}{R_2}$, so that

$$T = T_1 + T_2 = D\left(\frac{1}{R_1} + \frac{1}{R_2}\right) = \frac{D(R_1 + R_2)}{R_1 R_2}.$$

However, have students consider:

$$R = \frac{2D}{T} = \frac{2D}{D\left(\dfrac{1}{R_1} + \dfrac{1}{R_2}\right)} = \frac{2}{\dfrac{1}{R_1} + \dfrac{1}{R_2}} = \frac{2R_1 R_2}{R_1 + R_2} \quad (1)$$

They should notice that $\dfrac{2R_1 R_2}{R_1 + R_2}$ is actually the reciprocal of the average of the reciprocals of R_1 and R_2. Such an average is called the *harmonic mean*.

Perhaps a word about the harmonic mean would be in order. A progression of numbers is said to be harmonic if any three consecutive members of the progression, a, b and c have the property that:

$$\frac{a}{c} = \frac{a - b}{b - c} \quad (2)$$

This relationship may also be written as:

$$a(b-c) = c(a-b) \quad (3)$$

Dividing by abc we get:

$$\frac{1}{c} - \frac{1}{b} = \frac{1}{b} - \frac{1}{a} \quad (4)$$

This relationship shows that the reciprocals of a harmonic progression are in an arithmetic progression, as with $\dfrac{1}{a}$, $\dfrac{1}{b}$ and $\dfrac{1}{c}$. When three terms are in an arithmetic progression the middle term is their mean. Thus $\dfrac{1}{b}$ is the arithmetic mean between $\dfrac{1}{a}$ and $\dfrac{1}{c}$; b is the harmonic mean between a and c.

Expressing b in terms of a and c in equation (4):

$$\frac{2}{b} = \frac{1}{a} + \frac{1}{c}, \text{ and } b = \frac{2ac}{a + c} \quad (5)$$

Have students compare (1) with (5)!

In a similar manner you may wish to have the class consider the harmonic mean of three numbers, r, s and t:

$$\frac{3}{\dfrac{1}{r} + \dfrac{1}{s} + \dfrac{1}{t}} = \frac{3rst}{st + rt + rs}$$

Students may even wish to extend this to determine a "formula" for the harmonic mean of four numbers, k, m, n and p:

$$\frac{4}{\dfrac{1}{k} + \dfrac{1}{m} + \dfrac{1}{n} + \dfrac{1}{p}} = \frac{4kmnp}{mnp + knp + kmp + kmn}.$$

Have students consider the following problem: Lisa bought 2 dollars worth of each of three different kinds of pencils, priced at 2¢, 4¢ and 5¢ each respectively. What is the average price paid per pencil?

The answer to this question is $3\dfrac{3}{19}$, the harmonic mean of 2, 4 and 5. Stress the point that this was possible since each rate acted on the same base, 2 dollars. Similar problems (see the Posttest) may be posed and solved by the students at this time.

You may wish to consider a geometric illustration of the concept. Although the harmonic mean enjoys the most prominence geometrically in projective geometry, it might be more appropriate to give an illustration of the harmonic mean in synthetic geometry.

Have the students consider the length of the segment containing the point of intersection of the diagonals of a trapezoid and parallel to the bases, with its endpoints in the legs. (see $\overline{EGF}$ below.) The length of this segment, $\overline{EGF}$, is the harmonic mean between the lengths of the bases, $\overline{AD}$ and $\overline{BC}$. In the figure below, ABCD is a trapezoid, with $\overline{AD}$ // $\overline{BC}$ and diagonals intersecting at G. Also $\overline{EGF}$ // $\overline{BC}$, and $\overline{DEC}$ and $\overline{AFB}$.

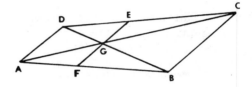

Since $\overline{GF}$ // $\overline{BC}$, $\triangle AFG \sim \triangle ABC$, and $\dfrac{AF}{FG} = \dfrac{AB}{BC}$. Similarly, since $\overline{GF}$ // $\overline{AD}$, $\triangle GBF \sim \triangle DBA$, and $\dfrac{BF}{FG} = \dfrac{AB}{AD}$. Therefore, $\dfrac{AF}{FG} + \dfrac{BF}{FG} = \dfrac{AB}{BC} + \dfrac{AB}{AD}$. Since AF + BF = AB, $\dfrac{AB}{FG} = \dfrac{AB}{BC} + \dfrac{AB}{AD}$, or FG $= \dfrac{(BC)\,(AD)}{BC + AD}$. In a similar manner it can be shown that EG $= \dfrac{(BC)\,(AD)}{BC + AD}$. Therefore, EF = FG + EG $= \dfrac{2(BC)\,(AD)}{BC + AD}$; hence, EF is the harmonic mean between BC and AD.

Postassessment

1) If a jet flies from New York to Rome at 600 mph and back along the same route at 500 mph, what is the average rate of speed for the entire trip?

2) Alice buys 2 dollars worth of each of three kinds of nuts, priced at 40¢, 50¢ and 60¢ per pound, respectively. What is the average price Alice paid per pound of nuts?

3) In June, Willie got 30 hits for a batting average of .300; however, in May he got 30 hits for a batting average of .400. What is Willie's batting average for May and June?

4) Find the harmonic mean of 2, 3, 5, 6, 2 and 9.

References:

Posamentier, Alfred S. *A Study Guide for the Mathematics Section of the Scholastic Aptitude Test,* Boston, Mass.: Allyn & Bacon, 1983.

Posamentier, Alfred S., and Charles T. Salkind. *Challenging Problems in Algebra, Volumes I and II.* New York: Macmillan Co., 1970.

Posamentier, Alfred S., and Charles T. Salkind.

Challenging Problems in Geometry, Volumes I and II. New York: Macmillan Co., 1970.

Posamentier, Alfred S., and Charles T. Salkind. *Uncommon Problems for Common Topics in Algebra.* Portland, Me.: J. Weston Walch, Publisher, 1981.

Posamentier, Alfred S., and Charles T. Salkind. *Unusual Topics for Usual Topics in Algebra.* Portland, Me.: J. Weston Walch, Publisher, 1981.

74   Howlers

In *Fallacies in Mathematics*, E.A. Maxwell refers to the following cancellations as *howlers:*

$$\frac{1\cancel{6}}{\cancel{6}4} = \frac{1}{4}$$

$$\frac{2\cancel{6}}{\cancel{6}5} = \frac{2}{5}$$

This unit will offer a method of presenting these howlers to elementary algebra students so students better understand number concepts.

Performance Objectives

1. *Students will develop a howler not already presented in class.*
2. *Students will explain why there are only four howlers composed of two-digit fractions.*

Preassessment

Students should be able to reduce fractions to lowest terms. They should also be familiar with such concepts as factor, prime number, and be able to perform all operations on fractions.

Teaching Strategies

Begin your presentation by asking students to reduce to lowest terms the following fractions: $\frac{16}{64}, \frac{19}{95}, \frac{26}{65}, \frac{49}{98}$. After they have reduced to lowest terms each of the fractions in the usual manner, tell them that they did a lot of unnecessary work. Show them the following cancellations:

$$\frac{1\cancel{6}}{\cancel{6}4} = \frac{1}{4}$$

$$\frac{1\cancel{9}}{\cancel{9}5} = \frac{1}{5}$$

$$\frac{2\cancel{6}}{\cancel{6}5} = \frac{2}{5}$$

$$\frac{4\cancel{9}}{\cancel{9}8} = \frac{4}{8} = \frac{1}{2}$$

At this point your students will be somewhat amazed. Their first reaction is to ask if this can be done to any

fraction composed of two-digit numbers. Challenge your students to find another fraction (comprised of two-digit numbers) where this type of cancellation will work. Students might cite $\frac{5\cancel{5}}{\cancel{5}5} = \frac{5}{5} = 1$ as an illustration of this type of cancellation. Indicate to them that although this will hold true for all multiples of eleven, it is trivial, and our concern will be only with proper fractions (i.e. whose value is less than one).

After they are thoroughly frustrated you may begin a discussion on why the four fractions above are the only ones (composed of two-digit numbers) where this type of cancellation will hold true.

Have students consider the fraction $\dfrac{10x + a}{10a + y}$.

The nature of the above four cancellations was such that when cancelling the a's the fraction was equal to $\dfrac{x}{y}$. Therefore $\dfrac{10x + a}{10a + y} = \dfrac{x}{y}$.

This yields: $y(10x + a) = x(10a + y)$

$$\text{or } 10xy + ay = 10ax + xy$$
$$9xy + ay = 10ax$$
$$\text{and } y = \frac{10ax}{9x + a}$$

At this point have students inspect this relationship. They should realize that it is necessary that x, y, and a be integers since they were digits in the numerator and denominator of a fraction. It is now their task to find the values of a and x for which y will also be integral.

To avoid a lot of algebraic manipulation you might have students set up a chart which will generate values of y from $y = \dfrac{10ax}{9x + a}$. Remind them that x, y and a must be *single digit* integers. Below is a portion of the table they will construct. Notice that the cases where $x = a$ are excluded since $\dfrac{x}{a} = 1$.

		x \ a	1	2	3	4	5	6	...	9
		1	////	$\frac{20}{11}$	$\frac{30}{12}$	$\frac{40}{13}$	$\frac{50}{14}$	$\frac{60}{15}=4$		
		2	$\frac{20}{19}$	////	$\frac{60}{21}$	$\frac{80}{22}$	$\frac{100}{23}$	$\frac{120}{24}=5$		
		3	$\frac{30}{28}$	$\frac{60}{29}$	////	$\frac{120}{31}$	$\frac{150}{32}$	$\frac{180}{33}$		
		:								
		.								
		9								

The portion of the chart pictured above already generated two of the four integral values of y; that is, when $x = 1$, $a = 6$, then $y = 4$, and when $x = 2$, $a = 6$ and $y = 5$. These values yield the fractions $\frac{16}{64}$, and $\frac{26}{65}$, respectively. The remaining two integral values of y will be obtained when $x = 1$, $a = 9$, then $y = 5$; and when $x = 4$, $a = 9$, then $y = 8$. These yield the fractions $\frac{19}{95}$ and $\frac{49}{98}$, respectively. This should convince students that there are only four such fractions composed of two-digit numbers.

Students may now wonder if there are fractions composed of numerators and denominators of more than two digits, where this strange type of cancellation holds true. Have students try this type of cancellation with $\frac{499}{998}$. They should find that, in fact,

$$\frac{499}{998} = \frac{4}{8} = \frac{1}{2}.$$

Soon they will realize that

$$\frac{49}{98} = \frac{499}{998} = \frac{4999}{9998} = \frac{49999}{99998} = \ldots$$

$$\frac{16}{64} = \frac{166}{664} = \frac{1666}{6664} = \frac{16666}{66664} = \frac{166666}{666664} = \ldots$$

$$\frac{19}{95} = \frac{199}{995} = \frac{1999}{9995} = \frac{19999}{99995} = \frac{199999}{999995} = \ldots$$

$$\frac{26}{65} = \frac{266}{665} = \frac{2666}{6665} = \frac{26666}{66665} = \frac{266666}{666665} = \ldots$$

Students with higher ability may wish to justify these extensions of the original howlers.

Students who at this point have a further desire to seek out additional fractions which permit this strange cancellation should be shown the following fractions. They should verify the legitimacy of this strange cancellation and then set out to discover more such fractions.

$$\frac{3\cancel{3}2}{8\cancel{3}0} = \frac{32}{80} = \frac{2}{5}$$

$$\frac{3\cancel{8}5}{8\cancel{8}0} = \frac{35}{80} = \frac{7}{16}$$

$$\frac{1\cancel{3}8}{\cancel{3}45} = \frac{18}{45} = \frac{2}{5}$$

$$\frac{27\cancel{5}}{7\cancel{7}0} = \frac{25}{70} = \frac{5}{14}$$

$$\frac{1\cancel{6}\cancel{3}}{\cancel{3}2\cancel{6}} = \frac{1}{2}$$

$$\frac{2\cancel{0}3}{6\cancel{0}9} = \frac{1}{3}$$

Postassessment

Have students:

a. Generate a "howler" not already presented in this discussion.

b. Explain why there are only four howlers, each composed of two-digit numbers.

75 Digit Problems Revisited

Problems involving the digits of a number as presented in the elementary algebra course are usually very straightforward and somewhat dull. Often they serve merely as a source of drill for a previously taught skill. This unit shows how digit problems (perhaps somewhat "off the beaten path" in nature) can be used to improve a student's concept of numbers.

Performance Objectives

1. *Students will solve problems involving the digits of a number.*

2. *Students will analyze a mathematical fact about the nature of certain numbers.*

Preassessment

Students should be able to solve simple linear equations as well as simple simultaneous equations.

Teaching Strategies

Begin your presentation by asking your students to select any three-digit number in which the hundreds digit and units digit are unequal. Then have them write the number whose digits are in the reverse order from the selected number. Now tell them to subtract these two numbers (the smaller number from the greater one). Once again tell them to take this difference, reverse its digits and add the "new" number to the *original difference*. They *all* should end up with 1,089.

For example, suppose a student selected the number 934. The number with the digits reversed is 439. The computation would appear as:

$$934$$
$$\underline{439}$$
$$\overline{495} \quad \text{(difference)}$$
$$\underline{594} \quad \text{(reversed digits)}$$
$$\overline{1089} \quad \text{(sum)}$$

When students compare results they will be amazed to discover uniformity in their answers. At this point they should be quite eager to find out why they all came up with the same result.

Begin by letting them represent the original number by $100h + 10t + u$, where h, t and u represent the hundreds, tens and units digits, respectively. Let $h > u$, which would have to be true in one of the original numbers. In subtracting, $u - h < 0$; therefore take 1 from the tens place to make the units place $10 + u$ (of the minuend).

Since the tens digits of the two numbers to be subtracted are equal, and 1 was taken from the tens digit of the minuend, then the value of this digit is $10(t - 1)$. The hundreds digit of the minuend is $h - 1$, since 1 was taken away to enable subtraction in the tens place, making the

value of the tens digit $10(t - 1) + 100 = 10(t + 9)$.
Pictorially this appears as:

$$100(h - 1) \quad + 10(t + 9) + (u + 10)$$
$$\underline{100u \quad\quad\quad + 10t \quad\quad\quad + h}$$
$$\overline{100(h - u - 1) \quad + 10(9) \quad\quad + u - h + 10}$$

reversing the digits of this difference yields

$$100(u - h + 10) + 10(9) + h - u - 1$$

Adding the last two lines yields:

$$100(9) + 10(18) + (10 - 1) = 1089$$

Another problem involving the digits of a number and presenting a somewhat unusual twist follows:

> Seven times a certain two-digit number equals a three-digit number. When the digit 6 is written after the last digit of the three-digit number, the three-digit number is increased by 1,833. Find the two-digit number.

The major obstacle students encounter in the solution of this problem is how to indicate placing a 6 after a number. Let students represent the two-digit number by a. Therefore the three-digit number is $7a$. Now to place a 6 after a number is to multiply the number by 10 and add the 6. The required equation is then $70a + 6 = 7a + 1833$, and $a = 29$.

To further exhibit the usefulness of working algebraically with a digital expression of a number, you may find it exciting to show students why a number is divisible by 9 (or 3) if the sum of its digits is divisible by 9 (or 3). Have them consider any five digit number, say, ab,cde, that is $10,000a + 1,000b + 100c + 10d + e$. Since this number may be rewritten as $(9,999 + 1)a + (999 + 1)b + (99 + 1)c + (9 + 1)d + e$, or $9,999a + 999b + 99c + 9d + a + b + c + d + e$, and the sum of the first four terms is divisible by 9 (or 3), the sum of the remaining terms must also be divisible by 9 (or 3). That is, in order for the number to be divisible by 9 (or 3), $a + b + c + d + e$ must be divisible by 9 (or 3).

Another digit problem with a rather nonroutine solution should now be presented. Students will find the following analysis a bit unusual.

> Find the two-digit number N such that when it is divided by 4 the remainder is zero, and such that all of its positive integral powers end in the same two digits as the original number, N.

Students will naturally want to begin solving this problem by letting $N = 10t + u$. Since $10t + u = 4m$ (i.e. a multiple of 4), u is even. Ask students which even digits have squares terminating with the same digit as the original digit. Once students establish that only 0 and 6 satisfy this property, therefore $u = 0$ or 6.

The case $u = 0$ implies that $t = 0$ so that N = 00, a trivial case, for if $t = 0$, N will terminate in 0 while its square will terminate in 00.

Now have students consider $u = 6$. Then N = $10t + 6 = 4m$, or $5t + 3 = 2m$. This indicates that $t = 1,3, 5,7$, or 9. But $N^2 = (10t + 6)^2 = 100t^2 + 120t + 36 = 100t^2 + 100d + 10e + 36$, where $120t = 100d + 10e$. Since the last two digits of N^2 are the same as those of N, $10e + 36 = 10t + 6$, and $t = e + 3$, so that $t \geq 3$. Also, $120t = 100d + 10(t-3)$, whereby $11t = 10d-3$, and $11t \leq 87$, or $t \leq 7$.

Have students try $t = 3$, $36^2 = 1296$ (reject) then try $t = 5$, $56^2 = 3136$ (reject). Finally try $t = 7$, then $76^2 = 5776$ (accept since N = 76).

There are many other problems involving the digits of numbers which you may wish to present to your class to advance the number theory introduction which this model provided.

Postassessment

1. Show, using a digital representation of a number, that a given number is divisible by 8, if the last three digits (considered as a new number) are divisible by 8.

2. There are two numbers formed of the same two digits—one in reverse of the other. The difference between the squares of the two numbers is 7,128 and the sum of the number is 22 times the difference between the two digits. What are the two numbers?

3. By shifting the initial digit 6 of the positive integer N to the end, we obtain a number equal to ¼N. Find the smallest possible value of N that satisfies the conditions.

76 Algebraic Identities

This unit will present a geometric process for carrying out algebraic identities. With only the representation of a number by a length, and lacking sufficient algebraic notation, early Greeks devised the method of application of areas to prove these identities.

Performance Objective
Students will geometrically establish algebraic identities using the method of application of areas.

Preassessment
1. Have students expand $(a+b)^2$.
2. Have students expand $a(b+c)$.
3. Have students expand $(a-b)^2$.
4. Elicit for what values of a and b each of the above generated equalities are true.

Teaching Strategies
After students have considered questions above, they should be reacquainted with the properties of an identity. Once students understand the concept of an identity, introduce the method of application of areas by illustrating geometrically the identity $(a+b)^2 = a^2 + 2ab + b^2$. To begin, have students draw a square of side length $(a+b)$. The square should then be partitioned into various squares and rectangles. (See Figure 1) The lengths of the various sides are appropriately labeled.

Figure 1

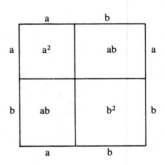

Students can easily determine the area of each region. Since the area of the large square equals the areas of the four quadrilaterals into which it was partitioned, students should get,
$(a+b)^2 = a^2 + ab + ab + b^2 = a^2 + 2ab + b^2$.
A more rigorous proof can be found in Euclid's *Elements*, Proposition 4, Book II.

Next illustrate geometrically the identity $a(b+c) = ab + ac$. To begin, have students draw a rectangle whose adjacent sides are of lengths a and $(b+c)$. The rectangle should then be partitioned into various rectangles. (See *Figure 2*) The lengths of these sides are also labeled.

Students can easily determine the area of each partition. Elicit from students that since the area of the large rectangle equals the areas of the two quadrilaterals into which it was partitioned, the diagram illustrates $a(b+c) = ab + ac$.

Figure 2

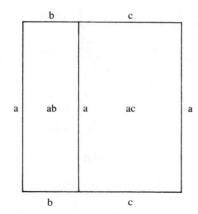

Have students consider the following identity $(a+b) \times (c+d) = ac + ad + bc + bd$. Guide students to draw the appropriate rectangle with side lengths $(a+b)$ and $(c+d)$. The rectangle should be partitioned into various rectangles. (See Figure 3) The lengths of sides and areas of regions have been labeled. As in the other cases, the area of the large rectangle equals the areas of the four quadrilaterals into which it was partitioned.

The diagram (Fig. 3) illustrates the identity $(a+b) \times (c+d) = ac+ad+bc+bd$. Explain to students that the method of application of areas can be used to prove most algebraic identities. The difficulty will lie in their choice of dimensions for the quadrilateral and the partitions made.

Figure 3

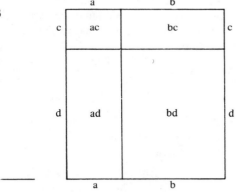

After students feel comfortable using areas to represent algebraic identities, have them consider the Pythagorean relationship, $a^2 + b^2 = c^2$. Although this is not an identity, the application of areas is still appropriate. Have students draw a square of side length $(a+b)$. Show students how to partition this square into four congruent triangles and a square. (See *Figure 4)* The lengths of the sides have been labeled.

Figure 4

The diagram (Fig. 4) illustrates:
1. Area DEFG = 4 × (Area of ΔGNM) + Area KLMN.

2. Therefore, $(a+b)^2 = 4(\frac{1}{2}ab) + c^2$

3. If we now substitute the identity for $(a+b)^2$, which was proven before, we obtain, $a^2 + 2ab + b^2 = 2ab + c^2$.

Elicit from students the remainder of the proof to conclude that $a^2 + b^2 = c^2$. Students should now be able to pose and solve geometrically their own identities.

Postassessment
1. Have students indicate how to establish the following algebraic identities geometrically.
   a). $(a-b)^2 = a^2 - 2ab + b^2$
   b). $a^2-b^2 = (a+b) \times (a-b)$
2. Have students determine other identities that can be proved using the method of application of areas.

77 A Method For Factoring Trinomials of the Form $ax^2 + bx + c$

This unit presents a rather unusual method for factoring, when possible, trinomials of the form $ax^2 + bx + c$, where a, b, and c are integers. This technique is especially helpful when the coefficient a of $ax^2 + bx + c$ is different from 1, because in this case the usual method based on trial and error is rather tedious for most of the trinomials.

Performance Objectives

1. Given various trinomials of the form $ax^2 + bx + c$, *students will analyze and factor them.*

2. Students will be able to apply this technique to the solution of quadratic equations.

Preassessment

Students should be familiar with multiplications and factorizations of binomials and with factorizations of perfect square trinomials.

Teaching Strategies

Begin this lesson by giving several examples of multiplications of binomials: $(x + 5)(x + 2)$, $(2x - 3)(x + 1)$, $(5x - 2)(3x - 7)$, etc. Have students notice the following properties of these multiplications:

(a) They always yield trinomials of the form $ax^2 + bx + c$, where a, b, and c are integers.

(b) The product of the first terms of the binomials is the first term of the trinomial.

(c) It is impossible for a to obtain the value of zero from the product of any two binomials. Thus a is always different from zero in the trinomial of the form $ax^2 + bx + c$.

Once students have practiced these multiplications, have them consider the inverse operation. That is, given trinomials of the form $ax^2 + bx + c$, have students factor them as the product of two binomials. Ask for suggestions on how to factor different trinomials; for example: $x^2 + 5x + 6$, $2x^2 - 7x - 4$, and so on. Then have students consider the factorization of the general trinomial $ax^2 + bx + c$ in the following fashion:

$$ax^2 + bx + c = \frac{a(ax^2 + bx + c)}{a} = \frac{a^2x^2 + abx + ac}{a},$$

this being possible because a is always different from zero.

If $a^2x^2 + abx + ac$ can be factored, one factorization could be: $(ax + y)(ax + z)$ where y and z are to be determined. Thus, we have:

$$ax^2 + bx + c = \frac{a^2x^2 + abx + ac}{a} = \frac{(ax + y)(ax + z)}{a}$$
$$= \frac{a^2x^2 + a(y + z)x + yz}{a}$$

If the second and fourth equalities are now compared, we notice that: $y + z = b$ and $yz = ac$. Thus, to factor a trinomial of the form $ax^2 + bx + c$, it is only necessary to express it as the product $\frac{(ax + y)(ax + z)}{a}$ where y and z can be determined by noticing that their sum must be b and their product must be ac. Also have students notice that because $\frac{(ax + y)(ax + z)}{a} = \frac{a^2x^2 + abx + ac}{a}$, it follows that the numerator is a multiple of a, and therefore, it will always be possible to cancel the constant a.

EXAMPLE 1.

Factor $5x^2 + 8x + 3$

We have $5x^2 + 8x + 3 = \frac{(5x + y)(5x + z)}{5}$ where $y + z = 8$ and $yz = (5)(3) = 15$. An analysis of the constant term 15 reveals that the possible pairs of numbers y and z whose product is 15 are: 15 and 1, -15 and -1, 5 and 3, and -5 and -3; but because their sum must be 8, the only possible combination of y and z is 5 and 3. Therefore,

$$5x^2 + 8x + 3 = \frac{(5x + 5)(5x + 3)}{5} = \frac{\cancel{5}(x + 1)(5x + 3)}{\cancel{5}}$$
$$= (x + 1)(5x + 3)$$

EXAMPLE 2.

Factor $6x^2 + 5x - 6$

We have: $(6x^2 + 5x - 6) = \frac{(6x + y)(6x + z)}{6}$, where $y + z = 5$ and $yz = (6)(-6) = -36$. An analysis of the product yz, that is, of -36 reveals that the possible pairs of numbers whose product is -36 are: 36 and -1, -36 and 1, 18 and -2, -18 and 2, 12 and -3, -12 and 3, 9 and -4, -9 and 4, and 6 and -6. But, because the algebraic sum of y and z must be $+5$, we have that the only possible combination is 9 and -4. Therefore,

$$6x^2 + 5x - 6 = \frac{(6x + 9)(6x - 4)}{6} = \frac{3(2x + 3)\,2(3x - 2)}{6}$$
$$= (2x + 3)(3x - 2)$$

If $a = 1$, we have the simpler form $x^2 + bx + c$. Thus,

$$x^2 + bx + c = \frac{(1x + y)(1x + z)}{1} = (x + y)(x + z)$$

where $y + z = b$ and $yz = c$.

EXAMPLE 3.
Factor $x^2 - 4x - 5$

We have: $x^2 - 4x - 5 = (x + y)(x + z)$ where $y + z$ is -4 and yz is -5. Thus, the possible pairs of numbers are: 5 and -1, and -5 and 1, but because the algebraic sum is -4 the only possible combination is -5 and $+1$. Therefore, $x^2 - 4x - 5 = (x - 5)(x + 1)$. This technique is also applicable to the solution of quadratic equations, that is, equations of the form $ax^2 + bx + c = 0$.

EXAMPLE 4.
Solve $2x^2 - 7x - 4 = 0$

We first factor $2x^2 - 7x - 4$. Thus, $2x^2 - 7x - 4 = \dfrac{(2x + y)(2x + z)}{2}$ where $y + z$ is -7 and yz is -8.

Because the product is -8, we find that the possible pairs are: 8 and -1, -8 and 1, 4 and -2, and -4 and 2. But because the algebraic sum is -7, the only pos-

sible combination is -8 and 1. Thus, $2x^2 - 7x - 4 = \dfrac{(2x - 8)(2x + 1)}{2} = (x - 4)(2x + 1)$. Therefore we have: $2x^2 - 7x - 4 = (x - 4)(2x + 1) = 0$ and the roots of this quadratic equation will be 4 and $-\frac{1}{2}$. It is important for students to understand that there is no guarantee that "any" given trinomials can be factored; $x^2 - 5x - 7$ and $x^3 - 5x - 6$ *cannot* be factored.

Postassessment
Students who have met the *Performance Objectives* should be able to do the following exercises:
1. Factor the following trinomials
   (a) $x^2 - 8x + 12$ (b) $4x^2 + 4x - 3$
   (c) $x^2 + 10x + 25$ (d) $3x^2 - 5x$
   (e) $2r^2 + 13r - 7$ (f) $9m^2 - 1$
2. Solve the following quadratic equations:
   (a) $x^2 - 3x - 4 = 0$
   (b) $6x^2 + x = 2$

78   Solving Quadratic Equations

This unit presents four new methods for solving quadratic equations.

Performance Objective
Students will solve a given quadratic equation in at least four different ways.

Preassessment
Students should be able to solve the equation:
$$x^2 - 7x + 12 = 0$$

Teaching Strategies
In all likelihood most of your students solved the above equation by the *Factoring* method. That is, to solve they performed the following operations:
$$x^2 - 7x + 12 = 0$$
$$(x - 3)(x - 4) = 0$$

$x - 3 = 0$ | $x - 4 = 0$
$x = 3$ | $x = 4$

This method cannot be used to solve all types of quadratic equations. If the trinomial $ax^2 + bx + c$ from the equation $ax^2 + bx + c = 0$ is not factorable, then this method cannot be used to solve the equation.

The rest of this lesson develops four new methods for solving quadratic equations.

Completing the Square

Consider the equation $ax^2 + bx + c = 0$, where a, b and c are integers and $a \neq 0$.
$$ax^2 + bx + c = x^2 + \frac{b}{a}x + \frac{c}{a} = 0$$

Add the square of one-half the coefficient of x to both sides:
$$x^2 + \frac{b}{a}x + \left(\frac{b}{2a}\right)^2 = -\frac{c}{a} + \left(\frac{b}{2a}\right)^2$$
$$\left(x + \frac{b}{2a}\right)^2 = -\frac{c}{a} + \frac{b^2}{4a^2}$$

Take the square root of both sides:
$$x + \frac{b}{2a} = \pm\sqrt{\frac{b^2 - 4ac}{4a^2}}$$
$$x = \frac{-b \pm \sqrt{b^2 - 4ac}}{2a}$$

This is the quadratic formula:

Example: Solve $x^2 - 7x + 12 = 0$
$$x^2 - 7x + \left(\frac{-7}{2}\right)^2 = -12 + \left(\frac{-7}{2}\right)^2$$
$$\left(x - \frac{7}{2}\right)^2 = -12 + \frac{49}{4} = \frac{-48 + 49}{4} = \frac{1}{4}$$
$$x - \frac{7}{2} = \pm\sqrt{\frac{1}{4}} = \pm\frac{1}{2}$$
$$x = \frac{7}{2} \pm \frac{1}{2} \qquad x = 3, 4$$

Splitting the Difference

Let x_1 and x_2 be the roots of the given equation $ax^2 + bx + c = 0$. Then $x^2 + \frac{b}{a}x + \frac{c}{a} = 0$ or
$$(x - x_1)(x - x_2) = 0$$

We know that the sum of the roots $x_1 + x_2 = \dfrac{-b}{a}$ and

that the product of the roots $x_1 x_2 = \dfrac{c}{a}$

Let $x_1 = \dfrac{-b}{2a} + N$, where N is some rational number

and $x_2 = \dfrac{-b}{2a} - N$

Then the product of the roots, $\dfrac{c}{a} = x_1 x_2 =$

$(-\dfrac{b}{2a} + N)(-\dfrac{b}{2a} - N)$

In solving for N, we get:

$$N = \pm \frac{\sqrt{b^2 - 4ac}}{2a}$$

Therefore the roots are $x = \dfrac{-b}{2a} \pm \dfrac{\sqrt{b^2 - 4ac}}{2a}$

Example: Solve $x^2 - 7x + 12 = 0$

Students will establish that the sum of the roots $x_1 + x_2$

$= 7$. Therefore one root must be $\dfrac{7}{2} + N$ and the other

must be $\dfrac{7}{2} - N$, where N is some rational number.

Since the produce of the roots is 12, $x_1 x_2 =$

$(\dfrac{7}{2} + N)(\dfrac{7}{2} - N) = \dfrac{49}{4} - N^2 = 12.$

Therefore $N^2 = \dfrac{1}{4}$. and $N = \pm \dfrac{1}{2}$

Thus the roots are: $x_1 = \dfrac{7}{2} + N = \dfrac{7}{2} + \dfrac{1}{2} = 4$

$x_2 = \dfrac{7}{2} - N = \dfrac{7}{2} - \dfrac{1}{2} = 3$

Method of Simultaneous Equations:

Rather than developing the general case first, we shall first solve the given equation $x^2 - 7x + 12 = 0$. This order should be easier to follow for this method.

Example: Solve $x^2 - 7x + 12 = 0$
Consider the sum and product of the roots: $x_1 + x_2 = 7$
and $x_1 x_2 = 12$
Square the sum: $(x_1 + x_2)^2 = 49$
Multiply the product by -4: $-4x_1 x_2 = -48$
By addition $(x_1 + x_2)^2 - 4x_1 x_2 = 49 - 48 = 1$
However, the left side simplifies to $(x_1 - x_2)^2$
Therefore $x_1 - x_2 = \pm \sqrt{1} = \pm 1$
Remember that $x_1 + x_2 = 7$
Now solving these equations simultaneously:
$$2x_1 = 8 \quad x_1 = 4 \quad x_2 = 3$$
The general case for $ax^2 + bx + c = 0$ follows:
The square of the sum of the roots,

$$(x_1 + x_2)^2 = x_1^2 + 2x_1 x_2 + x_2^2 = \frac{b^2}{a^2}$$

The product of the roots and -4 is:

$$-4x_1 x_2 = \frac{-4c}{a}$$

As above, we add these last two equations:

$$x_1^2 - 2x_1 x_2 + x_2^2 = \frac{b^2}{a^2} - \frac{4c}{a}$$

$$(x_1 - x_2)^2 = \frac{b^2 - 4ac}{a^2}$$

Therefore:

$$x_1 - x_2 = \pm \frac{\sqrt{b^2 - 4ac}}{a}$$

Since $x_1 + x_2 = \dfrac{-b}{a}$

$$x_1 \text{ or } x_2 = \frac{1}{2}\left(\frac{-b}{a} \pm \frac{\sqrt{b^2 - 4ac}}{a} \right)$$

$$= \frac{-b \pm \sqrt{b^2 - 4ac}}{2a}$$

Method of Root Reduction:

Again we start the discussion with the solution for a specific equation before considering the general form.

Example: Solve $x^2 - 7x + 12 = 0$
Let $r = x - n$, then $x = r + n$, and $x^2 = (r + n)^2 = r^2 + 2rn + n^2$

We now substitute the appropriate values in the original equation.

$$(r^2 + 2rn + n^2) - 7(r + n) + 12 = 0$$
$$r^2 + r(2n - 7) + (n^2 - 7n + 12) = 0$$

If $2n - 7 = 0$ then the r term is annihilated.

This will happen when $n = \dfrac{7}{2}$.

We then have $r^2 + (n^2 - 7n + 12) = 0$ or by substituting

$n = \dfrac{7}{2}$: $\quad r^2 + \left(\dfrac{49}{4} - 7(\dfrac{7}{2}) + 12 \right) = 0$

$r^2 = \dfrac{49}{4} - 12 = \dfrac{1}{4}$; and $r = \pm \dfrac{1}{2}$

Thus the roots $(x = r + n)$ are:

$$x_1 = +\frac{1}{2} + \frac{7}{2} = 4 \qquad x_2 = -\frac{1}{2} + \frac{7}{2} = 3$$

The general case proceeds in a similar manner. Consider the equation $ax^2 + bx + c = 0$. Let $r = x - n$, then $x = r + n$ and
$$x^2 = (r + n)^2 = r^2 + 2rn + n^2$$
Now substitute these values into the original equation:

$$x^2 + \frac{bx}{a} + \frac{c}{a} = 0$$

$$(r^2 + 2rn + n^2) + \frac{b}{a}(r + n) + \frac{c}{a} = 0$$

or $\quad r^2 + r(2n + \dfrac{b}{a}) + (n^2 + \dfrac{bn}{a} + \dfrac{c}{a}) = 0$

In order to annihilate the r term we let

$$2n + \frac{b}{a} = 0, \text{ or } n = \frac{-b}{2a}$$

This then gives us:

$$r^2 + (n^2 + \frac{b}{a}n + \frac{c}{a}) = 0$$

or $\quad r^2 = -(n^2 + \dfrac{b}{a}n + \dfrac{c}{a})$

However, since $n = \dfrac{-b}{2a}$

$$r^2 = -\left(\dfrac{b^2}{4a^2} - \dfrac{b^2}{2a^2} + \dfrac{c}{a}\right)$$

$r^2 = \dfrac{b^2 - 4ac}{4a^2}$ $\quad$ and $\quad$ $r = \pm\dfrac{\sqrt{b^2 - 4ac}}{2a}$

Therefore, since $x = r + n$, $x = \dfrac{-b}{2a} \pm \dfrac{\sqrt{b^2 - 4ac}}{2a}$

or $\qquad x = \dfrac{-b \pm\sqrt{b^2 - 4ac}}{2a}$

Although some of these methods for solving quadratic equations are not too practical, they do offer students a better understanding of many of the underlying concepts.

Postassessment

Ask students to use at least four of the methods presented in this lesson to solve the following equations.

1. $x^2 - 11x + 30 = 0$
2. $x^2 + 3x - 28 = 0$
3. $6x^2 - x - 2 = 0$

79   The Euclidean Algorithm

This unit presents a method of introducing students to the Euclidean Algorithm for finding the greatest common divisor of two given integers.

Performance Objectives

1. Given any two integers, students will determine the greatest common divisor of the two integers, regardless of the magnitude of the two integers.

2. Having determined the greatest common divisor, the students will then be able to express the greatest common divisor in terms of the two integers.

Preassessment

Ask students how they would weigh 12 ounces, 2 ounces, 3 ounces, 4 ounces, 1 ounce and 11 ounces using only a set of two pan balance scales and some 5 and 7 ounce weights.

Teaching Strategies

Students should be able to suggest weighing the weights in the following manner:

  a. 12 ounces: Place one 5 oz. and one 7 oz. weight on the same pan, and the 12 ounces can be weighed on the other pan.

  b. 2 ounces: Place one 7 oz. weight on one pan and a 5 oz. weight on the other pan. Then the desired 2 oz. weight is that which must be placed on the pan containing the 5 oz. weight in order to balance the scales.

  c. 3 ounces: Place two 5 oz. weights on one pan and a 7 oz. weight on the other pan. The desired 3 oz. weight is that which must be added to the 7 oz. weight in order to balance the scales.

  d. 4 ounces: Place two 5 oz. weights on one pan and two 7 oz. weights on the other. The desired weight is that which must be added to the two 5 oz. weights in order to balance the scales.

  e. 1 ounce: Place three 5 oz. weights on one pan and two 7 oz. weights on the other. The desired weight is that which must be added to the two 7 oz. weights in order to balance the scales.

  f. 11 ounces: Place five 5 oz. weights on one pan and two 7 oz. weights on the other pan. The desired weight is that which must be added to the two 7 oz. weights in order to balance the scales.

Students should then be asked to weigh one ounce, two ounces, three ounces and four ounces using other combinations of given weights. They should soon be able to discover that the smallest weight which can be weighed using any combination of given weights is equal to the *greatest common divisor* of the two weights:

Given Weights	G.C.D.	Minimum Weighable
2 and 3	1	1
2 and 4	2	2
3 and 9	3	3
8 and 20	4	4
15 and 25	5	5

The greatest common divisor of A and B will be referred to as either G.C.D. of A and B or (A,B).

In order to find (945, 219) we can use the *Euclidean Algorithm*. The Euclidean Algorithm is based on a lemma which states: A and B are integers where A does not equal zero. If B is divided by A a quotient Q and remainder R is obtained (B = QA+R), then (B,A) = (A,R). Using the following procedure the G.C.D. of 945 and 219 can be found:

Divide 945 by 219: $945 = (4)(219)+69$ (1)

Divide 219 by 69: $219 = (3)(69)+12$ now   (2)

continue this process

$69 = (5)(12)+9$ (3)

$12 = (1)(9)+3$ (4)

$9 = (3)(3)+0$ ... until R equals 0.

Therefore, the G.C.D. of 945 and 219 is 3, which was the last non-zero remainder in the successive divisions. This method may be used to find (A,B) where A and B are any two integers. Have students practice this algorithm with some exercises before continuing the lesson.

For stronger students in the class (or just for your interest) a proof of this algorithm is provided. The following is a statement and proof of the *Euclidean Algorithm:*

For given non-zero integers a and b, divide a by b to get remainder r_1; divide b by r_1 to get remainder r_2. This is continued so that when remainder r_k is divided by r_{k+1} the remainder r_{k+2} is obtained. Eventually there will be an r_n such that $r_{n+1} = 0$. It follows that $|r_n|$ is the greatest common divisor of a and b.

Proof: The division algorithm will determine integers $q_1, r_1, q_2, r_2, q_3, r_3, \ldots$ where

$$a = q_1b+r_1$$
$$b = q_2r_1+r_2$$
$$r_1 = q_3r_2+r_3$$
$$\cdot$$
$$\cdot$$
$$\cdot$$

and where $0\leq \ldots <r_3<r_2<r_1<|b|$. There are only $|b|$ non-negative integers less than $|b|$. Therefore there must be an $r_{n+1} = 0$ for $n+1\leq|b|$. If $r_1 = 0$ then $(a, b) = b$. If $r_1 \neq 0$ then:

$$a = q_1b+r_1$$
$$b = q_2r_1+r_2$$
$$r_1 = q_3r_2+r_3$$
$$\cdot$$
$$\cdot$$
$$\cdot$$

$$r_{n-2} = q_nr_{n-1}+r_n$$
$$r_{n-1} = q_{n+1}r_n$$

Let $d = (a,b)$. Since $d|a$, and $d|b$, then $d|r_1$. Similarly, since $d|b$ and $d|r_1$, then $d|r_2$. Again, since $d|r_1$ and $d|r_2$, then $d|r_3$. Continuing this reasoning eventually yields $d|r_{n-2}$, and $d|r_{n-1}$, then $d|r_n$.

Since $r_n\neq0$, $r_n \mid r_{n-1}$. Also $r_n \mid r_n$; therefore $r_n|r_{n-2}$. Similarly, $r_n|r_{n-3}$, $r_n|r_{n-4}$, $\ldots r_n|r_2$, $r_n|r_1$, $r_n|b$, and $r_n \mid a$. Since $r_n|a$ and $r_n|b$, therefore $r_n|d$. Thus, $r_n \mid d$ and $d|r_n$, it follows that $r_n = d$, or $r_n = (a,b)$.

At this juncture it would be nice to be able to express the G.C.D. of two integers in terms of the two integers, that is, $MA+NB = (A,B)$, where M and N are integers. In the earlier case of (945, 219), $3 = M(219) + N(945)$. By working backwards, ("up" the Euclidean Algorithm), we can accomplish the following:

From line (4) above: $3 = 12-9$

Substituting for 9 from line (3) above:

$3 = 12 - (69 - 5\cdot12)$, $3 = 6\cdot12 - 69$

Substituting for 12 from line (2):

$3 = 6(219 - 3\cdot69) - 69$

Substituting for 69 from line (1):

$3 = 6\cdot219 - 19(945 - 4\cdot219)$, or

$3 = 82(219) - 19(945)$.

Earlier students have determined the minimum which can be weighed by a 945 oz. and a 219 oz. weight by finding (945, 219). Now they can also determine how many 945 oz. weights to place on one pan and how many 219 oz. to place on the other pan, by expressing (945, 219) in terms of 945 and 219. That is, they must place 82 219 oz. weights on one pan and 19 945 oz. weights on the other pan. The desired weight is that which must be added to the 19 945 oz. weights in order to balance the weights. This scheme may be used to develop an understanding of Diophantine Equations.

Postassessment

Students should be able to compute the G.C.D. of the following pairs of integers and express the G.C.D. in terms of the two integers:

1) 12 and 18   2) 52 and 86

3) 865 and 312   4) 120 and 380

80   Prime Numbers

This unit will introduce students to fascinating facts concerning prime numbers.

Performance Objectives

1. Given a number, students will use Euler's ϕ function to find the number of positive integers less than the given number that are relatively prime to it.

2. Students will explain why it is not possible for a polynomial with integral coefficients to exist that will generate only primes.

Preassessment

Ask students to identify which of the following are prime numbers:

    a) 11   b) 27   c) 51

    d) 47   e) 91   f) 1

Teaching Strategies

Mathematicians have spent years trying to find a general formula that would generate primes. There have been many attempts, but none have succeeded.

Have students test the expression $n^2 - n + 41$ by substituting various positive values for n. Make a chart on the chalkboard recording their findings. As they proceed they should begin to notice that as n ranges in value from 1 through 40, only prime numbers are being produced. (If they have not substituted $n = 40$, have them do so.) Then ask them to try $n = 41$. The value of $n^2 - n + 41$ is $(41)^2 - 41 + 41 = (41)^2$ which is not prime. A similar expression, $n^2 - 79n + 1601$, produces primes for all values of n up to 80. But for $n = 81$, we have $(81)^2 - 79 \cdot 81 + 1601 = 1763 = 41 \cdot 43$ which is not a prime. Students might now wonder if it is possible to have a polynomial in n with integral coefficients whose values would be primes for every positive integer n. Advise them not to try to find such an expression; Leonhard Euler (1707-1783) proved that none can exist. Euler showed that any proposed expression will produce at least one non-prime.

Euler's proof follows. First, assume that such an expression exists, being in the general form: $a + bx + cx^2 + dx^3 + \ldots$ (understanding that some of the coefficients may be zero.) Let the value of this expression be s when $x = m$. Therefore: $s = a + bm + cm^2 + dm^3 + \ldots$. Similarly, let t be the value of the expression when $x = m + ns$: $t = a + b(m+ns) + c(m+ns)^2 + d(m+ns)^3 \ldots$ This may be transformed to:

$$t = (a + bm + cm^2 + dm^3 + \ldots) + A$$

where A represents the remaining terms all of which are multiples of s. But the expression within the parentheses is, by hypothesis, equal to s. This makes the whole expression a multiple of s, and the number produced is not a prime. Every such expression will produce at least one prime, but not necessarily more than one. Consequently, no expression can generate primes exclusively.

Although this last statement was recognized early in mathematical history, mathematicians continued to conjecture about forms of numbers that generated only primes.

Pierre de Fermat (1601-1665), who made many significant contributions to the study of number theory, conjectured that all numbers of the form $F_n = 2^{2^n} + 1$, where $n = 0, 1, 2, 3, 4, \ldots$ were prime numbers. Have students find F_n for $n = 0, 1, 2$. They will see that the first three numbers derived from this expression are 3, 5, and 17. For $n = 3$, students will find that $F_n = 257$; by telling them $F_4 = 65,537$, they should notice these numbers are increasing at a very rapid rate. For $n = 5$, $F_n = 4,294,967,297$, and Fermat could not find any factor of this number. Encouraged by his results, he expressed the opinion that all numbers of this form are probably also prime. Unfortunately he stopped too soon, for in 1732, Euler showed that $F_5 = 4,294,967,297 = 641 \times 6,700,417$ (not a prime!). It was not until 150 years later that the factors of F_6 were found: 18,446,744,073,709,551,617 = 247,177 $\times$ 67,280,421,310,721. As far as is now known, many more numbers of this form have been found but *none* of them have been prime. It seems that Fermat's conjecture has been completely turned around, and one now wonders if any primes beyond F_4 exist.

Euler also continued further into his study of primes. He began examining those integers that are *relatively prime* (two integers are relatively prime if they have no common positive factor except 1). Have students write down the number 12 and the positive integers less than 12. Tell them to cross out 12 itself and then all the integers that have a factor greater than 1 in common with 12.

$$1 \; \not2 \; \not3 \; \not4 \; 5 \; \not6 \; 7 \; \not8 \; \not9 \; \not{10} \; 11 \; \not{12}$$

They will see that 1, 5, 7, 11 are the only integers remaining. Therefore, there are four positive integers less than 12 which are relatively prime to it. The number of such integers is denoted by $\phi(n)$ and is known as Euler's ϕ function. For $n = 1$, obviously $\phi(n) = 1$. For $n > 1$, $\phi(n) =$ the number of positive integers less than n and relatively prime to it. Thus, as we just saw, $\phi(12) = 4$.

Let students now find values of $\phi(n)$ for $n = 1, 2, 3, 4, 5$. A chart, such as Figure 1 below is convenient for this.

n	integers relatively prime to and less than n	$\phi(n)$
1		1
2	1 2	1
3	1 2 3	2
4	1 2 3 4	2
5	1 2 3 4 5	4
6	1 2 3 4 5 6	2
7	prime	6
8	1 2 3 4 5 6 7 8	4
9	1 2 3 4 5 6 7 8 9	6
10	1 2 3 4 5 6 7 8 9 10	4
11	prime	10
12	1 2 3 4 5 6 7 8 9 10 11 12	4

Students should notice that when n is prime, it is not necessary to list all the numbers. Since a prime is relatively prime to all positive integers less than it, we therefore have $\phi(n) = n - 1$, for n a prime.

Have students continue to find $\phi(n)$ for $n = 6$ through 12. Looking down the $\phi(n)$ column, it does not seem that any particular pattern is emerging. We would like to, though, obtain an expression for the general term, so that $\phi(n)$ can be calculated for any number. We have already stated that if n is prime, then $\phi(n) = n - 1$. In order to discover an expression for $\phi(n)$ if n is not prime, we will look at a particular case. Let $n = 15$. Decomposing 15 into primes, we obtain $15 = 3 \cdot 5$. We can write this as $n = p \cdot q$, where $n = 15$, $p = 3$, and $q = 5$. Next, have students write down 15 and all positive integers less than 15. Have them cross out all integers having 3 (which is p) as a factor:

1 2 3̸ 4 5 6̸ 7 8 9̸ 10 11 12̸ 13 14 15̸

They will see that there are 5 or $5 = \frac{15}{3} = \frac{n}{p}$ of these. There are 10 numbers remaining or $10 = 15$

$- \frac{15}{3} = n - \frac{n}{p} = n\left(1 - \frac{1}{p}\right).$

From these 10 integers, have students cross out those having 5 (which is q) as a factor:

1 2 4 5̸ 7 8 10̸ 11 13 14

There are only 2 of these or $2 = \frac{1}{5}(10) = \frac{1}{q}[n$ $(1 - \frac{1}{p})]$. There are now 8 numbers left: $8 = 10$

$- \frac{1}{5}(10) = n(1 - \frac{1}{p}) - \frac{1}{q}[n(1 - \frac{1}{p})]$. $n(1 - \frac{1}{p})$ is a factor of both terms of the expression. We have therefore established a formula for the number of positive integers less than n and relatively prime to it:

$$\phi(n) = n(1 - \frac{1}{p})(1 - \frac{1}{q})$$

The number n, though, might have more than 2 factors in its prime decomposition, so let us now state a more general formula (given without proof). Let the number n be decomposed into its prime factors $p, q, r, \ldots, w$. Then $n = p^a \cdot q^b \cdot r^c \cdot \ldots w^h$, where $a, b, c, \ldots, h$ are positive integers (which may or may not be all 1's). Then $\phi(n) = n(1 - \frac{1}{p})$ $(1 - \frac{1}{q})(1 - \frac{1}{r}) \ldots (1 - \frac{1}{w})$. The teacher should also show the students that if n is a prime, the formula still holds since $\phi(n) = n - 1 = n(\frac{n-1}{n}) = n(1 - \frac{1}{n})$. To see how the formula works, work together with students in finding the following: $\phi(21), \phi(43), \phi(78)$.

Solutions: $\phi(21) = \phi(7 \cdot 3) = 21(1 - \frac{1}{7})(1 - \frac{1}{3}) = 21$

$(\frac{6}{7})(\frac{2}{3}) = 12$

$\phi(43) = 43 - 1$ (since 43 is a prime) $= 42$

$\phi(78) = \phi(2 \cdot 3 \cdot 13) = 78(1 - \frac{1}{2})(1 - \frac{1}{3})$

$(1 - \frac{1}{13}) = 78(\frac{1}{2})(\frac{2}{3})(\frac{12}{13}) = 24$

At this point, some students might have noticed that every value of $\phi(n)$ is even. Justification of this may serve as a springboard for further investigation.

Postassessment

1. Find each of the following:
a. $\phi(13)$ b. $\phi(14)$ c. $\phi(48)$ d. $\phi(73)$ e. $\phi(100)$
2. Have students explain why there is no polynomial with integral coefficients that will generate only primes.

81   Algebraic Fallacies

All too often students make errors in their mathematics work which are more subtle than an errors in computation or some other careless act. To prevent errors which are the results of violations of mathematical definitions of concepts, it would be wise to exhibit such flaws beforehand. This is the main mission of this unit.

Performance Objective
Given an algebraic fallacy, students will analyze and determine where the fallacy occurs in the algebraic "proof"

Preassessment
Students should be familiar with the basic algebraic operations normally taught in the high school elementary algebra course.

Teaching Strategy
When the theory behind mathematical operations is poorly understood, there exists the possibility that the operations will be applied in a formal and perhaps illogical way. Students, not aware of certain limitations on these operations, are likely to use them where they do not necessarily apply. Such improper reasoning leads to an absurd result called a fallacy. The following paradoxes will illustrate how such fallacies can arise in algebra when certain algebraic operations are performed without realizing the limitations upon those operations.

Almost everyone who has been exposed to elementary algebra will come across, at one time or another, a proof that $2 = 1$ or $1 = 3$, etc. Such a "proof" is an example of a fallacy.

"Proof":
1) Let $a = b$
2) Multiply both sides by a: $a^2 = ab$
3) Subtract b^2 from both sides: $a^2 - b^2 = ab - b^2$
4) Factoring: $(a + b)(a - b) = b(a - b)$
5) Dividing both sides by $(a - b)$: $(a + b) = b$
6) Since $a = b$, then $2b = b$
7) Dividing both sides by b: $2 = 1$

Ask the students to analyze the "proof" and find out where the reasoning breaks down. Of course, the trouble is in the fifth step. Since $a = b$, then $a - b = 0$. Therefore, division by zero was performed, which is *not permissible*. It would be appropriate at this time to discuss what division means in terms of multiplication. To divide a by b implies that there exists a number y such that $b \cdot y = a$, or $y = \dfrac{a}{b}$. If $b = 0$, there are two

possibilities, either $a \neq 0$ or $a = 0$. If $a \neq 0$, then $y = \dfrac{a}{0}$ or $0 \cdot y = a$. Ask your students if they can find a number which when multiplied by zero will equal a. Your students should conclude that there is no such number y. In the second case, where $a = 0$, $y = \dfrac{0}{0}$ or $0 \cdot y = 0$. Here any number for y will satisfy the equation, hence any number multiplied by zero is zero. Therefore we have the "rule" that division by zero is not permissible. There are other fallacies based on division by zero. Have your students discover for themselves where and how the difficulty occurs in each of the following examples.

1) To "prove" that any two unequal numbers are equal. Assume that $x = y + z$, and x,y,z are positive numbers. This implies $x > y$. Multiply both sides by $x - y$. Then $x^2 - xy = xy + xz - y^2 - yz$. Subtract xz from both sides:

$$x^2 - xy - xz = xy - y^2 - yz$$

Factoring, we get $x(x - y - z) = y(x - y - z)$.
Dividing both sides by $(x - y - z)$ yields $x = y$.
Thus x, which was assumed to be greater than y, has been shown to equal y. The fallacy occurs in the division by $(x - y - z)$, which is equal to zero.

2) To "prove" that all positive whole numbers are equal. By doing long division, we have, for any value of x

$$\frac{x - 1}{x - 1} = 1$$

$$\frac{x^2 - 1}{x - 1} = x + 1$$

$$\frac{x^3 - 1}{x - 1} = x^2 + x + 1$$

$$\frac{x^4 - 1}{x - 1} = x^3 + x^2 + x + 1$$

$$\vdots$$

$$\frac{x^n - 1}{x - 1} = x^{n-1} + x^{n-2} + \ldots + x^2 + x + 1$$

Letting $x = 1$ in all of these identities, the right side then assumes the values $1, 2, 3, 4, \ldots, n$. The left side members are all the same. Consequently, $1 = 2 = 3 = 4 = \ldots = n$. In this example, the left-hand side of each of the identities assumes the value $\dfrac{0}{0}$ when $x = 1$. This problem serves as evidence that $\dfrac{0}{0}$ can be any number.

Consider the following, and ask your students if they would agree with the following statement, "If two fractions are equal and have equal numerators, then they also have equal denominators." Let the students give illustrations using any fractions they choose. Then have them solve the following equation.

$$6 + \frac{8x - 40}{4 - x} = \frac{2x - 16}{12 - x} \qquad (1)$$

Add terms on the left-hand side, to get

$$\frac{6(4 - x) + 8x - 40}{4 - x} = \frac{2x - 16}{12 - x} \qquad (2)$$

Simplifying: $\dfrac{2x - 16}{4 - x} = \dfrac{2x - 16}{12 - x}$

Since the numerators are equal, this implies $4 - x = 12 - x$. Adding x to both sides, $4 = 12$. Again, as in some of the previous examples, the division by zero is disguised. Have students find the error. It should be pointed out that the axioms cannot be blindly applied to equations without considering the values of the variables for which the equations are true. Thus, equation (1) is not an identity true for all values of x, but it is satisfied only by $x = 8$. Have students solve $(12 - x)(2x - 16) = (4 - x) \times (2x - 16)$ to verify this. Thus $x = 8$, implies that the numerators are zero. You may also have the students prove the general case for $\dfrac{a}{b} = \dfrac{a}{c}$, to show that a cannot be zero.

Another class of fallacies includes those which neglect to consider that a quantity has two square roots of equal absolute value; however one is positive and the other is negative. As an example, take the equation $16 - 48 = 64 - 96$. Adding 36 to both sides gives $16 - 48 + 36 = 64 - 96 + 36$. Each member of the equation is now a perfect square, so that $(4 - 6)^2 = (8 - 6)^2$. Taking the square root of both sides, we get $4 - 6 = 8 - 6$, which implies $4 = 8$. Ask the students where the fallacy occurs. The fallacy in this example lies in taking the improper square root. The correct answer should be $(4 - 6) = -(8 - 6)$.

The following fallacies are based upon the failure to consider all the roots of a given example.

Have students solve the equation $x + 2\sqrt{x} = 3$ in the usual manner. The solutions are $x = 1$ and $x = 9$. The first solution satisfies the equation, while the second solution does not. Have students explain where the difficulty lies.

A similar equation is $x - a = \sqrt{x^2 + a^2}$. By squaring both sides and simplifying we get $-2ax = 0$, or $x = 0$. Substituting $x = 0$ in the original equation, we find that this value of x does not satisfy the equation. Have the students find the correct root of the given equation.

So far we have dealt with square roots of positive numbers. Ask the students what happens when we apply our usual rules to radicals containing imaginary numbers, in light of the following problem. The students have learned that $\sqrt{a} \cdot \sqrt{b} = \sqrt{ab}$, for example, $\sqrt{2} \cdot \sqrt{5} = \sqrt{2 \cdot 5} = \sqrt{10}$. But this gives then, $\sqrt{-1} \cdot \sqrt{-1} = \sqrt{(-1)(-1)} = \sqrt{1} = 1$. However $\sqrt{-1} \cdot \sqrt{-1} = (\sqrt{-1})^2 = -1$. It therefore may

be concluded that $1 = -1$, since both equal $\sqrt{-1} \times \sqrt{-1}$. Students should try to explain the error. They should realize that we cannot apply the ordinary rules for multiplication of radicals to imaginary numbers.

Another proof that can be used to show $-1 = +1$ is the following:

$$\sqrt{-1} = \sqrt{-1}$$
$$\sqrt{\frac{1}{-1}} = \sqrt{\frac{-1}{1}}$$
$$\frac{\sqrt{1}}{\sqrt{-1}} = \frac{\sqrt{-1}}{\sqrt{1}}$$
$$\sqrt{1} \cdot \sqrt{1} = \sqrt{-1} \cdot \sqrt{-1}$$
$$1 = -1$$

Have students replace i for $\sqrt{-1}$, and -1 for i^2 to see where the flaw occurs.

Before concluding the topic on algebraic fallacies, it would be appropriate to consider a fallacy involving simultaneous equations. The students, by now, should realize that in doing the preceding proofs a certain law or operation was violated. Consider an example where hidden flaws in equations can bring about ludicrous results. Have students solve the following pairs of equations by substituting for x in the first equation:

$2x + y = 8$ and $x = 2 - \dfrac{y}{2}$. The result will be $4 = 8$.

Have students find the error. When students graph these two equations, they will find the two lines to be parallel and therefore have *no* points in common.

Further exhibition of such fallacies will prove a worthwhile activity due to the intrinsically dramatic message they carry.

Postassessment

Have students determine where and how the fallacy occurs in the following examples.

1) a. $x = 4$
   b. $x^2 = 16$
   c. $x^2 - 4x = 16 - 4x$
   d. $x(x - 4) = 4(4 - x)$
   e. $x(x - 4) = -4(x - 4)$
   f. $x = -4$

2) a. $(y + 1)^2 = y^2 + 2y + 1$
   b. $(y + 1)^2 - (2y + 1) = y^2$
   c. $(y + 1)^2 - (2y + 1) - y(2y + 1) = y^2 - y(2y + 1)$
   d. $(y + 1)^2 - (y + 1)(2y + 1) + \dfrac{1}{4}(2y + 1)^2 =$
   $y^2 - y(2y + 1) + \dfrac{1}{4}(2y + 1)^2$
   e. $\left[(y + 1) - \dfrac{1}{2}(2y + 1)\right]^2 = \left[y - \dfrac{1}{2}(2y + 1)\right]^2$
   f. $y + 1 - \dfrac{1}{2}(2y + 1) = y - \dfrac{1}{2}(2y + 1)$
   g. $y + 1 = y$

82 Sum Derivations with Arrays

Performance Objectives

(1) *Students will derive the formula for the sum of the first n natural numbers, triangular numbers, square numbers, or pentagonal numbers.*

(2) *Given any integral value of n, students will apply the proper formula to find the sum of the first n figurate numbers.*

Preassessment

Before beginning this lesson, be sure students are familiar with the meanings of *figurate numbers* and *formation of sequences of figurate numbers*. They should also have some knowledge of elementary algebra.

Teaching Strategies

To begin to familiarize students with this topic, have them construct dot arrays on graph paper to illustrate the first few terms in the sequences of various figurate numbers.

Natural
numbers

1   2   3   4   5

Triangular
numbers

1   3   6   10   15

Square
numbers

1   4   9   16   25

Pentagonal
numbers

1   5   12   22   35

Discuss with the class the visual relationships. Most students will clearly see that we can represent the sum of the first *n* natural numbers as follows:

$N_n =$ Sum of the first *n* natural numbers
$$= 1 + 2 + 3 + \ldots + n$$
$$= 1 + (1+1) + (1+1+1) + \ldots + (1+1+ \ldots +1)$$
$$n$$

N_n can also be represented as the sum of the numbers in an array:

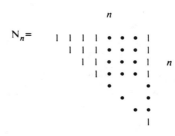

By switching the rows with the columns, N_n can be made to look slightly different:

These two representations of N_n in array form can now be combined to produce an array for $2N_n$ as shown below:

Students can distinctly see that $2N_n = n(n+1)$ from an inspection of the array for $2N_n$. We therefore have:

$$N_n = \frac{n(n+1)}{2}$$

This resulting formula for N_n can be applied whenever it is required to find the sum of the first *n* natural numbers.

Have students consider trying to derive a formula for the first *n* triangular numbers. Clearly, from the dot arrays presented earlier, the following can be established:

$T_n =$ Sum of the first *n* triangular numbers
$$= 1 + 3 + 6 + \ldots + N_n$$
$$= 1 + (1+2) + (1+2+3) + \ldots + (1+2+3+ \ldots +n)$$

T_n can now be represented as the sum of the numbers in an array:

$T_n =$

$$
\begin{array}{cccccc}
 & 1 & & & & \\
 & 1 & 2 & & & \\
 & 1 & 2 & 3 & & \\
n & 1 & 2 & 3 & 4 & \\
 & \bullet & \bullet & \bullet & \bullet & \bullet \\
 & \bullet & \bullet & \bullet & \bullet & & \bullet \\
 & \bullet & \bullet & \bullet & \bullet & & & \bullet \\
 & 1 & 2 & 3 & 4 & \bullet & \bullet & \bullet & n \\
 & & & n & & &
\end{array}
$$

By applying the previously determined formula for N to each row of this array we obtain:

$$
\begin{aligned}
T_n = \ & \frac{1(1+1)}{2} \\
+ \ & \frac{2(1+2)}{2} \\
+ \ & \frac{3(1+3)}{2} \\
+ \ & \frac{4(1+4)}{2} \\
+ \ & \ldots \\
+ \ & \frac{n(1+n)}{2}
\end{aligned}
$$

Students should now see that:
$$2T_n = 1(2) + 2(3) + 3(4) + 4(5) + \ldots + n(n+1)$$
which can be represented in a very convenient form as the sum of the numbers in an array:

$$
2T_n = \quad
\begin{array}{ccccccc}
2 & 3 & 4 & 5 & \bullet & \bullet & \bullet & (n+1) \\
 & 3 & 4 & 5 & \bullet & \bullet & \bullet & (n+1) \\
 & & 4 & 5 & \bullet & \bullet & \bullet & (n+1) \\
 & & & 5 & \bullet & \bullet & \bullet & (n+1) & n \\
 & & & & \bullet & & & \bullet \\
 & & & & & \bullet & & \bullet \\
 & & & & & & \bullet & (n+1)
\end{array}
$$

The combination of the array for T_n and the array for $2T_n$ produces an array for $3T_n$ which is easy to sum up:

$$
3T_n = \qquad\qquad (n+1)
$$

$$
\begin{array}{cccccccc}
1 & 2 & 3 & 4 & 5 & \bullet & \bullet & \bullet & (n+1) \\
1 & 2 & 3 & 4 & 5 & \bullet & \bullet & \bullet & (n+1) \\
1 & 2 & 3 & 4 & 5 & \bullet & \bullet & \bullet & (n+1) \\
1 & 2 & 3 & 4 & 5 & \bullet & \bullet & \bullet & (n+1) & n \\
\bullet & \bullet & \bullet & \bullet & \bullet & \bullet & & & \bullet \\
\bullet & \bullet & \bullet & \bullet & & & \bullet & & \bullet \\
1 & 2 & 3 & 4 & \bullet & \bullet & \bullet & n & (n+1)
\end{array}
$$

Our formula for N_n directly yields
$$3T_n = n \ \frac{(n+1)\ (1+[n+1])}{2}$$

$$
\boxed{T_n = \frac{n(n+1)\ (n+2)}{6}}
$$

Students are now ready to consider the sum of the first n square numbers.
$S_n =$ Sum of the first n square numbers
$= 1^2 + 2^2 + 3^2 + 4^2 + \ldots + n^2$
In array form this appears as:

$$
S_n = \quad
\begin{array}{ccccccc}
 & & & n & & & \\
1 & 2 & 3 & 4 & \bullet & \bullet & \bullet & n \\
 & 2 & 3 & 4 & \bullet & \bullet & \bullet & n \\
 & & 3 & 4 & \bullet & \bullet & \bullet & n \\
 & & & 4 & \bullet & \bullet & \bullet & n & n \\
 & & & & \bullet & & \bullet \\
 & & & & & \bullet & \bullet \\
 & & & & & & n
\end{array}
$$

Combining the array for T_n with this array for S_n, we obtain an array for $S_n + T_n$:

$$
S_n + T_n = \quad
\begin{array}{cccccccc}
 & & & & n & & & \\
1 & 2 & 3 & 4 & \bullet & \bullet & \bullet & n \\
1 & 2 & 3 & 4 & \bullet & \bullet & \bullet & n \\
1 & 2 & 3 & 4 & \bullet & \bullet & \bullet & n \\
1 & 2 & 3 & 4 & \bullet & \bullet & \bullet & n & (n+1) \\
1 & 2 & 3 & 4 & \bullet & & & \bullet \\
\bullet & \bullet & \bullet & \bullet & \bullet & & \bullet \\
\bullet & \bullet & \bullet & & & \bullet & n \\
1 & 2 & 3 & 4 & \bullet & \bullet & \bullet & n
\end{array}
$$

Students should observe that each row of the array for $S_n + T_n$ is the sum of the first n natural numbers. In the present notation, this is N_n. Since the array has $(n+1)$ rows, we clearly obtain
$$S_n + T_n = (n+1)N_n.$$
Substituting the formulas previously derived for T_n and N_n is an exercise in elementary algebra which quickly yields

$$
\boxed{S_n = \frac{n(n+1)\ (2n+1)}{6}}
$$

Postassessment

To measure students' attainment of the performance objective, have each student:

(1) Derive a formula for the sum of the first n pentagonal numbers using arrays.

(2) Apply the various formulas the class has derived to find the sum of the first n figurate numbers for several integral values of n.

83   Pythagorean Triples

While teaching the Pythagorean Theorem at the secondary school level, teachers often suggest that students recognize (and memorize) certain common ordered sets of three numbers which can represent the lengths of the sides of a right triangle. Some of these ordered sets of three numbers, known as Pythagorean triples, are: (3, 4, 5), (5, 12, 13), (8, 15, 17), (7, 24, 25). The student is asked to discover these Pythagorean triples as they come up in selected exercises. How can one generate more triples without a trial and error method? This question, often asked by students, will be answered in this unit.

Performance Objectives
1. *Students will generate six primitive Pythagorean triples using the formulas developed in this unit.*
2. *Students will state properties of various members of a primitive Pythagorean triple.*

Preassessment
Students should be familiar with the Pythagorean Theorem. They should be able to recognize Pythagorean triples and distinguish between primitive Pythagorean triples and others.

Teaching Strategies
Ask your students to find the missing member of the following Pythagorean triples:
1. (3, 4, _____)
2. (7, _____, 25)
3. (11, _____, _____)

The first two triples can be easily determined using the Pythagorean Theorem. However, this method will not work with the third triple. At this point you can offer your students a method for solving this problem. This is the topic of this unit.

Before beginning the development of the desired formulas, we must consider a few simple lemmas.

Lemma 1: When 8 divides the square of an odd number, the remainder is 1.

Proof: We can represent an odd number by $2k + 1$, where k is an integer.
$$(2k + 1)^2 = 4k^2 + 4k + 1 = 4k(k + 1) + 1$$
Since k and $k+1$ are consecutive, one of them must be even. Therefore $4k(k+1)$ must be divisible by 8.
Thus $(2k + 1)^2$, when divided by 8, leaves a remainder of 1.

The following lemmas follow directly.

Lemma 2: When 8 divides the sum of two odd square numbers, the remainder is 2.

Lemma 3: The sum of two odd square numbers cannot be a square number.

Proof: Since the sum of two odd square numbers, when divided by 8, leaves a remainder of 2, the sum is even but not divisible by 4. It therefore cannot be a square number.

We are now ready to begin our development of formulas for Pythagorean triples. Let us assume that (a, b, c) is a primitive Pythagorean triple. This implies that a and b are relatively prime. Therefore they cannot both be even. Can they both be odd?

If a and b are both odd, then by Lemma 3: $a^2 + b^2 \neq c^2$. This contradicts our assumption that (a, b, c) is a Pythagorean triple; therefore a and b cannot both be odd. Therefore one must be odd and one even.

Let us suppose that a is odd and b is even. This implies that c is also odd.

We can rewrite $a^2 + b^2 = c^2$ as
$$b^2 = c^2 - a^2$$
$$b^2 = (c + a) \cdot (c - a)$$

Since the sum and difference of two odd numbers is even,

$c + a = 2p$, and $c - a = 2q$ (p and q are natural numbers).

By solving for a and c we get:
$$c = p + q, \quad \text{and} \quad a = p - q$$

We can now show that p and q must be relatively prime. Suppose p and q were not relatively prime; say $g > 1$ was a common factor. Then g would also be a common factor of a and c. Similarly g would also be a common factor of $c + a$ and $c - a$. This would make g^2 a factor of b^2, since $b^2 = (c + a) \cdot (c - a)$. It follows that g would then have to be a factor of b. Now if g is a factor of b and also a common factor of a and c, then a, b, and c are not relatively prime. This contradicts our assumption that (a, b, c) is a *primitive* Pythagorean triple. Thus p and q must be relatively prime.

Since b is even, we may represent b as
$$b = 2r$$

But $b^2 = (c + a)(c - a)$.

Therefore $b^2 = (2p) \cdot (2q) = 4r^2$, or $pq = r^2$

If the product of two relatively prime natural numbers (p and q) is the square of a natural number (r), then each of them must be the square of a natural number. Therefore we let

$$p = m^2 \quad \text{and} \quad q = n^2$$

where m and n are natural numbers. Since they are factors of relatively prime numbers (p and q), they (m and n) are also relatively prime.

Since $a = p - q$ and $c = p + q$
$\qquad a = m^2 - n^2$ and $c = m^2 + n^2$

Also, since $b = 2r$ and $b^2 = 4r^2 = 4pq = 4m^2n^2$
$\qquad b = 2\,mn$

To summarize we now have formulas for generating Pythagorean triples:

$$a = m^2 - n^2 \qquad b = 2mn \qquad c = m^2 + n^2$$

The numbers m and n cannot both be even, since they are relatively prime. They cannot both be odd, for this would make $c = m^2 + n^2$ an even number, which we established earlier as impossible. Since this indicates that one must be even and the other odd, $b = 2mn$ must be divisible by 4. Therefore no Pythagorean triple can be composed of three prime numbers. This does *not* mean that the other members of the Pythagorean triple may not be prime.

Let us reverse the process for a moment. Consider relatively prime numbers m and n (where $m > n$) and where one is even and the other odd. We will now show that (a, b, c) is a primitive Pythagorean triple where $a = m^2 - n^2$, $b = 2mn$ and $c = m^2 + n^2$.

It is simple to verify algebraically that

$$(m^2 - n^2)^2 + (2mn)^2 = (m^2 + n^2)^2$$

thereby making it a Pythagorean triple. What remains is to prove that (a, b, c) is a *primitive* Pythagorean triple.

Suppose a and b have a common factor $h > 1$. Since a is odd, h must also be odd. Because $a^2 + b^2 = c^2$, h would also be a factor of c. We also have h a factor of $m^2 - n^2$ and $m^2 + n^2$ as well as of their sum, $2m^2$, and their difference $2n^2$.

Since h is odd, it is a common factor of m^2 and n^2. However m and n (and as a result m^2 and n^2) are relatively prime. Therefore h cannot be a common factor of m and n. This contradiction establishes that a and b are relatively prime.

Having finally established a method for generating primitive Pythagorean triples, students should be eager to put it to use. The table below gives some of the smaller primitive Pythagorean triples

Pythagorean Triples

m	n	a	b	c
2	1	3	4	5
3	2	5	12	13
4	1	15	8	17
4	3	7	24	25
5	2	21	20	29
5	4	9	40	41
6	1	35	12	37
6	5	11	60	61
7	2	45	28	53
7	4	33	56	65
7	6	13	84	85

A fast inspection of the above table indicates that certain primitive Pythagorean triples (a, b, c) have $c = b + 1$. Have students discover the relationship between m and n for these triples.

They should notice that for these triples $m = n + 1$. To prove this will be true for other primitive Pythagorean triples (not in the table), let $m = n + 1$ and generate the Pythagorean triples.

$$a = m^2 - n^2 = (n + 1)^2 - n^2 = 2n + 1$$
$$b = 2mn = 2n(n + 1) = 2n^2 + 2n$$
$$c = m^2 + n^2 = (n + 1)^2 + n^2 = 2n^2 + 2n + 1$$

Clearly $c = b + 1$, which was to be shown!

A natural question to ask your students is to find all primitive Pythagorean triples which are consecutive natural numbers. In a method similar to that used above, they ought to find that the only triple satisfying that condition is $(3, 4, 5)$.

Other investigations can be proposed for student consideration. In any case students should have a far better appreciation for Pythagorean triples and elementary number theory after completing this unit.

Postassessment

1. Find six primitive Pythagorean triples which are not included in the above table.

2. Find a way to generate primitive Pythagorean triples of the form (a, b, c) where $b = a + 1$.

3. Prove that every primitive Pythagorean triple has one member which is divisible by 3.

4. Prove that every primitive Pythagorean triple has one member which is divisible by 5.

5. Prove that for every primitive Pythagorean triple the product of its members is a multiple of 60.

6. Find a Pythagorean triple (a, b, c) where $a^2 = b + 2$.

84   Divisibility

The unit will present methods for finding divisors without doing division.

Performance Objectives
1. Given any integer, students will determine its prime factors, without doing any division.
2. Students will produce rules for testing divisibility by all natural numbers less than 49, and some greater than 49.

Preassessment
Have students indicate without doing any division which of the following numbers are divisible by 2, by 3, and by 5.
a) 792   b) 835   c) 356   d) 3890   e) 693   f) 743

Teaching Strategies
Students are probably aware that any even number is divisible by 2; hence of the above numbers, a, c, and d are divisible by 2. Many will also recognize that a number whose terminal digit (units digit) is either 5 or 0, is divisible by 5; hence, b and d are divisible by 5. At this point students will be eager to extend this rule to hold true for testing divisibility by 3. Of the above numbers, c, e, and f are the only numbers whose terminal digit is a multiple of 3; yet only one of these numbers, 693, is in fact divisible by 3. This should stir up sufficient curiosity so as to create a desire among the students to develop rules to test divisibility by numbers other than 2 and 5.

There are various ways to develop rules for testing divisibility by various numbers. They may be developed in order of magnitude of the numbers. This method may be appealing to some; however it detracts from the various patterns which students so often appreciate in the development of mathematics. In this unit we shall consider the rules in groups of related methods.

Divisibility by powers of 2: *A given number is divisible by 2^1 (or 2^2, 2^3, . . . 2^n, respectively) if the last 1 (or 2, 3, . . . n, respectively) digit(s) is (are) divisible by 2^1 (or 2^2, 2^3, . . . 2^n, respectively).*

Proof: Consider the following *n*-digit number:
$$a_{n-1}a_{n-2}a_{n-3} . . . a_2 a_1 a_0$$
which can be written as:
$$10^{n-1}a_{n-1} + 10^{n-2}a_{n-2} + . . . + 10^2 a_2 + 10^1 a_1 + 10^0 a_0$$
Since all terms except the last are always divisible by 2, we must be assured of the divisibility of the last term when testing divisibility by 2. Similarly, since all the terms except the last two are always divisible by 2^2, we must merely determine if the last two digits (considered as a number) is divisible by 2^2. This scheme may easily be extended to the nth case.

Divisibility by powers of 5: *A given number is divisible by 5^1 (or 5^2, 5^3, . . . 5^n, respectively) if the last 1 (or 2, 3, . . . n, respectively) digit(s) is (are) divisible by 5^1 (or 5^2, 5^3, . . . 5^n, respectively).*

Proof: The proof of these rules follows the same scheme as the proof for testing divisibility by powers of two, except the 2 is replaced by a 5.

Divisibility by 3 and 9: *A given number is divisible by 3 (or 9) if the sum of the digits is divisible by 3 (or 9).*

Proof: Consider the number $a_8 a_7 a_6 a_5 a_4 a_3 a_2 a_1 a_0$ (the general case $a_n a_{n-1} . . . a_3 a_2 a_1 a_0$ is similar). This expression may be written as $a_8(9 + 1)^8 + a_7(9 + 1)^7 + . . . + a_1(9 + 1) + a_0$. Using the expression $M_i(9)$ to mean a multiple of 9, for $i = 1, 2, 3, . . . , 7, 8$, we can rewrite the number as:
$$a_8[M_8(9) + 1] + a_7[M_7(9) + 1] + . . . + a_1[M_1(9) + 1] + a_0$$
(A mention of the binomial theorem may be helpful here.) The number equals $M(9) + a_8 + a_7 + a_6 + a_5 + a_4 + a_3 + a_2 + a_1 + a_0$, where $M(9)$ is a multiple of 9. Thus the number is divisible by 9 (or 3) if the sum of the digits is divisible by 9 (or 3).

A rule for testing divisibility by 11 is proved in a manner similar to the proof for divisibility by 3 and 9.

Divisibility by 11: *A given number is divisible by 11 if the difference of the two sums of alternate digits is divisible by 11.*

Proof: Consider the number $a_8 a_7 a_6 a_5 a_4 a_3 a_2 a_1 a_0$ (using the general case is similar). This expression may be written as:
$$a_8(11-1)^8 + a_7(11-1)^7 + . . . + a_1(11-1) + a_0$$
$$= a_8[M_8(11) + 1] + a_7[M_7(11) - 1] + . . . + a_1[M_1(11) - 1] + a_0$$
This expression then equals $M(11) + a_8 - a_7 + a_6 - a_5 + a_4 - a_3 + a_2 - a_1 + a_0$. Thus the number is divisible by 11 if $a_8 + a_6 + a_4 + a_2 + a_0 - (a_7 + a_5 + a_3 + a_1)$ is divisible by 11.

You would be wise to indicate the extensions in bases other than ten of each of the previously mentioned divisibility rules. Often students are able to make these generalizations on their own (especially with appropriate coaxing). The remainder of this Model will deal with rules for testing divisibility of primes ≥ 7 and composites.

Divisibility by 7: *Delete the last digit from the given number, then subtract* twice *this deleted* digit from the remaining number. *If the result is divisible by 7, the original number is divisible by 7. This process may be repeated if the result is too large for simple inspection of divisibility by 7.*

Proof: To justify the technique, consider the various possible terminal digits and the corresponding subtraction:

Terminal digit	Number subtracted from original	Terminal digit	Number subtracted from original
1	$20 + 1 = 21 = 3 \cdot 7$	5	$100 + 5 = 105 = 15 \cdot 7$
2	$40 + 2 = 42 = 6 \cdot 7$	6	$120 + 6 = 126 = 18 \cdot 7$
3	$60 + 3 = 63 = 9 \cdot 7$	7	$140 + 7 = 147 = 21 \cdot 7$
4	$80 + 4 = 84 = 12 \cdot 7$	8	$160 + 8 = 168 = 24 \cdot 7$
		9	$180 + 9 = 189 = 27 \cdot 7$

In each case a multiple of 7 is being subtracted one or more times from the original number. Hence, if the remaining number is divisible by 7, then so is the original number.

Divisibility by 13: *This is the same as the rule for testing divisibility by 7, except that the 7 is replaced by 13 and instead of subtracting* twice *the deleted digit, we subtract* nine times *the deleted digit each time.*

Proof: Once again consider the various possible terminal digits and the corresponding subtraction:

Terminal digit	Number subtracted from original	Terminal digit	Number subtracted from original
1	$90 + 1 = 91 = 7 \cdot 13$	5	$450 + 5 = 455 = 35 \cdot 13$
2	$180 + 2 = 182 = 14 \cdot 13$	6	$540 + 6 = 546 = 42 \cdot 13$
3	$270 + 3 = 273 = 21 \cdot 13$	7	$630 + 7 = 637 = 49 \cdot 13$
4	$360 + 4 = 364 = 28 \cdot 13$	8	$720 + 8 = 728 = 56 \cdot 13$
		9	$810 + 9 = 819 = 63 \cdot 13$

In each case a multiple of 13 is being subtracted one or more times from the original number. Hence, if the remaining number is divisible by 13, then the original number is divisible by 13.

Divisibility by 17: *This is the same as the rule for testing divisibility by 7 except that the 7 is replaced by 17 and instead of subtracting* twice *the deleted digit, we subtract* five times *the deleted digit each time.*

Proof: The proof for the rule for divisibility by 17 follows a similar pattern to those for 7 and 13.

The patterns developed in the preceding three divisibility rules (for 7, 13, and 17) should lead students to develop similar rules for testing divisibility by larger primes. The following chart presents the "multipliers" of the deleted digits for various primes.

To test divisibility by	7	11	13	17	19	23	29	31	37	41	43	47
Multiplier	2	1	9	5	17	16	26	3	11	4	30	14

To fill in the gaps in the set of integers, a consideration of divisibility of composites is necessary.

Divisibility by composites: *A given number is divisible by a composite number if it is divisible by each of its relatively prime factors.* The chart below offers illustrations of this rule. You or your students should complete the chart to 48.

To be divisible by	6	10	12	15	18	21	24	26	28
The number must be divisible by	2,3	2,5	3,4	3,5	2,9	3,7	3,8	2,13	4,7

At this juncture the student has not only a rather comprehensive list of rules for testing divisibility, but also an interesting insight into elementary number theory. Have students practice using these rules (to instill greater familiarity) and try to develop rules to test divisibility by other numbers in base ten and to generalize these rules to other bases. Unfortunately lack of space prevents a more detailed development here.

Postassessment

Students who have met the performance objectives should be able to do these exercises.
1. State a rule for testing divisibility by
   a) 8   b) 18   c) 13   d) 23   e) 24   f) 42
2. Determine the prime factors of
   a) 280   b) 1001   c) 495   d) 315   e) 924

Further references on this topic may be found in:

Posamentier, Alfred S. *A Study Guide for the Mathematics Section of the Scholastic Aptitude Test*, Boston, Mass.: Allyn & Bacon, 1983.

Posamentier, Alfred S. and Charles T. Salkind. *Challenging Problems in Algebra, Volumes I and II.* New York: Macmillan Co., 1970.

Posamentier, Alfred S., and Charles T. Salkind. *Uncommon Problems for Common Topics in Algebra.* Portland, Me.: J. Weston Walch, Publisher, 1981.

Posamentier, Alfred S., and Charles T. Salkind. *Unusual Topics for Usual Topics in Algebra.* Portland, Me.: J. Weston Walch, Publisher, 1981.

85 Fibonacci Sequence

Performance Objectives

Students will:
1. *define the Fibonacci Sequence.*
2. *find sums of various Fibonacci numbers.*
3. *find the sum of squares of the first Fibonacci numbers.*
4. *discover properties of Fibonacci numbers.*

Preassessment

Have students try to solve the following problem:
How many pairs of rabbits will be produced in a year, beginning with a single pair, if in one month each pair bears a new pair which becomes productive from the second month on?

Teaching Strategies

Italian mathematician Leonardo of Pisa (he was the son, figlio, of Bonaccio, hence the name Fibonacci) presented the above problem in his book *LIBER ABACI* published in 1202. Consider its solution with students. Begin by drawing a chart as pictured below.

Figure 1

let A = Adult pairs, B = Baby pairs

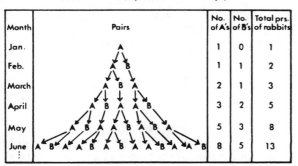

Month	Pairs	No. of A's	No. of B's	Total prs. of rabbits
Jan.		1	0	1
Feb.		1	1	2
March		2	1	3
April		3	2	5
May		5	3	8
June ⋮		8	5	13

Start with first month and proceed to the next months explaining the procedure as you go along. Remind students that a baby pair must mature one month before becoming productive.

Continue the chart until the twelfth month where it will be discovered that 377 pairs of rabbits are produced in a year. Now focus students' attention on the third column (Number of A), the Fibonacci Sequence. Have them try to discover a rule for continuing this sequence. Tell students to notice that each term is the sum of the two preceding terms. This can be written as a general expression: $f_n = f_{n-1} + f_{n-2}$, where f_n stands for the nth Fibonacci number. For example, $f_3 = f_1 + f_2$; $f_4 = f_2 + f_3$; $f_7 = f_5 + f_6$. Also $f_1 = f_2 = 1$.

The Fibonacci Sequence has many interesting properties that students can observe by studying the relationships between the terms. It can be proved that the sum of the first n Fibonacci numbers, $f_1 + f_2 + \ldots + f_n = f_{n+2} - 1$ (A)

It has already been noted that the following relations hold: $f_1 = f_3 - f_2$ (since $f_3 = f_1 + f_2$)
$$f_2 = f_4 - f_3$$
$$f_3 = f_5 - f_4$$
.
.
.
$$f_{n-1} = f_{n+1} - f_n$$
$$f_n = f_{n+2} - f_{n+1}$$

By *termwise* addition of all these equations it follows that $f_1 + f_2 + f_3 + \ldots + f_n = f_{n+2} - f_2$, but we know that $f_2 = 1$. Therefore $f_1 + f_2 + f_3 + \ldots + f_n = f_{n+2} - 1$.

In a similar manner we can find an expression for the sum of the first n Fibonacci numbers with odd indices: $f_1 + f_3 + f_5 + \ldots + f_{2n-1} = f_{2n}$ (B)
To do this we write:
$$f_1 = f_2$$
$$f_3 = f_4 - f_2 \text{ (since } f_4 = f_2 + f_3)$$
$$f_5 = f_6 - f_4$$
$$f_7 = f_8 - f_6$$
$$f_{2n-3} = f_{2n-2} - f_{2n-4}$$
$$f_{2n-1} = f_{2n} - f_{2n-2}$$
Again by termwise addition, we obtain:
$$f_1 + f_3 + f_5 + \ldots + f_{2n-1} = f_{2n}$$
The sum of the first n Fibonacci numbers with even indices is $f_2 + f_4 + f_6 + \ldots + f_{2n} = f_{2n+1} - 1$ (C)
To prove this we subtract equation (B) from twice equation (A), that is, $f_1 + f_2 + f_3 + \ldots + f_{2n} = f_{2n+2} - 1$, to obtain $f_2 + f_4 + \ldots + f_{2n} = f_{2n+2} - 1 - f_{2n} = f_{2n+2} - f_{2n} - 1 = f_{2n+1} - 1$ (since $f_{2n+2} = f_{2n} + f_{2n+1}$ and $f_{2n+1} = f_{2n+2} - f_{2n}$) which is what we wanted to prove.

By yet another application of the process of termwise addition of equations we can derive a formula for the sum of the squares of the first n Fibonacci numbers. We must first note that for $k > 1$:
$$f_k f_{k+1} - f_{k-1} f_k = f_k (f_{k+1} - f_{k-1}) = f_k \cdot f_k = f_k^2$$
This gives us the following relations:
$$f_1^2 = f_1 f_2 - f_0 f_1 \text{ (where } f_0 = 0)$$
$$f_2^2 = f_2 f_3 - f_1 f_2$$
$$f_3^2 = f_3 f_4 - f_2 f_3$$
.
.
.
$$f_{n-1}^2 = f_{n-1} f_n - f_{n-2} f_{n-1}$$
$$f_n^2 = f_n f_{n+1} - f_{n-1} f_n$$
By adding termwise we obtain:
$$f_1^2 + f_2^2 + f_3^2 + \ldots + f_n^2 = f_n \cdot f_{n+1}$$

The Fibonacci Sequence is also connected to a famous, ancient topic in mathematics. Examining the ratios of the first successive pairs of numbers in the sequence we obtain the following:

$\dfrac{1}{1}$ = 1.0000 $\dfrac{2}{1}$ = 2.0000

$\dfrac{3}{2}$ = 1.5000 $\dfrac{5}{3}$ = 1.6667

$\dfrac{8}{5}$ = 1.6000 $\dfrac{13}{8}$ = 1.6250

$\dfrac{21}{13}$ = 1.6154 $\dfrac{34}{21}$ = 1.6190

$\dfrac{55}{34}$ = 1.6176 $\dfrac{89}{55}$ = 1.6182

$\dfrac{144}{89}$ = 1.6180 $\dfrac{233}{144}$ = 1.6181

The ratios f_n/f_{n-1} $(n > 0)$ form a decreasing sequence for the odd values of n and an increasing sequence for the even values of n. Each ratio on the right hand side is larger than each corresponding ratio on the left hand side. The ratio approaches a limiting value between 1.6180 and 1.6181. It can be shown that this limit is $\dfrac{1 + \sqrt{5}}{2}$ or approximately 1.61803 to five decimal places.

The ratio was so important to the Greeks that they gave it a special name, the "Golden Ratio" or the "Golden Section." They did not express the relationship in decimal form but with a geometric construction in which two line segments are in the exact golden ratio, 1.61803 . . . to 1.

The golden ratio yields the basic connection between the Fibonacci Sequence and geometry. Consider again the ratios of consecutive Fibonacci numbers. As we said earlier, the table of fractions above seems to be approaching the golden ratio. Let us investigate this notion further by considering the line segment $\overline{APB}$, with P partitioning $\overline{AB}$ so that $\dfrac{AB}{AP} = \dfrac{AP}{PB}$.

A———————•———— B
                  P

Let $x = \dfrac{AB}{AP}$. Therefore $x = \dfrac{AB}{AP} = \dfrac{AP + PB}{AP} =$ $1 + \dfrac{PB}{AP} = 1 + \dfrac{AP}{AB} = 1 + \dfrac{1}{x}$. Thus $x = 1 + \dfrac{1}{x}$ or $x^2 - x - 1 = 0$.

The roots of this equation are:

$a = \dfrac{1 + \sqrt{5}}{2} \approx 1.6180339887$, and

$b = \dfrac{1 - \sqrt{5}}{2} \approx -.6180339887$

Since we are concerned with lengths of line segments, we shall use only the positive root, a. As a and b are roots of the equation $x^2 - x - 1 = 0$, $a^2 = a + 1$ (1) and $b^2 = b + 1$ (2).

Multiplying (1) by a^n (where n is an integer) $a^{n+2} = a^{n+1} + a^n$. Multiplying (2) by b^n (where n is an integer) $b^{n+2} = b^{n+1} + b^n$. Subtracting equation (2) from equation (1):

$$a^{n+2} - b^{n+2} = (a^{n+1} - b^{n+1}) + (a^n - b^n)$$

Now dividing by $a - b = \sqrt{5}$ (non-zero!):

$$\frac{a^{n+2} - b^{n+2}}{a - b} = \frac{a^{n+1} - b^{n+1}}{a - b} + \frac{a^n - b^n}{a - b}$$

If we now let $t_n = \dfrac{a^n - b^n}{a - b}$, then $t_{n+2} = t_{n+1} + t_n$ (same as the Fibonacci Sequence definition). All that remains to be shown in order to be able to establish t_n as the nth Fibonacci number, f_n, is that $t_1 = 1$ and $t_2 = 1$:

$$t_1 = \frac{a^1 - b^1}{a - b} = 1$$

$$t_2 = \frac{a^2 - b^2}{a - b} = \frac{(a - b)(a + b)}{a - b} = \frac{(\sqrt{5})(1)}{(\sqrt{5})} = 1$$

Therefore $f_n = \dfrac{a^n - b^n}{a - b}$, where $a = \dfrac{1 + \sqrt{5}}{2}$, $b = \dfrac{1 - \sqrt{5}}{2}$ and $n = 1, 2, 3, \ldots$

Postassessment

1. Find the sum of the first 9 Fibonacci numbers.
2. Find the sum of the first 5 Fibonacci numbers with odd indices.

References

Brother, U. Alfred, *An Introduction to Fibonacci Discovery*. San Jose, Calif.: The Fabonacci Association, 1965.

Bicknell, M. and Verner E. Hoggatt, Jr., *A Primer for the Fibonacci Numbers*. San Jose, California: The Fibonacci Association, 1972.

Hoggatt, Verner E., Jr., *Fibonacci and Lucas Numbers*. Boston: Houghton Mifflin, 1969.

Posamentier, Alfred S. *Excursions in Advanced Euclidean Geometry*. Menlo Park, Ca.: Addison-Wesley, 1984.

86 Diophantine Equations

This unit may be presented to any class having mastered the fundamentals of elementary algebra.

Performance Objectives

1. Given an equation with two variables, students will find integral solutions (if they exist.)

2. Given a verbal problem which calls for a solution of a Diophantine equation, students will determine (where applicable) the number of possible solutions.

Preassessment

Have students solve the following problem: Suppose you are asked by your employer to go to the post office and buy 6-cent and 8-cent stamps. He gives you 5 dollars to spend. How many combinations of 6-cent and 8-cent stamps could you select from to make your purchase?

Teaching Strategies

Most students will promptly realize that there are two variables which must be determined, say x and y. Letting x represent the number of 8-cent stamps and y represent the number of 6-cent stamps, the equation: $8x + 6y = 500$ should follow. This should then be converted to: $4x + 3y = 250$. At this juncture the student should realize that although this equation has an infinite number of solutions, it may or may not have an infinite number of *integral* solutions; moreover, it may or may not have an infinite number of *positive integral* solutions (as called for by the original problem). The first problem to consider is whether integral solutions, in fact, exist.

For this a useful theorem may be employed. It states that if the greatest common factor of a and b is also a factor of k, then there exist an infinite number of integral solutions for x and y in $ax + by = k$. Equations of this type whose solutions must be integers are known as *Diophantine equations* in honor of the Greek mathematician Diophantus, who wrote about them.

Since the greatest common factor of 3 and 4 is 1, which is a factor of 250, there exist an infinite number of integral solutions to the equation $4x + 3y = 250$. The question now facing your students is how many (if any) *positive* integral solutions exist?

One possible method of solution is often referred to as Euler's method (Leonhard Euler, 1707-1783). To begin, students should solve for the variable with the coefficient of least absolute value; in this case, y. Thus $y = \dfrac{250 - 4x}{3}$. This is to be rewritten as:

$$y = 83 + \frac{1}{3} - x - \frac{x}{3} = 83 - x + \frac{1 - x}{3}.$$

Now introduce another variable, say t; and let $t = \dfrac{1 - x}{3}$. Solving for x yields $x = 1 - 3t$. Since there is no fractional coefficient in this equation, the process does *not* have to be repeated as it otherwise would have to be (i.e., each time introducing new variables, as with t above). Now substituting for x in the above equation yields: $y = \dfrac{250 - 4(1 - 3t)}{3} = 82 + 4t$. For various integral values of t, corresponding values for x and y will be generated. A table of values such as that below might prove useful.

t	$\ldots$	-2	-1	0	1	2	$\ldots$
x	$\ldots$	7	4	1	-2	-5	$\ldots$
y	$\ldots$	74	78	82	86	90	$\ldots$

Perhaps by generating a more extensive table, students will notice for what values of t positive integral values for x and y may be obtained. However, this procedure for determining the number of positive integral values of x and y is not very elegant. The students should be guided to the following inequalities to be solved simultaneously:

$$1 - 3t > 0 \quad \text{and} \quad 82 + 4t > 0.$$

Thus $t < \dfrac{1}{3}$ and $t > -20\dfrac{1}{2}$,

or $-20\dfrac{1}{2} < t < \dfrac{1}{3}$. This indicates that there are 21 possible combinations of 6-cent and 8-cent stamps which can be purchased for 5 dollars.

Students might find it helpful to observe the solution to a more difficult Diophantine equation. The following is such an example:

Solve the Diophantine equation $5x - 8y = 39$.

1. Solve for x, since its coefficient has the lower absolute value of the two coefficients

$$x = \frac{8y + 39}{5} = y + 7 + \frac{3y + 4}{5}.$$

2. Let $t = \dfrac{3y + 4}{5}$, then solve for y:

$$y = \frac{5t - 4}{3} = t - 1 + \frac{2t - 1}{3}.$$

3. Let $u = \dfrac{2t - 1}{3}$, then solve for t:

$$t = \frac{3u + 1}{2} = u + \frac{u + 1}{2}.$$

4. Let $v = \dfrac{u + 1}{2}$, then solve for u:

$$u = 2v - 1.$$

We may now reverse the process since the coefficient of v is an integer.

5. Now substituting in the reverse order:

$$t = \frac{3u + 1}{2}$$

therefore: $t = \dfrac{3(2v - 1) + 1}{2} = 3v - 1.$

also: $y = \dfrac{5t - 4}{3}$

therefore: $y = \dfrac{5(3v - 1) - 4}{3} = \boxed{5v - 3 = y}$

Similarly: $x = \dfrac{8y + 39}{5}$

therefore: $x = \dfrac{8(5v - 3) + 39}{5} = \boxed{8v + 3 = x}$

v	...	-2	-1	0	1	2	...
x	...	-13	-5	3	11	19	...
y	...	-13	-8	-3	2	7	...

The above table indicates how the various solutions of this Diophantine equation may be generated. Students should be urged to inspect the nature of the members of the solution set.

Another method of solving Diophantine Equations is presented in Unit 87.

Postassessment

Have students solve each of the following Diophantine equations and then determine the number of positive integral solutions (if any.)

1. $2x + 11y = 35$ 3. $3x - 18y = 40$
2. $7x - 3y = 23$ 4. $4x - 17y = 53$

Reference: Related works by the author include: Posamentier, Alfred S. and Charles T. Salkind, *Challenging Problems in Algebra,* Volumes I and II. New York: Macmillan Co., 1970; *Uncommon Problems for Common Topics in Algebra* and *Unusual Topics for Usual Topics in Algebra.* Portland, Me.: J. Weston Walch, Publisher, 1981.

87 Continued Fractions And Diophantine Equations

This lesson should be considered after the accompanying unit, "Diophantine Equations" is presented. This unit describes another method of solving Diophantine equations.

Performance Objectives

1. Given an equation with two variables, students will find integral solutions (if they exist).

2. Given a verbal problem which calls for a solution of a Diophantine equation, students will determine (where applicable) the number of possible solutions.

3. Given an improper fraction, students will write an equivalent continued fraction.

Preassessment

Students should have successfully mastered the concepts of the unit "Diophantine Equations."

Teaching Strategies

Before discussing this method of solution of Diophantine equations, an excursion into continued fractions would be appropriate. Every improper fraction (reduced to lowest terms) has an equivalent continued fraction. For example:

$$\frac{11}{7} = 1 + \frac{4}{7} = 1 + \frac{1}{\dfrac{7}{4}} = 1 + \cfrac{1}{1 + \dfrac{3}{4}}$$

$$= 1 + \cfrac{1}{1 + \cfrac{1}{\dfrac{4}{3}}} = 1 + \cfrac{1}{1 + \cfrac{1}{1 + \dfrac{1}{3}}}$$

The last expression is called a *simple continued fraction*, since all the numerators after the first term are 1. These are the only types of continued fractions we shall consider here.

Consider a general improper fraction (reduced to lowest terms) and its equivalent simple continued fraction:

$$\frac{r}{s} = a_1 + \cfrac{1}{a_2 + \cfrac{1}{a_3 + \cfrac{1}{a_4 + \cfrac{1}{a_5}}}}$$

We shall call $c_1 = a_1$ the first convergent;

$c_2 = a_1 + \cfrac{1}{a_2}$ the second convergent;

$c_3 = a_1 + \cfrac{1}{a_2 + \cfrac{1}{a_3}}$ the third convergent;

$c_4 = a_1 + \cfrac{1}{a_2 + \cfrac{1}{a_3 + \cfrac{1}{a_4}}}$ the fourth convergent;

$c_5 = a_1 + \cfrac{1}{a_2 + \cfrac{1}{a_3 + \cfrac{1}{a_4 + \cfrac{1}{a_5}}}}$ the last convergent.

For example, for the above continued fraction equivalent to: $\frac{11}{7}$,

$$c_1 = 1; c_2 = 2; c_3 = \frac{3}{2}; c_4 = \frac{11}{7}$$

It would be appropriate at this juncture to derive a method for finding the nth convergent of a general continued fraction.

Let $c_n = \frac{r_n}{s_n}$ (the nth convergent)

$c_1 = a_1$, therefore $r_1 = a_1$ and $s_1 = 1$.

$c_2 = a_1 + \cfrac{1}{a_2} = \cfrac{a_1 a_2 + 1}{a_2}$

therefore $r_2 = a_1 a_2 + 1$, and $s_2 = a_2$.

$c_3 = a_1 + \cfrac{1}{a_2 + \cfrac{1}{a_3}} = a_1 + \cfrac{1}{\cfrac{a_2 a_3 + 1}{a_3}}$

$= a_1 + \cfrac{a_3}{a_2 a_3 + 1} = \cfrac{a_1 a_2 a_3 + a_1 + a_3}{a_2 a_3 + 1}$

$= \cfrac{a_3(a_1 a_2 + 1) + a_1}{a_3 a_2 + 1}$, since

$a_1 a_2 + 1 = r_2$; $a_1 = r_1$; $a_2 = s_2$; $1 = s_1$; we get

$c_3 = \cfrac{a_3 r_2 + r_1}{a_3 s_2 + s_1}$. Therefore, $r_3 = a_3 r_2 + r_1$,

and $s_3 = a_3 s_2 + s_1$.

Similarly $c_4 = \cfrac{a_4 r_3 + r_2}{a_4 s_3 + s_2}$. Following this pattern

$$\boxed{c_n = \frac{a_n r_{n-1} + r_{n-2}}{a_n s_{n-1} + s_{n-2}} = \frac{r_n}{s_n}}$$

(This can be proved by mathematical induction.)
Now consider the general case for $n = 2$:

$c_2 = \cfrac{a_2 r_1 + r_0}{a_2 s_1 + s_0}$. Earlier c_2 was found to

equal $\cfrac{a_1 a_2 + 1}{a_2}$.

Equating corresponding parts yields:
$a_2 r_1 + r_0 = a_1 a_2 + 1$
Therefore, $r_1 = a_1$ and $r_0 = 1$
also, $a_2 s_1 + s_0 = a_2$
Therefore, $s_1 = 1$ and $s_0 = 0$.
In a similar way consider the general case for $n = 1$:

$c_1 = \cfrac{a_1 r_0 + r_{-1}}{a_1 s_0 + s_{-1}}$ Earlier this was found

equal to $\cfrac{a_1}{1}$.

Equating corresponding parts yields:
$a_1 r_0 + r_{-1} = a_1$
Therefore, $r_0 = 1$ and $r_{-1} = 0$
also, $a_1 s_0 + s_{-1} = 1$
Therefore, $s_0 = 0$ and $s_{-1} = 1$

Have students convert $\frac{117}{41}$ to the equivalent

continued fraction, $2 + \cfrac{1}{1 + \cfrac{1}{5 + \cfrac{1}{1 + \cfrac{1}{5}}}}$

Now set up a table:

Convergents

n	-1	0	1	2	3	4	5
a_n			2	1	5	1	5
r_n	0	1	2	3	17	20	117
$c_n = \frac{r_n}{s_n}$	1	0	1	1	6	7	41

The first two columns for r_n and s_n are constant. However, the other values vary with the particular fraction. The values of a_n are taken directly from the continued fractions. Each value of r_n and s_n is obtained from the general formula derived earlier. To check if this chart was constructed properly students should notice that the last convergent is in fact the original improper fraction.

An inspection of the various cross-products suggests: $r_n \cdot s_{n-1} - r_{n-1} \cdot s_n = (-1)^n$
With this background material learned, the students are now ready to apply their knowledge of continued fractions to solving Diophantine equations of the form $ax + by = k$, where the greatest common factor of a and b is a factor of k. First they should form an *improper* fraction using the two coefficients, say $\frac{a}{b}$. Then convert this fraction to a

continued fraction: $\frac{a}{b} = \frac{r_n}{s_n}$

Using the previously developed formula:

$$r_n \cdot s_{n-1} - r_{n-1} \cdot s_n = (-1)^n$$

and substituting: $a \cdot s_{n-1} - b \cdot r_{n-1} = 1$
(or multiply by -1.)   Now multiplying by k:
$a(k \cdot s_{n-1}) - b(k \cdot r_{n-1}) = k$.
Thus, $x = k \cdot s_{n-1}$, and $y = -k \cdot r_{n-1}$ is a solution of the Diophantine equation.
For example, consider the Diophantine equation:
$$41x - 117y = 3.$$
After setting up the above table, the $n-1$ convergent is used. That is, $r_{n-1} = 20$ and $s_{n-1} = 7$. The above relationship:
$a(k \cdot s_{n-1}) - b(k \cdot r_{n-1}) = k$
yields with appropriate substitution:
$41(3 \cdot 20) - 117(3 \cdot 7) = 3$
Thus one solution of $41x - 117y = 3$ is $x = 60$ and $y = 21$.

In order to find the remaining solutions the following scheme is used.
Subtract $41(60) - 117(21) = 3$ from $41x - 117y = 3$ to obtain $41(x-60) - 117(y-21) = 0$
Therefore, $41(x-60) = 117(y-21)$;

$$\text{or} \quad \frac{x-60}{117} = \frac{y-21}{41} = t$$

Thus, $t = \dfrac{x-60}{117}$ and $\boxed{x = 117t + 60}$

Also $t = \dfrac{y-21}{41}$ and $\boxed{y = 41t + 21}$

A table of solutions may then be constructed.

t	...	-2	-1	0	1	2	...
x	...	-174	-57	60	177	294	...
y	...	-61	-20	21	62	103	...

Postassessment

Have students change each of the following improper fractions to equivalent continued fractions.

1. $\dfrac{37}{13}$ 2. $\dfrac{47}{23}$ 3. $\dfrac{173}{61}$

Have students solve each of the following Diophantine equations and then determine how many (if any) positive solutions exist.

4. $7x - 31y = 2$ 6. $5x - 2y = 4$
5. $18x - 53y = 3$ 7. $123x - 71y = 2$

88   Simplifying Expressions Involving Infinity

This unit presents simple algebraic methods (appropriate for elementary algebra students) to solve seemingly difficult problems involving infinity.

Performance Objective

Given an algebraic problem involving infinity, students will use a simple algebraic method to solve the problem.

Preassessment

Students should be able to work with radical equations and quadratic equations.

Teaching Strategies

Offer the following problem to your students for solution:
Find the value of x if

$$x^{x^{x^{x^{\cdot^{\cdot^{\cdot}}}}}} = 2.$$

Most students' first reaction will be one of bewilderment. Since they have probably never worked with an infinite expression they are somewhat overwhelmed. Students may try to substitute into the expression values for x, in order to estimate an answer to the problem. Before they are entirely frustrated, begin by

explaining the infinite nature of the expression. Explain also that

$$3^{3^{3}} \neq 27^{3} = 19{,}683 \text{ but rather } 3^{3^{3}} = 3^{27} = 7{,}625{,}597{,}484{,}989.$$

Now have your students inspect the original expression in the following way: if

$x^{x^{x^{x^{\cdot^{\cdot}}}}} = 2$, then, since there are an infinite number of x's, one x less would not affect the expression. Therefore the exponent of the first x (lowest base) is 2.

Thus, this expression simplifies to $x^2 = 2$, and $x = \sqrt{2}$. Students should be asked to consider the possibility of $x < 0$.

It would be natural for students to wonder if they could compose a similar problem by replacing 2 with, say, 5 or 7. Without elaborating, indicate to them that values to replace 2 may not be chosen at random, and that in fact these replacement values may not exceed e (i.e. the base of the natural system of logarithms, approximately 2.7182818284 . . .).

To reinforce the scheme used in the solution of the above problem, have students consider the value of the nest of radicals

$$\sqrt{5 + \sqrt{5 + \sqrt{5 + \sqrt{5 + \sqrt{5 + \ldots}}}}}$$

In order to find x, where

$x = \sqrt{5 + \sqrt{5 + \sqrt{5 + \sqrt{5 + \sqrt{5 + \ldots}}}}}$, have students realize that nothing is lost by deleting the first 5 of this nest of radicals, since there are an infinite number of them. Thus

$x = \sqrt{5 + \underbrace{\sqrt{5 + \sqrt{5 + \sqrt{5 + \sqrt{5 + \ldots}}}}}_{= x}}$

or $x = \sqrt{5 + x}$, which is a simple radical equation. Students merely square both sides of the equation and solve the resulting quadratic equation:

$$x^2 = 5 + x$$
$$x^2 - x - 5 = 0$$
$$x = \frac{1 \pm \sqrt{21}}{2}$$

Since x is positive, $x = \dfrac{1 + \sqrt{21}}{2} \approx 2.79$.

An alternative approach to evaluating a nest of radicals is to first square both sides of the original equation to get

$x^2 = 5 + \sqrt{5 + \sqrt{5 + \sqrt{5 + \ldots}}}$ . . . and then substitute x, so that $x^2 = 5 + x$. The rest is as in the previous method.

It is important that you stress inspecting the reasonability of the value of the nest of radicals. That is, should the value be positive or negative, real or imaginary, etc.

Another application of this method of evaluating expressions involving infinity is with continued fractions. Before introducing infinite continued fractions, you ought to refresh your students' memories about continued fractions. You may wish to have them write $\dfrac{13}{5}$ as a continued fraction:

$$\frac{13}{5} = 2 + \frac{3}{5} = 2 + \frac{1}{\frac{5}{3}} = 2 + \frac{1}{1 + \frac{2}{3}}$$

$$= 2 + \frac{1}{1 + \frac{1}{\frac{3}{2}}} = 2 + \frac{1}{1 + \frac{1}{1 + \frac{1}{2}}}$$

Further, you may also want to have them simplify the continued fraction $1 + \dfrac{1}{2 + \dfrac{1}{3 + \dfrac{1}{4}}}$

$$1 + \frac{1}{2 + \frac{1}{3 + \frac{1}{4}}} = 1 + \frac{1}{2 + \frac{1}{\frac{13}{4}}} = 1 + \frac{1}{2 + \frac{4}{13}}$$

$$= 1 + \frac{1}{\frac{30}{13}} = 1 + \frac{13}{30} = \frac{43}{13}$$

Now have students consider the infinite continued fraction: $1 + \dfrac{1}{1 + \dfrac{1}{1 + \dfrac{1}{1 + \dfrac{1}{1 + \ldots}}}}$

They will soon realize that the previous method of simplification will no longer work. At this point you would show them the following method:

Let $x = 1 + \dfrac{1}{1 + \dfrac{1}{1 + \dfrac{1}{1 + \ldots}}}$

Once again deleting the first "part" of the infinite continued fraction will not affect its value (because of the nature of infinity).

Therefore $x = 1 + \dfrac{1}{\underbrace{1 + \dfrac{1}{1 + \dfrac{1}{1 + \ldots}}}_{= x}}$

or $x = 1 + \dfrac{1}{x}$, which yields $x^2 = x + 1$

$$x^2 - x - 1 = 0$$

and $x = \dfrac{1 \pm \sqrt{5}}{2}$, however since $x > 0$, $x = \dfrac{1 + \sqrt{5}}{2}$. Some of your students may recognize this value as that of the golden ratio.

More advanced students might wonder how a non-repeating infinite expression is evaluated. For these students you may wish to present the following:

Evaluate $\sqrt{1 + 2\sqrt{1 + 3\sqrt{1 + 4\sqrt{1 + 5\sqrt{1 + \ldots}}}}}$.

To evaluate this expression some preliminary work must first be done. Since

$(n+2)^2 = n^2 + 4n + 4 = 1 + (n+1)(n+3)$,

$n + 2 = \sqrt{1 + (n+1)(n+3)}$.

$n(n+2) = n\sqrt{1 + (n+1)(n+3)}$

Let $f(n) = n(n+2)$

then $f(n+1) = (n+1)(n+3)$

Thus $f(n) = n\sqrt{1 + (n+1)(n+3)}$

$f(n) = n\sqrt{1 + f(n+1)}$

$f(n) = n\sqrt{1 + (n+1)\sqrt{1 + f(n+2)}}$

$f(n) = n\sqrt{1 + (n+1)\sqrt{1 + (n+2)\sqrt{1 + f(n+3)}}}$,
and so on.

Now if $n = 1$, then $f(n) = 1(1+2) = 3$ and $3 =$

$1\sqrt{1 + (1+1)\sqrt{1 + (1+2)\sqrt{1 + (1+3)\sqrt{1 + \ldots}}}}$

$= 1\sqrt{1 + 2\sqrt{1 + 3\sqrt{1 + 4\sqrt{1 + \ldots}}}}$

As a result of presenting the methods considered in this model, your students should have a more solid concept of infinite expressions.

Postassessment

1. Simplify: $\sqrt{7 + \sqrt{7 + \sqrt{7 + \sqrt{7 + \ldots}}}}$

2. Simplify: $2 + \cfrac{1}{3 + \cfrac{1}{3 + \cfrac{1}{3 + \cfrac{1}{3 + \ldots}}}}$

3. Simplify: $1 + \cfrac{1}{2 + \cfrac{1}{1 + \cfrac{1}{2 + \cfrac{1}{1 + \cfrac{1}{2 + \ldots}}}}}$

89 Continued Fraction Expansion of Irrational Numbers

Performance Objectives
1. Given an irrational number, students will write an equivalent continued fraction.
2. Given an infinite expansion, students will get back to the irrational number.
Preassessment
Students should be familiar with continued fractions.

Teaching Strategies
The procedure for expanding an irrational number is essentially the same as that used for rational numbers. Let x be the given irrational number. Find a_1, the greatest integer less than x, and express x in the form

$$x = a_1 + \frac{1}{x_2}, \quad 0 < \frac{1}{x_2} < 1$$

where the number

$x_2 = \dfrac{1}{x - a_1} > 1$ is irrational; for, if an integer is subtracted from an irrational number, the difference and the reciprocal of the difference are irrational.

Find a_2, the largest integer less than x_2 and express x_2 in the form

$$x_2 = a_2 + \frac{1}{x_3}, \quad 0 < \frac{1}{x_3} < 1, \quad a_2 \geq 1$$

where again the number

$$x_3 = \frac{1}{x_2 - a_2} > 1$$

This calculation may be repeated indefinitely, producing in succession the equations

$$x = a_1 + \frac{1}{x_2}, \quad x_2 > 1$$

$$x_2 = a_2 + \frac{1}{x_3}, \quad x_3 > 1, \quad a_2 \geq 1$$

$$x_3 = a_3 + \frac{1}{x_4}, \quad x_4 > 1, \quad a_3 \geq 1$$

$$\vdots \qquad \vdots \qquad \vdots$$

$$x_n = a_n + \frac{1}{x_{n+1}}, \quad x_{n+1} > 1, \quad a_n \geq 1$$

$$\vdots \qquad \vdots \qquad \vdots$$

where $a_1, a_2, a_3, \ldots, a_n, \ldots$ are all integers and the numbers $x, x_2, x_3, \ldots$ are all irrational. This process cannot end because the only way this could happen would be for some integer a_n to be equal to x_n. This is impossible since each successive x_i is irrational.

Substituting x_2 from the second equation above into the first equation, then x_3 from the third into this result, and so on, produces the required infinite simple continued fraction

$$x = a_1 + \frac{1}{x_2} = a_1 + \cfrac{1}{a_2 + \cfrac{1}{x_3}} = a_1 + \cfrac{1}{a_2 + \cfrac{1}{a_3 + \cfrac{1}{x_4}}}$$

or sometimes written as $x = [a_1, a_2, a_3, a_4, \ldots]$, where the three dots indicate that the process is continued indefinitely.

Example 1. Expand $\sqrt{3}$ into an infinite simple continued fraction.

Solution: The largest integer less than $\sqrt{3}$ is 1. Therefore, $a_1 = 1$ and

$$\sqrt{3} = 1 + \frac{1}{x_2}$$

Solving this equation for x_2, we get

$$x_2 = \frac{1}{\sqrt{3} - 1} \cdot \frac{\sqrt{3} + 1}{\sqrt{3} + 1} = \frac{\sqrt{3} + 1}{2}$$

Therefore: $\sqrt{3} = a_1 + \frac{1}{x_2} = 1 + \cfrac{1}{\cfrac{\sqrt{3} + 1}{2}}$

$x_2 = a_2 + \frac{1}{x_3}$ where $a_2 = 1$, since it is the largest integer less than $\frac{\sqrt{3} + 1}{2}$

Therefore:

$$x_3 = \cfrac{1}{\cfrac{\sqrt{3} + 1}{2} - 1} = \frac{2}{\sqrt{3} - 1} \cdot \frac{\sqrt{3} + 1}{\sqrt{3} + 1}$$

$$= \sqrt{3} + 1$$

$$\sqrt{3} = 1 + \cfrac{1}{1 + \cfrac{1}{\sqrt{3} + 1}}$$

Continuing this process:

$x_3 = 2 + \frac{1}{x_4}$, $a_3 = 2$ since 2 is the largest integer less than $\sqrt{3} + 1$.

$$x_4 = \frac{1}{\sqrt{3} - 1} \cdot \frac{\sqrt{3} + 1}{\sqrt{3} + 1} = \frac{\sqrt{3} + 1}{2}$$

$$\sqrt{3} = 1 + \cfrac{1}{1 + \cfrac{1}{2 + \cfrac{1}{\cfrac{\sqrt{3} + 1}{2}}}}$$

Since $x_4 = \frac{\sqrt{3} + 1}{2}$ is the same as $x_2 = \frac{\sqrt{3} + 1}{2}$, x_5 will produce the same result as x_3, namely $\sqrt{3} + 1$. All the following partial quotients will be 1,2,1,2 and the infinite expansion of $\sqrt{3}$ will be

$$\sqrt{3} = 1 + \cfrac{1}{1 + \cfrac{1}{2 + \cfrac{1}{1 + \cfrac{1}{2 + \cdots}}}} \qquad = [1,1,2,1,2,\ldots] = [1,\overline{1,2}].$$

The bar over the 1 and 2 indicates that the numbers 1 and 2 are repeated indefinitely.

Example 2. Find the infinite continued fraction expansion for

$$x = \frac{\sqrt{30} - 2}{13}$$

Solution: Since $\sqrt{30}$ is between 5 and 6, the largest integer less than x is $a_1 = 0$. Then

$$x = \frac{\sqrt{30} - 2}{13} = 0 + \frac{1}{x_2}$$

where $x_2 = \frac{1}{x} = \frac{13}{\sqrt{30} - 2} \cdot \frac{\sqrt{30} + 2}{\sqrt{30} + 2}$

$$= \frac{\sqrt{30} + 2}{2} > 1$$

The largest integer less than x_2 is $a_2 = 3$, therefore,

$$x_2 = a_2 + \frac{1}{x_3} = 3 + \frac{1}{x_3}$$

Therefore $x_3 = \cfrac{1}{x_2 - 3} = \cfrac{1}{\cfrac{\sqrt{30} + 2}{2} - 3}$

$$= \frac{2}{\sqrt{30} - 4} \cdot \frac{\sqrt{30} + 4}{\sqrt{30} + 4}$$

$$= \frac{2(\sqrt{30} + 4)}{14} = \frac{\sqrt{30} + 4}{7}$$

The largest integer less than x_3 is $a_3 = 1$.

Therefore $x_4 = \cfrac{1}{x_3 - 1} = \cfrac{1}{\cfrac{\sqrt{30} + 4}{7} - 1}$

$$= \frac{7}{\sqrt{30} - 3} \cdot \frac{\sqrt{30} + 3}{\sqrt{30} + 3} = \frac{\sqrt{30} + 3}{3}$$

In a similar way we get $x_5 = \frac{\sqrt{30} + 3}{7}$, $x_6 = \frac{\sqrt{30} + 4}{2}$, and $x_7 = \frac{\sqrt{30} + 4}{7} = x_3$

Further investigation will show that the sequence 1,2,1,4 repeats. The required expansion is

$$x = 0 + \frac{1}{x_2} = 0 + \cfrac{1}{3 + \cfrac{1}{x_3}} = 0 + \cfrac{1}{3 + \cfrac{1}{1 + \cfrac{1}{x_4}}}$$

$$= 0 + \cfrac{1}{3 + \cfrac{1}{1 + \cfrac{1}{2 + \cfrac{1}{x_5}}}} = 0 + \cfrac{1}{3 + \cfrac{1}{1 + \cfrac{1}{2 + \cfrac{1}{1 + \cfrac{1}{x_6}}}}}$$

$$= 0 + \cfrac{1}{3 + \cfrac{1}{1 + \cfrac{1}{2 + \cfrac{1}{1 + \cfrac{1}{4 + \cfrac{1}{x_7}}}}}}$$

so finally we obtain

$$x = \frac{\sqrt{30} - 2}{13} = [0,3,\overline{1,2,1,4}].$$

Students may prove that a given infinite continued fraction actually represents an irrational number. Consider showing that $[2,\overline{2,4}]$ represents $\sqrt{6}$. Begin by writing:

Let $x = 2 + \cfrac{1}{2 + \cfrac{1}{4 + \cfrac{1}{2 + \cfrac{1}{4 + \cdots}}}}$

where $y = 2 + \cfrac{1}{4 + \cfrac{1}{2 + \cfrac{1}{4 + \cdot}}}$

Therefore $y = 2 + \cfrac{1}{4 + \cfrac{1}{y}} = 2 + \cfrac{y}{4y + 1}$

Solving for y yields: $\dfrac{2 + \sqrt{6}}{2}$

However $x = 2 + \dfrac{1}{y} = 2 + \dfrac{2}{2 + \sqrt{6}}$

Hence, $x = 2 + \sqrt{6} - 2 = \sqrt{6}$

Postassessment

Have students change each of the following into an infinite simple continued fraction.

    1. $\sqrt{2}$ 2. $\sqrt{43}$ 3. $\dfrac{25 + \sqrt{53}}{22}$

Have students show that the infinite continued fraction $[\overline{3,6}] = \sqrt{10}$.

90   The Farey Sequence

This unit presents a discussion of a rather unusual sequence of numbers. This topic can be presented to students at various levels. However, the emphasis will change with the various ability and maturity levels of the students.

Performance Objectives

(1) Students will show that the fraction immediately before $\frac{1}{2}$ and its immediate successor of the Farey Sequence are complementary.

(2) Students will establish the relationship between π and the number of terms in the Farey Sequence.

Preassessment

Using the sequence of fractions below, have students find the sum of the two fractions:

a. fifth term to the left and fifth term to the right of $\frac{1}{2}$;

b. third term to the left and third term to the right of $\frac{1}{2}$;

c. second term to the left and second term to the right of $\frac{1}{2}$;

$$\frac{1}{7}, \frac{1}{6}, \frac{1}{5}, \frac{1}{4}, \frac{2}{7}, \frac{1}{3}, \frac{2}{5}, \frac{3}{7}, \frac{1}{2}, \frac{4}{7}, \frac{3}{5}, \frac{2}{3},$$
$$\frac{5}{7}, \frac{3}{4}.$$

Ask students to generalize their results.

Teaching Strategies

A review of the preassessment activity will indicate that the three sums students were asked to find all resulted in 1. That is,

$\dfrac{1}{4} + \dfrac{3}{4} = 1; \dfrac{1}{3} + \dfrac{2}{3} = 1$ and $\dfrac{2}{5} + \dfrac{3}{5} = 1$.

We shall refer to a pair of fractions whose sum is 1 as *complementary*. Let us now inspect the given sequence.

If we list all proper common fractions in their lowest terms in order of magnitude up to some arbitrarily assigned limit—such as with denominators not exceeding 7—we have the 17 fractions

$$\frac{1}{7}, \frac{1}{6}, \frac{1}{5}, \frac{1}{4}, \frac{2}{7}, \frac{1}{3}, \frac{2}{5}, \frac{3}{7}, \frac{1}{2}, \frac{4}{7}, \frac{3}{5}, \frac{2}{3},$$
$$\frac{5}{7}, \frac{3}{4}, \frac{4}{5}, \frac{5}{6}, \frac{6}{7}.$$

This is called the Farey Sequence. The Farey Sequence F_n, of order n, is defined as the *ordered set consisting of $\frac{0}{1}$, the irreducible proper fractions with denominators from 2 to* n, *arranged in order of increasing magnitude, and $\frac{1}{1}$*. There are many characteristic properties of the Farey Sequence. One is the relationship students discovered earlier: fractions equidistant from $\frac{1}{2}$ are complementary; that is, their sum equals one. Another interesting relationship involves the number of terms in the Farey Sequence of order n and π.

Before beginning a development of this sequence, students should be given some background on the Farey Sequence. They should be told that Farey, in 1816, discovered the sequence while perusing lengthy tables of decimal quotients. Apparently the numerator of any fraction in the Farey Sequence is obtained by adding the numerators of the fractions on each side of it, and similarly for the denominators. Since the result must be in lowest terms, this holds true for triplet:

$\frac{1}{3}, \frac{2}{5}, \frac{3}{7}$ where $\frac{3+1}{3+7} = \frac{4}{10} = \frac{2}{5}$.

Students will see that the sum of fractions equidistant from $\frac{1}{2}$ equals 1. This can be proved many ways.

Suppose that $\frac{\ell}{n}$ is a number of the series which is less than $\frac{1}{2}$ and such that ℓ and n are relatively prime. Comparing the corresponding number of the other side of $\frac{1}{2}$, we find $\frac{(n-\ell)}{n}$. Since this belongs to the Farey Sequence it is necessary that g.c.d. $(n-\ell,n) = 1$. Supposing that $(n-\ell)$ and n are not relatively prime, then $n - \ell = qd$ and $n = qd + \ell$. Also $n = rd$ and thus $rd = qd + \ell$. Therefore d divides ℓ and consequently d divides $(n-\ell)$ for d divides n. This however contradicts the fact that $((n-\ell)/n)$ was in its lowest terms (which is the definition of terms in the Farey Sequence) and therefore g.c.d. $(n-\ell,n) = 1$.

Now to prove that $\frac{\ell}{n} + \frac{a}{b} = 1$. Let $\frac{\ell}{n}$ be the immediate predecessor of $\frac{1}{2}$. If there was another term immediately succeeding $\frac{1}{2}$ and belonging to F_n, then the fractions are arranged as follows:

$$\frac{\ell}{n}, \frac{1}{2}, \frac{a}{b} \text{ where } \frac{1}{2} = \frac{\ell + a}{n + b}$$

(one of the properties of the sequence). To prove that $\frac{\ell}{m} + \frac{a}{b} = 1$, $\frac{a}{b}$ must be in lowest terms if it belongs to F_n. If two fractions whose sum is 1 are in lowest terms, then their denominators are equal. Thus if $\frac{\ell}{n} + \frac{a}{b} = 1$, b must equal n. Therefore $\frac{\ell + a}{n} = 1$ and $\ell + a = n$, or $a = n - \ell$. But $\frac{\ell}{n}$ was the immediate predecessor of $\frac{1}{2}$ and $\frac{a}{b} = \frac{n - \ell}{n}$. Thus the immediate predecessor of $\frac{1}{2}$ and its immediate successor are complementary since their sum equals 1.

Another very interesting property results between π and the sum of the terms in the Farey Sequence. The number of fractions of order n is obtained as follows. Since the fractions are all in lowest terms, it follows that for a given denominator b, the number of numerators is the number of integers less than, and prime to, b. Students should then see the number of fractions N, in the Farey Sequence is equal to $\phi 2 + \phi 3 + \phi 4 + \ldots + \phi n$, where ϕn is the number of positive integers less than or equal to n that are relatively prime to n. If $n = 7$, we have N $= \phi 2 + \phi 3 + \phi 4 + \phi 5 + \phi 6 + \phi 7 = 1 + 2 + 2 + 4 + 2 + 6$. The value of N increases rapidly as n increases and when $n = 100$, N $= 3043$. Thus there are many irreducible common fractions with numerators and denominators not exceeding 100.

There is a remarkable formula involving the ϕ function and π (the ratio of the circumference to the diameter of the circle).

The ϕ function refers to Euler's function. The sum of the Farey Sequence can be written by using a formula in terms of Euler's function ϕ. If $\frac{h}{k}$ is a term in the Farey Sequence then g.c.d. $(h,k) = 1$. For any fixed number $k > 1$ the number of terms of the form $\frac{h}{k}$ is ϕk. It can be demonstrated that the sum $\phi(1) + \phi(2) + \ldots + \phi(n)$ is approximated by the expression $3n^2/\pi^2$, the approximation becoming more and more accurate as n increases. Except for the first term this sum represents the number of terms, N in a Farey Sequence of order n. Since we know the value of π to any desired degree of accuracy, this means we can find approximately the number of terms in a Farey Sequence without evaluating separately $\phi(1)$, $\phi(2)$, $\phi 3 \ldots \phi(n)$. Thus for $n = 100$ we would have N $= 3 \cdot 100^2/\pi^2 = 3039.6355 \ldots$ whereas the true value is 3043.

Thus the number of terms of the Farey series approaches $\frac{3n^2}{\pi^2}$.

Postassessment

1. Given $n = 200$, $n = 8$, find the number of terms in the Farey Sequence using the expression $\frac{3n^2}{\pi^2}$.

2. Have students find other properties of the Farey Sequence.

91   The Parabolic Envelope

This unit describes briefly the mechanical construction of the parabolic envelope and shows how students can use the envelope to derive a host of related curves.

Performance Objectives

Using the envelope as a foundation, students will draw a variety of curves by different techniques without point by point plotting from an equation. In the process, they will be introduced to the visual concepts of an envelope, evolute and pedal to a given curve.

Preassessment

Students should have completed a basic geometry course and be familiar with the conic sections.

Teaching Strategies

Have your students construct tangents to a parabola in the following manner:

Draw an angle of any measure, and divide each side of the angle into the same number of equally-spaced intervals. In Figure 1, we have an angle, A, of measure 50°, divided on each side into 17 equally-spaced, numbered intervals. Starting, as we did, at the lower left of the angle, lines were drawn connecting points 1

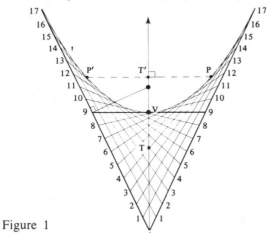

Figure 1

to 17, 2 to 16, 3 to 15, and so on, terminating with 17-1, (where the notation "17-1" means the segment connecting point 17 to point 1, or conversely). The resulting array of lines are tangents which *envelope* a parabola.

The midpoint, V, of the line 9-9, is the *vertex* of the parabola, and 9-9 is the tangent to the parabola at V. A line from A to V, extended beyond V, is the parabola's *axis of symmetry,* and is also included in Figure 1. Ask students why 9-9 is the tangent perpendicular to AV.

Erect a perpendicular to either side of the angle at point 9. We state without proof that the intersection of this perpendicular with the axis of symmetry determines the *focus*, F, of the parabola. More ambitious students may wish to prove this. At any rate, it would be meaningful to mention the reflective and locus properties of the focus.

Specific points of tangency on the parabola can be visually approximated directly from Figure 1. They can be more exactly located from the fact that a tangent to the parabola intersects the axis at a distance from the vertex equal to the ordinate of the point of tangency. As an example in Figure 1, tangent 14-4 intersects the axis at T. Locate a point T′ on the axis above V such that TV = VT′. Draw a line through T′ parallel to 9-9 so as to intersect the envelope at P and P′, then P and P′ are the points on the parabola where 14-4 and 4-14 are tangent. Other points on the parabola can be determined in the same manner.

Evolute to the Parabola

Having located all such points of tangency P and P′ on the parabola, use a right-angled triangle or carpenter's square to erect perpendiculars at each of these points. These perpendiculars to a curve at the point of tangency are called *normals*. The envelope of all such normals defines the *evolute* to the curve; that is, the normals are then tangents to the evolute of the given curve. Thus, the evolute to the parabola can be shown to be a one-cusped curve called a *semi-cubic parabola*. This is shown in Figure 2.

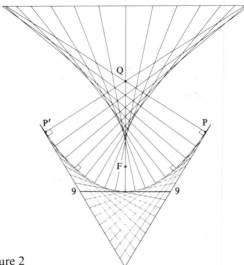

Figure 2

To realize an accurately drawn evolute, utilize the symmetry of the parabola about the axis. Hence, normals to P and P intersect at Q on the axis of symmetry.

Pedal Curves to the Parabola

Figure 3 shows a given curve, C, and a fixed point, F, on or in the neighborhood of C. Dropping perpendiculars from F to each of the tangents to the curve, we find that the locus of the feet of the perpendiculars, P, defines the *pedal curve* to the given curve with respect to F. For a given curve, different choices of F will result in different pedal curves.

Figure 3

Now let the focus, F, of the parabola in Figure 1 be the fixed point for consideration. If perpendiculars are dropped to each of the tangents, students will note that the locus of the feet of these perpendiculars is the line 9-9. That is, the tangent to the vertex is the pedal curve to a parabola with respect to its focus. Conversely, it can be shown that a perpendicular erected to a tangent with 9-9 will pass through F. This latter fact justifies the technique used earlier to locate the parabola's focus. (Students should recall that to prove a locus, a biconditional statement must be proved.)

Next let V be the fixed point. From V, we drop perpendiculars to each of the tangents obtained in Figure 1. The locus of the feet is shown in Figure 4 as a curve having a cusp at V, and symmetric to the axis. We state without proof that the locus is the *cissoid of Diocles*. Locate F' on the axis, below V, such that FV = VF'. Through F' draw a line parallel to 9-9. This line is the parabola's *directrix*, and can be shown to be the asymptotic line which the cissoid approaches.

At this point you may wish to discuss the various properties of a parabola, such as its reflective properties. You may also define the parabola in terms of a locus, now that the focus and direction have been determined. Thus, a parabola is the locus of points equidistant from a point (the focus), and a line (the directrix), not containing the point. Folding waxed paper clearly demonstrates this locus. Draw a line and an external point on a piece of wax paper. Fold the wax paper repeatedly in such a manner that the point is superimposed on the line. The creases produced form a parabolic envelope.

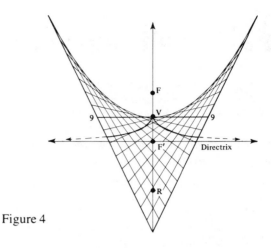

Figure 4

Postassessment

Have students draw two additional pedal curves to the parabola. Tell them to use the following as a guide:

a.) Let F' be the fixed point. The pedal curve will be seen to the *Right Strophoid*.

b.) Locate R (Figure 4), the reflection of F through the directrix such that FF' = F'R. Have R be the fixed point. The pedal curve is the *trisectrix of MacLaurin*.

c.) The *contrapedal* to a given curve is the locus of the feet of the perpendiculars from a given fixed point to the normals to a given curve. In Figure 2, with F as fixed point, determine the locus of the contrapedal. From F, drop perpendiculars to each of the normals you drew to obtain the evolute. The locus of the contrapedal is a parabola whose turning point concurs with F.

d.) Confirm by measurement that the contrapedal locus in c.) is identical to the locus of the midpoints of the segment of a normal from the point of tangency on the parabola to the point of intersection of the normal and the parabola's axis of symmetry.

References

Lockwood, E. H., *A Book of Curves*, Cambridge University Press, 1961.

Zwikker, C., *The Advanced Geometry of Plane Curves and their Applications*, Dover Publications, 1963.

92 Application of Congruence to Divisibility

Performance Objectives

1. *Given any integer, students will determine its prime factors without doing any division.*

2. *Students will produce rules for testing divisibility by natural numbers other than those presented in this unit.*

Preassessment

1. Have students find the prime factors of each of the following: (a) 144 (b) 840 (c) 360
2. Have students indicate, without doing any division, which of the following numbers are divisible by 2, 3, and 5: (1) 234 (b) 315

Teaching Strategies

Begin the lesson by introducing the concept of number congruences. Two numbers which have the same remainder when divided by 7 are said to be *congruent modulo 7.*

For example, 23 and 303 give the same remainder when divided by 7. Therefore, we say that 23 and 303 are congruent modula 7. This statement can be represented by symbols as follows: $23 \equiv 303$ (mod 7).

In general, two integers a and b are congruent modulo m (written as $a \equiv b$ (mod. m), if they give the same non-negative remainder when divided by the integer $m \neq 0$.

Because of this definition, we have the following double implication:

$$a \equiv b \pmod{m} \iff \begin{cases} a = mk + r \\ \\ b = mk' + r \end{cases} \quad 0 \leq r < |m|$$

The symbol "$\equiv$" was first used in 1801 by Karl Friedrich Gauss (1777—1855), the famous German mathematician. It is suggested by its similarity with the ordinary equality. It has nothing to do with geometric congruence. The sign $\not\equiv$ means "is not congruent to."

Example 1: $17 \equiv -4 \pmod{7}$

Because: $\begin{array}{l} 17 = 72 + 3 \\ -4 = 7 \cdot (-1) + 3 \end{array}$

In this example, we must use -1 as a quotient. If we use 0, the remainder would be negative against the definition of congruence.

Example 2: $a \equiv 0 \pmod{a}$ This is true because they both give the same remainder 0.

Another Definition of Congruences:

Two numbers are congruent modulo m, *if and only if their difference is divisible by* m. We want to prove that: $a \equiv b \pmod{m} \iff a - b = \overline{m}$ ($\overline{m}$ reads "a multiple of m.")

Proof

If $a \equiv b \pmod{m} \iff \begin{array}{l} a = mk_1 + r \\ b = mk_2 + r \end{array}$

Subtracting: $a - b = m(k_1 - k_2)$ or $a - b = \overline{m}$

Therefore: $a \equiv b \pmod{m} \Rightarrow a - b = \overline{m}$

Conversely: if $a - b = \overline{m} \Rightarrow a = b + \overline{m}$
$$\Rightarrow a = b + km \quad (1)$$

But $b = mk' + r$ (2). Thus, from (1) and (2) we have:
$$a = b + km = (mk' + r) + km$$
$$= m(k' + k) + r$$
$$= mk'' + r \,(3)$$

From (2) and (3) we then have:

$\begin{array}{l} a = mk'' + r \\ b = mk' + r \end{array}$ therefore: $a \equiv b \pmod{m}$

Thus, $a - b = \overline{m} \Rightarrow a \equiv b \pmod{m}$

Therefore, $a \equiv b \pmod{m} \Rightarrow a - b = \overline{m}$, *Q.E.D.*

Students should now be ready to consider the following:

Some Elementary Properties of Congruences

If $a \equiv b \pmod{m}$ and $c \equiv d \pmod{m}$, then:

   I) $a + c \equiv b + d \pmod{m}$

   II) $ac \equiv bd \pmod{m}$

   III) $ka \equiv kb \pmod{m}$ *for every integer k.*

These properties follow from the definition of congruences. We shall prove II); the others can be proved by following the same method:

Since $a \equiv b \pmod{m} \iff a = b + \overline{m}$ (1)

and $c \equiv d \pmod{m} \iff c = d + \overline{m}$ (2)

Then, multiplying (1) and (2):
$$ac = bd + b\overline{m} + d\overline{m}$$
$$= bd + (b + d)\overline{m}$$
$$= bd + \overline{m}$$

Therefore, $ac \equiv bd \pmod{m}$.

Another interesting aspect of modular system are *power residues*. The *power residues* of a number a with respect to another number m are *the remainders obtained when the successive powers a^0, a^1, $a^2, \ldots$, of a are divided by m.*

Example 3: Find the power residues of **5** with respect to 3. Since:

$5^0 : 3 = \quad 1 : 3 = \quad 0 \cdot 3 + 1$ therefore $r_0 = 1$.

$5^1 : 3 = \quad 5 : 3 = \quad 1 \cdot 3 + 2$ therefore $r_1 = 2$.

$5^2 : 3 = \quad 25 : 3 = \quad 8 \cdot 3 + 1$ therefore $r_2 = 1$.

$5^3 : 3 = 125 : 3 = 41 \cdot 3 + 2$ therefore $r_3 = 2$.

and so on.

Therefore, the power residues of 5 with respect to 3 will be: 1, 2, 1, 2, ... Have students consider why no number other than 1 or 2 appears in this sequence.

Example 4: Find the power residues of 10 modulo 2. Also indicate the different congruences. We have:

$10^0: 2 = 1 : 2 = 0 \cdot 2 + 1$ therefore $r_0 = 1$.
$10^1: 2 = 10 : 2 = 5 \cdot 2 + 0$ therefore $r_1 = 0$.
$10^2: 2 = 100 : 2 = 50 \cdot 2 + 0$ therefore $r_2 = 0$.
Therefore, the power residues are $1, 0, 0, \ldots$.
Thus, the congruences will be:

$$10^0 \equiv 1, \ 10^1 \equiv 0, \ 10^2 \equiv 0, \ldots, \ (\text{mod } 2)$$

Students should be able to justify the appearance of this sequence.

Once students have mastered the concept of power residues, they should be ready to consider various *properties of power residues*.

I) The power residue of a^0, when divided by m, is always 1.

Proof: We have that: $a^0 : m = 1 : m = 0 \cdot 1 + 1$. i.e., a remainder of 1. Hence, $a^0 \equiv 1 \ (\text{mod } m)$.

II) If a power residue is zero, then the following power residues are also zero.

Proof: Let a^h give a zero power residue when divided by m. Then, $a^h \equiv 0 \ (\text{mod } m)$ If both sides are multiplied by a, we have: $a \cdot a^h \equiv a \cdot 0 \ (\text{mod } m)$ or $a^{h+1} \equiv 0 \ (\text{mod } m)$ Therefore, $a^{h+1}, a^{h+2}, \ldots$ will give zero power residues also. This was evident in example 4 above.

Criteria for Divisibility

Have students consider any number $N = a_n a_{n-1} \ldots a_2 a_1 a_0$ written in base 10. Therefore: $N = a_0 10^0 + a_1 10^1 + a_2 10^2 + \ldots + a_n 10^n$. Let $r_0, r_1, \ldots, r_n$ be the power residues of 10 $(\text{mod } m)$ Therefore, $10^0 \equiv 1, 10^1 \equiv r_1, \ldots, 10^n \equiv r_n \ (\text{mod } m)$ Have students multiply each congruence by $a_0, a_1, \ldots, a_n$, respectively, to get:
$a_0 10^0 \equiv a_0, a_1 10^1 \equiv a_1 r_1, \ldots, a_n 10^n \equiv a_n r_n \ (\text{mod } m)$ If they are added in order, we will get: $a_0 10^0 + \ldots + a_n 10^n \equiv a_0 + a_1 r_1 + a_2 r_2 + \ldots + a_n r_n \ (\text{mod } m)$ Thus, $N \equiv a_0 + a_1 r_1 + a_2 r_2 + \ldots + a_n r_n$.

From this last congruence, N will be divisible by m if and only if $a_0 + a_1 r_1 + \ldots + a_n r_n$ is divisble by m. This statement can be used to find the different criteria for divisibility the following way:

Divisibility by 2 and 5

We have for any number N that:
$N \equiv a_0 + a_1 r_1 + \ldots + a_n r_n \ (\text{mod } m)$. If students consider $m = 2$ (or $m = 5$), they will have that $r_1 = 0$ because $10^1 \equiv 0 \ (\text{mod } 2)$ (or mod 5) therefore, $r_2 = 0, r_3 = 0, \ldots$ Hence they will have $N \equiv a_0 \ (\text{mod } 2 \text{ or } 5)$. This means that: *A number is divisible by 2 or 5, if and only if its last digit is divisible by 2 or 5.*

Divisibility by 3 and 9

We have that: $10^0 \equiv 1, \ 10^1 \equiv 1, \ldots \ (\text{mod } 3 \text{ or } 9)$. Since $N \equiv a_0 + a_1 r_1 + a_2 r_2 + \ldots + a_n r_n \ (\text{mod } m)$. Thus, $N \equiv a_0 + a_1 + a_2 + \ldots + a_n \ (\text{mod } 3 \text{ or } 9)$. Therefore, a given number is divisible by 3 or 9, if and only if the sum of its digits is divisible by 3 or 9.

Divisibility by 11

Since $10^0 \equiv 1, \ 10^1 \equiv -1, \ 10^2 \equiv 1, \ldots, \ (\text{mod } 11)$ Hence, $N \equiv a_0 - a_1 + a_2 - \ldots + (-1)^n a_n \ (\text{mod } 11)$ Therefore, a given number is divisible by 11 if and only if the difference of the two sums of the alternate digits is divisible by 11.

The previous method will lead students to develop similar rules for testing divisibility by other primes. It should be emphasized and justified that a number is divisible by a composite number if it is divisible by each of its *relative prime* factors.

Therefore, if we want to determine if a number is divisible by 6, we only have to test its divisibility by 2 and 3.

With sufficient discussion students should be able to establish a comprehensive list of rules for testing divisibility as well as develop insight into some elementary theory of congruences.

Postassessment

Have students perform these exercises:
1) State a rule for testing divisibility by:
   (a) 4 and 25   (b) 7 (c) 13 (d) 101
2) Determine the prime factors of:
   (a) 1220 (b) 315 (c) 1001
3) Find the criteria for divisiblity by 6 and 11 in base 7.

93 Problem Solving—A Reverse Strategy

Geometry teachers are frequently asked, "How did you know which approach to take in order to prove these two line segments parallel?" Generally, the teacher would like to think that experience prompted the proper conclusion. This would, of course, be of no value to the questioning student. He or she would like to learn a definite procedure to follow. The teacher would be wise to describe to the student a reverse strategy which would have the student begin with the desired conclusion and discover each preceding step in order.

Performance Objective

Given a problem situation which lends itself to a reverse strategy of solution, students will employ this strategy to successfully solve the problem.

Preassessment

Have students solve the following problem:

If the sum of two numbers is 2, and the product of the same two numbers is 3, find the sum of the reciprocals of these numbers.

Teaching Strategies

A reverse strategy is certainly not new. It was considered by Pappus of Alexandria about 320 A.D. In Book VII of Pappus' *Collection* there is a rather complete description of the methods of "analysis" and "synthesis". T.L. Heath in his book, *A Manual of Greek Mathematics* (Oxford University Press, 1931, p. 452-3) provides a translation of Pappus' definitions of these terms:

Analysis takes that which is sought as if it were admitted and passes from it through its successive consequences to something which is admitted as the result of synthesis; for in analysis we assume that which is sought as if it were already done, and we inquire what it is from which this results, and again what is the antecedent cause of the latter, and so on, until, by so retracing our steps, we come upon something already known or belonging to the class of first principles, and such a method we call analysis as being solution backwards.

But in *synthesis,* reversing the process, we take as already done that which was last arrived at in the analysis and, by arranging in their natural order as consequences what before were antecedents, and successively connecting them one with another, we arrive finally at the construction of that which was sought; and this we call *synthesis.*

Unfortunately, this method has not received its due emphasis in the mathematics classroom. This discussion will reinforce the value of reverse strategy in problem solving.

To better understand this technique for problem solving, a number of appropriate problems will be presented. Discussion of their solutions should help students attain a better grasp of this method.

Let us first consider the following simple problem from basic geometry.

Problem 1:

Given: $\overline{AB} \cong \overline{DC}$

$\overline{AB} // \overline{DC}$

$\angle BAH \cong \angle DCG$

$\overline{BEGHFD}$

$\overline{GE} \cong \overline{HF}$

Prove: $\overline{AE} // \overline{CF}$

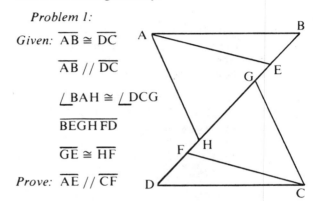

Solution: The first thoughts of a student trying to do this proof is to consider what information is given, and then what is to be proved. Having considered the given information, the poorly trained student will usually proceed blindly, proving segments, angles and triangles congruent until (if ever) he or she reaches the desired conclusion.

On the other hand, a well-trained student, after considering the given information, will immediately look at the desired conclusion and begin working in reverse from that conclusion ("analysis"). First this student will ask what methods there are for proving lines parallel. This will for the most part lead to proving angles congruent. In this proof clever students will realize that if they were able to prove $\angle AED \cong \angle CFB$, they would then be able to prove $\overline{AE}$ parallel to $\overline{CF}$. But how can they prove $\angle AED \cong \angle CFB$? Because of the type of training they receive, most students will generally react to this question by trying to find a pair of congruent triangles, which have $\angle AED$ and $\angle CFB$ as a pair of corresponding angles. Continuing this reverse approach, students must now locate such a pair of congruent triangles. It would be helpful if students could prove $\triangle AEH \cong \triangle CFG$, as these triangles have $\angle AED$ and $\angle CFB$ as a pair of corresponding angles. Can these triangles be proven congruent? Evidently not. All that students know about these triangles at this point is that $\overline{HE} \cong \overline{GF}$. Using this type of reasoning she or he soon will prove that $\triangle ABH \cong \triangle CDG$, which will help to prove $\triangle AEH$

$\cong \triangle CFG$. Then, by retracing steps of reverse reasoning in the opposite order ("synthesis") students will easily attain the desired conclusion. It is clear that reverse strategy was instrumental in formulating a path to the desired conclusion.

The reverse approach to solving a problem becomes dramatically stronger, when the resulting solution becomes significantly more elegant. As an example, let us consider the following problem offered in the preassessment.

Problem 2:

If the sum of two numbers is 2 and the product of these same two numbers is 3, find the sum of the reciprocals of these two numbers.

Solution: A first reaction after reading this problem would be to set up the equation: $x + y = 2$, and $xy = 3$. A well-trained student of algebra would promptly set out to solve these equations simultaneously. She or he may solve the first equation for y to get $y = 2 - x$, and then substitute appropriately in the second equation so that $x(2-x) = 3$ or $x^2 - 2x + 3 = 0$. As $x = 1 \pm \sqrt{-2}$ the two numbers are $1 + i\sqrt{2}$ and $1 - i\sqrt{2}$. Now the sum of their reciprocals is

$$\frac{1}{1+i\sqrt{2}} + \frac{1}{1-i\sqrt{2}} = \frac{(1-i\sqrt{2}) + (1+i\sqrt{2})}{(1+i\sqrt{2}) \cdot (1-i\sqrt{2})} = \frac{2}{3}$$

This solution is by no means elegant.

Had students used a reverse strategy ("analysis"), they would have first inspected the desired conclusion; that is, $\frac{1}{x} + \frac{1}{y}$.

The sum of these fractions is $\frac{x + y}{xy}$. The two original equations immediately reveal the numerator and the denominator of this fraction.

This produces the answer, $\frac{2}{3}$, immediately. It is quite obvious that for this particular problem, a reverse strategy was superior to more common, straightforward approach.

Problem 3: If the sum of two numbers is 2, and the product of the same two numbers is 3, find the sum of the squares of the reciprocals of these numbers.

Solution: To find the sum of the squares of the reciprocals (of the numbers described in the above problem) by a reverse approach, the student must first consider the conclusion, that is: $\left(\frac{1}{x}\right)^2 + \left(\frac{1}{y}\right)^2$ or $\frac{1}{x^2} + \frac{1}{y^2}$

Once again students would be required to add the fractions to get: $\frac{x^2 + y^2}{x^2y^2}$. Therefore the denominator of the answer is $(xy)^2 = 9$. However, the numerator is not as simple to evaluate as it was earlier. Students must now

find the value of $x^2 + y^2$. Once again students must look backward. How can they somehow generate $x^2 + y^2$? Students will be quick to suggest that $(x + y)^2$ will yield $x^2 + y^2 + 2xy$, which in part produces $x^2 + y^2$. Besides, $(x + y)^2 = (2)^2 = 4$ and $2xy = 2 \cdot 3 = 6$. Hence $x^2 + y^2 = -2$. The problem is therefore solved, as $\frac{1}{x^2} + \frac{1}{y^2} = \frac{x^2 + y^2}{x^2y^2} = \frac{-2}{9}$.

A similar procedure can be employed to find the value of $(\frac{1}{x})^3 + (\frac{1}{y})^3$ from the original two equations $x + y = 2$ and $xy = 3$. Once again beginning with the conclusion and working in reverse, $\frac{1}{x^3} + \frac{1}{y^3} = \frac{x^3 + y^3}{(xy)^3}$. Since students already know that $(xy)^3 = (3)^3 = 27$, they need only to find the value of $x^3 + y^3$. How can they generate $x^3 + y^3$? From: $(x + y)^3 = x^3 + y^3 + 3x^2y + 3xy^2$

We get: $x^3 + y^3 = (x + y)^3 - 3xy(x + y)$
$$x^3 + y^3 = (2)^3 - 3(3)(2)$$
$$x^3 + y^3 = -10$$

Therefore: $\frac{1}{x^3} + \frac{1}{y^3} = \frac{x^3 + y^3}{(xy)^3} = \frac{-10}{27}$

This procedure may also be used to find the sum of higher powers of these reciprocals.

Another problem whose solution lends itself nicely to a reverse strategy ("analysis") involves geometric constructions.

Problem 4: Construct a triangle given the lengths m_a and m_b, of two medians of a triangle and the length, c, of the side whose endpoints are each an endpoint of one of the medians.

Solution: Rather than immediately trying to perform the required construction, students would be wise to use a reverse strategy. They may assume construction and inspect the results.

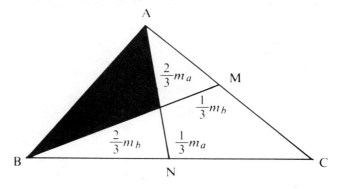

Students will soon realize that they would be able to construct the shaded triangle above as they can easily obtain the lengths of its sides (c, $\frac{2m_a}{3}$, $\frac{2m_b}{3}$). Points M and N can then be located using the property of the centroid. Then point C will be determined by the intersection of $\overrightarrow{AM}$ and $\overrightarrow{BN}$.

Having started from the conclusion and working in reverse, students have formulated a plan for constructing the required triangle, by merely retracing steps in the reverse direction ("synthesis").

Although there are many problems whose solutions can be significantly simplified by using a reverse strategy, there are also a great number of problems where a straightforward approach is best. It is natural for a student to approach a problem in a straightforward manner. Yet we as teachers must encourage our students to abandon the straightforward approach when a solution is not easily forthcoming, and attempt a reverse solution.

Some problems require only a partial reverse strategy. In such problems it is useful to begin with the conclusion and work backwards until a path to the conclusion is established. Let us consider the following problems.

Problem 5: Find the solution of the following: $(x - y^2)^2 + (x - y - 2)^2 = 0$, where x and y are real numbers.

Solution: Students of algebra might naturally use a straightforward approach to solve this equation. After squaring each of the polynomials as indicated, confusion would mount. Students previously exposed to a reverse strategy would then try to analyze the solution set of the equation. The values of x and y must be such that the sum of the squares of the polynomials equals zero. How can the sum of two positive numbers equal zero? Students can answer this question by saying that $x - y^2 = 0$ and $x - y - 2 = 0$. Up to this point students used a reverse strategy ("analysis"). However, now they must proceed in a straightforward manner ("synthesis") solving the equations $x - y^2 = 0$ and $x - y - 2 = 0$ simultaneously.

In his book *How to Solve It,* George Polya discusses a backward method of problem solving which is similar to a reverse strategy discussed in this article. Polya emphasizes the importance of the role of a teacher in presenting such methods to students when he states that "there is some sort of psychological repugnance to this reverse order which may prevent a quite able student from understanding the method if it is not presented carefully."

It is the responsibility of the mathematics teacher to make a conscious effort to stress the importance, benefits and possible limitations of a reverse strategy in problem solving.

Postassessment

1. If $x + y = 2$ and $xy = 3$, find $\dfrac{1}{x^4} + \dfrac{1}{y^4}$.

2. Construct a triangle given the lengths of two sides and the length of an altitude to one of these sides.

3. Have students use analysis and synthesis to prove the following:
"In right $\triangle ABC$, $\overline{CF}$ is the median drawn to hypotenuse $\overline{AB}$, $\overline{CE}$ is the bisector of $\angle ACB$, and $\overline{CD}$ is the altitude to $\overline{AB}$.
Prove that $\angle DCE \cong \angle ECF$.

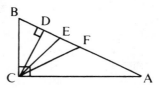

4. Evaluate $x^5 + \dfrac{1}{x^5}$, if $x^2 + \dfrac{1}{x^2} = 7$.

(Answer: $\pm\, 123$)

94 Decimals and Fractions in Other Bases

Performance Objectives

(2) Students will rationalize repeating decimals or repeating fractions in other bases.

Preassessment

Ask students to find the decimal number equivalent to $\dfrac{87}{99}\left(=\dfrac{87}{10^2-1}\right)$. Challenge students to represent a repeating decimal by a simple rational number.

Teaching Strategies

Decimal numbers are usually classified as repeating and non-repeating. Repeating decimals are further partitioned into terminating and non-terminating decimals. Students are usually readily aware that a terminating decimal represents a particular rational number. But the nature of a non-terminating decimal is more intriguing. We begin this exploration by confining ourselves to non-terminating repeating decimals. Consider the repeating decimal: $.1212\overline{12}$. (The bar over the last two digits indicates the repeating digits.) What we want to do is to represent this decimal by an equivalent rational simple fraction. If we let $x = .12\overline{12}\ldots$ and then $100x = 12.12\overline{12}\ldots$ subtracting the former from the latter yields the equation: $100x - x = 12$, or $x = \dfrac{12}{100-1} = \dfrac{12}{99}$.

We have now found a ratio representation for $.1212\ldots$.

Some further exploration is in order now. Notice that $\dfrac{12}{99} + \dfrac{88}{99} = 1$. However, if we add the equivalent decimal representations $\begin{array}{r}.1212\overline{12}\\+.8787\overline{87}\\\hline.9999\overline{99}\end{array}$ one would think that $.9999\overline{99} = 1$. Indeed, applying the above technique yields: $x = .9999\overline{9}$ and $10x = 9.9999\overline{9}$; therefore $10x - x = 9$, and $x = \dfrac{7}{10-1}$, $x = 1$.

This illustration leads us to an important theorem: any repeating decimal can be represented as a rational number (i.e., the *ratio* of two integers, the denominator not zero).

Proof:

Let the repeating decimal be represented by $.a_1a_2\ldots a_n \ldots$ where a_i is a digit and n is an integer that represents the length of the repetition. As before, let

$$x = .a_1a_2\ldots a_n\ldots$$
and
$$10^n x = a_1a_2\ldots a_n.a_1a_2\ldots a_n\ldots$$

Now
$$10^n x - x = a_1a_2\ldots a_n$$
$$x(10^n - 1) = a_1a_2\ldots a_n$$
$$x = \frac{a_1a_2\ldots a_n}{10^n - 1}$$

The repeating decimal is now represented by a rational number.

Students will now want to consider repeating fractions in bases other than 10 (no longer called decimals!). Suppose we have in base 3 the repeating fraction: $.12\overline{12}$. Students should be guided to asking the following:

(1) Can this repeating fraction be represented by a rational number in base 3?

(2) In general can *any* repeating fraction in *any* given base be represented by a rational number?

Begin by using the approach applied earlier to repeating decimals. Let $x = .12\overline{12}$. Ask students how the ternary point may be shifted two places to the right (note the ternary point in base 3 is analogous to the decimal point in base 10). How $3^2 x = 12.12\overline{12}$. By subtracting x we get: $3^2x - x = 12$, $x(3^2 - 1) = 12$, $x = \dfrac{12}{3^2-1} = \dfrac{12}{22}$. Thus the repeating fraction in base 3 can be represented by a rational number. Have students notice the analogous form in base 10.

Using these illustrations as models we shall prove that a repeating fraction in any base can be represented by a rational number in that base.

Proof:

Consider any base B and any repeating fraction in that base: $.a_1a_2\ldots a_n \ldots$ where a_i is a digit of the number and n is an integer that represents the length of the repetition $x = .a_1a_2\ldots a_n \ldots$

$$B^n x = a_1a_2\ldots a_n.a_1a_2\ldots a_n \ldots$$
$$B^n x - x = a_1a_2\ldots a_n$$
$$x = \frac{a_1a_2\ldots a_n}{B^n - 1}$$

This proves that any repeating fraction can be represented by a rational number.

Postassessment

Have students do the following exercises:

1. If $x = \dfrac{123}{10^3 - 1}$, what is its decimal representation?

2. If $x = \dfrac{11256}{7^4 - 1}$, represent x as a rational fraction.

3. Rationalize the repeating fraction $x = .23\overline{23}$ when x is in base 10, 8 and 5.

95 Polygonal Numbers

This unit can be taught to a class that has a reasonably good command of the basic algebraic skills. Since most of the unit employs intuitive thinking, a good degree of this training should result. It would be helpful if the students were familiar with arithmetic sequences and the formula for the sum of its series. However, if students are not familiar with this topic, essentials can be developed in a reasonably short time.

Performance Objectives
1. *Given the rank of any regular polygon, the student will find a number that corresponds to it.*
2. *The student will discover relations between two or more different polygonal numbers of given ranks.*

Preassessment
The ancient Babylonians discovered that some whole numbers can be broken down into patterns of units. This link between arithmetic and geometry was also of concern to the ancient Greeks. For example, the number 3 can be represented as three dots forming a triangle, as can the number 6.

Which regular polygon do you think the number 4 represents? The number 9? After the students have had some time to find such polygons, ask them to provide the answers.

Numbers that can be related to geometric figures are called *figurate* or *polygonal* numbers.

Teaching Strategies
Tell the students that it would be very easy to find the number which corresponds to a given regular polygon if we could find a formula such that given any regular polygon and its rank we could obtain that number from it.

Begin by telling the students what the rank of a regular polygon indicates. For any regular polygon, the rank indicates, in order, the corresponding polygonal number. For example, for a triangle, rank 1 = 3 (the first triangular number), rank 2 = 6 (the second triangular number), rank 3 = 10, etc.

Now draw five figures that will show how to get the first five ranks of the first five figurate numbers (triangular, square, pentagonal, hexagonal, heptagonal). To save time you may use an overhead projector instead, or you may distribute mimeographed sheets with the drawings. Make a corresponding table. Both the drawings and the table which follow indicate what might be shown to your students.

Table 1

Rank *r*

	1	2	3	4	5
Triangle					
Square					
Pentagon					
Hexagon					
Heptagon					

Table 2

Figure	No. sides			Rank *r*		
	N	1	2	3	4	5
Triangular	3	1	3	6	10	15
Square	4	1	4	9	16	25
Pentagonal	5	1	5	12	22	35
Hexagonal	6	1	6	15	28	45
Heptagonal	7	1	7	18	34	55

It should be clear to the student that making a figure to obtain every possible triangular, square, etc. number is a very tedious task. Instead we will study how consecutive polygonal numbers of a given polygon follow each other and, by looking at the sequence formed, try to obtain a formula for the rth rank of each given polygon.

If we look at the first row of figurate numbers corresponding to triangular numbers, and if we also look at their corresponding ranks (table 1) we will notice that they can be written as:

$$1 = r$$
$$3 = (r-1)+r$$
$$6 = (r-2)+(r-1)+r$$
$$10 = (r-3)+(r-2)+(r-1)+r$$
$$15 = (r-4)+(r-3)+(r-2)+(r-1)+r$$

If we look at the ranks we will also notice that their sequence forms an arithmetic sequence and that each triangular number of rank r is the sum of that arithmetic sequence $1, 2, 3, \ldots, r$ from 1 to r. Thus we can conclude that the rth triangular number is given by: $T_r = r(r+1)/2$

Next, let's look at the square numbers:

$$1 = r^2 = 1^2$$
$$4 = r^2 = 2^2$$
$$9 = r^2 = 3^2$$
$$16 = r^2 = 4^2$$
$$25 = r^2 = 5^2$$

It is clear that each square number is the square of its corresponding rank. So the r square number is r^2.

The formula for the rth pentagonal number can be obtained if we write each number in the following way:

$$1 = r^2 + 0 = 1 + 0$$
$$5 = r^2 + 1 = 2^2 + 1$$
$$12 = r^2 + 3 = 3^2 + 3$$
$$22 = r^2 + 6 = 4^2 + 6$$
$$35 = r^2 + 10 = 5^2 + 10$$

If we study the second part of the sums $0, 1, 3, 6, 10$, we will see that each of the numbers correspond to the sum of the arithmetic sequence $0, 1, 2, \ldots, (r-1)$ which is $(r-1)r/2$. So the rth pentagonal number is

$$r^2 + \frac{(r-1)r}{2} = \frac{2r^2 + (r-1)r}{2} = \frac{(2r^2 + r^2 - r)}{2}$$
$$= \frac{(3r^2 - r)}{2} = \frac{r(3r-1)}{2}$$

To find a formula for the rth hexagonal number, consider the first five as follows:

$$1 = 1r$$
$$6 = 3r = 3(2)$$
$$15 = 5r = 5(3)$$
$$28 = 7r = 7(4)$$
$$45 = 9r = 9(5)$$

An inspection of the coefficients of r: $1, 3, 5, 7, 9$, would reveal that each corresponds to the sum of the corresponding rank and the rank immediately before it. That is, each coefficient is equal to $r + (r-1)$. Therefore the rth hexagonal number is $[r + (r-1)]r = (2r-1)r$.

The rth heptagonal number is found as follows. Write the first seven heptagonal numbers in the following way:

$$1 = 2r^2 - 1 = 2(1)^2 - 1$$
$$7 = 2r^2 - 1 = 2(2)^2 - 1$$
$$18 = 2r^2 + 0 = 2(3)^2 + 0$$
$$34 = 2r^2 + 2 = 2(4)^2 + 2$$
$$55 = 2r^2 + 5 = 2(5)^2 + 5$$

It probably will be very difficult for the students to arrive at a formula for the second part X of each number $2r^2 + X$. Therefore after the students have looked at the numbers for a short time the teacher should immediately point out that each X is equal to the sum of the arithmetic sequence $-1, 0, 1, 2, 3, \ldots, (r-2)$ minus one, which is $\frac{(r-2)(r-1)}{2} - 1$.

Students should test the formula on each of the given numbers above. So the rth heptagonal number is

$$2r^2 + \frac{(r-2)(r-1)}{2} - 1 = 2r^2 + \frac{(r-2)(r-1) - 2}{2} =$$
$$2r^2 + \frac{r^2 - 3r + 2 - 2}{2} = \frac{r(5r-3)}{2}$$

Call attention to the fact that we now have a formula for the rth rank of each of the first 5 polygonal numbers. So we are now able to find any triangular, square, pentagonal, hexagonal and heptagonal number. But, there are regular polygons of $8, 9, \ldots 20, 100$, etc. sides and we would also like to have a formula for the rth rank of each of them. It is our next task to find such formulas.

To do this let's write the formulas we have already found as follows:

No. sides	Rank $= r$		
3	$\dfrac{r(r+1)}{2}$	$= \dfrac{r^2+r}{2}$	$= \dfrac{1r^2}{2} + \dfrac{r}{2}$
4	r^2	$= \dfrac{2r^2}{2}$	$= \dfrac{2r^2}{2} + \dfrac{0}{2}$
5	$\dfrac{r(3r-1)}{2}$	$= \dfrac{3r^2-r}{-2}$	$= \dfrac{3r^2}{2} - \dfrac{r}{2}$
6	$r(2r-1)$	$= \dfrac{4r^2-2r}{2}$	$= \dfrac{4r^2}{2} - \dfrac{2r}{2}$
7	$\dfrac{r(5r-3)}{2}$	$= \dfrac{5r^2-3r}{2}$	$= \dfrac{5r^2}{2} - \dfrac{3r}{2}$
.			
.			
.			
.			
.			
.			
.			
N			

Let's now look at the last column. We will notice that the coefficients of the $\frac{r^2}{2}$ terms can be written as $(N - 2)$. Also the coefficients of the $\frac{r}{2}$ terms can be written as $-(N-4)$. Therefore, the rth rank of a N-gonal number is

$$\frac{(N-2)r^2}{2} - \frac{(N-4)r}{2} = \frac{(N-2)r^2 - (N-4)r}{2} =$$
$$\left(\frac{r}{2}\right)\left[(N-2)r - (N-4)\right] = \left(\frac{r}{2}\right)\left[(r-1)N - 2(r-2)\right]$$

The completed table (including the first 5 ranks of the N-gonal number looks like this:

No. sides	1	2	3	4	5	. . . . .	r
3	1	3	6	10	15	. . . . .	$\frac{r(r+1)}{2}$
4	1	4	9	16	25	. . . . .	r^2
5	1	5	12	22	35	. . . . .	$\frac{r(3r-1)}{2}$
6	1	6	15	28	15	. . . . .	$\frac{r(2r-1)}{}$
7	1	7	18	34	55	. . . . .	$\frac{r(5r-3)}{2}$
.							
.							
.							
N	1		. . . . .				$\left(\frac{r}{2}\right)\left[(r-1)N - 2(r-2)\right]$

At this point it would be instructive for the students to work out some simple examples using the formula for the rth N-gonal number.

Example 1
Find the third octagonal number.
Solution: Let $N = 8$ and $r = 3$. Substitute these numbers in the formula $\frac{r}{2}\left[(r-1)N - 2(r-2)\right]$
$$= \frac{3}{2}\left[(3-1)8 - 2(3-2)\right] = \frac{3}{2}\ (2)8 - 2(1)$$
$$= \frac{3}{2}\left[16 - 2\right] = \frac{3 \times 14}{2} = 21$$

Example 2
To what regular polygon does the number 40 correspond if $r = 4$?
Solution: In this case we know the rank and the number, but we must find N. We substitute into and solve the following equation:

$$\left(\frac{r}{2}\right)\left[(r-1)N - 2(r-2)\right] = 40$$
$$\left(\frac{4}{2}\right)\left[(4-1)N - 2(4-2)\right] = 40$$
$$2\left[3N - 2(2)\right] = 40, \quad \text{and} \quad N = 8.$$

So the figure is a regular octagon.

The following examples are a little more difficult for they call for applications of the formulas to find relationships between different types of polygonal numbers.

Example 3
Show that the rth pentagonal number is equal to r plus three times the $(r - 1)$th triangular number.
Solution: In order to do this problem we must first write the formula for the rth pentagonal number:

$$P_r = \frac{r(3r-1)}{2} = \frac{3r^2}{2} - \frac{r}{2}$$

Rewrite $\frac{-r}{3}$ as $\frac{-3r}{2} + r$.

Now we have $\frac{3r^2}{2} - \frac{3r}{2} + r = \frac{3(r^2 - r)}{2} + r$

$$\frac{3r(r-1)}{2} + r = 3T_{r-1} + r, \text{ where}$$

T_{r-1} is the $(r-1)^{\text{st}}$ triangular number.

Example 4
Show that any hexagonal number is equal to the sum of a pentagonal number of the same rank and a triangular number of the preceding rank.

Solution: $(\text{Hex})_r = r(2r - 1) = 2r^2 - r$
$$= \frac{3r^2 - r}{2} + \frac{r^2 - r}{2}$$
$$= \frac{r(3r-1)}{2} + \frac{r(r-1)}{2} = P_r + T_{r-1}$$

Postassessment
After students have studied the previous examples they should be able to do the following problems:
1. Draw a regular octagon corresponding to the third octagonal number of example 1 (study the drawings of the first 5 figurate numbers before doing this problem).
2. Find the first 3 dacagonal (10 sides) numbers.
3. Show that any heptagonal number is equal to the sum of a hexagonal number of the same rank and a triangular number of the previous rank (i.e., show: $(\text{Hep})_r = (\text{Hex})_r + T_{r-1}$).

4. Show that any N-gonal number ($N \geqslant 5$) is equal to the sum of the $(N-1)$-gonal number of the same rank and a triangular number of the previous rank. (Hint: Begin with the $(N-1)$-gonal number of rank

r and T_{r-1}. Carry out the addition).

5. Show that the sum of any number of consecutive odd integers, starting with 1 is a perfect square (i.e., a square number).

96   Networks

This unit will serve as an introductory lesson in topology.

Performance Objective
Given a closed curve, students will determine if it is traversible or nontraversible.

Preassessment
Have students try to trace with a pencil each of the following configurations without missing any part and without going over any part twice.

Ask students to determine the number of arcs or line segments which have an endpoint at each of A, B, C, D, E.

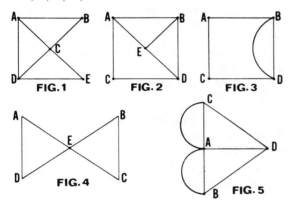

FIG. 1   **FIG. 2**   **FIG. 3**

FIG. 4   **FIG. 5**

Teaching Strategies
Configurations such as Figures 1-5, which are made up of line segments and/or continuous arcs are called *networks*. The number of arcs or line segments which have an endpoint at a particular vertex, is called the *degree* of the vertex.

After trying to trace these networks without taking their pencils off the paper and without going over any line more than once, students should notice two direct outcomes. The networks can be traced (or *traversed*) if they have (1) all even degree vertices or (2) exactly two odd degree vertices. The proof of these two outcomes follows.

There are an even number of odd degree vertices in a connected network.

Proof: Let V_1 be the number of vertices of degree 1, let V_3 be the number of vertices of degree 3, and

V_n the number of vertices of degree n. Also let $N = V_1 + V_3 + V_5 + \ldots + V_{2n-1}$. N is the number of odd degree vertices in a given connected network ("connected" meaning without loose ends). Since there are 3 arc endpoints at V_3, 5 at V_5 and n at V_n, the total number of arc endpoints in a connected network is $M = V_1 + 2V_2 + 3V_3 + 4V_4 + \ldots + 2nV_{2n}$.

$$M - N = 2V_2 + 2V_3 + 4V_4 + 4V_5 + \ldots +$$
$$(2n-2)V_{2n-1} + 2nV_{2n}$$
$$= 2(V_2 + V_3 + 2V_4 + 2V_5 + \ldots +$$
$$(n-1)V_{2n-1} + nV_{2n})$$

Since the difference of two even numbers is an even number, $M-(M-N) = N$ is an even number.

A connected network can be traversed, only if it has at most two odd degree vertices.

Proof: On a continuous path the inside vertices must be passed through. That is, if a line "enters" the point another must "leave" the point. This accounts for the endpoints. The only vertices which do not conform to this rule are the beginning and endpoints in the traversing. These *two* points may be of odd order. By the previous theorem, it was established that there must be an even number of odd vertices; therefore there can only be *two* or *zero* vertices of odd order in order to traverse a network.

Have students now draw both traversible and nontraversible networks (using these two theorems). Network 1 in the Preassessment has five vertices. Vertices B,C,E are of even degree and vertices A and D are of odd degree. Since Figure 1 has exactly two odd degree vertices as well as three even degree vertices it is traversible. If we start at A then go down to D, across to E, back up to A, across to B, and down to D we have chosen a desired route.

Network 2 has five vertices. Vertex C is the only even degree vertex. Vertices A,B,E, and D, are all of odd degree. Consequently, since the network has more than two odd vertices, it is not traversible.

Network 3 is traversible because it has two even vertices and exactly two odd degree vertices.

Network 4 has five even degree vertices and can be traversed.

Network 5 has four odd degree vertices and *cannot* be traversed.

To generate interest among your students present them with the famous Königsberg Bridge Problem. In the eighteenth century the small Prussian city of Königsberg, located where the Pregel River formed two branches, was faced with a recreational dilemma: Could a person walk over each of the seven bridges exactly once in a continuous walk through the city? In 1735 the famous mathematician Leonhard Euler (1707-1783) proved that this walk could not be performed. Indicate to students that the ensuing discussion will tie in their earlier work with networks to the solution of the Königsberg Bridge Problem.

FIG. 6

Tell pupils to indicate the island by A, the left bank of the river by B, the right one by C, and the area between the two arms of the upper course by D. If we start at Holzt and walk to Sohmede and then through Honig, through Hohe, through Kottel, through Grüne we will never cross Kramer. On the other hand if we start at Kramer and walk to Honig, through Hohe, through Kottel, through Sohmede, through Holzt we will never travel through Grüne.

The Königsberg Bridge Problem is the same problem as the one posed in Figure 5. Let's take a look at Figures 5 and 6 and note the similarity. There are seven bridges in Figure 6 and there are seven lines in Figure 5. In Figure 5 each vertex is of odd degree. In Figure 6 if we start at D we have three choices, we could go to Hohe, Honig, or Holzt. If in Figure 5 we start at D we have three line paths to choose from. In both figures if we are at C we have either three bridges we could go on or three lines. A similar situation exists for locations A and B in Figure 6 and vertices A and B in Figure 5. Emphasize that this network *cannot* be traversed.

Another example of a problem where the consideration of the traversibility of a network is important is the Five Room House Problem. Have

students consider the diagram of a five-room house.

Each room has a doorway to each adjacent room and a doorway leading outside the house. The problem is to have a person start either inside or outside the house and walk through each doorway *exactly once*.

FIG. 7a

Students should be encouraged to try various paths. They will realize that although the number of attempts is finite, there are far too many to make a trial-and-error solution practical. They should be guided to a network diagram analogous to this problem.

Figure 7b shows various possible paths joining the five rooms A, B, C, D, and E, and the outside F. The problem now reduces to merely determining if this network is traversible. There are

FIG. 7b

four vertices of odd degree and two vertices of even degree. Since there are not *exactly* two or zero vertices of odd order, this network *cannot* be traversed; hence the Five-Room House Problem does not have a solution path.

Other problems of a similar nature may now be presented to the students.

Postassessment

1. Have students find out if the following figures can be traced without removing their pencils from the paper and without going over any line twice. (i.e., traversed)

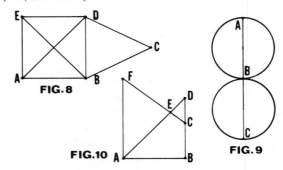

FIG. 8 FIG. 10 FIG. 9

2. Have students draw a house floor plan and then determine if one can walk through each doorway exactly once.

97   Angle Trisection—Possible or Impossible?

Of the Three Famous Problems of Antiquity, the one most instructive to a high school student is the angle trisection. This unit will present a discussion and proof that any angle cannot be trisected with only straightedge and compasses.

Performance Objective

Students will outline a proof that an angle of measure 120° cannot be trisected.

Preassessment

Students should be familiar with the basic geometric constructions.

Teaching Strategies

Ask students to trisect an angle of measure 90° using only straightedge and compasses. With little difficulty they ought to be able to construct an angle of measure 60° at the vertex of the given angle. This virtually completes the trisection. However, now ask students to trisect an angle of measure 120°. This will cause difficulty because it is impossible with straightedge and compasses. At this point, begin discussion of the impossibility of angle trisection using only straightedge and compasses.

With the aid of a unit length and an angle of measure A, it is possible to construct a line segment of length cos A. (see figure below)

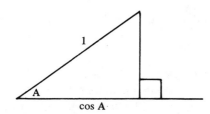

If we can trisect ∠A, then we can also construct the $\cos \frac{A}{3}$. If we can show that $\cos \frac{A}{3}$ cannot be constructed, then we have shown that ∠A cannot be trisected. Here we shall let $m\angle A = 120°$, and show ∠A cannot be trisected.

We shall first obtain an expression for cos A in terms of $\cos \frac{A}{3}$.

cos 3y = cos (2y+y) = cos 2y cos y − sin 2y sin y
But, cos 2y = 2 cos² y − 1.
Substituting:
cos 3y = cos y (2 cos²y − 1) − sin 2y sin y
= $\left[2 \cos^3 y - \cos y\right]$ − sin 2y sin y.

But, sin 2y = 2 sin y cos y
Therefore:

cos 3y = $\left[2 \cos^3 y - \cos y\right]$ − sin y (2 sin y cos y)
cos 3y = $\left[2 \cos^3 y - \cos y\right]$ − 2 sin²y cos y
cos 3y = $\left[2 \cos^3 y - \cos y\right]$ − 2 cos y(1 − cos²y)
cos 3y = $\left[2 \cos^3 y - \cos y\right]$ − 2 cos y + 2 cos³y
cos 3y = 4 cos³y − 3 cos y

Let 3y = A to obtain:

$\cos A = 4 \cos^3 \frac{A}{3} - 3 \cos \frac{A}{3}$

Multiply by 2 and replace $2 \cos \frac{A}{3}$ with x to get:

2 cos A = x³ − 3x.

Since $\cos 120° = -\frac{1}{2}$, $x^3 - 3x + 1 = 0$.

Students should now recall that one of the criteria of constructibility (see p. 256) indicates that constructible roots must be of the form $a + b\sqrt{c}$, where a and b are rational and c is constructible.

First, then, we must show that $x^3 - 3x + 1 = 0$ has no rational roots. To do this, we assume that there is a rational root, $\frac{p}{q}$, where p and q have no common factor greater than 1. Substituting for $\frac{p}{q}$, we have

$(\frac{p}{q})^3 - 3(\frac{p}{q}) + 1 = 0$
$p^3 - 3pq^2 + q^3 = 0$
$q^3 = 3pq^2 - p^3$
$q^3 = p(3q^2 - p^2)$

This means that q^3, and hence q, has the factor p. Therefore p must equal ±1. Also, solving for p^3
$p^3 = 3pq^2 - q^3$
$p^3 = q^2(3p - q)$
This means p and q must have a common factor, and hence q = ±1. We can conclude from this that the only rational root of $x^3 - 3x + 1 = 0$ is r = ±1. By substitution, we can show that neither +1 nor −1 is root.

Next, assume $x^3 - 3x + 1 = 0$ has a constructible root $a + b\sqrt{c}$. By substitution in the equation $x^3 - 3x + 1 = 0$, we can show that if $a + b\sqrt{c}$ is a root, then its conjugate, $a - b\sqrt{c}$, is also a root. The sum of the roots of the polynomial equation $x^n + a_1x^{n-1} + a_2x^{n-2} + \ldots + a_n = 0$ is $r_1 + r_2 + r_3 + \ldots + r_n = -a_1$.

It follows from this that the sum of the roots $x^3 - 3x + 1 = 0$ is zero. If two roots are $a + b\sqrt{c}$ and $a - b\sqrt{c}$, with the third root r, we have

$$a + b\sqrt{c} + a - b\sqrt{c} + r = 0$$
$$r = -2a$$

But a is rational and hence r is rational, and we have a contradiction. Hence the angle whose measure is $120°$ cannot be trisected. This essentially proves that any angle cannot be trisected with only straightedge and compasses.

Postassessment

Have students write an outline of the proof presented in this unit as well as a discussion of its significance.

98   Comparing Means

This unit can be used as a major part of a lesson on statistics.

Performance Objectives

1. Students will compare magnitudes of three means for any two or more numbers.

2. Students will prove comparison relationships between means.

Preassessment

After students have reviewed the arithmetic and geometric means, have students express h in terms of a and b, where a,h,b is a harmonic sequence.

Teaching Strategies

Begin by defining the three means (arithmetic, harmonic and geometric) in the following way.

Suppose a,m,b are an arithmetic sequence. The middle term (m) is said to be the *arithmetic mean*. Since a,m,b have a common difference $m - a = b - m$,

and $\boxed{m = \dfrac{a+b}{2} = \text{arithmetic mean (A.M.)}}$

Now suppose a,h,b are a harmonic sequence. The middle term (h) is said to be the *harmonic mean*. Since a,h,b have reciprocals with a common difference, $\dfrac{1}{h} - \dfrac{1}{a} = \dfrac{1}{b} - \dfrac{1}{h}$ and

$\boxed{h = \dfrac{2ab}{a+b} = \text{harmonic mean (H.M.)}}$

Finally suppose a,g,b are a *geometric sequence*. Since a,g,b have a common ratio, $\dfrac{g}{a} = \dfrac{b}{g}$ and

$\boxed{g = \sqrt{ab} = \text{geometric mean (G.M.)}}$

Since often a pictorial model crystalizes understanding, a geometric interpretation is appropriate here. Consider the semicircle with diameter $\overline{AOPB}$ with $\overline{AO} \cong \overline{OB}$ and $\overline{PR} \perp \overline{APB}$. (R is on the semicircle). Also $\overline{PS} \perp \overline{RSO}$. Let $AP = a$ and $PB = b$.

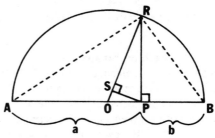

Since $RO = \frac{1}{2}AB = \frac{1}{2}(AP + PB) = \frac{1}{2}(a+b)$, RO is the *arithmetic mean* (A.M.) between a and b.

Consider right $\triangle ARB$. Since $\triangle BPR \sim \triangle RPA$, $\dfrac{PB}{PR} = \dfrac{PR}{AP}$ or $(PR)^2 = (AP) \cdot (PB) = ab$. Therefore $PR = \sqrt{ab}$. Thus PR is the *geometric mean* (G.M.) between a and b.

Since $\triangle RPO \sim \triangle RSP$, $\dfrac{RO}{PR} = \dfrac{PR}{RS}$. Therefore $RS = \dfrac{(PR)^2}{RO}$. But $(PR)^2 = ab$ and $RO = \frac{1}{2}AB = \frac{1}{2}(a+b)$. Thus $RS = \dfrac{ab}{\frac{1}{2}(a+b)} = \dfrac{2ab}{a+b}$ which is the *harmonic mean* (H.M.) between a and b.

This geometric interpretation lends itself quite well to a comparison of the magnitudes of these three means. Since the hypotenuse of a right triangle is its longest side, in $\triangle ROP$, $RO > PR$ and in $\triangle RSP$, $PR > RS$. Therefore, $RO > PR > RS$. However, since it is possible for these triangles to degenerate, $RO \geq PR \geq RS$ which implies that A.M. $\geq$ G.M. $\geq$ H.M.

Since the student is familiar with both arithmetic mean and geometric mean (sometimes called the mean proportional), a brief introduction to the harmonic mean would be in order.

The *harmonic mean* between two numbers is the *reciprocal of the arithmetic mean between the reciprocals* of these two numbers. This is because a harmonic sequence is a sequence of reciprocals of members of an arithmetic sequence. For a and b,

$$\text{H.M.} = \cfrac{1}{\cfrac{\cfrac{1}{a}+\cfrac{1}{b}}{2}} = \frac{2ab}{a+b}$$

Example 1: Find the harmonic mean of $a, b,$ and c.
Solution: by the definition

$$\text{H.M.} = \cfrac{1}{\cfrac{\cfrac{1}{a}+\cfrac{1}{b}+\cfrac{1}{c}}{3}} = \frac{3abc}{ab+ac+bc}$$

Both the arithmetic mean and the geometric mean have popular applications in secondary school curriculum. The harmonic mean also has a very useful and often neglected application in elementary mathematics. The harmonic mean is the "average of rates." For example, suppose the average rate of speed for the trip to and from work is desired, when the rate of speed to work is 30 m.p.h. and returning (over the same route) is 60 m.p.h. The average speed is the harmonic mean between 30 and 60; that is, $\frac{(2)(30)(60)}{30+60} = 40$.

To show that the average rate of speed of two (or more) speeds is in fact the harmonic mean of these speeds, consider rates of speed $r_1, r_2, r_3, \ldots, r_n$, each traveled for a time $t_1, t_2, t_3, \ldots, t_n$, respectively and *each* over a distance d.

$$t_1 = \frac{d}{r_1}, t_2 = \frac{d}{r_2}, t_3 = \frac{d}{r_3}, \ldots t_n = \frac{d}{r_n}$$

The average speed (for the entire trip) is

$$\frac{\text{total distance}}{\text{total time}} = \frac{nd}{t_1+t_2+t_3+\ldots+t_n}$$

$$= \frac{nd}{\dfrac{d}{r_1}+\dfrac{d}{r_2}+\ldots+\dfrac{d}{r_n}} = \frac{n}{\dfrac{1}{r_1}+\dfrac{1}{r_2}+\dfrac{1}{r_3}+\ldots+\dfrac{1}{r_n}},$$

which is the harmonic mean.

Example 2: If Lisa bought $1.00 worth of each of three kinds of candy, 15¢, 25¢ and 40¢ per pound, what was her average price paid per pound?
Solution: Since the harmonic mean is the average of rates (taken over the same base), the average price per pound was

$$\frac{(3)(15)(25)(40)}{(15)(25)+(15)(40)+(25)(40)} = 22\frac{62}{79}¢$$

To complete the discussion of a comparison of the magnitude of the three means, consider with the class a more general (algebraic) discussion.

In general terms,

$$\text{A.M.} = \frac{a_1+a_2+a_3+\ldots+a_n}{n}$$

$$\text{G.M.} = \sqrt[n]{a_1 \cdot a_2 \cdot a_3 \cdot \ldots \cdot a_n}$$

$$\text{H.M.} = \frac{n}{\dfrac{1}{a_1}+\dfrac{1}{a_2}+\dfrac{1}{a_3}+\ldots+\dfrac{1}{a_n}}$$

Theorem 1: A.M. $\geq$ G.M.

Proof: Let $g = \sqrt[n]{a_1 \cdot a_2 \cdot a_3 \cdot \ldots \cdot a_n}$;

then $1 = \sqrt[n]{\dfrac{a_1}{g} \cdot \dfrac{a_2}{g} \cdot \dfrac{a_3}{g} \cdot \ldots \cdot \dfrac{a_n}{g}}$

Therefore $1 = \dfrac{a_1}{g} \cdot \dfrac{a_2}{g} \cdot \dfrac{a_3}{g} \cdot \ldots \cdot \dfrac{a_n}{g}$

However $\dfrac{a_1}{g} + \dfrac{a_2}{g} + \dfrac{a_3}{g} + \ldots + \dfrac{a_n}{g} \geq n$ since if the product of n positive numbers equals 1, their sum is *not* less than n. Therefore

$$\frac{a_1+a_2+a_3+\ldots+a_n}{n} \geq g$$

Hence $\dfrac{a_1+a_2+a_3+\ldots+a_n}{n} \geq \sqrt[n]{a_1 \cdot a_2 \cdot a_3 \cdot \ldots \cdot a_n},$
or A.M. $\geq$ G.M.

This proof for two numbers a and b $(a > b)$ is rather cute:

Since $a - b > 0$, $(a-b)^2 > 0$, or $a^2 - 2ab + b^2 > 0$.
By adding $4ab$ to both sides of the inequality:

$$a^2 + 2ab + b^2 > 4ab$$

Taking the positive square root yields:

$$\frac{a + b}{2} > \sqrt{ab}$$

Hence A.M. > G.M. (Note: if $a = b$ then A.M. = G.M.)

Theorem 2: G.M. $\geq$ H.M.

Proof: Since A.M. $\geq$ G.M. for $a_1^b, a_2^b, a_3^b \ldots, a_n^b$

$$\frac{a_1^b + a_2^b + a_3^b + \ldots + a_n^b}{n} \geq \sqrt[n]{a_1^b \cdot a_2^b \cdot a_3^b \ldots a_n^b}.$$

when $\dfrac{1}{b} < 0$, $\left[\sqrt[n]{a_1^b \cdot a_2^b \cdot a_3^b \cdot \ldots \cdot a_n^b}\right]^{\frac{1}{b}} \geq$

$$\left[\frac{a_1^b + a_2^b + a_3^b + \ldots + a_n^b}{n}\right]^{\frac{1}{b}}$$

Take $b = -1$, then $\sqrt[n]{a_1 \cdot a_2 \cdot a_3 \ldots a_n} \geq$

$$\left[\frac{a_1^{-1} + a_2^{-1} + a_3^{-1} + \ldots + a_n^{-1}}{n}\right]^{-1}$$

Hence; $\sqrt[n]{a_1 \cdot a_2 \cdot a_3 \ldots a_n} \geq$

$$\frac{n}{\dfrac{1}{a_1} + \dfrac{1}{a_2} + \dfrac{1}{a_3} + \ldots + \dfrac{1}{a_n}}, \text{ or G.M.} \geq \text{H.M.}$$

Once again for two numbers a and b $(a > b)$ the proof becomes much simpler:

Since (from above) $a^2 + 2ab + b^2 > 4ab$,
$ab(a+b)^2 > (4ab)(ab)$

Therefore $ab > \dfrac{4a^2b^2}{(a+b)^2}$, or $\sqrt{ab} > \dfrac{2ab}{a+b}$

Hence, G.M. > H.M. (Note if $a = b$ then G.M. = H.M.)

Postassessment
1. Find the A.M., G.M., and H.M. for each of the following:
   a) 20 and 60;   b) 25 and 45   c) 3, 15 and 45.
2. Arrange the G.M., H.M., and A.M. in ascending order of magnitude.
3. Show that for two given numbers the G.M. is the geometric mean between the A.M. and H.M.
4. Prove that the G.M. > H.M. for a, b, and c.

99 Pascal's Pyramid

The ability to expand and generalize is one of the most important facilities a teacher can help a student develop. In this unit, the familiar application of Pascal's triangle to determine the coefficients of a binomial expansion $(a + b)^n$ is expanded by the use of "Pascal's pyramid" to consider the coefficients of $(a + b + c)^n$.

Performance Objectives
1) *Students will evaluate trinomial expansions* (a + b + c)^n *of lower powers.*
2) *Students will discover important relationships between Pascal's triangle and Pascal's pyramid.*

Preassessment
If your students are familiar with Pascal's triangle, have them perform the following expansions:
   a) $(a + b)^3$; b) $(a - b)^4$; c) $(x + 2y)^5$.
Ask your students to test their algebraic multiplication (and patience) by evaluating:
a) $(a + b + c)^3$; b) $(a + b + c)^4$.

Teaching Strategies
Begin by reviewing Pascal's triangle. You might mention that this triangle is not Pascal's alone. In fact, the triangle was well known in China before 1300 and was also known to Omar Khayyam, author of the *Rubiyat,* almost 600 years before Pascal. Historical accuracy aside, each row of Pascal's (or Khayyam's or Ying Hui's) triangle yields the coefficients of $(a + b)^n$.

$$
\begin{array}{ll}
1 & (a + b)^0 \\
1\ 1 & (a + b)^1 \\
1\ 2\ 1 & (a + b)^2 \\
1\ 3\ 3\ 1 & (a + b)^3 \\
1\ 4\ 6\ 4\ 1 & (a + b)^4 \\
1\ 5\ 10\ 10\ 5\ 1 & (a + b)^5
\end{array}
$$

For example, to find $(a + b)^4$ use the coefficients in row 5 of the triangle: $a^4 + 4a^3b + 6a^2b^2 + 4ab^3 + b^4$:

Whereas a binomial expansion can be represented by a readily visible triangle, the trinomial expansion is represented by the more complex pyramid. The first expansion $(a + b + c)^0$ has the single coefficient 1. We can visualize this as the vertex of the pyramid. Each succeeding expansion is then represented by a triangular cross section of the pyramid with the coefficient 1 at each of the vertices.

Figure 1

Therefore each of the lateral edges of the pyramid consists of a sequence of 1's. The second expansion $(a + b + c)^1$ has coefficients: $1a + 1b + 1c$, which are represented by the first layer triangle with entries only at the vertices,   1
    1   1.

There are two methods of generating the coefficients of higher powers by means of the pyramid. In the first, again consider each expansion as a triangular cross-section of a pyramid. The numbers on the outer edge of each layer (the numbers between the vertices) are found by adding the two numbers that lie directly above. For example, $(a + b + c)^2$ has 1's at each vertex, and 2's between   1
            2   2
        1   2   1

To determine the terms in the interior of the triangle, add the three terms that lie above; for example, $(a + b + c)^3$ has the following coefficients:

```
        1
     3     3
  3     6     3
1     3     3     1
```

or referring to the pyramid:

Figure 2

To assign these coefficients to the correct variables:

1) let the coefficient in the first row of the pyramid be "*a*" to the highest power of that expansion;

2) let the elements of the second row be the coefficients of the product of "*a*" to the second highest power and the other variables to the first power;

3) in the third row again decrease the power of "*a*" and arrange the other variables such that the sum of the exponents of each term equals the power the original expansion was raised to;

4) within each row the powers of "*a*" remain the same while ths power of "*b*" decreases left to right and the power of "*c*" increases.

Specifically, consider $(a + b + c)^3$ which has a coefficient configuration:

```
        1
     3     3
  3     6     3
1     3     3     1
```

The full expansion would then be: $a^3 + 3a^2b + 3a^2c + 3ab^2 + 6abc + 3ac^2 + b^3 + 3b^2c + 3bc^2 + c^3$.

In working with these pyramids students may notice that the edge of each triangle corresponds exactly to a row of the Pascal triangle i.e., the edge of $(a + b + c)^3$,

1 3 3 1, is the same as the fourth row in Pascal's triangle. This observation leads to the second method of deriving the pyramid.

Let the left edge of the trinomial expansion be represented by the corresponding row of Pascal's triangle. Then multiply each row of Pascal's triangle by the number on the left edge to generate the coefficients for the trinomial expansion. For example, the left edge of $(a + b + c)^4$ will be 1 4 6 4 1, corresponding to the fifth row of Pascal's triangle.

```
        1                    (1×1)
      1   1              (4×1) (4×1)
    1   2   1          (6×1) (6×2) (6×1)
  1   3   3   1      (4×1) (4×3) (4×3) (4×1)
1   4   6   4   1  (1×1) (1×4) (1×6) (1×4) (1×1)
```

Multiplying these elements along the edge by the consecutive rows of the triangle yields $(a + b + c)^4$.

```
           1
          4  4
         6 12 6
       4 12 12 4
      1  4  6  4  1
```

This may at first appear to be a complicated procedure, but practice in its use will clear up intitial confusion and introduce an intriguing and useful technique.

Postassessment

Students should perform the following exercises:

1) Have the students compare the time required to expand $(a + b + c)^4$ algebraically versus the pyramid expansion.

2) Expand $(a + b + c)^5$, $(a + b + c)^6$.

3) Expand $(a + 2b + 3c)^3$, $(a + 4b + c)^4$.

4) Some students may be interested in constructing a working model of the pyramid, composed of detachable triangular sections with the appropriate coefficients noted on each surface.

100   The Multinomial Theorem

This unit should be used with a class which has already studied the Binomial Theorem.

Performance Objectives

1. *Students will find the coefficient of any given term of a given multinomial expansion without actually expanding it.*

2. *Students will justify the existence of the coefficients of the multinomial expansion.*

3. *Students will successfully apply Multinomial Theorem to a given trinomial.*

Preassessment

Have students expand $(a + b)^4$ by using the Binomial Theorem. Ask students to determine the number of different arrangements which can be formed from the letters AAABBBCC.

Teaching Strategies

Begin by reviewing student responses concerning the number of arrangements of AAABBBCC. They should realize that this problem differs from asking them to determine the number of arrangements of ABCDEFGH (where each symbol to be arranged is different from the rest). In the latter case the first place (of the eight places) can be filled in any one of eight ways, the second place can be filled in any one of seven ways, the third in six ways, the fourth in five ways, . . . , the eighth in only one way. Using the counting principle, the total number of ways is $8 \cdot 7 \cdot 6 \cdot 5 \cdot 4 \cdot 3 \cdot 2 \cdot 1 = 8!$ (read "8 factorial").

Having already studied Binomial Theorem, students should be familiar with the basic concepts of *combinations*. That is, $_nC_r = \binom{n}{r} = \dfrac{_nP_r}{r!}$

$= \dfrac{n!}{r! \, (n-r)!}$

Students should now be ready to consider the original problem, finding the number of arrangements of AAABBBCC. They should be carefully led through the following development.

Let #(A) represent the "number of ways of selecting positions for the A's." Since there are three A's, from the 8 positions 3 must be selected. This can be done $_8C_3$ or $\binom{8}{3}$ ways. Hence #(A)

$= \binom{8}{3} = \dfrac{8!}{3! \cdot 5!}$

Similarly $\#(B) = \binom{5}{3} = \dfrac{5!}{3! \cdot 2!}$, since 3 posi-

tions for the three B's must be selected from the remaining 5 positions. This leaves 2 positions to be selected for the two C's. Since only 2 positions remain, there is only one way of selecting these 2 positions, that is $\binom{2}{2} = \dfrac{2!}{2! \cdot 0!} = 1$. Indicate that $0! = 1$ by definition. By using the counting principle, #(A and B and C) = #(A)·#(B)·#(C) =

$$\dfrac{8!}{3! \cdot 5!} \cdot \dfrac{5!}{3! \cdot 2!} \cdot \dfrac{2!}{2! \cdot 0!} = \dfrac{8!}{3! \cdot 3! \cdot 2!}$$

This last expression is usually symbolized as $\binom{8}{3,3,2}$ which represents the number of ways of arranging eight items consisting of repetitions of 3 items, 3 items and 2 items.

To reinforce this technique, ask your students to determine the number of ways in which the letters of *Mississippi* can be arranged. Taking into consideration the repetitions (i.e. 1-M, 4-I's, 4-S's, 2-P's) students should obtain

$$\dfrac{11 \; 10 \; 9 \; \cancel{8} \; 7 \; \cancel{6} \; 5 \; \cancel{4} \; \cancel{3} \; \cancel{2} \; \cancel{1}}{1 \; \cancel{4} \; \cancel{3} \; \cancel{2} \; 1 \; \cancel{4} \; \cancel{3} \; \cancel{2} \; 1 \; \cancel{2} \; \cancel{1}} = 34,650.$$

Students should now be guided to generalizing this scheme for counting to n items which include n_1 items of one kind, n_2 items of another, n_3 items of a third kind, . . . , n_r items of a last kind. Clearly $n_1 + n_2 + n_3 + \ldots + n_r = n$. Applying the scheme from before, #(N₁) shall represent "the number of ways in which n_1 positions may be selected from the n positions available." Hence $\#(N_1) = \dfrac{n!}{n_1! \, (n - n_1)!}$

Similarly, $\#(N_2) = \dfrac{(n - n_1)!}{n_2!(n - n_1 - n_2)!}$, since only $n - n_1$ places remained from which to select n_2 positions. Similarly, $\#(N_r) =$

$\dfrac{(n - n_1 - n_2 - \ldots - n_{r-1})!}{n_r!(n - n_1 - n_2 - \ldots - n_r)!}$. Since $n_1 + n_2 + n_3 + \ldots + n_r = n$, $\#(N_r) \ldots 1$, $\dfrac{n_r!}{n_r! \cdot 0!} = 1$

Using the counting principle for these r cases the numbers of ways of arranging these n items (with r items being repeated) is obtained:

$$\dfrac{n!}{n_1!(n - n_1)!} \cdot \dfrac{(n - n_1)!}{n_2!(n - n_1 - n_2)!} \cdot \dfrac{(n - n_1 - n_2)!}{n_3!(n - n_1 - n_2 - n_3)!}$$

$$\ldots \cdot 1 = \dfrac{n!}{n_1! \cdot n_2! \cdot n_3! \ldots n_r!} = \binom{n}{n_1, n_2, n_3, \ldots, n_r}$$

which is a convenient symbol to use here.

Students should apply this general formula to the case where $r = 2$. They will get:

$\binom{n}{n_1 n_2} = \dfrac{n!}{n_1! \cdot n_2!} = \dfrac{n!}{n_1!(n-n_1)!}$, which is the familiar $_nC_{n_1}$ or $\binom{n}{n_1}$.

The students should now be ready to tackle Multinomial Theorem. In the preassessment they were asked to expand $(a+b)^4$. They should note that certain terms appear more than once. For example, the term *aaab*, commonly written a^3b, appears $\binom{4}{3}$ times. This corresponds to the number of arrangements of aaab. For each such term the same argument holds.

Students should now consider the expansion of $(a+b+c)^4$. To actually compute this expansion, students may multiply a different combination of the members of each of the factors to obtain each term. For example, some of the 81 terms will appear as *aaaa, aaab, aabb, abac, abab, cbcb*, ... These are commonly written as a^4, a^3b, a^2b^2, a^2bc, a^2b^2, b^2c^2. In the above list a^2b^2 appeared twice; however, in the complete expansion (of 81 terms) it would appear $\binom{4}{2,2,0} = \dfrac{4!}{2!\ 2!\ 0!}$ = 6 times. Thus if a student were asked to find the coefficient of the term a^3bc^2 in the expansion $(a+b+c)^6$, he would merely evaluate $\binom{6}{3,1,2} = \dfrac{6!}{3! \cdot 1! \cdot 2!} = 60$. Hence the entire expansion may be written as: $(a+b+c)^4 =$

$$\sum_{n_1 + n_2 + n_3 = 4} \dfrac{4!}{n_1! \cdot n_2! \cdot n_3!} \cdot a^{n_1} \cdot b^{n_2} \cdot c^{n_3}.$$

From here the general Multinomial Theorem follows easily: $(a_1 + a_2 + a_3 + \ldots + a_r)^n =$

$$\sum_{n_1 + n_2 + \ldots + n_r = n} \dfrac{n!}{n_1! \cdot n_2! \cdot \ldots \cdot n_r!} \cdot a_1^{n_1} \cdot a_2^{n_2} \cdot a_3^{n_3} \cdot \ldots \cdot a_r^{n_r}$$

Although rather cumbersome, some students might wish to prove this theorem by mathematical induction.

Following are two applications of the Multinomial Theorem.

1) Expand and simplify: $(2x + y - z)^3$

$$= \binom{3}{3,0,0}(2x)^3(y)^0(-z)^0 + \binom{3}{0,3,0}(2x)^0(y)^3(-z)^0$$

$$+ \binom{3}{0,0,3}(2x)^0(y)^0(-z)^3 + \binom{3}{2,1,0}(2x)^2(y)^1(-z)^0$$

$$+ \binom{3}{2,0,1}(2x)^2(y)^0(-z)^1 + \binom{3}{1,1,1}(2x)^1(y)^1(-z)^1$$

$$+ \binom{3}{0,2,1}(2x)^0(y)^2(-z)^1 + \binom{3}{0,1,2}(2x)^0(y)^1(-z)^2$$

$$+ \binom{3}{1,2,0}(2x)^1(y)^2(-z)^0 + \binom{3}{1,0,2}(2x)^1(y)^0(-z)^2$$

$(2x + y - z)^3 = 8x^3 + y^3 - z^3 + 12x^2y - 12x^2z + 6xy^2 + 6xz^2 - 12xyz - 3y^2z + 3yz^2.$

2) Find the term in the expansion of $(2x^2 - y^3 + \frac{1}{2}z)^7$ which contains x^4 and z^4. The general term of the expansion is: $\binom{7}{a,b,c}(2x^2)^a\,(-y^3)^b\left(\frac{1}{2}z\right)^c$, where $a + b + c = 7$. Thus the terms containing x^4 and z^4 have $a=2$ and $c=4$, $\therefore b=1$. Substituting in the above gives:

$$\binom{7}{2,1,4}(2x^2)^2(-y^3)^1\left(\frac{1}{2}z\right)^4 = \dfrac{7!}{2!1!4!}(4x^4)(-y^3) \times$$

$$\left(\dfrac{1}{16}z^4\right) = \dfrac{-105}{4}x^4y^3z^4.$$

Postassessment

1. Have students find the coefficient of a^2b^5d in the expansion of $(a+b-c-d)^8$.

2. Ask students to explain how the coefficients for any term of a multinomial expansion are derived.

3. Have students expand $(2x + y^2 - 3)^5$

101 Algebraic Solution of Cubic Equations

Man's interest in cubic equations can be traced back to the times of the early Babylonians about 1800–1600 B.C. However, the algebraic solution of third degree equations is a product of the Italian Renaissance.

The algebraic solution of cubic equations is thus associated with the names of the Italian mathematicians: Scipione del Ferro, Nicolo de Brescia (called Tartaglia), Girolamo Cardan, and Rafael Bombelli.

Performance Objectives

1. *Given some cubic equations, students will find their solutions.*
2. *Given a verbal problem which calls for a solution of a cubic equation, students will determine (where applicable) the real solutions to the problem.*

Preassessment

Students should have mastered operations with quadratic equations. They should also have a solid background in complex numbers and trigonometry.

Teaching Strategies

Review roots of complex numbers in the following fashion:

The nth root of a complex number z is obtained by taking the nth root of the absolute value r, and dividing the amplitude ϕ by n. This will give you the principal value of that root. The general formula to get all the roots of z is:

$$\sqrt[n]{z} = \sqrt[n]{r}\,[\mathrm{Cos}\,\frac{\phi + 2k\pi}{n} + i\,\mathrm{Sin}\,\frac{\phi + 2k\pi}{n}\,]$$

For $k = 0$, this yields the principal value, and for $k = 1, 2, 3, \ldots, n-1$, we get the rest of the roots.

Example 1: Find the cube roots of unity. We have that $1 = \mathrm{Cos}\,0° + i\,\mathrm{Sin}\,0°$, therefore, $\phi = 0°$ and $r = 1$.

The general formula is then, $z = \mathrm{Cos}\,\frac{2k\pi}{3} + i\,\mathrm{Sin}\,\frac{2k\pi}{3}$ where $k = 0, 1,$ and 2.

If $k = 0, z_1 = \mathrm{Cos}\,0 + i\,\mathrm{Sin}\,0 = 1$ (Principal value)

If $k = 1, z_2 = \mathrm{Cos}\,\frac{2\pi}{3} + i\,\mathrm{Sin}\,\frac{2\pi}{3} = \mathrm{Cos}\,120°$
$+ i\,\mathrm{Sin}\,120°$
$= -\mathrm{Cos}\,60° + i\,\mathrm{Sin}\,60° = -\frac{1}{2} + \frac{\sqrt{3}}{2}i$

If $k = 2, z_3 = \mathrm{Cos}\,\frac{4\pi}{3} + i\,\mathrm{Sin}\,\frac{4\pi}{3} = \mathrm{Cos}\,240° +$
$i\,\mathrm{Sin}\,240°$
$= -\mathrm{Cos}\,60° - i\,\mathrm{Sin}\,60° = -\frac{1}{2} - \frac{\sqrt{3}}{2}i$

Notice that each one of the complex roots of unity generates the other roots. To do so, we only have to take the second and third powers of those roots. For example, if we take $\alpha = z_2 = -\frac{1}{2} + \frac{\sqrt{3}}{2}i$, we get:

$\alpha^2 = (-\frac{1}{2} + \frac{\sqrt{3}}{2}i)^2 = (-\frac{1}{2})^2 + 2(-\frac{1}{2})(\frac{\sqrt{3}}{2}i)$
$+ (\frac{\sqrt{3}}{2}i)^2$

$\alpha^2 = \frac{1}{4} - \frac{\sqrt{3}}{2}i + \frac{3}{4}i^2$, but $i^2 = -1$, thus,

$\alpha^2 = \frac{1}{4} - \frac{3}{4} - \frac{\sqrt{3}}{2}i = -\frac{1}{2} - \frac{\sqrt{3}}{2}i = z_3$

Similarly,

$\alpha^3 = \alpha^2 \cdot \alpha = (-\frac{1}{2} - \frac{\sqrt{3}}{2}i)(-\frac{1}{2} + \frac{\sqrt{3}}{2}i)$

$\alpha^3 = (-\frac{1}{2})^2 - (\frac{\sqrt{3}}{2}i)^2 = \frac{1}{4} - \frac{3}{4}i^2$

$= \frac{1}{4} + \frac{3}{4} = 1 = z_1$

Therefore, the three roots of unity are: 1, α. and α^2 where α can be either $z_2 = -\frac{1}{2} + \frac{\sqrt{3}}{2}i$ or $z_3 = -\frac{1}{2} - \frac{\sqrt{3}}{2}i$.

Example 2: Find the cubic roots of the real number a. We have that $a = a\,(\mathrm{Cos}\,0° + i\,\mathrm{Sin}\,0°)$, therefore, $\sqrt[3]{a} = \sqrt[3]{r}\,(\mathrm{Cos}\,\frac{2k\pi}{3} - i\,\mathrm{Sin}\,\frac{2k\pi}{3})$, where $k = 0, 1,$ or 2. But, $\mathrm{Cos}\,\frac{2k\pi}{3} - i\,\mathrm{Sin}\,\frac{2k\pi}{3}$ where $k = 0,$ 1 or 2, will give the three roots of unity (see Example 1). Thus, if the real root of a is a', the three roots of a will be: a', $a'\alpha$, and $a'\alpha^2$, where α can be either $-\frac{1}{2} + \frac{\sqrt{3}}{2}i$, or $-\frac{1}{2} - \frac{\sqrt{3}}{2}i$.

Let us now consider the general cubic equation:
$$ax^3 + bx^2 + cx + d = 0,$$
where $a, b, c,$ and d are arbitrary complex numbers. This equation can be reduced to a simpler form without the second degree term, by making the transformation $x = y - \frac{b}{3a}$. Thus, we have:

$$a\left(y - \frac{b}{3a}\right)^3 + b\left(y - \frac{b}{3a}\right)^2 + c\left(y - \frac{b}{3a}\right) + d = 0$$

$$a\left(y^3 - \frac{b}{a}y^2 + \frac{b^2}{3a^2}y - \frac{b}{27a^3}\right) + b\left(y^2 - \frac{2b}{3a}y + \right.$$

$$\left.\frac{b^2}{9a^2}\right) + c\,(y - \frac{b}{3a}) + d = 0, \text{ and we have,}$$

$$ay^3 + \left(\frac{b^2}{3a} - \frac{2b^2}{3a} + c\right)y + \left(-\frac{b^3}{27a^2} + \frac{b^3}{9a^2} - \frac{bc}{3a} + d\right) = 0$$

Now, if we make:

$$\frac{b^2}{3a} - \frac{2b^2}{3a} + c = c' \quad \text{and} \quad \frac{-b^3}{27a^2} + \frac{b^3}{9a^2} - \frac{bc}{3a} + d = d',$$

the general equation will become:

$$ay^3 + c'y + d = 0$$

To avoid fractions in the solution of this equation, we divide it by a, and write it in the following fashion:

$$y^3 + 3py + 2q = 0$$

This last equation is called the reduced cubic equation and, as we have shown, any cubic equation can be reduced to that form.

To solve the reduced equation, the following identity is considered:

$$(a+b)^3 - 3ab\,(a+b) - (a^3+b^3) = 0$$

If this identity is compared with the reduced equation, we have that:

$$a + b = y, \quad ab = -p, \quad \text{and} \quad a^3 + b^3 = -2q$$

From these equations, we see that we only have to find the values of a and b to find y. This can be done by solving the system:

$$ab = -p \qquad \text{or} \qquad a^3b^3 = -p^3$$
$$a^3 + b^3 = -2q \qquad\qquad a^3 + b^3 = -2q$$

From the second equation we have that: $b^3 = -2q - a^3$, and substituting this value in the first equation, we have: $-a^3(2q + a^3) = -p^3$, therefore, $a^6 + 2a^3q - p^3 = 0$

If we make $a^3 = v$, we obtain the following quadratic equation: $v^2 + 2qv - p^3 = 0$.

The roots of this quadratic equation are:

$$v_1 = -q + \sqrt{q^2 + p^3} \quad \text{and}$$
$$v_2 = -q - \sqrt{q^2 + p^3}.$$

Because of the symmetry of a and b in the system, we can take v_1 or v_2 to be a^3 or b^3 randomly.

So, $a^3 = -q + \sqrt{q^2 + p^3}$ and
$$b^3 = -q - \sqrt{q^2 + p^3}$$

Therefore, $a = \sqrt[3]{-q + \sqrt{q^2 + p^3}}$ and
$$b = \sqrt[3]{-q - \sqrt{q^2 + p^3}},$$

But $y = a + b$, thus,

$$y = \sqrt[3]{-q + \sqrt{q^2 + p^3}} + \sqrt[3]{-q - \sqrt{q^2 + p^3}},$$

which is called Cardan's formula for the cubic.

Since a^3 and b^3 have three roots each, it seems, that y has nine roots. This is not the case, for since $ab = -p$, the cubic roots of a^3 and b^3 are to be taken in pairs so that their product (which is ab) is a rational number $-p$.

Now, we know that the cubic roots of a^3 are: a (the principal value), $a\alpha$, and $a\alpha^2$, where α is one of the complex roots of unity. Similarly, the cubic roots of b^3 are: b, $b\alpha$, and $b\alpha^2$.

However, if the product of a and b must be rational, we have that the only admissible solutions are: (a,b), $(a\alpha, b\alpha^2)$, and $(a\alpha^2, b\alpha)$, because:

$$ab = -p$$
$$a\alpha \cdot b\alpha^2 = ab\alpha^3 = ab = -p \quad \text{(because } \alpha^3 = 1\text{)}$$
$$a\alpha^2 \cdot b\alpha = ab\alpha^3 = ab = -p$$

Therefore, the values of y are:
$$a + b, \quad a\alpha + b\alpha^2, \quad \text{and} \quad a\alpha^2 + b\alpha.$$

But $x = y - \dfrac{b}{3a}$ and so, the roots of the general cubic equation will be found once we know y.

Example 3: Solve the equation $x^3 + 3x^2 + 9x - 13 = 0$. First, we must reduce this equation to eliminate the second degree term. The transformation is: $x = y - \dfrac{b}{3a}$. In this example, $a = 1$, $b = 3$, $c = 9$, and $d = -13$. Therefore, $x = y - \dfrac{3}{3(1)} = y - 1$.

Thus, substituting $y - 1$ for x in the equation, $(y-1)^3 + 3(y-1)^2 + 9(y-1) - 13 = 0$, or $(y^3 - 3y^2 + 3y - 1) + 3(y^2 - 2y + 1) + 9(y-1) - 13 = 0$
So, $y^3 - 6y - 20 = 0$ is the reduced equation.

Therefore,
$$3p = 6, \; p = 2, \; \text{and} \; p^3 = 8$$
$$2q = -20, \; q = -10, \; \text{and} \; q^2 = 100.$$

Thus, $\sqrt{q^2 + p^3} = \sqrt{108} = 6\sqrt{3}$, and,

$$a = \sqrt[3]{10 + 6\sqrt{3}} = \sqrt[3]{1 + 3\sqrt{3} + 9 + 3\sqrt{3}}$$
$$= \sqrt[3]{(1+\sqrt{3})^3} = 1 + \sqrt{3}$$
$$b = \sqrt[3]{10 - 6\sqrt{3}} = \sqrt[3]{1 - 3\sqrt{3} + 9 - 3\sqrt{3}}$$
$$= \sqrt[3]{(1 - \sqrt{3})^3} = 1 - \sqrt{3}$$

The solutions for the reduced equation are then,

$$y_1 = a + b = (1 + \sqrt{3}) + (1 - \sqrt{3}) = 2$$
$$y_2 = a\alpha + b\alpha^2 = (1 + \sqrt{3})\left(-\frac{1}{2} + \frac{\sqrt{3}}{2}i\right)$$
$$+ (1 - \sqrt{3})\left(-\frac{1}{2} - \frac{\sqrt{3}}{2}i\right) = -1 + 3i$$
$$y_3 = a\alpha^2 + b\alpha = (1 + \sqrt{3})\left(-\frac{1}{2} - \frac{\sqrt{3}}{2}i\right)$$
$$+ (1 - \sqrt{3})\left(-\frac{1}{2} + \frac{\sqrt{3}}{2}i\right)$$
$$= -1 - 3i.$$

But, $x = y - 1$. Therefore:

$$x_1 = y_1 - 1 = 2 - 1 = 1$$
$$x_2 = y_2 - 1 = -1 + 3i - 1 = -2 + 3i$$
$$x_3 = y_3 - 1 = -1 - 3i - 1 = -2 - 3i$$

Thus, in this example, we have for solutions one real and two conjugate complex roots. In this first of two units, we have studied the general solution of the cubic. In a second, we will study the different cases, reducible and irreducible, in the solution of Cardan's formula.

Students who have met the performance objectives should be able to do the following exercises:
1) Find the roots of $x^3 + 6x^2 + 17x + 18 = 0$
2) Solve: $x^3 - 11x^2 + 35x - 25 = 0$
3) Find the solution of $x^3 - 3x^2 + 3x - 1 = 0$

102 **Solving Cubic Equations**

In the first of two units on cubic equations, we have studied the general solution of the cubic. In this second, we will study the different cases, reducible and irreducible, in the solution of Cardan's formula for the cubic.

Performance Objectives

1. *Given some cubic equations, students will analyze them to see the kind of solutions they are going to obtain when the equation is solved.*

2. *Students will solve given cubic equations.*

Preassessment

Students should have mastered operations with complex numbers and quadratic equations. They should also have a solid background in trigonometry.

Teaching Strategies

Review the content of the previous unit on cubic equations in the following fashion: Given a general cubic equation $Ax^3 + Bx^2 + Cx + D = 0$, it is always possible to eliminate the second degree term by making the change of variables $x = y - \dfrac{B}{3A}$. This transformation will lead to an equation of the form $y^3 + 3py + 2q = 0$, which is called the reduced or normal cubic equation.

The solution of the reduced equation is given by the Cardan's formula $y = \sqrt[3]{-q + \sqrt{q^2 + p^3}} + \sqrt[3]{-q - \sqrt{q^2 + p^3}}$. If $a = \sqrt[3]{-q + \sqrt{q^2 + p^3}}$ and $b = \sqrt[3]{-q - \sqrt{q^2 + p^3}}$, the roots of the reduced equations are: $y_1 = a + b$, $y_2 = a\alpha + b\alpha^2$, and $y_3 = a\alpha^2 + b\alpha$ where $\alpha = -\dfrac{1}{2} + \dfrac{\sqrt{3}}{2} i$ and $\alpha^2 = \dfrac{1}{2} - \dfrac{\sqrt{3}}{2} i$ are cube roots of unity.

Once the values y_1, y_2, and y_3 are found, the solutions of the general cubic equation will be obtained by using the transformation $x = y - \dfrac{B}{3A}$.

From the Cardan's formula, it is obvious that the nature of the solutions will depend on the value of $q^2 + p^3$ which for this reason is called the discriminant of the cubic. This is so, because $q^2 + p^3$, being under a square root will yield real or imaginary values according to the sign of the sum $q^2 + p^3$.

Before discussing the discriminant, it is useful to rewrite solutions of the reduced equation in the following fashion:

$$y_1 = a + b; \quad y_2 = a\alpha + b\alpha^2 = a(-\frac{1}{2} + \frac{\sqrt{3}}{2} i)$$
$$+ b(-\frac{1}{2} - \frac{\sqrt{3}}{2} i); y_3 = a\alpha^2 + b\alpha = a(-\frac{1}{2} - \frac{\sqrt{3}}{2} i)$$
$$+ b(-\frac{1}{2} + -\frac{\sqrt{3}}{2} i)$$

and simplifying:

$$y_1 = a + b; \quad y_2 = -\frac{a + b}{2} + \frac{a - b}{2} \sqrt{3} i;$$
$$y_3 = -\frac{a + b}{2} - \frac{a - b}{2} \sqrt{3} i.$$

Let us now consider the discriminant $q^2 + p^3$.

I) If $q^2 + p^3 > 0$, a and b have each one real value, then we can suppose a and b will be real also. Consequently, $a + b$ and $a - b$ will be real also. Therefore, we have that if $a + b = m$ and $a - b = n$, the solutions of the reduced equation are:

$$y_1 = a + b = m; \quad y_2 = -\frac{m}{2} + \frac{n}{2}\sqrt{3} i; \quad y_3 = -\frac{m}{2} - \frac{n}{2}\sqrt{3} i.$$

Thus, if $q^2 + p^3 > 0$, we have one real root and two conjugate imaginary.

Example 1: Solve $x^3 - 6x^2 + 10x - 8 = 0$
First, we must eliminate the square term. The transformation for this example is:

$$x = y - \frac{B}{3A} = y - \frac{-6}{3} = y + 2$$

Thus, substituting $y + 2$ for x in the equation:

$(y + 2)^3 - 6(y + 2)^2 + 10(y + 2) - 8 = 0$

$y^3 + 6y^2 + 12y + 8 - 6y^2 - 24y - 24 + 10y$
$\quad + 20 - 8 = 0$

$y^3 - 2y - 4 = 0$ (Reduced equation)

Therefore:

$$3p = -2 \quad p = -\frac{2}{3} \quad \text{and} \quad p^3 = -\frac{8}{27}$$

$$2q = -4 \quad q = -2 \quad \text{and} \quad q^2 = 4$$

Thus, $q^2 + p^3 = 4 - \dfrac{8}{27} = \dfrac{100}{27} > 0.$

Therefore, we know that in the solution one root must be real and two conjugate imaginary.

The values for a and b are:

$$a = \sqrt[3]{-q + \sqrt{q^2 + p^3}} = \sqrt[3]{2 + \sqrt{\frac{100}{27}}} = \sqrt[3]{2 + \frac{10}{3\sqrt{3}}}$$

$$b = \sqrt[3]{-q - \sqrt{q^2 + p^3}} = \sqrt[3]{2 - \sqrt{\frac{100}{27}}} = \sqrt[3]{2 - \frac{10}{3\sqrt{3}}}$$

and simplifying:

$$a = \sqrt[3]{\frac{6\sqrt{3} + 10}{3\sqrt{3}}} = \sqrt[3]{\frac{3\sqrt{3} + 9 + 3\sqrt{3} + 1}{\sqrt{27}}} = \sqrt[3]{\frac{(3 - 1)^3}{\sqrt{27}}}$$

$$b = \sqrt[3]{\frac{6\sqrt{3} - 10}{3\sqrt{3}}} = \sqrt[3]{\frac{3\sqrt{3} - 9 + 3\sqrt{3} - 1}{\sqrt{27}}} = \sqrt[3]{\frac{(\sqrt{3} - 1)^3}{\sqrt{27}}}$$

$$a = \frac{\sqrt{3} + 1}{\sqrt{3}} \quad \text{and} \quad b = \frac{\sqrt{3} - 1}{\sqrt{3}}$$

The solutions for the reduced equation are then:

$$y_1 = a + b = \frac{\sqrt{3} + 1}{\sqrt{3}} + \frac{\sqrt{3} - 1}{\sqrt{3}} = 2$$

$$y_2 = a\alpha + b\alpha^2 = \left(\frac{\sqrt{3} + 1}{\sqrt{3}}\right)\left(-\frac{1}{2} + \frac{\sqrt{3}}{2}i\right)$$
$$+ \left(\frac{\sqrt{3} - 1}{\sqrt{3}}\right)\left(-\frac{1}{2} - \frac{\sqrt{3}}{2}i\right)$$

$$y_3 = a\alpha^2 + b\alpha = \left(\frac{\sqrt{3} + 1}{\sqrt{3}}\right)\left(-\frac{1}{2} - \frac{\sqrt{3}}{2}i\right)$$
$$+ \left(\frac{\sqrt{3} - 1}{3}\right)\left(-\frac{1}{2} + \frac{\sqrt{3}}{2}i\right)$$

and simplifying

$y_1 = 2; \, y_2 = -1 + i; \, y_3 = -1 - i.$

Therefore the solutions of the general equation are:

$x_1 = y_1 + 2 = 2 + 2 = 4$

$x_2 = y_2 + 2 = -1 + i + 2 = 1 + i$

$x_3 = y_3 + 2 = -1 - i + 2 = 1 - i$

II) If $q^2 + p^3 = 0$, a and b are equal; therefore if m represents the common real value of a and b, we have:

$$y_1 = m + m = 2m$$

$$y_2 = -\frac{m + m}{2} + \frac{m - m}{2}\sqrt{3}\,i = -m$$

$$y_3 = -\frac{m + m}{2} - \frac{m - m}{2}\sqrt{3}\,i = -m$$

Thus, in this case we have that all the roots are real and two are equal.

Example 2: Find the roots of $x^3 - 12x + 16 = 0$

In this example we already have the reduced equation, therefore:

$3p = -12 \quad p = -4 \quad \text{and} \quad p^3 = -64$

$2q = 16 \quad q = 8 \quad \text{and} \quad q^2 = 64$

thus, $q^2 + p^3 = 64 - 64 = 0$. This means that the solution will have three real roots, two of them equal. The values of a and b are:

$$a = \sqrt[3]{-q + \sqrt{q^2 + p^3}} = \sqrt[3]{-8} = -2$$

$$b = \sqrt[3]{-q - \sqrt{q^2 + p^3}} = \sqrt[3]{-8} = -2$$

Therefore the roots are:

$y_1 = a + b = -4$

$y_2 = a\alpha + b\alpha^2 = -2(\alpha + \alpha^2)$

$$= -2\left(-\frac{1}{2} + \frac{\sqrt{3}}{2}i - \frac{1}{2} - \frac{\sqrt{3}}{2}i\right) = 2$$

$y_3 = a\alpha^2 + b\alpha = -2(\alpha^2 + \alpha)$

$$= -2\left(-\frac{1}{2} - \frac{\sqrt{3}}{2}i - \frac{1}{2} + \frac{\sqrt{3}}{2}i\right) = 2$$

III) If $q^2 + p^3 < 0$, a and b will be complex numbers because of the square root of the discriminant which is negative in this case. Therefore, if the values a and b are $a = M + Ni$ and $b = M - Ni$, the solutions of the reduced equation will be:

$y_1 = a + b = 2M$

$$y_2 = -\frac{2M}{2} + \frac{2Ni}{2}\sqrt{3}i = -M - \sqrt{3}\,N$$

$$y_3 = -\frac{2M}{2} - \frac{2Ni}{2}\sqrt{3}i = -M + \sqrt{3}\,N$$

which are all real roots and unequal.

However, there is no general arithmetic or algebraic method of finding the exact value of the cubic root of complex numbers. Therefore, Cardan's formula is of little use in this case, which for this reason is called the irreducible case.

The solution of this case can be obtained with the use of trigonometry. Thus, when the Cardan's formula has the form $y = \sqrt[3]{u + vi} + \sqrt[3]{u - vi}$ we call

$r = \sqrt{u^2 + v^2}$ and $\tan \Theta = \dfrac{v}{u}$; therefore, the cubic root of them will be:

$$y = \sqrt[3]{r}\left[\text{Cos}\frac{\Theta + 2k\pi}{3} + i\,\text{Sin}\frac{\Theta + 2k\pi}{3}\right]$$
$$+ \sqrt[3]{r}\left[\text{Cos}\frac{\Theta + 2k\pi}{3} - i\,\text{Sin}\frac{\Theta + 2k\pi}{3}\right]$$

where $k = 0, 1,$ and 2.

If we simplify this expression we obtain:

$$y = 2\sqrt[3]{r}\,\text{Cos}\frac{\Theta + 2k\pi}{3} \quad \text{where } k = 0, 1, \text{ and } 2.$$

Therefore the three roots are:

$$y_1 = 2\sqrt[3]{r}\,\text{Cos}\frac{\Theta}{3}; \, y_2 = 2\sqrt[3]{r}\,\text{Cos}\frac{\Theta + 2\pi}{3};$$

$$y_3 = 2\sqrt[3]{r}\,\text{Cos}\frac{\Theta + 4\pi}{3}.$$

Example 3: Solve $x^3 - 6x - 4 = 0$

From this equation we have: $3p = -6$ and $2q = -4$; therefore, $p^3 = -8$, $q^2 = 4$, $p^3 + q^2 = -4$ and $\sqrt{p^3 + q^2} = 2i$

The solution then would be: $y = \sqrt{2 + 2i} + \sqrt{2 - 2i}$,

thus, $r = \sqrt{4 + 4} = \sqrt{8}$, $\tan \Theta = \frac{2}{2}$ or $\tan \Theta = 1$ and $\Theta = \frac{\pi}{4}$. Therefore, the roots of the equation are:

$$x_1 = 2\sqrt[3]{r} \; \text{Cos} \; \frac{\Theta}{3} = 2\sqrt[3]{\sqrt{8}} \; \text{Cos} \; \frac{\pi}{12} = 2\sqrt{2} \; \text{Cos} \; 15°$$

$$x_2 = 2\sqrt[3]{r} \; \text{Cos} \; \frac{\Theta + 2\pi}{3} = 2\sqrt{2} \; \text{Cos} \; \frac{\pi/4 + 2\pi}{3} = 2\sqrt{2} \; \text{Cos} \; 135°$$

$$x_3 = 2\sqrt[3]{r} \; \text{Cos} \; \frac{\Theta + 14\pi}{3} = 2\sqrt{2} \; \text{Cos} \; \frac{\pi/4 + 4\pi}{3} = 2\sqrt{2} \; \text{Cos} \; 255°$$

But,

$$\text{Sin} \; \frac{y}{2} = \sqrt{\frac{1 - \text{Cos} \, x}{2}} \quad \text{and} \quad \text{Cos} \; \frac{x}{2} = \sqrt{\frac{1 + \text{Cos} \, x}{2}}$$

Therefore,

$$\text{Sin} \; 15° = \sqrt{\frac{1 - \text{Cos} \, 30°}{2}} = \sqrt{\frac{1 - \sqrt{3}/2}{2}} = \frac{\sqrt{2 - \sqrt{3}}}{2}$$

and

$$\text{Cos} \; 15° = \sqrt{\frac{1 + \text{Cos} \, 30°}{2}} = \sqrt{\frac{1 + \sqrt{3}/2}{2}} = \frac{\sqrt{2 + \sqrt{3}}}{2}$$

Thus, the roots are:

$$x_1 = 2\sqrt{2} \; \sqrt{\frac{2 + \sqrt{3}}{3}} = \sqrt{4 + 2\sqrt{3}} = \sqrt{1 + 2\sqrt{3} + 3}$$
$$= \sqrt{(1 + \sqrt{3})^2} = 1 + \sqrt{3}$$

$$x_2 = 2\sqrt{2} \; \text{Cos} \; 135° = 2\sqrt{2}(-\text{Cos}\,45°) = 2\sqrt{2}(-\sqrt{2}) = -2$$

$$x_3 = 2\sqrt{2} \; (-\text{Sin} \; 15°) = 2\sqrt{2} \; (-\sqrt{\frac{1 - \sqrt{3}/2}{2}}) = -\sqrt{(1 - \sqrt{3})^2} = \sqrt{1 - 3}$$

The reducible cases may also employ the aid of trigonometry.

Postassessment

Students who have met the performance objectives should be able to do the following exercises: Analyze and then solve the following cubics:

1) $x^3 - 6x^2 + 11x - 6 = 0$
2) $x^3 - 5x^2 + 9x - 9 = 0$
3) $x^3 - 75x + 250 = 0$
4) $x^3 - 6x^2 + 3x + 10 = 0$

103 Calculating Sums of Finite Series

Mathematical induction has become thoroughly entrenched in secondary school curricula. Many textbooks provide a variety of applications of this technique of proof. Most popular among these applications is proving that specific series have given formulas as sums. Although most students merely work the proof as required, some may question how the sum of a particular series was actually generated.

This unit will provide you with a response to students' requests for deriving formulas for certain series summations.

Performance Objectives

1. Given some finite series, students will find their sum.

2. Students will develop formulas for determining the sum of various finite series.

Preassessment

Students should have mastered operations with algebraic expressions, functions, and concepts of finite sequence and series.

Teaching Strategies

Review concepts of sequences and series in the following fashion.

A *finite sequence* is a finite set of ordered elements or terms, each related to one or more of the preceding elements in some specifiable way.

Examples: 1) $1, 3, 5, 7, \ldots, 19$
2) $\sin x, \sin 2x, \sin 3x, \ldots, \sin 20x$
3) $2, 4, 6, 8, \ldots, 2n$

Let us now consider any finite sequence of elements $u_1, u_2, \ldots, u_n$. We can obtain the following partial sums:

$$s_1 = u_1$$
$$s_2 = u_1 + u_2$$
$$s_3 = u_1 + u_2 + u_3$$
$$\cdots\cdots\cdots\cdots\cdots\cdots\cdots$$
$$s_n = u_1 + u_2 + \ldots + u_n$$

We call this sum $u_1 + u_2 + \ldots + u_n$ a *finite series* of the elements of the sequence $u_1, u_2, \ldots, u_n$. S_n represents the total sum of these elements. For example, if we have the sequence 1, 2, 3, 4, the series is $1 + 2 + 3 + 4$, and the sum S_4 is 10.

This example is a simple one. However, if instead of considering four terms 1, 2, 3, and 4, we consider "n" terms 1, 2, 3, ..., n, it will not be that simple to calculate their sum $S_n = 1 + 2 + 3 + \ldots + n$. Sometimes, there are easy ways to calculate the sum of a specific series, but we cannot apply that particular method to all the series.

For example, the previous series $1 + 2 + 3 + \ldots + n$, could be calculated by using the following artifice:

$$1 = 1 = \frac{1 \cdot 2}{2}$$

$$1 + 2 = 3 = \frac{2 \cdot 3}{2}$$

$$1 + 2 + 3 = 6 = \frac{3 \cdot 4}{2}$$

$$\cdots\cdots\cdots\cdots\cdots\cdots\cdots$$

$$1 + 2 + \ldots + n = \frac{n(n + 1)}{2}$$

which is the total sum of the series.

This means that if we want to calculate the sum of the series $1 + 2 + 3 + \ldots + 10$, we will have:

$$S_{10} = \frac{10(10 + 1)}{2} = \frac{10 \cdot 11}{2} = 55.$$

We cannot apply this artifice to every series, therefore, we must find a more general method which permits us to calculate the sum of several series. This method is given by the following theorem:

Theorem: Let us consider a finite series $u_1 + u_2 + u_3 + \ldots + u_n$ If we can find a function $F(n)$ such that $u_n = F(n + 1) - F(n)$ then, $u_1 + u_2 + \ldots + u_n = F(n + 1) - F(1)$.

Proof: We have by hypothesis that: $u_n = F(n + 1) - F(n)$; therefore, if we apply it for $n - 1, n - 2, \ldots, 3, 2, 1$, we will get the following relations:

$$u_n = F(n + 1) - F(n)$$
$$u_{n - 1} = F(n) - F(n - 1)$$
$$u_{n - 2} = F(n - 1) - F(n - 2)$$

$$\begin{matrix} \cdot & \cdot & \cdot \\ \cdot & \cdot & \cdot \\ \cdot & \cdot & \cdot \end{matrix}$$

$$u_2 = F(3) - F(2)$$
$$u_1 = F(2) - F(1)$$

If we now add these relations, we will get: $u_1 + u_2 + u_3 + \ldots + u_n = F(n + 1) - F(1)$ which proves the theorem.

Before having students embark on applications, have them consider the following examples:

1. Find the sum of the series $1 + 2 + 3 + \ldots + n$. Because $u_n = n$, we consider $F(n) = An^2 + Bn + C$.

(A polynomial one degree higher than u_n should be used.) Therefore, $F(n + 1) = A(n + 1)^2 + B(n + 1) + C$. According to the theorem above, we must have:

$$u_n = F(n + 1) - F(n)$$
$$n = [A(n + 1)^2 + B(n + 1) + C] - [An^2 + Bn + C]$$
$$n = 2An + (A + B)$$

Therefore, by equating coefficients of powers of n we get: $2A = 1$, and $A + B = 0$. By solving these simultaneously we get: $A = \frac{1}{2}$ and $B = -\frac{1}{2}$

Therefore, $F(n) = \frac{1}{2}n^2 - \frac{1}{2}n + C$,
$$F(n + 1) = \frac{1}{2}(n + 1)^2 - \frac{1}{2}(n + 1) + C,$$
and $F(1) = C$

Thus, $1 + 2 + 3 + \ldots + n = F(n + 1) - F(1)$
$$= \frac{1}{2}(n + 1)^2 - \frac{1}{2}(n + 1)$$
$$= \frac{1}{2}n(n + 1).$$

2. Find the sum of the series $1^2 + 2^2 + 3^2 + \ldots + n^2$. Since $u_n = n^2$, we consider $F(n) = An^3 + Bn^2 + Cn + D$ (One degree higher than u_n, since the highest power of $F(n)$ will be annihilated in $F(n + 1) - F(n)$. Thus $F(n + 1) = A(n + 1)^3 + B(n + 1)^2 + C(n + 1) + D$.

Now, $u_n = n^2 = F(n + 1) - F(n)$
$$n^2 = [A(n + 1)^3 + B(n + 1)^2 + C(n + 1) + D] - [An^3 + Bn^2 + Cn + D]$$
$$n^2 = 3An^2 + (3A + 2B)n + (A + B + C)$$

By equating coefficients of powers of n, we get
$$3A = 1; \quad 3A + 2B = 0; \quad \text{and} \quad A + B + C = 0$$
and solving simultaneously:

$$A = 1/3; \quad B = -1/2; \quad C = 1/6$$

Thus, $F(n) = \frac{1}{3}n^3 - \frac{1}{2}n^2 + \frac{1}{6}n + D$

$$F(n + 1) = \frac{1}{3}(n + 1)^3 - \frac{1}{2}(n + 1)^2 + \frac{1}{6}(n + 1) + D$$

$$F(1) = \frac{1}{3} - \frac{1}{2} + \frac{1}{6} + D = D$$

Hence, $1^2 + 2^2 + 3^2 + \ldots + n^2$
$$= F(n + 1) - F(1)$$
$$= \frac{1}{3}(n + 1)^3 - \frac{1}{2}(n + 1)^2 + \frac{1}{6}(n + 1)$$
$$= \frac{n(n + 1)(2n + 1)}{6}$$

3. Find the sum of the series $1^3 + 3^3 + 5^3 + \ldots + (2n - 1)^3$. Since u_n is of third degree, $F(n) = An^4 + Bn^3 + Cn^2 + Dn + E$ and $F(n + 1) = A(n + 1)^4 + B(n + 1)^3 + C(n + 1)^2 + D(n + 1) + E$.

Thus, $u_n = (2n - 1)^3 = F(n + 1) - F(n)$; or $8n^3 - 12n^2 + 6n - 1 = 4An^3 + (6A + 3B)n^2 + (4A + 3B + 2C)n + (A + B + C + D)$.

Equating coefficients:
$4A = 8$, and $A = 2$; $6A + 3B = -12$, and $B = -8$;
$4A + 3B + 2C = 6$; and $C = 11$; $A + B + C + D = -1$, and $D = -6$

Therefore, $F(n) = 2n^4 - 8n^3 + 11n^2 - 6n + E$;
$$F(n + 1) = 2(n + 1)^4 - 8(n + 1)^3$$
$$+ 11(n + 1)^2 - 6(n + 1) + E;$$
and $\quad F(1) = -1 + E$.
Thus,
$$1^3 + 3^3 + 5^3 + \ldots + (2n - 1)^3 = F(n + 1) - F(1)$$
$$= 2(n + 1)^4 - 8(n + 1)^3 + 11(n + 1)^2 - 6(n + 1)$$
$$+ E - (-1 + E) = 2n^4 - n^2 = n^2(2n^2 - 1).$$

4. Find the sum of the series $\frac{1}{2} + \frac{1}{4} + \ldots + \frac{1}{2^n}$
Let us consider $F(n) = \dfrac{A}{2^n}$ and therefore, $F(n + 1)$
$= \dfrac{A}{2^{n+1}}$ Hence, $u_n = F(n + 1) - F(n)$. Thus,
$\dfrac{1}{2^n} = \dfrac{A}{2^{n+1}} - \dfrac{A}{2^n}$, therefore $A = -2$. Hence,
$F(n + 1) = -\dfrac{1}{2^n}$; and $F(1) = -1$. Therefore,

$$\frac{1}{2} + \frac{1}{4} + \ldots + \frac{1}{2^n} = F(n + 1) - F(1)$$
$$= -\frac{1}{2^n} + 1$$
$$= 1 - \frac{1}{2^n}$$

After sufficient practice students should be able to find $F(n)$ more easily.

Postassessment
Students who have met the performance objectives should be able to do the following exercises:
1) Find the sum of the series $1 + 8 + 27 + \ldots + n^3$.
2) Find the sum of the series $1/5 + 1/25 + 1/125 + \ldots + 1/5^n$.
3. Find the formula for the sum of a finite arithmetic progression.

104 A General Formula For The Sum Of Series Of The Form $\sum\limits_{t=1}^{n} t^r$

The calculation of the sum of convergent series is an important topic. There is not, however, a general formula to calculate the sum of any given convergent series.

This unit will provide you with a general formula to calculate the sum of series of the specific type $\sum\limits_{t=1}^{n} t^r$.

Performance Objectives
1. Given some infinite series of the form $\sum\limits_{t=1}^{n} t^r$, students will find their sum.
2. Students will demonstrate an understanding of the technique used to find general formulas for certain specific series.

Preassessment
Students should know the Binomial Theorem and have a fair knowledge of series and elementary linear algebra.

Teaching Strategies
Review the concept of series and the Binomial Theorem in the following fashion.

A series is a sum of the elements of a given sequence. · For example, if we have the sequence of elements $u_1, u_2, \ldots, u_n$, the series is $u_1 + u_2 + \ldots + u_n$. This series can also be represented by the symbol $\sum\limits_{r=1}^{n} u_r$. Thus, the symbol $\sum\limits_{n=1}^{n} k^2$ means $1^2 + 2^2 + \ldots + n^2$.

Another example of series is the one represented by $\sum\limits_{m=0}^{k} \binom{k}{m} a^{k-m} b^m$, where a and b are arbitrary real numbers, k is any positive integer, and $\binom{k}{m} = \dfrac{k!}{m!(k-m)!}$. This series can be proved to be equal to $(a + b)^k$, and this fact is known as the *Binomial Theorem*.

There is also a less known but important theorem from the theory of series whose proof we are going to give in this unit. We are going to use this theorem and the Binomial Theorem in the development of our discussion.

Lemma: Let us consider a finite series $\sum\limits_{r=1}^{n} u_r$. If we can find a function $f(n)$ such that $u_n = f(n+1) - f(n)$, then $\sum\limits_{r=1}^{n} u_r = f(n+1) - f(1)$

Proof: We have by hypothesis that: $u_n = f(n+1) - f(n)$; therefore, if we apply it for $n-1, n-2, \ldots, 3, 2, 1$, we will get the following relations:
$$u_n = f(n+1) - f(n)$$
$$u_{n-1} = f(n) - f(n-1)$$
$$u_{n-2} = f(n-1) - f(n-2)$$
$$\ldots\ldots\ldots\ldots\ldots\ldots\ldots$$
$$u_2 = f(3) - f(2)$$
$$u_1 = f(2) - f(1)$$

If we now add these relations, we will get $\sum_{r=1}^{n} u_r$ equal to $f(n+1) - f(1)$ which proves the theorem.

Let $\sum_{t=1}^{n} t^r$ be the series whose sum we want. In order to apply the previous Lemma to this series, we may consider the arbitrary function $f(n) = \sum_{k=0}^{r+1} b_k n^k$ where b is any real number and n is any positive integer. Thus, $f(n+1) = \sum_{k=0}^{r+1} b_k (n+1)^k$. If we now impose the condition of the hypothesis of the Lemma to this function for the series $\sum_{t=1}^{n} t^r$, we have:

$$u_n = f(n+1) - f(n)$$

or

$$n^r = \sum_{k=0}^{r+1} b_k (n+1)^k - \sum_{k=0}^{r+1} b_k n^k$$

$$n^r = \sum_{k=0}^{r+1} b_k [(n+1)^k - n^k] \qquad \text{(I)}$$

But according to the Binomial Theorem,

$$(n+1)^k = \sum_{m=0}^{k} \binom{k}{m} n^{k-m} \text{ and thus,}$$

$$(n+1)^k - n^k = \sum_{m=1}^{k} \binom{k}{m} n^{k-m}.$$

Therefore in (I) we have:

$$n^r = \sum_{k=0}^{r+1} b_k \left[\sum_{m=1}^{k} \binom{k}{m} n^{k-m} \right]$$

This equation leads to the following system of equations:

$$\binom{r+1}{1} b_{r+1} = 0$$

$$\binom{r+1}{2} b_{r+1} + \binom{r}{1} b_r = 0$$

$$\binom{r+1}{3} b_{r+1} + \binom{r}{2} b_r + \binom{r-1}{1} b_{r-1} \ldots \ldots = 0$$

$$\ldots \ldots \ldots \ldots \ldots \ldots \ldots \ldots \ldots \ldots = 0$$

$$\binom{r+1}{m} b_{r+1} + \binom{r}{m-1} b_r + \binom{r-1}{m-2} b_{r-1} + \ldots = 0$$

$$\ldots \ldots \ldots \ldots \ldots \ldots \ldots \ldots \ldots \ldots = 0$$

$$\binom{r+1}{r+1} b_{r+1} + \binom{r}{r} b_r + \ldots \ldots + \binom{1}{1} b_1 \ldots = 0$$

This system of equations can be expressed in matrix form as follows:

$$\begin{bmatrix} \binom{r+1}{1} & 0 & 0 & 0 & \ldots & 0 \\ \binom{r+1}{2} & \binom{r}{1} & 0 & 0 & \ldots & 0 \\ \binom{r+1}{3} & \binom{r}{2} & \binom{r-1}{1} & 0 & \ldots & 0 \\ \vdots & \vdots & \vdots & \vdots & & \vdots \\ \binom{r+1}{m} & \binom{r}{m-1} & \binom{r-1}{m-2} & 0 & \ldots & 0 \\ \vdots & \vdots & \vdots & \vdots & & \vdots \\ \binom{r+1}{r+1} & \binom{r}{r} & \binom{r-1}{r-1} & \binom{r-2}{r-2} & \ldots & 1 \end{bmatrix} \begin{bmatrix} b_{r+1} \\ b_r \\ b_{r-1} \\ \vdots \\ b_m \\ \vdots \\ b_1 \end{bmatrix} = \begin{bmatrix} 1 \\ 0 \\ 0 \\ \vdots \\ 0 \\ \vdots \\ 0 \end{bmatrix}$$

If we call these three matrices A, X, and B respectively, we have that $AX = B$. But A is a diagonal matrix, thus, $\det A = \prod_{s=1}^{r+1} \binom{s}{1} = 0$ and therefore A^{-1} exists. (Det A is the determinant of A, which for a simple case is $\begin{vmatrix} a_1 & b_1 \\ a_2 & b_2 \end{vmatrix} = a_1 b_2 - a_2 b_1$. The $\prod$ represents "product," in the way the $\sum$ represents "sum.") Thus we have $X = A^{-1}B$. If a_{ij} represents any element of A^{-1}, that implies that $X = A^{-1}B = \begin{pmatrix} a_{11} \\ a_{21} \\ \vdots \\ a_{r+1,1} \end{pmatrix}$ because

B is a column vector. Thus,

$$\begin{pmatrix} b_{r+1} \\ b_r \\ \vdots \\ b_1 \end{pmatrix} = \begin{pmatrix} a_{11} \\ a_{21} \\ \vdots \\ a_{r+1,1} \end{pmatrix}$$

But this means that: $b_{r+2-i} = a_{i,1}$ for all $i \in \{1, 2, 3, \ldots, r+1\}$.

Therefore in equation $f(n) = \sum_{k=0}^{r+1} b_k n^k$ we have:

$$f(n+1) = \sum_{k=0}^{r+1} b_k (n+1)^k \text{ and } f(1) = \sum_{k=0}^{r+1} b_k \text{ where } b_{r+2-i}$$

$$= a_{i,1} \text{ for all } i \in \{1, 2, 3, \ldots, r+1\}$$

Thus, by the previous Lemma,

$$\sum_{t=1}^{n} t^r = \sum_{k=0}^{r+1} b_k (n+1)^k - \sum_{k=0}^{r+1} b_k \text{ or}$$

$$\sum_{t=1}^{n} t^r = \sum_{k=0}^{r+1} b_k [(n+1)^k - 1] \qquad \text{(II)}$$

But by the Binomial Theorem we have that:

$$(n+1)^k - 1 = \binom{k}{0} n^k + \binom{k}{1} n^{k-1} + \ldots + \binom{k}{k-1} n$$

Thus, in (II)

$$\sum_{t=1}^{n} t^r = \sum_{k=0}^{r+1} b_k [\binom{k}{0} n^k + \binom{k}{1} n^{k-1} + \ldots + \binom{k}{k-1} n]$$

or

$$\sum_{t=1}^{n} t^r = n \sum_{k=0}^{r+1} [b_k \binom{k}{0} n^{k-1} + b_k \binom{k}{1} n^{k-2} + \ldots + b_k \binom{k}{k-1}]$$

And if we call $b_k \binom{k}{j} = c_j$, we have $\sum_{t=1}^{n} t^r =$

$n \sum_{j=0}^{r} c_j n^j$ because when $k = 0$, $b_0 \binom{0}{j} = c_j = c_0$

which implies that $j = 0$ and when $k = r+1$, b_{r+1}

$\binom{r+1}{j} = c_j$, which implies that $j = r$. Thus:

Theorem: The general formula for series of the form $\sum_{t=1}^{n} t^r$ is $n \sum_{j=0}^{r} c_j n^j$ where $c_j = b_k \binom{k}{j}$ for all $j \in \{0,1,3, \ldots , r\}$ and $b_{r+2-i} = a_{i,1}$ for all $i \in \{1,2,3, \ldots , r+1\}$

Example 1. Find $\sum_{t=1}^{n} t^2$.

In this example $r = 2$, therefore we have

$$\begin{pmatrix} \binom{3}{1} & 0 & 0 \\ \binom{3}{2} & \binom{2}{1} & 0 \\ \binom{3}{3} & \binom{2}{2} & \binom{1}{1} \end{pmatrix} \begin{pmatrix} b_0 \\ b_1 \\ b_2 \end{pmatrix} = \begin{pmatrix} 1 \\ 0 \\ 0 \end{pmatrix}$$

Thus, $A = \begin{pmatrix} 3 & 0 & 0 \\ 3 & 2 & 0 \\ 1 & 1 & 1 \end{pmatrix}$ and A^{-1} is

$$A^{-1} = \frac{(\text{Adj. } A)'}{\text{Det. } A} = \frac{\begin{pmatrix} 2 & -3 & 1 \\ 0 & 3 & -3 \\ 0 & 0 & 6 \end{pmatrix}'}{\begin{vmatrix} 3 & 0 & 0 \\ 3 & 2 & 0 \\ 1 & 1 & 1 \end{vmatrix}} \quad \text{or}$$

$$A^{-1} = \frac{\begin{pmatrix} 2 & 0 & 0 \\ -3 & 3 & 0 \\ 1 & -3 & 6 \end{pmatrix}}{6}$$

Therefore,

$$X = \frac{1}{6} \begin{pmatrix} 2 & 0 & 0 \\ -3 & 3 & 0 \\ 1 & -3 & 6 \end{pmatrix} \begin{pmatrix} 1 \\ 0 \\ 0 \end{pmatrix} = \frac{1}{6} \begin{pmatrix} 2 \\ -3 \\ 1 \end{pmatrix}$$

and $\begin{pmatrix} b_0 \\ b_1 \\ b_2 \end{pmatrix} = \frac{1}{6} \begin{pmatrix} 2 \\ -3 \\ 1 \end{pmatrix}$ implies that $\begin{cases} b_0 = \frac{1}{6} (2) \\ b_1 = \frac{1}{6} (-3) \\ b_2 = \frac{1}{6} (1) \end{cases}$

Thus, $f(n) = \frac{1}{6} [2n^3 - 3n^2 + n + a_3]$

$f(n+1) = \frac{1}{6} [2(n+1)^3 - 3(n+1)^2 + (n+1) + a_3]$

and, $f(1) = \frac{1}{6} (a_3)$

Hence, the sum of the series will be:
$k^2 = f(n+1) - f(1)$
$= \frac{1}{6} [2(n+1)^3 - 3(n+1)^2 + (n+1)]$
$= \frac{1}{6} n(n+1)(2n+1)$

Example 2. Find the sum of $1 + 2 + 3 + \ldots + n$

In this example the series is $\sum_{k-1}^{n} k$ and $r = 1$. Thus, the equation will be:

$$\begin{pmatrix} \binom{2}{1} & 0 \\ \binom{2}{2} & \binom{1}{1} \end{pmatrix} \cdot \begin{pmatrix} b_0 \\ b_1 \end{pmatrix} = \begin{pmatrix} 1 \\ 0 \end{pmatrix} \quad \text{Then, } A = \begin{pmatrix} 2 & 0 \\ 1 & 1 \end{pmatrix}$$

The inverse of A will then be, $A^{-1} = \frac{\begin{pmatrix} 1 & 0 \\ -1 & 2 \end{pmatrix}}{2}$ and

$$X = \frac{1}{2} \begin{pmatrix} 1 & 0 \\ -1 & 2 \end{pmatrix} \begin{pmatrix} 1 \\ 0 \end{pmatrix} = \frac{1}{2} \begin{pmatrix} 1 \\ -1 \end{pmatrix}$$

This implies that $b_0 = \frac{1}{2} (1)$ and $b_1 = \frac{1}{2} (-1)$

Then, $f(n) = \frac{1}{2} (n^2 - n + a_2)$

$f(n+1) = \frac{1}{2} [(n+1) - (n+1) + a_2]$

and $f(1) = \frac{1}{2} (a_2)$

Then, $\sum_{k=1}^{n} k = f(n+1) - f(1) = \frac{1}{2} [(n+1)^2 - (n+1)]$
$= \frac{1}{2} n (n+1)$

After sufficient practice students should be able to do the following exercises.

Postassessment
Have students complete the following exercises:
1) Find the sum of $1^3 + 2^3 + \ldots + n^3$
2) Find the sum of $\sum_{k=1}^{n} k^5$
3) What are the changes in the general theorem if in $\sum_{r=1}^{n} t^r$, t is an even number, $2m$?

105 A Parabolic Calculator

After having taught the properties of the parabola to an eleventh grade mathematics class, the teacher might want to discuss some applications of the parabola. The teacher may discuss the reflective properties of a parabolic surface such as a searchlight or the mirror in a telescope. The light source at the focus of a parabolic reflecting surface (fig. 1) reflects its rays off the surface in *parallel paths*. It may be noted that the angle of incidence, $\angle$FTP, equals the angle of reflection, $\angle$FTQ.

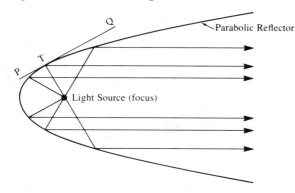

Figure 1

The same principal is used in a telescope (fig. 2) (or radar unit). However here the rays are generated from external sources and reflected off the mirror (or radar screen) to the focus, which may consist of a camera or other sensing device.

Other applications such as the parabolic path of a thrown object may be considered. However a rather unusual application of the parabola involves its properties on the Cartesian plane. This model will present a method of using a parabola on the Cartesian plane as a calculating device for performing multiplication and division. The only supplies students will need are graph paper and a straightedge.

Performance Objectives

• *Students will draw an appropriate parabola, and perform a given multiplication with it.*
• *Students will draw an appropriate parabola and perform a given division with it.*
• *Students will justify (analytically) why the multiplication method presented in this unit "works."*

Preassessment

Before presenting this unit to the class the teacher should be sure that students are able to graph a

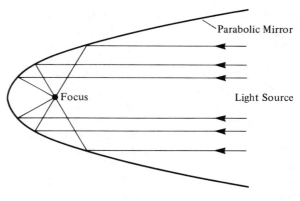

Figure 2

parabola and are able to find the equation of a line, given two points on the line.

Teaching Strategies

On a large sheet of graph paper (preferably one with small squares) have students draw coordinate axes and graph the parabola $y = x^2$. This must be done very accurately. Once this has been completed students are ready to perform some calculations. For example, suppose they wish to multiply 3×5. They would simply draw the line joining the point on the parabola whose abscissa is 3 with the point whose abscissa is -5. The point product of 3 and 5 is the ordinate of the point where this line intersects the y-axis. (Figure 3, AB)

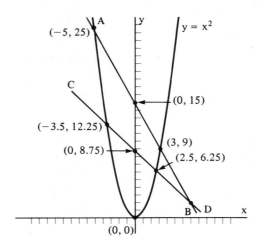

Figure 3

For further practice have students multiply 2.5 $\times$ 3.5. Here they must draw the line containing the points (2.5, 6.25) and (−3.5, 12.25). (These are the points on parabola $y = x^2$, whose abscissas are 2.5 and −3.5) The ordinate of the point where this line (Figure 3, $\overleftrightarrow{CD}$) intersects the y-axis is the product of 2.5 and 3.5, that is, 8.75. Naturally the size of the graph will determine the degree of accuracy which can be obtained. Students should realize that the points on the parabola whose abscissas were −2.5 and 3.5 could just as well have been used in place of the points whose abscissas were 2.5 and −3.5 in the past example.

At this point the teacher may ask students how this same scheme can be used to do division. Students, noting that division is the inverse operation of multiplication, should suggest that $\overleftrightarrow{CD}$ could have been used to divide the following: 8.75 ÷ 3.5. The other point of intersection which $\overleftrightarrow{CD}$ makes with the parabola, point (2.5, 6.25) yields the answer 2.5.

The teacher would be wise to offer students a variety of drill exercises to better familiarize them with this technique. Students can use a straightedge (without drawing a line) to read the answers from the graph.

After sufficient drill, students may become curious about the reason why this technique of calculation actually "works." To prove that it does work, have the class consider the following general case (Figure 4).

Let $\overleftrightarrow{PQ}$ intersect the parabola $y = x^2$ at points (x_1, y_1) and (x_2, y_2), and intersect the y-axis at $(0, y_3)$. This proof must conclude that $y_3 = |x_1 x_2|$.

Proof:

The slope of $\overleftrightarrow{PQ} = \dfrac{y_2 - y_1}{x_2 - x_1} = \dfrac{x_2^2 - x_1^2}{x_2 - x_1} = $

$x_1 + x_2$ (since $y_2 = x_2^2$, and $y_1 = x_1^2$).

The slope of $\overleftrightarrow{PQ}$ expressed with any point (x, y) is $\dfrac{y - y_1}{x - x_1}$.

Therefore $\dfrac{y - y_1}{x - x_1} = x_1 + x_2$ is the equation of $\overleftrightarrow{PQ}$.

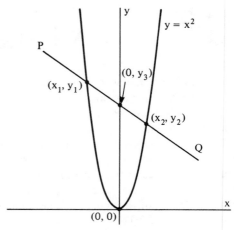

Figure 4

At the point $(0, y_3)$ $\dfrac{y_3 - y_1}{0 - x_1} = x_1 + x_2$ and

$y_3 = - x_1^2 - x_1 x_2 + y_1$.

But $y_1 = x_1^2$, thus $y_3 = -x_1 x_2$, but this is positive, so $y_3 = |x_1 x_2|$.

With a knowledge of this proof students may wish to experiment with other parabolas in an attempt to replace $y = x^2$ with a more "convenient" parabola.

This scheme also provides the student with a host of further investigations. For example, it may be used to "construct" a line of length $\sqrt{a}$. The student need only construct a line parallel to the x-axis and intersecting the y-axis at $(0, a)$. The segment of that line which is between the y-axis and the parabola has length $\sqrt{a}$. Further student investigations should be encouraged.

Postassessment

1. Have students draw the parabola $y = x^2$ and then use it to do the following exercises:
   a) 4 × 5 b) 4.5 × 5.5 c) 4 ÷ 2.5 d) 1.5 ÷ .5
2. Have students show how $y = \frac{1}{2}x^2$ may be used to perform multiplication and division operations.

106 Constructing Ellipses

This unit provides a means of constructing ellipses using a straightedge and a compass.

Performance Objectives

1. Students will plot points on an ellipse without the use of an equation.

2. The relation of the circle to the ellipse will be used by students.

Preassessment

Students should have completed tenth year mathematics and be familiar with fundamental trigonometric identities. Knowledge of analytic geometry is helpful, but not necessary. Ask students to construct an ellipse using any method (i.e., analytically or with special tools).

Teaching Strategies

After inspecting student attempts to construct an ellipse, have them consider the accuracy of their work. Some students may have attempted a "freehand" drawing, while others may have plotted an appropriate curve on a piece of graph paper. This should lead comfortably to Method I.

Method I: Point-by-point construction. One of the definitions of an ellipse is: *the locus of a point,* P, *which moves such that the sum of its distances from two given fixed points,* F *and* F′, *is a constant.* From Figure 1, the definitions just given implies that PF + PF′ = a constant. (1)

Figure 1

Customarily, this constant is given the value 2a, and it is not too difficult to derive from this definition the equation of the ellipse:

$$\frac{x^2}{a^2} + \frac{y^2}{b^2} = 1 \qquad (2)$$

Indeed, the popular thumbtack and string-loop construction is directly based on this definition (where a string-loop is held taut between two thumbtacks and a pencil which changes position).

Procedure: Place an 8½″ × 11″ sheet in the horizontal position and center on it a 4″ horizontal line whose endpoints F and F′ are the ellipse's foci (see

Figure 2). Let the constant in (1) equal 6″. Thus, PF + PF′ = 6″. (3)

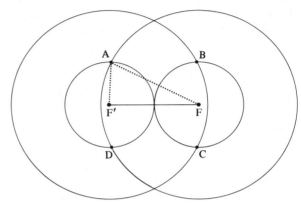

Figure 2

With F as center, draw a circle of 4″ radius. Do likewise with F′ as center. Next, again use F and F′ as centers for circles of 2″ radius. Note that these four circles intersect in four points A, B, C and D which lie on the ellipse. For, if point A is arbitrarily chosen, by construction FA = 2″ and F′A = 4″; hence FA + F′A = 6″, satisfying (3).

A rather accurate construction can be made by using increments of ¼″ for the radii of each circle centered on F and F′, starting with $5\frac{1}{4}$″ and $\frac{3}{4}$″ radii. The next set of four points on the ellipse would be obtained by drawing two circles of 5″ and 1″ radius, both on F and F′. These two pairs of circles would be followed by another two pairs of radii $4\frac{3}{4}$″ and $1\frac{1}{4}$″, and so on, as indicated in Figure 3. Indeed, additional ellipses can then be sketched from Figure 3.

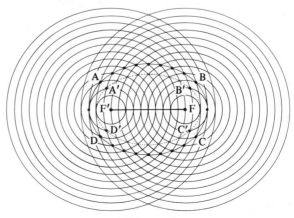

Figure 3

Assume that PF + PF′ = 5″.   (4)

Then, one need only mark the intersections of those circles centered on F and F′, the sum of whose radii is 5. For example, in constructing (3) by using the suggested ¼″ increment, it was necessary at some point to use a radius of 3½″ centered on F and F′ and another radius of 1½″ again centered on F and F′. The intersection of these four circles, A′, B′, C′ and D′, provide four points on *another* ellipse such that, using A′ arbitrarily, FA′ + F′A′ = 5″.

Figure 3 thus shows the two ellipses sketched, both of which have F and F′ as their foci. Other ellipses can be sketched in a similar manner from the same figure.

Method II: Tangent construction. Centered on an 8½″ by 11″ sheet of paper, have students draw a circle of radius 3″. Locate a point F in the interior of the circle 2¼″ from the center (see Figure 4).

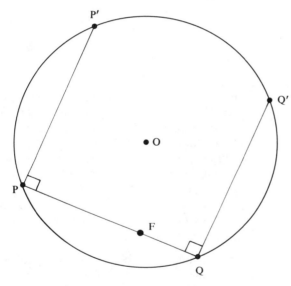

Figure 4

Through F draw a chord to intersect the circle at P and Q. Using a right triangle template or carpenter's T-square, erect perpendiculars at P and Q to meet the circle at P′ and Q′, respectively. Then $\overleftrightarrow{PP'}$ and $\overleftrightarrow{QQ'}$ are each tangents to an ellipse having F as one of its foci. Continue this procedure for many such chords $\overline{PQ}$, obtaining a diagram similar to that shown in Figure 5.

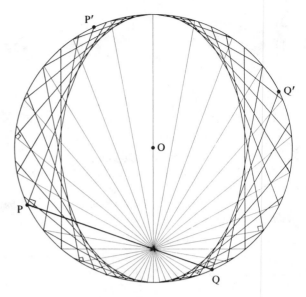

Figure 5

The proof of this construction is based on the converse of the following theorem: *The locus of the intersection of the tangent to an ellipse with the perpendicular on it from either focus is a circle.* A proof of this theorem can be found in Bowser's *An Elementary Treatise on Analytic Geometry,* pages 139-140.

Varying the position of F will change the size and shape of the ellipse. Furthermore, the second focus, F′ is located on $\overrightarrow{FO}$ extended through O its own distance.

Postassessment

1. Have students draw Figure 3 on a larger scale, such as FF′ = 6″. Coloring in the numerous regions formed by the intersections of the circles may prove quite satisfying.

2. Have students draw a circle of radius *r,* with O as center. They then locate a fixed point, F, inside the circle, and draw $\overline{OF}$. Clearly, *r* > OF. Then have them draw an arbitrary radius OQ. Connect FQ, and construct its midpoint, M. At M, they should erect a perpendicular to intersect $\overline{OQ}$ at P. Then P lies on an ellipse with F as one of its foci. Moreover, $\overleftrightarrow{MP}$ extended through P is a tangent to the same ellipse. Have students complete this construction and justify it.

107 Constructing the Parabola

Performance Objective
With straightedge and compasses, students will construct a parabola without using an equation.

Preassessment
Ask students to construct the parabola $y = x^2$ on a sheet of graph paper. When this has been done, have them draw any other parabola on a sheet of "blank" paper.

Teaching Strategies
In all likelihood students will be unable to draw a parabola without use of graph paper. At this point the teacher may define the parabola in terms of locus. That is, it is the locus of points equidistant from a fixed point and a fixed line. Perhaps students will find this a useful hint in deriving a method of construction of a parabola. After considering students' suggestions, have them consider the following methods.

Method I. Point-by-point Construction. Towards the left of an 8½-by-11-inch sheet of paper held horizontally, lightly draw about 15 vertical parallel lines each spaced ½ inch apart (see Figure 1). Each line segment should be eight inches long. Draw the

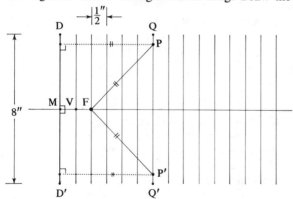

Figure 1

common perpendicular bisector of these lines. Label your drawing as shown in Figure 1, being sure to place F at the intersection of the third parallel line and the perpendicular bisector. Let $\overleftrightarrow{QQ'}$ be any arbitrary parallel line, say the sixth one from $\overleftrightarrow{DD'}$. By construction, $\overleftrightarrow{QQ'}$ is $(6 \cdot \frac{1}{2}) = 3''$ from $\overleftrightarrow{DD'}$. Maintaining this distance, using F as center, swing an arc with your compasses cutting $\overleftrightarrow{QQ'}$ above and below the perpendicular bisector at P and P'. Then P and P' are on the parabola with F as the *focus* of the parabola. Repeat this procedure for the other parallel lines, joining all the points so determined (see Figure 2).

Discussion: By construction, the perpendicular distance of either P or P' from $\overleftrightarrow{DD'}$ is equal to FP

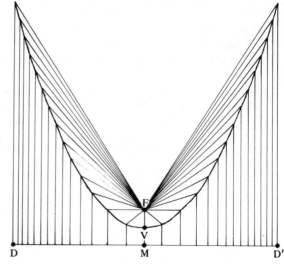

Figure 2

or FP'. The definition of a parabola is based on such an equivalence of distance of a varying point from a fixed line and a fixed point. A parabola is the locus of points each of whose distances from a fixed point equals its distance from a fixed line. The line $\overleftrightarrow{DD'}$ is referred to as the *directrix* and its perpendicular bisector is the *axis* of the parabola. If M is the intersection of the axis and the directrix $\overleftrightarrow{DD'}$, by letting FM = $2p$, it is not difficult, using the distance formula and the above definition, to show that the parabola's equation is $y^2 = 4px$. (1) The midpoint, V, of $\overline{MF}$ is the parabola's *vertex*, and is often referred to as the parabola's turning point.

Method II. Point-by-point Construction. Draw a rectangle ABCD (see Figure 3), letting V and G be the midpoints of $\overline{AD}$ and $\overline{BC}$, respectively.

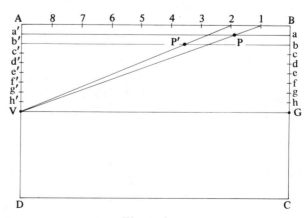

Figure 3

Divide $\overline{AB}$ and $\overline{BG}$ into the same *number* of equal parts. Starting from B, let the successive points of equal division be 1, 2, 3, . . . on $\overline{AB}$ and *a, b, c* . . . on $\overline{BG}$. Draw $\overline{aa'}$ perpendicular to $\overline{BG}$. Note that *a'*, *b', c'* . . . . are points on $\overline{AV}$). Draw $\overline{V1}$, meeting $\overline{aa'}$ at P. Similarly, draw $\overline{bb'}$ perpendicular to $\overline{BG}$ and draw $\overline{V2}$, meeting $\overline{bb'}$ at P'. Continue this for the other points. Then P and P', and other points so obtained are on a parabola with V as its vertex and $\overline{VG}$ as its axis.

Proof: From Figure 3, let $\overleftrightarrow{AD}$ be the *y*-axis and $\overleftrightarrow{VG}$ the *x*-axis (see Figure 4). Let *b* on $\overline{BG}$ now be called

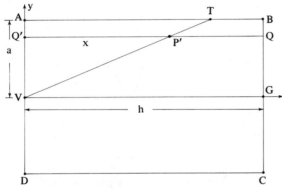

Figure 4

Q, *b'* on $\overline{AV}$ to be labelled Q'. Similarly, let point 2 in Figure 3 be called T. Draw $\overline{VT}$ and $\overline{QQ'}$, meeting at P'. Let VQ' = GQ = *y*, Q'P' = *x*, VG = *h*, AV = *a*.

By construction (i.e., points T and Q were selected with this property),

$$\frac{AT}{AB} = \frac{GQ}{GB}, \text{ or } \frac{AT}{h} = \frac{y}{a}. \qquad (2)$$

From similar triangles VQ'P' and VAT, $\dfrac{x}{y} = \dfrac{AT}{AV}$

$$= \frac{AT}{a}, \text{ or } AT = \frac{ax}{y}. \qquad (3)$$

Substituting this value of AT in (2), $\dfrac{\frac{ax}{y}}{h} = \dfrac{y}{a}$, or

$$\frac{a^2 x}{y} = hy. \qquad (4)$$

Solving (4) for y^2 yields $y^2 = \dfrac{a^2 x}{h}$, $\qquad$ *(5)*

which is of the same form as (1) in which

$$4p = \frac{a^2}{h}. \qquad (6)$$

Since *p* is the distance from the vertex to the focus, solving (6) for *p* will locate the focus in terms of *a* and *h* of the original rectangle.

Method III. Envelope construction. Near the bottom edge of a vertically-held 8½x11-inch sheet of paper, draw a horizontal line the full width of the paper (see Figure 5). Label this line $\overleftrightarrow{AA'}$. Draw the perpendicular bisector of $\overline{AA'}$, with midpoint V. Locate F on the perpendicular bisector, one inch above V. On $\overline{AA'}$, on either side of V, mark off points Q, Q', Q'', ..., gradually increasing, by a very small increment, the successive distances from V to Q, Q to Q', Q' to Q'', ... Place a right triangle template or carpenter's T-square such that a leg passes through F and the vertex of the right angle is concurrent with

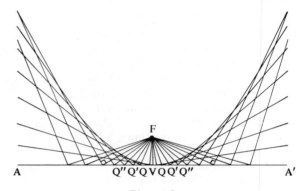

Figure 5

any of the points Q, Q', Q'', ... Construct a right angle with one ray $\overrightarrow{FQ}$ and drawing an extended line to the edge of the paper with the other ray of the right angle. Repeat this procedure for other points Q', Q'', ... The resulting diagram should be similar to Figure 5, and the shape "enveloped" by all these lines is a parabola.

Postassessment

Have your students draw an angle of any measure, making both sides equal in length. Starting from the vertex, have them measure off equally spaced intervals along each side, labeling the intervals on each side 1, 2, 3, 4, . . . , 10, with the vertex labelled 0. Then ask them to connect point 10 on one side with point 1 on the other side. See that they do likewise for points 9 and 2, 8 and 3, and so forth, always being sure that the sum of the numbers joined is 11. The resulting appearance will be somewhat similar to Figure 5. Students will have drawn an envelope to a parabola. Have students attempt to justify this construction, as well as that for Figure 5.

108 Using Higher Plane Curves to Trisect an Angle

This unit will introduce two higher plane algebraic curves, showing analytically and visually (experimentally) how the trisection is done.

Performance Objective

1. Given a certain locus condition, students will learn how to sketch a curve directly from the locus without using an equation.

2. Given a polar equation, students will plot the curve on polar coordinate paper.

3. Given one of the curves discussed in this unit, students will trisect any angle.

Preassessment

Students should have done some work with polar coordinates.

Teaching Strategies

The trisection of an angle can be considered a consequence of the following locus problem: Given ΔOAP with fixed base $\overline{OA}$ and variable vertex P, find the locus of points P such that $m\angle OPA = 2m\angle POA$. (See figure 1.) Let O be the pole of a polar coordinate system and $\overrightarrow{OA}$ the initial line, with A having coordinate $(2a,0)$.

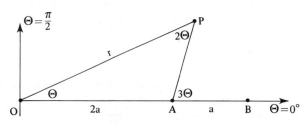

Figure 1

Let $m\angle AOP = \theta$ and $OP = r$. Then by hypothesis, $m\angle APO = 2\theta$, from which it follows $m\angle OAP = \pi - 3\theta$, ($\pi$ radians = 180°). Extend $\overline{OA}$ through A a distance of a units, thereby locating point B. Then $m\angle BAP = 3\theta$. By the law of sines,

$$\frac{r}{\sin(\pi-3\theta)} = \frac{2a}{\sin2\theta} \quad (1)$$

from which it follows $r = \dfrac{2a\cdot\sin(\pi-3\theta)}{\sin2\theta} \quad (2)$

Since $\sin(\pi-3\theta) = \sin3\theta$ and $\sin2\theta = 2\sin\theta\cos\theta$, the appropriate substitutions for equation (2) yield

$$r = \frac{a\cdot\sin3\theta}{\sin\theta\cos\theta} \quad (3)$$

With $\sin3\theta = 3\sin\theta - 4\sin^3\theta = \sin\theta(3 - 4\sin^2\theta)$,

(3) yields $r = \dfrac{3a - 4a\cdot\sin^2\theta}{\cos\theta} \quad (4)$

Letting $\sin^2\theta = 1 - \cos^2\theta$ in (4),

$r = \dfrac{-a + 4a\cdot\cos^2\theta}{\cos\theta}$, which can easily be simplified, by letting $\dfrac{1}{\cos\theta} = \sec\theta$, to $r = a(4\cos\theta - \sec\theta)$

$$(5)$$

the required polar equation for the *Trisectrix of Maclaurin.*

By placing P on the other side of $\overleftrightarrow{OA}$ (Fig. 1) a similar derivation will yield

$$r = a(4\cos\theta + \sec\theta) \quad (6)$$

Since $\cos(-\theta) = \cos\theta$ and $\sec(-\theta) = \sec\theta$, it follows that (5) is symmetric with respect to $\overleftrightarrow{OA}$. Thus, as confirmed by (6), for all points of the locus above $\overleftrightarrow{OA}$, there are corresponding points below it as well. (These corresponding points are reflections in $\overleftrightarrow{OA}$.)

To sketch the locus, assigning values to θ in (5) and (6) will, of course, furnish points of the Trisectrix. Have students make an exact copy of ΔAOP on polar coordinate graph paper, so that O is at the origin and $\overrightarrow{OA}$ is on the horizontal axis (at θ radians.) Then students should plot various points of the curve and draw the curve.

Students may now use the original diagram (on regular paper.) A novel approach to curve sketching would be to plot points and draw lines directly from the given locus condition. One need only assign various values to θ and a corresponding 3θ value to $\angle BAP$. With $\overrightarrow{OB}$ a fixed base for each of these angles, the intersection of the second side of each angle will yield point P. Figure 2 shows such a construction for values of $0° \le \theta \le 55°$ in 5° intervals.

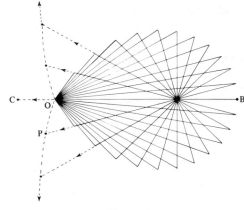

Figure 2

For $\theta = 0°$ and 60°, there is no triangle, merely $\overline{OB}$. For $\theta > 60°$, consider some arbitrary point C such that $\overleftrightarrow{COA}$. Let the measure of reflex

$m \angle \text{BAP} = 195°$, thus placing P below $\overleftrightarrow{\text{COA}}$. Then $m \angle \text{COP} = 65°$, preserving the trisection property. Note that for $|\Theta| \angle 60°$, there will be two asymptotic branches above and below $\overrightarrow{\text{OB}}$.

Conversely, given (5), it is a bit more difficult to show that for any point P on the Trisectrix, $m \angle \text{BOP} = \frac{1}{3} \cdot m \angle \text{BAP}$. The proof rests on showing that $m \angle \text{OPA} = 2\Theta$, from which it follows that $m \angle \text{BAP} = 3\Theta$.

Equation (5) for the Trisectrix of Maclaurin can also be obtained from the following locus problem (see Figure 3):

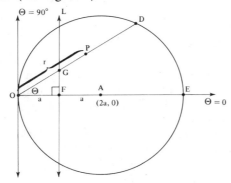

Figure 3

Given O, the pole of a polar coordinate system and E $(4a,0)$. At A $(2a,0)$ as center, draw a circle of radius $2a$. Through F $(a,0)$ draw a line L perpendicular to $\overleftrightarrow{\text{OE}}$. Locate an arbitrary point D on the "upper" semicircle's circumference and draw $\overrightarrow{\text{OD}}$, intersecting L at G. Arbitrarily locate P on $\overrightarrow{\text{OD}}$. As D varies along the semicircle, find the locus of P on $\overrightarrow{\text{OD}}$ such that OP = GD. The resulting polar equation will be identical to (5). (*Hints for solution:* Let $m < \text{AOD} = \Theta$, OP = r = GD. Draw $\overline{\text{DE}}$, forming right triangle ODE. Express OD in terms of a and $\cos\Theta$, and express OG in terms of a and $\sec\Theta$).

The student now has a method for trisecting an angle (using an additional tool, a curve.) Once students have grasped the above, they may consider another curve, the Limacon of Pascal, which also

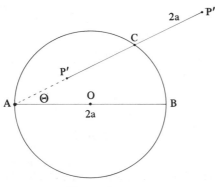

Figure 4

can be used to trisect an angle. However, the following construction for the Limacon should be attempted first.

Draw a circle of diameter AB = $2a$, center O. Locate an arbitrary point C, distinct from A or B, on the circle's circumference. Place the edge of a ruler at C in such a way that the ruler's midpoint rests on C and that the same edge passes through A. Locate two points P and P' at a distance of a units on either side of C. Repeat this for different positions of C. P and P' are then points on the Limacon.

For a visual effect analogous to Figure 2, divide the circle's circumference into 18 evenly spaced arcs. Repeat the procedure in the preceding paragraph for each of these 18 points, thereby yielding 36 points on the Limacon's circumference. Be sure to draw a line to connect all corresponding points P and P', taking note of the loop that occurs *inside* the Limacon. A suggested diameter for the base circle O is $3''$, making $P'C = CP = 1\frac{1}{2}''$.

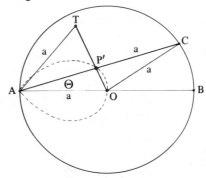

Figure 5

Figure 5 shows the base circle O, the Limacon's inner loop, as well as a few other points and lines used for the following trisection: Let $\angle$ BAT be congruent to the angle to be trisected, making AT = a. Draw $\overline{\text{TO}}$, intersecting the loop at P', and then draw $\overline{\text{AP}'}$. We now show that $m \angle \text{BAT} = 3$ times $m \angle \text{BAP}'$.

Extend $\overline{\text{AP}'}$ to intersect the circle at C. Since P' is a point on the Limacon, CP' = a, from the above construction. Draw $\overline{\text{OC}}$ and let $m \angle \text{OAP}' = \Theta$. Immediately, OA = OC, $m \angle \text{C} = \Theta$, therefore $m \angle \text{AOC} = \pi - 2\Theta$. Since $\Delta\text{OCP}'$ is isosceles, each of its base angles has measure $\frac{\pi}{2} - \frac{1}{2}\Theta$. $m \angle \text{AP}'\text{O} = \frac{\pi}{2} + \frac{1}{2}\Theta$, and it follows that $m \angle \text{AOP}' = \frac{\pi}{2} - \frac{3}{2}\Theta$.

However, ΔATO is also isosceles, hence $m \angle \text{T} = \frac{\pi}{2} - \frac{3}{2}\Theta$, from which it follows that $m \angle \text{BAT} = 3\Theta$, which was to be proved.

Postassessment

Construct the Limacon of Figure 4 by locating P and P' a distance of $2a$ units on either side of c.

109 Constructing Hypocycloid and Epicycloid Circular Envelopes

In this unit, two elementary cycloidal curves will be related to each other. Students will then create a circular envelope which will simultaneously encompass both curves.

Performance Objectives

1. Students will define: hypocycloid and epicycloid.

2. Students will construct a hypocycloid and an epicycloid.

3. Students will generalize these constructions to other hypocycloids and epicycloids.

Preassessment

Tenth year mathematics is necessary. A minimal knowledge of polar coordinates is helpful.

Teaching Strategies

Initiate the introduction of hypocycloid and epicycloid curves by rolling varying sized circular discs about the interior and exterior circumference, respectively, of a fixed circular disc of constant radius. If possible, let the radius of the fixed circle be some integral multiple of the radius of the rolling circle. Have your students speculate on the loci obtained by a fixed point on the circumference of the varying sized rolling circles. For the interior rotations, it will be necessary for the fixed circle to be hollowed out. A Spirograph Kit, if available, is an excellent motivational source.

This unit analyzes the case when the interior and exterior rolling circles each have radius $b = \dfrac{a}{3}$, as shown in Figure 1 (next column). 0 is the center of the fixed circle, radius a, and is also the pole of a polar coordinate system. C and C' are the centers, respectively, of the interior and exterior rolling circles. We will assume that both rotating circles are continuously in tangential contact with each other at T. Therefore, $\overrightarrow{OT}$, making an angle of measure Θ with the initial line, intersects circles C and C' at I, T, and I', and contains the centers, C and C'. It is understood that initially each circle was tangent to the fixed circle at B; furthermore, P and P' are respectively fixed points on the circumference of circles C and C'. At the instant both circles began their circuits, P and P' were coincident with B. The partial loci from B to P and P' are shown in Figure 1.

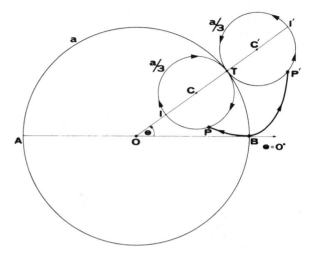

Figure 1

In Figure 2, we show the complete loci swept out by each fixed point. The locus of P is a *hypocycloid of three cusps*, often called the *deltoid;* whereas the locus of P' is an *epicycloid of three cusps*. Each circle requires three complete rotations before returning to point B. The fixed circle is then a circumcircle for the deltoid and an incircle for the three-cusped epicycloid.

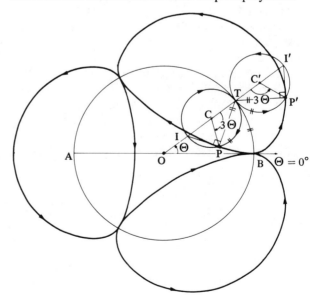

Figure 2

The following lines are drawn in each circle: $\overline{IP}$, $\overline{CP}$ and $\overline{TP}$ for circle C; $\overline{TP'}$, $\overline{C'P'}$ and $\overline{I'P'}$ for circle C'. Have your students explain why

length $\overset{\frown}{TP}$ = length $\overset{\frown}{TB}$ = length $\overset{\frown}{TP'}$.   (1)
Then show that
m $\angle$ TCP = 3Θ = m $\angle$ TC'P'.   (2)
Since the radii of circles C and C' are equal, ΔTPC $\cong$ ΔTP'C' (SAS); and corresponding sides,
TP = TP'.   (3)
Observe that m $\angle$TPI = 90 = m$\angle$TP'I'. Furthermore, we state without proof that $\overline{PI}$ and $\overline{P'I'}$ are respectively tangents to the deltoid at P and the epicycloid at P'. Further details can be found in reference (2).

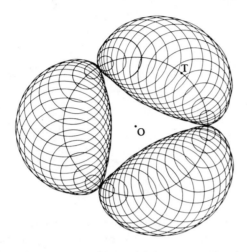

Figure 3

The above equation (3) implies that a circle centered at T, with radius TP = TP' will be tangent to each curve at P and P'. Certainly, as T varies, there is a corresponding change in the length of $\overline{TP'}$ (or $\overline{TP}$). We show in Figure 3 the final result obtained when circles are drawn for 60 equally spaced positions of T along the fixed circle. We utilize symmetry properties of each curve to minimize the work required to determine the varying lengths of $\overline{TP}$: since each curve repeats itself every 120°, and $\overline{OI'}$ divides the curve symmetrically at m$\angle\Theta$ = 60, it is only necessary to obtain those lengths of $\overline{TP}$ between 0°≤Θ≤60°, in intervals of measure 6. These lengths were obtained by making an

accurate drawing of the required ten positions of either rolling circle.

Postassessment

To test student comprehension of hypocycloids and epicycloids, have them complete the following exercises.

1. Figure 4 (below) shows the results obtained when $b = \dfrac{a}{4}$. Justify the occurrence of a four cusped hypocycloid and a four cusped epicycloid.

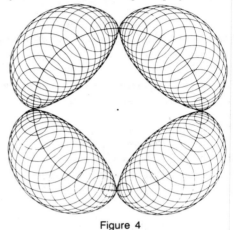

Figure 4

2. Generalize for $b = \dfrac{a}{n}$, $n = 5, 6, \ldots$
3. Make a drawing for the case $b = \dfrac{a}{2}$ (the *nephroid*). Visually show that the locus of a fixed point on the interior rolling circle is a diameter of the fixed circle.
4. Repeat for $b = a$, the *cardioid*. Show that all the circles centered on T pass through a fixed point; i.e., one of the loci degenerates to a point.

References

Beard, Robert S., *Patterns in Space,* Creative Publications, 1973.
Lockwood, E. H., *A Book of Curves,* Cambridge University Press, 1961.

110 The Harmonic Sequence

This unit is best presented to a class after arithmetic and geometric sequences have been mastered.

Performance Objectives

1. *Students will define harmonic sequence.*

2. *Students will illustrate a harmonic sequence geometrically.*

3. *Students will solve simple problems with harmonic sequences.*

Preassessment

Ask students to find the fourth term of the sequence:

$$1\frac{1}{3}, \; 1\frac{11}{17}, \; 2\frac{2}{13}.$$

Teaching Strategies

A natural response on the part of your students is to try to find the fourth term of the above sequence by trying to find a common difference, and when that fails, a common ratio. In a short time your students will feel frustrated. This will offer you a good opportunity to motivate your students towards a "new" type of sequence. Ask students to write each term in improper fraction form and then write its reciprocal. This will yield: $\frac{3}{4}, \frac{17}{28}, \frac{13}{28}$ or $\frac{21}{28}, \frac{17}{28}, \frac{13}{28}$. Further inspection of this new sequence will indicate it to be an arithmetic sequence with a common difference of $\frac{-4}{28}$. Students will now easily obtain the required fourth term, $\dfrac{1}{\frac{9}{28}} = \frac{28}{9} = 3\frac{1}{9}$.

Students should now be motivated to learn more about the harmonic sequence.

Consider three or more terms in an arithmetic sequence: for example, $a_1, a_2, a_3 \ldots, a_n$. The sequence of reciprocals of these terms, $\frac{1}{a_1}, \frac{1}{a_2}, \frac{1}{a_3}$, $\ldots, \frac{1}{a_n}$ is called a harmonic sequence. The term "harmonic" comes from a property of musical sounds. If a set of strings of uniform tension whose lengths are proportional to $1, \frac{1}{2}, \frac{1}{3}, \frac{1}{4}, \frac{1}{5}, \frac{1}{6}$ are sounded together, the effect is said to be "harmonious" to the ear. This sequence is harmonic, as the reciprocals of the terms from an arithmetic sequence, 1, 2, 3, 4, 5, 6.

There is no general formula for the sum of the terms in a harmonic series. Problems dealing with a harmonic sequence are generally considered in terms of the related arithmetic sequence.

Two theorems would be useful to consider:

Theorem 1: If a constant is added to (or subtracted from) each term in an arithmetic sequence, then the new sequence is also arithmetic (with the same common difference.)

Theorem 2: If each term in an arithmetic sequence is multiplied (or divided) by a constant, the resulting sequence is also arithmetic (but with a different common difference).

The proofs of these theorems are left as exercises.

The proofs of these theorems are simple and straightforward and do not merit special consideration here. However, the following example will help students gain facility in work with harmonic sequences.

Example: If a, b, c forms a harmonic sequence, prove that $\dfrac{a}{b+c}, \dfrac{b}{c+a}, \dfrac{c}{a+b}$ also forms a harmonic sequence.

Solution: Since $\dfrac{1}{a}, \dfrac{1}{b}, \dfrac{1}{c}$ forms an arithmetic sequence, $\dfrac{a+b+c}{a}, \dfrac{a+b+c}{b}, \dfrac{a+b+c}{c}$ also forms an arithmetic sequence. This may be written as $1 + \dfrac{b+c}{a}$, $1 + \dfrac{a+c}{b}, 1 + \dfrac{a+b}{c}$. Therefore $\dfrac{b+c}{a}, \dfrac{a+c}{b}, \dfrac{a+b}{c}$. forms an arithmetic sequence. Thus $\dfrac{a}{b+c}, \dfrac{b}{a+c}, \dfrac{c}{a+b}$ forms a harmonic sequence.

Perhaps one of the more interesting aspects of any sequence is to establish a geometric model of the sequence.

One geometric interpretation of a harmonic sequence can be taken from the intersection points of the interior and exterior angle bisectors of a triangle with the side of the triangle.

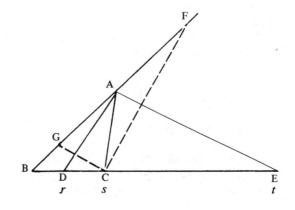

Consider $\triangle ABC$, where $\overline{AD}$ bisects $\angle BAC$ and $\overline{AE}$ bisects $\angle CAF$, and B, D, C, and E are collinear. (see fig. a) It can easily be proved that for exterior angle bisector $\overline{AE}$, $\frac{BE}{CE} = \frac{AB}{AC}$ (i.e. draw $\overline{GC}//\overline{AE}$;

$AG = AC$; also $\frac{BE}{CE} = \frac{AB}{AG} = \frac{AB}{AC}$.)

Similarly for interior angle bisector $\overline{AD}$,

$$\frac{BD}{CD} = \frac{AB}{AC}.$$

(The proof is done by drawing $\overline{CF}//\overline{AD}$; $AF = AC$;

$\frac{BD}{CD} = \frac{AB}{AF} = \frac{AB}{AC}$.)

Therefore $\frac{BE}{CE} = \frac{BD}{CD}$ or $\frac{CD}{CE} = \frac{BD}{BE}$. It is then said that the points B and C separate the points D and E harmonically.

Now suppose $\overleftrightarrow{BDCE}$ is a number line with B as the zero point, point D at coordinate r, point C at coordinate s, and point E at coordinate t. Therefore $BD = r$, $BC = s$, and $BE = t$. We shall show that

r, s, t forms a harmonic sequence. Since $\frac{CD}{CE} = \frac{BD}{BE}$,

$\frac{BC - BD}{BE - BC} = \frac{BD}{BE}$, or $\frac{s - r}{t - s} = \frac{r}{t}$. Therefore $t(s - r) = r(t - s)$ and $ts - tr = rt - rs$. Dividing each term by rst, we get $\frac{1}{r} - \frac{1}{s} = \frac{1}{s} - \frac{1}{t}$, which indicates that $\frac{1}{t}, \frac{1}{s}, \frac{1}{r}$ forms an arithmetic sequence. Thus, r, s, t forms a harmonic sequence.

Students should now have reasonably good insight into a harmonic sequence.

Postassessment

1. Set up an equation with the terms of the harmonic sequence a, b, c. (Use the definition.)
2. Find the 26th term of the sequence:

$$2\frac{1}{2}, \ 1\frac{12}{13}, \ 1\frac{9}{16}, \ 1\frac{6}{19} \ \cdots$$

3. Prove that if a^2, b^2, c^2 forms an arithmetic sequence, then $(b + c)$, $(c + a)$, $(a + b)$ forms a harmonic sequence.

111   Transformations and Matrices

This unit will algebraically formalize a discussion of geometric transformations by use of matrices.

Performance Objectives

1. *Given a particular geometric transformation, students will name the 2 × 2 matrix that effects this transformation.*
2. *Given certain 2 × 2 matrices, students will, at a glance, name the transformation each matrix effects.*

Preassessment

1. On a cartesian plane, graph $\triangle ABC$ with vertices at A(2,2), B(4,2), C(2,6). Write the coordinates of A', B', C' which result when $\triangle ABC$ undergoes each of the following transformations:
   a. Translation by -5 units in the x direction tion and 2 units in the y direction.
   b. Reflection across the x-axis.
   c. Rotation of 90° about the origin.
   d. Enlargement scale factor 2 with center at (2,2).
2. Given an equilateral triangle as shown with each vertex the same distance from the origin, list geometric transformations which leave the position of the

triangle unchanged, assuming the vertices are indistinguishable.

Figure 1

Teaching Strategies

The teacher should first make students aware of a matrix array of numbers. Tell the students that a matrix of size $a \times b$ has a rows and b columns enclosed in brackets. When $a = b$ the matrix is said to be *square*. The class should see that adding matrices involves adding the numbers in corresponding positions in each matrix, for example

$$\begin{bmatrix} a \\ b \end{bmatrix} + \begin{bmatrix} c \\ d \end{bmatrix} = \begin{bmatrix} a + c \\ b + d \end{bmatrix} \quad \text{and the students must}$$

see that matrices must be of the same size (dimension) to be added.

When showing students how to multiply matrices you should use the following general form. Note carefully the column-row relationship between the two matrix factors in the product.

$$\begin{bmatrix} a & b \\ c & d \end{bmatrix} \cdot \begin{bmatrix} x \\ y \end{bmatrix} = \begin{bmatrix} ax + by \\ cx + dy \end{bmatrix}$$

Students may now describe the position of a point either by its coordinates (x,y) or by a 2×1 matrix, called a *position vector*, $\begin{bmatrix} x \\ y \end{bmatrix}$, which represents the vector from the origin to the point.

You may find it effective to use the phrase "is mapped onto" when describing the effect of a transformation. The symbol for this phrase using matrices is "$\longrightarrow$."

Translations provide a simple introduction into the use of matrices.

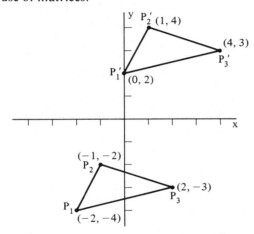

A translation of the triangle $P_1P_2P_3$ to $P'_1P'_2P'_3$ can be generalized in matrix form

$$\begin{bmatrix} x \\ y \end{bmatrix} \longrightarrow \begin{bmatrix} x \\ y \end{bmatrix} + \begin{bmatrix} 2 \\ 6 \end{bmatrix}$$

$\begin{bmatrix} 2 \\ 6 \end{bmatrix}$ represents here a "translation vector," meaning it translates (x,y) 2 units in the x direction and 6 units in the y direction. Students should readily see that by matrix addition each point P_1, P_2, P_3 is mapped onto P'_1, P'_2, P'_3 respectively. That is,

$P_1 \begin{bmatrix} -2 \\ -4 \end{bmatrix} + \begin{bmatrix} 2 \\ 6 \end{bmatrix} = P'_1 \begin{bmatrix} 0 \\ 2 \end{bmatrix}, P_2 \begin{bmatrix} -1 \\ -2 \end{bmatrix} + \begin{bmatrix} 2 \\ 6 \end{bmatrix} = P'_2 \begin{bmatrix} 1 \\ 4 \end{bmatrix}, P_3 \begin{bmatrix} 2 \\ -3 \end{bmatrix} + \begin{bmatrix} 2 \\ 6 \end{bmatrix} = P'_3 \begin{bmatrix} 4 \\ 3 \end{bmatrix}$ Matrix addition of 2×1 position vectors can therefore describe any translation in the two-dimensional plane. Students should be given several examples and exercises where a particular point (x_1, y_1) is translated into any other point (x_2, y_2) by a suitable

choice of 2×1 matrix $\begin{bmatrix} x \\ y \end{bmatrix}$ such that

$$\begin{bmatrix} x_1 \\ y_1 \end{bmatrix} + \begin{bmatrix} x \\ y \end{bmatrix} = \begin{bmatrix} x_2 \\ y_2 \end{bmatrix}$$

Rotations, reflections and *enlargements* are more interesting, and to describe them algebraically requires 2×2 matrices. Students should first be given two or three examples of the type $\begin{bmatrix} 2 & 3 \\ -1 & 2 \end{bmatrix} \cdot \begin{bmatrix} 3 \\ 2 \end{bmatrix} = \begin{bmatrix} 12 \\ 1 \end{bmatrix}$ for two reasons. For one, they may need practice in matrix multiplication, a skill they must master before embarking on the rest of this topic, and second, and most important in this strategy, is that students begin to think of the matrix $\begin{bmatrix} 2 & 3 \\ -1 & 2 \end{bmatrix}$ (or any 2×2 matrix) as a transformation of the point $P(3,2)$ onto the point $P'(12,1)$. Each example of this type should be accompanied by an illustration, as in Figure 2.

Figure 2

When the students are familiar with the notion that any 2×2 matrix represents a transformation, the teacher should be ready to show them that some 2×2 matrices represent special transformations with which they are familiar. For example, the teacher may give them the matrix and point, respectively (which follow):

1. $\begin{bmatrix} -1 & 0 \\ 0 & 1 \end{bmatrix} \cdot \begin{bmatrix} 2 \\ 3 \end{bmatrix} = \begin{bmatrix} -2 \\ 3 \end{bmatrix}$ and

2. $\begin{bmatrix} 0 & -1 \\ 1 & 0 \end{bmatrix} \cdot \begin{bmatrix} 3 \\ 1 \end{bmatrix} = \begin{bmatrix} -1 \\ 3 \end{bmatrix}$ and

3. $\begin{bmatrix} 3 & 0 \\ 0 & 3 \end{bmatrix} \cdot \begin{bmatrix} -2 \\ -1 \end{bmatrix} = \begin{bmatrix} -6 \\ -3 \end{bmatrix}$

Students may have recognized the transformations in these examples as (1) a reflection (across the y axis), (2) a positive rotation of 90°, and (3) an enlargement, scale factor 3. To emphasize the point that it was not merely by chance that the matrices accomplished these transformations, ask the students to take the general point $\begin{bmatrix} x \\ y \end{bmatrix}$ and multiply it by each of the matrices. The students' answers will be, respectively, $\begin{bmatrix} -x \\ y \end{bmatrix}$, $\begin{bmatrix} -y \\ x \end{bmatrix}$, $\begin{bmatrix} 3x \\ 3y \end{bmatrix}$. Students will therefore see (the second case may require some insight) that the matrices $\begin{bmatrix} -1 & 0 \\ 0 & 1 \end{bmatrix}$, $\begin{bmatrix} 0 & -1 \\ 1 & 0 \end{bmatrix}$, and $\begin{bmatrix} 3 & 0 \\ 0 & 3 \end{bmatrix}$ do indeed accomplish, in the general case, the transformations they recognized in the particular examples.

To achieve performance objectives, whereby matrices provide a handy tool in transformational work, show what 2×2 matrices do to the unit vectors i $\begin{bmatrix} 1 \\ 0 \end{bmatrix}$ and j $\begin{bmatrix} 0 \\ 1 \end{bmatrix}$.

Choose any 2×2 matrix, as in the previous example, $\begin{bmatrix} 2 & 3 \\ -1 & 2 \end{bmatrix}$, and ask your students to multiply the unit vectors i and j by this matrix.

$$\begin{bmatrix} 2 & 3 \\ -1 & 2 \end{bmatrix} \cdot \begin{bmatrix} 1 \\ 0 \end{bmatrix} = \begin{bmatrix} 2 \\ -1 \end{bmatrix},$$

$$\begin{bmatrix} 2 & 3 \\ -1 & 2 \end{bmatrix} \cdot \begin{bmatrix} 0 \\ 1 \end{bmatrix} = \begin{bmatrix} 3 \\ 2 \end{bmatrix}$$

Use another example:

$$\begin{bmatrix} -1 & 0 \\ 0 & -1 \end{bmatrix} \cdot \begin{bmatrix} 1 \\ 0 \end{bmatrix} = \begin{bmatrix} -1 \\ 0 \end{bmatrix},$$

$$\begin{bmatrix} -1 & 0 \\ 0 & -1 \end{bmatrix} \cdot \begin{bmatrix} 0 \\ 1 \end{bmatrix} = \begin{bmatrix} 0 \\ -1 \end{bmatrix}$$

Continue with more examples until it is obvious to the students that

In any 2×2 matrix $\begin{bmatrix} a & b \\ c & d \end{bmatrix}$, multiplying by $\begin{bmatrix} 1 \\ 0 \end{bmatrix}$ gives the first column $\begin{bmatrix} a \\ c \end{bmatrix}$ and multiplying by $\begin{bmatrix} 0 \\ 1 \end{bmatrix}$ gives the second column $\begin{bmatrix} b \\ d \end{bmatrix}$. In other words, the matrix maps the base vectors $\begin{bmatrix} 1 \\ 0 \end{bmatrix}$ and $\begin{bmatrix} 0 \\ 1 \end{bmatrix}$ onto $\begin{bmatrix} a \\ c \end{bmatrix}$ and $\begin{bmatrix} b \\ d \end{bmatrix}$ respectively.

When this conclusion is reached and appreciated by each student, the class then holds the key to reaching the performance objectives. Check whether the class can answer each of the following two types of problems:

1. Which transformation is performed by applying the matrix $\begin{bmatrix} 2 & 0 \\ 0 & 2 \end{bmatrix}$ to the unit vectors?

Show them that $\begin{bmatrix} 2 & 0 \\ 0 & 2 \end{bmatrix} \cdot \begin{bmatrix} 1 \\ 0 \end{bmatrix} = \begin{bmatrix} 2 \\ 0 \end{bmatrix}$

and so $\begin{bmatrix} 1 \\ 0 \end{bmatrix}$ has been mapped onto $\begin{bmatrix} 2 \\ 0 \end{bmatrix}$

and $\begin{bmatrix} 2 & 0 \\ 0 & 2 \end{bmatrix} \cdot \begin{bmatrix} 0 \\ 1 \end{bmatrix} = \begin{bmatrix} 0 \\ 2 \end{bmatrix}$.

and so $\begin{bmatrix} 0 \\ 1 \end{bmatrix}$ has been mapped onto $\begin{bmatrix} 0 \\ 2 \end{bmatrix}$.

Conclude that $\begin{bmatrix} 2 & 0 \\ 0 & 2 \end{bmatrix}$ is therefore an enlargement, scale factor 2.

2. Which matrix effects the transformation: rotation by 180°, centered at the origin? Ask the students to draw the effect of 180 rotation on the base vectors. Check with them that $\begin{bmatrix} 1 \\ 0 \end{bmatrix} \rightarrow \begin{bmatrix} -1 \\ 0 \end{bmatrix}$ and $\begin{bmatrix} 0 \\ 1 \end{bmatrix} \rightarrow \begin{bmatrix} 0 \\ -1 \end{bmatrix}$. Ask them what 2×2 matrix will give the results $\begin{bmatrix} a & d \\ c & d \end{bmatrix} \cdot \begin{bmatrix} 1 \\ 0 \end{bmatrix} = \begin{bmatrix} -1 \\ 0 \end{bmatrix}$ and $\begin{bmatrix} a & b \\ c & d \end{bmatrix} \cdot \begin{bmatrix} 0 \\ 1 \end{bmatrix} = \begin{bmatrix} 0 \\ -1 \end{bmatrix}$. They should by now know that $\begin{bmatrix} -1 \\ d \end{bmatrix}$ gives the first column of the 2×2 matrix and $\begin{bmatrix} 0 \\ -1 \end{bmatrix}$ gives the second column.

Therefore the desired matrix is $\begin{bmatrix} -1 & 0 \\ 0 & -1 \end{bmatrix}$.

Numerous examples and exercises should follow, such as those found in the posttest.

Depending on his aims, the teacher may want to go on at this point to discuss inverse transformations (i.e., ones that reverse the effect of the original transformation) and transformations followed in the same problem by other transformations. The teacher should be aware here too of the value of using matrices, for the inverse of a matrix represents the inverse of a transformation, and multiplying two 2×2 matrices represents the effect of one transformation followed by another.

Postassessment

1. What transformation does the matrix a.) $\begin{bmatrix} 0 & 1 \\ -1 & 0 \end{bmatrix}$ b.) $\begin{bmatrix} 2 & 0 \\ 0 & -2 \end{bmatrix}$ c.) $\begin{bmatrix} 0 & -1 \\ -1 & 0 \end{bmatrix}$ represent?

2. Find the matrix of each of the following transformations:
   a.) Reflection across the line y = x.
   b.) Enlargement with center at the origin, scale factor ½.
   c.) Rotation by −90°.

112 The Method of Differences

Many students familiar with arithmetic and geometric progressions will welcome the opportunity to extend their knowledge of sequences and series to a much broader class of simple functions.

Performance Objectives

(1) Given sufficient terms of a sequence whose *nth* term is a rational, integral function of n, students will form an array consisting of the successive orders of differences.

(2) Given such an array, students will then use the method of differences to find expressions for the *nth* term and the sum of the first n terms.

Preassessment

Students should be acquainted with the Binomial Theorem for positive, integral exponents as it is ordinarily taught in high schools.

Teaching Strategies

Begin the lesson by challenging the class to find the general term of the sequence 2, 12, 36, 80, 150, 252 . . . After initial efforts of most students to find the familiar arithmetic and geometric progressions have proved unsuccessful hint that sequences of this sort might be generated by single polynomials e.g. n^2 (1, 4, 9, . . .) or n^3 (1, 8, 27, . . .). One student or another may shortly recognize that the *n*th term is given by $n^3 + n^2$.

Elicit that an infinite number of such sequences could be produced by using familiar polynomial functions. Then explain that a simple method exists for finding both the general term and the sum of these sequences. It is called the ''Method of Differences'' and although it is not generally taught to high school students, it is nonetheless well within their grasp.

Have the class form the ''difference between successive terms'' of the above sequence, and then continue the process as shown below.

$$
\begin{array}{ccccccc}
2 & 12 & 36 & 80 & 150 & 252 & \ldots \\
& 10 & 24 & 44 & 70 & 102 & \ldots \\
& & 14 & 20 & 26 & 32 & \ldots \\
& & & 6 & 6 & 6 & \ldots
\end{array} \quad (1)
$$

Observe that we reach a line of differences in which all terms are equal. To test whether this occurrence is merely accidental, have the students form sequences from polynomials such as $n^3 + 5n$, $2n^3 + 3$, and so forth, and then repeat the process of taking successive differences. A consensus will soon emerge that an eventual line of equal terms is indeed characteristic of such sequences. The formal proof of this proposition (although simple) is not necessary at this time. Suffi-

cient motivation will have been produced to examine the general case shown below.

Given sequence: $U_1, U_2, U_3, U_4, U_5, U_6, \ldots$

1st order of difference: $\Delta U_1, \Delta U_2, \Delta U_3, \Delta U_4, \Delta U_5, \ldots \quad (2)$

2nd order of difference: $\Delta_2 U_1, \Delta_2 U_2, \Delta_2 U_3, \Delta_2 U_4, \ldots$

3rd order of difference: $\Delta_3 U_1, \Delta_3 U_2, \Delta_3 U_3, \ldots$

. . . .

The notation will be self-evident to all who have written out several previous arrays. Thus: $\Delta U_3 = U_4 - U_3$, $\Delta_2 U_3 = \Delta U_4 - \Delta U_3$, etc. If the delta symbol, Δ, appears too forbidding for some, it can simply be replaced by the letter D.

From the method of forming each entry in (2) it can be seen that: any term is equal to the sum of the term immediately preceding it added to the term below it on the left.

Using nothing more than this simple observation, we will now express each term of the given sequence as a function of the descending terms making up the left-hand boundary. Thus: $\boxed{U_2 = U_1 + \Delta U_1}$ (3)

Also, $U_3 = U_2 + \Delta U_2$ with $\Delta U_2 = \Delta U_1 + \Delta_2 U_1$.
$U_3 = (U_1 + \Delta U_1) + (\Delta U_1 + \Delta_2 U_1)$
$\boxed{U_3 = U_1 + 2\Delta U_1 + \Delta_2 U_1}$ (4)

By referring to (2) students should be able to follow the reasoning that leads to an expression for U_4 in terms of U_1.
$U_4 = U_3 + \Delta U_3$; however, $\Delta U_3 = \Delta U_2 + \Delta_2 U_2$.
But, $\Delta U_2 = \Delta U_1 + \Delta_2 U_1$, and $\Delta_2 U_2 = \Delta_2 U_1 + \Delta_3 U_1$.
Therefore, $\Delta U_3 = \Delta U_1 + 2\Delta_2 U_1 + \Delta_3 U_1$
Now, using (3) and (4):
$U_4 = (U_1 + 2\Delta U_1 + \Delta_2 U_1) + (\Delta U_1 + 2\Delta_2 U_1 + \Delta_3 U_1$
$\boxed{U_4 = U_1 + 3\Delta U_1 + 3\Delta_2 U_1 + \Delta_3 U_1}$ (5)

Calling attention to the boxed expressions for U_2, U_3, U_4 the teacher can elicit the fact that the numerical coefficients involved are those of the Binomial Theorem. Note, however, that the coefficients used for the *fourth* term (1, 3, 3, 1) are those found in a binomial expansion for the exponent *three*. If this remains true generally, we shall be able to write:

$$\boxed{U_n = U_1 + (n-1)\Delta U_1 + \frac{(n-1)(n-2)}{1 \cdot 2}\Delta_2 U_1 + \ldots + {}_{n-1}C_r\Delta_r U_1 + \ldots + \Delta_{n-1}U_1} \quad (6)$$

If desired, the formal proof of (6) can be easily obtained by mathematical induction once the identity $_nC_r + {}_nC_{r-1} = {}_{n+1}C_r$ is established.

Some teachers may wish to rewrite (6) so as to resemble the notation typically used in treating arithmetic progressions. To do this, let the first term of the sequence be "a", while the first terms of each successive order of difference are $d_1, d_2, d_3 \ldots$. Then the *nth* term will be:

$$\ell = a + (n-1)d_1 + \frac{(n-1)(n-2)}{1 \cdot 2} d_2 + \ldots \quad (7)$$

Finding the Sum of the First n-Terms

Examine the following array, in which $U_1, U_2 \ldots$ are again the terms of the given sequence we wish to sum.

$$
\begin{array}{llllll}
0_1 & S_2 & S_3 & S_4 & S_5 & \ldots \\
U_1 & U_2 & U_3 & U_4 & \ldots \\
\Delta U_1 & \Delta U_2 & \Delta U_3 & \ldots
\end{array} \quad (8)
$$

Observe that the S-terms are formed by relations such as

$S_2 = 0 + U_1 = U_1$
$S_3 = S_2 + U_2 = U_1 + U_2$
$S_4 = S_3 + U_3 = U_1 + U_2 + U_3$
$S_5 = S_4 + U_4 = U_1 + U_2 + U_3 + U_4$

Thus, if we can find an expression for S_{n+1} we will have also found the sum of the first *n*-terms. To find S_{n+1} one simply applies the previously determined equation (6) to the above array (8). Before doing so, students should carefully compare (8) with (2). Then

it should become evident that the proper application of equation (6) yields:

$$S_{n+1} = 0 + nU_1 + \frac{n(n-1)}{1 \cdot 2}\Delta U_1 + \ldots + \Delta_n U_n \text{ or}$$

$$\boxed{U_1 + U_2 + \ldots + U_n = nU_1 + \frac{n(n-1)}{1 \cdot 2}\Delta U_1 + \ldots + \Delta_n U_n} \quad (9)$$

As an illustration, let us sum the first *n* squares of the integers.

$$
\begin{array}{ccccc}
1, & 4, & 9, & 16, & 25 \ldots \\
 & 3, & 5, & 7, & 9 \ldots \\
 & & 2, & 2, & 2 \ldots
\end{array}
$$

$$\text{Sum of } n^2 = n \cdot 1 + \frac{n(n-1)}{1 \cdot 2} \cdot 3 + \frac{n(n-1)(n-2)}{1 \cdot 2 \cdot 3} \cdot 2$$

$$= \frac{6n + 9n(n-1) + 2n(n-1)(n-2)}{6} = \frac{n}{6}(n+1)(2n+1)$$

Students may readily confirm the validity of this expression. Again, as before, the teacher may elect to rewrite (9) in terms of $a, d_1, d_2, \ldots$ and so forth.

Postassessment

Have students find the *nth* term and the sum of *n* terms for

1) 2, 5, 10, 17, 26 . . .
2) 1, 8, 27, 64, 125 . . .
3) 12, 40, 90, 168, 280, 432 . . .

Have students create sequences of their own from simple polynomials, and then challenge their classmates to discover the general term.

113 Probability Applied To Baseball

Each year the first months of school coincide with the last months of major league baseball. The playing of the World Series in October normally provides a source of distraction. For mathematics teachers, however, this event can be harnessed to provide useful motivation for a host of probability applications that have high intrinsic academic value.

Performance Objectives

1) *Given odds for opposing World Series teams, students will calculate the expected number of games to be played.*

2) *Given the batting average of any hitter, students will estimate the probability of his attaining any given number of hits during a game.*

Preassessment

Previous study of permutations and probability is not necessary if some introductory discussion is provided. The topic is thus suitable for younger senior high school students (who have not yet learned the binomial theorem). Older students need even less preparation.

Teaching Strategies

The lesson should begin with an informal, spirited discussion of which team is likely to win the World Series. Newspaper clippings of the "odds" should be brought in. This leads directly to the question of how many games will be required for a decision.

Length of Series

If the outcome of a World Series is designated by a sequence of letters representing the winning team (NAANAA means National League won the first and fourth games while losing the rest), challenge the class to find the total number of possible outcomes.

Discuss the solution in terms of "permutations of objects that are not all different." Observe that separate cases of four, five, six, or seven objects must be considered. Elicit that a constraint in the problem is that the winning team must always win the last game. The results can be tabulated as:

No. of Games Played	4	5	6	7
No. of Sequences	2	8	20	40

Table 1

As to the probabilities that the series will actually last four, five, six or seven games, these clearly depend on the relative strengths of the teams. Most students will recognize intuitively that the prospects for a long series increase when the teams are closely matched, and vice versa.

If newspaper "odds" are available these should be translated into the probability of A's winning (p) and N's winning ($q = 1 - p$). If the odds are m:n then $p = m/(m + n)$.

After a brief discussion reviewing the principle that governs the probability of independent events (perhaps illustrated by coin throws), it should become clear that the probability of an American League sweep is P(A in 4) $= p \cdot p \cdot p \cdot p = p^4$. Similarly P(N in 4) $= q^4$ and the overall probability of a four-game series is simply $p^4 + q^4$.

It is rewarding for students to find their intuitions confirmed, so it will be illuminating to substitute the various values for p and q that result from different odds, as shown by Table 2 below.

If odds favoring A are	1:1	2:1	3:1
P (4-game series)	.13	.21	.32

Table 2

Students should be encouraged to extend this table of values.

Before calculating the likelihood of a five-game series, recall work done at the outset to determine the number of possible five-game sequences. There were eight such sequences (NAAAA, ANAAA, AANAA, AAANA, ANNNN and so forth) and the probability associated with *each* of the first four is given by $q \cdot p \cdot p \cdot p \cdot p = p \cdot q \cdot p \cdot p \cdot p = p \cdot p \cdot q \cdot p \cdot p = p \cdot p \cdot p \cdot q \cdot p = p^4 q$
Since these outcomes are mutually exclusive, the probability of P(A in 5) $= 4p^4q$. In identical fashion P(N in 5) $= 4pq^4$ and the overall chance for a five-game series is: $4p^4q + 4pq^4 = 4pq (p^3 + q^3)$.

Similarly, by falling back on the work done on permutations at the start of the lesson, it is simple to show that P(six-game series) $= 10p^2q^2 (p^2 + q^2)$ and P(seven-game series) $= 20p^3q^3 (p + q) = 20 p^3q^3 [p + q = 1]$

As more complete information is derived, Table 2 can be extended to five, six, and seven games for various initial odds.

At this point, students may be introduced to (or reminded of) the important concept of Mathematical Expectation, E(X). With probabilities available for each outcome, E(X) for the length of the series can be calculated

Odds 1:1

X — no. of Games .	4	5	6	7
P(X)	.13	.24	.31	.31

$$E(X) = \Sigma X_i P(X_i) = 5.75$$
[Σ notation can be avoided]

Table 3

Batting Probabilities

Most students who follow baseball believe they have a clear understanding of the meaning of "batting average", and its implications for a hitter going into a game. Challenge the class to estimate the chances of a player getting at least one hit in four times at bat if his season-long batting average has been .250. Some may feel there is a virtual certainty of a hit since $.250 = \frac{1}{4}$.

Begin the analysis, as before, by using a sequence of letters to denote the hitter's performance (NHNN means a hit the second time up). Again, calculate the total number of possible sequences, which will be seen to be 16. Weaker students would be advised to write out each of these permutations.

Select the simplest case of NNNN. From previous work, the probability of this outcome should be evident to the class as P(hitless) $= \frac{3}{4} \cdot \frac{3}{4} \cdot \frac{3}{4} \cdot \frac{3}{4} = \frac{(3)^4}{(4)} = \frac{81}{256} = 0.32$ (Recall: P(H) $= \frac{1}{4}$ and P(N) $= \frac{3}{4}$.) Since all other sequences involve at least one hit, their combined probability is $1 - .32 = 0.68$. Thus there is only a 68 percent chance that the batter will achieve at least one hit in four times. While this result is not startling, it may definitely entail some readjustment in the thinking of some students.

In a similar manner, probabilities can be calculated for the cases of one hit (four possible sequences), two hits (six possible sequences), and so on.

The above topics represent examples of Binomial Experiments and Bernouilli Trials. Discuss with the class the definition of a Bernouilli Trial and the criteria for a Binomial Experiment, using illustrations from dice tossing, coin throwing and so forth. Elicit their estimation of whether these concepts might be usefully applied to other real life events such as gamete unions in genetics; the success of medical procedures such as surgery, and finally, the success of a batsman in baseball.

There are inherent limitations in attempting to treat baseball performances as Bernouilli Trials, especially in a unique situation like a World Series. Nonetheless, there is value in having students acquire a sense of "first-order approximations".

At the same time, their insight into the applications of mathematics can be deepened by confronting a topic with which they feel familiar and are competent to evaluate.

Postassessment

Have students:
(1) Extend Table 2 for P(five-game series), P(6), P(7) for the odds shown, as well as other realistic odds.

(2) Reconstruct Table 3 for odds of 2:1, 3:1 and then calculate E(X) for these cases.

114 Introduction to Geometric Transformations

Beginning with an introduction to the three basic rigid motion transformations, this unit will show how a group can be developed, where the elements are transformations.

Performance Objectives

1. Students will define translation, rotation, and reflection.

2. Students will identify the appropriate transformation from a diagram showing a change of position.

3. Students will produce a group of transformations.

Preassessment

This unit should be presented when students have mastered the basics of geometry. They should be familiar with the concept of group, but do not need to have had any exposure to transformations prior to this unit. A knowledge of functions is also helpful for this unit.

Teaching Strategies

The first part of this unit will concern itself with a brief introduction to the three basic rigid motion transformations: translations, rotations, and reflections.

Students should recall that a one-to-one and onto function is a congruence. That is, $\overline{AB} \xrightarrow[\text{onto}]{1=1} \overline{CD}$ implies that $\overline{AB} \cong \overline{CD}$.

Translations

Consider $T: \alpha \xrightarrow[\text{onto}]{1=1} \alpha$, that is, a mapping of the entire plane onto itself in the direction of a given vector **v**.

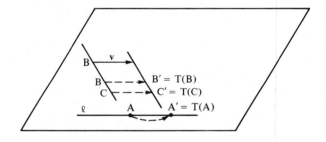

In the figure above each point in the plane is taken to a new point in the plane in the direction and distance of the translation vector **v**. Here T(B)=B′, B′ is the image of B under the translation. Points along line ℓ, which is parallel to **v**, are mapped onto other points of ℓ. To insure a good understanding of this type of transformation ask your students the following questions:

1. Which lines are mapped onto themselves? (those parallel to the translation vector)
2. Which points are mapped onto themselves? (none)
3. Which vector determines the inverse of T? (the negative of **v**)

Rotations

Consider R: $\alpha \xrightarrow[\text{onto}]{1-1} \alpha$, that is a mapping of the entire plane onto itself as determined by a rotation of any angle about a point. We shall agree to consider only counterclockwise rotations unless specified otherwise.

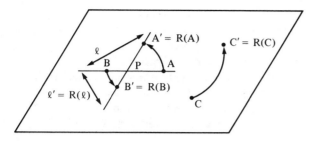

In the figure above R represents a rotation of 90° about P. The following questions should help your students understand this transformation:

1. Are any points mapped upon themselves by a rotation R? (yes, P)
2. Are any lines mapped upon themselves by a rotation R? (No, unless the rotation is 180°, written R_{180}, then any line through the center of rotation (P) is mapped upon itself.)
3. If ℓ is in the plane, how are ℓ and $\ell' = R_{90}(\ell)$ related? (perpendicular)
4. What is the inverse of R_{90}? (either R_{270}, or R_{630}, etc., or R_{-90}.)
5. What is the inverse of R_{180}? (R_{180})
6. If $R_a\,R_b$ means a rotation of $b°$ followed by a rotation of $a°$, describe R^2, R^3, R^4.
7. Simplify $R_{200} \cdot R_{180}$.   ($R_{380} = R_{380-360} = R_{20}$)
8. Simplify $R_{90} \cdot R_{270}$.   ($R_{360} = R_0$)
9. Simplify R_{120}^4.   ($R_{480} = R_{480-360} = R_{120}$)

Reflections

Consider M_ℓ: $\alpha \xrightarrow[\text{onto}]{1=1} \alpha$, a mapping of the entire plane onto itself as determined by a reflection in a point or a line.

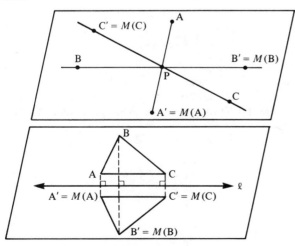

To find the reflection of a point A in a given point P, simply locate the point A′ on ray $\overrightarrow{AP}$ (on the opposite side of P as is A) so that A′P = AP. In the top figure above, A′ is the image (or reflection) of A.

To find the reflection of a point A in a given line ℓ, locate the point A′ on the line perpendicular to ℓ and

containing A, at the same distance from ℓ as A, but on the opposite side. In the bottom figure above, the points of a triangle (and hence the triangle itself) are reflected in ℓ.

Once again some questions for your students:

1. What is the inverse of M_ℓ?   (M_ℓ)
2. How does an image differ from its pre-image? (different orientation, or "mirror image")
3. How does the reflection of a line in a given point change the line's orientation? (changes the order of points on the line from given to the reverse of that)
4. Describe each of the following:
   a) $M_\ell(m)$, where $\ell\,/\!/\,m$.
      ($m'\,/\!/\,\ell$ on the opposite side of ℓ as is m)
   b) $M_\ell(n)$, where $\ell \perp n$.
      (n' is the same line as n)
   c) $M_\ell(k)$, where ℓ is oblique to k.
      (k' forms the same angle with ℓ as does k at the same point as k but on the opposite side of ℓ)

Groups

In order to discuss a group of transformations it would be helpful to review the definition of a group.

1. A set with one operation.
2. Associative property must hold true.
3. An identity element must exist.
4. Every element must have an inverse.

To consider the elements as the three types of transformations would be confusing. We shall therefore show that (I) any translation is the product of two reflections, and (II) any rotation is the product of two reflections. This will enable us to work exclusively with reflections. The word "product" as it was used above refers to the "composition" of transformations; that is, one transformation performed after the other.

I. To show that any translation $T_\mathbf{v}$ is equivalent to the composition of two reflections consider the figure below.

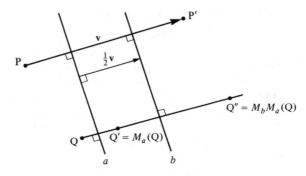

At either end of any vector $\frac{1}{2}\,\mathbf{v}$ consider the lines perpendicular to $\mathbf{v}$. By reflecting any point Q in line a

and then in line *b* (the order of reflections is not important), Q'' is obtained, which is $T_v(Q)$. That is, $M_a(Q) = Q'$ and $M_b(M_a(Q)) = Q'' = M_bM_a(Q)$.

II. To show that any rotation R_Θ is equivalent to the composition of two reflections consider the figure below.

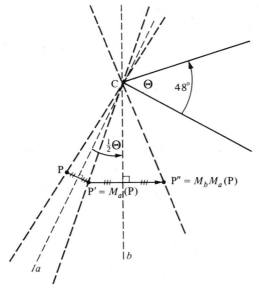

Through the center of rotation, C, draw two lines forming an angle of measure $\frac{1}{2}\Theta$. Select any point P and reflect it through line *a* and then reflect that image through line *b*. Once again the order of reflections is

not important, but for convenience we shall use line *a* before line *b*. Using the two pairs of congruent triangles in the figure above, we can easily prove that $M_bM_a(P) = P''$ is in fact equal to $R_\Theta(P)$.

Now that we can replace translations and rotations with combinations of reflections, ask your students to verify that a group of transformations is at hand. They must demonstrate *all* four properties listed above.

Postassessment

1. Define translation, rotation, and reflection.
2. Describe each of the following as a single transformation.
3. Show that reflections form a group under the operation of composition.

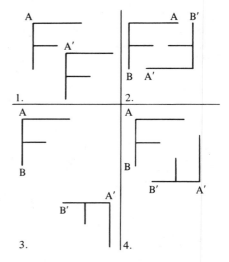

115   The Circle and the Cardioid

Performance Objectives

1. *Given a circle, students will be able to draw a cardioid without using an equation.*

2. *Students will be able, by experimentation, to generate curves other than the cardioid.*

Preassessment

Introduce students to the cardioid by having them set up a table of values for $r = 2a(1 + \cos\theta)$ Then have students locate the corresponding points on a polar coordinate graph. After they have constructed this curve, which was first referred to as a *cardioid* (heart-shaped) by de Castillon in 1741, students should be enticed to consider some rather unusual methods for constructing this curve.

Teaching Strategies

Method I. Ask the students to draw a base circle, O, of diameter 3 inches, centered evenly on an

8½″ × 11″ sheet. With a protractor, divide the circumference into 36 equally spaced points (see figure 1.) Through any of these 36 points, T, con-

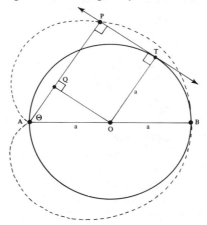

Figure 1

struct a tangent, *t*, to the circle. This need not necessarily be constructed in the classical way using straightedge and compasses, but rather with a right triangle template, or a carpenter's T-square, in which one leg of the triangle passes through the center of the circle. Drawing a tangent to a circle in this manner is based on the fact that the tangent to a circle is perpendicular to the radius at the point of tangency. From a *fixed* point, A, on the circle's circumference (where A is one of the 36 points), drop a perpendicular to meet *t* at P. Now construct tangents to all the remaining points (except through A), to each tangent repeating the preceding step of dropping a perpendicular from A

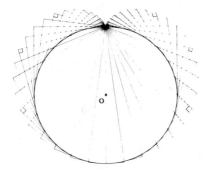

Figure 2

to *t*. The resulting figure will appear as shown in figure 2; the locus of all such points P is a cardioid. Point A is then the cardioid's *cusp*. In figure 2, certain construction lines from figure 1 were eliminated so as to enhance the final drawing. Also, 48 points were used along the base circle in figure 2 for a more compact appearing effect. Finally, note that the orientation of the cardioid in figure 2 differs from that in figure 1 by a 90° clockwise rotation of the cardioid about A.

Proof: In figure 1, let A be the fixed point on the circle 0. Let A also be the pole, and diameter $\overline{AB}$ the initial line, of a polar coordinate system. Draw $\overline{OT}$. Thus, $\overline{AP} \parallel \overline{OT}$. From 0, drop a perpendicular to meet $\overline{AP}$ at Q.
Then $\overleftrightarrow{OQ} \parallel \overleftrightarrow{TP}$ and OTPQ is a rectangle. Let OT = OP = *a*, *r* = AP and m ∠ BAP = *θ*. Then, from figure 1, *r* = AQ + QP.   (1)

In right △ AQO, $\cos\theta = \dfrac{AQ}{a}$, so that

    AQ = *a* · cos*θ*.   (2)
With QP = *a*, and using (2), (1) becomes
    r = *a* · cos*θ* + *a*, or
    r = *a*(1 + cos*θ*),   (3)
which is the polar equation of a cardioid.

The procedure given above is an example of how a *pedal* curve to a given curve is generated (i.e., the cardioid is referred to as the *pedal* to circle O with respect to A). All pedal curves are obtained in this manner: Some arbitrary fixed point is chosen, often

on the curve itself, and from that point perpendiculars are dropped to various tangents to the particular curve. The locus of the intersection of the perpendiculars to each tangent from a fixed point defines the pedal curve. Though the tangent to a circle can easily be constructed, and hence a pedal curve drawn, further pedal constructions of a visual nature can prove challenging.

Method II. As in Method I, draw a base circle of diameter 3 inches, except that the circle should be placed about one inch left of center on a vertically-held 8½″x11″ sheet (see figure 3). Divide the circle into 18 equally spaced points. Label the diameter AB =2a, with A once again a fixed point. Let M be one of these 18 points, distinct from A. Place the edge of a

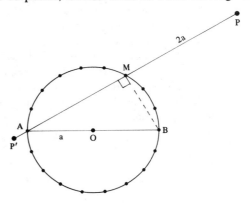

Figure 3

marked straightedge on M, being sure that the straightedge also passes through A. Locate two points of $\overleftrightarrow{AM}$, P and P′, on either side of M, at a distance of 2a units from M. Thus M is the midpoint of $\overline{PP'}$. Continue for all such points M, as M is allowed to move to each of the remaining points (of the originally selected 18 points) around the circumference. The locus of all such points P and P′ is a cardioid (see figure 4).

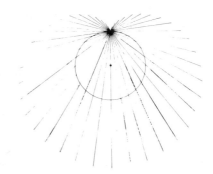

Figure 4

Proof: In figure 3, draw $\overline{MB}$, let AP = *r*, and let m ∠ BAM = *θ*. Since △AMB is a right triangle,

AM = $2a \cdot \cos\theta$.   (4)

But r = AM + MP,   (5)

and by construction, MP = $2a$. Substituting this, as well as (4), into (5), we get

$r = 2a \cdot \cos\theta + 2a$,

or $r = 2a(1 + \cos\theta)$,   (6)

a form identical with (3) except for the constant $2a$. For $\theta + 180°$, we obtain P′, so that r = AP′. Since cos $(\theta + 180°) = -\cos\theta$, we would have obtained

$r = 2a(1 - \cos\theta)$ (7)

had we repeated the above steps.

The cardioid construction given here is an example of a *conchoid* curve. Using this technique with an ellipse, the choice of a fixed point could be an extremity of the major or minor axis. Varying the length of the line on either side of M to equal the major or minor axis creates several interesting combinations of conchoid curves for the ellipse.

Method III. The cardioid can also be generated as the locus of a point, P, on the circumference of a rolling circle which rolls, without slipping on a fixed circle of equal diameter.

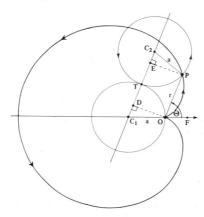

Figure 5

Proof: Let the fixed circle, C_1, of radius a, be centered at the pole of a polar coordinate system.

Let O be the intersection of circle C_1 with the initial line. Circle C_2, whose initial position was externally tangent to circle C_1 at O, has now rolled to the position shown in figure 5, carrying with it fixed point P. The locus of P is desired.

Circle C_2 is now tangent to circle C_1 at T. A line joining C_1 to C_2 will pass through T. Since $\overset{\frown}{PT} \cong \overset{\frown}{OT}$, m $\angle OC_1T = m \angle PC_2T$. If $C_2P = a$ is drawn, as well as $\overline{OP}$, we obtain isosceles trapezoid OC_1C_2P, and hence m $\angle POF = \theta$.

Drop perpendiculars from O and P to $\overleftrightarrow{C_1C_2}$, meeting $\overleftrightarrow{C_1C_2}$ at D and E, respectively. Immediately, $\triangle ODC_1 \cong \triangle PEC_2$, from which it follows that $C_1D = EC_2$ and DE = OP. In triangles ODC_1 and PEC_2,

$C_1D = a \cdot \cos\theta$,   (8)

and $C_2E = a \cdot \cos\theta$.   (9)

Now $C_1C_2 = 2a = C_1D + DE + C_2E$.   (10)

Substituting (8) and (9) into (10), and remembering that DE = OP = r,

$2a = a \cdot \cos\theta + r + a \cdot \cos\theta$,   (11)

which yields, upon simplification

$r = 2a(1 - \cos\theta)$.   (12)

This is identical with (7).

The concept of a circle rolling smoothly on the circumference of another, fixed, circle, has been well studied. The locus of a point on the circumference of the rolling circle gives rise to a curve called an *epicycloid*, of which the cardioid is a special case. Changing the ratio of the fixed circle's radius to that of the radius of the rolling

Postassessment

Refer to Method I for drawing the following two variations, and in so doing, possibly obtain equations similar to (3):

(a) choose the fixed point A *outside* the circle at a distance of $2a$ units from O;

(b) choose A *inside* the circle, at a distance of $\frac{a}{2}$ units from 0.

116 Complex Number Applications

The number system we presently use has taken a long time to develop. It proceeded according to the necessity of the time. To early man, counting numbers was sufficient to meet his needs. Simple fractions, such as the unit fractions employed by the Egyptians followed. While the early Greeks did not recognize irrational numbers, their necessity in geometric problems brought about their acceptance. Negative numbers, too, were used when their physical application became apparent, such as their use in temperature. Complex numbers, however, are studied because the real number system is not algebraically complete without them. Their application to the physical world is not explored by most mathematics students. This unit introduces students to some physical applications of complex numbers.

Performance Objectives

Students will be able to solve some physics problems involving complex numbers and vector quantities.

Preassessment

Students should be familiar with operations with complex numbers and vector analysis. A knowledge of basic physics is also recommended.

Teaching Strategies

In algebra, a complex plane is defined by two rectangular coordinate axes in which the real parts of the complex numbers are plotted along the horizontal axis and the imaginary parts are plotted along the vertical axis. This complex plane can be developed if we take an approach in which i is treated as the "sign of perpendicularity" as an operator functioning to rotate a vector through an angle of 90°.

To develop this idea we begin with any vector quantity, A, which is represented by a vector ——————→ whose length indicates the magnitude and whose arrow tip indicates sense. (To distinguish between vector and scalar quantities, a bar is placed over the symbol to indicate a vector quantity, $\overline{A}$, while a symbol without a bar indicates a scalar quantity, A). Now, if $\overline{A}$ is operated upon by -1 (multiplied by -1), we have $-\overline{A}$ whose graphical representation is ←——————. Thus, operating upon the vector $\overline{A}$ by -1 rotates it through 180° in the positive sense. Now, since $i^2 = -1$, i must represent rotating the vector through an angle of 90°, since two applications of 90° will result in a rotation of 180°. Therefore, operating

upon a vector by i^3 rotates the vector through 270°, and so on. Similarly we can consider using as operators higher roots of -1, which will rotate the vector through a smaller angle. So $\sqrt[3]{-1} = (i^2)^{\frac{1}{3}} = i^{\frac{2}{3}}$ will rotate a vector through an angle of 60° since three applications of this operator is equivalent to operating by -1. We can show this in a vector diagram. Given a vector $\overline{A}$, with magnitude A, we operate upon it by $i^{\frac{2}{3}}$, i.e., we rotate the vector through 60°. This, of course,

Figure 1

does not change its magnitude, A. Therefore, the real component is $A \cos 60° = \frac{1}{2}A$ and the imaginary component is $A \sin 60° = \sqrt{\frac{3}{2}}A$. So $\sqrt[3]{-1}\,\overline{A} = i^{\frac{2}{3}}\,\overline{A} = A \cos 60° + iA \sin 60°$, which indicates the position of the vector. In this way $\sqrt[n]{-1}\,\overline{A} = i^{\frac{2}{n}}\,\overline{A} = \overline{A} \cos \frac{\pi}{n} + i\,A \sin \frac{\pi}{n}$. To generalize, to rotate a vector A through the angle Θ we use the operator $\cos \Theta + i \sin \Theta$.

Now, if we are given a vector $\overline{A}_1 = a + bi$, we can graph it on the complex plane. The position of the

Figure 2

vector is given by $\Theta_1 = \arctan \frac{b}{a}$. Its magnitude is $A_1 = \sqrt{a^2 + b^2}$. Vector $\overline{A}_1$ is pictured in figure 2. Similarly vector $\overline{A}_2 = -a - bi$ has magnitude $A_2 = \sqrt{(-a)^2 + (-b)^2}$, the same as that of vector A_1. Its position is given by $\Theta_2 = \arctan \frac{-b}{-a}$ and is located in the third quadrant as pictured in Figure 3.

Now, we can explore a physical interpretation of these operators. In physics books $\sqrt{-1}$ is represented

Figure 3

by the letter j and electrical current by the letter I. Since this paper is written for mathematics students, we used i to represent $\sqrt{-1}$ and, for the sake of clarity, we will use the letter J to represent the electrical current.

In the study of alternating currents, we have for the current the vector $\overline{J} = j_1 + ij_2$. The voltage $\overline{E}$ of this frequency can be represented by $E = \epsilon_1 + \epsilon_2 i$. The impedance (effective resistance of the current) of the circuit, *not* a vector, can be represented by $Z = r \pm ix$ where r is the ohmic resistance and x is the reactance. The angle between $\overline{E}$ and $\overline{J}$ is the phase angle (the angle by which the current lags behind the electromotive force, emf) and is represented by $\phi = \text{arc tan } \frac{r}{x}$.

We can obtain mathematically the product of two impedances, but it has no physical meaning. The product of the voltage and the current, although it has no physical meaning, is referred to as apparent power. If, however, we take the product of the current and the impedance $Z\overline{J} = (r + ix)(j_1 + ij_2) = (rj_1 + xj_2) + i(rj_2 + xj_1)$, we have a voltage of the same frequency as the current, *the actual voltage*, i.e., $Z\overline{J} = \overline{E}$. This is Ohm's law in the complex form (recall that Ohm's law states that for direct currents the voltage is equal to the product of the resistance and the current). So, in direct currents one deals with scalar quantities while in alternating current circuits the quantities are vectors expressable as complex numbers obeying the laws of vector algebra. In the following diagrams for Ohm's law, the first diagram (Figure 4) has $\overline{J}$ on the real axis, the second diagram (Figure 5) does not.

Let us now try some problems.

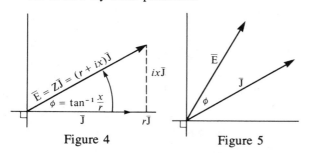

Figure 4   Figure 5

Example 1. Let $r = 5$ ohms, $x = 4$ ohms and the current J is 20 amperes. Take J on the real axis

Given this information we have the impedance, $Z = 5 + 4i$. The inductive circuit is $\overline{E} = \overline{J}Z = 20(5 + 4i) = 100 + 80i$. Therefore $E = \sqrt{100^2 + 80^2} = 128$ volts. The angle $\overline{E}$ makes with the real axis is $\Theta = \text{arc tan } \dfrac{80}{100} =$

$38°40'$, which also happens to be the phase angle for this problem. The vector diagram is shown in Figure 6.

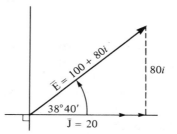

Figure 6

Example 2. Let us change the above example slightly by letting the angle that the current vector $\overline{J}$ makes with the real axis be 30°. We will let the remaining data be as before.

We still have $Z = 5 + 4i$. We now have $\overline{J} = 20(\cos 30° + i \sin 30°) = 20(.866 + .5i) = 17.32 + 10i$
$\overline{E} = \overline{J}Z = (17.32 + 10i) \cdot (5 + 4i) = 46.6 + 119.28i$
$E = \sqrt{(46.6)^2 + (119.28)^2} = 128$ volts, just as before
The angle E makes with the real axis is $\theta = \text{arc tan } \dfrac{119.28}{46.6} = 68°40'$.
The phase angle ϕ remains the same, $\phi = \text{arc tan } \dfrac{4}{5} = 38°40'$.

The vector diagram for this problem is:

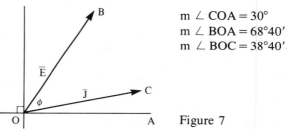

m $\angle$ COA $= 30°$
m $\angle$ BOA $= 68°40'$
m $\angle$ BOC $= 38°40'$

Figure 7

Students should now be able to solve similar physics problems involving complex numbers.

Postassessment

1. Let r $= 3$ ohms and x $= 4$ ohms. Take $\overline{J}$ on the real axis, $J = 3$. Find the impedance Z, the complex expression for $\overline{E}$ and the magnitude of E. What is Θ, the angle $\overline{E}$ makes with the real axis? What is ϕ, the phase angle? Draw a vector diagram for this problem.

2. Use the data for the above problem, letting $\overline{J}$ make an angle of 20° with the real axis. Recalculate all quantities, both the complex expressions and the magnitudes. Draw the vector diagram.

3. Let $\overline{E} = 4 + 14i$ and $\overline{J} = 2 + 3i$. Find the complex expression for Z and its magnitude. What is the phase angle? Draw a vector diagram.

Reference

Suydam, Vernon A. *Electricity and Electromagnetism.* New York: D. Van Nostrand Company, 1940.

117   Hindu Arithmetic

The mathematics curriculum may be enriched for students on many levels by the study of a number system and its arithmetic. An investigation into the mechanics of the system, its contribution to our own system, and other suitable tangents may be entered upon by a student on a high level. For other students it can serve as practice in basic skills with integers, as students check the answers they obtain in working out problems. This unit introduces students to the ancient Hindu numerical notation and system of adding, subtracting, multiplying and dividing (circa 900, India).

Performance Objectives

1. *Given an addition problem, students will find the answer using a Hindu method.*

2. *Given a subtraction problem, students will find the answer using a Hindu method.*

3. *Given a multiplication problem, students will find the answer using a Hindu method.*

4. *Given a division problem, students will find the answer using a Hindu method.*

Preassessment

Students need only be familiar with the basic operations of integers, i.e., addition, subtraction, multiplication and division.

Teaching Strategies

The symbols of the nine numerals used in Hindu reckoning in ascending order are: ? , ? , ? , ? , ? , ? , ? , ? , ? , o This system included a symbol for zero, o. This, then, was a positional system, as in our own, as opposed to a grouping system such as that used by the ancient Egyptians. Therefore, similar to our modern system, 5639 would be represented as ? .

At this point we can discuss the importance of the Hindu symbol for zero. A comparison with the Egyptian numeral system might be instructive (see Unit 14 on Ancient Egyptian Arithmetic). The historical importance of zero could be investigated. Without a zero numbers were cumbersome, and intricate computations were difficult. In the Hindu system, record keeping and other computations necessary for commerce, astronomical computations, and mathematical tables were advanced, for with the existence of a placeholder numbers are easier to write and read, and can be manipulated with greater ease.

Hindu computation was generally written upon surfaces where corrections and erasures were easily done. For our purposes, instead of erasing numbers

we will cross out numbers so that the methods discussed will be more easily followed.

Hindu addition, though set up vertically as in our method, was done from left to right. Consider the problem: 6537 + 886. The addition begins on the left with 8 being added to the 5. The 1 of this 13 is added to the numeral on the left, 6, changing it to 7, and the 5 is now changed to a 3. This process continues, from left to right. Thus, the solution would look like this:

```
7 4 2
7 3 1 3
6 5 3 7        The result is 7423.
  8 8 6
```

Subtraction was also done from left to right, the larger number being placed above the smaller one. To subtract 886 from 6537, we begin by subtracting 8 from 5. Since this is not possible, we subtract the 8 from 65, leaving 57. We put the 5 in place of the 6, and the 7 in place of the 5. We continue this process by subtracting 8 from 3 using the described method. The solution of the entire problem would look like this:

```
6
5 7 5 1
6 5 3 7        The result is 5651.
  8 8 6
```

To multiply as the Hindus did, we begin by placing the units' digit of the multiplier under the highest place of position of the multiplicand. To multiply 537 by 24 we begin this way:

```
    5 3 7
  2 4
```

We multiply 2 by 5 and place the resulting 0 above the 2, and the 1 to the left. We now multiply 4 by the 5, placing the resulting 0 in place of the 5 above the 4, and adding the 2 to the 0 we now have 2 in the next place:

```
  2 0
1 0 5 3 7
  2 4
```

Now that we have finished with the 5, we shift the multiplier one place to the right, the 4 now being below the 3, indicating 3 is the number we are now concerned with.

```
  2 0
1 0 5 3 7
    2 4
```

We multiply as before, first the 2 by the 3, then the 4, and when finished shift again to the right. When we have done the entire problem it will look like this:

$$\begin{array}{r}
8 \\
\not7\ 8 \\
6\ 6 \\
2\ \not0\ \not2\ 8 \\
1\ \not0\ \not8\ \not3\ \not7 \\
\not2\ \not4 \\
\not2\ \not4 \\
2\ 4
\end{array}$$

The answer is 12,888.

It can be seen that crossing out, instead of erasing, requires space. As division is the most complex of the basic operations, the problem will be done step by step, instead of crossing out, substituting new results for the old numbers.

To divide, we place the divisor below the dividend, aligning them on the left. Thus, we begin the problem $5832 \div 253$ as $\begin{smallmatrix} 5 & 8 & 3 & 2 \\ 2 & 5 & 3 & \end{smallmatrix}$. As 253 is below 583, we seek a number to multiply 253 by so that the product will be as close as possible to 583 without exceeding it. The number we seek here is 2, and it is placed thus:

$$\begin{array}{c}
2 \\
5\ 8\ 3\ 2 \\
2\ 5\ 3
\end{array}$$

We now multiply 253 by 2 (as the Hindus did) and subtract the result from 583 (as the Hindus did). This gives us 77, which we put in the place of 583. So we now have:

$$\begin{array}{c}
2 \\
7\ 7\ 2 \\
2\ 5\ 3
\end{array}$$

The divisor is shifted to the right to get:

$$\begin{array}{c}
2 \\
7\ 7\ 2 \\
2\ 5\ 3
\end{array}$$

The process continues as above until we reach the results

$$\begin{array}{c}
23 \\
13 \\
253
\end{array}$$

which shows the quotient to be 23 and the remainder 13.

Investigate these processes with your students to the extent you feel necessary. You will find instructive the similarity of these algorithms to ours.

Postassessment

1. Have students write the following numbers using Hindu numerals:
   a) 5342   b) 230796
2. Have students solve the following problems using Hindu methods:
   a) $3567 + 984$ b) $8734 - 6849$
   c) 596×37 d) $65478 \div 283$

Suggested References

Waerden, B. L. van der. *Science Awakening*. New York: John Wiley & Sons, 1963

Eves, Howard. *An Introduction to the History of Mathematics*, 4th ed. New York: Holt, Rinehart and Winston, 1976.

118 Proving Numbers Irrational

When high school students are introduced to irrational numbers, they are usually asked to accept the fact that certain numbers like $\sqrt{2}$, sin 10°, and so on are irrational. Many students wonder, however, how it could be proved that a given number is irrational. This unit presents a method to prove the irrationality of certain algebraic numbers.

Performance Objectives

1. Given certain algebraic numbers students will be able to prove their irrationality.

2. Students will find some specific patterns that will determine in advance whether a given algebraic number is irrational.

Preassessment

Students should be familiar with the concepts of irrational numbers and algebraic numbers. They should also have a general background in algebraic equations, radicals, trigonometry and logarithms.

Teaching Strategies

Begin the lesson by asking students to give examples of irrational numbers. Ask them how they are sure these numbers are irrational. Then have them define irrational numbers. Students will be curious enough at this point to want to investigate the following theorem.

Theorem:

Consider any polynomial equation with the integer coefficients, $a_n x^n + a_{n-1}x^{n-1} + \ldots + a_1 x + a_0 = 0$. If this equation has a rational root p/q, where p/q is in its lowest terms, then p is a divisor of a_0 and q is a divisor of a_n.

Proof:

Let p/q be a root of the given equation. Then it satisfies the equation and we have:

$a_n(p/q)^n + a_{n-1}(p/q)^{n-1} + \ldots + a_1(p/q) + a_0 = 0$ (I)

We now multiply (I) by q^n to obtain

$a_n p^n + a_{n-1}p^{n-1}q + \ldots + a_1 pq^{n-1} + a_0 q^n = 0$

This equation can be rewritten as

$a_n p^n = -a_{n-1}p^{n-1}q - \ldots - a_1 pq^{n-1} - a_0 q^n$

or

$a_n p^n = q(-a_{n-1}p^{n-1} - \ldots - a_1 pq^{n-2} - a_0 q^{n-1})$

This shows that q is a divisor of $a_n p^n$. But if p/q is in its lowest terms, then p and q are relatively prime and therefore q is a divisor of a_n. Likewise, if we rewrite equation (I) as

$a_0 q^n = p(-a_1 q^{n-1} - \ldots - a_{n-1}p^{n-2}q - a_n p^{n-1})$

we see that p is a divisor of $a_0 q^n$. Again, because p and q are relatively prime, we have that p is a divisor of a_0. This completes the proof of the theorem.

Example 1. Prove that $\sqrt{5}$ is irrational.

$\sqrt{5}$ is a root of $x^2 - 5 = 0$. Then according to the notation used for the theorem, $a_2 = 1$ and $a_0 = -5$. Now any rational root, p/q, of this equation will have to be of such a nature that p will have to divide -5, and q will have to divide 1. This is so because of the previous theorem. But the only divisors of 1 are $+1$ and -1. Thus q must be either $+1$ or -1, and the rational root of the equation must be an integer. This integer p, according to the theorem must divide -5, and the only divisors of -5 are: $-1, 1, 5$ and -5. However none of these is a root of the equation $x^2 - 5 = 0$, that is $(1)^2 - 5 = 0$; $(-1)^2 - 5 = 0$ $(5)^2 - 5 = 0$; and $(-5)^2 - 5 = 0$, are *all false*. Hence $x^2 - 5 = 0$ has no rational root, and $\sqrt{5}$ is therefore an irrational number.

Example 2. Prove that $\sqrt[3]{2}$ is irrational.

$\sqrt[3]{2}$ is a root of $x^3 - 2 = 0$. Then p must divide -2, and q must divide 1. Thus, if this equation has a rational root, this root must be an integer and a divisor of -2. Now the only divisors of -2 are: $2, -2, 1$, and -1. But none of these is a root of the equation $x^3 - 2 = 0$, because $(2)^2 - 2 = 0$, $(-2)^2 - 2 = 0$, $(1)^2 - 2 = 0$, and $(-1)^2 - 2 = 0$ are all false. Hence, $\sqrt[3]{2}$ is irrational.

Example 3. Prove that $\sqrt{2} + \sqrt{3}$ is irrational.

If we write $x = \sqrt{2} + \sqrt{3}$, we have that $x - \sqrt{2} = \sqrt{3}$. Now, square both sides and obtain $x^2 - 1 = 2x\sqrt{2}$

Squaring again gives us $x^4 - 2x^2 + 1 = 8x^2$ or $x^4 - 10x^2 + 1 = 0$.

This equation has been so constructed that $\sqrt{2} + \sqrt{3}$ is a root. But the only possible rational roots of this equation are those integers that are divisors of 1, that is, -1 and 1. But none of these is root of the equation because $(1)^4 - 10(1)^2 + 1 = 0$ and $(-1)^4 - 10(-1)^2 + 1 = 0$ are both false. Hence this equation has no rational roots and consequently $\sqrt{2} + \sqrt{3}$ is irrational.

Example 4. Prove the sin 10° is irrational.

We have the identity $\sin 3\Theta = 3\sin\Theta - 4\sin^3\Theta$. Now if we replace Θ by 10°, and notice that

$\sin 30° = \frac{1}{2}$, we get

$\frac{1}{2} = 3 \sin 10° - 4 \sin^3 10°$.

If we now make $\sin 10° = x$, we obtain

$\frac{1}{2} = 3x - 4x^3$ or

$8x^3 - 6x + 1 = 0$.

According to the theorem, p must be a divisor of 1, and q must be a divisor of 8, thus the only possible rational roots are $\pm\frac{1}{8}$, $\pm\frac{1}{4}$, $\pm\frac{1}{2}$ and ± 1. But none of these eight possibilities is a root of the equation, as can be seen by substitution into the equation obtained. Therefore, this equation has no rational roots, and since sin 10° is a root of the equation, it must be irrational.

Students should now be able to prove irrational those numbers that occur most frequently in high school text books and that students are *told* are irrational. It is important to have students understand why a mathematical concept is true after they have comfortably worked with the concept. All too often students accept the irrationality of a number without question. This unit provides a method which should bring some true understanding to the average high school mathematics student. In addition to the problems posed in the *Postassessment*, students should be encouraged to use the technique presented here when the need arises.

Postassessment

Those students who have mastered the technique learned through the previous examples, should be able to complete the following exercises:
1. Prove that $\sqrt{2}$ is irrational.
2. Prove that $\sqrt[3]{6}$ is irrational.
3. Prove that $\sqrt[3]{3} + \sqrt{11}$ is irrational.
4. Prove that Cos 20° is irrational.
5. Prove that a number of the form $\sqrt[n]{m}$, where n and m are natural numbers, is either irrational or an integer.

119 How to Use a Computer Spreadsheet to Generate Solutions to Certain Mathematics Problems

This unit presents some simple examples of how spreadsheets, such as Multiplan and Visicalc, can be used to generate solutions to certain mathematics problems. A computer with an appropriate spreadsheet must be available and pupils should be familiar with its operation. Secondary school students of any grade should find this challenging as well as fascinating.

Performance Objectives
1. *Students will generate a Fibonacci sequence on a spreadsheet.*
2. *Students will create a Pascal triangle on a spreadsheet.*
3. *Students will list other mathematical problems appropriate for spreadsheet solution.*

Preassessment

Students need to review Enrichment Units 85 (Fibonacci sequence) and 99 (Pascal's pyramid — especially the first part, which discusses the Pascal triangle.) Students should also be familiar with basic operations on a microcomputer and electronic spreadsheets.

Teaching Strategies

An electronic spreadsheet is an array that appears on the screen of a microcomputer. Most spreadsheets have built-in mathematical functions so that elements in the ith row, j^{th} column can be easily accessed for any given i or j. For example, show students how maximum value, minimum value, average value, median, mode, standard deviation, and so on, can be determined for a set of numbers listed on a spreadsheet. Point out that other mathematical applications may be found for spreadsheets in addition to those already in the program.

One interesting application is to generate a Fibonacci sequence as well as a sequence of ratios of successive pairs of numbers. Pay special attention to the formula used to generate a Fibonacci sequence as it is listed in Enrichment Unit 85: $f(n) = f(n-1) + f(n-2)$.

One way this formula can be translated to "spreadsheet language" is, "For a given row, the number in the nth column is equal to the sum of the numbers in the two previous columns."

Together with the students, use "indirect addressing" to develop the formula that a given cell's contents should equal the sum of the entries of the two columns to its left in the same row. Thus, for a given cell,

$$entry = RC[-1] + RC[-2].$$

This technique may be used to write as many terms as will fit onto one row. Then, if you like, develop a variation of this formula that will permit continuation of the sequence to the next row for as many places as you want, considering the physical limitations of the computer.

A second sequence of ratios of successive pairs of terms, as indicated in the enrichment unit, may be generated with this formula:

$$entry = R[-1]C[+1]/R[-1]C.$$

The following sample was produced on an Apple IIe computer on a Multiplan spreadsheet.

	1	2	3	4	5	6	7	8	9	10
1										
2		FIBONACCI SEQUENCE								
3										
4										
5	1	1	2	3	5	8	13	21	34	55
6		2	1.5	1.667	1.6	1.625	1.615	1.619	1.618	

Now suggest a second application that might be of interest: the Pascal triangle. After some discussion of Enrichment Unit 99, especially the rule for generating the triangle, suggest that the triangle be written as follows:

```
1   1
1   2    1
1   3    3    1
1   4    6    4    1
1   5    10   10   5    1
. . . . . . . . . . . . . . . . . . . .
```

Ask pupils to suggest an appropriate spreadsheet formula that would generate this triangle. Point out that the first and last entry of each row is 1 and that each of the other entries is the sum of the number in the row above and the number in that same row but one column to its left.

Postassessment

Ask the class to prepare a list of mathematical topics that might be appropriate for development via a spreadsheet, and solve some of them. You might suggest topics taken from the enrichment units in this book.

The following could prove to be challenging:

Magic squares
Palindromic numbers
The Sieve of Eratosthenes
Solving a quadratic equation
Pythagorean triples
Continued fractions

INDEX

Absentees
  homework assignments for, 49
  tests and, 68
Acceleration of gifted students, 149
Administrative details, 178–79
Algebra, history of, 145–47
Algebraic exercises on tests, 65
  point value for, 66
Algebraic problems, solving, 114–16
Algorithms, 146
Al-Jabr W'al Mukabala, (al-Khowarizmi) 146
al-Khowarizmi, Mohammed ibn Musa, 146
Almagest, The (Ptolemy), 143, 144
Always-sometimes-never questions, 64–65
  point value for, 66
Ambiguous questions, 29–30
Anecdotal record reports, 76
Apperceptive basis of lesson plans, 4
Applications in School Mathematics (NCTM), 130
Archimedes, 142
Arithmetic Teacher, The, 80, 182
Assignment sheets, 50–52
Attendance in class, 175
  student responsibility for, 74
Attitudinal assessment instruments, 93–94
Average ability students
  enrichment for, 148–49
  problem solving and, 111

Backward work in problem solving, 112
Behavioral objectives. *See* Performance objectives
Bulletin boards, 101, 176

CAI. *See* Computer assisted instruction
Calculators, 128
  advanced mathematics courses and, 130
  calculator-assisted instruction, 129
  checking arithmetic, 128–29
  mathematical curiosities and, 130
  mathematics concepts and, 129
  problem solving and, 129–30

remediation and, 100
California Achievement Tests, 93
Cassettes for remediation, 100
Cassette tape recorders, 132
Cathode ray tubes (CRT), 130, 132
Chalkboards, 50, 54, 66, 101
Challenge and motivation, 39
Cheating
  on homework, 56
  mathematics anxiety and, 195
  on tests, 67, 175
Checking homework assignments, 55–56
Chorus response questions, 30
Class ability, questions keyed to, 31–32
Class participation, student responsibility for, 74
Classroom
  arrangement for tests, 67
  computers in, 135–36
  remediation in, 101–2
  tidiness of, 174
Classroom management, 174–76
  administrative details, 178–79
  discipline, 176–78
Competitiveness and math anxiety, 196
Completion questions, 65
  point value for, 66
Computer assisted instruction (CAI), 99, 130–31
Computers
  computer equipment, 132
  computer literacy, 131
  creativity and, 136
  extracurricular activities and, 163
  lesson ideas, 132–35
  in mathematics classes, 135–36
  multiple choice tests and, 70
  problem solving with, 114
  programming in curriculum, 131–32
  recreational mathematics and, 131
  remediation and, 100, 130
  types of, 130
Creativity
  computers and, 136
  in problem solving, 123
Criterion-referenced grading system, 77
Criterion-referenced tests, 93
Cubicles and remediation, 101
Curriculum, basic, 92
Curriculum guides, 182

Data organization in problem solving, 113

Descartes, René, 146
Developmental-drill lessons, 18
Developmental lesson plans, 7–17
Development and methods in lesson plans, 6
Dewey, John, 106
Diagnostic-prescriptive approach to remediation, 94, 96
Diagnostic procedures for remediation, 93–94
Digression from topics for gifted students, 151
Diophantus, 146
Discipline, 176–77
  handling problems, 177–78
  student responsibility for, 74, 178
  unacceptable teacher practices, 178
Discovery approach homework assignment, 46–47
Disk operating systems (DOS), 132
Do-now exercises, 6
Drill
  camouflaged drill, 98
  in lesson plans, 6–7, 18
Duplicator stencils, 54, 66

Elements (Euclid), 140–41, 143, 146
el-Hasib, 144
Elliptical questions, 29
Enrichment
  historical approach, 140–47
  for slow learners, 147–48
Equipment in lesson plans, 7
Euclid, 140–41, 143, 146
Expansion of topics for gifted students, 149–51
Extracurricular activities
  bulletin boards, 163–64
  computers, 163
  field trips, 162–63
  guest speakers programs, 162
  mathematics assembly programs, 161–62
  mathematics clubs, 156
  mathematics contests, 158, 159
  mathematics fairs, 159, 161
  mathematics magazines, 161
  mathematics projects, 159, 160
  mathematics teams, 156–57, 159
  peer teaching program, 163

Factual problems, point values for, 66
Factual questions, 28–29
Field trips
  extracurricular activities, 162–63
  remediation and, 98

for slow learners, 148
Framing answers on homework
papers, 53

Games
  problem solving in, 111
  remediation and, 101
Gauss, Carl Friedrich, 143
Generalizations, strategies for
  discovering, 17–18
Geometric problems, solving, 116
  algebraic method, 119–20
  analytic method, 117–18
  "brute force," 118–19
Geometric proofs on tests, 65
  point values for, 66
Geometry
  history of, 140–43
  reasons omitted from
    chalkboard proofs, 175
Geometry of Compasses, The
  (Mascheroni), 141
Gifted students, enrichment for,
  149. *See also* High ability
  classes
Grading
  honors or slow classes, 76–77
  parental responsibilities, 74–75
  student responsibilities, 74
  techniques for, 75–76
Grouping for remediation, 97
Guessing, correction of test scores
  for, 70
Guessing questions, 29
Guest speakers programs, 162

Heuristic methods, 106
High ability classes, 55
  calculators and, 130
  computers in, 135–36
  grading of, 76–77
Hipparchus, 143
Historical enrichment
  mathematics anxiety and, 196
  motivation and, 41–42
  for slow learners, 148
Homework assignments
  anticipation of, 46
  assignment sheets, 50–52
  cheating, 56
  checking, 55–56
  collecting, 55–56
  discovery approach, 46–47
  format of, 52–53
  frequency of, 49
  lesson plans for, 7
  long term assignments, 52
  objectives for, 48
  punitive homework, 46
  quizzes and, 56

reasons for, 46
relevance of, 175
reviewing, 53–55
spiraled assignment, 48
student attitude re, 48, 49
student responsibility for, 74
time allotted to, 48
time of assignment, 49–50
uniform v individualized, 48–49
How To Solve It (Polya), 106–7, 157
How We Think (Dewey), 106
Hypatia, 146

"If time" exercises in lesson plans,
  7
Impulsive responding and
  mathematics anxiety, 194
Incorrect answers, response to, 32
Individualization
  of homework assignments, 48–49
  of lesson plans, 21
  of remediation, 94, 96–97, 99
Individual tutoring for
  remediation, 102
Internal bisectors problem, 107–8
Item analysis of test questions, 70

*Journal for Research in
  Mathematics Education, The*,
  80

Language of questions, 31
Leading questions, 30–31
Lecture approach, lesson plans
  for, 18
Lesson plans
  adjusting during class, 176
  daily plans, 4–7
  developmental lessons, 7–17
  drill lessons, 18
  generalizations, strategies for
    discovering, 17–18
  individualized lessons, 21
  lectures, 18
  for new courses, 182
  review lessons, 19–20
  unit plans, 4
Letter grades, 75
Library and media center
  resources, 183
Logical sequence of questions, 31
Long term assignments, 52. *See
  also* Projects, long term
Low ability classes, 55
Low ability classes
  enrichment for, 147–48
  grading of, 76–77
  See also Remediation

Margins on homework papers,
  52–53

Mascheroni, Lorenzo, 141–42
Matching questions, 65
Materials
  classroom distribution and
    collection, 174
  motivation and, 42–43
Mathematical Association of
  America, 80
Mathematical curiosities
  calculators and, 130
  motivation and, 42
Mathematical retardation, 94
Mathematics anxiety
  sources of, 194
  strategies for reducing, 194–96
Mathematics assembly programs,
  161–62
Mathematics clubs, 156
Mathematics contests, 158, 159
Mathematics courses
  long-range preparation, 182–83
  short-range preparation, 183
  textbook selection, 183–85
Mathematics fairs, 159, 161
Mathematics magazines, school
  publication of, 161
Mathematics skills laboratories,
  100
Mathematics Teacher, The, 80, 182
Mathematics teams, 156–57, 159
  notes for, 165–69
Meaning of questions, 31
Medial summary in lesson plans, 7
Menelaus, 143
Minimum competency tests, 92
Monroe *Classmate-88*, 129, 130
Motivation
  challenge and, 39
  in lesson plans, 6
  mathematical curiosities and, 42
  recreational math and, 40–41
  sequential achievement and,
    38–39
  stories and, 41–42
  students' knowledge, void in,
    38
  teacher-made and commercially
    prepared materials and, 42–43
  topic usefulness and, 39–40
Muller, Johann, 143
Multiple choice questions, 65
Multiple choice tests, 70
Multiple questions, 28

National Council of Teachers of
  Mathematics, 1, 80, 105, 128,
  130, 182–83
National Science Foundation, 80
News Bulletin, 80
Norm-referenced grading system,
  77

Northrop, E. P., 162
Notebooks for homework, 53
Number grades, 75
Numerical exercises on tests, 65
  point values for, 66

Overhead projectors, 54, 66
Overlaid questions, 28

Paper, format for homework, 52, 53
Parental responsibilities, 74–75
Partial credit for test questions, 68–69
Pascal, Blaise, 142
Pass-fail reports, 76
Patterns in problem solving, 112–13
Peer group tutoring, 98–99
Peer teaching programs, 163
Performance objectives, 188–89
  using, 189, 191
  writing, 189
Phobias, mathematics, 194
Pictures and diagrams in problem solving, 112
Plan books, 4
Polya, George, 106–7, 157
Pre-test cards, 93
Printers for computers, 130, 132
Problem solving
  algebraic problems, 114–16
  calculators and, 129–30
  creating problems, 122–23
  creativity in, 123
  critical and analytic thought in, 110–11
  geometric problems, 116–20
  non-academically oriented students and, 111
  non-routine problems, 120–22
  pride in, 109–10
  psychological view, 106–7
  reading mathematics for, 108–9
  rote responses, 106
  strategies, 111–16
Proctoring tests, 67, 175
Professional conventions, 184
Professional literature, 182–83
Projects
  long term, 159, 160
  remediation and, 97
Ptolemy, 143, 144–45
Punitive homework, 46
Punitive use of mathematics, 194, 196
Pythagoras, 140

Quadratic equations, history of, 146–47

Questions
  features to develop, 31–34
  types on tests, 64–66
  types to avoid, 28–31
  wait-time after, 33–34
  writing in homework, 52
Quizzes, 56, 60, 96

Reading mathematics, 20
  mathematics anxiety and, 196
  problem solving and, 108–9
Recorde, Robert, 146
Recreational mathematics, 101
  computers and, 131
  motivation and, 40–41
  for remediation, 98
  for slow learners, 147–48
Relevance
  in enrichment for slow learners, 147
  of homework, 175
  remediation and, 99
Remediation, 92–94
  diagnostic procedures for, 93–94
  handicapped students, 102
  methods of, 94, 96–99
  physical arrangements for, 100–102
Repetition
  in questions, 32
  of student answers, 32–33
Report cards, 75
Review lesson plans, 19–20
Riddles in Mathematics (Northrop), 162
Rigidity of Behavior (Luchins and Luchins), 106
Rote responses in problem solving, 106
Routine, classroom, 174
Rowe, Mary Budd, 33–34

Scales for the Measurement of Attitudes (Shaw and Wright), 94
School Science and Mathematics, 183
School Science and Mathematics Association, 80, 183
"Scientific" formula for grading, 76
Sequential achievement and motivation, 38–39
Shaw, M. E., 94
Spatial relations and mathematics anxiety, 196
Spiraled homework assignment, 48
Standardized tests, 56, 87
  diagnosing remediation, 93
Student attitudes
  remediation and, 93–94

student responsibility for, 74
Student identification on homework, 52
Student improvement and grading, 76
Student interest, questions for maintaining, 32
Student interests and remediation, 99
Student involvement in class, 176
Student performance and grading, 76
Students
  absences from tests, 68
  assessment of progress, 76
  backgrounds of, 183
  critical and analytic thought and problem solving, 110–11
  discipline responsibilities, 74, 178
  effort, praise for, 196
  finishing early on tests, 67
  girls and boys treated equally, 196
  grouping by ability, 175
  knowledge and motivation, 38
  names, techniques for learning, 174
  neatness of work, 174–75
  performance objectives, 188–89, 191
  problem solving, pride in, 109–10
  teacher evaluations by, 81
Summary in lesson plans, 7
Supplies, classroom, 174, 183
Survey tests diagnosing remediation, 93

Teacher-centered questions, 31
Teacher-made materials
  diagnosing remediation, 93
  motivation and, 42–43
Teacher performance
  formal observations, 82–84
  informal evaluations, 81–82
  tenure and, 84, 87
Teachers
  classroom movement of, 175
  correct English usage, 175
  discipline problems, practices provoking, 178
  humor of, 196
  observation of, 182
  professional growth, 80, 183
  as role models, 196
  strictness of, 174
  students called on, 33, 176
Television for remediation, 100
Tenure and teacher performance, 84, 87

Test files, 60, 65
Tests
    administering, 66–68
    cheating on, 67, 175
    construction of, 60–61, 64
    correction of, 64
    grading, 68–69
    interpreting results, 69–70
    mathematics anxiety and, 195
    minimum competency, 92
    multiple choice, 70
    point values for, 66
    presenting, 66
    questions, types of, 64–66
    speed tests/timed tests, 196
    student responsibility for, 74
    time limits for, 66
    topic choice, 64

    types of, 64
Texas Instruments, 128
Textbooks
    examination in preparation for
        teaching, 182
    for remediation, 100
    selection of, 183–85
Thales, 140
Topics
    choice for tests, 64
    usefulness and motivation, 39–40
Trial and error in problem solving,
    114
Trigonometry, history of, 143–45
True-false questions, 64
    point values for, 66
Tutoring
    individual, 102

    peer, 98–99, 163

Uniform motion problems, 108

Variety
    in homework assignments, 48
    in questioning, 34
Verbal problems on tests, 66
Video-tape equipment for teacher
    evaluation, 82

Whetstone of Witte, The
    (Recorde), 146
Whiplash questions, 30
Work folders for remediation, 101
Wright, J. M., 94

Yes-no questions, 29

Dr. Alfred S. Posamentier is professor of mathematics education and Associate Dean of Education at The City College of The City University of New York. Although he is intensely involved in the preparation and education of teachers of secondary school mathematics, both at the undergraduate and graduate levels, he is also very much involved with mathematics curriculum development for the secondary schools.

Professor Posamentier has directed numerous programs for teachers sponsored by the National Science Foundation (NSF). Some programs focused on using topics and concepts from higher mathematics to improve and enliven the instruction of mathematics at all secondary school levels.

He has been chairman of the Department of Secondary and Continuing Education and coordinator of the NSF Northeast Resource Center in Science and Engineering at City College. Among the many activities he conducted in this program was one designed to help teachers enrich their instruction by introducing them to topics in mathematics generally considered "off the beaten path." Many of the topics presented in that program are found in Part 2 of this book. Refinements of this material resulted from the comments of many teachers who have been enrolled in this program over the years.

His extensive prior experience as both a secondary school mathematics teacher and supervisor is useful when he serves as a mathematics consultant to many school systems (both urban and suburban).

One of Dr. Posamentier's recent direct involvements with secondary school students has been through the Select Program in Science and Engineering (SPISE), which he developed at The City College in 1978, supported largely through corporate funds. SPISE is designed to motivate and prepare about 500 disadvantaged high school sophomores for careers in science and engineering.

While teaching in secondary school, Dr. Posamentier has taught all mathematics courses and students at all levels of ability. During this time he also developed new courses for both enrichment and remediation.

In addition to his articles that have appeared in professional journals and the many presentations he has made at mathematics teachers conferences, Dr. Posamentier has written several mathematics books for secondary school students and their teachers. This book ties together much of his earlier work.

Jay Stepelman has had over twenty years of experience as a mathematics supervisor at George Washington High School and Yeshiva University High School in New York City. He is directly involved with on-the-job teacher training and curriculum development in a practical rather than a theoretical setting. His experience ranges from planning, supervising, and teaching regular, honors, and remedial mathematics programs to developing a unique individualized algebra program that has found special success with inner-city students, pupils with certain emotional handicaps, youngsters with limited reading ability, and bilingual students.

Mr. Stepelman is the author of *Milestones in Geometry* (Macmillan, 1970) and the *Algebra Tutor* series for the Apple II family of computers (Learning Well, 1985), and has lectured at professional meetings of the National Council of Teachers of Mathematics, the Association of Teachers of Mathematics of New York State, and the New York City Mathematics Chairmen's Association. He has received numerous awards, including Outstanding Secondary School Educator of 1974, Exemplary Supervisory Service Award in 1985, has been named as the one person most influential in the success of several Westinghouse scholarship winners, and has been honored by having at least three doctoral theses in mathematics dedicated to him by his former students.

Mr. Stepelman has been called upon to evaluate mathematics programs and teachers at various private schools. He has served with the Board of Examiners of the City of New York in the area of teacher certification for the city. His academic training includes mathematics and education work at the City College of New York, Courant Institute of Mathematics, New York University, and Adelphi University.